DEPARTMENT OF EDUCATION AND SCIENCE

Children and their Primary Schools

A Report of the Central Advisory Council for Education (England)

VOLUME 2: RESEARCH AND SURVEYS

LONDON
HER MAJESTY'S STATIONERY OFFICE
1967

First published 1967
Third impression 1969

SBN 11 270140 X

Foreword

In this volume we have brought together accounts of some of the more detailed studies that have been made on our behalf, most of which have been commissioned, designed and written up within a period of two years.

The larger part of the volume consists of accounts of surveys and research commissioned at our request by the Department of Education and Science. We are grateful to the Department for meeting our requests for finance for this purpose. Most of all, however, we express our gratitude to the researchers who responded and produced studies, often at short notice within a given time limit. This has imposed great burdens on everybody concerned, including members of our own Secretariat. We should particularly like to refer to the distinguished contribution made to some of the studies by Mr. G. F. Peaker, C.B.E., who, although retired from H.M. Inspectorate, was retained by the Department to help us with our National Survey and to advise on other research matters. From amongst our full time Secretariat, Miss S. M. C. Duncan, H.M.I., bore a heavy burden in contributing to and helping to carry out some of the research. Substantial help was also given by members of the Statistics Branch of the Department.

The research studies have enabled us to examine, in some depth, several issues within our field of interest. We are glad to learn that some of the research projects described in this volume will continue, and are pleased that the Central Advisory Council have been instrumental in helping them to get started. At the same time, it will be understood that because almost all the work here described has been done quickly, many of the conclusions must be regarded as provisional. In some cases we have published abridged versions in the knowledge that fuller accounts are to be published at about the same time as this volume.

In Volume 1 we have written of the contribution which research can make to primary education: the research described in Volume 2 illustrates the slow process by which knowledge is built up and forms the basis for further investigation.

Table of Contents

APPENDIX 1

A Questionnaire to Some Teachers, and Tables of Replies

1. We decided to send a questionnaire to a random sample of some 3,000 primary and secondary school teachers in order to canvass their views on some of the major issues in our enquiry, and to supplement our evidence from other sources. Many of their replies proved illuminating and have been referred to in different chapters of our Report.

2. We reproduce here the questionnaire sent to the teachers and the tables of replies that have proved to be of interest. Detailed analyses (between men and women and head and assistant teachers, teachers in infant, junior and junior and infant schools) have been omitted except where the groups diverged substantially in the opinions offered.

3. Because of the smallness of the sample detailed breakdowns were not made of secondary teachers' opinions according to their type of school. For the same reason the separate analyses of opinion are of no value in the case of men in infant schools, women heads of junior schools and untrained graduates (shown in the tables by *), and of doubtful value in the case of unqualified teachers (shown in the tables by +). Percentages in the tables are rounded to one decimal place and consequently do not always total exactly 100.

4. The identifying numbers of the tables reproduced in this Appendix are those of the questions in the questionnaire to which the tables show the answers.

5. We are grateful to the large number of teachers who replied to our questionnaire. Their replies supplement, although they in no way replace, the considered views of their professional associations which were all carefully argued and documented statements reinforced by discussion with the full Council.

1

Letter Sent to Teachers in Sample

CENTRAL ADVISORY COUNCIL FOR EDUCATION (ENGLAND)

Replies to the
Secretary of the
Central Advisory Council
HYDe Park 7070 ext.

Curzon Street House,
LONDON, W.1

C.A.C. letter No. 18   16th November, 1964

IN CONFIDENCE

Dear Sir/Madam,

As you probably know, the Central Advisory Council for Education (England) are considering, under the Chairmanship of Lady Plowden, the following terms of reference:—

"To consider primary education in all its aspects and the transition to secondary education"

The Council are very anxious to consult fully the opinions of teachers, and they have decided that this might be done in two ways. First, they have sought evidence from the principal teachers' associations as well as from other organisations and individual witnesses, including many teachers from various types of school, who may be able to help them in their task and this will be the main source from which evidence will be received. But, secondly, they feel that they ought to supplement this evidence by seeking the views of a much larger number of teachers throughout the country, and for this purpose they have selected on a sample basis 2,500 teachers in primary and secondary schools who have been chosen to constitute as complete a range as possible of serving teachers. The sample has been drawn in such a way that the final analysis should represent the views of all teachers employed by local education authorities in all types and sizes of maintained primary and secondary schools. The sample includes teachers from schools in both urban and rural areas.

The Council would be most grateful if you would send your views on the questions to be found in the attached questionnaire; these have been selected as being the main issues upon which teachers' opinions ought to be sought in this way. They are not intended, of course, to represent all of the main issues with which the Council are concerned or on which they expect that teachers will have views; the questionnaire is restricted to issues to which a comparatively unambiguous answer can be given. It is important that the views expressed should be your own and that you should not consult your colleagues on them; otherwise the sample may become unrepresentative. The Council would emphasise, however, that the replies received will be used to provide a national analysis only: no analyses are to be prepared about individual teachers, schools or local education authorities. Your views will be treated as confidential, and the Council hope that you will feel able to make a full and free reply.

Would you please complete the questionnaire carefully and return it in the enclosed envelope not later than 1st December, 1964. The Council hope that all of the teachers invited will fill in and return the questionnaire.

Yours faithfully,

M. KOGAN,
Secretary.

CENTRAL ADVISORY COUNCIL FOR EDUCATION (ENGLAND)

QUESTIONNAIRE TO TEACHERS

Instructions

1. Please read each question carefully.
2. Each question should be answered by placing a tick (√) in the appropriate box. Some questions are "multiple" and require more than one answer; these can be identified by the col. number against each box. " Single" questions which require only one answer are those with the boxes bracketed and one col. number. An example of each type of question is given below.

EXAMPLES—*Multiple question*

Question 31. Should part-time teachers be encouraged to teach in primary schools as a ..	YES	NO	UN	
	1	2	3	
(a) temporary measure? ..		√		Col. 61
(b) permanent measure? ..		√		Col. 62

(A tick should be placed in the third column, marked UN, if you are undecided what answer to give to the question.)

Single question

Question 4. If you think nursery education should be generally available, should this be from

age 2? ..	2		
age 3? ..	3		Col. 24
age 4? ..	4	√	
Undecided ..	5		

The questions which follow have to be put in simple terms in order to permit accurate statistical analysis of the very large number of replies that will be received. If you feel that *none* of the answers available for a particular question represents your views, please add a further note in Section H at the end of the questionnaire.

APPENDIX 1

LEAVE
BLANK | | | | |

QUESTIONNAIRE

SECTION A. PERSONAL DETAILS

(i) In which type of school are you at present employed?

Infant	1	
Infant/Junior ..	2	
Junior	3	Col. 12
Secondary Modern	4	
Other Secondary	5	

(ii) By which L.E.A. are you at present employed?

LEAVE BLANK

.... | | | | Cols. 13/14/15

(iii) Sex

Man	1	Col. 16
Woman	2	

(iv) What is your age in years? .. .. .. | | | Cols. 17/18

(v) What is your present Grade?

Head Teacher ..	1	Col. 19
Assistant Teacher	2	

(vi) What is your qualification?

Teacher's Certificate ..	1	
Trained Graduate ..	2	
Untrained Graduate ..	3	Col. 20
Unqualified	4	

SECTION B. ORGANISATION OF PRIMARY EDUCATION

1. Should all children enter school at the beginning of the school year?

YES	1		
NO	2		Col. 21
UND	3		

2. Should nursery education

    (a) be available only for those with special needs? **1**

    (b) be available for all children whose parents wish it?   ..   ..   **2**   Col. 22

    (c) not be available? **3**

        Undecided **4**

3. Should nursery education be part-time for most children?

YES	1		
NO	2		Col. 23
UND	3		

4. If you think nursery education should be generally available, should this be from

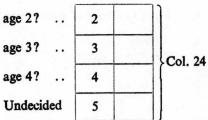

age 2? ..	2		
age 3? ..	3		Col. 24
age 4? ..	4		
Undecided	5		

5. Should full-time education (nursery and infant) be generally available, but not necessarily compulsory, from

age 2? ..	2	
age 3? ..	3	
age 4? ..	4	
age 5? ..	5	
age 6? ..	6	
Undecided	7	

Col. 25

6. Should full-time education be compulsory at

age 4? ..	4	
age 5? ..	5	
age 6? ..	6	
age 7? ..	7	
Undecided	8	

Col. 26

7. Should there be provision for part-time attendance by children beginning school?

YES	1	
NO	2	
UND	3	

Col. 27

8. Are you in favour of a four-term year?

YES	1	
NO	2	
UND	3	

Col. 28

9. Do you favour

    (a) separate infant and junior schools?   .. | 1 | |

    (b) combined infant/junior schools? ..   .. | 2 | |

    (c) some of each according to circumstances? | 3 | |

         Undecided ..   .. | 4 | |

Col. 29

10. Where there is a separate infant school should transfer to the junior stage be at

            age 7? .. | 7 | |

            age 8? .. | 8 | |

            age 9? .. | 9 | |

            Undecided | 10 | |

Col. 30

SECTION C. TRANSITION TO SECONDARY EDUCATION

11. Should the transition to secondary school be at

            age 11? .. | 1 | |

            age 12? .. | 2 | |

            age 13? .. | 3 | |

            Undecided | 4 | |

Col. 31

12. Taking into account the raising of the school leaving age to 16 in 1971, do you consider the minimum length of time necessary for a secondary course to be

            3 years? .. | 3 | |

            4 years? .. | 4 | |

            5 years? .. | 5 | |

            Undecided | 6 | |

Col. 32

13. Should secondary schools be common to all children other than those requiring special educational treatment?

YES	1	
NO	2	
UND	3	

} Col. 33

14. Do you think that the age of beginning secondary education should, apart from flexibility for individual pupils, be uniform throughout the country?

YES	1	
NO	2	
UND	3	

} Col. 34

SECTION D. THE WORK OF THE PRIMARY SCHOOLS

15. Please show by ranking 1, 2, 3, (1 scores highest) the relative importance which you place on

	1	2	3
(a) factual instruction			
(b) training in skills of reading, writing and computation			
(c) creative work in English, art, etc., in the primary school			

Col. 35

Col. 36

Col. 37

(Ties can be allowed but are to be avoided if possible. If there are two "1s", last figure should be 3.)

16. Please show by ranking 1, 2, 3 (1 scores highest) the relative amount of time you would give in the primary school to

	1	2	3
(a) class instruction			
(b) group teaching			
(c) individual work			

Col. 38

Col. 39

Col. 40

(Ties can be allowed but are to be avoided if possible. If there are two "1s", last figure should be 3.)

17. Are satisfactory standards of performance and attainment being reached with

	YES	NO	UND	
	1	2	3	
(a) children of exceptional ability? ..				Col. 41
(b) children of average ability? ..				Col. 42
(c) children of low ability?				Col. 43

18. What is the *maximum* reasonable size of primary school class for teaching purposes (indicate nearest figure to that considered reasonable):—

40? ..	1	
35? ..	2	
30? ..	3	
25? ..	4	Col. 44
below 25?	5	
Undecided	6	

19. Is any classification made by ability desirable in junior schools?

YES	1	
NO	2	Col. 45
UND	3	

20. If answer to question 19 is Yes, is it desirable

(a) at all or most ages?	1	
(b) for older pupils only?	2	Col. 46
Undecided	3	

21. Do you think the use of corporal punishment in primary schools should be

(a) a regular means of discipline?	1
(b) a last resort only?	2
(c) forbidden?	3
Undecided	4

Col. 47

22. Should the organization of the primary school be based on the class teacher

(a) entirely?	1
(b) mainly?	2
(c) partially?	3
Undecided	4

Col. 48

23. Do you think children in the first two years of the secondary school should have

(a) a general class teacher?	1
(b) a gradual introduction to specialisation?	2
(c) full specialist teaching from the first? ..	3
Undecided	4

Col. 49

SECTION E. TEACHERS AND THEIR TRAINING

24. Do you think that students in training are or were prepared adequately for work in primary schools by

	YES	NO	UND	
	1	2	3	
(a) 3-year (or until recently 2-year) training college courses?				Col. 50
(b) combination of graduate and professional courses?				Col. 51

25. Do you think there should be more in-service courses for teachers?

YES	1	
NO	2	
UND	3	

Col. 52

26. Does in-service training at present deal with the aspects of education in which teachers need most help?

YES	1	
NO	2	
UND	3	

Col. 53

27. Is sufficient care taken in placing probationer teachers?

YES	1	
NO	2	
UND	3	

Col. 54

28. Do you think that men should be encouraged to teach infants?

YES	1	
NO	2	
UND	3	

Col. 55

29. Do you think that there should be

	YES	NO	UND
	1	2	3
(a) more posts of responsibility in primary schools?			
(b) a higher basic scale?			
(c) financial reward for long service in the profession?			

Col. 56

Col. 57

Col. 58

30. Should part-time teachers be encouraged to teach in primary schools as a

	YES	NO	UND
	1	2	3
(a) temporary measure?				Col. 59
(b) permanent measure?				Col. 60

31. Do you think that there is a place for non-qualified assistants in primary schools:—

	YES	NO	UND
	1	2	3
(a) for activities outside the classroom?				Col. 61
(b) for helping in the classroom under the general supervision of a qualified teacher?				Col. 62

SECTION F. SCHOOL, HOME AND COMMUNITY

32. Please show by ranking 1, 2, 3, 4, 5, 6 (1 is first in order of importance) which of the following methods of contact with parents you think are most important:—

	1	2	3	4	5	6	
(a) opportunities for individual interview of head with parents							Col. 63
(b) opportunities for individual interview of class teacher with parents							Col. 64
(c) written reports							Col. 65
(d) circular letter to parents ..							Col. 66
(e) meetings to explain educational policy							Col. 67
(f) special occasions, sports day, carol concert, harvest festival, etc.							Col. 68

33. Is collaboration between home and school best achieved

   (a) by an established organisation such as a
       Parent/Teacher Association?   ..   ..

   (b) by the initiative of the head teacher?   ..

   (c) by a combination of (a) and (b)?   ..

       Undecided ..   ..

1	
2	
3	
4	

Col. 69

34. Should parents have more freedom
    in their choice of

	YES	NO	UND
	1	2	3
(a) Primary school?				Col. 70
(b) Secondary school?				Col. 71

35. Is information about local educational facilities easily available
    to parents in your area?

YES	1
NO	2
UND	3

Col. 72

36. Do the social welfare services such as children's officers and
    probation officers work closely with the schools?

YES	1
NO	2
UND	3

Col. 73

SECTION G. THE STATUS AND RESPONSIBILITIES OF TEACHERS

37. Do heads

YES	NO	UND
1	2	3

    (a) consult assistant teachers about the running of the school?   ..   ..   Col. 74

    (b) allow assistant teachers sufficient freedom to organise the work within their own classes? ..   ..   ..   Col. 75

38. Have you had a recent opportunity to see the work of other schools?

YES	1	
NO	2	
UND	3	

     Col. 76

39. Is the status of primary education, compared with that of secondary education,

    (a) higher?   ..   .. | 1 |

    (b) equal?   ..   .. | 2 |

    (c) lower?   ..   .. | 3 |

         Undecided ..   .. | 4 |

     Col. 77

40. Are L.E.A. administrators and inspectors accessible

YES	NO	UND
1	2	3

    (a) to heads?   ..   ..   Col. 78

    (b) to assistant teachers?   ..   ..   Col. 79

41. Are Managing Bodies helpful to primary schools?

YES	1	
NO	2	
UND	3	

     Col. 80

SECTION H

Please enter here any additional points you wish to bring to the notice of the Council or any clarification that you wish to make of your answers given in Sections B to G above. (Please answer as briefly as possible.)

Teachers who Answered the Questionnaire, Analysed by Sex, Type of School, Grade, Age and Qualification.

Table A[1]

	Men				Women				Men and women			
	Head	Assistant	†	Total	Head	Assistant	†	Total	Head	Assistant	†	Total
Type of school												
Infant	4	2	—	6	135	215	2	352	139	217	2	358
Infant/Junior	185	158	—	343	111	354	—	465	296	512	—	808
Junior	125	305	—	430	17	224	1	242	142	529	1	672
Secondary modern	55	76	—	131	13	41	—	54	68	117	—	185
Other secondary	24	95	—	119	13	49	—	62	37	144	—	181
All-age	3	3	—	6	4	4	—	8	7	7	—	14
Peripatetic	—	—	—	—	—	1	—	1	—	1	—	1
Not employed	—	—	3	3	—	9	2	11	—	9	5	14
Unknown	1	—	3	4	1	1	—	2	2	1	3	6
Total	397	639	6	1,042	294	898	5	1,197	691	1,537	11	2,239
Age[2]												
20–29	—	87	3	90	2	225	1	228	2	312	4	318
30–49	173	410	1	584	113	383	3	499	286	793	4	1,083
50 and over	223	137	—	360	175	288	1	464	398	425	1	824
Unknown	1	5	2	8	4	2	—	6	5	7	2	14
Total	397	639	6	1,042	294	898	5	1,197	691	1,537	11	2,239
Qualification												
Teachers certificate	317	532	1	850	268	816	2	1,086	585	1,348	3	1,936
Trained graduate	70	79	1	150	25	41	—	66	95	120	1	216
Untrained graduate	10	24	—	34	1	8	—	9	11	32	—	43
Unqualified	—	4	2	6	—	33	3	36	—	37	5	42
Unknown	—	—	2	2	—	—	—	—	—	—	2	2
Total	397	639	6	1,042	294	898	5	1,197	691	1,537	11	2,239

Graduates in primary schools	Trained graduates	Untrained graduates
Infant	6	1
Infant/Junior	26	9
Junior	39	4
Total	71	14

† Grades unknown
(1) Table numbers throughout this Appendix refer to the section and question in the questionnaire.
(2) The youngest teacher was 20 years old; the oldest was 68.

Notes on Interpretation

Tables B6 and B7

1. Opinion expressed on one question would have been influenced by opinion on the other, but because of the form in which the questions were phrased, a viable cross-analysis could not be made.

Tables D15, D16 and F32

2. In questions D15, D16 and F32 teachers were invited to show their order of preference on three or six point scales. The counting of replies has been undertaken as follows:

Main Preference

The alternative shown as the main preference is that which attracted the highest number of first votes.

Weighted Scores

(a) Each weighted score has been calculated by adding together the first, second and subsequent votes recorded with weights of 3, 2 and 1 (6, 5, 4, 3, 2 and 1 in the case of Table F32) respectively. Weighted scores thus indicate the relative importance placed by the teachers on these propositions.

(b) For simplicity of processing, the answers were analysed in exactly the manner in which they had been recorded by the respondents; thus, for example, where two or three first choices had been given each of them has been so recorded.

(c) A subsequent re-valuation of the answer totals on statistically more elaborate lines has produced results which for none of the propositions differ by more than three per cent (and in only one case by more than two per cent) from the answers as given in the analyses.

Should all children enter school at the beginning of the school year?

	Percentage of teachers		
	Yes	No	Undecided
Teachers in primary schools			
Infant	60·2	34·7	5·1
Infant/Junior	54·2	41·5	4·3
Junior	62·3	31·5	6·3
All primary	58·3	36·6	5·1

Source B1 by A (i)

Should nursery education (a) be available only for those with special needs, (b) be available for all children whose parents wish it, (c) not be available?

	Percentage of teachers			
	Only for those with special needs	For all children whose parents wish it	Not available	Undecided
Teachers in primary schools				
Infant	25·0	71·2	1·9	1·9
Infant/Junior	21·4	73·8	3·4	1·3
Junior	21·8	72·9	2·1	3·2
All primary	22·3	72·9	2.7	2·1

Source B2 by A (i)

Should nursery education be part-time for most children?

	Percentage of teachers		
	Yes	No	Undecided
Teachers in primary schools			
Infant	66·3	26·0	7·7
Infant/Junior	73·0	18·8	8·2
Junior	71·0	18·4	10·6
All primary	70·8	20·3	8·9

Source B3 by A (i)

Table B4

From what age should nursery education be available to most children?

Percentage of teachers

	Age of commencement			
	2	3	4	Undecided
Teachers in primary schools				
Infant	2·8	41·9	39·3	16·1
Infant/Junior	3·3	36·0	42·7	18·1
Junior	1·3	35·0	44·2	19·4
All primary	2·5	36·9	42·5	18·1

Source B4 by A (i)

Table B5

From what age should full time education (nursery and infant) be available, but not necessarily compulsory?

Percentage of teachers

	Age of commencement					
	2	3	4	5	6	Undecided
Teachers in primary schools						
Infant	2·3	22·0	43·8	24·4	1·2	6·3
Infant/Junior	2·2	16·8	45·4	27·3	1·0	7·3
Junior	0·9	16·6	44·2	26·9	1·7	9·7
All primary	1·7	17·9	44·7	26·5	1·3	7·9

Source B5 by A (i)

Table B6(1)

From what age should education be compulsory and full time?

Percentage of teachers

	Age of commencement				
	4	5	6	7	Undecided
Teachers in primary schools					
Infant	3·7	77·4	17·5	0·5	0·9
Infant/Junior	2·5	77·2	17·4	0·3	2·6
Junior	3·6	77·5	16·6	1·0	1·2
All primary	3·1	77·4	17·2	0·6	1·8

Source B6 by A (i)
(1) See note on page 17

Table B7(^{1})

Should there be provision for part-time attendance by children beginning school?

Percentage of teachers

Teachers in primary schools	Head teachers			Assistant teachers			Head and assistant teachers		
	Yes	No	Un-decided	Yes	No	Un-decided	Yes	No	Un-decided
Men									
*Infant	—	100·0	—	100·0	—	—	33·3	66·7	—
Infant/Junior	45·4	48·1	6·5	52·5	39·9	7·6	48·7	44·3	7·0
Junior	44·8	51·2	4·0	50·5	43·6	5·9	48·8	45·8	5·3
All primary	44·6	50·0	5·4	51·4	42·2	6·5	48·7	45·3	6·0
Women									
Infant	60·7	34·8	4·4	54·0	41·4	4·7	55·6	39·8	4·6
Infant/Junior	51·4	42·3	6·3	54·5	37·6	7·9	54·1	38·2	7·7
Junior	*64·7	*23·5	*11·8	46·0	42·9	11·2	46·7	42·2	11·2
All primary	57·0	37·3	5·7	52·0	40·1	7·9	52·7	39·7	7·6
Men and women									
Infant	59·0	36·7	4·3	54·2	41·2	4·6	55·3	40·1	4·6
Infant/Junior	47·6	45·9	6·4	54·2	38·0	7·9	52·5	40·0	7·5
Junior	47·2	47·9	4·9	47·8	43·2	9·0	47·7	43·9	8·4
All primary	50·3	44·2	5·5	51·8	40·6	7·6	51·5	41·4	7·2

Source B7 by A (i), (iii), (v)
(^{1})See note on page 17

Should there be four terms in the school year?

		Percentage of teachers	
	Yes	No	Undecided
Teachers in primary schools			
Infant	45·0	36·1	18·9
Infant/Junior	51·6	33·5	14·9
Junior	49·1	38·0	13·0
All primary	49·3	35·6	15·1

Source B8 by A (i)

How should infant and junior education be organised?

			Percentage of teachers	
	Separate infant and junior schools	Combined infant/junior schools	Some of each according to circumstances	Undecided
Teachers in primary schools				
Men				
*Infant	50·0	33·3	16·7	—
Infant/Junior	8·7	51·3	39·1	0·9
Junior	21·9	31·2	46·5	0.5
All primary	16·3	40·1	43·0	0·6
Women				
Infant	48·0	16·4	34·6	1·1
Infant/Junior	14·4	45·5	39·3	0·7
Junior	27·7	27·9	42·3	2·1
All primary	28·0	32·2	38·6	1·2
Men and women				
Infant	48·0	16·6	34·4	1·0
Infant/Junior	12·7	47·2	39·2	0·8
Junior	24·9	29·5	44·3	1·3
All primary	24·6	34·5	39·9	1·0
Teachers aged:				
20–29	20·2	40·6	37·5	1·8
30–49	22·2	36·5	40·9	0·5
50 and over	29·5	29·1	40·0	1·4
All ages	24·6	34·5	39·9	1·0
Teachers in:				
Counties (including London)	22·6	35·6	40·9	1·0
County Boroughs	29·2	32·0	37·6	1·2
Total	24·6	34·5	39·9	1·0

Source B9 by A (i), (ii), (iii), (iv)

Table B10

At what age should children transfer from separate infant school to the junior stage?

Percentage of teachers

Teachers in primary schools	Men				Women				Men and women			
	7	8	9	Undecided	7	8	9	Undecided	7	8	9	Undecided
Head teachers												
Infant	*50·0	*50·0	*—	*—	28·9	65·9	4·4	0·7	29·5	65·5	4·3	0·7
Infant/Junior	65·4	28·1	2·7	3·8	50·5	38·7	3·6	7·2	59·8	32·1	3·0	5·1
Junior	68·8	28·0	1·6	1·6	*82·4	*17·6	*—	*—	70·4	26·8	1·4	1·4
All primary	66·6	28·3	2·2	2·9	41·4	51·3	3·8	3·4	55·1	38·8	2·9	3·1
Assistant teachers												
Infant	*—	*100·0	*—	*—	46·5	51·6	—	1·9	46·3	51·9	—	1·9
Infant/Junior	62·7	32·3	1·3	3·8	53·7	38·4	3·1	4·8	55·3	37·3	2·8	4·6
Junior	70·5	23·9	3·3	2·3	70·1	27·7	0·9	1·3	70·3	26·2	1·9	1·7
All primary	67·5	27·1	2·6	2·8	56·4	39·0	1·6	3·0	58·9	36·3	1·9	3·0
Head and assistant teachers												
Infant	*33·3	*66·7	*—	*—	42·3	55·0	1·1	1·6	42·2	55·2	1·1	1·6
Infant/Junior	64·1	30·0	2·0	3·8	53·2	38·5	3·2	5·1	56·5	36·0	2·8	4·7
Junior	70·0	25·1	2·8	2·1	70·5	27·3	0·9	1·3	70·3	26·3	1·8	1·7
All primary	67·1	27·6	2·4	2·8	54·2	40·7	1·9	3·1	58·1	36·8	2·1	3·0

Source B10 by A (i), (iii), (v)

Table C11

At what age should children transfer from the junior to the secondary school?

				Percentage of teachers
	11	12	13	Undecided
Teachers in primary schools				
Men				
*Infant	16·7	50·0	16·7	16·7
Infant/Junior	32·7	44·6	18·1	4·7
Junior	39·3	40·7	15·1	4·9
All primary	36·2	42·5	16·4	4·9
Women				
Infant	27·1	44·6	14·7	13·6
Infant/Junior	39·9	36·0	12·6	11·5
Junior	40·6	35·1	17·6	6·7
All primary	36·2	38·4	14·5	10·9
Men and women				
Infant	27·0	44·7	14·7	13·7
Infant/Junior	37·8	38·6	14·2	9·5
Junior	40·0	37·8	16·4	5·8
All primary	36·2	39·6	15·1	9·1
Head teachers	29·5	45·4	16·6	8·5
Assistant teachers	38·1	38·0	14·6	9·3
Head and assistant teachers	36·2	39·6	15·1	9·1
Teachers aged: 20–29	39·7	31·8	18·4	10·1
30–49	34·0	40·4	17·5	8·1
50 and over	37·5	42·4	10·2	9·8
All ages	36·2	39·6	15·1	9·1
Teachers in secondary schools				
Head teachers	62·5	21·4	11·2	5·0
Assistant teachers	53·4	22·7	18·8	5·2
Head and assistant teachers	53·8	22·6	18·4	5·2

Source C11 by A (i), (iii), (iv), (v)

Table C12

What is the minimum length of time necessary for a secondary course, taking into account the raising of the school leaving age in 1971?

			Percentage of teachers	
	3 years	4 years	5 years	Undecided
Teachers in primary schools				
Infant	11·3	51·8	23·6	13·3
Infant/Junior	9·3	51·7	28·5	10·5
Junior	10·4	50·9	29·7	9·0
All primary	10·1	51·5	27·8	10·6
Teachers in secondary schools	12·0	38·4	44·1	5·5

Source C12 by A (i)

Table C13

Should secondary schools be common to all children other than those requiring special educational treatment?

		Percentage of teachers	
	Yes	No	Undecided
Teachers in primary schools			
Teachers aged:			
20–29	54·6	30·3	15·1
30–49	56·7	33·3	10·0
50 and over	59·7	24·9	15·3
All ages	57·3	29·8	12·9
Teachers in:			
Counties (including London)	58·1	29·4	12·5
County Boroughs	55·5	30·7	13·8
Total	57·3	29·8	12·9
Teachers in secondary schools	56·6	32·4	11·0

Source C13 by A (i), (ii), (iv)

Table C14

Should there be a national age of transfer to secondary education?

Percentage of teachers

	Head teachers			Assistant teachers			Head and assistant teachers		
	Yes	No	Undecided	Yes	No	Undecided	Yes	No	Undecided
Teachers in primary schools									
Infant	89·9	2·2	7·9	94·0	2·8	3·2	93·0	2·6	4·4
Infant/Junior	94·3	3·4	2·4	92·5	4·6	2·9	92·9	4·3	2·8
Junior	96·5	3·5	—	95·4	2·9	1·7	95·5	3·0	1·5
All primary	93·8	3·1	3·1	93·9	3·6	2·5	93·8	3·5	2·7
Teachers in secondary schools	87·6	11·2	1·2	95·1	3·8	1·1	94·8	4·1	1·1

Source C14 by A (i), (v)

What is the relative importance in the primary school of:—(a) factual instruction (b) training in skills of reading, writing and computation (c) creative work in English, art, etc.?

	Main preference[1] (percentage of teachers)		Weighted scores[1]		
			Factual instruction	Training in skills	Creative work
Teachers in primary schools					
Teachers aged:					
20–29	(b)	83·6	566	1,280	959
30–49	(b)	88·0	1,396	3,432	2,493
50 and over	(b)	90·7	1,227	2,758	1,822
Teachers by qualification:					
Teachers certificate	(b)	88·7	2,979	7,025	4,957
Trained graduates	(b)	84·1	103	248	173
*Untrained graduates	(b)	73·7	31	50	36
+Unqualified	(b)	81·5	89	183	131
Teachers in secondary schools					
Men	(b)	86·3	9,281	19,853	13,076
Women	(b)	91·7	4,351	9,772	6,363
Men and women	(b)	88·1	13,632	29,625	19,439
Head teachers	(b)	86·4	562	1,405	979
Assistant teachers	(b)	88·1	13,070	28,220	18,460
Head and assistant teachers	(b)	88·1	13,632	29,625	19,439

Source D15 by A (i), (iii), (iv), (v), (vi)

[1] See note on page 17

Table D16

In the primary school, what time should be given relatively to (a) class instruction (b) group teaching (c) individual work?

	Main preference(1) (percentage of teachers)		Weighted scores(1)		
			(a) Class instruction	(b) Group teaching	(c) Individual work
Teachers in primary schools					
Men					
Head teachers					
*Infant	(c)	50·0	6	8	10
Infant/Junior	(c)	48·1	248	437	427
Junior	(b)	53·6	206	292	245
All primary	(b)	49·7	460	737	682
Assistant teachers					
*Infant	(c)	100·0	2	4	6
Infant/Junior	(b)	50·6	251	370	317
Junior	(a) &				
	(b)	34·4	555	631	601
All primary	(b)	39·8	808	1,005	924
Head and assistant teachers					
*Infant	(c)	66·7	8	12	16
Infant/Junior	(b)	49·0	499	807	744
Junior	(b)	40·0	761	923	846
All primary	(b)	43·8	1,268	1,742	1,606
Women					
Head teachers					
Infant	(b)	54·1	148	338	328
Infant/Junior	(b)	55·0	140	275	250
*Junior	(b)	58·8	21	42	34
All primary	(b)	54·8	309	655	612
Assistant teachers					
Infant	(b)	52·3	558	1,042	996
Infant/Junior	(b)	47·7	1,004	1,662	1,584
Junior	(b)	43·4	782	935	879
All primary	(b)	47·8	2,344	3,689	3,459
Head and assistant teachers					
Infant	(b)	52·7	706	1,380	1,324
Infant/Junior	(b)	48·7	1,144	1,937	1,834
Junior	(b)	14·0	803	1,027	913
All primary	(b)	48·8	2,653	4,344	4,071
Men and women teachers aged:					
20–29	(b)	47·4	645	1,067	1,034
30–49	(b)	48·2	1,716	2,783	2,623
50 and over	(b)	45·8	1,539	2,201	1,998
Teachers by qualification					
Teachers certificate	(b)	47·8	3,641	5,709	5,313
Trained graduates	(b)	39·8	158	188	169
*Untrained graduates	(c)	52·6	33	37	44
+Unqualified	(c)	52·3	89	152	151

Source D16 by A (i), (iii), (iv), (v), (vi)   (1) See note on page 17

B

Table D17

Are satisfactory standards of performance and attainment being reached with:—
(a) children of exceptional ability (b) children of average ability (c) children
of low ability?

Percentage of teachers

	Exceptional ability			Average ability			Low ability		
	Yes	No	Un-decided	Yes	No	Un-decided	Yes	No	Un-decided
Teachers in primary schools									
Men									
*Infant	16·7	50·0	33·3	50·0	33·3	16·7	66·7	16·7	16·7
Infant/Junior	45·5	37·9	16·6	74·3	17·8	7·9	20·7	61·8	17·5
Junior	46·0	40·9	13·0	73·7	20·9	5·3	23·3	59·3	17·4
All primary	45·6	39·7	14·8	73·8	19·6	6·5	22·5	60·1	17·5
Women									
Infant	52·6	31·0	16·5	76·6	15·8	7·6	18·2	60·2	21·6
Infant/Junior	58·0	28·2	13·8	77·5	14·4	8·1	19·2	57·3	23·6
Junior	50·3	31·6	18·1	73·1	15·9	11·0	22·2	48·6	29·2
All primary	54·4	29·9	15·7	76·1	15·2	8·7	19·6	56·0	24·4
Men and women									
Head teachers									
Infant	46·0	30·2	23·7	69·8	18·7	11·5	26·6	49·6	23·7
Infant/Junior	49·0	31·8	19·3	78·4	12·5	9·1	27·7	49·0	23·3
Junior	48·6	40·8	10·6	76·8	19·0	4·2	22·5	62·0	15·5
All primary	48·2	33·6	18·2	75·9	15·6	8·5	26·2	52·3	21·5
Assistant teachers									
Infant	54·2	31·5	14·4	78·5	15·0	6·5	16·2	63·0	20·8
Infant/Junior	56·1	30·8	13·0	76·0	16·4	7·6	16·9	61·9	21·2
Junior	48·2	35·2	16·6	72·8	18·2	9·0	22·7	52·2	25·1
All primary	52·8	32·6	14·6	75·3	16·8	7·9	18·9	58·6	22·6
Head and assistant teachers									
Infant	52·2	31·2	16·6	76·4	15·9	7·7	18·7	59·7	21·5
Infant/Junior	54·3	31·1	14·6	76·6	15·4	8·0	19·6	58·6	21·8
Junior	48·3	36·1	15·6	73·4	18·3	8·3	22·7	53·7	23·6
All primary	51·8	32·8	15·4	75·5	16·5	8·0	20·5	57·2	22·3
Teachers in secondary schools									
Men	44·1	30·7	25·2	44·7	35·9	19·4	5·7	65·9	28·4
Women	53·1	17·5	29·4	41·1	27·1	31·9	11·6	48·5	39·9
Men and women									
Head teachers	50·7	24·0	25·3	42·1	42·3	15·6	11·0	62·9	26·1
Assistant teachers	46·9	26·5	26·6	43·6	32·5	23·9	7·5	60·0	32·5
Head and assistant teachers	47·1	26·4	26·6	43·5	33·0	23·5	7·6	60·1	32·2

Source D17 by A (i), (iii), (v)

What is the maximum reasonable size of primary school class?

					Percentage of teachers	
	40	35	30	25	Under 25	Undecided
Teachers in primary schools						
Head teachers						
Infant	—	6·5	67·6	22·3	2·2	1·4
Infant/Junior	0·3	7·4	53·7	33·8	4·1	0·7
Junior	0·7	14·1	64·1	16·2	2·1	2·8
All primary	0·3	8·8	59·6	26·7	3·1	1·4
Assistant teachers						
Infant	—	11·5	57·8	28·8	1·8	—
Infant/Junior	—	9·0	62·1	24·2	4·2	0·5
Junior	0·1	12·6	61·5	23·3	1·5	0·9
All primary	—	10·9	61·0	24·9	2·7	0·5
Head and assistant teachers						
Infant						
20–29	—	4·6	58·6	34·5	2·3	—
30–49	—	12·2	55·5	30·2	1·6	0·4
50 and over	—	10·5	65·0	21·9	2·1	0·4
Total	—	10·3	60·2	27·2	1·9	0·3
Infant/Junior						
20–29	—	11·7	60·7	23·5	4·1	—
30–49	0·2	9·2	58·4	27·8	3·7	0·7
50 and over	—	6·5	61·4	26·9	4·8	0·5
Total	0·1	8·6	60·0	26·7	4·1	0·5
Junior						
20–29	—	9·8	54·9	32·9	1·2	1·2
30–49	0·2	12·7	64·4	20·0	1·2	1·4
50 and over	0·3	14·5	62·5	19·4	2·3	1·0
Total	0·2	12·8	61·9	22·2	1·6	1·2
All primary						
20–29	—	9·6	58·1	29·2	2·6	0·4
30–49	0·2	11·0	59·9	25·6	2·4	0·9
50 and over	0·1	10·0	62·6	23·3	3·3	0·6
Total	0·1	10·4	60·7	25·3	2·8	0·7
Teachers in:						
Counties (including London)	—	8·8	60·8	26·4	3·1	0·9
County Boroughs	0·4	14·2	60·4	22·6	2·1	0·3
Total	0·1	10·4	60·7	25·3	2·8	0·7

Source D18 by A (i), (ii), (iv), (v)

Is any classification by ability desirable in junior schools?

Percentage of teachers

	Undecided	No	Yes		
			For all or most ages	For older pupils only	Undecided
Teachers in primary schools					
Head teachers					
Infant	18·0	39·6	16·5	23·7	2·2
Infant/Junior	9·1	40·9	22·6	26·7	0·7
Junior	6·3	25·4	35·9	30·3	2·1
All primary	10·6	36·7	24·4	26·9	1·4
Assistant teachers					
Infant	14·3	28·8	33·9	22·1	0·9
Infant/Junior	8·9	34·2	29·6	26·4	0·9
Junior	7·0	20·0	46·6	24·4	2·0
All primary	9·3	27·8	36·7	24·8	1·3
Head and assistant teachers					
Infant					
Teachers aged: 20–29	20·7	33·3	29·9	16·1	—
30–49	10·2	33·9	29·8	24·9	1·2
50 and over	17·3	28·3	30·0	22·8	1·7
All ages	15·2	31·4	29·7	22·5	1·2
Infant/Junior					
Teachers aged: 20–29	12·2	36·2	20·9	30·6	—
30–49	9·4	39·0	26·0	24·9	0·7
50 and over	7·0	32·1	33·3	26·1	1·4
All ages	9·0	35·9	27·8	26·5	0·9
Junior					
Teachers aged: 20–29	8·1	25·4	39·9	25.4	1·2
30–49	6·0	24·0	45·0	23·6	1·4
50 and over	7·6	13·8	47·4	28·0	3·3
All ages	6·9	20·9	44·9	25·3	2·0
All primary					
Teachers aged: 20–29	12·3	31·6	29·8	25·9	0·4
30–49	8·4	32·8	33·3	24·4	1·1
50 and over	9·7	25·4	37·0	25·9	2·1
All ages	9·6	29·8	34·0	25·2	1·3
Teachers in:					
Counties (including London)	9·6	32·3	31·1	25·6	1·4
County Boroughs	9·6	23·9	41·0	24·3	1·2
Total	9·6	29·8	34·0	25·2	1·3
Teachers in secondary schools					
Head teachers	14·0	28·5	14·4	41·1	2·0
Assistant teachers	14·0	31·0	24·9	28·5	1·6
Head and assistant teachers	14·0	30·9	24·4	29·1	1·6

Source D19, 20 by A (i), (ii), (iv), (v)

Table D21

Should corporal punishment be used in primary schools?

Percentage of teachers

	Regular means of discipline	Last resort only	Forbidden	Undecided
Teachers in primary schools				
Infant	1·9	84·8	9·3	4·0
Infant/Junior	2·7	89·3	5·2	2·8
Junior	4·7	89·2	4·2	1·9
Men	5·1	90·2	3·1	1·5
Women	2·4	87·5	6·9	3·2
Head teachers	1·9	91·7	4·3	2·1
Assistant teachers	3·6	87·3	6·2	2·9
Teachers aged:				
20–29	3·7	84·6	6·4	5·3
30–49	2·9	88·6	5·8	2·7
50 and over	3·2	89·7	5·4	1·7
All teachers in primary schools	3·2	88·3	5·8	2·7

Source D21 by A (i), (iii), (iv), (v)

Table D22

Should the organisation of the primary school be based on the class teacher?

		Percentage of teachers		
	Entirely	Mainly	Partially	Undecided
Teachers in primary schools				
Men				
*Infant	—	83·3	16·7	—
Infant/Junior	6·7	76·7	15·5	1·2
Junior	7·4	77·4	13·7	1·4
All primary	7·1	77·2	14·5	1·3
Women				
Infant	5·1	57·0	35·6	2·3
Infant/Junior	2·9	66·1	27·4	3·7
Junior	4·3	63·4	29·7	2·6
All primary	3·9	62·6	30·4	3·0
Men and women				
Infant	5·1	57·3	35·4	2·3
Infant/Junior	4·0	69·2	23·8	2·9
Junior	5·0	70·2	22·0	2·0
All primary	4·9	66·9	25·7	2·5
Head teachers	5·2	70·2	23·2	1·4
Assistant teachers	4·8	66·0	26·4	2·8
Head and assistant teachers	4·9	66·9	25·7	2·5
Teachers aged:				
20–29	4·8	68·4	23·7	3·1
30–49	5·0	68·5	24·6	1·9
50 and over	4·8	64·6	27·8	2·8
All ages	4·9	66·9	25·7	2·5

Source D22 by A (i), (iii), (iv), (v)

Table D23

Should children in the first two years of the secondary school have (a) a general class teacher, (b) a gradual introduction to specialisation or (c) full specialist teaching from the first?

	General class teacher	Gradual introduction to specialisation	Full specialist teaching from the first	Undecided
				Percentage of teachers
Teachers in primary schools				
Head teachers				
Infant	13·7	69·8	7·2	9·4
Infant/Junior	11·8	81·4	4·1	2·7
Junior	13·4	74·6	9·9	2·1
All primary	12·7	76·9	6·2	4·2
Assistant teachers				
Infant	12·0	65·3	15·7	6·9
Infant/Junior	13·3	70·3	13·0	3·3
Junior	9·2	74·2	13·1	3·5
All primary	11·5	70·7	13·7	4·1
Head and assistant teachers				
Infant	12·4	66·4	13·7	7·5
Infant/Junior	12·9	73·1	10·8	3·2
Junior	9·8	74·3	12·6	3·2
All primary	11·8	72·1	12·0	4·1
Teachers by qualification				
Teachers certificate	11·9	72·2	11·7	4·2
Trained graduate	8·0	71·6	15·9	4·5
*Untrained graduate	5·3	78·9	10·5	5·3
+Unqualified	12·5	64·1	20·3	3·1
Total	11·8	72·1	12·0	4·1
Teachers in secondary schools				
Head teachers	5·0	61·9	29·1	4·0
Assistant teachers	5·4	48·1	43·5	3·1
Head and assistant teachers	5·3	48·8	42·8	3·1

Source D23 by A (i), (v), (vi)

APPENDIX 1

Table E24

Are or were students in training prepared adequately for work in primary schools by (a) 3-year (or until recently 2-year) training college courses (b) combination of graduate and professional training?

Percentage of teachers

	3 (or 2) year certificate course			Graduate and professional course		
	Yes	No	Undecided	Yes	No	Undecided
Teachers in primary schools						
Head teachers						
Infant	43·9	42·4	13·7	12·2	30·9	56·8
Infant/Junior	53·7	32·1	14·2	15·9	40·5	43·6
Junior	48·6	38·7	12·7	14·1	47·2	38·7
All primary	50·1	36·2	13·7	14·6	39·9	45·6
Assistant teachers						
Infant	58·8	28·2	13·0	13·9	25·9	60·2
Infant/Junior	57·4	32·2	10·4	11·0	34·8	54·3
Junior	57·9	31·2	10·9	13·8	40·4	45·8
All primary	57·9	31·0	11·1	12·6	35·0	52·4
Head and assistant teachers						
Infant	55·2	31·7	13·1	13·5	27·1	59·4
Infant/Junior	56·5	32·2	11·4	12·2	36·2	51·5
Junior	56·4	32·4	11·2	13·9	41·5	44·7
All primary	56·2	32·2	11·7	13·1	36·0	50·9
Teachers by qualification						
Teachers certificate	56·2	32·9	10·9	12·5	36·4	51·1
Trained graduate	59·1	28·4	12·5	27·3	45·5	27·3
*Untrained graduate	26·3	36·8	36·8	5·3	26·3	68·4
+Unqualified	60·9	6·3	32·8	15·6	12·5	71·9
Total	56·2	32·2	11·7	13·1	36·0	50·9

Source E24 by A (i), (v), (vi)

Table E25

Should there be more in-service courses for teachers?

| | Percentage of teachers | | |
	Yes	No	Undecided
Teachers in primary schools			
Head teachers			
Infant	87·8	5·0	7·2
Infant/Junior	78·7	12·8	8·4
Junior	83·8	7·0	9·2
All primary	82·1	9·5	8·3
Assistant teachers			
Infant	81·9	6·5	11·6
Infant/Junior	80·6	10·9	8·5
Junior	76·5	9·8	13·7
All primary	79·4	9·6	11·1
Head and assistant teachers			
Infant	83·4	6·1	10·5
Infant/Junior	80·1	11·4	8·5
Junior	77·7	9·4	13·0
All primary	80·0	9·6	10·5
Teachers by qualification			
Teachers certificate	80·6	9·4	9·9
Trained graduate	69·3	15·9	14·8
*Untrained graduate	73·7	5·3	21·1
+Unqualified	71·9	6·3	21·9
Total	80·0	9·6	10·5

Source E25 by A (i), (v), (vi)

Does in-service training at present deal with the aspects of education in which teachers need most help?

Table E26

Percentage of teachers

Teachers in primary schools	Head teachers			Assistant teachers			Head and assistant teachers		
	Yes	No	Undecided	Yes	No	Undecided	Yes	No	Undecided
Infant	45·3	28·1	26·6	30·8	37·3	31·9	34·3	35·0	30·6
Infant/Junior	44·3	26·0	29·7	33·5	35·5	31·1	36·2	33·0	30·7
Junior	38·0	31·0	31·0	35·6	31·1	33·3	36·0	31·1	33·0
All primary	43·0	27·7	29·3	33·7	34·2	32·1	35·7	32·8	31·5

Source E26 by A (i), (v)

Is sufficient care taken in placing probationer teachers?

	Percentage of teachers		
	Yes	No	Undecided
Teachers in primary schools			
Head teachers			
Infant	29·5	47·5	23·0
Infant/Junior	18·6	49·3	32·1
Junior	23·2	53·5	23·2
All primary	22·4	49·9	27·7
Assistant teachers			
Infant	16·2	52·3	31·5
Infant/Junior	13·5	56·9	29·6
Junior	15·8	57·1	27·1
All primary	14·9	56·0	29·1
Head and assistant teachers			
Infant	19·4	51·1	29·4
Infant/Junior	14·8	55·0	30·2
Junior	17·0	56·5	26·5
All primary	16·6	54·7	28·8
Teachers aged:			
20–29	14·5	62·5	23·0
30–49	16·8	54·7	28·5
50 and over	17·0	51·2	31·8
All ages	16·6	54·7	28·8

Source E27 by A (i), (iv), (v)

Should part-time teachers be encouraged to teach in primary schools as a
(a) temporary measure (b) permanent measure?

Percentage of teachers

	Temporary measure			Permanent measure		
	Yes	No	Undecided	Yes	No	Undecided
Teachers in primary schools						
Men						
*Infant	66·7	16·7	16·7	—	83·3	16·7
Infant/Junior	67·9	24·5	7·6	19·2	68·5	12·2
Junior	61·4	30·7	7·9	17·4	72·8	9·8
All primary	64·3	27·9	7·8	18·1	71·0	10·9
Women						
Infant	71·3	19·4	9·3	21·0	57·3	21·7
Infant/Junior	70·9	18·6	10·5	25·6	57·0	17·3
Junior	63·7	25·5	10·7	28·8	59·0	12·2
All primary	69·2	20·6	10·2	25·0	57·6	17·4
Men and women						
Infant	71·2	19·4	9·4	20·8	57·6	21·6
Infant/Junior	70·1	20·3	9·6	23·8	60·4	15·8
Junior	62·6	28·0	9·4	23·3	65·6	11·0
All primary	67·8	22·7	9·5	23·0	61·6	15·5
Head teachers	70·7	20·3	9·0	23·6	59·8	16·6
Assistant teachers	66·9	23·5	9·7	22·8	62·1	15·1
Head and assistant teachers	67·8	22·7	9·5	23·0	61·6	15·5
Teachers aged: 20–29	65·1	22·6	12·3	30·5	55·0	14·5
30–49	65·6	25·0	9·4	22·1	65·4	12·5
50 and over	71·9	19·8	8·2	20·7	60·1	19·2
All ages	67·8	22·7	9·5	23·0	61·6	15·5
Primary teachers in:						
Counties (incl. London)	68·3	22·4	9·3	23·4	61·0	15·6
County Boroughs	66·5	23·4	10·1	21·9	63·0	15·1
Total	67·8	22·7	9·5	23·0	61·6	15·5

Source E30 by A (i), (ii), (iii), (iv), (v)

Table E31

Is there a place for non-qualified assistants in primary schools (a) for activities outside the classroom (b) helping in the classroom under the general supervision of a qualified teacher?

Percentage of teachers

	Outside classroom			In classroom		
	Yes	No	Undecided	Yes	No	Undecided
Teachers in primary schools						
Men						
*Infant	83·3	16·7	—	50·0	16·7	33·3
Infant/Junior	71·4	23·6	5·0	39·7	50·7	9·6
Junior	66·0	27·0	7·0	26·3	65·6	8·1
All primary	68·5	25·4	6·0	32·3	58·7	9·0
Women						
Infant	80·7	13·1	6·2	48·7	39·8	11·5
Infant/Junior	75·3	15·6	9·0	45·4	46·8	7·8
Junior	73·5	21·1	5·4	29·2	59·1	11·6
All primary	76·5	16·2	7·2	42·3	47·8	9·9
Men and women						
Infant	80·7	13·1	6·1	48·7	39·6	11·7
Infant/Junior	74·2	18·0	7·8	43·7	47·9	8·3
Junior	69·9	23·9	6·1	27·8	62·2	9·9
All primary	74·2	18·9	6·9	39·4	51·0	9·6
Head teachers	74·7	17·7	7·6	49·4	40·7	9·9
Assistant teachers	74·0	19·3	6·7	36·6	53·9	9·6
Head and assistant teachers	74·2	18·9	6·9	39·4	51·0	9·6
Teachers aged:						
20–29	80·0	12·7	7·2	42·5	48·5	9·0
30–49	73·3	20·7	6·0	36·0	54·7	9·3
50 and over	72·4	19·8	7·7	42·5	47·5	10·0
All ages	74·2	18·9	6·9	39·4	51·0	9·6

Source E31 by A (i), (iii), (iv), (v)

What, in order of importance, are the schools' most important methods of contact with parents?

Teachers in primary schools		Main preference[1] (percentage of teachers)	Weighted scores[1]					
			(a) Opportunities for individual interview of head with parents	(b) Opportunities for individual interview of class teacher with parents	(c) Written reports	(d) Circular letter to parents	(e) Meetings to explain educational policy	(f) Special occasions, sports day, carol concert, harvest festival, etc.
Men								
Head teachers								
*Infant	(a)	75·0	23	19	12	6	12	12
Infant/Junior	(a)	68·6	1,038	925	424	399	575	537
Junior	(a)	72·0	706	612	336	235	346	363
All primary	(a)	70·1	1,767	1,556	772	640	933	912
Assistant teachers								
Infant	(b)	100·0	6	12	5	3	8	8
Infant/Junior	(b)	58·2	803	844	396	314	482	434
Junior	(b)	67·9	1,498	1,685	817	606	954	829
All primary	(b)	64·7	2,307	2,541	1,218	923	1,444	1,271
Head and assistant teachers								
Infant	(a)	50·0	29	31	17	9	20	20
Infant/Junior	(a)	53·1	1,841	1,769	820	713	1,057	971
Junior	(b)	56·0	2,204	2,297	1,153	841	1,300	1,192
All primary	(b)	49·4	4,074	4,097	1,990	1,563	2,377	2,183

		%						
Women								
Head teachers								
Infant	(a)	77·0	769	660	214	317	411	433
Infant/Junior	(a)	68·5	606	524	250	227	323	384
*Junior	(a)	82·4	99	82	41	35	50	52
All primary	(a)	73·8	1,474	1,266	505	579	784	869
Assistant teachers								
Infant	(b)	61·9	2,110	2,358	830	888	1,408	1,404
Infant/Junior	(b)	62·1	3,412	3,822	1,682	1,404	2,374	2,166
Junior	(b)	63·4	2,176	2,424	1,164	818	1,422	1,346
All primary	(b)	62·4	7,698	8,604	3,676	3,110	5,204	4,916
Head and assistant teachers								
Infant	(b)	52·7	2,879	3,018	1,044	1,205	1,819	1,837
Infant/Junior	(b)	56·8	4,018	4,346	1,932	1,631	2,697	2,550
Junior	(b)	61·7	2,275	2,506	1,205	853	1,472	1,398
All primary	(b)	56·8	9,172	9,870	4,181	3,689	5,988	5,785
Men and women								
Head teachers								
Infant	(a)	77·0	792	679	226	323	423	445
Infant/Junior	(a)	68·6	1,644	1,449	674	626	898	921
Junior	(a)	73·2	805	694	377	270	396	415
All primary	(a)	71·8	3,241	2,822	1,277	1,219	1,717	1,781
Assistant teachers								
Infant	(b)	62·0	2,116	2,370	835	891	1,416	1,412
Infant/Junior	(b)	61·4	4,215	4,666	2,078	1,718	2,856	2,600
Junior	(b)	65·2	3,674	4,109	1,981	1,424	2,376	2,175
All primary	(b)	62·9	10,005	11,145	4,894	4,033	6,648	6,187
Head and assistant teachers								
Infant	(b)	52·5	2,908	3,049	1,061	1,214	1,839	1,857
Infant/Junior	(b)	52·2	5,859	6,115	2,752	2,344	3,754	3,521
Junior	(b)	59·0	4,479	4,803	2,358	1,694	2,772	2,590
All primary	(b)	54·6	13,246	13,967	6,171	5,252	8,365	7,968

Source F32 by A (i), (iii), (v)
(1)See note on page 17

How is collaboration between home and school best achieved?

Percentage of teachers

	(a) Established organisation	(b) Initiative of head teacher	(c) Both (a) and (b)	(d) Undecided
Teachers in primary schools				
Men				
Head teachers				
*Infant	—	50·0	50·0	—
Infant/Junior	0·5	54·6	43·2	1·6
Junior	—	61·6	38·4	—
All primary	0·3	57·3	41·4	1·0
Assistant teachers				
*Infant	50·0	—	50·0	—
Infant/Junior	5·7	50·0	38·0	6·3
Junior	4·6	45·6	45·6	4·3
All primary	5·2	46·9	43·0	4·9
Head and assistant teachers				
*Infant	16·7	33·3	50·0	—
Infant/Junior	2·9	52·5	40·8	3·8
Junior	3·3	50·2	43·5	3·0
All primary	3·2	51·1	42·4	3·3
Women				
Head teachers				
Infant	0·7	68·9	28·1	2·2
Infant/Junior	1·8	48·6	43·2	6·3
*Junior	—	82·4	17·6	—
All primary	1·1	61·2	33·8	3·8
Assistant teachers				
Infant	4·7	44·2	48·4	2·8
Infant/Junior	4·8	37·9	53·1	4·2
Junior	3·6	40·2	49·1	7·1
All primary	4·4	40·2	50·7	4·7
Head and assistant teachers				
Infant	3·7	50·1	43·5	2·7
Infant/Junior	4·4	39·3	51·8	4·5
Junior	3·4	41·7	48·0	6·9
All primary	3·9	43·2	48·3	4·5
Men and women				
Head teachers				
Infant	0·7	68·3	28·8	2·2
Infant/Junior	1·0	52·4	43·2	3·4
Junior	—	64·1	35·9	—
All primary	0·7	59·1	38·0	2·3

continued on next page

Table F33 continued

Percentage of teachers

	(a) Established organisation	(b) Initiative of head teacher	(c) Both (a) and (b)	(d) Undecided
Assistant teachers				
Infant	4·9	44·0	48·4	2·8
Infant/Junior	5·0	40·1	50·3	4·6
Junior	4·0	42·4	47·7	6·0
All primary	4·6	41·7	49·0	4·7
Head and assistant teachers				
Infant	3·9	49·9	43·6	2·6
Infant/Junior	4·0	43·2	48·5	4·3
Junior	3·4	45·8	45·8	5·0
All primary	3·7	45·5	46·5	4·2
Teachers aged:				
20–29	4·4	29·4	61·2	5·0
30–49	3·2	45·3	48·2	3·4
50 and over	4·2	53·2	37·8	4·8
Total	3·7	45·5	46·5	4·2

Source F33 by A (i), (ii), (iv), (v)

Table F34

Should parents have more freedom in their choice of primary and secondary schools?

Percentage of teachers

	More freedom of choice of primary school			More freedom of choice of secondary school		
	Yes	No	Undecided	Yes	No	Undecided
Teachers in primary schools						
Head teachers						
Infant	53·2	35·3	11·5	59·7	13·7	26·6
Infant/Junior	44·3	43·6	12·2	53·4	29·7	16·9
Junior	45·8	43·7	10·6	57·7	31·0	11·3
All primary	46·8	41·6	11·6	56·0	26·2	17·9
Assistant teachers						
Infant	61·6	28·2	10·2	65·3	16·7	18·1
Infant/Junior	58·7	30·9	10·4	67·7	20·7	11·7
Junior	52·3	39·4	8·2	60·6	29·1	10·4
All primary	56·9	33·5	9·6	64·6	22·9	12·5
Head and assistant teachers						
Infant	59·5	29·9	10·5	63·9	15·9	20·1
Infant/Junior	55·0	34·2	10·8	64·0	23·0	13·0
Junior	51·3	40·1	8·6	60·1	29·4	10·5
All primary	54·7	35·3	10·0	62·7	23·6	13·7

Source F34 by A (i), (v)

Table F35

Is information about local educational facilities easily available to parents?

Percentage of teachers

Primary school teachers	Head teachers			Assistant teachers			Head and assistant teachers		
	Yes	No	Un-decided	Yes	No	Un-decided	Yes	No	Un-decided
Teachers in:									
Counties (including London)	79·5	11·5	9·0	60·4	16·8	22·8	65·0	15·5	19·5
County Boroughs	86·6	6·0	7·5	73·0	9·7	17·2	75·4	9·1	15·5
Total	81·1	10·2	8·7	64·4	14·6	21·1	68·0	13·6	18·3

Source F35 by A (i), (ii), (v)

Table F36

Do the social welfare services (such as children's officers, probation officers) work closely with the schools?

Percentage of teachers

Primary school teachers	Head teachers			Assistant teachers			Head and assistant teachers		
	Yes	No	Un-decided	Yes	No	Un-decided	Yes	No	Un-decided
Teachers in:									
Counties (including London)	75·8	12·9	11·3	62·4	14·1	23·5	65·6	13·8	20·6
County Boroughs	80·6	14·9	4·5	72·1	11·6	16·3	73·6	12·2	14·2
Total	76·9	13·3	9·7	65·4	13·3	21·3	68·0	13·3	18·7

Source F36 by A (i), (ii), (v)

Do head teachers (a) consult assistant teachers about running of the school (b) allow assistant teachers sufficient freedom to organise the work within their own classes?

Percentage of teachers

	Consult assistant teachers about running of the school			Allow assistant teachers freedom in classes		
	Yes	No	Undecided	Yes	No	Undecided
Teachers in primary schools						
Men						
Head teachers						
*Infant	100·0	—	—	100·0	—	—
Infant/Junior	90·8	4·9	4·3	92·4	4·9	2·7
Junior	90·4	3·2	6·4	94·4	0·8	4·8
All primary	90·8	4·1	5·1	93·3	3·2	3·5
Assistant teachers						
*Infant	50·0	50·0	—	100·0	—	—
Infant/Junior	69·0	23·4	7·6	86·1	7·6	6·3
Junior	64·3	26·9	8·9	87·2	6·2	6·6
All primary	65·8	25·8	8·4	86·9	6·7	6·5
Head and assistant teachers						
*Infant	83·3	16·7	—	100·0	—	—
Infant/Junior	80·8	13·4	5·8	89·5	6·1	4·4
Junior	71·9	20·0	8·1	89·3	4·7	6·0
All primary	75·9	17·1	7·1	89·5	5·3	5·3
Women						
Head teachers						
Infant	87·4	6·7	5·9	94·1	0·7	5·2
Infant/Junior	81·1	6·3	12.6	86·5	4·5	9·0
*Junior	100·0	—	—	100·0	—	—
All primary	85·6	6·1	8·4	91·3	2·3	6·5
Assistant teachers						
Infant	61·9	23·3	14·9	89·3	4·2	6·5
Infant/Junior	67·2	20·9	11·9	89·0	5·6	5·4
Junior	63·4	25·4	11·2	86·2	7·1	6·7
All primary	64·7	22·8	12·5	88·3	5·7	6·1
Head and assistant teachers						
Infant	68·0	19·3	12·7	90·4	3·4	6·2
Infant/Junior	69·1	18·9	12·0	88·6	5·5	5·9
Junior	64·7	24·5	10·8	86·7	6·9	6·5
All primary	67·7	20·4	11·9	88·7	5·2	6·1

continued on next page

Table G37—continued

Percentage of teachers

	Consult assistant teachers about running of the school			Allow assistant teachers freedom in classes		
	Yes	No	Undecided	Yes	No	Undecided
Teachers in primary schools (*continued*)						
Men and women						
Head teachers						
Infant	87·8	6·5	5·8	94·2	0·7	5·0
Infant/Junior	87·2	5·4	7·4	90·2	4·7	5·1
Junior	91·5	2·8	5·6	95·1	0·7	4·2
All primary	88·4	5·0	6·6	92·4	2·8	4·9
Assistant teachers						
Infant	61·8	23·4	14·8	89·4	4·2	6·5
Infant/Junior	67·6	21·4	11·1	88·5	6·0	5·5
Junior	63·7	26·0	10·2	86·6	6·8	6·6
All primary	64·9	23·5	11·6	88·0	5·9	6·1
Head and assistant teachers						
Infant	68·1	19·3	12·6	90·5	3·3	6·1
Infant/Junior	72·5	17·3	10·2	88·9	5·7	5·4
Junior	68·2	22·3	9·5	87·9	5·8	6·3
All primary	70·1	19·4	10·5	88·9	5·2	5·9
Head teachers aged:						
20–29	100·0	—	—	100·0	—	—
30–49	88·2	6·8	5·1	94·1	3·4	2·5
50 and over	88·9	3·3	7·8	91·6	2·1	6·3
Total	88·4	5·0	6·6	92·4	2·8	4·9
Assistant teachers aged:						
20–29	55·9	31·5	12·6	89·0	6·6	4·4
30–49	67·6	22·1	10·4	88·6	4·9	6·5
50 and over	67·0	20·2	12·8	86·2	6·9	6·9
Total	64·9	23·5	11·6	88·0	5·9	6·1
Head and assistant teachers aged:						
20–29	56·1	31·4	12·5	89·0	6·6	4·4
30–49	71·6	19·1	9·3	89·7	4·6	5·7
50 and over	74·6	14·3	11·1	88·1	5·2	6·7
Total	70·1	19·4	10·5	88·9	5·2	5·9

Source G37 by A (i), (iii), (iv), (v)

Table G38

Has there been recent opportunity for teachers to see the work of other schools?

	Percentage of teachers		
	Yes	No	Undecided
Teachers in primary schools			
Head teachers			
Infant	57·6	38·8	3·6
Infant/Junior	50·3	48·3	1·4
Junior	62·7	35·9	1·4
All primary	55·1	43·0	1·9
Assistant teachers			
Infant	38·9	59·3	1·9
Infant/Junior	37·6	59·7	2·7
Junior	38·5	59·1	2·4
All primary	38·2	59·4	2·4
Head and assistant teachers			
Infant	43·4	54·3	2·3
Infant/Junior	40·9	56·8	2·3
Junior	42·3	55·4	2·2
All primary	41·9	55·8	2·3

Source G38 by A (i), (v)

APPENDIX 1

What is the status of primary education compared with that of secondary education?

				Percentage of teachers
	Higher	Equal	Lower	Undecided
Teachers in primary schools				
Men				
Head teachers				
*Infant	—	50·0	50·0	—
Infant/Junior	3·2	16·2	75·7	4·9
Junior	5·6	13·6	73·6	7·2
All primary	4·1	15·6	74·5	5·7
Assistant teachers				
*Infant	—	—	100·0	—
Infant/Junior	3·2	17·7	72·8	6·3
Junior	4·6	16·7	71·8	6·9
All primary	4·1	17·0	72·3	6·7
Head and assistant teachers				
*Infant	—	33·3	66·7	—
Infant/Junior	3·2	16·9	74·3	5·5
Junior	4·9	15·8	72·3	7·0
All primary	4·1	16·4	73·2	6·3
Women				
Head teachers				
Infant	3·0	12·6	68·1	16·3
Infant/Junior	5·4	20·7	61·3	12·6
*Junior	5·9	23·5	58·8	11·8
All primary	4·2	16·7	64·6	14·4
Assistant teachers				
Infant	5·1	18·1	59·1	17·7
Infant/Junior	5·9	24·0	59·0	11·0
Junior	4·0	21·9	65·6	8·5
All primary	5·2	21·8	60·9	12·1
Head and assistant teachers				
Infant	4·6	16·8	61·2	17·3
Infant/Junior	5·9	23·6	59·3	11·2
Junior	4·1	21·9	65·4	8·6
All primary	5·0	21·1	61·4	12·4
Men and women				
Head teachers				
Infant	2·9	13·7	67·6	15·8
Infant/Junior	4·1	17·9	70·3	7·8
Junior	5·6	14·8	71·8	7·7
All primary	4·2	16·1	70·0	9·7
Assistant teachers				
Infant	5·1	18·1	59·3	17·6
Infant/Junior	5·4	22·9	61·5	10·2
Junior	4·2	19·8	68·1	7·8
All primary	4·9	20·7	63·5	10·9

continued on next page

Table G39—continued

Percentage of teachers

	Higher	Equal	Lower	Undecided
Head and assistant teachers				
Infant	4·6	17·0	61·3	17·2
Infant/Junior	5·1	21·6	63·8	9·6
Junior	4·5	19·0	68·7	7·8
All primary	4·8	19·7	64·9	10·6
Teachers by qualification				
Teachers certificate	4·9	19·6	64·9	10·5
Trained graduate	4·5	19·3	67·0	9·1
*Untrained graduate	—	5·3	78·9	15·0
+Unqualified	—	28·1	57·8	14·1
Total	4·8	19·7	64·9	10·6
Teachers in secondary schools				
Head teachers	4·0	36·1	46·9	13·0
Assistant teachers	3·0	27·3	54·7	15·0
Head and assistant teachers	3·1	27·7	54·3	14·9

Source G39 by A (i), (iii), (v), (vi)

Table G40

Are L.E.A. administrators and inspectors accessible to teachers?

Percentage of teachers

	Accessible to head teachers			Accessible to assistant teachers		
	Yes	No	Undecided	Yes	No	Undecided
Teachers in primary schools						
Head teachers						
Infant	92·1	3·6	4·3	62·6	14·4	23·0
Infant/Junior	90·9	6·1	3·0	68·2	16·6	15·2
Junior	91·5	5·6	2·8	69·0	12·7	18·3
All primary	91·3	5·4	3·3	67·1	15·1	17·9
Assistant teachers						
Infant	81·5	3·2	15·3	52·5	25·7	21·8
Infant/Junior	79·3	4·0	16·6	52·4	24·9	22·6
Junior	78·6	3·2	18·2	54·3	28·2	17·5
All primary	79·5	3·6	16·9	53·1	26·3	20·6
Head and assistant teachers						
Infant	84·1	3·3	12·6	55·0	22·9	22·1
Infant/Junior	82·3	4·6	13·2	56·5	22·8	20·7
Junior	80·7	3·6	15·8	56·6	25·7	17·7
All primary	82·1	4·0	13·9	56·2	23·8	20·0
Primary teachers in:						
Counties (incl. London)	82·0	4·2	13·8	54·0	24·6	21·4
County Boroughs	82·5	3·4	14·1	61·5	22·0	16·5
Total	82·1	4·0	13·9	56·2	23·8	20·0

Source G40 by A (i), (ii), (v)

Are managing bodies helpful to primary schools?

		Percentage of teachers	
	Yes	No	Undecided
Teachers in primary schools			
Head teachers			
Infant	53·2	18·7	28·1
Infant/Junior	61·8	22·6	15·5
Junior	57·0	21·1	21·8
All primary	58·6	21·3	20·1
Assistant teachers			
Infant	40·3	26·9	32·9
Infant/Junior	38·7	34·4	26·9
Junior	31·9	33·2	34·9
All primary	36·5	32·4	31·1
Head and assistant teachers			
Infant	43·4	24·9	31·7
Infant/Junior	44·6	31·4	24·0
Junior	35·9	31·3	32·8
All primary	41·4	29·9	28·7
Primary teachers in:			
Counties (incl. London)	44·1	31·0	24·9
County Boroughs	34·8	27·5	37·7
Total	41·4	29·9	28·7

Source G41 by A (i), (ii), (v)

APPENDIX 2

HEALTH OF SCHOOL CHILDREN AND THE SCHOOL HEALTH SERVICE

PART I

THE HEALTH OF PRIMARY SCHOOL CHILDREN AND THE EARLY DEVELOPMENT OF THE SCHOOL HEALTH SERVICE

The Early Years

1. At the turn of the century, allegations (1) that 40 to 60 per cent of men enlisting in the army were unfit for military service led to the appointment of the Inter-Departmental Committee on Physical Deterioration. Their report in 1904 was instrumental in the establishment of the School Medical Service. The Committee made a number of recommendations of which two were that:

(1) "A systematical medical inspection of children at school should be imposed as a public duty on every school authority"; and that

(2) ". . . definite provision should be made by the various local authorities for dealing with the question of underfed children".

2. In fact, in 1905 periodic medical inspections were being carried out in 85 local authorities and a number of charitable organisations were providing school meals. But the arrangements for medical inspection and school meals were such that the Inter-Departmental Committee on Medical Inspection and Feeding of Children Attending Public Elementary Schools, set up in 1905, reported that there was "much opening for improvement", and subsequent legislation did not permit local authorities to miss these openings.

3. The Education (Provision of Meals) Act, 1906, allowed education authorities to provide meals free or at a reduced cost to necessitous children. The Education (Administrative Provisions) Act, 1907, imposed on local education authorities the duty to provide for the medical examination of children in public elementary schools and allowed them to make any necessary arrangements for treatment.

Table 1

Recorded Incidence per 100 Children Examined of Certain Diseases and Defects Found at Periodic Medical Inspections to Require Treatment, 1915–1963

Condition	1915†	1931	1963
Malnutrition	13·3	1·2	0·5
Unclean heads	14·2 ⎫ 20·4	14·0	1·7
Unclean bodies	6·2 ⎭		
Skin disease	1·8	1·2	1·4
Cardiac defect	3·6	0·2	0·2
Lung disease	3·6	Not available	0·5
Disease of nose and throat	20·7	7·0	1·5
Middle ear infection	2·5	0·5	0·3
Defective hearing	11·1	0·4	0·6
Defective speech	1·3	⌈Not available⌉ 1·0 in 1932 ⌊ ⌋	0·5
Defective vision (including squint)	17·3*	9·6*	7·8
Dental disease	69·1	68·0	62·0

* excluding entrants to school.   † among pupils in 90 areas only.

4. By 1915 routine periodic medical inspections had identified some important defects common to many school children (Table 1). That year, one third of the school population of 5·3 millions were examined and about 35 per cent of the children examined had a defect requiring treatment. Equally disturbing was the discovery that many of these defects were not being treated, partly on account of the poverty of the parents and partly because of inadequate treatment facilities.

5. It was intended that the rôle of the school medical service should be mainly preventive (2). But so many children required treatment for defects that hampered their progress in school that the authorities were obliged either to make arrangements for treatment with voluntary associations or local hospitals, or to make use of their power under the Education Act of 1907 to organise their own treatment service. In 1913 Exchequer Grants were made available for this purpose, and by 1915 450 clinics had been established; most of these were single school clinics, but some were part of a comprehensive system of clinics undertaking the treatment of all kinds of defects.

6. The outbreak of war in 1914 interrupted the development of the school medical service. The medical examination of close on two-and-a-half million men had resulted in the rejection of one-third as unfit for military service. This was a spur to renewed activity on the part of those who championed the service. Regulations under the Education Act, 1918, required authorities to arrange for the treatment of children attending public elementary schools and the medical inspection of children in the secondary schools; authorities were also allowed to provide treatment for these older pupils.

7. However, the expansion of the school medical service was again curtailed by the economic difficulties of the early 1920s and the continuing need for the service was closely questioned. But a marked improvement in the health of the nation's children had already been achieved, and this continued over the next decade.

Child Health in 1931

8. In the period 1906–1910 the mortality rate for infants was 118 per thousand live births. It fell to 76 per thousand for children aged 1–4, 3·7 per thousand for those aged 5–9 and 2·12 per thousand for older school children aged 10–14. Nevertheless, in 1905, 193,913 children died and 19,655 of them were children of school age.

9. By 1931 infant mortality was down to 66·4 per thousand live births, and the age specific death rate per thousand for children aged 5–14 stood at 1·9 for the period 1926–1930. In 1931, 71,990 infants and children 0–14 died, including 11,813 school children. Respiratory diseases claimed 14 per cent of these deaths, and accidents another 12 per cent, but specific infections, included in Table 2, were still responsible for nearly half the deaths.

10. Seven infections that together caused 90 per cent of the deaths from specific infectious diseases are listed in Table 3. The highest tolls among school children were due to tuberculosis (1,744 deaths) and diphtheria (1,339 deaths). Methods of protecting children against these infections were not

then available. The total number of children who survived after contracting a specific infection cannot be known, but it is certain that these diseases attacked several hundred thousands of children and left a trail of ill-health in very many of them.

11. Routine medical inspections revealed, however, that the school child was in a better physical state than in previous years and only one in five of those examined had a defect, excluding dental disease, requiring treatment (Table 1). In spite of increasing unemployment between 1920 and 1930, malnutrition reached a record low level of one per cent of pupils, although in areas in which there was exceptional social distress, for example, in the Rhondda Valley, malnutrition was five times more prevalent than in the country as a whole. Classical rickets was rarely seen, although special surveys showed that the condition was by no means uncommon in a mild form (3). Only 9·6 per cent of the children examined needed spectacles. Seven per cent of the children required treatment for a condition of the nose and throat, whilst less than one per cent had organic heart disease (Table 1).

12. The improvement in health was encouraging but still left much to be desired. For instance, contrary to common belief at the time, children living in rural areas were by no means healthier than urban children. Medical

Table 2

Main Causes and Numbers of Deaths in Children Under 15—1931 and 1963
(with percentages of total deaths in brackets)

Causes of Death	1931		1963	
	Age 1–4	Age 5–14	Age 1–4	Age 5–14
All causes	18,038	11,813	2,780	2,437
Tuberculosis (all forms)	1,600	1,744	22	10
	(9%)	(15%)	(1%)	(0·4%)
Other infectious diseases	5,524	2,708	175	82
	(30%)	(23%)	(6%)	(3·3%)
Respiratory diseases	6,704	1,680	676	242
	(37%)	(14%)	(24%)	(10%)
Malignant disease (including leukaemia)	Not recorded		307	449
			(11%)	(14%)
Congenital defects	207	86	249	233
	(1%)	(0·7%)	(9%)	(9%)
Accidental (including traffic accidents)	1,135	1,442	626	836
	(6%)	(12%)	(22%)	(34%)
Cardio-vascular diseases	103	1,138	17	33
Rheumatic fever	42	401	6	15
Digestive disease	649	111	94	16
Diabetes	11	99	8	21
Age specific death rate per 1,000 total population	7·53	1·80	0·86	0·38
School population in millions	—	5·57	—	7·09

Table 3

Number of Deaths and Notifications* of Illness for Certain Infectious Diseases in Children Aged 1–14: 1931 and 1963

INFECTIOUS DISEASE	1931 School Population 5,570,142		1963 School Population 7,095,106			
	Deaths		Deaths		Notifications	
	Age 1–4	Age 5–14	Age 1–4	Age 5–14	Age 1–4	Age 5–14
Tuberculosis (all forms)	1,600	1,744	22	10	753†	1,198
Diphtheria	1,025	1,339	1	1	6	26
Measles	2,210	321	59	29	304,867	266,370
Meningococcal Infection	272	206	51	6	363	113
Scarlet Fever	209	198	nil	1	5,304	11,404
Whooping Cough	1,292	88	6	1	17,070	12,750
Acute Poliomyelitis	27	21	nil	1	21	15

† Children under five.

inspection showed that as many of them were physically unfit as elsewhere in the country, while arrangements for their treatment were less effective and facilities for school meals were poorer. Even though severe malnutrition was seen in only one per cent of the nation's children who were examined, nutrition was sub-normal in another 15 per cent. A similar proportion of children were verminous on arrival at school. Dental disease was still rife, and of the children inspected 68 per cent were in need of treatment. The medical inspection of children attending secondary schools had confirmed that many defects detected at a younger age persisted through later school life and others appeared then for the first time. Nineteen per cent of school leavers were still in need of some kind of treatment, half of them because of defective vision.

13. It had also become clear that children would not benefit fully from the medical services unless their physical environment also improved. The basic requirements for healthy growth—suitable and adequate food, fresh air, appropriate amounts of exercise and rest, and a minimum standard of personal hygiene—were too often absent. The slums that were the children's homes and the streets that were their playgrounds, even the unhealthy conditions of many school premises, encouraged the diseases, accidents and ailments which it was the aim of the school medical service to eradicate or prevent. A considerable amount of school building and renovation had been carried out immediately before and after the war, but, by 1928, there still

*   Throughout this appendix 'notifications' means statutory notifications made to Medical Offices of Health.

remained in many areas "grave defects in the structure and sanitation of the schools, and in some a deplorable lack of the common necessities of decency and cleanliness . . ." (4).

14. The health of the children when first admitted to school, between the ages of three and six, was another matter for concern. Although the death rate for children aged one to four had been more than halved in 30 years, it was still 7·5 per 1,000 (Table 2). Three quarters of these deaths were due to infections, commonly of the respiratory tract.

15. The medical inspection of entrants had shown that they had a higher prevalence of disease and impaired physique than older school children. Reports of three special studies of young children (5) (6) (7), issued in 1931, revealed that 27 per cent of children aged two to six had physical or mental defects (excluding dental disease and visual defects). The nutrition of nearly two per cent was "seriously affected", 10 per cent had obvious nose and throat disease, and five per cent had clinical evidence of bronchitis; three per cent had signs of organic heart disease, while signs or symptoms of rheumatism were present in half that number. Many school entrants had discharging ears. Only a quarter of them had perfect teeth and many of the remainder were urgently in need of dental treatment. More than one third of those requiring medical treatment had not received it.

16. Maternity and Child Welfare Centres and day nurseries, and nursery schools and classes were the only form of public service, either municipal or voluntary, available to these children. But more than half of them had never attended a Welfare Clinic, those that had did not continue to attend for long enough, and there was a "deplorable absence of following up the sick child until it received treatment" (8).

17. There was also a growing realisation of the need for early medical assessment of school children. "The whole trend of modern medicine is the early detection of the beginnings of the disease and the fortifying of the normal person" (9). Principal school medical officers were exhorted to consider and investigate the possibility of making tests of visual acuity in children before they reached the age of eight. At that age all school children had a routine vision test, but examination of their hearing was omitted. Very few authorities had anything approaching an efficient system for discovering children's loss of hearing. But the gramophone audiometer had recently been invented and this had made possible the scientific assessment of the hearing of a complete school population.

Child Health Between 1931 and 1963

18. The first half of this period was overshadowed by six years of war. Between 1939 and 1945 the school medical service aimed to keep the bare essentials of the pre-war service functioning with the minimum of staff. It is remarkable that the nutritional level of the children was raised in spite of food rationing, and the prevalence of specific infectious diseases declined in spite of the mass evacuation of thousands of children from target areas.

Declining Mortality of School Children

19. Mortality rates in children from 1–14 have fallen sharply since 1931 (Table 2). The rate for children aged one to four in 1963 was 0·86 per 1,000

and twice that for school children (0·38 per 1,000). The improvement since 1931 has been more striking among the younger children. Although two million more children attended school in 1963 than in 1931, the number of school children who died in 1963 (2,347) was a fraction of the figure for 1931. The rate for schoolboys (0·44—1,528 deaths) was still appreciably higher than the rate for schoolgirls (0·28—909 deaths), largely because a greater number of boys die as a result of accidents and malignant conditions.

20. The chief reason for the fall in mortality has been the great reduction in deaths from infectious diseases. In 1963 fewer than 50 school children died from the seven infections specified in Table 3, compared with nearly 4,000 in 1931. Measles alone accounted for 29 of the deaths, three times as many as were due to the formerly dreaded tuberculosis. Even chicken-pox (five deaths) killed more pupils than diphtheria, scarlet fever, whooping cough and poliomyelitis together. Acute infective encephalitis and infective hepatitis, newly identified since 1931, caused the deaths of respectively 11 and nine school children.

The Control of Infectious Diseases

21. During the early years of the period 1931 to 1963, diphtheria was brought under control and the effects of other infections were appreciably mitigated. This was achieved largely by specific immunising programmes on a national scale and the control by drugs of certain infections and their complications.

22. The annual number of notifications of diphtheria in all ages in the first 40 years of the century was around 50,000 and it reached a peak of almost 65,000 in 1938. Immunisation against diphtheria became available a number of years before the 1939 war, but it was not until 1941 that a national scheme was adopted. So successful was it that by 1948 almost six million children under the age of 15 had been immunised and notifications for that year were a tenth of what they had been. Even so, 1,606 children of school age had diphtheria in 1948 and 69 of them died. In 1963, 26 school children were notified and only one died.

23. It is a matter for some concern that only 57 per cent of children under 15 were known, in 1963, to be adequately protected against diphtheria, compared with 63·5 per cent in 1948. It is still a deadly disease that showed a 3·8 per cent case fatality rate in 1963.

24. Almost 7,000 pupils were known to have been absent from school during 1930 because of tuberculosis; in about one-third of cases infection was due to bovine tubercle bacilli in milk (10). In the following year 1,744 pupils died from the disease and, in a special survey of children in ten areas, 13 per cent of children ascertained as physically handicapped were crippled by tuberculosis.

25. In 1950, in a nation-wide survey of 16,719 physically handicapped pupils (11), 1 per cent had tubercular disease. In 1963, 1,198 school children contracted tuberculosis; most of the cases were of a pulmonary type, and 10 children died. Twenty-two children aged one to four died, compared with 1,600 in 1931.

26. This change has resulted from better living conditions and an improved level of nutrition in children as well as from the specific effects of the modern treatment and prophylaxis. A marked reduction in surgical tuberculosis

followed the pasteurisation of milk. Bovine infection has virtually been eliminated now that tuberculosis has been eradicated from the nation's herds of cows.

27. Mass miniature radiography, the compulsory chest X-ray examination of students in colleges of education (introduced in 1952), the X-ray examination of all contacts of new cases and B.C.G. vaccination have all helped to reduce the incidence of tuberculosis in school children.

28. However, it is apparent from the tuberculin-testing of school entrants in many areas that between five and 10 per cent of children have the infection in pre-school years, commonly in a sub-clinical form. On the other hand, pre-vaccination testing has shown that by the age of 13, 15 per cent of children may be tuberculin positive. The number of notifications of tuberculosis among young people between 15 and 24 is still one-and-a-half times as great as the number among children up to the age of 14. The interim report (12) of the Medical Research Council's Tuberculosis Research Unit gave early confirmation of the substantial degree of protection that B.C.G. vaccination offered adolescents for at least the following two to three years. Yet, in spite of these facts, in 1962 the parents of one in four children did not accept the offer of B.C.G. vaccination, and over 10 per cent of the negative reactors to pre-vaccination testing were not subsequently vaccinated.

29. Scarlet fever is another disease whose power and prevalence have waned since the turn of the century. For example, in 1863 of every thousand children born in Liverpool 27 died of the infection before their fifth birthday (13). Even 15 years ago 45,482 school children in the country were infected, of whom seven died, but in 1963 there were no deaths among 11,406 pupils notified. The reduction of case fatality has been attributed to a number of general social and medical factors, but particularly to an alteration in the virulence of the organism concerned and the introduction of chemotherapy.

30. There has been a parallel decline in the incidence of rheumatic fever, the most dangerous after-effect of scarlet fever. In 1931 the incidence of rheumatism in school children was 2·2 per cent and 401 children died from rheumatic fever. Special rheumatism clinics had been established and some of these were diagnosing 100–150 new cases a year. Accommodation in special hospitals for prolonged convalescence had more than doubled. Since 1948 the condition has been seen much less. Rheumatic fever with joint involvement is now rare, as also are cases of severe rheumatic carditis and chorea. Units that have specialised in the treatment of rheumatism now cater for children with other defects, especially congenital heart conditions, and the number of children with rheumatic hearts in schools for delicate children and in those for the physically handicapped has shown a marked decline (Table 6). In 1963 15 school children died of rheumatic fever; for those that survived, there is now the chance of a functional cure as a result of the skill of the modern cardiac surgeon.

31. The mortality and prevalence of measles and whooping cough are still highest in children under five (Table 3), but many children contract these infections during their early primary school years. For example, in 1944, when the total number of notifications of whooping cough was 94,044, there were 31,930 cases among school children, and 30 of them died. Whooping

cough immunisation was not then nationally organised and the search for an effective therapeutic agent had not yet been successful. Nowadays, each year between 600 and 700 thousand children complete primary courses of vaccination against the disease. In 1963 the total notifications numbered 33,937; over one third of these were of children of school age, but only one pupil died.

32. Generally, there are epidemics of measles every two years, and the great majority of children have the infection as soon as they are exposed to it. In their study of children growing up in Newcastle-upon-Tyne, Miller and his co-workers (14) found it was the commonest of the infectious illnesses of the first five years, affecting two out of three children, that most of the remainder were infected during their first year at school (raising the proportion infected at six years to four out of five) and that it was spread mainly by pre-school children, with most of its transmission independent of school attendance. It is also the commonest specific infectious disease of childhood occurring in children of school age, although almost all episodes are confined to infant school children. 1963 was an epidemic year (Table 3) and over a quarter-of-a-million children of school age had the infection, and 29 died. The number of school children notified during epidemic years has tended to be greater than 20 years ago. In the non-epidemic year of 1962 notifications were as low as 85,167 and deaths were 15. A fatal outcome is more common among children already handicapped by chronic disability or recent acute illness (15).

33. Measles is still a major cause of ill-health in childhood, especially in young children. In a study of 53,008 cases in 1961, Miller (16) found seven per cent of the children had a potentially severe complication, commonly broncho-pneumonia or otitis media, and one per cent were admitted to hospital. A break-through against measles is now within sight, for a vaccine has been discovered, but it remains to be decided how best to apply vaccination on a national scale if this is found to be justified (17).

34. The most recently introduced national scheme of immunisation is vaccination against poliomyelitis. Only 15 cases occurred in children of school age in 1963, of whom one died; in 1931 there were 400 cases and 21 deaths.

Accidents and Malignant Diseases

35. Today one in every three deaths in school children is the result of an accident, although the total of accidental deaths is lower than it was in 1931 (Table 2). In 1963 836 school children were accidentally killed. More than 60 per cent of them (534) were killed on the roads, as a pedestrian in 280 cases and as a pedal cyclist in 117 cases. Of the remainder, 130 were drowned and 108 died from burns. The number of other children who were injured or maimed by accident is not known, but it may be judged from the fact that on the roads alone for every one that died 18 were seriously injured (9,865 in all). There is no evidence of an increased road accident rate during school holidays, but casualties are more frequent during the four summer months than in the preceeding and following periods of four months. Twice as many girls (72) as boys (36) were burned to death, while other accidental deaths in 1963 concerned four times as many boys as girls.

36. Fortunately, the actual number of children who die from all forms of accident is smaller each year (Table 2). On the other hand, cancerous conditions are disturbingly a main cause of death of young people. In 1963 these

diseases caused more deaths of school children than motor accidents; leukaemia was responsible for half of them.

37. In 1963 15 per cent of the children examined were found to have a defect requiring treatment, but this represented a 50 per cent improvement on the situation 60 years ago. Among school children as a whole dental and visual defects are still the commonest to be detected, orthopaedic defects are the next commonest, followed by diseases of the nose and throat, ears and skin. Table 4 shows how the prevalence of certain defects varies according to age. It also shows that, in general terms, half the defects (excluding those affecting the eyes and skin) found to require treatment in children on entry to school have been successfully dealt with by the time the children are ready to leave school.

Defects of Vision

38. Diminished visual acuity is almost always due to mild developmental deviations rather than physical ailments or ill-health. A study, carried out in 1960 (18), of defects of vision among 2,262 children in primary and secondary schools found that about half the defects were myopia or myopic astigmatism and about one-third were hypermetropia or hypermetropic astigmatism.

39. Cataract is the most frequent and myopia the second most frequent visual defect requiring ascertainment of a school child as partially sighted. The prevalence of partial sight is today 0·3 per 1,000 school children, compared with one per 1,000 in 1934 (19).

Table 4

Recorded Incidence of Certain Defects and Diseases Requiring Treatment per 1,000 Children Examined, in Age Groups—1963

Defect	Entrants Aged 5–7		Intermediate Ages		Leavers Aged 14–16	
Nose and Throat		26		12·7		5·6
Orthopaedic:						
Feet	14·2 }	21·4	13·8 }	21·1	6·5 }	12·6
Other	7·2		7·3		6·1	
Ears:						
Hearing	8·3		6·5		3·3	
Otitis media	4·2 }	15·0	2·5 }	11·7	2·0 }	7·9
Other	2·5		2·7		2·6	
Speech		8·5		4·8		1·1
Lungs		8·0		5·5		2·7
Developmental (physical)		4·6		5·6		2·3
Heart		2·4		1·9		1·7
Neurological (including epilepsy)		2·4		3·5		1·9
Postural		2·2		4·9		4·2
Others		17·8		26·2		13·5
SUB-TOTAL		108·3		97·9		52·5
Skin		9·9		15·5		17·3
Eyes:						
Vision	29·6 }	45·7	102·4 }	113·1	85·0 }	87,1
Squint	16·1		10·7		2·1	
ALL DEFECTS		163·9		226·5		156·9

C

40. Blindness in children has declined with the prevention of such infectious diseases as ophthalmia neonatorum, and nowadays it is mainly due to congenital hereditary and environmental abnormalities. Between 1948 and 1954 there was a temporary increase in blindness due to the occurrence of retrolental fibroplasia in premature infants.

Orthopaedic Defects

41. Excluding dental diseases, orthopaedic defects are the second commonest defects found in children between eight and 13, but the third commonest in entrants and leavers (Table 4).

42. The work of the orthopaedic clinics has changed greatly in recent years. One surgeon commented (20) that, before the last war, attention was given largely to discovering the more serious ailments and making sure that they were given adequate treatment; it was not unusual during a session to find cases of bone and joint tuberculosis that required in-patient treatment. Until only a few years ago poliomyelitis also accounted for many new cases at orthopaedic clinics each year. Since tuberculosis has come under better drug control and vaccination against poliomyelitis has been available to young children, the number of children crippled by these two diseases has fallen substantially. The great majority of the children attending school orthopaedic clinics today have only minor defects of posture and feet. For example, in Stoke-on-Trent during 1958 (21), over 1,000 children attended the authority's orthopaedic clinics, but 600 had flat feet and about 300 faulty posture. With the establishment of more chiropody and remedial exercise clinics (Table 14), it has become possible to concentrate on the prevention and early treatment of foot and postural defects. Special surveys have shown that about 30 per cent of the population have foot defects which originated in childhood. Hallux valgus and cramping of the toes are the two commonest conditions. Specific foot-fitting research has demonstrated a clear association between hallux valgus and the wearing of ill-fitting shoes (22) (23) (24). While minor degrees of this condition occur naturally in some children after the age of seven, more severe deformity, and in adult life the presence of bunions, commonly follow the persistent wearing of shoes of an unsuitable shape, type or fitting.

43. Rickets is often thought of as an evil of the past, but it still exists in special circumstances in this country. Among the Stoke-on-Trent children previously referred to, 20 were treated for the effects of rickets, and it was reported in 1963 (25) that 32 children with rickets were admitted to a Glasgow hospital during the four years 1959–1962, compared with only 12 during the prior six years. The virtual disappearance of nutritional rickets has given prominence to the problem of vitamin D resistant forms (26). A survey by the British Paediatric Association indicated that present measures are keeping these diseases under control in all ordinary circumstances.

44. Within the last 15 years there have been striking changes in the numbers of children attending special schools for physically handicapped pupils (Table 5) and in the nature of their chief disabilities.

Table 5

Physically Handicapped Children 1951 and 1963

	1951	1963
Children who were attending special schools for the physically handicapped:		
Day schools	3,499	4,848
Boarding schools	1,543	2,486
Hospital schools	6,123	1,231
Total	11,165	8,365
Incidence per 10,000 school population	19·4	11·7
Receiving home tuition	Not available	1,334
Otherwise placed or awaiting such placement	Not available	1,368
Total physically handicapped pupils in 1963:		11,067
and incidence per 10,000 school population:		15·6

45. Congenital and rheumatic heart disease and cerebral palsy were the pathological conditions most frequently present among 16,719 school children known to be physically handicapped in 1951. Nowadays, more than half the pupils in these schools have neurological disorders, including cerebral palsy.

46. Since 1951 the trend has been for children with quite seriously disabling conditions to be taught in an educational environment, with appropriate medical treatment, rather than in a strictly medical setting with educational help. In 1951 there were more of these children in hospitals than in special schools, but in 1963 there were six times as many in the special schools as in the hospitals (Table 5). There are now more places in special schools, but this reversal also reflects the diminished severity of many of the disorders as well as the increasing ability of special schools to manage the more severely handicapped children. Today some children with the great disability of congenital deformity or absence of limbs are attending ordinary schools. The modern trend is to keep handicapped children in ordinary schools so far as possible (see Chapter 21, Vol. 1).

Congenital Abnormalities

47. With declining child mortality and disability due to conditions arising after birth, the relative importance and incidence of congenital abnormalities have increased. In Great Britain today one-fifth of all stillbirths and one-fifth of infant deaths under one year are due to congenital malformation, as are one-seventh of the deaths of children aged one to four years and one-eleventh of the deaths of children of school age (Table 2). They are the one remaining major cause of serious physical disability in children, for not all the children afflicted die.

48. A national system of notification of congenital abnormalities as observed at birth was instituted in 1964, and during 1965 13,599 notifications were made, giving a reported incidence of 18·9 per 1,000 live and stillbirths (27) in England and Wales. This may well prove to be an underestimate. For instance, the incidence in Birmingham in 1950–52 (28) rose from 17·3 to 23·1 per 1,000 when the children were kept under observation until the age of five. The incidence appears, however, to vary from place to place (29). Stevenson has estimated (30) that about 50 per 1,000 liveborn infants have disabling congenital defects; 25 of them will have actual malformations, of which 15 will be recognisable at birth and the majority by five years.

49. Neurological abnormalities form the largest single group, and one of the most disabling of such disorders is spina bifida. As a result of early surgery and improved medical and nursing care, many more children with spina bifida are surviving. Nash (31) (32) gives the number of deaths in 1942 as 1,400 and in 1961 as 653. Special surveys in Sheffield and Liverpool (33) suggest that the prevalence of the condition may be as high as one per 1,000 children, five times that of blind children in the country. Experience in Sheffield indicates that two out of three children surviving with spina bifida may be mentally normal and that one in three may be able to attend ordinary schools. Children with spina bifida represented 8·5 per cent of pupils in special schools for the physically handicapped in 1963, but this percentage is rising sharply.

50. There have always been a number of children born each year with con- genital absence or deformity of one or more limbs. A Ministry of Health survey (34) showed that between January 1960 and August 1962 894 such babies were born in England, Scotland and Wales. This large number, over a relatively short period of time, was in part due to the toxic effect of the drug thalidomide taken by some of the mothers (certainly 237, possibly 349) during a phase of pregnancy which is critical for the normal development of limbs. Six hundred and ninety-five of these babies survived.

Respiratory Diseases

51. It has been said that respiratory diseases are the most important and the least understood of all diseases of early childhood. They are the chief single cause of death before the age of five, and half the children at risk in this age range attend their family practitioner every year because of them (35). In the five to 14 age group respiratory disease accounts for 10 per cent of deaths and causes one third of all children at risk to attend their family doctor annually; in some practices (36) (37) the number is nearer two thirds.

52. There is a low incidence of tonsillitis and pharyngitis in early life which may, however, partly be due to the inability of the young child to complain of sore throat. In contrast, there is a heavy concentration of the more serious respiratory illnesses, acute bronchitis and pneumonia, during the first three years of life. By the age of five respiratory illnesses begin to decrease and, as a child gets older, diseases of the lower respiratory tract (lungs and bronchi) become less frequent and cause less constitutional disturbance, whilst catarrhal symptoms associated with upper respiratory tract infections become more prominent.

53. Within this general epidemiological pattern a second peak incidence of both upper and lower respiratory infections has been noted as a child extends his social contacts. After two or three years of mixing in a group of children, during which there is an increase in the prevalence of these infections, there is a marked decline. The timing of the secondary wave may vary. Among the children in Newcastle-upon-Tyne (38) and Paddington, London (39), who start their social mixing long before school age, it occurs between two and four years. When appreciable group activities are postponed until school entry, as in Cleveland, Ohio (40) and Beckenham, Kent (41), it occurs between the ages of five to eight.

54. Among school entrants, diseases of the nose and throat are second only to diminished visual acuity among the conditions requiring treatment (excluding dental treatment). The removal by operation of tonsils and adenoids has for long been a feature in the treatment of these respiratory diseases. The frequency of operation has always shown wide geographical and social differences. The operation has been performed most often between the ages of four and six (42) (43), but a national survey among over a million school children in 1958 (44) showed that by the age of 10 to 12, 18·6 per cent of children had been operated on. In 1931, 11,023 school children underwent tonsillectomy. Recurrent tonsillitis is nowadays more often treated conservatively, and for the last few years 65,000 pupils in each year have had the operation.

55. As a result of better therapy and a waning of virulence of the haemolytic streptococcus, severe complications of acute throat infections occur less frequently. Over a ten year period reviewed by Fry (45) there were no cases of quinsy (peri-tonsillar spread of infection), no cases of rheumatic fever and only two cases of acute nephritis among 1,566 episodes of acute tonsillitis.

56. Throughout the school years a significant amount of lung disease is found in children examined at routine and special medical inspections (Table 6). It has not diminished since 1953: of every 1,000 children examined that year, 15·4 were found with lung disease and the figure was even higher (17·3) in 1963. In very many children these conditions were bronchitis and asthma: bronchiectasis is fast disappearing from among school children.

57. It may not be surprising that, in an average year, 57 per cent of children of primary school age may be examined by their family doctor for coughs, colds or catarrh. It may be less commonly realised that, among all children at risk over a period of three years, as many as 37 per cent may have an attack of bronchitis (46). In one practice survey among children under the age of ten (47), two out of every three episodes of respiratory illness occurred in school children. In spite of an appreciable reduction in the notifications of acute pneumonia, acute chest illnesses are seen by the general practitioner as frequently as ever (48) and in some practices rather more often than before (49), while the mortality from acute bronchitis and pneumonia was the same in 1963 as it was ten years ago.

Table 6

Respiratory Disease in Children, 1931–1963

	1931		1963	
	Under 5	5–14	Under 5	5–14
Notification of Acute Pneumonia	—	—	2,382	1,395
Total	Not available		3,777	
Deaths due to respiratory diseases:	0–4	5–14	0–4	5–14
Bronchitis	2,128	117	586	47
Pneumonia	12,634	1,111	3,323	151
Other respiratory diseases	8	8	265	44
	15,560	1,236	4,174	242
Totals	16,796		4,416	
Deaths due to Asthma	28	17	37 9	41

Respiratory diseases found at medical inspections to require:	Entrants	Intermediate Ages	Leavers	All ages at Special Examinations
Treatment	5,372	4,002	1,655	4,305
Total	15,334			
Observation	20,093	3,940	5,382	8,494
Total	46,403			
Prevalence per 1,000 children examined	17·3			

58. A sizeable proportion of children have more than one attack of bronchitis (11 per cent of Fry's series and 43 per cent of the Newcastle children), and in a minority of children chronic disabling respiratory disease develops. Home child care factors are important in determining the course of an acute respiratory illness, especially in infants, but in the few children who subsequently suffer recurrent attacks there seems to be an individual predisposition to pulmonary disease.

59. It has been estimated that about one in five children experience one or more attacks of wheezing associated with a respiratory infection (50). Most of these children cease to react in this way to these infections by the end of their primary school years, and only five to 10 per cent of them are diagnosed as asthmatics. But asthma can still kill children of school age (Table 6). Asthma and bronchitis have now become the commonest conditions for which children are admitted to special schools for delicate pupils.

Diseases of the Ear and Deafness

60. Infection of the middle ear (otitis media) is always a risk when a young child has an upper respiratory infection because of the anatomical relationship between the middle ear and the pharynx at this period of growth. As a result, the disease is predominantly one of young school children (Table 4). 75 per cent of all acute middle ear infections occur in children under the age of ten; the highest rates were among six year olds in the 1955 Medical Research Council Survey (51). In 1958, in Plymouth (52), among over 11,000 children examined most of those requiring treatment were school entrants. In a South London practice 42 per cent of the children at risk had sought treatment for at least one attack by the age of ten. Ear-ache and diminished hearing are more often symptoms than discharge from the ear (53).

61. The introduction of the National Health Service made it easier for children to receive prompt and effective initial treatment. Complications are now less common and the condition is less often seen in its chronic form. In the 1930s as many as one in ten children might be operated on for mastoiditis, but by 1955 the rate was one in a thousand. Nevertheless, there are still some parents who are ignorant of the significance of painless ear discharge, and in some parts of the country, especially in industrial areas, suppurative otitis media continues to be a considerable problem. The severity and outcome of the condition are related to social patterns of child care, though not the actual incidence of the disease (54) (55).

62. One of the serious dangers of continuing ear discharge is permanent damage to the middle ear and progressive diminution of hearing. In 1952 all nine year old children in Sheffield were tested with a gramophone audiometer (56), and 313 of the 6,346 children had impaired hearing; on medical examination 112 of these children were found to have otitis media. In another joint study by members of the staffs of the Department of Otalaryngology and Education of the Deaf in Manchester University (57), it was found that of 354 children examined, including 288 of school age, 52 (14 per cent) had conductive deafness due to chronic suppurative otitis media.

63. Great strides have been made since 1944 in the organisation of services for deaf and partially hearing children. These have developed as advances in

electronics have led to improved hearing aids and better instruments for use in testing and training children whose hearing is impaired.

64. The testing of pre-school children by health visitors and doctors instructed in the appropriate methods has helped in the earlier detection of significant hearing loss in very young children. The gramophone audiometer has been generally superseded by the pure tone audiometer for screening tests of hearing of school children, and all local education authorities had their own audiometers by 1963 or had alternative arrangements for the testing of pupils. Many new audiology units have been established (Table 13) for the full investigation of children who fail these screening tests, and it is now possible to ensure the optimum known conditions for enabling deaf and partially hearing children to learn to communicate.

65. Perceptive or nerve deafness is a much greater handicap than conductive deafness. It is more common than conductive deafness in young children and hence a serious impediment to the development of speech. It also causes greater educational problems, and many of the children in the special schools for deaf children suffer from perceptive deafness.

66. Since 1949 the number of deaf children in special schools has fallen from 5·7 to 4·7 per 10,000 school population. But during the same period the proportion of school children classified as partially hearing, and who needed special oral teaching methods, has increased from 1·3 to 3·0 per 10,000 school population (Table 7). This is, however, a measure of progress rather than the reverse. It results from fewer children passing through school with hearing loss undetected; it is also a consequence of the earlier recognition of hearing loss in young children, better diagnosis and treatment of some of the causes, early and more effective auditory training, and use of hearing aids, so that many children are now classified as partially hearing who, not so long ago, would have been regarded as deaf.

Table 7

Deaf and Partially Hearing Children in Special Schools and Special Classes in Ordinary Schools, 1930–1963

	Number of children and (in brackets) prevalence per 10,000 school population		
	1930	1948	1963
DEAF			
Special schools	3,245 (5·8)	3,065 (5·7)	3,356 (4·7)
PARTIALLY HEARING			
Special schools	706 (1·3)	751 (1·3)	2,104 (3·0)
Special classes	Nil	Nil	916 (1·3)
TOTAL	3,951 (7·1)	3,816 (7·0)	6,376 (9·0)

67. The cause of deafness is usually unknown in one third of deaf and partially hearing children; in about half of them pre-natal factors have been responsible, including genetic factors and virus infections during pregnancy (for example, rubella). Meningitis and other acute infections, and the toxic effects of the drugs used in their treatment, account for only one in six of all cases. Quite a number of children in ordinary schools have a slight loss of hearing which is, nevertheless, sufficient to retard their educational progress. In many of these children the defect can be remedied by medical or surgical treatment.

Speech Disorders

68. The number of children referred from routine medical inspections for speech therapy has steadily increased, from 1·5 per 1,000 children in 1938 to 4·9 in 1963. This does not mean that a defect of speech is more common than it was 25 years ago. The difference is due to more complete discovery of the children who need therapy and more therapists to provide it.

69. Morley's intensive study (58) of speech defects in children in Newcastle revealed a prevalence of three per cent among the city's 12,000 school children. A small number of these children had a severe speech disability resulting from aphasia, dysarthria or a functional disorder; the majority had a developmental speech defect, of the kind that most children have during the normal course of speech development. Treatment was required for this latter group of children (and many more were boys than girls) because the deviation from normal speech was either excessive or prolonged beyond the age of six or seven, by which time most children have acquired normal speech. Among all the children studied by Morley, 14 per cent had a serious defect of articulation at the age of five, but only three per cent had a defect persisting after the age of six and a half. Of the seven year olds in the N.C.D.S. sample (Appendix 8, Table 18), 14 per cent had speech not fully intelligible on testing by school doctors. An experienced school doctor and speech therapist, in a study based on personal interviews of 2,000 four year olds in Leicester (59), found that only 2·7 per cent had an obvious speech defect necessitating further investigation. Table 4 also shows how the need for speech therapy diminishes with age.

70. Since 1951 the number of speech therapy clinics has more than doubled and so has the number of children treated (Table 9). However, there is still an acute shortage of speech therapists, especially in the north of the country and in the Midlands. The equivalent of 220 full-time therapists were employed in the school health service in 1951 but, in spite of there being training places for about 80–100 therapists a year, in the 12 years up to 1963 the national increase has been only 172.

Diabetes

71. The discovery of insulin in 1922 transformed the prognosis of diabetes, which until then had been virtually hopeless (Table 8). In the absence of accurate information about its incidence in children in this country a survey was made in 1948 (60). It covered 21 counties and county boroughs with a total child population of 540,000 aged under four and 767,000 aged five to 15. Only three children under five years were found (one case in 180,000 children), but 180 children of school age (one case in 4,250). On this basis there must be at the present time at least 1,650 pupils with diabetes, but recent small surveys of school children in one English county have found an incidence more than twice as great.

Table 8

Deaths in Children due to Diabetes, 1921–1963

	Age 0–4	Age 5–14
1921	17	135
1931	13	137
1948	9	15
1963	10	13

Epilepsy

72. Epilepsy is a symptom rather than a disease in itself. The two most important reasons for the apparently unprovoked epileptic seizures of childhood are brain damage sustained by the child at an earlier age and a genetic predisposition. Age modifies fits, and the seizure patterns in children differ in certain respects from those in older people.

73. The earlier the age of onset of seizures the more likely they are to be major ones and the more likely they are to be the result of brain injury. Trauma in itself, however, seldom causes epilepsy: young children frequently survive quite severe brain injury without fits, and many children with cerebral palsy do not have seizures.

74. Some children, possibly two per cent of those under five (61), have a short major seizure at the onset of a rapidly rising temperature, but such febrile convulsions are extremely rare outside the age range of one to three years since this effect of fever is limited to immature brains. Only a few of these children have epilepsy in later childhood (62). Of 120 children in Cooper's series (63) who had their first fit before the age of two years, only six children were still having fits at the age of six and only three went on to have epilepsy in later childhood. Another 45 children had their first fit after the age of two, but for 28 of them this was their one and only fit. In a recent survey in three general practices (64), over 60 per cent of new cases of epilepsy were in children aged 14 or under.

75. Petit mal is classically an epilepsy of childhood, with a peak age of onset between five and ten. It is commonly stated that petit mal tends to cease as the child reaches adolescence, but this is by no means always so (65).

76. The prevalence of epilepsy in school children is probably in the region of eight per 1,000 (66) (67) (68) (69). There is no evidence of any real increase. The steadily mounting number of children known by school doctors to be under treatment for epilepsy (1,307 in 1947, but 3,251 in 1963) is but evidence of better understanding between parents, teachers and doctors and more complete ascertainment. Many of these children never have fits in school, and some parents are reticent about mentioning that their child has epilepsy when it does not apparently interfere with the child's work at school. Convulsions in childhood are still a serious matter and they may be fatal. In 1963 60 children of school age died as a result of epilepsy.

Diseases of the Skin

77. Skin diseases are the only ones that occur with increasing frequency as school children grow up (Table 4). They are also more prevalent. They were found in 17,728 children among approximately one and a half million children examined in 1947 and in 28,523 among two million examined in 1963. The detailed returns of treatment carried out in minor ailment clinics tell a similar story in that almost as many children were treated for "other skin conditions" in 1963 as were treated in 1947 (Table 9).

Table 9

Number of Children Known to Have Received Treatment for Certain Defects, 1947–1963

	1947	1951	1963
Skin diseases:			
Ringworm—scalp	5,454	2,365	137
body	6,654	4,847	612
Scabies	38,577	4,723	3,499
Impetigo	64,129	27,191	8,239
Sub-total	114,814	39,126	12,487
Other skin diseases	156,892	169,595	144,045
TOTAL	271,706	208,721	156,532
External eye diseases (excluding hospital treatment)	74,795	91,741	47,570
Miscellaneous conditions	773,060	938,628*	960,020**
TOTAL with MINOR AIL-MENTS	1,190,754	1,239,090	1,164,122
Diseases of ear, nose or throat (excluding operation)	107,539	108,703	52,779
Speech defects	Not available	28,132	61,279
Children treated under Child Guidance Arrangements	Not available	25,123	49,133

* Including children who received convalescent treatment.
** Including 416,904 children who received B.C.G. vaccination.

78. Against this may be put the remarkable change in the prevalence of the former "terrible trio"; scabies, ringworm and impetigo. In all, 114,814 children were treated for those conditions in 1947, but only 12,487 in 1963. These are family diseases or infestations usually associated with overcrowding, insanitary living conditions and with poor personal hygiene.

79. An increase in the incidence of scabies has always followed closely upon the outbreak of a major war, and the Second World War was no exception. By 1947 the amount of scabies in school children had returned to its pre-war level. Within another five years it was down to a little more than 3,000 cases a year, and there has been little change since then. Ringworm was at one time a major problem to be dealt with by the school medical service; the first school nurse in London was called the "Ringworm Nurse". Now ringworm of the scalp is hardly ever seen and ringworm of the body is mostly confined to the feet. Impetigo is diagnosed eight times less frequently than in former years.

80. No doubt general practitioners treat a certain number of school children for these three skin conditions, but the sharp decline in the numbers known to have actually received treatment indicates a satisfactory improvement in the personal hygiene of children.

81. Among entrants to school the frequency of skin diseases is almost half that among older children, and especially school leavers. It is not known how much this reflects the reduced prevalence of scabies, ringworm and impetigo; there is little detailed information about the ages of the children treated for these, although impetigo is particularly contagious among young children. There is also little information about the nature of the "other skin conditions" known to have been treated (Table 9), beyond the fact that the most frequently occurring conditions are acne, warts and psoriasis. Thus, it may well be that the majority of these other conditions occur predominantly in older children.

Gastro-intestinal Disorders

82. Dysentery has occurred with increasing frequency in recent years. Approximately 11,000 children, most of them of primary school age, have been notified annually since 1958, compared with a total among all ages of 800 per annum in 1931–33. These figures draw attention to the need for high standards of personal hygiene which are encouraged by the modernisation of school lavatory and sanitary facilities. The great increase in the number of school meals, which are prepared in bulk, has been a factor also in the increase in the number of outbreaks of food poisoning.

Absence from School

83. Absence from school is usually due to illness. In a study during 1947/48 (70), respiratory diseases accounted for most of this absence, but much of it was also due to intestinal infections. In the 1947/48 study 26 per cent of infant school children and approximately 15 per cent of junior and senior school pupils were absent for practically one sixth of their possible attendance during a year. In the recent study of absence among 3,273 primary school children taking part in the National Survey of Health and Development (71) 37,832 weeks of school were lost in the four years between the ages of six and a half and ten and a half. At this rate over seven million weeks of school would have been lost by junior school children during 1963. Frequent episodes of absence have been found to be educationally more harmful than an occasional long one (72).

Dental Health

84. The prevalence of dental disease today is little less than in 1907. When the first school dental clinic was opened that year in Cambridge the dentist found only one in ten of three to four year old children and none of the children over ten had sound teeth.

85. The Education Act of 1918 had made it a duty for authorities to provide dental treatment for children in public elementary schools, but progress in establishing this service was slow. In his report for 1929, the Chief Medical Officer to the Board of Education stated that existing services covered less than half the need. The chief reason was the shortage of dentists. By the end of 1937, however, every authority had established a scheme of dental inspection and treatment.

86. The lack of dental officers was again acute by the end of the war in 1945. Fortunately, the demand for their services was to some extent less because of an apparent reduction since 1942 in the incidence of dental caries among the children (73). In 1944 the number of children found at routine dental inspections to require treatment had fallen to one of the lowest figures recorded, 58 per cent; 20 per cent of five year old children had sound teeth (74).

87. The introduction of the National Health Service in 1946 did not affect the administrative structure under which the school dental service worked, although in practice its effect was serious because of the higher incomes obtainable by dentists under the new general dental service. It was another four years before the strength of the service approached the pre-war level and, in the meantime, there had been another change for the worse in the prevalence of dental caries.

88. This reverse coincided with the gradual removal of food rationing. It has been noted that the consumption per head of sugar has closely followed the fluctuations in the prevalence of dental caries (Table 11), and there is now strong evidence that sweet, sticky articles of food are a major cause of dental decay, although their effect can be modified considerably by other factors, including diets enriched by vitamin D.

89. Quinquennial surveys since 1948 (Table 10) have shown that only within the last five years has there been any appreciable change for the better among five year old pupils and a slowing down of the deterioration among twelve year olds. Some 60 per cent of children inspected were found to need treatment in 1963. The improvement in dental health in five and twelve year old children in 1963 has, however, occurred in spite of a stationary consumption of sugar, and there is good reason to believe that parents and children are now more aware of the benefits of dental fitness and are more ready to seek and accept conservative treatment of early caries. The amount of treatment provided by the School Dental and Joint Dental Services has greatly reduced the number of emergency treatments needed.

Table 10

Incidence of Dental Caries in School Children, 1948–1963

	Quinquennial Surveys				% Requiring Treatment at Routine Dental Inspections
	Age 5 years		Age 12 years		
	Average Number DMF* per Child	% children showing no DMF*	Average Number DMF* per Child	% children showing no DMF*	
1948	4·3	21·7	2·9	19·2	60%
1953	5·1	14·8	3·8	12·0	68%
1958	5·7	12·8	5·5	5·0	66%
1963	5·1	17·4	5·6	3·8	62%

* Number DMF = Number of teeth decayed, missing or filled.

Table 11

Sugar Consumption per Capita in the United Kingdom
("Group" Figures include Sugar, Glucose, Honey)

Year	Consumption in lbs.
Pre-war	108·7
1943	71·9
1948	88·3
1953	103·1
1958	121·9
1963	119·9

90. The fluoridation of water supplies has been shown (75) to reduce substantially the amount of dental caries in children's teeth, but it is clear that this must be considered a useful adjunct to traditional health education methods and effective treatment services. It is encouraging that by the end of 1963 the equivalent number of full-time dental officers had reached the highest recorded figure of 1,215, a ratio of one to 5,840 pupils. However, the distribution of school dentists is still uneven throughout the country.

Improvement in the Physical Health of School Children

91. This chronicle of diminishing ill health and diminishing prevalence of ailments and defects seen by school doctors has been matched by more positive evidence of an improvement in the health of school children, in the form of accelerated physical growth (see Table 12) and better general physical condition. The result of all these has been a noticeable increase in the liveliness and physical activity of contemporary primary school children.

Table 12

Average Height of London School Children, 1905–1959

Year	Average height (cms.)			
	Age 5·5 years		Age 13·5 years	
	Boys	Girls	Boys	Girls
1905–12	104·0	103·0	143·1	146·8
1938	109·1	108·4	149·0	152·2
1959	110·9	110·2	155·8	156·4

92. In the early days of the school medical service a general estimate of the quality of nutrition was recorded at medical inspections. As malnutrition in school children became rare a wider assessment of their general physical health was required. Their general physical condition is now classified as "satisfactory" or "unsatisfactory" (School Health Service and Handicapped Pupils Regulations, 1953). This has focused attention upon the need mainly to consider whether there is any way in which a particular child's physical condition and health can be improved as a result of treatment following investigation. The physical condition of more than 99 per cent of school children is nowadays assessed as satisfactory.

The School Meals Service

93. The School Meals Service has made an important contribution to this state of affairs. By 1930 almost half of the 317 authorities were providing school dinners and 320,000 pupils were eating them. Many of the authorities were also assisting in schemes for "milk clubs", enabling some 800,000 children to have one third of a pint of milk daily at school at the cost of one penny.

94. The Education Act, 1944, made it a duty of local education authorities to provide school meals and milk, and since 1946 every school child has been entitled to one third of a pint of milk per day, free of charge. Consequently, during the last 20 years or so the annual number of children having school dinners has increased to 3,849,401 (59 per cent of the children at school), of whom 4·4 per cent were given free dinners. And in 1963 over 90 per cent of primary school pupils and two thirds of secondary school children—5,855,307 pupils in all—had milk each day.

95. These figures relate the increasing use made of the school meals service. They do not reveal the change that has taken place in the character of the service during the last 25 years. "Feeding centres" have given place to school canteens, many schools have their own kitchens and dining facilities, and school dinners have become an integral part of the school day. There is, however, some difference of opinion about the social value of the school meal in present conditions and about the desirability of the younger children staying at school for their dinner.

96. So much has the nutritional state of school children improved that it is now the fat boy who is beginning to present more of a problem to school doctors than the under-nourished child. For example, in 1960, in Wakefield (76), as many as 2·7 per cent of children examined by school doctors were considered obese. The increase in obesity prompted the thought in 1962 that school children were getting too much to eat as a result of school meals. However, the Standing Committee on Medical and Nutritional Aspects of Food Policy of the Ministry of Health knew of no evidence from the health records of the school population or elsewhere that this was so, save perhaps in a minority of cases of obesity—a conclusion supported by a Departmental Working Party in their Report on the Nutritional Standard of the School Dinner and the Type of Meal (77). Even in these cases such factors as the diet at home and the sweets consumed, in relation to the amount of exercise taken, were considered to be causally more important than the lunches and milk taken at school. School milk and meals provide those who take them with a substantial part of their daily food requirements. One third of a pint of milk gives a primary school child about 10 per cent of the recommended daily allowance of protein, 23 per cent of his calcium and six per cent of his calories (78). A school dinner is intended to have an energy value of 650–1,000 calories, according to the age of the child, and supplies on average 20 gms. (0·44 lbs.) of animal protein and 25–30 gms. (0·55 lbs.–0·66 lbs.) of fat; thus, it provides about a third of the total protein and calories required daily. There are still some children whose nutrition is likely to be dependent on food provided in school. Recent studies (79 and 80) have indicated that the diets that are least likely to be adequate are those of families with three or more children. Between 1950 and 1959 these and other groups showed appre-

ciable reductions in protein intake associated with increased consumption of sugar and fat, both largely conveyors of "empty calories". About 1959 there was, however, some improvement both absolutely and in terms of the percentage of calories derived from protein. While no one would advocate a return to the austerities of rationing, it had at least the virtue that money spent on food was spent in ways that were nutritionally above reproach.

Infestation of Children

97. In 1963 1·7 per cent of children (187,354) inspected by the school nurses were found to be verminous, compared with 14 per cent in 1931, and in many schools all the children have remained clean for year after year. Infestation has always been more prevalent in poor areas with bad social conditions and in densely populated industrial and urban areas than in rural parts of the country. It is essentially a social and family problem that has become less prominent as living standards have improved and as cleanliness has been promoted by health education in schools. The greater efficiency of the newer insecticides has also helped.

Summary

98. In this Section, against the background of the early development of the School Health Service since its origin as a School Medical Service, we have traced the changing physical health of children of primary school age. In particular, we have noted:

(a) the remarkable reduction in mortality due to the effective control of certain infectious diseases;

(b) that far fewer children are physically handicapped by crippling disorders resulting from some of these infections, though congenital disorders are now more apparent;

(c) that accidents and cancerous conditions are now the chief remaining causes of death of school children;

(d) a striking improvement in their cleanliness and health, as shown by their better physical condition, their rate of growth and the reduction, in general, of the number of defects found at school medical inspections and the amount of treatment they require;

(e) the continuation of respiratory disease as a major cause of illness and its relationship to ear disease leading to loss or impairment of hearing;

(f) the amount of absence from school due to respiratory disease and gastro-intestinal disorder.

PART II

DEVELOPMENT OF THE SCHOOL HEALTH SERVICES SINCE 1944

99. It is a truism that poor health in children may limit the influence of education. School doctors have always preferred to interpret health in terms of function; their concern has been less with diseases of childhood than that children should be functioning normally and living and growing in harmony with their environment. The responsibility of the school health service has therefore been to see that school children are not denied through unrecognised or untreated ill health the opportunity to make the most of what school can offer. This is as clearly the rôle of the service today as it was nearly 60 years ago.

100. By the Education Act of 1944, the School Medical Service was renamed the School Health Service. The present era of the service may be said to date from this Act and the National Health Service Act of 1946.

101. Under the Education Act parents of children in maintained schools were obliged to submit their children to medical inspection. The same facilities for free medical treatment that were already available to primary school children were extended to secondary school children.

102. The principal effect for children of the National Health Service Act was to entitle them to free medical attention from the general practitioner and hospital specialist services. Circular 179, issued by the Ministry of Education in 1948, broadly indicated the principles that were to underly the co-ordination of the health and education services. In fact, local authorities now largely rely upon the National Health Service in discharging their obligations under the Education Act to provide free medical treatment for school children, and Regional Hospital Boards usually provide the services of specialists attending local education authority clinics. The clinics chiefly affected have been opthalmic, orthopaedic and ear, nose and throat clinics; while these have continued mostly to be held in local authority premises they have some-times been transferred to hospital premises. The provision of spectacles for school children has become the responsibility of the Supplementary Ophthal-mic Service. Hearing aids are also provided by the National Health Service, except when an authority considers it is in the interests of a pupil to be supplied with a special aid.

103. The full range and number of clinical services provided by local educa-tion authorities and the special clinics arranged for school children in hospital out-patient departments are detailed in Table 13. There are now about 2,700 school clinic premises. Some of these are large with a wide range of services, others are small branch clinics with limited services. Some of the clinics are in fine modern buildings, but many are in adapted premises, quite a number of which are out of date, inconvenient for children and parents and poorly equipped and furnished.

104. The need for a special health service for children at school was admirably expressed in Circular 576, issued in 1907. It defined the purpose of school medical inspection as "the medical examination and supervision not only of children known, or suspected, to be weakly or ailing, but of all children in the elementary schools, with a view to adapting and modifying the system of

education to the needs and capacities of the child, securing the early detection of unsuspected defects, checking incipient maladies at their onset, and furnishing the facts which will guide education authorities in relation to physical and mental development during school life". That there is still need for such a service today was emphasised in the Report (81), published in 1962, of a Joint Medical Committee appointed by the profession to review the work of the health services in Britain.

105. The function of the school health service is primarily preventive and advisory. It was not, and is not, a rival to the domiciliary and hospital medical services. This fact has sometimes been overlooked since, in its early years, the service was preoccupied with arranging treatment that was otherwise unavailable for the unfit child. However, the introduction of the National Health Service in 1948 enabled the school health service for the first time to concentrate on its primary objectives.

106. Table 13 also shows something of the changing nature of the work of the school health service since 1938. There are more audiology, speech therapy, child guidance, chiropody and remedial exercise clinics. There are fewer heart and rheumatism clinics. There are more clinics for asthmatic children and newly established clinics for enuretic children. Minor ailment clinics are more numerous, but the work is rather different. Practically all the skin diseases and external eye conditions referred to in Table 9 were treated in minor ailment clinics, and the "Miscellaneous Conditions" in 1963 included many special examinations of children as well as B.C.G. vaccinations given to 10 to 14 year old children.

Table 13
Type and Number of Clinic Services, 1938–1963

Type of Clinic	1938	1963	
	L.E.A.	L.E.A.	Under arrangements with Hospital authorities
Minor ailments	1,279	1,895	1
Speech therapy	—	1,330	9
*Immunisation and vaccination	—	1,122	92
Ophthalmology	774	562	420
Orthoptic	—	64	73
Orthopaedic	382	222	231
Physiotherapy	—	436	52
Remedial exercises	121	188	29
Artificial light	—	220	24
Chiropody	—	180	2
Ear, nose and throat	57	118	110
Audiology	—	299	23
Asthma	—	45	12
Heart and rheumatism	—	26	25
Enuresis	—	75	4
Ringworm	31	—	—
Specialist paediatric	—	41	62
Miscellaneous	—	24	6
Child Guidance	—	325	—

* A local health authority activity.

107. These changes have occurred in response to a change in need, and the change in need is but a reflection of continuing improvement in the physical health of school children during this period. This has now reached the point when the school health service can justifiably pay much more attention to the mental health of school children. One of the most important changes in clinic services has been the establishment by local education authorities of child guidance clinics.

108. The detection and treatment of illness neither modify nor reduce their causes when these are environmental. In the last 30 years much has been done to combat and reduce the social evils which contribute to physical ill-health, but much remains to be done. Poverty has not been eliminated. Not all parents can afford sufficient clothes for their children and, in Bootle, for example, in 1958 (82), free clothing and footwear were provided for 898 school children. In 1963 well over a quarter of a million needy children were given free meals in school, 4·4 per cent of those taking school meals compared with 3·7 per cent five years previously. The living conditions of many children have improved beyond recognition—but not of all of them. Of the 5,000 children followed over 18 years since 1946, in the National Survey of Health and Development (83), more than 12 per cent always shared their bed with another child or adult, seven per cent lived throughout in homes that lacked several essential amenities and two per cent in homes that during the whole of their childhood were consistently over-crowded and lacked amenities. In terms of total population, two per cent of children under the age of 15 amount to nearly a quarter of a million children.

109. The rôle of the school in minimising the effects of such standards of living is made immeasurably more difficult when the hygienic arrangements in the school are themselves sub-standard. In 1962, amongst other deficiencies, one primary school in four lacked a hot water supply and two out of three had only outdoor sanitation (84).

110. Attention is now turning to the effects of the environment on mental health. Health is viewed in terms of mental harmony as well as adequate growth in size and stature and freedom from physical illness. It is acknowledged that the origin of some of the recurrent disorders in childhood lies in emotional disturbance rather than physical pathology. Such diverse conditions as alimentary infections, accidents, retarded growth and enuresis have been grouped together as diseases of the social environment (85), while others may form part of a family pattern of reaction to environmental stress (86). The physical health of a child is only a part of his total adjustment and adaptation to continually changing circumstances.

Mental Health

111. The prevalence of mental disturbance in school children is not accurately known; statistical assessment bristles with difficulties, from an elementary lack of definition of terms to the elusiveness of standardised measurements of personality and behaviour. When the Underwood Committee (87) commissioned enquiries in three areas in 1955, the estimates ranged from 0·3 per cent to nine per cent. On the other hand, surveys of the problem in rural and urban areas (88) (89) have put the figure as high as 20 to 30 per cent. In an

educational and medical survey of children aged nine to ten, 6·3 per cent were found to be in need of psychiatric advice or treatment, including 2·2 per cent with severe disorders (90).

112. The increasing number of children attending child guidance clinics each year is a corollary to the increased number of such clinics available. Demand continually outstrips provision and the service is still at the stage when provision actually stimulates demand. In fact, this has been the case since the pioneer East London Clinic was opened in 1926. There are now 325 clinics, but the opening of additional clinics has been mainly limited by insufficient staff (Table 14).

113. Although some authorities have excellent child guidance clinic services many have none at all: others operate well below the optimum strength. In most areas the Regional Hospital Boards have provided at least a minimal child psychiatric service based on a hospital. As the usual arrangement in local authority child guidance clinics is for the Boards to provide the services of the psychiatrist, the governing factor remains the lack of these consultants. However, 40 local authorities are still without the services of a psychologist. On the whole, the South East and East are better provided for than the rest of the country.

Table 14

Local Authority Child Guidance Clinic Staff (in full-time equivalents)

Year	Psychiatrists	Educational Psychologists	Psychiatric Social Workers
1965	101	151	140
Underwood Committee Objective 1965	140	280	420

114. The local authority clinic has always worked closely with the school, the educational psychologists sharing their time between the clinic and the school psychological service. By contrast, the hospital services have commonly had closer links with the general practitioners than with the schools, their interests being more towards family psychiatry. Whatever may be the cause of a child's disturbance, the influence of the school is considerable in either aggravating or modifying it. It is rare for children with recognised and significant behaviour disorders or physical symptoms of a predominantly neurotic nature not to experience difficulties in school, though their problems may be due as much to parental mis-management as to their own constitution. The educational element is thus an exceedingly important one when dealing with maladjustment in school children. Nevertheless, a disturbed child comes so often from a disturbed family that local authority clinics are adopting increasingly a family approach to diagnosis and therapy, while maintaining their relationships with the schools.

115. Although the child guidance service aims, through family and child therapy, to prevent mental ill health in adolescence and adult life, it is not a truly preventive service because it is used only when a parent or teacher

needs guidance in the care of a child already showing disturbance. True preventive work is a matter of education and involves teachers, school doctors and health visitors. The special contribution of the child guidance service might be in educating such staff in mental health, about which there is a large reservoir of knowledge which is hardly used in this direction (91). In-service training for school doctors and health visitors, as already provided by some clinics, is necessary if their rôle is to change from passive observer to that of effective worker at an appropriate level.

116. The rate at which this change is proceeding is still slow. The chief reasons are the shortage of clinic staff and pressure of other work upon an understaffed school health service. But there is a problem here which has yet to be resolved by many authorities: the selection of priorities and the organisation of the work accordingly.

The Work of the School Health Service

117. The work of the school health service today consists principally of:
   (a) the medical examination of children in school;
   (b) the detection, assessment and medical supervision of handicapped pupils in school;
   (c) the advising of teachers and counselling of parents;
   (d) health education;
   (e) the control of infectious diseases in school.

Routine Medical Inspections of School Children

118. The classical measure for detecting diseases and defects in school children has been the periodic medical inspection. Circular 576 of 1907 proposed four inspections during the school years: on entry, at the ages of seven and 11, and just before the child left school. The recommended conduct of the medical inspections would not be considered sufficient today: each inspection was to occupy on the average not more than a few minutes, and it was expected that as a rule the child would only need to have its clothes loosened or be partially undressed; children under six were not to have their vision tested, and tests of hearing were only to be given in a general way. However, the point was made even then that "needless medical examination of healthy children should, for obvious reasons, be avoided" (92). Nevertheless, this remained the pattern for many years, and about two million children were examined annually. Almost the only new development was an increasing use of special examinations in clinics, which allowed a more thorough investigation of a child than was possible in a school inspection.

119. Thirty years ago some experienced school doctors began to question the need for so many medical inspections. It seemed to them that as a method of detecting the earliest deviations from normal health it could be improved upon and that the superficial examination of hundreds of thousands of normal healthy children was an uneconomical use of limited staff. Part of the case for modifying routine inspections still rests upon the need to concentrate the special skills of overtaxed staff on the children whose problems most require them. For this reason the revised School Health Service and Handicapped Pupils Regulations of 1953 and 1959 allowed authorities to experiment with less than three inspections during the school years.

Staffing

120. The number of doctors employed in the school health service at various times since 1931 is given below (Table 15). In 1931 there was the equivalent of one whole-time school doctor for every 7,500 pupils. The situation is little better today. It is estimated that for the school health service to perform its proper function one school doctor is required for every 6,000 school children, a ratio only once achieved after the war.

121. The ratio of school nurses to school children is only a little more encouraging (Table 16). Although lower than desirable, it has remained stationary for ten years. Following the report of the Working Party on Health Visiting, published in September 1953 (93), an increasing number of school nurses have been qualified health visitors working in both local health and local education authority services. But relatively unskilled duties at clinics and medical inspections, and the simple screening tests for hearing and vision, are now being delegated to suitably instructed but unqualified assistant staff, leaving the school health visitor free to concentrate on the work for which she is especially trained.

122. There are no ancillary workers able to relieve the school doctor of his routine work. With so much to be done in the field of mental health and in the comprehensive assessment of handicapped children, and with so few doctors to do it, there must perforce be some modification of the routine work which does not give full value in terms of the time and skill employed. In the social circumstances prevailing in Britain today it is even more difficult than it was 30 years ago to justify the routine examination every year of one and a quarter million healthy children in the intermediate and school-leaving age groups.

Table 15

Number of Doctors in the School Health Service, 1931–1963

YEAR	Whole-time in school health service	Whole-time school health and local health authority services		General Practitioners and married women doctors		TOTAL		Ratio: Full-time School Doctor to pupils
No.	No.	No.	Equiv. number working whole-time in school health service	No.	Equiv. number working whole-time in school health service	No.	Equiv. number working whole-time in school health service	
1931	277	676	—	386	—	—	662	1:7,500
1938	266	903	—	349	—	—	728	1:6,220
1947	276	1,332	—	—	—	—	832	1:6,000
1955	198	1,477	654	578	95	2,253	947	1:7,040
1963	146	1,752	733	623	103	2,521	982	1:7,250

Table 16

Number of School Nurses, 1931–1963

	Number of nursing staff	Number of nursing staff who were trained health visitors	Resultant equivalent number of whole-time school nurses	Ratio: nurse to pupils
1931	3,230	—	2,235	1:2,300
1938	3,313	—	2,398	1:2,000
1947	3,857	—	2,297	1:2,200
1955	6,276	4,561	2,548	1:2,600
1963	7,449	5,749	2,667	1:2,600

123. This view is now receiving much wider support. By 1964 more than a third of education authorities had adopted, to some extent if not throughout their school health service, a system of selecting for special examination only those children whose symptoms or behaviour indicate the need for it. A variety of selection methods has now been used (94) (95), including question-naires completed by parents and teachers, special requests to teachers and health visitors for the names of children known to be causing concern either at home or in school, and perusal of attendance registers. Children whose names are brought forward, and returned questionnaires, are usually dis-cussed by the school doctor, head.teacher and health visitor before parents are advised of the need for selected children to be examined. These will include children noted at the school entry examination to need following closely. A number of authorities also invite parents to request a medical examination if they wish this for any reason.

124. In areas where a selective procedure has been carefully thought out, and introduced with conviction, it has been welcomed by parents, teachers and doctors. It has brought parents and teachers into closer touch with the school health service and focused attention on the children causing concern. It has commonly been accompanied by more frequent visits of the school doctor and, almost without exception, teachers prefer these new arrangements.

125. At present, selective medical inspections are used mainly as an alter-native to the routine examination of all children either at the age of eight or between 10 and 12, or both. Only rarely have they replaced the routine examination of school leavers.

126. There is universal agreement on the value of a routine examination on entry to school. Almost invariably mothers accompany their children on this occasion. A full medical history may be obtained from the parent which adds to the value of the physical examination. Many thousands of young children already show by the age of five the marks of their brush with disease and a faulty environment. The interview of the child and his mother is also an occasion for a functional assessment of the growth and development of the child involving all aspects of his behaviour, and it should be as much con-cerned with a search for reasons why the child might have learning difficulties as for the presence of physical defects.

127. A comprehensive assessment and examination such as this cannot be done in a few minutes. All too often 20 to 25 children are called for in a session of two and a half to three hours, although the recommendation has been made (96) that 10–12 are quite sufficient for a session of this length. An appointment system is necessary when children are examined at intervals of 15 minutes. It has the added advantage of making some privacy possible for the interview with the parent, especially in those schools that do not have a Medical Inspection room. The Standards for School Premises Regulations 1959 do not require that a school has a Medical Inspection room, but that a room should always be immediately available for inspection and treatment of pupils. The introduction of selective medical examinations and the more frequent and regular attendance of the doctor at the school make it even more necessary that each school should have suitable accommodation available for such purposes as visits by the school doctor, nurse and the educational psychologist. As it is, there are many schools where inspections are done under deplorable conditions.

The Assessment of Handicapped Pupils

128. The importance of the early discovery of children with mental or physical handicaps was fully realised 20 years ago. The Education Act, 1944, requires parents to submit their children for medical examination at any time after the age of two, if it is considered necessary by an education authority in order to carry out its duty of ascertaining which children may need special educational treatment as handicapped pupils. Many children with severe disabilities are referred by health visitors for assessment before they reach school age and even before the age of two. This may occur as a result of home visits by the health visitor or by the increasingly popular measure of the maintenance, by health departments, of a risk register of children in whom certain physical disorders are more likely to be present than is normally the case. Special diagnostic clinics and facilities for parent guidance have been arranged for children with certain specific disabilities, such as deafness, blindness and cerebral palsy. Ascertainment and counselling are a major responsibility of the school health service as well as the maternity and child welfare services (see Volume 1, Chapter 21).

Health Education

129. In the primary school, health education is mainly concerned with elementary personal hygiene and the prevention of infection, with dental hygiene, first aid and the prevention of accidents especially in the home. It is carried out mostly by teachers and health visitors. When school doctors are involved they usually undertake more responsibility for it in secondary schools, in the form of counselling of adolescents. Earlier maturity means that teachers in primary schools may expect more questions than formerly on the facts of reproduction and on personal relationships.

Control of Infectious Diseases in School

130. The decline in severity and frequency of most of the specific infections, especially those of childhood, has led to a change in the pattern of infections seen in school children. Infective hepatitis, chicken pox and rubella remain

and are not yet controlled by immunisation. The suppression of one disease has given added importance to the remaining ones. Less clearly defined infectious illnesses are now receiving more attention. Some of these are due to viruses which have been identified. The causes of others, such as winter vomiting, are not yet known.

131. The control of infectious diseases rests with the local authority, but principal school medical officers also have responsibilities to the education authorities. School doctors play a valuable rôle in supervising the hygiene of school premises, especially of canteens. They also assist in immunisation procedures. Vigilance is still needed against the specific infectious diseases described in Part I of this Appendix. Defence against several of these infections lies in the maintenance of an adequate state of immunity among a sufficiently high proportion of the susceptible population and a high level of personal hygiene among the children.

Future Trends Affecting Primary School Children

132. For children below secondary school age it is recognised that trends in the school health service must be towards the earlier identification of the less severe disabilities in children which impede their growth and development and their education in school; an extension of screening procedures towards this end; a wider functional assessment of children around the age of entry to school; a more complete assessment of handicapped pupils with regard as much for residual abilities as for primary disabilities; and a greater participation by school doctors and nurses in the management of incipient maladjustment and in its prevention. Mental health depends to a large extent upon personal relationships. In the necessary expansion of advisory work with teachers and parents of all children, but especially of handicapped children, attention needs to be given to difficulties in emotional development that are associated with personal relations as well as to guidance regarding any specific disability when one is present.

133. The prime responsibility for health, and specifically sex education, rests with teachers, although school doctors may well have a part to play in advisory work. While at present children of secondary school age receive advice on personal relationships more than younger children, any raising of the age of transfer from primary to secondary education would mean that opportunities for dealing with this topic would have to be provided in the primary school. All schools need a policy for ensuring that children know the facts of reproduction before they leave the primary school and that questions including those touching on personal relationships are answered when they are raised. Health education to curb the increase in smoking amongst school children must begin in the primary school. Already 10 per cent of 12 year old schoolboys smoke regularly and some do so from as early as nine or ten (97). The recent anti-smoking campaigns, however, are having some effect. In recent years there has been some cessation of smoking in adolescents (98).

134. It is highly significant for the school health service that both research and clinical experience have clearly shown that the disturbance in mental health of many of the school children attending child guidance clinics (even of the 10 per cent of them who are of secondary school age) has its origin

during the formative years before the child first goes to school. The amount of intellectual under-functioning in children is not known, but it is thought to be considerable. That failure in children, either social or educational, may profoundly affect their personality and produce behaviour disorders, is better understood than how much failure is due to preceding personality disturbance. This subject has recently been discussed in detail (99) in an international report which adds to the weight of evidence that experiences during the early years of childhood, especially the amount and quality of environmental stimulation, are as important for the realisation of full intellectual potential in later years as they are for emotional stability (see Volume 1, Chapter 2).

135. These facts point the way to measures which have as yet hardly begun to be exploited for the prevention and the early detection of emotional and intellectual handicaps. Regular developmental examinations during infancy and pre-school years can form the basis of an observation register, which can include the names of children still requiring to be kept under observation following examination because they have been in a peri-natal "at risk" group. Such registration might take account of the emotional vulnerability of some children during biologically sensitive periods of growth and development (100), and of others who are likely to have emotional difficulties as a result of bereavement or belonging to broken homes or families with special problems.

136. The observation register has the advantage over the risk register of being compiled from a screening procedure applied to a total age group. Screening tests are not intended to be diagnostic tests identifying those requiring treatment. Their value lies in their ability to detect potential disabilities at the pre-symptomatic stage for subsequent observation. For example, hearing loss of many children will fail to be revealed by reliance on a risk register alone. There is need for both kinds of approach to the discovery of children with handicaps.

137. The health services already use a number of screening procedures, including vision and hearing (audiometric) tests, measurements of height and weight, tuberculin tests and health questionnaires. These are not, however, being applied extensively. For instance, vision tests are not always given annually and hearing tests never are. The exact value of some of these screening tests, and how often they should be given, have yet to be determined in terms of their rôle in the continuing supervision of children in primary schools after an initial comprehensive assessment. It is necessary to search for and try out new screening devices. Limited experience with group tests of attainment or non-verbal intelligence justifies their wider application as a screening test for mental retardation and maladjustment. The results of current research (for example, The Isle of Wight Educational and Medical Survey, and The National Child Development Study) may result in the use of standardised questionnaires to identify children with learning and emotional difficulties in school.

138. It is disquieting that an assessment of developmental need for the child is so seldom made before he goes to school, except when he has a severe mental or physical disability. Thus, it is not possible to attempt any modifi-

cation of the educational environment until after the child has been exposed to the risk of failure at an exceedingly vulnerable stage of life. Accordingly, a few authorities have experimented with a scheme for the routine medical inspection of children during the term before they are due to enter school (101).

139. Children's needs cannot be met by a single examination, whether this is just before or just after the child's admission to school. They result from insufficient demand for medical supervision during the years between infancy and school attendance, unless a severe mental or physical disorder in the child forces the parents to seek help. Parents are not obliged to use the services provided, in contrast to the situation when the child reaches school age. Supervision ought to be a continuing process, irrespective of the child's age. This means that the health service for children should be co-ordinated.

The Need for a Co-ordinated Health Service for Children

140. In the local authority services the duties of assistant medical officers and school medical officers already overlap. There is, indeed, almost complete integration of local health and school health services in all but a handful of authorities. The health visitors are school nurses in most authorities, and approximately 1,750 of the 1,900 doctors employed by local authorities work in both services. In addition, in many areas there is zoning of staff providing these services, so that a doctor will work with one or more health visitors and school nurses in a team based on a clinic and the surrounding infant and junior schools. He can then examine at medical inspections in schools the children he has seen as infants in the child welfare centres.

141. Close co-operation has not yet been achieved between general practitioners and the school health service. Yet in some parts of the country general practitioners are already working in the school health service on a sessional basis, and in one county this has been the pattern for nearly 60 years. In their report published in 1963 (102), The Gillie Committee observed that ". . . as family doctors find an increasing interest in the environmental circumstances of their patients, they will participate more fully in clinic work among those groups which are the responsibility of the health departments". In 1963 there were 623 general practitioners and married women doctors engaged in school health service work, compared with 386 in 1931 (Table 15). This trend is welcomed in turn by the school health service. It is the most natural and satisfactory method of ensuring continuity of medical care and treatment for individual children throughout their childhood, and it increases the understanding and co-operation between doctors in the family practitioner and school health services. Furthermore, it allows for the fullest and most economical use of the time and particular skills of the doctors working full-time in the local authority child health services.

142. The work of these services involves knowledge of child development and psychology, of health and disease in children, of child neurology and child psychiatry. It is therefore regrettable that this work is not more widely recognised as a branch of paediatrics. If it were, much closer links might be forged between the school health service and the hospital paediatric service.

143. One of the recommendations of the Platt Committee (103) was that a new type of post of unlimited tenure—that of Medical Assistant—should be

established in the hospital staffing structure. When this recommendation is implemented the further suggestion of the Platt Committee that some medical assistants might also be employed part-time in the local authority health services could well be adopted by the joint appointment of a doctor as medical assistant to a paediatric department in a hospital and as a senior medical officer in the school health service.

144. Herein lies a great opportunity to bring paediatric departments of hospitals into active collaboration with general practitioners and school doctors. In this way it would be possible to provide a continuous and co-ordinated health service for children, from infancy, through school years and adolescence.

145. The better physical health enjoyed by the majority of school children, and the facilities for treatment now provided by the National Health Service, mean that the School Health Service should take up the challenge presented by the various environmental factors that today disturb the development and learning of the children. The Service should be able to attend to its primary function of providing an advisory service for children, their parents and teachers within the school setting.

LIST OF REFERENCES

(1) *Report of Inter-Departmental Committee on Physical Deterioration.* 1904. H.M.S.O.
(2) Circulars 576, 582 and 596. Board of Education. 1907. H.M.S.O.
(3) *Report of Chief Medical Officer, Board of Education.* 1931. H.M.S.O.
(4) *Report of Chief Medical Officer, Board of Education.* 1928. H.M.S.O.
(5) See (3) above.
(6) See (4) above.
(7) *On the State of Public Health.* 1931. H.M.S.O.
(8) See (3) above.
(9) See (3) above.
(10) Memorandum on Bovine Tuberculosis in Man. *Ministry of Health Report on Public Health and Medical Subjects.* No. 63. 1931. H.M.S.O.
(11) *Report of the Chief Medical Officer, Ministry of Education.* 1952/53. H.M.S.O.
(12) Report of the Medical Research Council's Tuberculosis Research Unit. 1956. *Brit. Med. J.* i. 413.
(13) *Monthly Bulletin of the Ministry of Health.* Vol. 14. July 1955. London: H.M.S.O.
(14) MILLER, F. J. et al. 1960. *Growing up in Newcastle-upon-Tyne.* Oxford University Press.
(15) *Monthly Bulletin of the Ministry of Health.* 1963, 22, 167.
(16) MILLER, D. L. 1964. *Brit. Med. J.*, 11th July.
(17) Report of Measles Vaccine Committee, Medical Research Council. 1965. *Brit. Med. J.* 1, 817.
(18) *Report of Chief Medical Officer, Ministry of Education.* 1960/61. H.M.S.O.
(19) *Report of the Committee of Enquiry into Problems Relating to Partially Sighted Children.* 1934. H.M.S.O.
(20) *Report of the Chief Medical Officer, Ministry of Education.* 1954/55. H.M.S.O.
(21) *Report of the Principal School Medical Officer, Stoke-on-Trent.* 1958.
(22) SHINE, I. B. 1965. *Brit. Med. J.* 1, 1,648.
(23) CRAIGMILE, D. A. 1953. *Brit. Med. J.* 2, 749.
(24) BURRY, H. S. *Brit. Boot, Shoe and Allied Trades Rs. Ass. Report.* No. 147.
(25) ARNEIL, G. C. and CROSBIE, J. C. 1963. *Lancet,* 31st August.
(26) STEWART, W. K. et al. 1964. *Lancet,* 28th March.
(27) *Report of Chief Medical Officer, Ministry of Health.* 1965.
(28) McKEOWN, T. and RECORD, R. G. 1960. In: Ciba Foundation Symposium on Congenital Malformations. London.
(29) LAURENCE, M. 1965. *Arch. Dis. Childh.* 40, 451.
(30) STEVENSON, A. C. 1961. *British Medical Bulletin* 17, No. 3.
(31) NASH, E. 1956. *Brit. J. of Urology.* Vol. XXVIII, No. 4. December.
(32) NASH, E. 1963. *Proc. Roy. Soc. Med.* Vol. 56, No. 6. June.
(33) *Report of the Chief Medical Officer, Department of Education and Science.* 1962/63. H.M.S.O.
(34) Deformities Caused by Thalidomide. *Ministry of Health Report on Public Health and Medical Subjects.* No. 112. 1964. H.M.S.O.

(35) FRY, J. 1958. Morbidity Statistics in General Practice, Vol. I. *Medical and Population Subjects*. No. 14. H.M.S.O.

(36) COOK, N. 1954. *Medical World*. **80**, 539.

(37) FRY, J. 1961. *The Catarrhal Child*. London. Butterworth.

(38) See (14) above.

(39) CRUICKSHANK, R. 1958. *Brit. Med. J*. **1**, 119.

(40) DINGLE, J. *et al*. 1953. *Ann. Intern. Med*. **43**, 518.

(41) See (37) above.

(42) GLEN, J. A. 1938. *Proc. Soc. Med*. **31**, 1,219.

(43) CARNE, S. 1956. *Brit. Med. J*. **2**, 19.

(44) *Report of the Chief Medical Officer, Ministry of Education*. 1958/59. H.M.S.O.

(45) See (37) above.

(46) See (36) above.

(47) See (37) above.

(48) See (37) above.

(49) BEAUCHAMP, A. 1958. *Brit. Med. J*. **2**, 234.

(50) See (37) above.

(51) Report of Medical Research Council's Working Party for Research in General Practice: Acute Otitis Media in General Practice. *Lancet*, 1957. **2**, 510.

(52) *Report of Principal School Medical Officer, Plymouth*. 1958.

(53) See (51) above.

(54) DOUGLAS, J. W. B. and BLOMFIELD, J. M. 1958. *Children Under Five*. London: Allen and Unwin.

(55) FRY, J. 1960. Morbidity Statistics in General Practice, Vol. II. *Medical and Population Subjects*. No. 14. London: H.M.S.O.

(56) *Report of the Principal School Medical Officer, Sheffield*. 1952.

(57) See (44) above.

(58) MORELY, M. E. 1957. *The Development and Disorder of Speech in Childhood*. Edinburgh and London: Livingstone.

(59) *Report of Chief Medical Officer, Department of Education and Science*. 1964/65. H.M.S.O.

(60) *Report of Chief Medical Officer, Ministry of Education*. 1948/49. H.M.S.O.

(61) LENNOX, W. G. 1960. *Epilepsy and Related Disorders*. Churchill, Vol. 1.

(62) MELIN, K. A. 1954. *Mschr. Kinderheilk*. **102**, 62.

(63) COOPER, J. E. 1965. *Brit. Med. J*. **1**, 1,020.

(64) POND, D. A. *et al*. 1960. Psychiat. Neurol. *Neurochir*. (Amst.) **63**, 217.

(65) LEES, F. and LIVERSEDGE, L. A. 1962. *Lancet*, **ii**, 797.

(66) See (63) above.

(67) See (64) above.

(68) Report by Research Committee of the College of General Practitioners. 1960. *Brit. Med. J*. **2**, 416.

(69) RUTTER, M. *et al*. 1966. Severe Reading Retardation: its relationship to maladjustment, epilepsy and neurological disorders (Isle of Wight Survey). Paper read at Association for Special Education International Conference, London.

(70) BRANSBY, E. R. 1951. *Med. Off*. 1st and 8th December.

(71) DOUGLAS, J. W. B. 1964. Papers prepared at the request of the Central Advisory Council.

(72) See (71) above.

(73) *Report of the Principal School Medical Officer, London County Council.* 1943.

(74) *Report of the Chief Medical Officer, Ministry of Education.* 1939–45, H.M.S.O.

(75) *The Conduct of Fluoridation Studies in the United Kingdom and the Results Achieved After Five Years.* 1962. H.M.S.O.

(76) *Report of the Principal School Medical Officer, Wakefield.* 1960.

(77) *The Nutritional Standard of the School Dinner. Report of the Departmental Working Party.* 1965. H.M.S.O.

(78) *British Medical Association Committee on Nutrition.* 1950. H.M.S.O.

(79) *The National Food Surveys,* 1950–1963.

(80) ABEL-SMITH, B. and TOWNSEND, P. *The Poor and the Poorest.* Occasional Papers on Social Administration. No. 17. Bell. 1965. LAMBERT, R. "Nutrition in Britain', 1950–1960. Occasional Papers. No. 6.

(81) *A Review of the Medical Services in Great Britain.* 1962. *Social Assay.* (Porritt Committee Report).

(82) *Report of the Principal School Medical Officer, Bootle.* 1958.

(83) DOUGLAS, J. W. B. 1964. *Public Health.* 4, 196.

(84) *The School Building Survey.* 1962. H.M.S.O.

(85) See (14) above.

(86) APLEY, J. 1963. *Lancet,* 12th January.

(87) *Report of the Committee on Maladjusted Children.* 1955. London: H.M.S.O.

(88) *Report of the Principal School Medical Officer, Somerset.* 1952.

(89) *Report of the Principal School Medical Officer, Birmingham.* 1953.

(90) RUTTER, M. and GRAHAM, P. 1966. *Proc. Roy. Soc. Med.* Vol. 59, No. 4. 382–387 (Section of Psychiatry, 30–35).

(91) *Expert Committee on Mental Health: Tech. Rep. Ser.* No. 9 1950, No. 31 1951 and No. 73 1953. W.H.O.: Geneva.

(92) See (2) above.

(93) *An Enquiry into Health Visiting.* 1956. H.M S.O.

(94) See (18) above.

(95) See (33) above.

(96) See (18) above.

(97) See (33) above.

(98) *Report of Chief Medical Officer to Ministry of Health.* 1965. Page 90.

(99) WALL, W. D., SCHONELL, F. J. and OLSEN, W. C. 1962. *Failure in School.* UNESCO.

(100) *Chronicle of World Health Organisation.* September 1955.

(101) MELLOR, M. R., JONES, J. T. and PEARSON, R. C. M. 1964. *Med. Off.* 20th November.

(102) The Field Work of the Family Doctor. *Report of the Sub-Committee of the Standing Medical Advisory Committee, Ministry of Health.* 1963. H.M.S.O.

(103) *Report of the Joint Working Party on the Medical Staffing Structure in the Hospital Service.* 1961. H.M.S.O.

1964 National Survey of Parental Attitudes and Circumstances Related to School and Pupils Characteristics

The Survey consists of:

FOREWORD

APPENDIX 3: Survey Among Parents of Primary School Children by Roma Morton-Williams, The Government Social Survey.

APPENDIX 4: The Regression Analyses of the National Survey by G. F. Peaker.

APPENDIX 5: The National Survey: Data from the Schools.

APPENDIX 6: The National Survey: Infant Starters.

APPENDIX 7: Standards of Reading of Eleven-Year-Olds, 1948–1964, by G. F. Peaker.

Annexes to the National Survey.

1964 NATIONAL SURVEY OF PARENTAL ATTITUDES AND CIRCUMSTANCES RELATED TO SCHOOL AND PUPIL CHARACTERISTICS

FOREWORD

1. The surveys carried out for the last three reports of the Central Advisory Council, and other research, have provided powerful evidence linking home circumstances with the pupils' educational progress. Parental occupation was used as the measure of home circumstances because it was easily ascertainable. But it was clear that the association between the occupation of the parent and the achievement in school of the child must arise, at any rate in part, from the association between occupations and attitudes, and that the variation in attitudes might account for a good deal more of the variation in achievement. It therefore seemed desirable to attempt to estimate the influence of occupation, irrespective of attitudes, and of attitudes, irrespective of occupation.

2. With this end in view, the Council requested the Department of Education and Science to commission the Social Survey Division of the Central Office of Information to interview the parents of a representative national sample of primary school children. The children were at three stages of the primary school, "top" infant, first year junior and fourth year junior. The evidence obtained by the Social Survey from the parents covered aspects both of parental circumstances and parental attitudes. The opportunity was also taken to find out the attitude of parents on aspects of school organisation on which the Council might wish to recommend changes and to obtain information about facilities for children in the neighbourhood of the schools. The report of the Social Survey follows this foreword and is Appendix 3.

3. The regression analyses, reported in Appendix 4, formed the core of the enquiry. The evidence from the Social Survey interviews with parents has been linked with evidence from the schools that the children attended. The evidence from the schools included the children's performance in tests of reading comprehension (and also a picture test for the youngest) their rank order and many facts about their teachers and the school organisation. Estimates are made of the part played by parental attitudes, independently of their circumstances, and by circumstances, independently of attitudes, in influencing the children's achievement in school. There are also estimates of the effect of variation in schools and teaching, independently of parental attitudes and circumstances.

4. Just as parental attitudes were tested on matters not immediately relevant to the main enquiry, so information was obtained from the schools, which was too detailed—or otherwise unsuitable—for use in the regression analyses but was of general interest for the Council's Report. Evidence about the staffing and organisation of schools and the attendance of teachers at short courses is reported and tabulated in Appendix 5 (Data from the Schools).

D   91

5. Information was needed by the Council about the way in which beginners at school settled down. In infant schools and junior mixed and infant schools included in the main sample, a sample was drawn of those children who began school in the summer term of 1964. Their parents were interviewed by the Social Survey interviewers and information was obtained from the schools. The results of this enquiry are reported in Appendix 6.

6. One of the criterion variables used for the analyses relating to fourth-year juniors was the Watts-Vernon Reading Test. This is the test that was used for the Department's chain of surveys of reading ability from 1948–1956. It was therefore possible to compare the reading standards of children of 11 in 1964 with those of earlier years since 1948. The results are reported in Appendix 7.

7. To supplement the work on the representative sample a special group of schools was selected by H.M. Inspectorate. This group consisted of a dozen schools where the relation with parents was thought to be particularly good. The Social Survey interviewed the parents of a sample of children from these schools. The evidence from the interviews vindicated the judgements that led to the selection of the schools, but there was no perceptible difference between the average of the children's achievements and the general average.

8. The Social Survey also interviewed the parents of a sample of children drawn from the Manchester schools on which Professor Wiseman reports in Appendix 9.

9. Finally, they interviewed the parents of selected children from four schools, two streamed and two unstreamed, in the sample of schools from which the evidence was drawn for the interim report on streaming contained in Appendix 11 by the N.F.E.R.

10. We believe that the data collected from the Survey may be of use to research workers and are glad to hear that the Department of Education and Science have made arrangements for the material to be preserved in a form accessible to research workers and institutions.

11. It remains only to thank all those who collaborated in the National Survey: the parents who were ready to give their time to the interviews; the teachers who returned much information about school organisation and about individual pupils and, at short notice, tested the pupils in the sample; and, finally, the research workers and those who helped them. We are much indebted to the Social Survey, to their interviewers and their staff and, in particular, to Miss R. Morton-Williams who describes the results of the interviews with parents. We also wish to thank Mrs. E. Fisher who gave much help with the Survey. The main plan of the enquiry was designed by Mr. G. F. Peaker, C.B.E., and Miss S. M. C. Duncan, H.M.I. To Mr. Peaker, also, we owe the design and analysis of the standards of reading survey.

APPENDIX 3

SURVEY AMONG PARENTS OF PRIMARY SCHOOL CHILDREN

by Roma Morton-Williams
Government Social Survey

CONTENTS

LIST OF TABLES

I. THE METHOD OF ENQUIRY

1.1. This survey among parents of primary school children investigated their attitudes towards the education their children were receiving and their relationships with the teaching staff of their children's schools. It also obtained information about the interest displayed by parents in their children's education and the hopes they had for their future. In addition, facts were collected about the socio-economic status of the families, the physical conditions of the homes, and neighbourhood amenities of these primary school children.

(a) The sampling procedure

1.2. The sampling procedure had two stages. First a random sample was taken from all types of maintained primary schools in England. Then a random selection was made of children within these schools. The parents of these children formed the interview sample. Full details of the method of sampling are given in Annex I.

1.3. A total of 173 schools were selected in the first stage of the sampling. In the second stage within these schools four, eight or 12 children, depending on the size of the school, were selected from each of the three forms. In the junior with infants schools all three forms would of course be present. In the juniors only two forms, top and bottom juniors and in the infants only the top infants form. This procedure gave an interview sample of 3,237 parents. The interview achievement was as follows—

	Number	Percentage
Interviews achieved	3,092	95
Refused	87	3
Non-contacts	58	2
Total interview sample	3,237	100

1.4. It should be borne in mind that the sample for this survey is of children in primary schools whose parents were interviewed. Parents' chances of coming into the sample were related to the number of children they had in primary schools. This inquiry is, however, about the backgrounds of children at school and it seemed right, therefore, that the sampling design should give each child an equal probability of being selected, regardless of the size of family to which he or she belonged.

1.5. At the time of the survey the majority of the top juniors were 11, the bottom juniors eight and the top infants seven years old.

(b) The interviewing

1.6. The structured questionnaire shown in Annex III was used for the interviewing. There were two stages in its development, the first was to establish what were the most important topics to cover in the interview, the second was to test the actual wording of questions and the structure of the questionnaire. In the first stage advice was sought from heads and other teachers in primary schools, care committee workers and child welfare officers. Discussions were held with four groups of parents and freely-ranging individual interviews with approximately fifty parents. In the second stage the questionnaire was tried out in interviews with approximately 200 parents. Thanks are very much due here to H.M.I. Miss S. M. C. Duncan of the Central Advisory Council for Education who contributed greatly to the planning of the survey and the design of the questionnaire.

1.7. The parents were interviewed in their homes by Social Survey interviewers. The interviews took place over the period June 22 to July 31 1964. Within the time available for the inquiry it would not have been feasible to interview both parents separately and as it is extremely difficult to carry out an interview with two people together it was decided as far as possible to see the mother of the selected child alone. The mother was chosen rather than the father because it was thought that in the majority of families she would be the parent having most direct contact with the school, at least when the child was at the primary stage. The interviews were in fact carried out with the following members of the children's families:

Table 1

Member of child's family interviewed, analysed by form

Member of family interviewed	Form			
	Top juniors	Bottom juniors	Top infants	Total
Child's natural mother	95	96	97	96
Foster or adopted mother	2	2	1	1
Child's natural father	3	2	1	2
Other person	1	—	1	1
Number interviewed (100%)	(1,023)	(1,016)	(1,053)	(3,092)

1.8. The interviewers were instructed to make every effort to interview the mother on her own. In 43 per cent of the interviews however at least one other person was present for part or the whole of the interview. Table 2 shows the relationship to the selected child of other people present.

Table 2

Other people present during interview, analysed by form

Other people present during whole or part of interview	Form			
	Top juniors	Bottom juniors	Top infants	Total
Informant interviewed alone	59	56	55	57
Selected child present	11	12	12	12
Child's father present	17	18	16	17
Other children present	20	23	23	22
Other adults present	7	6	6	7
*Total percentage	114	115	112	115
Number interviewed	(1,023)	(1,016)	(1,053)	(3,092)

*In some instances more than one other person was present.

1.9. The parents showed great interest in the inquiry and were very ready to give their views. Over half of the interviews lasted for an hour or longer. (See Table 3).

Table 3

Length of time interviews lasted, analysed by form

Length of time interviews lasted	Form			
	Top juniors	Bottom juniors	Top infants	Total
Less than ¾ of an hour	7	6	7	6
¾ but less than 1 hour	33	36	38	36
1 but less than 1¼ hours	35	35	32	34
1¼ but less than 1½ hours	17	14	16	16
1½ hours or longer	8	8	7	8
Number interviewed (100%)	(1,023)	(1,016)	(1,053)	(3,092)

II. THE HOME BACKGROUNDS OF PRIMARY SCHOOL CHILDREN

2.1. Parents' attitudes towards the education their children are receiving, the sort of relationship they have with the schools and the rôle they expect or wish the schools to take in the upbringing of their children are of course likely to be related to characteristics of the parents themselves, such as their own level of education, and also to home circumstances such as the financial position of the family. In presenting the results of this survey, therefore, we look first at the home backgrounds of these children in primary schools and then at parental attitudes towards their schooling.

2.2. In this section we examine the socio-economic status of these families; the incidence of working mothers and broken homes and how these are related to economic circumstances; parents' education and reading habits; the amount of educational support which appeared to be given to the children in their homes, parents' aspirations for their children and, finally, the physical conditions and amenities of the homes and the neighbourhoods.

(a) Social class and economic position of the families

(i) Social class

2.3. The social class grouping used in this inquiry was the Registrar General's classification based on occupations, 1960 edition. The social class of the family was determined by the occupation of the father or father substitute. If there was no father or father substitute in the household at the time of the interview then the classification was based on the occupation of the father or father substitute when last in the household. If the father was unemployed, then his last occupation was used. Only one per cent of the families could not be classified by paternal occupation. The proportions of the sample falling into each social class group are given overleaf. For comparison is given the social class distribution of married males aged 20 to 64 in the general population at the time of the 1961 census.

	Fathers of primary school children	Married males aged 20 to 64, general population
	%	%
I Professional	4	4
II Managerial, includes self-employed	14	16
III Non-manual, clerical, includes minor supervisory grades	11 ⎫ 59	51
III Skilled manual, includes foreman	48 ⎭	[ ]
IV Semi-skilled	16	19
V Unskilled, labourers	6	7
Unclassified	1	3
Number interviewed (100%)	(3,092)	

2.4. The social class distributions of these families in the 10 Department of Education Divisions in England are given in Table 4. It must be remembered that the distribution within a Division is based on a relatively small sample of schools. The Divisions with the lowest proportion of these families in social classes I and II were the North West, North Midlands, Midlands and Northern. The highest proportion were in the South Western. The Metropolitan division had the highest proportion of fathers who were in unskilled and labouring occupations. The highest proportion of skilled manual workers were in the North Midland and the lowest in the South Eastern.

Table 4

Social class distribution of family by Department of Education Division

Department of Education Division	SOCIAL CLASS							Total Number (100%)
	I Profes-sional	II Mana-gerial	III Non-Manual	III Skilled Manual	IV Semi-Skilled	V Un-Skilled	Un-Clas-sified	
Northern	% 4	11	13	49	14	9	1	(257)
E. and W. Riding	% 4	17	9	51	11	6	2	(393)
N. West	% 2	9	10	54	17	8	1	(510)
N. Midland	% 2	12	10	56	16	3	1	(250)
Midland	% 3	11	10	49	23	4	2	(260)
Eastern	% 3	18	8	47	19	5	2	(374)
Metropolitan	% 5	15	13	42	11	11	2	(255)
S. Western	% 5	19	16	44	12	3	1	(177)
S. Eastern	% 4	15	13	41	18	8	1	(343)
Southern	% 6	15	11	44	20	3	1	(273)
Total	% 4	14	11	48	16	6	1	(3,092)

2.5. In Table 5 is shown the social class distribution in this sample of the children in the three different primary school forms included in the inquiry. In examining social class and form differences in later tables it should be borne in mind that, in this sample, social class I parents had a slightly lower proportion of children in the top juniors and social class V a slightly higher proportion than did the other social class groups.

Table 5

Child's form by social class

Child's form	SOCIAL CLASS							
	I Profes- sional	II Manag- erial	III Non- Manual	III Skilled Manual	IV Semi- Skilled	V Un- Skilled	Un- Clas- sified	Total
	%	%	%	%	%	%	%	%
Top Juniors	26	33	34	33	33	40	35	33
Bottom Juniors	38	32	33	33	33	28	28	33
Top Infants	36	35	33	34	34	32	37	34
Total number (100%)	(110)	(430)	(338)	(1,486)	(499)	(189)	(40)	(3,092)

(ii) *Income level*

2.6. Two measures of the economic levels of the families were obtained. Firstly the net income of the father, or if there was no father, of the head of the household. This was his income for the week before the interview, including any overtime or bonuses and excluding income tax, national insurance deductions and family allowances. The second measure was the total of the net incomes of the father plus the mother, if she had any, plus family allowances and any other income apart from money received from other working members of the family living in the household. The latter contributions were not included because it was not possible to determine what proportion went to raising the standard of living of the family in general and what was spent directly on the person who had made the contribution.

2.7. Table 6 shows the relationship between social class and income of father. For each social class group the salary band in which the median salary falls is marked with dotted lines. Although there was a wide spread of incomes within each social class group, there was nevertheless a marked difference between the general income levels of the different groups with the median salaries of those in social classes IV and V being in the £12 10s. 0d. to £15 per week range, and of the class I's being £25 to £30.

Table 6

Net income of father, analysed by social class

Net income of father	SOCIAL CLASS							
	I Profes- sional	II Manag- erial	III Non- Manual	III Skilled Manual	IV Semi- Skilled	V Un- Skilled	Un- Clas- sified	Total
	% out of total giving father's income							
Up to £7 10s. 0d. p.w.	—	1	1	2	3	3	43	2
Over £7 10s. 0d. to £10	—	1	2	3	9	14	23	5
Over £10 to £12 10s. 0d.	1	3	6	13	24	28	20	13
Over £12 10s. 0d. to £15	2	7	17	28	33	34	9	24
Over £15 to £20	7	28	43	37	22	19	3	31
Over £20 to £25	21	28	21	12	7	1	3	14
Over £25 to £30	22	14	8	3	1	—	—	5
Over £30	47	17	2	2	1	1	—	5
Total giving income (100%)	(107)	(391)	(322)	(1,380)	(469)	(184)	(35)	(2,888)
% of interviews in which income information was refused or not known by inform ant	3	9	5	7	6	3	13	6

2.8. The way in which the father's or head of the household's income is aug-mented by the addition of income from the mother, family allowances, and income from other sources is shown below and in more detail in Table 7. It must be remembered that any contributions made by members of the family other than father and mother are not included. In subsection (c) of this section it is shown that in almost half the families with incomes of £10 or less per week there was either no father or no mother in the household.

	Net income of father or head of household	Total net income of father plus mother plus family allowances
Up to £7 10s. 0d. p.w. ..	2	1
Over £7 10s. 0d. to £10 ..	5	3
Over £10 to £12 10s. 0d. ..	13	8
Over £12 10s. 0d. to £15 ..	24	18
Over £15 to £20	31	34
Over £20 to £25	14	21
Over £25 to £30	5	9
Over £30	5	7

Table 7

Income of father only, by income of father plus mother plus family allowances

Net income of father or head of household	Total net income of father plus mother plus family allowances								Total Number giving income (100%)
	Up to £7.10	Over £7.10 –£10	Over £10– £12.10	Over £12.10 –£15	Over £15– £20	Over £20– £25	Over £25– £30	Over £30	
	%	%	%	%	%	%	%	%	
Up to £7.10	37	34	15	10	2	2	—	—	(62)
Over £7.10 to £10	—	39	42	10	7	1	1	—	(134)
Over £10 to £12.10	—	—	40	42	16	1	1	—	(386)
Over £12.10 to £15	—	—	—	50	43	6	1	—	(685)
Over £15 to £20	—	—	—	—	67	28	4	—	(908)
Over £20 to £25	—	—	—	—	—	74	20	5	(401)
Over £25 to £30	—	—	—	—	—	—	79	20	(157)
Over £30	—	—	—	—	—	—	—	100	(155)
Total giving income	1	3	8	18	34	21	9	7	(2,888)

2.9. The numbers of dependent children in families of different income level are given in Table 8. Dependent children were taken as those who had not started school or were still in full-time education. Apart from the lowest incomes, that is £10 per week or less, there was very little difference between family income level and the numbers of dependent children in the family. At the £10 a week or lower income level there were slightly lower proportions of families with more than three dependent children but even so 18 per cent of these families had four or more children not yet at school or still in full-time education. (This latter finding is based on only 103 cases however.)

Table 8

Total net income of father and mother and number of dependent children

Income of father and mother plus family allowances	Number of dependent children							Total (100%)
	1	2	3	4	5	6	7 or more	
	%	%	%	%	%	%	%	
Up to £10 p.w.	32	28	22	9	7	1	1	(103)
Over £10 to £12.10	19	33	19	14	10	3	3	(219)
Over £12.10 to £15	19	33	24	11	8	3	3	(526)
Over £15 to £20	18	36	24	12	6	2	3	(976)
Over £20 to £25	13	39	26	12	4	3	2	(593)
Over £25 to £30	20	35	22	11	8	2	3	(253)
Over £30	10	39	28	14	5	2	1	(214)
Not given	21	40	18	10	8	3	—	(208)
Total	17	36	24	12	6	2	2	(3,092)

(iii) *Working mothers*

2.10. At the time of the survey over one-third of the mothers were in paid employment. For 17 per cent their work took them away from home for five hours or more a day. The lowest proportion of working mothers was in social class I, 18 per cent. In the other social class groups the proportions of working mothers varied only from 34 per cent in class II to 44 per cent in class IV. (See Table 9.) Thirty-four per cent of mothers of children in the top infants forms worked, the proportion rose to 46 per cent with children in the top juniors.

Table 9

Mothers' hours of work, analysed by social class

Mothers' hours of work	Social class							
	I Profes- sional	II Mana- gerial	III Non- Manual	III Skilled Manual	IV Semi- Skilled	V Un- Skilled	Un- Clas- sified	Total
	%	%	%	%	%	%	%	%
Not working	83	66	64	59	56	61	30	60
Worked variable hours or on premises	3	9	4	4	5	2	8	5
Away from home under five hours per day	9	11	16	18	20	20	2	17
Away from home five hours or over per day	6	14	16	19	19	17	58	17
No mother	—	1	1	1	1	2	2	1
Total number (100%)	(110)	(430)	(338)	(1,486)	(499)	(189)	(40)	(3,092)

2.11. There was a marked association between the income of the father (or head of the household) and the likelihood both of the mother being in paid employment and of working away from home for five hours or more a day. Approximately half of the mothers in the £10 a week or lower income category were working and the proportion of working mothers fell steadily through the income groups to a quarter in the £25 a week or higher category. (See Table 10.)

Table 10

Mothers' hours of work analysed by income of father or head of household

Mothers' hours of work	Income of father or head of household								
	Up to £10	Over £10– £12.10	Over £12.10 –£15	Over £15– £20	Over £20– £25	Over £25– £30	Over £30	Not known	Total
Not working	50	54	56	60	70	75	74	65	60
Hours variable or on premises	6	4	4	4	5	5	7	10	5
Away from home under five hours per day	18	20	22	18	11	10	9	12	17
Away from home five hours or over per day	23	21	18	18	14	11	10	14	17
No mother	2	1	—	1	1	—	—	—	1
Total number (100%)	(196)	(386)	(685)	(908)	(401)	(157)	(155)	(204)	(3,092)

(iv) *Broken homes*

2.12. One or both of the natural parents was missing from at least eight per cent of the homes in which interviews were conducted. The true figure might well be higher than this because informants may not always have told interviewers whether either or both parents were not the child's natural parents. The interviewers were instructed not to press the checking of this point if to do so was likely to cause resentment or distress. In the sample of children selected for this survey 0·3 per cent were found to be living in institutions or group homes. No interviews were attempted for these children. The parental situation where both natural parents were not in the household was as follows:

	Percentage of total sample
Natural mother only, no father or father substitute	4
Natural father only, no mother or mother substitute	1
Natural mother, substitute father	1
Natural father, substitute mother	1
Neither natural parent	1
Total	8

2.13. There was no significant association between the proportion of broken families and social class. However in 47 of the 103 families with incomes of £10 a week or less there was either no father or no mother in the household. The fatherless families were the only group large enough to examine further. Tables 11 and 12 compare family incomes and the employment position of the mother in fatherless and normal families. Fifty-six per cent of the fatherless families had an income of £12 10s. 0d. per week or less compared with seven per cent of the normal families. A larger proportion of these mothers were working and 41 per cent of them were away from home for over five hours a day compared with 16 per cent of mothers in the normal families.

Table 11

Comparison of family incomes of fatherless and normal families

Family income	Fatherless families	Natural father and mother in family
Up to £10 p.w.	35	1
Over £10 to £12.10	21	6
Over £12.10 to £15	16	17
Over £15 to £20	11	33
Over £20 to £25	5	20
Over £25 to £30	2	9
Over £30	2	7
Not given	8	7
Total number (100%)	(130)	(2,845)

Note.—Broken families other than fatherless ones are omitted from Tables 11 and 12.

Table 12

Comparison of employment position of mothers in fatherless and normal families

Employment position of mother	Fatherless families	Natural father and mother in family
Not working	43	62
Works variable hours, or on premises	7	4
Away from home under five hours per day	9	18
Away from home over five hours per day	41	16
Total number (100%)	(130)	(2,845)

(b) The educational level of the homes

2.14. There is no doubt that the type of education which parents have themselves had is likely to colour their attitudes in one way or another towards the value of education in general and to affect their aspirations for their children. Parents' own educational experience may well also affect their understanding of what the schools are trying to achieve now and may limit the extent to which they are able to follow what their children are doing, irrespective of how interested they are or how anxious to encourage their children in their school work.

2.15. It is important then to note that over half of these children's parents had completed their continuous full-time formal education by the age of 14. Sixty-three per cent of the fathers and 81 per cent of the mothers had had no further education after leaving school. Further education is defined here as professional, academic, trade or vocational courses taken full or part-time or by correspondence but lasting for at least a session; completion of full-apprenticeship or qualification as state registered nurse is included. (See Tables 13 and 14 at the end of Section II.)

2.16. As would be expected there was a very close association between level of parents' education, particularly father's, and the occupation of the father. Only a very small proportion of the fathers in social classes IV and V, that is those who were doing semi- or unskilled work, had stayed at school beyond the age of 14 or taken any further education. In the large skilled-manual occupational category further education of fathers had mainly taken the form of apprenticeships. The majority of mothers in this group had had no further education after leaving school.

Further information about the family's educational experience is obtained by considering whether at least one member, that is father, mother, brother or sister of the selected child had been to a selective secondary school. A selective secondary school is taken as one in which there is some selection of entrants by ability. Included here are state grammar and technical schools, private grammar schools, and pre-1947 secondary, central, intermediate and higher grade schools. Comprehensive schools have also been included as they provide a wide range of courses. The proportion of families who, in this sense, had had some experience of selective secondary education ranged from only 15 per cent in social class V to 88 per cent in social class I. (See Table 15.)

2.17. Apart from further educational courses as already defined only a small proportion of the parents had taken any recreational or leisure time courses for interest. Sixteen per cent of the fathers and 26 per cent of the mothers had taken such courses. Again there was a marked difference between the social class groups but in each class a higher proportion of mothers than fathers had taken some type of leisure course.

2.18. The probability is that if parents have firm habits of reading their children also will be more likely to develop similar interests. The majority of these parents said that they liked to do some reading when they had time for relaxing. The wives of manual workers, however, tended to read as a form of relaxation rather less than their husbands. The main form of reading was of newspapers and magazines.

2.19. Less than half of the parents belonged to a lending library of any sort at the time of the interview and in approximately a third of the families neither parent had ever belonged to a library. Twenty-nine per cent of the parents possessed less than six books apart from children's books. There was a marked increase with social class both in the incidence of library membership among parents and in the number of books they possessed. (See Tables 16 and 17.)

(c) The educational support given to children in their homes

2.20. In this section are considered some aspects of child upbringing and parental attitudes which seem likely to support or to hinder the primary schools in what they are trying to achieve. We examine the extent to which parents spend time with their children and the interest taken by fathers in their children's upbringing. We also consider the amount of reading children do at home, parental attitudes towards children of these ages doing any school work at home and whether any help with school work is given outside school.

(i) *Time spent by parents with their children*

2.21 We look first at the extent to which parents said that they had any time free to join in activities with their children, should their children wish it, such as playing or reading with them, taking them out or showing them how to do things. Approximately half of the mothers were able to spend time with their children on most evenings during the week. The others were free only occasionally or not at all on weekday evenings. Whether mothers were available in the evenings was related to the form the child was in. Fifty-eight per cent of the mothers of children in the top infants were free most evenings compared with 42 per cent with children in the top juniors. (See Table 18.) Whether mothers were working or not and the hours worked made little difference to their being able to give time to their children in the evenings.

2.22. A quarter of the fathers were not able to join in activities with their children on weekday evenings and almost a third were only available occasionally if at all at weekends. In families in which the father was a manual worker there was a slight tendency for the parents to be less often available to spend time with their children than in other families. Over a quarter of the fathers in skilled and semi-skilled manual occupations were on shift work or permanent night work or were regularly working away from home for at least two nights each week. (See Tables 19 and 20.)

2.23. There was a marked social class difference in the proportions of families which went for outings together, that is other than visits to relatives or to church or out shopping. The families with fathers in the non-manual occupations were more inclined than the manual worker families to go on outings together and also to have had their last outing more recently.

(ii) *Interest taken by fathers in their children's education and upbringing*
2.24. The social class groups showed very different patterns in the responsibility taken by fathers over the educational progress of their children at the primary stage. The proportion of mothers who said that their husbands had taken an interest in the schools their children went to increased markedly with social class. Over 40 per cent of the fathers in manual occupations had left the starting of their children at the sampled school entirely to their wives. Almost half of these fathers had not been to the child's present school at all and less than a quarter of them had talked to the heads; on the other hand not a very high proportion of fathers in any social class had talked with the heads. (See Table 21.)

2.25. The majority of mothers in all social classes said that their husbands were taking an interest in how their children were getting on at school but again rather more of the manual occupation fathers left this responsibility to their wives.

(iii) *Reading habits of children*
2.26. The very great majority of children did some reading at home apart from homework. The frequency of reading increased with social class as also did the tendency for the children to read books and not just magazines or comics.

2.27. Approximately half of the children took books home from school to read and over half borrowed books from libraries, other than the school's. In all 80 per cent borrowed books from one or other sources. The proportion borrowing books increased both for school and library books as the children moved up the school. (See Table 22.)

2.28. In the social class V families there was a slight dropping off compared with other families in the proportion of children taking books home from school. The children from manual working families were less likely than those from non-manual to borrow books from libraries (see Table 23). Taking both sources of book borrowing together there was a marked relationship between the proportion of children borrowing books and social class, the percentages ranging from 73 per cent in social class V to 95 per cent in class I. (See Table 24.)

2.29. Parents whose children did not borrow books were asked if they would be quite happy if their children were to bring books home to read or whether they would be worried that these books might get spoilt. In all five per cent of the mothers from the manual worker families said that in fact they would be worried about this.

(iv) *Parents' attitudes towards school work being done at home and towards helping their children with school work*
2.30. We now consider parents' views on whether their children should be given any school work to do at home at the primary stage of their education. Over the school years covered in this sample there were marked increases both in the proportions of children already doing some school work at home and of parents approving of their doing so. In the top juniors 61 per cent of children were already given work to do at home and 75 per cent of parents wanted some homework for their children. Of the top juniors' parents whose children already had homework, 11 per cent thought that they should not be given any at

all and 26 per cent thought that they should have more. Among the top infants children 26 per cent already had homework and 46 per cent of parents approved of the idea. Of the top infants' parents whose children had homework 16 per cent did not want them to have any and 19 per cent wanted them to have more. (See Table 25.)

2.31. It is of interest that the children of manual workers were slightly less likely than other children to be given any school work to do at home but that there was little social class difference in the proportions of parents wanting their children to be given some homework. (See Table 26.)

2.32. Almost a third of the parents had asked for their children to be given some school work to do at home or had asked the teachers to show them how they could help their children at home. The proportions asking increased slightly with social class. Just over a third had bought copies, to have at home, of some of the textbooks their children were using in school. Considerably higher proportions of parents from the non-manual than manual worker families had done this.

2.33. Parents' attitudes towards helping their children at home with school work were related to social class and to the stages the children had reached in their primary schools. The proportions who considered that parents should leave all teaching and helping with school subjects to the teachers ranged from 30 per cent in social class I to 49 per cent in class V. Seventy-six per cent of those in class I said that their children were given help with school work outside school compared with 57 per cent in class V. Thirteen per cent of the mothers said that they had too much to do to spend time on helping their children with school work (three per cent in class I, 23 per cent in class V). There was however no difference here between working and non-working mothers.

2.34. The lower children were in the school the more likely they were to be helped with school work at home. Seventy-three per cent of those in the top infants were helped compared with 42 per cent in the top juniors. This may well be related to the difficulties that some parents said that they had in helping their children because methods of teaching had changed so much since they themselves were at school. In all social classes help was given mainly by the child's mother and/or father.

(d) Parental aspirations for their children

(i) *School leaving age*

2.35. At the time this inquiry was carried out approximately half of the young people in maintained secondary schools stayed at school beyond the statutory leaving age and the trend was for this proportion to increase. The government had already announced their decision to raise the school leaving age to 16 in 1970. In general this would affect all the children in the top infants classes of our sample, most of those in the bottom juniors but none of the top juniors.

2.36. In view of the government's decision it is an important finding that three-quarters of the parents in this sample had positive hopes at this stage in their children's lives that they would stay at school longer than the minimum leaving age which would apply to them. Only seven per cent definitely wanted their children to leave as soon as possible (see Table 27). Parents may become less keen, for financial or other reasons, for their children to stay on at school as they approach the permitted age of leaving. On the other hand there have been steady increases in the proportions of pupils staying on at school voluntarily and staying on right into the sixth forms and it seems likely therefore that parents' attitudes towards the value of a longer school life are changing. If this is so, these younger parents might be expected to be in the forefront of any general change in this area of attitudes.

2.37. There were some social class differences in parents' attitudes towards their children staying on at school. Virtually none of the non-manual occupation parents wanted their children to leave as soon as possible and over half hoped that they would stay until 18 or over. Among the manual workers the proportions of parents definitely wanting their children to leave at the minimum age possible ranged from eight per cent of the skilled manual to 15 per cent of the unskilled. From 17 to 21 per cent of these parents would not say at that stage whether they wanted their children to leave early or to stay on. It is noteworthy however that over a third of the social class V parents hoped that their children would stay at school till 17 or over; the proportions hoping this increased through the other social class groups.

2.38. There was little difference between the attitudes towards age of leaving school of parents with children in the different forms included in the sample, or towards the leaving age thought appropriate for boys compared with girls.

(ii) *Secondary school preferences*

2.39. The children in the top junior classes had already mostly been allocated to their secondary schools by the time the interviewing was carried out. Twenty-three per cent were going to grammar schools, 61 per cent to secondary modern and seven per cent to comprehensive. The other nine per cent were going to technical or independent schools or the type of secondary school was not known. We now compare this actuality with the hopes parents had had for their children's secondary education. Approximately half of all parents hoped, or had hoped, that their children would go to grammar schools. Twenty-four per cent of parents of top junior children said that they had wanted their children to go to secondary modern schools compared with 12 per cent of the parents with children in the earlier stages of the primary school. As would be expected a larger proportion of the parents of the younger children had not thought about the type of secondary school preferred. A comparison is made below between the hopes of parents at different stages and the actual allocation of the top juniors to secondary school.

	Parents' hopes		
Types of secondary school	Bottom junior and top infants	Top juniors	Allocation made Top juniors
Grammar	49	51	23
Secondary modern	12	24	61
Comprehensive	8	5	7
Technical	9	5	2
Independent	2	2	1
No opinion, no knowledge of different types of schools	13	13	6
Had not thought about it	7	—	—
Total number (100%)	(2,069)	(1,023)	(1,023)

2.40. There were marked social class differences in the proportions both of parents hoping that their children would go to grammar schools and of those achieving their ambitions. Of the top juniors whose parents had wanted them to go to grammar schools 52 per cent of the children of non-manual occupation fathers had gained grammar school places and 36 per cent of the manual workers. (See Tables 28, 29 and 30.)

2.41. The reasons for wanting their children to go to grammar schools which were given most frequently by parents were, firstly, that they considered that the standard of teaching and of education was better and that their children would learn more than at other schools (65 per cent), and secondly that a grammar school education led to better career prospects (60 per cent). Other reasons mentioned less frequently were that the grammar school curriculum was better and offered subjects in which their children were interested (22 per cent), or that their children had intellectual or academic abilities and that they hoped that a grammar school course would enable them to go to university (19 per cent). Seventeen per cent referred to what they felt to be the social advantages of going to grammar schools arising from their traditions and reputations. They cited the character training and general preparation for life given at grammar schools and the type of pupils with whom their children would be associating. (See Table 31.)

2.42. The parents who said that they would like their children to go to secondary modern schools mentioned most frequently the varied, interesting and wide curricula and the type of subjects offered as being attractive (41 per cent). Thirty-seven per cent knew of other children who were happy there or said that their children would be helped by having friends or relatives already there. Twenty-seven per cent thought that their children would learn more in a secondary modern school and that the education and teaching given was better.

2.43. Comprehensive schools were the preferred secondary schools of less than one in ten of the parents. This cannot be taken as a judgement on comprehensive schools however as it was found at the pilot stage of the survey that many parents did not know what they were. The attractions of these schools were the wide curricula offered (69 per cent), the standard of education and teaching (30 per cent), the social advantages in mixing with different types of pupils and the general preparation for life which they felt their children would have (17 per cent).

2.44. Technical schools were liked for the better career opportunities they offered (63 per cent), the subjects covered (50 per cent) and the standard of education and teaching (23 per cent).

2.45. Only three per cent of the total sample hoped to send their children to independent schools at the secondary stage. These parents thought particularly that their children would have a better standard of education and would also have social and career advantages from going to this type of school.

2.46. Parents in the non-manual occupational groups were considerably more likely than those in manual work to be positively opposed to their children going to some schools. (See Table 32.) The most disliked type of schools were secondary moderns and the criticisms most frequently made of them were of the behaviour of the pupils; that they were rough, bad mannered, poorly disciplined or lax in morals. Next in number came comments about the teaching, that the pupils did not seem to learn anything and that their progress was slow. (See Table 33.)

(e) Physical conditions of the home and neighbourhood amenities

(i) *Physical conditions and amenities of the home*

2.47. Some physical conditions of the home which seem likely to have an adverse influence on children's development are overcrowdedness, which may result in ill health and fatigue both of parents and children, lack of play space and of variety of stimulation, impermanent tenancy of accommodation and lack of, or sharing of, basic facilities such as running hot water and a fixed bath or shower.

2.48. We consider now the type of accommodation in which these families were living. The great majority (91 per cent) were in whole houses. More of those with fathers in non-manual than manual occupations were in detached or semi-detached houses. Eight per cent of the families overall were in self-contained flats and one per cent in rooms or caravans. Of the families in social class V however 15 per cent were accommodated in flats and five per cent in rooms or caravans. There was a close association between ownership of dwelling and social class with 84 per cent of social class I owning or buying their dwellings compared with 15 per cent of class V.

2.49. The measure of crowdedness of the home which we have used is the bedroom deficiency index devised by P. G. Gray of the Government Social Survey. This index is calculated by comparing the number of bedrooms possessed by a household with the standard given below. This standard has no statutory standing but seemed to us to be the most useful measure of crowdedness for this inquiry.

A standard number of bedrooms has been allocated to each household, the number of bedrooms being allocated in the following order:

(i) Each married couple was given one bedroom.

(ii) Any other persons aged 21 or over were each given a bedroom.

(iii) Persons aged 10 to 20 years, inclusive, of the same sex were paired off and a bedroom was given to each pair.

(iv) Any person aged 10–20 years left over after this pairing was paired with a child under 10 of the same sex. If no pairing of the latter kind was possible, such a person was given a separate bedroom.

(v) Any remaining children under 10 years were paired and a bedroom was given to each pair. Any remaining child was given an additional room.

2.50. On the bedroom deficiency index the children of manual workers were very much worse off than those of non-manual. There was a steady deterioration in standards from the social class I families, only three per cent of which had one or more bedrooms less than the standard considered satisfactory, to the social class Vs with 43 per cent of families having too few bedrooms. Among the non-manual occupational groups the proportions of families which had *two* or more bedrooms less than the standard were negligible. In the manual workers groups the proportions ranged from six per cent of the skilled workers to 11 per cent of the unskilled. (See Table 34.)

2.51. The bedroom accommodation situation of this sample of families with children in primary schools was in general lower than that of the general population in 1960, recorded in Social Survey Report SS 319 "The Housing Situation in 1960" by P. G. Gray and R. Russell. In that survey, it was found that 15 per cent of households in Greater London had fewer bedrooms than the standard. For the rest of England and Wales the proportion was 11 per cent. Our figure for households with children in primary schools in England is 25 per cent. This difference between the general population and our figures is not unexpected as under-occupied property tends to be lived in mainly by older people whose families have grown up and moved away.

2.52. Other amenities of the home which give an indication of the standard of living of families are whether their accommodation has hot water from a tap, a fixed bath or shower and whether the family owns or has the use of a car. Seven per cent of the families had no running hot water in their homes and 10 per cent no fixed bath or shower. The proportion sharing a hot water tap or a fixed bath or shower with other households was one per cent for each. In respect of these facilities the families of manual workers were again worse off than the non-manual, the proportions with no running hot water rising to 17 per cent in social class V, and with no fixed bath or shower to 19 per cent.

2.53. Just over half of the families owned or had the use of a car but again there was a marked difference between the social classes with the proportions with a car ranging from 93 per cent in class I to 17 per cent in class V.

(ii) *Neighbourhood amenities for children*

2.54. We look now at the information on the playing areas and facilities available for and used by these children. Only five per cent of the homes had no garden, yard, or play space, either for their sole use or shared, which the child could use. Again however the manual workers' families were worse off and 11 per cent of social class V had no play area for their children. The family's own garden or open space round or between dwellings were the main areas used by just over half the children when playing out of doors.

2.55. The next most common type of play areas were parks, heaths, commons, or fields. Thirteen per cent of the children played mainly in streets which were not specifically designated "play" streets. Expectedly, larger proportions of those in the higher social classes tended to play mainly in their own gardens or areas round their homes, and smaller proportions of them than in the lower social classes went to parks, commons or fields, played in the street or used outdoor playgrounds or recreation grounds.

2.56. Parents were asked what recreational facilities there were in the neighbourhood within easy distance of their homes, that is easy distance for a child to get to by himself or, if too young, for the parent or other adult to take the child. It was left to the parents to decide whether in their particular circumstances they felt that the various facilities were readily accessible to their children. It is possible that some amenities might have been available but not known about by parents.

2.57. The great majority of these families had public libraries with children's books within easy reach of their homes. The next most commonly found facility in the neighbourhood were outdoor open spaces such as parks, heaths, fields, or public gardens where children were allowed to play (81 per cent of families). Seventy-seven per cent had, locally, children's clubs or societies such as cubs, brownies, youth clubs or church clubs for young people. Proper playgrounds or outdoor play centres, children's cinema shows, and indoor or outdoor swimming pools were each available to approximately half of the families. Only four per cent said they had any indoor recreational or play centres available for children of primary school age. (See Tables 35 and 36.)

2.58. The facilities which had been used during the previous year by the largest numbers of children were the outdoor open spaces such as parks (69 per cent of all children in the sample), the libraries (57 per cent), and outdoor playgrounds (41 per cent). The swimming pools had been attended by 33 per cent, the children's clubs by 32 per cent and the children's cinema shows by 23 per cent.

2.59. The amenities for children which were lacking from the neighbourhoods and were wanted by the largest numbers of parents were swimming pools (32 per cent of all parents in the sample), proper outdoor playgrounds (27 per cent), and indoor recreational centres for children (27 per cent).

2.60. From social class I to class V there were slightly increasing proportions of parents saying that there were proper playgrounds available in the neighbourhood and also that their children used them. With children's clubs and societies the trend was in the opposite direction. Slightly higher proportions of the children of manual than non-manual workers had been to children's film shows during the year. Rather less of them had used the children's libraries.

2.61. Understandably there was a tendency for a higher proportion of the parents of the older children to feel that there were open spaces like parks, swimming pools, children's clubs, cinema shows and libraries which could readily and safely be used by their children. The proportions of children actually using these facilities also increased with age. Children's playgrounds and the very few indoor play centres were the only amenities used equally by all age groups.

Table 13

Age parents completed formal education, by social class

Age father completed formal education	Social class							Total
	I Profes-sional	II Manag-erial	III Non-manual	III Skilled manual	IV Semi-skilled	V Un-skilled	Un-classi-fied	
14 years and under	6	38	44	73	79	85	30	64
15 years but under 16	12	15	19	16	13	9	2	15
16 years but under 17	29	22	25	6	4	1	10	10
17 years but under 18	19	10	7	2	1	1	2	4
18 years and over	34	13	3	1	1	1	8	4
Not known	0	2	2	2	2	3	48	3
Total number (100%)	(110)	(430)	(338)	(1,486)	(499)	(189)	(40)	(3,092)

Age mother completed formal education								
14 years and under	13	43	50	64	69	76	48	59
15 years but under 16	19	22	25	24	22	19	22	23
16 years but under 17	27	16	15	8	6	3	15	10
17 years but under 18	21	10	7	2	2	0	5	4
18 years and over	20	9	3	2	1	1	8	4
Not known	0	0	0	0	0	1	2	0
Total number (100%)	(110)	(430)	(338)	(1,486)	(499)	(189)	(40)	(3,092)

Table 14

Whether parents had any further education after leaving school, by social class

| | Social class | | | | | | | |
Father's further education	I Profes- sional	II Manag- erial	III Non- manual	III Skilled manual	IV Semi- skilled	V Un- skilled	Un- classi- fied	Total
No further education	3	42	60	62	87	94	40	63
Part-time or correspondence course pursued	36	27	24	10	4	1	0	13
Full apprenticeship or S.R.N. completed	6	10	7	22	5	2	5	14
Full-time course at university, college or other education institution	54	18	4	3	1	2	10	7
Not known	1	3	5	3	3	1	45	3
Total number (100%)	(110)	(430)	(338)	(1,486)	(499)	(189)	(40)	(3,092)

Mother's further education								
No further education	42	65	76	85	89	94	80	81
Part-time or correspondence course pursued	15	15	15	9	8	3	7	10
Full apprenticeship or S.R.N. completed	12	5	3	2	1	1	5	3
Full-time course at university, college or other education institution	28	13	5	3	2	2	8	5
Not known	3	2	1	1	0	0	0	1
Total number (100%)	(110)	(430)	(338)	(1,486)	(499)	(189)	(40)	(3,092)

Table 15

Whether any members of family had been to a selective secondary school, by social class

| | Social class | | | | | | | |
Whether any member of family had been to a selective secondary school	I Profes- sional	II Manag- erial	III Non- manual	III Skilled manual	IV Semi- skilled	V Un- skilled	Un- classi- fied	Total
At least one member attended selective secondary school	88	69	68	32	23	15	45	41
None attended a selective secondary school	5	24	24	56	66	71	28	48
Not known whether any attended selective secondary schools	7	7	8	12	11	14	27	11
Total number (100%)	(110)	(430)	(338)	(1,486)	(499)	(189)	(40)	(3,092)

Table 16

Whether parents belonged to a lending library or either had belonged to one within the last 10 years, by social class

Q.59. Whether parents belonged to a library	Social class							
	I Profes-sional	II Manag-erial	III Non-manual	III Skilled manual	IV Semi-skilled	V Un-skilled	Un-classi-fied	Total
One or both belonged at time of interview	79	61	67	40	33	24	40	45
Neither belonged when interviewed, but one or both belonged in previous 10 years	11	18	18	25	21	29	28	23
Neither belonged within previous 10 years	10	21	15	35	46	47	32	32
Total number (100%)	(110)	(430)	(338)	(1,486)	(499)	(189)	(40)	(3,092)

Table 17

Number of books in home apart from children's books, by social class

Q.61. Number of books in home	Social class							
	I Profes-sional	II Manag-erial	III Non-manual	III Skilled manual	IV Semi-skilled	V Un-skilled	Un-classi-fied	Total
More than five books	95	88	85	67	61	43	55	70
One to five books	4	4	9	12	17	14	18	11
No books	1	7	6	21	22	42	27	18
Not known	0	1	0	0	0	1	0	1
Total number (100%)	(110)	(430)	(338)	(1,486)	(499)	(189)	(40)	(3,092)

Table 18

Whether parents had any time free to do things with child, by form

Q.51(a). Whether mother was free to do things with child in evenings	Top Juniors	Bottom Juniors	Top Infants	Total
Yes, free most evenings	42	53	58	51
Yes, but only on occasional evenings	44	38	36	39
Not free on weekday evenings	14	9	7	10
Total number (100%)	(1,023)	(1,016)	(1,053)	(3,092)

Q.52. Whether father could spend time with child in evenings	Top Juniors	Bottom Juniors	Top Infants	Total
Yes, most evenings	30	33	37	34
Yes, occasional evenings	40	37	33	36
Not on weekday evenings	24	24	25	24
No husband/wife or not answered	6	5	5	6
Total number (100%)	(1,023)	(1,016)	(1,053)	(3,092)

Q.52(b). Whether father could spend time with child at weekends	Top Juniors	Bottom Juniors	Top Infants	Total
Yes, most weekends	57	65	67	63
Yes, occasional weekends	26	21	20	22
No	11	9	7	9
No husband/wife	6	5	5	6
Total number (100%)	(1,023)	(1,016)	(1,053)	(3,092)

Table 19

Whether parents had any free time to do things with child, by social class

| | Social class | | | | | | | |
Q.51. Whether mother was free to do things with child in evenings	I Profes-sional	II Manag-erial	III Non-manual	III Skilled manual	IV Semi-skilled	V Un-skilled	Un-classi-fied	Total
Yes, did things with child most evenings	55	59	53	50	52	39	30	51
Yes, but only on occasional evenings	36	36	38	40	37	44	58	39
Not free on weekday evenings	9	5	9	10	11	16	12	10
Total number (100%)	(110)	(430)	(338)	(1,486)	(499)	(189)	(40)	(3,092)
Q.52(a). Whether father could spend time with child in evenings								
Yes, most evenings	31	42	40	33	28	28	2	34
Yes, occasional evenings	41	36	34	37	40	37	2	36
Not on weekday evenings	26	18	22	26	28	29	0	24
No husband/wife	3	4	4	5	4	6	95	6
Total number (100%)	(110)	(430)	(338)	(1,486)	(499)	(189)	(40)	(3,092)
Q.52(b). Whether father could spend time with child at weekends								
Yes, most weekends	74	75	72	62	57	49	2	63
Yes, occasional weekends	21	14	18	24	27	30	0	22
No	3	7	5	9	12	15	0	9
No husband/wife	3	5	5	4	4	6	98	6
Total number (100%)	(110)	(430)	(338)	(1,486)	(499)	(189)	(40)	(3,092)

Note — It should be borne in mind that only 26% of the children of the class I parents were in the top juniors compared with 40% of the class V.

Table 20

Whether father was on shift work, etc., by social class

| | Social class | | | | | | | |
Whether father was on shift work, permanent night work or working away from home for at least two nights each week	I Profes-sional	II Manag-erial	III Non-manual	III Skilled manual	IV Semi-skilled	V Un-skilled	Un-classi-fied	Total
Father was on shift work, etc.	10	8	19	25	36	15	0	22
Father not on shift work	86	88	78	70	58	70	0	71
Father sick/unemployed/retired	0	0	0	2	3	11	5	2
Father temporarily away from household	1	1	1	1	1	0	2	1
Father deceased/permanently separated/left household	3	3	2	2	2	4	92	3
Total number (100%)	(110)	(430)	(338)	(1,486)	(499)	(189)	(40)	(3,092)

Table 21

Interest taken by father in child's education and upbringing, by social class

	Social class							
Q.12. Whether husband took interest in which school child went to	I Profes-sional	II Manag-erial	III Non-manual	III Skilled manual	IV Semi-skilled	V Un-skilled	Un-classi-fied	Total
Husband took an interest	84	74	70	53	47	40	8	56
Left to mother	15	22	27	43	48	56	2	38
No husband/wife or not answered	1	4	3	4	5	4	90	5
Total number (100%)	(110)	(430)	(338)	(1,486)	(499)	(189)	(40)	(3,092)
Q.20. Whether husband had been to child's school and, if so, whether he had talked to the head								
Husband had been to school and talked to head	49	50	39	24	24	17	2	30
Husband had been to school but had not talked to head	30	24	32	27	24	14	0	25
Husband had not been to school	19	23	26	45	48	65	0	40
No husband	2	2	3	4	4	4	98	5
Total number (100%)	(110)	(430)	(338)	(1,486)	(499)	(189)	(40)	(3,092)
Q.33. Whether husband took much interest in how child was getting on at school								
Husband took an interest	94	88	86	77	77	68	2	79
Left to wife	3	9	10	19	19	28	0	16
No husband/wife	3	3	4	4	4	4	98	5
Total number (100%)	(110)	(430)	(338)	(1,486)	(499)	(189)	(40)	(3,092)
Q.53. Whether husband took a big part in controlling the children								
Husband took big part or equal part with wife	77	78	81	72	74	73	2	73
Husband took very small part in control of children, or left it to wife	20	19	15	24	22	23	0	22
No husband/wife	3	3	4	4	4	4	98	
Total number (100%)	(110)	(430)	(338)	(1,486)	(499)	(189)	(40)	(3,092)

Table 22

Whether child borrowed books from school or public libraries to read at home,
by form

Q.58(*a*). Whether child borrowed books from school	Top Juniors	Bottom Juniors	Top Infants	Total
Yes	61	48	46	52
No	39	52	54	48
(*b*). Whether child borrowed books from libraries				
Yes	72	61	48	60
No	28	39	52	40
Total number (100%)	(1,023)	(1,016)	(1,053)	(3,092)

Table 23

Whether child borrowed books from school or public libraries to read at home,
by social class

	Social class							
Q.58(*a*). Whether child borrowed books from school	I Profes-sional	II Manag-erial	III Non-manual	III Skilled manual	IV Semi-skilled	V Un-skilled	Un-classi-fied	Total
Yes	54	52	50	52	53	48	45	52
No	46	48	50	48	47	51	55	48
(*b*). Whether child borrowed books from libraries								
Yes	86	69	70	57	52	54	62	60
No	14	31	30	43	48	46	38	40
Total number (100%)	(110)	(430)	(338)	(1,486)	(499)	(189)	(40)	(3,092)

Table 24

Whether borrowed books from school or other libraries or, if not, whether parent would have been worried if child had done so, by social class

Q.58. Whether child borrowed books or parent would have been worried if child had done so	Social class							Total
	I Profes-sional	II Manag-erial	III Non-manual	III Skilled manual	IV Semi-skilled	V Un-skilled	Un-classi-fied	
Child already borrowed books from school or other library	95	88	84	78	75	73	80	80
Parent would have been quite happy if child had borrowed books	5	9	15	17	18	14	8	15
Parent would have been worried if child had borrowed books	0	3	2	4	5	11	12	4
Other answers	0	0	0	1	1	2	0	1
Total number (100%)	(110)	(430)	(338)	(1,486)	(499)	(189)	(40)	(3,092)

Table 25

Whether children were given school work to do at home and what parents felt about it, by form

Q.29 and 30. (a) Whether given school work to do at home	Top Juniors	Bottom Juniors	Top Infants	Total
Given work to do at home	61	39	26	42
Not given work to do at home	39	61	74	58
(b) Whether parent approved of child being given school work to do at home				
Liked child to have school work to do at home	75	59	46	60
Child should be free of school work at home	23	39	53	39
No answer	2	2	1	2
Total number (100%)	(1,023)	(1,016)	(1,053)	(3,092)
(c) If child was given work to do at home, whether parent thought this was the right amount				
Should not be given it	11	15	16	13
Given right amount	58	57	62	58
Given too much	3	2	0	2
Given too little	26	23	19	24
No answer	2	3	3	3
Number of parents whose children had homework (100%)	(621)	(394)	(271)	(1,286)
(d) Whether parents ever asked for child to be given work to do at home or how they could help child at home				
Yes, asked for work for child to do at home	34	27	29	30
Work to do at home already given	12	4	4	7
No, never asked for homework for child or how to help child at home	54	69	67	63
Total number (100%)	(1,023)	(1,016)	(1,053)	(3,092)

Table 26

Whether children were given school work to do at home and what parents felt about it, by social class

Q.29 and 30. (a) Whether given school work to do at home	I Profes- sional	II Manag- erial	III Non- manual	III Skilled manual	IV Semi- skilled	V Un- skilled	Un- classi- fied	Total
Given work to do at home	52	47	47	41	35	39	38	42
Not given work to do at home	48	53	53	59	65	61	62	58
(b) Whether parent approved of child being given school work to do at home								
Liked child to have school work to do at home	63	63	59	60	60	54	58	60
Child should be free of school work at home	36	36	40	39	39	43	42	39
No answer	1	1	1	1	1	3	0	1
Total number (100%)	(110)	(430)	(338)	(1,486)	(499)	(189)	(40)	(3,092)
(c) If child was given work to do at home, whether parent thought this was the right amount								
Should not be given it	12	14	13	13	10	18	20	13
Given right amount	53	60	56	58	64	55	53	58
Given too much	2	2	2	2	1	3	0	2
Given too little	26	24	27	23	23	19	27	24
No answer	7	0	2	4	2	5	0	3
Total number (100%)	(57)	(202)	(158)	(604)	(177)	(73)	(15)	(1,286)
(d) Whether parents ever asked for child to be given work to do at home or how they could help child at home								
Yes, asked for work for child to do at home	40	37	34	28	27	23	18	30
Work to do at home already given	9	7	10	7	5	5	7	7
No, never asked for homework for child or how to help child at home	51	56	56	65	68	72	75	63
Total number (100%)	(110)	(430)	(338)	(1,486)	(499)	(189)	(40)	(3,092)

Table 27

Parents' attitudes towards their children staying on at school, by social class

Q.48. Would like child to:		I Profes- sional	II Manag- erial	III Non- manual	III Skilled manual	IV Semi- skilled	V Un- skilled	Un- classi- fied	Total
1. Stay on longer	18 and over	68	59	54	37	32	25	45	42
	17	13	12	14	16	14	11	12	14
	16	3	6	9	12	16	17	8	11
	No age given	7	8	9	10	7	11	5	9
2. Could not say whether they would like their child to stay on longer		9	13	12	17	20	21	25	17
3. Leave at statutory age		0	1	0	3	4	7	0	3
4. Leave earlier than statutory age		0	1	2	5	7	8	5	4
Total number (100%)		(110)	(430)	(338)	(1,486)	(499)	(189)	(40)	(3,092)

Table 28

Children in last year of juniors. Type of secondary school child was actually going to and type of secondary school parents hoped child would go to, by social class

Q.43(a). Type of secondary school child was going to	Social class							Total
	I Profes- sional	II Manag- erial	III Non- manual	III Skilled manual	IV Semi- skilled	V Un- skilled	Un- classi- fied	
Grammar	52	33	39	18	18	7	22	23
Secondary Modern	21	50	42	66	68	81	64	61
Comprehensive	10	4	9	7	6	4	0	7
Technical	0	2	4	3	1	1	0	2
Independent	14	5	1	0	1	0	0	1
Not known	3	6	5	6	6	7	14	6
(b). Type of secondary school parents hoped child would go to								
Grammar	69	66	68	48	42	30	43	51
Secondary Modern	14	15	10	25	30	45	7	24
Comprehensive	3	3	8	4	7	3	7	5
Technical	0	1	6	7	8	3	0	5
Independent	14	6	2	1	1	0	0	2
No opinion, whichever child most suited to	0	9	6	15	12	19	43	13
Total number (100%)	(29)	(141)	(115)	(484)	(165)	(75)	(14)	(1,023)

Table 29

Children in last year of juniors. Type of secondary school child was going to by type of school parents had hoped for

Q.43(a). Type of second- ary school child was going to	Type of secondary school hoped for						Total
	Grammar	Secondary Modern	Compre- hensive	Technical	Independent	No opinion	
					Nos.		
Grammar	42	1	2	2	(3)	5	23
Secondary Modern	45	96	31	70	(6)	73	61
Comprehensive	5	1	65	2	(1)	4	7
Technical	2	0	0	23	—	2	2
Independent	1	0	0	0	(9)	0	2
Not known	6	2	2	4	—	17	6
Total number (100%)	(522)	(242)	(52)	(57)	(19)	(131)	(1,023)

Table 30

Children in bottom junior or top infants classes. Type of secondary school parents hoped they would go to, by social class

Q.44. Type of secondary school parents hoped child would go to	Social class							Total
	I Profes- sional	II Manag- erial	III Non- manual	III Skilled manual	IV Semi- skilled	V Un- skilled	Un- classi- fied	
Grammar	64	61	69	45	38	31	42	49
Secondary Modern	4	4	5	15	14	27	15	12
Comprehensive	12	12	7	7	7	4	16	8
Technical	1	5	7	10	11	7	15	9
Independent	9	5	1	1	2	0	4	2
Hasn't thought yet	3	4	5	8	12	10	8	7
Did not know about different types of schools	7	9	6	14	16	21	0	13
Total number (100%)	(81)	(289)	(223)	(1,002)	(334)	(114)	(26)	(2,069)

Table 31

Type of secondary school parents wanted child to go to and the advantages of that type

Q.43 and 44. Advantages:	Type of school wanted					
	Grammar	Secondary Modern	Compre-hensive	Technical	Independent Fee-paying Public	Total
Will lead to a good or better job, trade or profession. Good future prospects	60	12	14	63	37	46
Better standard of education, better teaching, learn more there	65	27	30	23	64	51
Child has academic or intellectual bias, want him/her to go to university	19	—	2	1	20	12
Have varied, interesting, wide curriculum, subjects in which child is interested	22	41	69	50	20	32
Knows other children are happy there; friend, relatives there	8	37	9	13	21	15
Social advantages of this type of school	17	6	17	5	46	14
School nearer home, more convenient for travel, can come home to lunch, etc.	—	6	—	—	—	1
It is a church school; wanted to send him/her to a R.C. school	1	1	—	—	2	1
More or better discipline, more strict, etc.	1	1	—	—	9	1
Better buildings, surroundings, sporting facilities	1	3	4	1	2	2
Prefers mixed schools, boys and girls in one school	—	1	2	2	—	1
Prefers single-sexed schools	—	—	—	—	2	—
Other specific advantages	1	7	1	3	14	3
Did not know any specific relevant advantages, but wanted child to go there nevertheless	2	8	4	1	—	3
Total number (100%)	(1,530)	(497)	(221)	(238)	(56)	(2,552)†

† Parents who had no particular type of secondary school in mind for their child are omitted from this table

Table 32

Whether any type of secondary school was particularly disliked for child, by social class

Q.45. Whether any type of secondary school was particularly disliked	Social class							
	I Professional	II Managerial	III Non-manual	III Skilled manual	IV Semi-skilled	V Un-skilled	Un-classified	Total
No	54	70	74	84	85	91	78	79
Yes	46	30	26	16	15	9	22	20
Type disliked:								
Grammar	—	1	1	2	1	1	—	1
Secondary Modern	26	14	13	6	6	3	12	8
Comprehensive	7	3	3	1	1	—	—	2
Independent public	2	1	—	1	—	—	—	1
Mixed schools (co-ed.)	8	7	6	3	4	3	2	4
Religious schools	2	2	2	2	1	2	8	2
Others	1	2	1	1	2	—	—	2
Total number (100%)	(110)	(430)	(338)	(1,486)	(499)	(189)	(40)	(3,092)

E

Table 33

The type of secondary school parents would have disliked their child to attend and the things disliked most about that kind of school

Q.45. Reasons for dislike	Type of school disliked					
	Grammar School	Secondary Modern	Compre-hensive	Mixed schools (co-ed.)	Religious schools	Total
Does not seem to teach them anything (poor teaching), slow	19	43	11	4	19	26
Type of pupil, rough, bad-mannered, illiterate, bad discipline, bad behaviour, lax morals	33	69	23	32	2	45
Too much religion	0	0	0	0	83	9
School too large, impersonal	0	3	68	1	0	8
Classes too large	0	2	8	1	0	2
Children find it too much of a distraction to be with member of opposite sex	2	0	8	57	0	15
Child emotionally unsuited to that type of school	2	0	0	2	0	1
School not suitable for ordinary working-class people	19	0	2	0	0	4
Standard too high for child, children feel sense of failure	26	2	2	0	2	3
School should be single sex only	0	0	2	17	0	4
Other answers	14	6	9	2	14	7
Total disliking a particular type of school (100%)	(43)	(257)	(53)	(132)	(59)	(544)

Note.—Reasons for disliking independent, non-catholic and single-sex schools are omitted because these schools were mentioned as disliked by very few parents.

Table 34

Bedroom deficiency, by social class

Bedroom deficiency	Social class							
	I Profes-sional	II Manag-erial	III Non-manual	III Skilled manual	IV Semi-skilled	V Un-skilled	Un-classi-fied	Total
3 or more bedrooms less than standard	0	0	0	1	2	2	5	1
2 bedrooms less than standard	0	1	1	5	6	9	10	4
1 bedroom less than standard	3	10	15	22	25	32	28	20
Equal to standard	44	44	52	49	48	42	52	48
1 bedroom more than standard	38	37	28	21	18	14	0	23
2 bedrooms more than standard	14	6	3	1	1	0	2	2
3 bedrooms more than standard	1	2	1	0	0	0	0	1
No answer	0	0	0	1	0	1	3	1
Total number (100%)	(110)	(430)	(338)	(1,486)	(499)	(189)	(40)	(3,092)

Table 35

Comparison of facilities for children present, used and wanted in the neighbour-hood

Q.50. Facilities for children in neighbourhood	Present	Used	Wanted
Park, heath, common, fields where children allowed to play	81	69	9
Proper playground or outdoor play centre	51	41	27
Swimming pools or baths	44	33	32
Indoor sports, recreational, play centre	4	2	27
Children's clubs or societies	77	32	10
Cinema or other place which has children's film shows	45	23	9
Public library, mobile library, with children's books	88	57	4

Table 36

Facilities present, used and wanted, by social class

	Social class							
Q.50. 1. Facilities present	I Profes-sional	II Manag-erial	III Non-manual	III Skilled manual	IV Semi-skilled	V Un-skilled	Un-classi-fied	Total
Park, heath, common, fields, gardens where children allowed to play	76	78	87	80	80	84	82	81
Proper playground or outdoor play centre	46	49	51	52	52	54	58	51
Swimming pools and baths	44	43	42	44	44	46	40	44
Indoor sports, recreational, play centre	2	1	2	4	4	11	5	4
Children's clubs or societies	84	81	81	78	74	70	68	77
Cinema or other place which has children's film shows	47	39	46	45	47	48	62	45
Public library, mobile library, with children's books	93	89	90	87	85	88	92	88
2. Facilities used								
Park, heath, common, fields, gardens where children allowed to play	61	66	73	69	68	75	65	69
Proper playground or outdoor play centre	33	36	37	43	42	46	48	41
Swimming pools and baths	32	31	31	34	31	35	28	33
Indoor sports, recreational, play centre	2	1	1	2	2	6	2	2
Children's clubs or societies	46	38	67	32	26	23	22	32
Cinema or other place which has children's film shows	13	15	18	25	27	32	30	23
Public library, mobile library, with children's books	73	66	64	54	48	53	60	57
3. Facilities wanted								
Park, heath, common, fields, gardens where children allowed to play	14	9	7	10	9	9	5	9
Proper playground or outdoor play centre	27	27	25	28	26	25	22	27
Swimming pools and baths	38	34	30	31	31	30	38	32
Indoor sports, recreational, play centre	17	23	25	30	26	29	38	27
Children's clubs or societies	6	6	10	10	12	10	15	10
Cinema or other place which has children's film shows	4	6	6	11	10	12	8	9
Public library, mobile library, with children's books	4	4	3	4	5	6	2	4
Total number (100%)	(110)	(430)	(338)	(1,486)	(499)	(189	(40)	(3,092)

III. PARENTAL ATTITUDES TO PRIMARY EDUCATION

(a) School starting age. Changes of and parental choice of primary school

3.1. We now examine parents' experience of and attitudes towards various aspects of primary education. In this section are considered parental prefer-ences, firstly, concerning the age of starting school and, secondly, for their children to attend school for a full or half day on first starting. We look also at the extent of parental choice of primary school, reasons for choices made and the amount of and reasons for changing schools at the primary stage.

(i) *Starting age, actual and preferred*

3.2. Just over half of these children had started attending school, either nursery or primary, for a full day before the age of five. Eleven per cent had started before four-and-a-half. Only two per cent had not started until they were five-and-a-half or older. Sixteen per cent had attended a nursery school or nursery class. Children in the Metropolitan Division of Education were more likely than those in other Divisions to have attended a nursery school or class or to have started school at a younger age. Slightly higher proportions of the children of professional and of unskilled parents had been to nursery schools. Rather smaller proportions of children of professional and managerial than of other parents had started school before four-and-a-half. (See Tables 37 to 40 and 43 at the end of Section III.)

3.3. A comparison is now made of the actual ages at which children started full time schooling with the ages preferred by parents. A prevalent tendency found in surveys is for people to express contentment with their actual circumstances rather than to want something different. An overall figure of a third of parents preferring their children to have started school at an earlier age than they did is therefore quite striking. The proportions preferring their children to have started earlier were closely related to the actual ages of starting and ranged from five per cent among parents whose children started at three-and-a-half to almost a half of those whose children started at five or older. On the other hand, over 10 per cent of those whose children started under four would have preferred them to have had a later start. (See Table 41.) There was little difference between the social classes in the proportions who would have liked their children to have started school earlier or later than they did.

3.4. The great majority of parents who would have preferred an earlier start for their children were not in fact thinking of a very markedly earlier starting age as is shown in Table 42. The overall differences between the actual starting ages and those parents would have preferred are shown below. In considering these figures we must of course remember that our sample consists only of parents with experience of having children actually at primary schools and does not include any whose children have not yet reached that stage. In all over two-thirds of the parents would have liked their children to have started full-time school before the age of five.

	Actual starting age	Preferred starting age
Under 3½ years old	3	4
3½ but under 4	2	4
4 but under 4½	6	24
4½ but under 5	42	36
5 but under 5½	45	26
5½ or older	2	4
No answer	—	2
Sample	(3,092)	(3,092)

(ii) *Full and half day starting*

3.5. Only one per cent of the children had started school by going for only half a day in the first instance. Approximately a quarter of the parents thought that it would have been better for their children to have attended school only in the mornings or the afternoons at first. The proportions preferring a half rather than a full day start for their children were very markedly associated with social class and ranged from 15 per cent of class V to 42 per cent of class I. (See Tables 43 and 44.)

(iii) *Changes of school and parental choice of school*

3.6. The proportions of children who had changed primary school at some stage rose from 18 per cent of those in the top form of the infants to 68 per cent of the top juniors. Fifteen per cent of children in the juniors had attended three or more primary schools including the one they were at when their parents were interviewed; only three per cent had been to four or more schools (See Table 45.) The lengths of time children had been at the schools in the sample are shown in Table 46.

3.7. The main reason for change of school was transfer from a separate infants to a junior school. The only other reason which was given with any frequency was that the family had moved to a different district; this accounted for over a third of the changes of school.

3.8. Just over half the parents felt that they had had a choice of primary school for their children and said that there was another school near their homes to which their children could have gone if they had wished. Private schools were not included. It needs to be borne in mind however that this was the position as the parents saw it but that they may not have known whether in fact the local education authority would have permitted their children to attend other schools in the neighbourhood. There was little difference either by social class or child's form in the proportions of parents saying that they had a choice of school.

3.9. The reasons given most frequently for selecting the school chosen were, firstly, that it was the most convenient for the child to get to, it was the nearest or safest to reach or there were no main roads to cross (49 per cent of parents who had a choice of school). Secondly came religious reasons, either that the school was chosen because it was a church school or an alternative was rejected for the same reason (30 per cent). Thirdly, parents chose primary schools because they had heard good reports about them (24 per cent) and, fourthly, because their other children or other relatives or friends of the sampled children were there or had been previously (23 per cent). Seven per cent of the parents specifically mentioned that there were better educational standards in the chosen schools and six per cent that the atmosphere seemed happier and more homely and friendly.

3.10. It is interesting that almost three-quarters of the children had had other relatives attending the sampled schools either at the time of the survey or previously. Sixty-two per cent had, or had had, brothers or sisters there and as many as 20 per cent of the selected children's fathers or mothers had been at the same schools. In manual worker families children were rather more likely to have had parents, siblings or other relatives at the same school than in non-manual worker homes. (See Table 47.)

3.11. Six per cent of the parents had at some stage asked the Education Office or someone in authority for permission for the selected child to go to a different school from the one to which he or she had been allocated. Of these half had obtained and a third failed to obtain permission for the child to go to the desired school; the other cases were still undecided at the time of the interview.

(b) Parental contacts with the primary schools

3.12. This section discusses the amount and type of parental contact with the primary schools. We examine the extent to which parents showed interest in their children's education by visiting the schools and discussing their children's progress with the teachers, the variety of opportunities provided by the schools for parents to see what the schools were doing and the proportions of parents who took advantage of them and, finally, parental satisfaction with the school's arrangements for seeing the staff.

(i) *Enquiries made and interest taken by parents when children started in school*

3.13. Just over half of the parents said that they had made enquiries about the sampled school or visited it *before* sending the first of their children there. If parents had themselves been at the school, they were asked whether they had taken steps to find out what it was like when their children were ready to start there. The proportions who had made enquiries or visited the schools increased with social class from 50 per cent of parents in class V to 80 per cent of those in class I. It must be remembered here that there was a greater likelihood among the manual than non-manual worker classes for other relatives to have attended the same school and there might therefore have been less need for these parents to make specific inquiries when they first sent any of their own children to the school.

3.14. Enquiries about the school were made most frequently of the head or other teachers at the school and next most often of friends, relatives or neighbours whose children were already at the school or had been recently.

3.15. Over a third of the parents had not had an actual talk with the head when the selected child first started in the school which he or she was attending at the time of the survey. By a talk we mean something more than the minimum communication necessary for the child's enrolment, the head would have told the parents something about the school or discussed the child. The proportions of parents who had talked to the heads when their child started at the school was higher among those with children in the infants than in the junior forms. Again there were differences between the social class groups with the proportions varying from 78 per cent of the parents in class I having had an initial talk with the head to 60 per cent of those in class V. (See Table 48.)

3.16. Among the parents who had talked to the heads when their children started at school the majority had been seen on their own by the heads. Fourteen per cent had seen the heads together with other parents. There was no social class difference in the proportions of parents who had talked on their own with the heads.

(ii) *Talks with teachers; frequency and subjects discussed.*

3.17. We look now at the frequency with which parents had discussed their children with the heads or class teachers in their children's schools. As would be expected this was related to the length of time the child had been at the school. (See Table 50.) In all eight per cent of the parents had had no talks at all about their children with the heads or class teachers. Forty-five per cent had

had four talks or more. The frequency with which parents discussed their children with the school staff was not related to whether mothers were working or not but it was markedly associated with social class. (See Tables 49 and 50.) As Table 46 shows there was little difference between the lengths of time that children in the various social classes had been at these schools.

3.18. This tendency for the amount of contact with the school staff to increase with social class is found again when we compare the proportions of parents in the different groups who had had a talk about the selected child with any of the child's own class teachers. Only six per cent of the parents in class I had not talked with the child's class teacher compared with 27 per cent of those in class V. (See Table 51.)

3.19. In their talks with heads or class teachers parents had most frequently discussed their children's progress educationally or the teaching methods used at the school (83 per cent). Over a quarter of the parents had talked about some behavioural problems of their children such as nervousness, anxiety or bad behaviour. The other main purpose of parents' talks with the head or class teachers was to notify them of children's illness or absence from school for other reasons.

(iii) *Opportunities provided for parents to visit the schools and advantage taken of them by parents*

3.20. It may be assumed that the provision of opportunities for parents to visit the schools has three main purposes, firstly to facilitate meetings between parents and teachers so that both come to know each other better, secondly to enable parents to see for themselves what the schools are doing and how their children are progressing and, thirdly, so that children feel that their parents are interested in and know what happens at school and that home and school are not separate worlds. It seems likely that in these respects some types of school activities to which parents are invited will be more valuable than others. We now compare the extent to which various opportunities for parents to visit the schools are provided and are taken advantage of by parents. Table 52 following shows the proportions of parents who said that they had been invited to various school functions and the proportions who attended.

Table 52

Comparison between opportunities provided for parents to visit the schools and parents' attendance

School activities to which parents were invited	Percentages of parents	
	Invited	Attended
Open days and evenings	81	72
Prize days	14	10
Sports days, swimming galas	55	39
School plays, shows, concerts, services	75	64
Parent/teacher association meetings, activities	25	13
School outings	14	4
Jumble sales, social evenings to raise money for school	65	49
Medical or dental examinations	88	72

3.21. Open days or evenings in general provide opportunities both for parents to see children's work and to talk to class teachers. Eighty-one per cent of the parents said that they had been invited to them. There was no social class difference in the provision made but the parents in the manual worker classes were rather less likely to attend them than those in the non-manual groups. (See Table 53.) Working mothers were just as likely to go to their children's open days as those not working.

3.22. During the course of the survey very different opinions were expressed to us about the value of parent/teacher associations. A quarter of these parents said that there was a P.T.A. attached to their children's schools. There was again a marked relationship between attendance and social class. Twenty per cent of social class I had attended P.T.A. meetings or activities but only five per cent of class V. During the preliminary stages of the enquiry working class mothers who had been to P.T.A. meetings had several times said that they did not care for them as the more fluent and confident parents dominated the meetings and they themselves were not able to express their views.

3.23. The great majority of parents had been invited to attend school medical or dental examinations of their children. Sixteen per cent in all had not done so. There was no social class difference either in the proportions who had been invited to or who had attended these examinations.

3.24. Three-quarters of the parents had had the opportunity of going to school plays, shows or concerts or to school carol or other services. Sixty-four per cent had been to at least one of these functions. Fifty-five per cent had been invited to sports days or swimming galas and 14 per cent to prize days. Thirty-nine per cent had been to the former and 10 per cent to the latter. The only social class difference evident here was a tendency for parents in class I to be the most likely to attend and those in class V the least likely. Fourteen per cent of parents could have gone on school outings with the children but only four per cent did so. Two-thirds of the parents, a slightly higher proportion in the non-manual than manual worker classes, said that the schools had organised jumble sales, bazaars or social evenings to raise money for the schools.

(iv) *Parental satisfaction with arrangements for seeing the school staff and opinion of their contacts with teachers*

3.25. In general these parents were satisfied with the arrangements at their children's schools for seeing the head or the class teachers and with the reception they had when they visited the schools. The proportions making any criticisms of contacts between themselves and the staff were small. Only 11 per cent were not completely satisfied about the arrangements for seeing the head or class teacher. Nine per cent felt that it was not easy to see the teachers whenever they wanted to, seven per cent did not think that the teachers seemed very pleased when they went to the schools and 11 per cent considered that the teachers would prefer to keep parents out of the school.

3.26. Social class differences found here were that parents in the professional and managerial classes tended to be slightly more critical of the school's arrangements for seeing the head or class teacher. As we have already seen they were more likely to want to visit the schools. On the other hand parents in the manual occupational categories were more inclined than the non-manual to consider that the teachers had favourites among the parents. In all 19 per cent of the parents felt this.

3.27. Suggestions made for improving the arrangements for seeing the staff were that it should be easier to see the *class* teachers (four per cent of the total sample) and that there should be a parent/teacher association (three per cent). The latter was raised more often by the professional and managerial class parents than the others. Other suggestions, each made by one or two per cent of the parents, were that it should be easier for them to see the head or class teacher in private, that the head should be more readily available for parents to see, that more open days should be arranged at convenient times, that parents should be given more information when they went to the schools and that they should be able to make appointments or have definite times for seeing the heads or other teachers.

3.28. It was clear in the preliminary stages of this inquiry that some parents were reluctant to go to the schools unless they were invited to some school function or were specifically asked by the heads in order to discuss their children. The impression gained from talking to these parents was not that they were uninterested in their children's schooling but that they were confident that the heads would let them know when they needed to visit the school for any reason. Approximately a quarter of the parents said that they felt that they were interfering if they went to the school uninvited. This attitude was not related to social class. Twenty-nine per cent considered that teachers had enough to do already without having to talk to parents.

3.29. Half of the parents had in fact been to have a talk with the head or another teacher on their own initiative. The highest proportions of parents who had been to see the staff without an invitation were in the professional and in the unskilled occupational classes. There was some association between parents going to school on their own initiative and their making a complaint to the head or class teacher on some issue. Twenty per cent of those who had been to the school uninvited had made a complaint compared with seven per cent of those who had been to the school only on invitation.

3.30. The findings discussed in this section point strongly to the importance of the initiative being taken by the school staff in inviting parents to the schools if close contacts are to be maintained between parents and teachers.

(iv) *Communication between parents and teachers*

3.31. The first step in establishing relations between parents and teachers is for parents to visit their children's schools. After that the important issue is that the contact established should be helpful to both groups. We now consider whether the results of this survey give any indications of the value of contacts between parents and teachers.

3.32. Approximately half of the parents said that they would have liked to be told more about how their children were getting on at school. Almost a third thought that the teachers should have asked them more about their children. A fifth considered that if they went up to the school the teachers only told them what they knew already. Each of these points tended to be made more frequently by parents in the manual than non-manual occupations, suggesting that satisfactory communication between parent and teacher is considerably easier for the latter category of parents.

3.33. An important finding of this enquiry is that, within the social class groups, parents were *less* likely to say that they wanted to be told more about how their children were getting on or that they thought that the teachers should ask them, the parents, more about their children if open days were arranged by the school or if parents had had several talks with the heads or class teachers.

3.34. These findings indicate the value of talks between parents and teachers and of open days in making parents feel better informed about their children's school life and also that their contribution towards their children's progress is of importance and is considered to be so by the schools.

(c) Parents' views on school organisation and teaching methods

3.35. In this section are discussed parents' preferences for combined and separate schools for infants and juniors, their views on the advantages and disadvantages of streamed and mixed ability classes in the primary schools and their satisfaction generally with the methods of teaching and the progress of their children at school.

(i) *Parental preferences for combined or separate schools for infants and juniors*

3.36. In the preferences expressed by parents for separate or combined schools for juniors and infants we find again the tendency for people to like the arrangement with which they are familiar. Taken overall however separate schools for juniors and infants were rather more frequently preferred. Separate schools were thought to be better by over 60 per cent of parents with children in separate schools and by 26 per cent of those with children in combined schools. Forty per cent of those with children in combined schools liked the arrangement they had but only 14 per cent with children in separate junior schools and 17 per cent with children in separate infants would have preferred a combined primary school. (See Table 54.)

3.37. The main advantages seen in having the juniors and infants in separate schools were that the older children tended to be rough and to bully the younger if they were together (given by 58 per cent of the parents who preferred separate schools). Separate schools were thought to provide a greater incentive for children to grow up and to help them to develop (29 per cent). There was considered to be more likelihood of having specialised teachers for different age groups if the juniors and infants were separate and it was thought that teachers in such schools were more able to concentrate on and so understand the special needs of different age groups (25 per cent). Some parents felt that older children tended to be a bad influence on the younger ones and taught them bad language and habits (14 per cent).

3.38. Three reasons for preferring combined juniors and infants schools were given frequently. One was that the change between the infants and junior stages was more gradual if the children were in one school; it was less upsetting because infants knew more what to expect in the higher classes from mixing with juniors (45 per cent of parents who preferred combined schools). The second most frequently mentioned reason was that it was useful if brothers, sisters or friends were in the same school because they could go to school together and see each other in break and generally look after each other (42 per cent). Thirdly these parents considered that it was better for older and younger children to mix together and that the older ones helped the younger (41 per cent).

(ii) *Parental preferences for streamed or mixed ability classes*

3.39. The ways in which these children were allocated to their classes, that is whether they were in streamed or mixed ability groups, were related to the stage they were at in the primary school. Fifty-three per cent of the parents of children in the top juniors said that their children were in streamed classes compared with 16 per cent of those with children in the top infants. Thirteen per cent of parents were not sure how their children were assigned to classes. Taken overall just over half the children were thought to be in classes according to their ages, these would have been of mixed ability. (See Table 55.)

3.40. There was a clear preference among the majority of parents for their children, at whatever age they were at the time of the survey, to be taught with other children of the same capacity, that is for the quicker and slower children to be allocated to separate classes rather than mixed together. Separate ability groups were preferred by as many as 59 per cent of the parents with children in the top infants class and by 70 per cent of those whose children were in the top juniors form. (See Table 56.)

3.41. What is striking is the large proportion of parents, 61 per cent, whose children were in mixed forms who would have preferred them to be in separate ability groups. Seventy-six per cent of parents with children in streamed classes considered that it was better for the quicker and slower children to be separated. (See Tables 57 and 58.)

3.42. There were no clear social class differences either in the ways in which these children were allocated to their classes or in parental preferences for streamed or mixed ability classes. (See Tables 59 and 60.)

3.43. The two most frequently mentioned advantages of streaming by ability were, firstly, that the slow children would then have more attention and tuition and greater opportunities for being brought on in their work (68 per cent of those who preferred streaming) and, secondly, that the bright children would not be held back academically by the slower children and could be given more attention by teachers (57 per cent). It is of interest that a greater proportion of the manual occupation parents were concerned about the advantages of streaming for the teaching of slower children whereas more of the non-manual groups mentioned the help to the brighter child. (See Table 61.)

3.44. Thirty per cent of the parents said that in separate ability classes the slow child was less likely to feel inadequate and ashamed of his slowness. Thirteen per cent said that streaming helped and made life easier for the teachers.

3.45. The majority of parents who thought that it was better for pupils of their children's ages to be in mixed ability classes were in favour of the sense of competition that this gave and considered that the slower and more backward pupils would be spurred on by being with brighter children (68 per cent of those preferring mixed ability classes). Thirty-seven per cent thought that mixed classes prevented feelings of difference developing among the children and the brighter or quicker looking down on the slower or duller. Seventeen per cent considered that the brighter, quicker ones would help the slower to learn and to develop. (See Table 62.)

(iii) *Parents' satisfaction with the teaching methods and with their children's progress at school*

3.46. Parents were asked whether they were quite happy with the methods of teaching used at their children's schools and with the way the children were progressing in their work. No attempt was made to separate parents' views on methods of teaching from concern about school progress because it was found in the preliminary trial interviews that in general parents saw these as aspects of one issue and could not assess them separately.

3.47. A third of the parents did have some worries about their children's progress or the teaching methods. The proportion was the same for each of the forms included in the survey. The non-manual occupation parents were somewhat more inclined to be anxious about these matters than the manual.

3.48. The anxieties most frequently expressed by parents were that they thought that their children were not being brought on fast enough or were not up to standard for their ages. This was mentioned by 15 per cent of the total sample of parents. Next came mention of too little individual attention being given to pupils, that classes were too large or that teachers were not interested in the children's progress. Points falling in this category were made more frequently by parents with children in the higher classes (13 per cent overall). Criticisms or anxiety specifically about new methods of teaching were expressed by seven per cent of all parents, rather more frequently by parents of younger children. In addition seven per cent of parents with children in the top infants class considered that too much time was spent on play and other activities which did not help the child with his work progress (see Table 63). There was no clear association between the type of worries expressed by parents and social class.

3.49. Heads or other teachers had talked to just over a quarter of the parents about the teaching methods which were used in the sampled schools. Rather more of the non-manual than manual occupation parents had had such a talk. The proportion of parents who were anxious about their children's progress or the methods of teaching was no lower among those who had than those who had not had a talk about the methods of teaching used in the school. The proportion who were worried was also no lower among parents who had attended open days and was not related to the number of talks parents had had with heads or class teachers.

3.50. These findings do not appear surprising in view of the fact that this assessment of satisfaction or anxiety covers a very wide range of issues many of which would not be affected by attendance at open days or talks between parents and teachers. For the same reason they are not thought to conflict with the conclusion reached in paragraph 3.34 on the value of contacts between parents and teachers.

3.51. Anxiety about the methods of teaching and their children's progress was to a certain extent related to parents' educational aspirations for their children. Among parents whose children had not at the time of the enquiry been allocated to their secondary schools, those who hoped that their children would go to a type of school other than secondary modern were slightly more inclined to worry about their children's progress than those who considered that secondary modern schools would suit their children. This relationship was not found, however, among parents of top junior children who had already been allocated to their secondary schools. Higher proportions of parents who were worried about their children's progress or the teaching methods had bought copies of the school text books to have at home.

(d) Behaviour training and discipline of children

3.52. The great majority of these parents considered that teaching children to behave was a joint responsibility of parents and the schools and did not think that it should be left mainly to the teachers.

3.53. On the whole parents thought that the control exercised by the schools over the children was about right but practically all of those who would have preferred it to be different in any way would have liked the teachers to be firmer and not less firm with the pupils. As children progressed up the schools parents were rather more inclined to want firmer discipline than the school provided. Parents who themselves found their children difficult to control were more likely to want the schools to be firmer with the children. There were no clear social class differences in parents' attitudes towards the teachers' control of the children.

3.54. Parents were asked for their views on corporal punishment. A quarter thought that children needed to be smacked quite often. Almost three-quarters said that they would agree to the school using the cane occasionally. Fifty-two per cent however considered that having the cane was very bad for most children and it follows that they would consider that it would need to be used with careful discrimination if at all. Thirty-eight per cent disagreed that the cane was very bad for most children (see Table 64). Parents in the manual and clerical occupational categories were slightly more inclined than those in the professional or managerial to think that children need to be smacked fairly frequently. Apart from this there were no marked social class differences in parental attitudes to these issues.

(e) Other general comments about primary schooling

3.55. Besides the specific questions put to parents about different aspects of primary education the answers to which we have already discussed, opportunities were also given to parents to raise any other issues they wished. After answering specific questions about the school they were asked whether there was anything which they were not happy about or which worried them about their children's schools which they had not already mentioned. The proportions of parents who wished to make additional comments varied markedly with social class and ranged from two-thirds of class I parents to less than one-third of class V.

3.56. The most frequently made complaints, and particularly by the professional and managerial class parents, were firstly of bad, old-fashioned school buildings, lack of facilities or poor equipment in their children's schools. Secondly about the size of classes, shortage of teachers and general overcrowding. (See Table 65.)

3.57. Next came comments about the discipline, control and general behaviour of the children and about teachers' relations with the pupils. Equally frequently mentioned were worries about the standard of teaching, the progress made by their child, and about various aspects of the curriculum. Criticism of the liaison between home and school were made more frequently by the professional and managerial than other parents. The school meals and the uniforms and other clothing required for school were each criticised by only one per cent of the parents.

3.58. At the end of their interviews parents were again asked whether they had anything else they wished to say about their children's schools or about primary schooling in general. This question produced a very similar distribution of comments about the schools. In addition however some points were made about primary schooling in general but only by small proportions of parents. For example four per cent considered that 11 was not a good age for transfer to secondary education. Three per cent commented on the unfairness resulting in some instances from children having to start or change schools according to the month of their birth. Other comments were made by even smaller proportions of parents. (See Table 66.)

Table 37

Whether child went to a nursery school or nursery class, by social class

Q.1. Whether child attended a nursery school	Social class							
	I Profes- sional	II Mana- gerial	III Non- Manual	III Skilled Manual	IV Semi- skilled	V Un- skilled	Un- classi- fied	Total
Yes	25	16	16	15	12	20	38	16
No	75	84	83	85	88	79	62	84
Not known	0	0	1	0	0	1	0	0
Total number (100%)	(110)	(430)	(338)	(1,486)	(499)	(189)	(40)	(3,092)

Table 38

Whether child went to a nursery school or nursery class, by Department of Education Division

Q.1. Whether child attended a nursery school	South West	North- ern	East/ West Riding	North West	North Mid- land	Mid- land	East- ern	Metro- politan	South East	South- ern	Total
Yes, in this country	14	18	9	15	20	10	8	34	12	12	15
Yes, abroad only	2	0	2	0	1	0	1	2	0	2	1
No	85	82	89	84	79	88	91	64	88	85	84
Not known	0	0	0	0	0	1	0	0	0	1	0
Total number (100%)	(177)	(257)	(393)	(510)	(250)	(260)	(374)	(255)	(343)	(273)	(3,092)

Table 39

Age at which child started at school, by social class

Q.2. Age of starting school for full day	Social class							
	I Profes- sional	II Mana- gerial	III Non- manual	III Skilled manual	IV Semi- skilled	V Un- skilled	Un- classi- fied	Total
Under 3½ years old	2	1	2	4	3	3	12	3
3½ but under 4	0	2	3	2	2	2	5	2
4 but under 4½	2	3	6	6	5	12	10	6
4½ but under 5	44	46	42	43	40	39	33	42
5 but under 5½	46	47	46	44	48	41	38	45
5½ or older	4	1	1	1	2	3	2	2
Not known	2	0	0	0	0	0	0	0
Total number (100%)	(110)	(430)	(338)	(1,486)	(499)	(189)	(40)	(3,092)

Table 40
Age at which child started at school, by Department of Education Division

Q.2. Age of starting school for full day	South West	North-ern	East/West Riding	North West	North Mid-land	Mid-land	East-ern	Metro-politan	South East	South-ern	Total
Under 3½ years old	2	2	4	8	5	4	1	2	1	2	3
3½ but under 4	1	3	1	3	5	2	1	4	1	1	2
4 but under 4½	1	7	4	8	8	2	1	20	6	2	6
4½ but under 5	42	54	39	50	26	42	40	34	42	46	42
5 but under 5½	52	35	51	31	52	49	56	36	48	46	45
5½ or older	1	0	2	0	4	0	1	4	2	2	2
Not known	1	0	0	0	0	0	0	0	0	1	0
Total number (100%)	(177)	(257)	(393)	(510)	(250)	(260)	(374)	(255)	(343)	(273)	(3,092)

Table 41
Whether earlier or later start preferred, by actual starting age

	Actual age of starting							
Q.3. Whether different starting age preferred	Under 3½	3½ under 4	4 under 4½	4½ under 5	5 under 5½	5½ or over	No Answer	Total
Earlier start preferred	5	8	14	30	43	60	—	34
Good age to start	78	76	74	65	53	32	—	60
Later start preferred	15	13	8	5	4	6	—	5
Not known	2	3	4	—	—	2	—	1
Total number (100%)	(100)	(63)	(178)	(1,300)	(1,395)	(47)	(9)	(3,092)

Table 42
Starting age preferred, by actual starting age

	Actual age of starting							
Starting age preferred	Under 3½	3½ under 4	4 under 4½	4½ under 5	5 under 5½	5½ or over	No Answer	Total
Under 3½ years old	83	8	8	1	1	0	—	4
3½ but under 4	0	76	5	3	1	0	—	4
4 but under 4½	6	2	75	24	22	6	—	24
4½ but under 5	3	3	1	68	18	13	—	36
5 but under 5½			6	6	2	53	36	—	26
5½ or over	0	2	1	2	4	40	—	4
No answer	2	3	4	0	1	4	—	2
Total number (100%)	(100)	(63)	(178)	(1,300)	(1,395)	(47)	(9)	(3,092)

Note.—Some of the percentages within the dotted lines in Table 42 are higher than those shown in Table 41 as saying that the actual starting age was a good age to start. This is because some of the preferred earlier or later starts come within the same age grouping as the actual starting age.

Table 43
Whether child attended school for a full or half day when he or she started in the infants, by social class

	Social class							
Q.4. Whether child attended for full or half-day on starting in the infants	I Profes-sional	II Mana-gerial	III Non-manual	III Skilled manual	IV Semi-skilled	V Un-skilled	Un-classi-fied	Total
Attended mornings AND afternoons immediately	96	98	98	99	99	99	98	99
Attended mornings or afternoons only at first	3	2	1	1	1	0	2	1
Not known	1	0	1	0	0	1	0	0
Total number (100%)	(110)	(430)	(338)	(1,486)	(499)	(189)	(40)	(3,092)

Table 44

Whether parents preferred child to start school by attending for a full or half day, by social class

Q.5. Whether better to have started full or half day in the infants' school	Social class							
	I Profes-sional	II Mana-gerial	III Non-manual	III Skilled manual	IV Semi-skilled	V Un-skilled	Un-classi-fied	Total
Better to have attended school:								
In morning and afternoon when starting	57	69	73	78	78	83	75	76
Only in mornings or afternoons	42	30	26	21	20	15	23	23
Not known	1	1	1	1	2	2	2	1
Total number (100%)	(110)	(430)	(338)	(1,486)	(434)	(189)	(40)	(3,092)

Table 45

Number of primary schools attended, by form

Q.6. Number of schools attended	Top Juniors	Bottom Juniors	Top Infants	Total
Present school only attended	32	35	82	50
Two schools attended	53	52	15	39
Three schools attended	11	10	2	8
Four schools attended	2	2	1	2
Five or more schools attended	2	1	0	1
Total number (100%)	(1,023)	(1,016)	(1,053)	(3,092)

Table 46

Length of time child had been at sampled school, by social class

Q.7. Length of time at sampled school	Social class							
	I Profes-sional	II Mana-gerial	III Non-manual	III Skilled manual	IV Semi-skilled	V Un-skilled	Un-classi-fied	Total
One term or less	0	2	3	1	2	2	3	2
Over one term, up to and exactly one school year	22	19	21	19	20	18	22	20
Over one school year, up to and exactly two years	16	13	14	14	13	14	10	13
Over two school years, up to and exactly three school years	31	30	26	28	28	28	30	28
Over three school years	31	36	36	38	37	38	35	37
Total number (100%)	(110)	(430)	(338)	(1,486)	(499)	(189)	(40)	(3,092)

Table 47

Whether other members of the family had attended child's present school, by social class

Q.8. Whether other members of family attended child's present school	Social class							
	I Profes-sional	II Mana-gerial	III Non-manual	III Skilled maual	IV Semi-skilled	V Un-skilled	Un-classi-fied	Total
No	40	31	34	25	21	22	35	27
Yes, brothers, sisters of selected child	56	62	57	63	66	67	48	62
Yes, father, mother	7	14	13	23	21	26	20	20
Yes, other relatives	8	9	12	18	18	27	20	17
Total number (100%)	(110)	(430)	(338)	(1,486)	(499)	(189)	(40)	(3,092)

Table 48

Whether parents had a talk with the head when child first went to present school, by social class

| | Social class | | | | | | | |
Q.14. Whether parents talked to head when child started at this school	I Profes-sional	II Mana-gerial	III Non manual	III Skilled manual	IV Semi-skilled	V Un-skilled	Un-classi-fied	Total
Yes	78	67	65	61	59	60	60	62
No	21	32	34	39	40	39	40	37
Not known	1	1	1	1	1	1	0	1
Total number (100%)	(110)	(430)	(338)	(1,486)	(499)	(189)	(40)	(3,092)

Table 49

Number of talks parents had had with school staff, by social class

| | Social class | | | | | | | |
Q.16. Number of talks parents had with heads or class teachers	I Profes-sional	II Mana-gerial	III Non manual	III Skilled manual	IV Semi-skilled	V Un-skilled	Un-classi-fied	Total
No talks with head or teacher	2	5	7	8	11	15	8	8
One talk	8	11	12	14	15	16	20	13
Two talks	9	13	15	17	15	16	12	15
Three talks	17	17	18	18	18	16	20	18
Four to six talks	29	23	24	21	21	18	20	22
More than six talks	35	31	24	22	20	18	20	23
Total number (100%)	(110)	(430)	(338)	(1,486)	(499)	(189)	(40)	(3,092)

Table 50

Number of talks parents had had with school staff, by length of time child had been at the school and by social class

| | Time child had been at the school, and social class | | | | | | | | | |
| | 1 year or less | | Over 1 yr–2 yrs. | | Over 2 yrs.–3 yrs. | | Over 3 yrs. | | Total | |
Number of talks parents had with heads or class teachers	Non-manual	Manual	Non-manual	Manual	Non-manual	Manual	Non-manual	Manual	Non-manual	Manual
No talks	13	21	3	5	2	6	4	7	5	9
One talk	30	28	11	16	4	11	4	9	11	14
Two talks	25	25	24	20	9	16	5	10	13	16
Three talks	14	16	28	24	21	21	12	17	17	18
Four to six talks	11	7	22	21	30	26	29	24	24	21
More than six talks	7	2	12	14	33	19	46	34	29	21
Total number (100%)	(197)	(450)	(119)	(294)	(250)	(604)	(312)	(826)	(878)	(2,174)

Table 51

Whether parents had had a talk with any of the class teachers since child had been at sampled school, by social class

| | Social class | | | | | | | |
Q.15. Whether parents had had a talk with their child's class teacher	I Profes-sional	II Mana-gerial	III Non manual	III Skilled manual	IV Semi-skilled	V Un-skilled	Un-classi-fied	Total
Yes	94	86	85	82	78	72	80	82
No	6	13	15	18	22	27	20	18
Not known	0	1	0	0	0	1	0	0
Total number (100%)	(110)	(430)	(338)	(1,486)	(499)	(189)	(40)	(3,092)

Table 53

Opportunities provided for parents to visit the schools and advantage taken of them by parents, by social class

		Social class							
School activities to which parents invited—		I Profes-sional	II Mana-gerial	III Non-manual	III Skilled manual	IV Semi-skilled	V Un-skilled	Un-classi-fied	Total
(1) Open days and evenings	Provided	78	81	82	81	82	82	85	81
	Attended	77	76	76	70	70	65	62	72
(2) Prize days	Provided	12	16	17	13	16	16	8	14
	Attended	11	13	12	9	9	11	8	10
(3) Sports days, swimming galas	Provided	51	56	56	54	58	51	42	55
	Attended	42	39	43	39	42	28	33	39
(4) School plays, shows, concerts, school carol and other services	Provided	81	80	77	74	72	71	72	75
	Attended	74	73	68	62	61	55	55	64
(5) Parent/teacher association meetings or other activities	Provided	24	28	26	26	23	16	28	25
	Attended	20	19	15	12	11	5	8	13
(6) School outings	Provided	12	17	14	14	13	12	15	14
	Attended	4	7	5	4	4	3	8	4
(7) Jumble sales, bazaars, social evenings to raise money for the school	Provided	72	70	68	64	61	62	62	65
	Attended	54	50	55	49	39	44	35	49
(8) Medical or dental examinations	Provided	88	89	87	88	88	89	92	88
	Attended	75	77	75	76	71	75	57	75
Total number (100%)		(110)	(430)	(338)	(1,486)	(499)	(189)	(40)	(3,092)

Note.—The percentages who said that the activities were provided and the percentages who attended are both out of the total sample.

Table 54

Whether parents preferred juniors and infants to be in same or separate schools, by type of school child was at

	Type of school			
Q.35. Parents' preferences for juniors and infants	Junior and Infants	Juniors only	Infants only	Total
Better in same school	40	14	17	25
Better in separate schools	26	64	61	48
Does not matter, depends on school	14	9	7	10
No opinion, had not thought about it	20	12	15	16
Total number (100%)	(1,256)	(1,178)	(658)	(3,092)

Q.35a. If better in same school, advantages—

Change between infants and juniors more gradual, know what to expect, less upsetting, know children in junior school	41	50	56	45
Useful if brothers, sisters, friends, would be in the same school, can go to and from school together; look after and see each other in break	37	56	43	42
Better for children of different age groups to mix together, older children can help younger	47	31	30	41
Children become used to, get to know teachers	3	4	4	3
Head gets to know children well from an early age	3	4	3	3
Other answers	6	6	12	7
Total number (100%)	(497)	(172)	(112)	(781)

Q.35b. If better in separate schools, advantages—

Older children rough, bullying	52	57	64	58
Older children can have a bad influence on younger, can pick up bad ways, habits, language	10	14	19	14
Have specialised teachers for the different age groups, teachers can concentrate on, understand different age groups better	28	24	24	25
An incentive for the child, stops them being babyish, helps them to develop, to grow up	28	31	26	29
Juniors do more serious work, work harder than infants	6	10	10	9
Discipline is different for juniors and infants	1	2	2	2
Small classes/more space	2	2	1	2
Brothers and sisters can be separated	2	1	—	1
Other answers	5	5	4	5
Total number (100%)	(332)	(758)	(401)	(1,491)

Table 55

Method of allocation to classes, by form

Q.27. Method of allocation into classes	Top Juniors	Bottom Juniors	Top Infants	Total
In classes by age	38	51	69	53
In class by ability/streamed	53	36	16	35
Not known	9	12	15	13
Total number (100%)	(1,023)	(1,016)	(1,053)	(3,092)

Table 56

Whether parents preferred streaming by ability or not, by form

Q.28. Parents' preferences	Top Juniors	Bottom Juniors	Top Infants	Total
For quicker and slower children to be in one class	24	26	34	28
For streaming by ability	70	68	59	66
No preference, depended on child	6	6	7	6
Total number (100%)	(1,023)	(1,016)	(1,053)	(3,092)

Table 57

Whether parents preferred streaming by ability or not, by method of allocation to classes

	Present method of allocation to classes			
Q.28. Parents' preference	In classes by age	In classes by ability/ streamed	Not known	Total
For the quicker and slower children to be in same class	32	20	32	28
For streaming by ability	61	76	58	66
No preference, depended on child	7	4	10	6
Total number (100%)	(1,638)	(1,078)	(376)	(3,092)

Table 58

Whether parents preferred streaming or not, by method of allocation to classes and by form

	Present method of allocation to class by form									
	By age			By ability			Not known			
Q.28. Parents' preferences	Top Jun.	Bottom Jun.	Top Inf.	Top Jun.	Bottom Jun.	Top Inf.	Top Jun.	Bottom Jun.	Top Inf.	Total
For the quicker and slower children to be in one class	27	29	37	20	19	21	33	32	31	28
For streaming by ability	67	64	56	75	77	75	55	58	60	66
No preference, depended on child	7		7	5	4	4	13	10	8	6
Total number (100%)	(387)	(523)	(728)	(541)	(366)	(171)	(95)	(127)	(154)	(3,092)

Table 59

Method of allocation to classes, by social class

	Social class							
Q.27. Method of allocation into classes	I Profes- sional	II Mana- gerial	III Non- manual	III Skilled manual	IV Semi- skilled	V Un- skilled	Un- classi- fied	Total
In classes by age	56	57	53	52	54	47	38	53
In classes by ability/streamed	34	35	36	35	32	40	35	35
Not known	9	8	11	12	14	13	27	13
Total number (100%)	(110)	(430)	(338)	(1,486)	(499)	(189)	(40)	(3,092)

Table 60

Whether parents prefer streaming by ability or not, by social class

Q.28. Parents' preferences	Social class							
	I Profes-sional	II Mana-gerial	III Non-manual	III Skilled manual	IV Semi-skilled	V Un-skilled	Un-classi-fied	Total
For quicker and slower children to be in one class	30	27	28	28	27	30	22	28
For streaming by ability	64	67	67	65	66	63	68	66
No preference, depended on child	6	6	4	7	7	7	10	6
Total number (100%)	(110)	(430)	(338)	(1,486)	(499)	(189)	(40)	(3,092)

Table 61

Advantages of streaming by ability, by social class

Q.28b. Advantages of streaming by ability	Social class							
	I Profes-sional	II Mana-gerial	III Non-manual	III Skilled manual	IV Semi-skilled	V Un-skilled	Un-classi-fied	Total
Slow ones can have more attention, tuition; can be brought on	59	64	61	70	74	71	—	68
Bright child not held back academically by slow children. Teachers can give time to bright child	68	66	63	54	55	49	—	57
Slow children not made to feel slow, dunces, ashamed	28	29	35	30	28	29	—	30
Helps the teacher, makes life easier for teachers	25	12	17	12	12	8	—	13
Slow children work better apart	1	3	4	3	2	2	—	3
Slow children copy from bright children, pick their brains	—	—	—	1	1	2	—	1
Total number (100%)	(71)	(290)	(227)	(972)	(329)	(119)	(27)	(2,035)

Table 62

Advantages of quicker and slower children in one class, by social class

Q.28(a). Advantages of mixed ability classes	Social class							
	I Profes-sional	II Manag-erial	III Non-manual	III Skilled manual	IV Semi-skilled	V Un-skilled	Un-classi-fied	Total
Avoids feeling of difference and of brighter, quicker looking down on slower, duller	30	42	38	37	36	27	—	37
Gives a sense of competition, spurs on the slower, backward	67	64	67	70	59	77	—	68
Brighter, quicker children can help the slower ones to develop	18	10	15	15	27	21	—	17
It is too early to judge child's capabilities, ability at this early stage	6	8	5	2	2	—	—	3
It steadies/slows down the quicker ones	12	2	6	2	1	2	—	3
Children have got to know one another, made friends at this stage	3	2	1	2	1	2	—	2
Slower children have better education if with bright ones, streaming is unfair to slower children	—	10	9	6	4	4	—	6
Children vary, slow in some subjects, quick in others	3	1	2	2	1	—	—	2
Total number (100%)	(33)	(115)	(96)	(415)	(137)	(56)	(9)	(861)

Table 63

Whether parents were satisfied with methods of teaching, and child's progress at school, by form

Q.26. Parents' views on methods of teaching and child's progress	Top Juniors	Bottom Juniors	Top Infants	Total
Quite happy with methods and progress	67	67	67	67
Worried about methods and/or progress. Including worried because did not know how child was getting on	33	33	33	33
Total number (100%)	(1,023)	(1,016)	(1,053)	(3,092)

Parental worries about methods of teaching and progress	Percentages of total sample			
Felt child not up to standard for his/her age, not being brought on fast enough	15	16	14	15
Not enough individual attention, classes too large, teachers not interested in child's progress	17	13	10	13
Too much time spent on play, other subjects, parents felt not useful for child's work or progress	4	4	7	5
Criticisms of or anxiety about new methods of teaching, e.g., reading, spelling, arithmetic	4	6	9	7
Not know how child was getting on. Liked to be told more, have reports on child's progress	4		5	5
Fault in child, untidy, wouldn't pay attention, lazy, too talkative	3	4	5	4
Staff problems at school	2	1	1	1
Equipment, methods used at school old fashioned, out of date	0	1	0	0
All worries about age groupings of children within classes	1	1	1	1
Criticisms, worries, suggestions, directly related to specific aspects of schooling	2	3	2	2

Table 64

Parental attitudes to corporal punishment, by social class

	Social class							
Q.39 (ii), (iii), (v). Parental attitudes to corporal punishment	I Profes-sional	II Manag-erial	III Non-manual	III Skilled manual	IV Semi-skilled	V Un-skilled	Un-classi-fied	Total
(ii) Most children need to be smacked quite often								
Parent agrees	21	19	28	28	31	32	25	27
Parent cannot say	5	8	6	6	7	7	8	7
Parent disagrees	74	73	66	66	62	61	67	66
Total number (100%)	(110)	(430)	(338)	(1,486)	(499)	(189)	(40)	(3,092)
(iii) Having the cane is very bad for most children								
Parent agrees	52	52	49	52	51	56	50	52
Parent cannot say	11	11	12	10	9	7	10	10
Parent disagrees	37	37	39	38	40	37	40	38
Total number (100%)	(110)	(430)	(338)	(1,486)	(499)	(189)	(40)	(3,092)
(v) I would agree to the school using the cane occasionally								
Parent agrees	62	72	73	73	74	77	75	73
Parent cannot say	9	4	4	3	3	3	5	3
Parent disagrees	29	24	23	24	23	20	20	24
Total number (100%)	(110)	(430)	(338)	(1,486)	(499)	(189)	(40)	(3,092)

Table 65
Whether there was anything else parents were not happy about or which worried them about child's school, by social class

Q.40. Other things that worried parents about child's school	I Profes-sional	II Manag-erial	III Non-manual	III Skilled manual	IV Semi-skilled	V Un-skilled	Un-classi-fied	Total
Nothing else about which unhappy or worried	34	50	56	64	68	70	60	61
Bad, old-fashioned buildings, lack of facilities, poor equipment	30	20	14	11	11	7	5	13
Too large classes, shortage of teachers	28	15	12	8	6	8	10	10
Criticisms of discipline, insufficient control of child's social behaviour (e.g., manners, hygiene, etc.). Bad teacher-pupil relationship	12	10	10	9	9		12	9
Criticisms of standard of teaching, amount of progress made by child or content of curriculum	17	10	12	8	6	6	10	9
Poor liaison between school and home	11	7	5	4	2	2	—	4
Other children rough, bullying; badly behaved or spoken	3	2	3	3	3	3	5	3
Other difficulties arising from geographical position, locality or situation of school	1	2	2	2	2	3	—	2
Complaints about school dinners	—	1	1	1	1	2	2	1
School uniform, clothing required by school	—	1	1	—	1	2	5	1
Criticisms of holidays (e.g., too many)	—	1	—	1	—	—	2	—
Other specific criticisms or worries	3	3	2	2	2	1	—	2
Total number (multi-coded)	(110)	(430)	(338)	(1,486)	(499)	(189)	(40)	(3,092)

Table 66
Whether there was anything else parent wanted to say about child's school or infants or junior schooling in general, by social class

Q.62. Other comments about school or primary schooling in general	I Profes-sional	II Manag-erial	III Non-manual	III Skilled manual	IV Semi-skilled	V Un-skilled	Un-classi-fied	Total
Nothing else to say about school or schooling in general	40	44	46	56	63	66	55	54
Criticisms of large classes, over-crowding, shortage of teachers	27	22	18	14	10	11	18	15
Criticisms of standard of teaching, or child's progress, or content of curriculum	17	17	15	13	9	6	10	13
Criticisms of school buildings, accommodation, facilities, equipment	16	15	12	9	8	6	12	10
Criticisms of discipline, or insufficient control of child's social behaviour, or of bad teacher-pupil relations		8	5	8	6	7	10	7
Poor liaison between school and home	6	7	7	4	4	1	5	5
Criticism of 11 as age of transfer to or selection for secondary school	7	5	4	3	4	1	—	4
Adverse comments about 11+ selection or secondary or further education	9	4	5	3	2	2	2	3
Starting, changing schools by month of birthday unfair, a problem in infants or junior schools	2	3	4	3	2	—	—	3
Complaints about the start of schooling	4	2	3	3	2	2	—	2
Holidays too long, too many	1	2	1	2	1	1	2	2
Other difficulties arising from geographical, locality or situation of schools	2	2	2	2	1	3	—	2
Criticisms of school meals; food or drink provided at breaks	—	2	2	2	1	2	—	2
Complaints about school uniform, clothing required for school	—	1	1	1	1	1	—	1
Complaints about the choice of infant or primary schools	2	1	1	—	1	1	2	1
There should be (more) nursery schools	1	1	1	1	—	2	2	1
Children should be segregated by sex in infants or junior schools	—	—	1	1	—	—	5	1
Other specific answers	7	1	1	1	2	4	2	2
Total number (100%)	(110)	(430)	(338)	(1,486)	(499)	(189)	(40)	(3,092)

IV. A SUMMARY OF SOME OF THE INTERRELATIONS BETWEEN PARENTAL
ATTITUDES TO EDUCATION, HOME CIRCUMSTANCES AND SOCIAL CLASS

4.1. As was mentioned in the foreword to these appendices this survey had two broad purposes. The first was to collect information about the home backgrounds of children in primary schools and parental attitudes towards primary education and the upbringing of children; this has been presented in sections II and III of this report. The second purpose was to relate this information to children's achievement in schools. This latter analysis is reported in Appendix 4. For this second part of the enquiry it was desirable to group together questions which tended to be answered in the same way, or in statistical terms were correlated. (For example, parents who said that it was very easy to see the teachers whenever they wanted also tended to say that the teachers seemed very pleased when parents went along to see them. Other parents tended to disagree with both statements.) To find which questions in the interview tended to be answered similarly a statistical analysis (factor analysis) was carried out on 80 items of the interview data. The items included in this analysis are given in Annex II.

4.2. Some of the main groupings of items are worth discussing here because they serve to summarise some of the information presented in this report. The first group of items which tended to be answered in the same way appears to indicate the extent to which parents took responsibility and initiative over their children's education. At one extreme were parents who had talked to the head when their child first started in school, had talked with their child's class teacher, in all had had a large number of talks with the head or class teacher and had discussed educational matters and teaching methods with them. These parents were also likely to have asked for work for their child to do at home or for advice on how they could help their child at home. They had attended a large proportion of the different types of school functions to which parents were invited and in many cases the father as well as the mother had been to the school and had a talk with the head. At the other extreme were mothers who had never or rarely been to the child's school or, if they had been, were unlikely to have talked to the child's class teacher or to have discussed educational matters. They had attended few or none of the different types of school functions offered and the husbands were unlikely to have been to the school.

4.3. Another set of items which clustered together bear upon the relations between parents and teachers. Answers expressing a favourable attitude were that parents felt it was easy to see the teachers whenever they wanted to and that the staff seemed very pleased when parents went along to see them. They considered that the teachers seemed really interested in all the children and that they definitely seemed interested in what parents thought about their children's education. These parents tended to be happy with the school's arrangements for seeing the head or class teachers. They did not feel that they were interfering if they went to the school uninvited nor did they have the impression that teachers would have liked to have kept parents out of the school.

4.4. The interest and part taken by fathers in educational decisions and in the upbringing of their children is indicated by the following items. Whether the father took much part in the control of the children, how much spare time he had and whether he spent any of it with the child in the evenings or at week-ends, whether he had taken an interest in which school the child went to and had visited it and talked with the head and whether he was concerned to know how the child was progressing there.

4.5. Other items associated together appear to relate to the extent to which mothers devoted time and attention to their children's development. The least favourable extreme was expressed by those who felt that they should leave all teaching and helping with school subjects to teachers and that teaching children to behave should also be mainly the school's job. These mothers rarely spent time with their children in the evenings. The children were unlikely to get any help with school work at home and the mothers tended to say that they were too busy to give such help.

4.6. Another group of items which clustered together were somewhat similar to those just discussed but seemed related rather more to parents' interest in and knowledge of the work the child was doing at school. The favourable extremes of these items were that the children often talked to their parents about school work, they brought books home from school to read, they read frequently and their mothers spent time with them on most evenings. These parents were satisfied with their children's progress at school and the teaching methods used. They felt that they were told enough about how their children were getting on at school and that the teachers consulted them sufficiently as parents.

4.7. The final cluster of items to be discussed in this section gives an assessment of the level of literate interest in the home. Included here are whether the husband or wife belonged to a library or liked reading, the number of books possessed by the parents, how much reading the child did at home and whether he or she used a library.

4.8. In order to see whether parental behaviour and attitudes in these six areas varied with social class, scores were calculated for all parents on each of the six item clusters. In Table 67 are given the average scores on each of these indices for the different social class groups. The items are scored so that a low average indicates a favourable position. The association between social class and, for example, the responsibility and initiative taken by parents over their children's education can be seen by comparing the average scores of the various social class groups on item cluster (1). (There is no significance in the variations in scores between the indices, i.e. the fact that the average total score of cluster (1) is 16·6 and for cluster (4) is 7·5 is an artefact of the number of items making up the cluster and the scoring system used.)

4.9. On these indices associations were found between social class and the responsibility and initiative taken by parents over their children's education, in the interest shown and support given by fathers over their education and upbringing, in the time and attention parents devoted to their children's development and in their interest in and knowledge of the work their children were doing at school. In respect of each of these factors the home situation was likely to be more favourable the higher the social class of the home. What might be termed the literacy of the homes, that is the extent to which the families had firm habits of reading, increased very markedly with social class.

4.10. The index of satisfaction with parent-teacher relations showed little variation between the social class groups. As discussed in paragraph 3.25 the proportions who had criticisms of their relationships with the school were not large. The parents from the professional and managerial occupational categories had had more contacts with their children's schools and they tended to be more aware of and critical of any difficulties in meeting the teachers they wished to see but they were also more able than less educated parents to have discussions with members of the staff which they found satisfactory and informative.

Table 67

Average scores on item clusters, analysed by social class

Item clusters	Social class						Total
	I Profes-sional	II Mana-gerial	III Non-manual	III Skilled manual	IV Semi-skilled	V Un-skilled	
(1) Responsibility and initiative taken by parents over child's education.	15·9	15·7	16·5	16·7	16·9	17·1	16·6
(2) Relations between parents and teachers.	11·1	10·7	10·6	10·9	11·1	10·8	10·9
(3) Paternal interest and support.	9·9	10·0	10·2	11·4	12·7	12·1	11·2
(4) Whether parents devoted time and attention to child's development.	7·0	7·2	7·4	7·6	7·9	7·8	7·5
(5) Parental interest in and knowledge of the work child was doing.	10·2	10·4	10·4	10·9	10·9	11·4	10·8
(6) Literacy of home.	8·8	9·7	9·6	10·9	11·3	12·0	10·7
Number of parents (100%)	(110)	(430)	(338)	(1,486)	(499)	(189)	(3,092)

Notes.—(1) A low average indicates a favourable position.
(2) The 40 parents for whom social class information was not available are included in the total column but excluded from the body of the table.

ANNEX I

THE SAMPLE DESIGN

The enquiry was conducted amongst the parents of a sample of children of certain age-groups in maintained primary schools in England.

The sample design was a stratified random one in two stages with maintained primary schools in England as the primary sampling units. At the second stage, a sample of children in the specified age-groups was selected such that the overall probability of selection of each child was uniform.

In designing the sampling frame the maintained primary schools were divided into four main size strata:

    (i) schools with 25 or less pupils
    (ii) schools with 26 to 50 pupils
    (iii) schools with 51 to 200 pupils
and (iv) schools with 201 and more pupils.

As the population of the first stratum, i.e. schools with 25 or less pupils being under 0·5 per cent of the total primary schools population it was decided to exclude this stratum from the frame. Within the remaining three size strata, schools were broken down into the four types:

(*a*) infants only
(*b*) junior with infants
(*c*) junior without infants
(*d*) all-age.

An estimate of the population of each of the 12 cells was obtained by taking the mid-point of each of the size-bands as given in Table II of *Statistics of Education, 1963*, multiplying these by the number of schools in each of the size groups and adding together to form the strata given by type and size of school. A sample of approximately 3,500 was distributed between the cells in proportion to the estimated populations.

From the junior with infants and all-age schools, the sample was to consist of children in three age-bands defined as "top infants", "bottom juniors" and "top juniors". From the "junior only" schools only two age-bands could be selected and the third—"top infants"—was to be selected from the "infants only" schools feeding the selected "junior only" schools. From selected schools in the largest size stratum it was decided that 12 children per age group would be selected; from schools in the 51–200 size group eight children per age-group would be selected and in the smallest size stratum four children would be selected from each size stratum.

The theoretical distribution of the sample of children and the number of schools selected in each cell is shown in the following table.

THEORETICAL DISTRIBUTION OF SAMPLE

Type of school	School size stratum			Total
	26–50 pupils	51–200 pupils	201+ pupils	
Infants only	1 school 4 per age-group 1 age-group 4 pupils	38 schools 8 per age-group 1 age-group 304 pupils	37 schools 12 per age-group 1 age-group 444 pupils	76 schools 752 pupils
Junior without infants	— —	9 schools 8 per age-group 2 age-groups 144 pupils	44 schools 12 per age-group 2 age-groups 1,056 pupils	53 schools 1,200 pupils
Junior with infants	7 schools 4 per age-group 3 age-groups 84 pupils	15 schools 8 per age-group 3 age-groups 360 pupils	25 schools 12 per age-group 3 age-groups 900 pupils	47 schools 1,344 pupils
All-age	— —	4 schools 8 per age-group 3 age-groups 96 pupils	3 schools 12 per age-group 3 age-groups 108 pupils	7 schools 104 pupils
Total	8 schools 88 pupils	66 schools 904 pupils	109 schools 2,508 pupils	183 schools 3,500 pupils

Then within each of the cells, other than "infants only", from which the primary units, schools, were to be selected, the schools were arranged by local education authority and in size order and the requisite number selected with probability proportionate to their size. One hundred and seven schools were selected in this manner. The total number of schools in the sample were increased to 173 by taking the "infants only" schools from which the selected "juniors only" schools recruited their intake. The actual distribution of the sample is shown in the following table.

Type of school		School size stratum			
		26–50	51–200	201+	Total
Infants only	schools	1	26	39	66
	pupils	4	208	468	680
Junior without infants	schools	—	9	45	54
	pupils		144	1,080	1,224
Junior with infants	schools	8	13	25	46
	pupils	93 (1)	287 (2)	900	1,280
All-age	schools	—	5	2	7
	pupils	—	117	48 (3)	165
Total	schools	9	53	111	173
	pupils	97	756	2,496	3,349

Notes—(1) Insufficient children in age-range in one school

(2) One school was found to be in the 26–50 size group. One school was found to be all-age girls only from the ages 8 years to 15 years.

(3) Only one age-stratum could be taken from those schools which were classified as all-age but took girls only from the age of eight years and upwards.

It can be seen from the figures in the above table that the distribution of "infants only" schools obtained by taking those feeding the "juniors only" schools does not conform with the theoretical distribution, that is the distribution which would have been obtained if the "infants only" schools had been selected in the same way as the other schools. This is accounted for by the fact that for such selected "juniors only" school a sample of infants was drawn from only one feeding infants school. This resulted in a reduction of 10 in the number of schools selected and a reduction of 72 in the number of infants.

At the second stage a systematic sample of children was selected for each of the three age-groups, 4, 8 or 12 children being selected from each dependent upon the size-stratum into which the school fell. Before selecting the sample of children's names all those comprising the survey population were arranged within each age-group:

(i) by class

(ii) by stream or group, where the school adopts this procedure

and (iii) by sex within.

The age-groups taken were those defined as:—

1. Top juniors—in general those born between 1/9/1952 and 31/8/1953 (both dates inclusive).
2. Bottom juniors—in general those born between 1/9/1955 and 31/8/1956 (both dates inclusive).
3. Top infants—in general those born between 1/9/1956 and 31/8/1957 (both dates inclusive).

The design produced a set sample of 3,349 children in 173 schools distributed by age-group as follows:

1. Top juniors	..	1,104
2. Bottom juniors	..	1,086
3. Top infants	..	1,159

From this selected sample children living in institutions or who had parents teaching in the sampled school were withdrawn. When more than one child in a family had been selected one child was picked at random as the subject of the interview. For one or other of these reasons 112 names (i.e. three per cent of the total) were deleted from the original sample, leaving an interview sample of 3,237.

The extent to which the sample was representative of the population of primary school children in respect of type of school attended and Department of Education Division is shown below. The sex distribution was the same in the sample as in the total population of children. The population figures are taken from *Statistics of Education Part 1 1964*, and refer to the position in January, 1964. The sample was drawn in April/May, 1964.

Type of school attended					*Sample* %	*All primary children* %
Juniors with infants	..	..	..	..	41	42
Juniors only	..	..	..	..	38	33
Infants only	..	..	..	..	21	23
All-age	..	..	..	..	*	2

Department of Education Division					*Sample* %	*All primary children* %
Northern ..	..	..	..	..	8	9
Yorks., E. and W. Riding	..	..	..	13	10
North Western ..	..	..	..	..	16	16
North Midlands ..	..	..	..	..	8	9
Midlands ..	..	..	..	..	8	12
Eastern ..	..	..	..	..	12	12
Metropolitan	..	..	..	..	8	10
South Eastern	..	..	..	..	11	9
Southern ..	..	..	..	..	9	6
South Western	..	..	..	..	6	8

Total   .. (3,092)

Note—In the sample two of the all-age schools had no infants classes—these are classified with the junior only schools. The other five all-age schools are classified with the juniors with infants schools.

TECHNICAL NOTE ON THE FACTOR ANALYSIS OF INFORMATION FROM
THE PARENTAL INTERVIEWS

This annex gives some technical details of the factor analysis which is discussed in section IV. The factor analysis was carried out with a computer programme devised by H. H. Harman and modified by C.E.I.R. (U.K.) Ltd. The results given are an orthogonal rotated solution using H. F. Kaiser's varimax criterion.

Varimax is specifically designed to break up any large general factors in the data and to produce factors which are more equal in size. The purpose of the factor analysis in this inquiry was to produce measures of parents' attitudes and home circumstances and generally to structure information about the homes so that this data could be related to children's school achievement in a multiple regression analysis. It was considered that if large general factors were included in the regression analysis the results might be very difficult to interpret because of the problem of deciding what broadly described factors are assessing. It was decided that the narrower and more precisely defined factors resulting from the varimax criterion would be more suitable for this study.

Eighty variables were included in the factor analysis. These variables are listed in the table at the end of this annex together with their loadings on the 14 factors which appeared meaningful and the percentage of the variance accounted for by each factor. The inclusion of this many variables, which covered many different aspects of parents' attitudes and home circumstances, and the use of the varimax criterion produced a large number of factors, each of which accounts for a very small proportion of the variance. A number of the factors also have very few items with reasonable loadings. For the multiple regression analysis it was decided nevertheless that combining the items with the highest loadings on each of these 14 factors would be likely to give results which were easier to interpret than including a large number of items separately which were known to be correlated.

For inclusion in the multiple regression each factor was scored by summing each individual's score on the items with the highest loading on that factor. The items used to form each factor score are given following.

FACTOR 1

Responsibility and initiative taken by parents over child's education

- —·81   Whether parent has talked to class teacher.
-   ·80   Number of talks with head or class teacher.
- —·76   Whether parent has seen head or class teacher about educational matters.
- —·33   Whether had talk about teaching methods used.
- —·32   Whether talked to head when child started school.
-   ·32   Whether husband has been to child's school and talked to the head.
- —·30   Whether asked for work for child or how to help child at home.
-   ·30   Number of possible types of school function attended.

FACTOR 2

Relations between parents and teachers

- ·70   It's very easy to see the teachers whenever you want to.
- ·70   The teachers seem very pleased when parents go along to see them.
- ·68   Whether parent happy with arrangements for seeing head or class teacher.
- —·65   I feel that teachers would like to keep parents out of the school.
- ·60   The teachers definitely seem interested in what you think about your child's education.
- —·49   I would feel that I was interfering if I went to the school uninvited.
- —·48   If you go up to the school they only tell you what you know already.
- ·47   The teachers seem really interested in all the children.

FACTOR 3

Paternal interest and support

- ·75   Whether husband helps with control of children.
- ·69   Whether husband takes interest in how child is progressing at school.
- ·68   Whether husband does things with child at weekends.
- ·65   Whether husband plays with child in evenings.
- ·53   Whether husband took an interest in school child went to.
- ·47   Husband's hours away from home at work.
- —·40   Whehter husband has been to child's school and talked to head.

FACTOR 4

Attitude to corporal punishment

- ·70   Having the cane is very bad for most children.
- —·69   I would agree to the school using the cane occasionally.
- —·31   Most children need to be smacked quite often.

FACTOR 5

Physical amenities of home

- —·86   Whether fixed bath or shower.
- —·84   Whether hot water from a tap.
- ·39   Whether child usually plays in street or not.
- —·35   Whether dwelling has garden or yard child can use.

FACTOR 6

Whether parents devote time and attention to child's development

- ·59   Parents should leave all teaching and helping with school subjects to the teachers.
- ·57   Whether help with school work given to child at home.
- ·53   I have too much to do to spend time on helping with school work.
- —·46   Whether mother plays with child in the evenings.
- ·27   Teaching children to behave should be mainly the school's job.

FACTOR 7

Educational aspirations for child

- ·80   Whether particular type of secondary school wanted for child.
- ·78   Whether grammar school wanted for child.
- —·41   Preferred age of leaving school.

FACTOR 8

Whether parents have taken any recreational or leisure courses
- ·80   Whether father has taken any recreational/leisure courses.
- ·78   Whether mother has taken any recreational/leisure courses.

FACTOR 9

Whether parents took steps to find out about school when child was starting there
- —·66   Whether made inquiries about school.
- —·52   Whether knew what school was like before child started.
- —·47   Whether parent talked to head when child started school.

FACTOR 10

Whether active antagonism shown to the school or not
- ·60   Whether parent has complained to head or class teacher.
- ·58   Whether parent has seen head or class teacher on own initiative.
- —·37   Whether teachers treat all children fairly.
- ·31   The teachers have favourites among the parents.

FACTOR 11

Literacy of home
- ·67   Whether husband or wife belong to library.
- ·63   Whether wife reads.
- ·54   Number of books in home.
- ·51   Whether husband reads.
- ·41   Whether child has library books at home.
- ·33   Whether child reads at home.

FACTOR 12

Parental interest in and knowledge of work child is doing at school
- —·55   Whether child talks to parent about school work.
- —·51   Whether child brings books home from school to read.
- —·50   Whether child reads at home.
- —·33   Whether mother plays with child in evenings.
- —·31   Whether parent happy about teaching methods used.
- ·29   I would like to be told more about how my child is getting on.
- ·27   I think that the teachers should ask me more about my child.

FACTOR 13

Attitude to starting age
- ·65   Starting age preferred.
- ·54   Whether better for child to have started mornings or afternoons or not.

FACTOR 14

Whether school should be stricter or freer
- ·74   The schools should be stricter with the children.
- —·71   Whether teachers should be firmer/less firm with children.
- ·48   The teachers should try to get the children on faster in their work.

VARIABLES INCLUDED IN THE FACTOR ANALYSIS AND THEIR FACTOR LOADINGS

Size of sample = 3,092

Note.—The description given for the variable is in each case the end of the scale scored lowest.

Variables	Factor loadings													
	1	2	3	4	5	6	7	8	9	10	11	12	13	14
1. Under 3½ starting age preferred	—06	—00	—02	—04	·07	·00	·08	·01	·01	—01	—03	·05	·65	·05
2. Better for child to have started mornings and afternoons	·04	·04	—01	—15	—02	·09	—05	—11	·03	—01	—06	—09	·54	—01
3. Knew what school was like before child started	·07	·05	—01	—15	·07	—09	—00	·12	—52	·09	·03	·01	—07	—17
4. Made inquiries about school	—11	·04	·02	·01	—02	—12	·11	—01	—66	—03	·11	—07	—04	—02
5. Husband took interest in school child went to	—08	—00	·53	·03	—01	—07	·08	·09	—22	—05	—08	—01	—09	—01
6. Talked to head when child started school	—32	·09	·09	·08	—04	—01	·02	—08	—47	—06	—00	—13	—05	—01
7. Talked to class teachers	—81	·12	·04	·04	—01	—04	—03	·02	·01	·14	—04	—01	—04	—01
8. No talks with head or class teacher	·80	—15	—09	—01	·08	·04	—03	—00	·10	—20	—05	·06	·02	·02
9. Saw head or class teacher on own initiative	—26	·08	·05	—04	·04	—09	·02	—03	—12	·58	·12	—02	—06	—05
10. Saw head or class teacher about educational matters	—76	·07	·05	·02	—03	—02	·03	—04	—00	—05	·02	—01	—06	·02
11. Complained to head or class teacher	—12	—16	—03	—08	·02	—02	—04	—06	—01	·60	—01	·03	—10	—03
12. Attended few of school functions open to parents	·30	—01	—08	—01	—01	·23	—08	—03	—10	—00	—05	—10	—05	—01
13. Husband had not been to child's school and talked to head	·32	—04	—40	—08	·08	·02	—08	—06	·20	·05	—12	·04	·12	—03
14. Happy with arrangements for seeing head, class teacher	·07	·68	—00	—02	·04	·11	—04	—04	—02	·07	—06	—06	—03	·02
15. It is very easy to see teachers whenever parents want to	·01	·70	·05	·05	·01	·05	·04	·05	·05	·22	—03	—04	—00	·06
16. Parents would feel that they were interfering if they went to the school uninvited	—01	—49	—04	—08	·04	·08	—01	—02	—02	—24	—05	·02	—09	·01
17. Parents feel that if they go to the school they are only told what they already know	·07	—48	·01	·03	·02	—08	—04	—08	·10	·03	—09	·11	—09	·17
18. Teachers seem very pleased when parents go along to see them	—16	·70	·01	—01	—01	—01	·02	—00	·02	—06	—00	—02	—01	·05

Factor loadings

Variables	1	2	3	4	5	6	7	8	9	10	11	12	13	14
19. Parents feel that the teachers have enough to do already without having to talk to them	·06	−·17	−·02	−·15	−·05	·22	−·05	−·07	·01	−·12	−·03	·04	−·14	−·01
20. The teachers have favourites among the parents	·12	−·41	−·04	·08	−·04	·01	·02	·08	·01	·31	−·12	·06	−·03	·18
21. The teachers definitely seem interested in what parents think about their child's education	−·12	·60	·00	−·03	−·02	−·05	−·02	−·04	−·06	−·22	·02	−·06	−·04	−·10
22. Parents feel that the teachers would like to keep them out of the school	·08	−·65	−·03	−·00	·01	·10	−·03	−·02	·01	·09	−·07	−·06	−·02	·06
23. Had a talk about teaching methods used	−·33	·12	−·00	·03	−·07	−·11	−·01	·08	−·15	−·04	·07	−·10	−·06	−·09
24. Child talks to parent about school work	·04	·14	·06	·04	−·01	−·12	·04	·08	−·15	·00	−·02	−·55	·04	−·03
25. Happy about teaching methods used	·05	·20	−·00	−·06	·02	·18	·01	−·04	−·07	−·27	−·14	−·31	·00	−·36
26. Streaming not preferred	·05	·06	·04	·18	·06	−·05	−·04	·07	−·15	−·00	−·01	−·06	·02	·14
27. Child should be given homework	−·03	−·07	·01	−·02	·00	−·23	·09	−·01	−·01	−·02	−·03	−·10	−·04	·14
28. Asked for work for child, or how to help child at home	−·30	·03	·07	−·01	−·07	−·24	·03	·09	−·03	·15	·10	·03	−·14	·03
29. Parents bought copies of school books	−·18	−·03	−·04	·02	−·10	−·25	·08	·18	−·01	−·01	·15	−·04	·03	·05
30. No help with school work given to child at home	·02	−·01	−·11	−·02	−·02	·57	·09	−·08	·12	·01	−·07	·04	−·04	−·05
31. Husband takes interest in how child is progressing at school	−·03	·01	·69	·01	·03	−·13	·08	·02	−·01	−·02	·06	−·06	·04	−·07
32. The teachers seem really interested in all the children	−·07	·47	·03	−·10	−·01	−·01	−·03	−·08	−·11	−·31	−·04	−·09	−·05	−·28
33. Parents would like to be told more about how child is getting on	·21	−·38	·02	·05	·00	−·15	·06	−·03	−·03	·07	−·01	·29	·09	·29
34. Teachers should try to get the children on faster in their work	·06	−·17	−·01	·08	−·00	−·07	−·03	−·01	·11	·17	·08	·20	·06	·48
35. Parents should leave all teaching and helping with school subjects to the teachers	−·00	−·02	−·01	−·10	·01	·59	·00	−·03	·13	−·04	−·07	−·08	·04	−·01
36. There is too much concentration on working for eleven plus exam.	·04	−·06	·00	·12	·02	·06	−·06	−·08	−·22	−·05	−·07	·12	−·13	·13
37. Parents feel teachers should ask them more about their child	·08	−·31	−·01	·09	−·00	−·11	·06	·01	−·01	·17	−·04	·27	−·04	·33

F

| Variables | \multicolumn{14}{c}{Factor loadings} | | | | | | | | | | | | |
	1	2	3	4	5	6	7	8	9	10	11	12	13	14
38. Parents have too much to do to spend time on helping with school work	·12	-·02	-·10	-·01	-·01	·53	-·11	·04	-·01	-·02	-·11	·13	·06	·05
39. Teachers should be less firm with children	·03	·01	·06	·14	-·04	-·02	·03	·02	-·04	-·05	·00	-·08	-·01	-·71
40. Teachers treat all children fairly	-·05	·35	·05	-·23	·02	-·12	·02	-·09	-·06	-·37	·06	-·00	-·02	-·14
41. Parents find child easy to control	·03	·08	·05	-·04	-·06	-·06	·14	-·08	·23	·01	·01	-·20	-·27	-·09
42. Teaching children to behave should be mainly school's job	·04	-·04	-·04	·15	·06	·27	-·05	-·05	-·05	·04	-·09	-·02	·08	·10
43. Most children need to be smacked quite often	·07	-·06	·01	-·31	·02	·14	-·14	-·06	-·23	-·00	·00	·02	·16	·24
44. Parents feel having the cane is very bad for most children	-·06	-·05	-·00	·70	-·06	·00	-·02	-·02	·06	-·02	·00	·01	-·04	-·12
45. Parents feel schools which give children a lot of freedom are good	·04	·08	-·01	·18	·05	-·01	·01	·02	·04	·02	-·01	·03	·03	-·19
46. Parents would agree to the school using the cane occasionally	·04	·07	·01	-·69	-·04	·02	·07	·06	-·04	·02	·00	·06	-·07	·10
47. Parents feel schools should be stricter with the children	-·01	-·11	-·02	-·19	·03	-·05	-·01	·00	·00	-·07	-·07	-·01	-·01	·74
48. A particular type of secondary school wanted for child	·03	·02	·01	-·07	-·02	·05	·80	·03	-·00	·04	·04	-·05	-·02	-·04
49. Grammar school wanted for child	-·07	·01	·07	-·01	-·01	-·03	·78	·00	-·07	-·02	·09	-·00	-·03	-·01
50. Grammar school particularly disliked for child	·04	·00	·02	-·01	·00	-·06	-·02	·06	·10	-·03	-·04	-·16	·18	-·04
51. Type of secondary school should be decided mainly by teachers	-·13	·03	-·06	-·12	·01	-·03	-·10	-·04	·02	-·08	·11	·10	-·21	-·09
52. Wishes child could leave school below statutory age	-·20	·01	·10	-·02	·12	-·23	-·41	-·07	-·08	-·11	-·20	·03	-·05	-·02
53. Child plays mainly in street	·01	·01	-·00	-·02	·39	-·02	-·00	-·10	·03	-·00	-·15	·16	-·23	-·09
54. Few amenities in neighbourhood used	·02	-·07	-·01	-·05	-·01	-·03	·02	-·02	-·05	-·02	·03	-·11	-·02	·03
55. Few amenities in neighbourhood used	·04	-·02	-·03	-·03	·02	-·01	-·01	-·01	-·01	·02	-·08	-·01	-·04	·02
56. Mother plays with child most evenings	-·10	·02	·20	-·11	-·04	-·46	·01	-·04	-·01	·10	·00	-·33	-·04	-·01
57. Husband plays with child most evenings	-·04	·05	·65	-·08	-·04	-·19	·02	-·02	-·02	·11	-·01	-·17	·02	-·02
58. Father does things with child most weekends	-·10	·03	·68	-·04	-·03	-·27	·02	-·02	-·08	·01	·07	-·05	-·02	-·06

Variables	Factor loadings													
	1	2	3	4	5	6	7	8	9	10	11	12	13	14
59. Husband takes big or equal part in control of children	—·01	·02	·75	·01	·01	·02	—·04	·00	·07	—·07	·06	·06	·01	—·03
60. Husband strict with children	—·06	—·05	·36	—·13	—·04	·03	—·03	—·00	—·01	—·08	—·08	—·08	—·03	—·03
61. Family has been on outings since Christmas	—·09	·02	·21	·05	—·07	—·23	·02	—·03	—·03	·00	·13	—·04	—·07	—·05
62. Family owns a car	—·10	—·01	·18	·11	—·09	·00	—·03	·10	—·09	—·13	·11	—·06	—·06	—·04
63. Child reads at home	—·09	—·03	—·07	·05	—·01	—·13	—·08	—·01	—·04	—·05	—·33	—·50	—·07	—·01
64. Child brings books home from school to read	—·06	·10	·06	·03	—·01	·01	—·03	—·03	—·01	—·00	·00	·51	·05	—·02
65. Child has library books at home	—·06	—·03	·04	·10	—·06	·02	·14	—·01	—·08	—·07	·41	—·20	—·04	—·04
66. Either husband or wife belong to library	—·04	—·03	·08	·06	—·07	—·03	—·14	—·10	—·04	—·05	·67	—·03	—·06	—·01
67. Husband reads non-fiction	—·01	·01	·36	·01	—·01	—·04	—·03	—·07	—·02	—·02	·51	—·00	—·07	—·01
68. Wife reads non-fiction	—·02	·06	·02	—·04	—·09	—·15	·03	—·04	—·08	—·05	·63	—·03	—·03	—·00
69. More than five books in the home	—·13	·03	—·08	—·08	—·14	·04	—·06	—·02	—·01	—·54	—·07	—·07	—·07	—·01
70. Family lives in whole house	·02	—·01	—·03	—·06	—·04	·03	·05	—·03	·04	—·04	—·00	·03	—·03	—·02
71. Dwelling has garden or yard child can use	—·01	—·03	—·07	—·04	—·35	—·04	—·03	—·08	·08	·03	—·06	—·13	—·17	—·03
72. Dwelling has fixed bath or shower	—·06	—·00	—·01	·02	—·86	·00	—·06	—·02	·08	—·06	—·08	·07	—·00	—·05
73. Dwelling has hot water from a tap	—·05	·00	·02	—·00	—·84	—·00	·02	—·03	—·00	—·02	—·08	·06	—·07	—·08
74. Family own or are buying dwelling	—·08	—·01	·13	—·06	—·01	—·05	·07	·17	—·14	—·03	·15	·13	—·08	—·03
75. Father on shift work or permanently away	·03	—·01	—·28	—·03	—·02	—·12	—·01	—·05	—·12	—·10	—·03	—·09	·24	—·04
76. Father spends less than 10 hours at work away from home	—·05	·05	·47	—·04	—·03	·11	—·00	—·02	—·07	—·06	—·03	—·08	—·02	·06
77. Mother not working	—·01	—·00	·15	—·01	—·11	—·18	—·05	—·01	—·09	—·02	—·02	—·08	—·18	—·01
78. Father has taken recreational/leisure courses	·01	—·02	—·07	—·05	—·02	—·03	—·01	·80	—·04	—·01	·01	—·05	—·04	—·03
79. Mother has taken recreational/leisure courses	—·12	—·02	·04	—·01	—·07	—·04	·07	·78	·02	—·02	·10	·02	—·06	—·01
80. Has asked permission for child to go to a different school	·04	—·04	—·08	—·02	—·07	·11	—·01	—·04	—·19	·17	—·04	·01	—·25	·05
Percentage of the variance accounted for	4	5	4	2	2	3	2	2	2	2	3	2	2	3

Total amount of variance accounted for by these factors = 38%

ANNEX III

S.S. 365. SURVEY OF PARENTS OF PRIMARY SCHOOL CHILDREN

(i) Serial Number: School...................... (a)

Child .... (b)

(ii) Interviewer's Name... (iii) Auth: Number (write in column)

(iv) Date of interview...

(v) Time of **starting interview**:

Before 11 am.................................	1
11 am up to just before 1 pm...........	2
1 pm up to just before 3 pm...........	3
3 pm up to just before 5 pm...........	4
5 pm up to just before 7 pm...........	5
7 pm or after	6

(vi) Time interview took:

Less than three-quarters of an hour...........	1
$\frac{3}{4}$ but less than 1 hour......................	2
1 hour but less than 1$\frac{1}{4}$ hours..........	3
1$\frac{1}{4}$ hours but less than 1$\frac{1}{2}$ hours...............	4
1$\frac{1}{2}$ hours but less than 2 hours...............	5
2 hour or longer.................................	6

RING ALL THAT APPLY

(vii) Whether anyone other than informant present during interview:

DO NOT COUNT ADULTS OR CHILDREN WHO WERE PRESENT FOR LESS THAN FIVE MINUTES

No, only informant present............................	1
Selected child present.................................	2
Child's father present.................................	3
Other children present, relatives or not.............	4
Other adults present, relatives or not...............	5

(viii) Relationship of person interviewed to selected child

Child's natural mother..............	1
Foster or adopted mother........	2
Other (specify)	

INTERVIEWER: THE HOUSEHOLD BOX, PAGE 175, CAN BE COMPLETED AT WHICHEVER POINT IN THE INTERVIEW IS MOST SUITABLE.

1. I would like to ask you first about the schools .... has been to so far.
Did he/she go to a **nursery** school or nursery class?

CODE AS 'NO-3' IF ATTENDED NURSERY FOR LESS THAN ONE MONTH IN TOTAL

PROBE IF NEC.
Yes, in this country..................	1
Yes, abroad only.....................	2
No	3
D.K.	4

(a) If Yes, in this country (1) and child is now in infants:
Was this a nursery class in his/her **present** school?

Yes	1
No	2

2. How old was he/she when he/she first started to go to school in the mornings **and** afternoons?

INCLUDE NURSERY SCHOOL OR CLASS IF ATTENDED IN THE MORNINGS AND AFTERNOONS

Under 3$\frac{1}{2}$ years old..................	1
3$\frac{1}{2}$ years but less than 4.........	2
4 years but less than 4$\frac{1}{2}$...........	3
4$\frac{1}{2}$ years but less than 5...........	4
5 years but less than 5$\frac{1}{2}$...........	5
5$\frac{1}{2}$ years but less than 6...........	6
6 or older............................	7
D.K.	8

3. Was that a good age for him/her to start or would you have liked him/her to have started earlier or later?

THIS REFERS TO STARTING IN THE MORNINGS AND AFTERNOONS

Good age to start..................	2	
Earlier start preferred.............	1	ask (a
Later start preferred................	3	
D.K./Not sure	4	

(a) If earlier/later start preferred (1 or 3): At what age would you have liked .... to have started?

THIS REFERS TO MORNINGS AND AFTERNOONS AT SCHOOL

Under 3$\frac{1}{2}$ years old..................	1
3$\frac{1}{2}$ years but less than 4.........	2
4 years but less than 4$\frac{1}{2}$...........	3
4$\frac{1}{2}$ years but less than 5...........	4
5 years but less than 5$\frac{1}{2}$...........	5
5$\frac{1}{2}$ years but less than 6...........	6
6 or older............................	7
D.K.	8

4. When .... first went to **infants** school did he/she attend school **in the mornings and** afternoons, or only in the mornings **or** the afternoons?
        Attended mornings and afternoons immediately............................... 1
        Attended mornings only or afternoons only at first...................... 2
        D.K., Can't remember... 3

5. Which do you think would have been better for .... when he/she first started in the infants:—
RUNNING   {   to have attended school in the mornings **and** afternoons................... 1
PROMPT   {   or to have attended school **only** in the mornings or the afternoons....... 3
        D.K., Can't say...................... 2

THROUGHOUT THE REST OF THE SCHEDULE THE **PRESENT** SCHOOL IS THE SCHOOL WHICH THE SELECTED CHILD IS NOW ATTENDING.
CHECK FROM YOUR ADDRESS LIST WHETHER THIS IS AN INFANTS, A JUNIOR, OR A COMBINED INFANTS AND JUNIOR SCHOOL.
THROUGHOUT MAKE CLEAR TO THE INFORMANT TO WHICH SCHOOL YOU ARE REFERRING.

---

6. When .... first went to **infants** school, which school did he/she go to?
COUNT INFANTS AND JUNIOR SCHOOL AS SEPARATE IF SEPARATE HEADS
        Present school............... 1 go to Q7
        Other school................ 2 ask (a) to (d)

If **other** school (2)   COMPLETE A SEPARATE COLUMN BELOW FOR EACH INFANT OR JUNIOR SCHOOL ATTENDED. PRESENT SCHOOL AND NURSERY SCHOOLS ARE EXCLUDED.

(a) What type of school was that?	1st School	2nd School	3rd School	4th School
(i) Was it:—				
State { Non-Church?	1	1	1	1
R.C.	2	2	2	2
C of E or other church?	3	3	3	3
PROMPT AS NEC: Private	4	4	4	4
School abroad (state or private)?	5	5	5	5
Other (describe)				
(ii) Was it:—				
PROMPT AS NEC: Infants only?	1	1	1	1
Infants and Juniors combined (one head)	2	2	2	2
Juniors only	3	3	3	3
School abroad	4	4	4	4
D.K.	5	5	5	5
(b) How old was he/she when he/she left there? (GIVE IN WHOLE YEARS OMIT MONTHS)	Yrs.	Yrs.	Yrs.	Yrs.
(c) Why did he/she leave that school? To go to the juniors	1	1	1	1
Family moved house/district, came to this country	2	2	2	2
New school built nearer home, old school closed	3	3	3	3
Other (describe)				
(d) Which school did he/she go to next? Present	1	1	1	1
Other	2	2	2	2
IF 'OTHER' COMPLETE NEXT COLUMN				
OFF: USE				
	a b	c d	e f	g h

TO ALL
7. How long has .... been at (PRESENT SCHOOL)?
One term or less... 1
Over 1 term, up to and exactly 1 school year............................ 2
Over 1 school year, up to and exactly 2 school years.................. 3
Over 2 school years, up to and exactly 3 school years................ 4
Over 3 school years... 5
D.K. 6

8. Have any other members of your family been to (PRESENT SCHOOL)?   RING ALL
THAT APPLY
No, not as far as parent knows.. 1
PROMPT   Yes, brothers, sisters of selected child (include step, etc.)............ 2
AS NEC: Yes, father, mother.. 3
Yes, other relatives, e.g. uncle, aunts, cousins........................... 4

9. 'X' IN THIS QUESTION AND Q.10 REFERS TO SELECTED CHILD OR TO
HIS/HER ELDER BROTHER OR SISTER, WHICHEVER STARTED FIRST IN
PRESENT SCHOOL.
Before X started at (PRESENT SCHOOL) did you know anything about what the
school was like (now)?
CODE AS 2 IF KNOWLEDGE   Knew something about what school was like... 1
OF SCHOOL IS ONLY OF   Did not know what school was like.............. 2
WHAT IT WAS LIKE IN   New school, child started in first term
PARENTS' TIME   opened 3

10. Were you (or your husband) able to make any inquiries about the school, or to visit it,
before deciding to send X there?
IF PARENTS' GENERATION THERE,   Yes, made inquiries, or visited school........ 1 ask (a)
WERE ANY INQUIRIES OR VISITS   No inquiries or visit made...................... 2
MADE TO FIND OUT WHAT   No inquiries needed, worked there.......... 3
SCHOOL IS LIKE NOW?
(a) If Yes (1): Who did you talk to about the school?
Head, or other teacher from the school 1
Education Office official............................ 2
Friends, relatives, neighbours with
children in school, or previously.......... 3
Friends, relatives, neighbours without
children in school, or previously 4

Other (specify)

11. Was there any other school near here that .... could have gone to if you had
wanted him/her to?
CODE 1 IF THERE IS A POSSIBLE SCHOOL   Yes .... 1 ask (a)
ALTHOUGH RELIGION OF PARENT OR SCHOOL WOULD   No 2
DETER PARENT FROM SENDING CHILD TO IT   D.K. 3

(a) If Yes (1): What were your reasons for choosing this particular school?
No particular reasons/D.K.. 1
Nearest, most convenient, safest, no main roads to cross............ 2
Religious reasons (Catholic, other church school).................... 3
Nice buildings, new buildings, modern, beautiful grounds.......... 4
Other children, relatives, friends, parents there, or had been...... 5
Had heard good reports about it, told it was a good school........ 6
Other (specify)

12. IF HUSBAND AND WIFE IN HOUSEHOLD
Was your husband able to take much interest in which school .... went to or did
he leave that to you?   D.N.A. No husband/wife.................... 3
Husband took an interest................ 1
Left to mother............................... 2

13. We have been talking about when .... started at (PRESENT SCHOOL)
Could you tell me now whether you have at any time asked the Education Office or
anyone else in authority for permission for .... to go to a different school from
the one he/she was to have gone to?

(IF NO, CHECK PROBE: Have you ever asked the Education Office, or anyone else
in authority, to allow you to send .... to a particular school, or to allow ....
to change schools?

Yes, asked Ed. Office or other authority for permission for child to go to a differ-   ask (a) (i)
ent school, to change schools, or go to a particular school................................ 1   & (ii)

No, never asked for permission for child to go to different school, D.K................ ... 2
Other (specify)

(a) If Yes (1): (i). At what stage in ....'s schooling was this?

RECORD EACH OCCASION IN SEPARATE COL., EARLIEST IN COL. (1)
PROMPT PRECODES AS NEC: (1)   (2)   (3)

	(1)	(2)	(3)
When child first started in infants school	1	1	1
When wanting child to transfer between infants schools/depts	2	2	2
When child was transferring from infants to juniors	3	3	3
When wanting child to transfer between junior schools/depts	4	4	4
When child was transferring from junior to secondary school	5	5	5

ASK FOR EACH OCCASION & RECORD IN APPROP. COL.

(ii) Did you get permission to send .... to the school you
wanted?   Yes ....1........1..... ... 1
                                                    No ....2........2..... ... 2
Not heard yet; no decision made, parent moved...................3........3..... ... 3

14. Can we talk now about the contacts parents have with the teachers at ....'s
present school? Did you have a talk with the head when .... first went to
(PRESENT SCHOOL)?

CODE 1 IF TALKED TO HEAD JUST   Yes .... 1 ask (a)
BEFORE   CHILD   STARTED,   IF   No 2
TALKED TO DEPUTY OR ASSISTANT   D.K. Can't
HEAD, OR IF PARENT KNEW HEAD   remember 3
PERSONALLY   AT   THAT   TIME

(a) If Yes (1): Apart perhaps from .... being there, did the head talk to you on
your own or with other parents?

Talked to mother and/or father on own (or knows head personally)....... 1
Talked to mother/father with other parents... 2
D.K. Can't remember 3

15. Have you had a talk with any of ....'s class teachers since he/she has been at
(PRESENT SCHOOL)?

Yes 1
No 2
D.K. Can't remember...... 3

16. About how often have you had a talk about .... with the head, or with ....'s class teacher since he/she started there?

No talk with head or teacher....................... 6

INCLUDE ANY TALK
WHEN CHILD STARTED.
IF TALKED TO HEAD AND
CLASS TEACHER ON SAME
VISIT, COUNT AS ONE TALK.

One talk with head or teacher........................ 1 ⎱
Two talks with head or teacher....................... 2 ⎰
Three talks with head or teacher..................... 3 ⎱ ask (a)
Four to six talks with head or teacher.............. 4 ⎰ and (b)
More than six talks with head or teacher.......... 5 ⎰

(a) If had a talk with head or class teacher (1 to 5): Have you ever been to see the head without him/her asking you to go?

Yes 1
No 2
D.K. Can't remember........ 3

(b) We would like to know what sort of things parents want to be able to see the teachers about. Would you mind telling me what sort of things you have been to see the head or ....'s teacher about?

RING ALL
THAT APPLY

INCLUDE ALL
VISITS, WHETHER
INITIATED BY
THE HEAD OR
PARENT

Child's progress educationally, teaching methods used...... 1
To notify school of illness, holiday, other absence from school 2
Bullying behaviour of other children........................... 3
Behavioural problems of informant's child, e.g. nervousness, worry, bad behaviour................................. 4
To discuss or look for lost items of clothing and other property 5
Other (specify)

17. INTERVIEWER CODE:—
Informant has made a complaint to head or class teacher.. 1
Informant has not complained to or has not talked to head or class teacher................. 2
D.K. Can't say................. 3

18. I am going to read out a list of things which some schools provide for parents.
   (a) I would like you to tell me whether (PRESENT SCHOOL) has had any of these since .... started there: PROMPT LIST BELOW AND RECORD IN (a).
   (b) FOR EACH ITEM CODED 1 IN (a) ASK: Have you (or your husband) been able to go to any of these? RECORD IN (b).

PROMPT LIST	(a) Whether school has this:—			(b) Whether attended:—		
	Yes	No	D.K.	Mother and/or Father attended	Neither attended or D.K.	
(i) Open days (include open evenings)	1	2	3	1	2	(i)
(ii) Prize days	1	2	3	1	2	(ii)
(iii) Sports days, swimming galas............	1	2	3	1	2	(iii)
(iv) School plays, shows, concerts, school carol and other services	1	2	3	1	2	(iv)
(v) Parent/teacher association meetings or other activities	1	2	3	1	2	(v)
(vi) School outings	1	2	3	1	2	(vi)
(vii) Jumble sales, bazaars, social evenings to raise money for school	1	2	3	1	2	(vii)
(viii) Medical or dental examinations	1	2	3	1	2	(viii)
OFF: USE						
	a	b	c	d	e	

19. Are there any (other) things which you have been to at (PRESENT SCHOOL) which
     I haven't mentioned?
     INTERVIEWER SEE INSTRUCTIONS AND BACK CODE INTO Q.18 IF
     APPROPRIATE, DELETING FROM THIS QUESTION

20. IF HUSBAND AND WIFE IN HOUSEHOLD
     Has your husband been able to go to ....'s school at all?

     D.N.A. No husband/wife 3
     Yes .... 1 ask (a)
     No, D.K. Can't remember 2

     (a) If Yes (1): Has he talked with the head at all?   Yes 1
                                                               No 2
                                                               D.K. 3

21. What do you think of the arrangements at (PRESENT SCHOOL) for seeing the head
O   or class teacher? Are you quite happy with the present arrangements or not?
     Completely happy with present arrangements, no reservations.............. 1
     Not completely happy with present arrangements............................ 2 ask (a)
     D.K. Can't say............. 3

     (a) If not completely happy (2): Could you tell me what sort of arrangements you would
         prefer?
         Should be able to/easier to see class teacher 1
         Should be able to see head, class teacher in private 2
         Should be a parent/teacher association 3
         Other (specify)

22. INTERVIEWER CODE: (SEE Q.7 PAGE 160)
     CHILD STARTED IN INFANTS THIS TERM (I.E. IN
     RECEPTION CLASS) .... 1 ask (a) & (b)

     CHILD NOT IN RECEPTION CLASS .... 2 go to Q23.
     (a) This is/was ....'s first term in the infants school then. Have you been quite
         happy with the way the teachers have helped him/her to settle in or not?

         Parent quite happy with settling in 1
         Parent has some worries, complaints, criticisms .... 2 ask (i)
         D.K. Can't say............. 3

         (i) If has any worries, criticisms (2): What is it that has worried you

     (b) Has .... been quite happy in infants school this term or has he/she been
         worried or disturbed by it at all?
                                                 Child has been quite happy.......... 1
                                                 Child worried or disturbed.......... 2 ask (i)
                                                 D.K. Can't say 3

         (i) If child worried or disturbed (2): In what way has he/she been worried or
             disturbed?

23. TO ALL.

O   I am going to read out some things that parents have said about going to their children's schools. I would like you to tell me whether you feel the same way or not about (PRESENT SCHOOL).

	Feels the same. Agrees	Does not feel this, disagree	D.K. Neither agrees nor disagrees. No personal experience. Can't answer	
(i) It's very easy to see the teachers whenever you want to	1	3	2	(i)
(ii) I would feel that I was interfering if I went to the school uninvited	1	3	2	(ii)
(iii) If you go up to the school they only tell you what you know already	1	3	2	(iii)
(iv) The teachers seem very pleased when parents go along to see them	1	3	2	(iv)
(v) I feel that teachers have enough to do already without having to talk to parents	1	3	2	(v)
(vi) The teachers have favourites among the parents	1	3	2	(vi)
(vii) The teachers definitely seem interested in what you think about your child's education	1	3	2	(vii)
(viii) I feel that the teachers would like to keep parents out of the school	1	3	2	(viii)

24. Can we talk now about the methods of teaching which they use at (PRESENT SCHOOL)?

Has the head, or have any of the other teachers talked to you about the methods they use at (PRESENT SCHOOL)?

(e.g. about the way they teach different subjects, or what they are trying to do in the school).

Yes, parent had a talk alone, or in a group of parents 1
Parent has received leaflet, but not had a talk 2
No, no leaflet or talk 3
D.K. Can't remember 4

25 Does .... talk to you much about the work he/she does in school, or show you the sort of things he/she does?

IF NOT GIVEN SPONTANEOUSLY, PROMPT WHETHER THIS HAPPENS OFTEN OR OCCASIONALLY.

Yes, often 1
No, only occasionally, or hardly ever ... 2

26. Do you feel quite happy about the methods of teaching used at (PRESENT SCHOOL)
O   and the way .... is getting on in his/her work, or is there anything which worries
     you at all?

    Quite happy with methods and with child's progress.....................................… 1

    Worried about methods and/or child's progress, including worried because
    does not know how child is getting on...… 2 ask (a)

	RING ALL THAT APPLY

(a) If worried (2): What is it that worries you?

    Feels that child is not up to standard for his/her age, not being brought on fast
    enough ....… 1

    Not enough individual attention given, particularly to backward, slow pupils,
    classes too large, teacher not interested in child's progress.............................… 2

    Too much time spent on play or other subjects which parent feels are not useful
    for child's work progress...… 3

    Criticisms of or anxiety about new methods of teaching.....................................… 4
    e.g. of reading, spelling, arithmetic

    Does not know how child is getting on. Would like to be told more about, to have
    reports on, child's progress..… 5

    Fault in child, untidy, won't pay attention, lazy, too talkative.............................… 6

    Other (specify)

27. Do you know how the children of ....'s age are put into classes at (PRESENT
     SCHOOL)?

     Are they put into classes by age or do they put the quicker ones into one class and the
     slower into another?

IF GROUPED BY ABILITY WITHIN A CLASS, CODE AS 1. IF CLASSED BY AGE EXCEPT FOR OCCASIONAL BRIGHT OR SLOW CHILD, CODE AS 1.	⟶ In classes by age.............................… 1 In classes by ability/streamed.............… 2 D.K., Can't say ....… 3 Other (specify)

28. For children of ....'s age could you tell me which of these you think is better?
O RUNNING ⌠   For the quicker and slower children to be mixed together in one
     PROMPT ⎨   class.. 1 ask (a)
             ⎩   or For the quicker children to be put in one class and the slower in
                  another .... 3 ask (b)

                  D.K. No opinion; can't generalise, depends entirely on child.......... 2
(IF THINKS THEY SHOULD BE DIVIDED INTO GROUPS BY ABILITY
WITHIN CLASS, CODE 1 TO MAIN).

(a) If better for quicker and slower to be mixed (1): What do you think are the advantages   **CODE ALL**
    of having the quicker and slower children mixed together in one class?   **THAT APPLY**

            Avoids feeling of difference and of brighter/quicker looking down
            on slower/duller 1

            Gives a sense of competition, spurs on the slower/backward............. 2

            Other (specify)

(b) If better for quicker and slower to be separated (3): What do you think are the   **CODE ALL**
    advantages of having the quicker in one class and the slower in another?   **THAT APPLY**

            The slow ones can have more attention/tuition; can be brought on....... 1

            The bright child is **not** held back academically by slow children,
            teachers can give time to the bright child...................................... 2

            Slow children are not made to feel slow/dunces/ashamed................. 3

            Helps the teacher, makes life easier for the teachers.......................... 4

            Other (specify)

29. Have the teachers at (PRESENT SCHOOL) given .... any work to do at home?
     READING AND PROJECTS   Yes, given work to do at home.......................... 1 ask (a)
     SHOULD BE CODED 1   Not given work to do at home, D.K................. 2 ask (b)

     a) If Yes (1): (i) Do you think that it is a good thing for .... to be given some
                         school work to do at home, or do you think that he/she should be
                         free from it at home?
                         Should be given some school work to do at home.............. 1 ask (ii)
                         Should be free from school work at home......................... 2
                         D.K., Can't say.. 3

                    (ii) If should have work to do at home (1 to (a)):
                         Do you think that .... is given about the right amount of
                         school work to do at home at present, or does he/she get too much
                         or too little?
                                     Given right amount of work to do at home...................... 1
                                     Given too much work to do at home.............................. 2
                                     Given too little work to do at home.............................. 3
                                     D.K., Can't say.. 4

     (b) If No (2) to main: Would you like the school to give .... any work to do at
         home or do you think he/she should be free from school work at home?
                         Would like school work given to do at home...................... 1
                         Should be free from school work at home......................... 2
                         D.K., Can't say.. 3

30. Have you ever asked the teachers to give .... some work to do at home, or have you asked them to show you how you could help him/her at home with his/her school work?

IF PARENT ASKED BUT SCHOOL REFUSED, CODE 1

Yes, asked for work for child to do at home, or asked how to help child at home.. 1
Work to do at home already given, no need to ask................. 2
No, not asked for work to do at home, nor how to help child (include can't remember)... 3

31. Have you bought copies at any time of any of the text books .... uses in school, for example readers or arithmetic books?

CODE 1 ONLY IF BOUGHT COPIES, NOT IF BORROWED THEM.
CODE 1 EVEN IF THE COPIES WERE ACTUALLY BOUGHT FOR AN ELDER CHILD.

Yes 1
No 2
D.K. 3

32. Outside school does .... get any help with school work from anyone, including yourself or your husband?

CODE AS NO (1) IF ONLY HELP IS VERY OCCASIONAL ANSWERING OF CHILD'S QUESTIONS ABOUT SCHOOL WORK

No 1
Yes, from both wife and husband............. 2
Yes, from wife (but not husband)............. 3
Yes, from husband (but not wife)............. 4
Yes, from brothers and sisters.................. 5
Other (specify)

33. IF HUSBAND/WIFE
Is your husband able to take much interest in how .... is getting on at school now or is that your job?

D.N.A. No husband/wife............. 3
Husband takes an interest........... 1
Left to wife 2

34. I want to read out some things that parents have said about the schools their children are attending
O I would like you to tell me whether you feel the same way or not about ....'s school

	Feels same/ agrees	Does not feel this/ disagrees	D.K. Neither agrees nor disagrees No personal knowledge can't say	
(i) The teachers seem really interested in all the children	1	3	2	(i)
(ii) I would like to be told more about how my child is getting on	1	3	2	(ii)
(iii) The teachers should try to get the children on faster in their work	1	3	2	(iii)
(iv) Parents should leave all teaching and help- ing with school subjects to the teachers	1	3	2	(iv)
(v) There is too much concentration on work- ing for the eleven plus exam	1	3	2	(v)
(vi) I think that the teachers should ask me more about my child	1	3	2	(vi)
(vii) I have too much to do to spend time on helping with school work	1	3	2	(vii)

35. Do you think that it is better for juniors and infants to be in the same or separate
O   schools; (PAUSE) or haven't you really thought about this?

Better in same school .... 1 ask (a)
Better in separate schools............................... 4 ask (b)
Doesn't matter depends on school.................... 2
D.K. Haven't thought about it 3

(a) **If better in same school (1): What do you think are the advantages of this?**

Change between infants and juniors more gradual/know what to
expect, less upsetting, know children in junior school......................... 1
Useful if brothers, sisters, friends would be in the same school, can go
to/from school together; look after/see each other in break/play........... 2
Better for children of different age groups to mix together, older
children can help younger.. 3
Other (specify)

(b) **If better in separate schools (4): What do you think are the advantages of this?**

Older children rough, bullying.. 1
Older children can have a bad influence on younger/can pick up bad
ways/habits/language 2
Have specialized teachers for the different age groups, teachers can
concentrate on, understand the different age groups better.................... 3
An incentive for the child, stops them being babyish, helps them to
develop, to grow up.. 4
Other (specify)

36. What do you feel about the way the teachers control the children at (PRESENT
O   SCHOOL)? Are you quite happy about this or do you feel that they should be firmer or
less firm with the children?

Quite happy, or can't say.. 2
Should be firmer with the children 3
Should be less firm with the children... 1

37. On the whole do the teachers seem to treat all the children pretty fairly or not?
O   CODE AS UNFAIR IF THINKS   Children treated fairly......................... 1
SOME CHILDREN PICKED UPON,   Children not treated fairly 3
OR IF SOME NEGLECTED.   D.K. Can't say, no opinion.................... 2

38. Do you find that .... is an easy or difficult child to control on the whole?
O
Easy to control................................... 1
In some ways easy/some difficult............. 2
Difficult to control............................. 3
Can't say 4

39. I am going to read out some things that parents have said about teaching children to behave. I would like
O   you to say whether you feel the same or not.

Some parents say that:—	Feels same/ agrees	Does not feel this/disagrees	D.K. Neither agrees nor disagrees, can't say	
(i) Teaching children to behave should be mainly the school's job	1	3	2	(i)
(ii) Most children need to be smacked quite often	1	3	2	(ii)
(iii) Having the cane is very bad for most children	1	3	2	(iii)
(iv) I think schools which give children a lot of freedom are good	1	3	2	(iv)
(v) I would agree to the school using the cane occasionally	1	3	2	(v)
(vi) The schools should be stricter with the children	1	3	2	(vi)

40. Is there anything which you are not happy about or which worries you about
    (PRESENT SCHOOL) which you haven't already mentioned?

    Other children rough, bullying; badly
    behaved/spoken 1
    Bad, old fashioned buildings, lack of
    facilities, poor equipment...................... ... 2
    Too large classes, shortage of teachers... ... 3
    Other (specify)

41. INTERVIEWER CODE:
    Child is in last year of juniors (i.e. 10/11 years old)...................................... ... 1 ask Q.42
    and 43
    Child is in bottom class of juniors (i.e. about 8 years old) or in infants........................... ... 2 go to
    Q.44

42. ASK ONLY IF CHILD IS IN LAST YEAR OF JUNIORS
    I would like to talk now about the type of school .... will be going to, when he/she
    leaves (PRESENT SCHOOL).
    Some Education Offices send round a letter to mothers asking them which school they
    would like their child to go to at 11. Have you received one of these?
    Yes .... 1 ask (a)
    No 2
    D.K. Can't remember........................ ... 3
    (a) IF YES (1): Was there anything that wasn't clear to you in it?
    Yes .... 1 ask (i)
    No 2
    (i) If Yes (1): What was that?

43. ASK ONLY IF CHILD IS IN LAST YEAR OF JUNIORS.

I expect you know that the main types of secondary schools are grammar schools and secondary modern schools. In some districts there are comprehensive and technical schools as well.

(a) Can you tell me what **type** of secondary school .... is going to when he/she leaves (PRESENT SCHOOL)? RECORD IN COL. (a) BELOW.

(b) What **type** of secondary school did you hope he/she would go to? RECORD IN COL. (b) BELOW.

	(a) Going to	(b) Hoped for
Grammar	1	1
Secondary Modern	2	2
Comprehensive	3	3 } Ask
Technical	4	4 } (i)
Independent, fee paying, public.	5	5
{ D.K. Can't say, didn't mind, whichever child most suited to	6	6 go to
{ Doesn't know anything about the different schools		

Other (specify): Ask (i)

(i) **If particular type of school hoped for (1 to 5 or 'other' to (b)):**
What did you think would be the advantages of this type of school?

Will lead to a good/better job/trade/profession: good future prospects...... ... 1
Better standard of education, better teaching, learn more there.................. ... 2
Child has academic/intellectual bias, want him/her to go to university.......... ... 3
Have varied, interesting, wide curriculum, subjects child interested in.......... ... 4
Knows other children are happy there, friends, relatives there.................. ... 5
Other (specify)

---

44. ASK ONLY IF CHILD NOT IN LAST YEAR OF JUNIORS (I.E. ASK IF IN FIRST YEAR OF JUNIORS, OR IN INFANTS).

Can we talk now about the different types of secondary schools children go to when they are 11. I expect you know that the main types of secondary schools are grammar schools and secondary modern schools. In some districts there are comprehensive and technical schools as well.

If you had the choice, what type of secondary school would you like .... to go to when he/she is 11?

Grammar .... 1 ⎤
Secondary Modern .... 2 ⎥
Comprehensive .... 3 ⎬ Ask (a)
Technical .... 4 ⎥
Independent, fee-paying, public..................... ... 5 ⎦
Has not thought about it yet, child too young... ... 6
{ Doesn't mind, doesn't make any difference,
{ whichever suits child, doesn't know anything
{ about different schools............................... ... 7
Other specify: Ask (a)

(a) **If particular kind of school wanted (1 to 5 or 'other'):**
What do you think would be the advantages for .... of that type of school?

Will lead to a good/better job/trade/profession, good future prospects............ ... 1
Better standard of education, better teaching, learn more there........................ ... 2
Child has academic/intellectual bias, want him/her to go to university................. ... 3
Have varied, interesting, wide curriculum, subjects child is interested in............ ... 4
Knows other children are happy there; friends, relatives there........................ ... 5
Other (specify)

45. TO ALL.
Is there any type of secondary school which you would particularly dislike .... to go to?

Yes	... 1 ask (a) &
No	... 3 (b)
D.K. Haven't thought about it............	... 2

——(a) If Yes (1): What kind of school is that?

Grammar	... 1
Secondary Modern	... 2
Comprehensive	... 3
Independent, fee-paying, public	... 4
Mixed schools, co-ed.	... 5
Religious schools	... 6
Other (specify)	

——(b) What would you dislike most about this kind of school?

Don't seem to teach them anything/poor teaching/slow..................	... 1
Type of child that goes there, rough, bad mannered, illiterate, bad discipline, bad behaviour, lax morals..	... 2
Too much religion...	... 3
School too large, impersonal	... 4
Classes too large	... 5
Other (specify)	

46. Is (was) there one particular secondary school which you would like (would have liked) ....to go at 11?

IF YES: PROMPT 'Would you prefer that school very much or just slightly?'	Yes, one school very much preferred.................	... 1
	Yes, one school slightly preferred......................	... 2
	No, no one school preferred............................	... 4
	Doesn't know enough about the schools to say...	... 3

47. Do you think that the type of secondary school your child goes to at 11 should be
O   decided mainly by his/her teachers or mainly by an examination like the 11+?

Mainly by teachers	... 1
Mainly by examination	... 3
By both equally...............................	2
D.K., no opinion	... 4

48. I know it's early yet but have you thought about what you would like .... to do later on? Would you like to see .... leave school as soon as possible or stay on longer?

	Would like child to:—	
(SCHOOL LEAVING AGE WILL BE 15 FOR 9–11's, 16 for 7–8- YEAR-OLDS IN GENERAL)	Leave as soon as possible (provided child wants to..	... 1 ask (a
	To stay on longer (provided child wants to)......	... 3 ask (b)
	Can't say at all, depends on child's ability.........	... 2

(a) If would like child to leave as soon as possible (1):
Would you prefer it if .... could leave at:—
(FOR 9–11's)   14 instead of having to stay till 15?
(FOR 7–8's   15 instead of having to stay till 16?
OR YOUNGER)

Yes	... 1
No	... 2
D.K.	... 3

(b) If would like child to stay on longer (3):
Up to what age would you like to see him/her staying?

IF RANGE GIVEN, TAKE HIGHEST AGE, AVOID USING CODE 4 IF POSSIBLE		
	16............................	... 1
	17............................	... 2
	18 and over..............	... 3
	No age given, as long as possible, up to child entirely, can't say.............................	... 4

49. We are interested to know what children like to do out of school, and the sort of places there are in the area where children can play or go to out of school.
Apart from indoors, where does .... play most of the time?

		CODE ONE ONLY
ONLY ONE TO BE CODED.	Own garden/yard/play space, open space round/between flats......................	... 1
IF PARENT CANNOT GIVE	Friends'/neighbours' garden or yard.......	... 2
ONE ONLY, PRIORITY	Park, heath, common, fields...................	... 3
CODE 1 DOWNWARDS	{Playground, outdoor play centre, recreation grounds, 'play' street...............	... 4
	Bombed site, car park, waste land..........	... 5
	Street (excluding 'play' streets).............	... 6
	D.K.	... 7
	Other (specify)	

50. A. I am going to read out a list of things and I would like you to tell me whether you have any of these within easy distance of your home (i.e. easy distance for a child to get to by himself/herself or, if too young, easy for a parent or other adult to take child to).

   RECORD PRESENCE BY RINGING CODE IN COL. A.
   B. Has .... used this at all this year (i.e. SINCE THIS TIME LAST YEAR).
   RECORD ITEMS USED BY RINGING CODE IN COL. B.

   C. Is there anything else that you wish there were round here for ....? RECORD BY RINGING APPROPRIATE CODE IN COL. C OR WRITING IN 'OTHERS' BELOW BOX.

PROMPT LIST FOR A AND B	A. Present	B. Used	C. Wanted
	(CODE ALL THAT APPLY)		
(1) A park, public garden, heath, common or fields where children are allowed to play......................	1	1	1
(2) A proper playground or outdoor play centre (OTHER THAN SCHOOL)	2	2	2
(3) Swimming or paddling places which are safe for children	3	3	3
(4) An indoor play centre....................................	4	4	4
(5) Any children's clubs or societies (e.g. Cubs, Brownies, Scouts, Guides, church clubs, youth clubs for young children, sports clubs)...................	5	5	5
(6) A cinema or other place which has children's film shows	6	6	6
(7) A public library...	7	7	7
C. Other (specify) Off. Use			
	a	b	c

51. (I realise from what you have told me that you are very busy). In the evenings when .... comes home from school do you have any time free to do things with him/her if he/she wants you to? (Such as playing or reading with him/her, taking him/her out, showing him/her how to do things).

THIS REFERS TO WEEKDAY EVENINGS, NOT WEEKENDS.	Yes, does things with child most evenings.......	... 1
	Yes, but only on occasional evenings..............	... 2
IF YES, PROMPT 'Is this most evenings or just occasionally?'	No	... 3

IF HUSBAND AND WIFE
What about your husband? (a) Does he have any time to do things with .... on weekday evenings?
RECORD BELOW.
(b) What about at weekends?

	(a) Week day evenings	(b) Weekends
IF YES, PROMPT: 'Does he spend time with .... just on occasional evenings/ weekends or on most?'		
D.N.A. No husband/wife............	4	4
Yes: most	1	1
Yes: occasional	2	2
No	3	3

53. IF HUSBAND AND WIFE
Does your husband take a big part in controlling the children or does he leave that to you mainly?

CODE 2 IF HUSBAND TAKES SMALL PART BECAUSE AWAY A LOT	
D.N.A. No husband/wife............	3
Husband takes big part, or equal part with wife............	1
Husband takes very small part in control of children, or leaves to wife............	2

54. IF HUSBAND AND WIFE
Would you say that your husband was on the strict or lenient side with the children?

IF LENIENT, PROMPT: 'Would you say that he is fairly lenient or very lenient?'	
D.N.A. No husband/wife............	5
Husband on the strict side............	1
Moderate in some ways, strict, some lenient...	2
Husband fairly lenient	3
Husband very lenient	4

55. Do you ever manage to go for outings together as a family? I mean any sort of outings apart from visits to relatives or going to church or going shopping. (For example picnicking, going to the theatre or cinema).

Yes .... 1 ask (a)
No 2

(a) If Yes (1): When was the last time you had an outing together as a family?

About three weeks ago or less............ 1
In Christmas holiday or since, but more than three weeks ago............ 2
Before last Christmas 3
Other (specify)

56. Does the family have a car, or the use of a car?

Yes 1
No 2

57. (Apart from homework) does .... do any reading at home or does anyone read to him/her?

CODE ONE ONLY

IF YES, PROBE WHETHER READS BOOKS OR ONLY COMICS OR MAGAZINES.

Yes, reads, or is read to: { Books with or without comics............ 1 ask (a)
Comics or magazines only............ 2
No reading (apart from homework)............ 3

(a) If reads Books (1): Not counting comics, about how often does he/she read books, or have them read to him/her?

Usually every day/night/evening............ 1
Two or three times a week............ 2
Less than twice a week............ 3
Other (specify)

ASK (a) AND (b)

58. (a) Does .... bring any books home from school to read?
    CODE AS YES (1)   Yes 1
    BOOKS FROM SCHOOL LIBRARY   No 2
    AND CLASS READERS   D.K. 3

    (b) Does .... ever have any books to read at home from the public library or any
        other library?
    CODE AS YES (1) IF CHILD   Yes 1
    BORROWS BOOKS OR IF SOMEONE   No 2
    ELSE BRINGS THEM FOR CHILD   D.K. 3

    (c) If No (2) to (a) and (b): Would you be quite happy if .... borrowed books to
        read at home or would you be worried that they might get spoilt?
                                    Would be happy if books borrowed........ 1
                                    Would be worried if books borrowed..... 2
                                    D.K. Can't say 3
                                    Other (specify)

59. Do you (or your husband) belong to a lending library, or have either of you belonged to   CODE ONE
    one within the last 10 years?   ONLY
                        One or both belongs now... 1
                        Neither belongs now, but one or both belonged within last 10 years......... 2
                        Neither belongs now nor within last 10 years as far as informant knows.... 3

60. If you (or your husband) have any time for relaxing, do you do any reading?

	(a) Husband	(b) Wife
D.N.A. No husband/wife.............................	3	3
Yes, likes reading	1	1
No, doesn't like reading, or no time for relaxing	2	2

(a) If Yes (1) to either or both:
    What sort of things do you/does he like to read?

	CODE ALL THAT APPLY	
	(a) Husband	(b) Wife
Does he/Do you like Newspapers or magazines	3	3
to read:—		
PROMPT { Detectivestories, westerns,		
{ novels or other fiction	2	2
{ Non-fiction books (e.g.		
{ biographies or technical books) .	1	1
(D.N.A. Code 2 in Main).........	A	A

61. IF MORE THAN FIVE BOOKS IN ROOM, CODE FROM OBSERVATION,
    OTHERWISE ASK AS SEEMS MOST TACTFUL:—

    Do you (or your husband) have any books?
    OR About how many books do you and (your husband) have?

    EXCLUDE MAGAZINES AND   Wife and/or husband has:—
    CHILDREN'S BOOKS. COUNT   More than five books...................... 1
    A SET OF ENCYCLOPAEDIAS   One to five books........................... 2
    AS ONE BOOK   No books 3
                                       D.K. 4

CLASSIFICATION SECTION

I   Household Composition

N.B.   1.   Complete this box at the most suitable point in the interview.

2.   Note that relationship to selected child (not H.O.H.) is required.

3.   On this survey, any paid work of 10 hours or less per week is to be included in 'Part-time' and anyone unemployed is to be included in 'Not Working.'

Person No.	Relationship to child selected	OFF. USE	Sex M F	Age last birth-day	Marital Status M. S. W. D/S.	Working Status Full- Part- Not time time Work-ing
1......	...Child selected	......	... 1 ... 2 ...	......	... 1 ... 2 ... 3 ... 4 ...	... 1 ...... 2 3
2......	...(H.O.H.)	......	... 1 ... 2 ...	......	... 1 ... 2 ... 3 ... 4 ...	... 1 ...... 2 3
3......		......	... 1 ... 2 ...	......	... 1 ... 2 ... 3 ... 4 ...	... 1 ...... 2 3
4......		......	... 1 ... 2 ...	......	... 1 ... 2 ... 3 ... 4 ...	... 1 ...... 2 3
5......		......	... 1 ... 2 ...	......	... 1 ... 2 ... 3 ... 4 ...	... 1 ...... 2 3
6......		......	... 1 ... 2 ...	......	... 1 ... 2 ... 3 ... 4 ...	... 1 ...... 2 3
7......		......	... 1 ... 2 ...	......	... 1 ... 2 ... 3 ... 4 ...	... 1 ...... 2 3
8......		......	... 1 ... 2 ...	......	... 1 ... 2 ... 3 ... 4 ...	... 1 ...... 2 3
9......		......	... 1 ... 2 ...	......	... 1 ... 2 ... 3 ... 4 ...	... 1 ...... 2 3
10...		......	... 1 ... 2 ...	......	... 1 ... 2 ... 3 ... 4 ...	... 1 ...... 2 3
11...		......	... 1 ... 2 ...	......	... 1 ... 2 ... 3 ... 4 ...	... 1 ...... 2 3
12...		......	... 1 ... 2 ...	......	... 1 ... 2 ... 3 ... 4 ...	... 1 ...... 2 3
13...		......	... 1 ... 2 ...	......	... 1 ... 2 ... 3 ... 4 ...	... 1 ...... 2 3
14		......	... 1 ... 2 ...	......	... 1 ... 2 ... 3 ... 4 ...	... 1 ...... 2 3
15...		......	... 1 ... 2 ...	......	... 1 ... 2 ... 3 ... 4 ...	... 1 ...... 2 3
OFFICE USE						

a   b   c   d   e   f   g   h

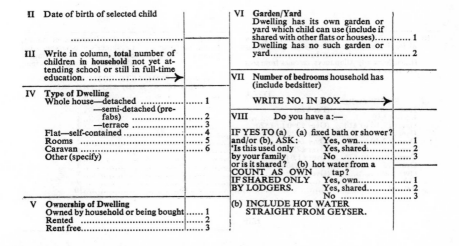

II   Date of birth of selected child

....

III   Write in column, total number of children in household not yet attending school or still in full-time education. ....➔

IV   Type of Dwelling
Whole house—detached 1
                    —semi-detached (pre-
                               fabs)   2
                    —terrace 3
Flat—self-contained 4
Rooms 5
Caravan 6
Other (specify)

V   Ownership of Dwelling
Owned by household or being bought 1
Rented 2
Rent free.. 3

VI   Garden/Yard
Dwelling has its own garden or yard which child can use (include if shared with other flats or houses)......... 1
Dwelling has no such garden or yard.. 2

VII   Number of bedrooms household has (include bedsitter)

WRITE NO. IN BOX————➔

VIII   Do you have a:—

IF YES TO (a)   (a) fixed bath or shower?
and/or (b), ASK: Yes, own.................. 1
'Is this used only   Yes, shared.............. 2
by your family   No 3
or is it shared?   (b) hot water from a
COUNT AS OWN   tap?
IF SHARED ONLY   Yes, own.................. 1
BY LODGERS.   Yes, shared.............. 2
                              No 3
(b) INCLUDE HOT WATER
      STRAIGHT FROM GEYSER.

N.B.   UNLESS OTHERWISE INDICATED, IN SUBSEQUENT SECTIONS INFORMATION SHOULD
       BE GIVEN ABOUT **PARENT WHO IS IN HOUSEHOLD**, IRRESPECTIVE OF WHETHER THE
       CHILD'S OWN PARENT OR A SUBSTITUTE, IF NO SUCH PERSON CURRENTLY IN
       HOUSEHOLD, ABOUT THE LAST PARENT OR PARENT SUBSTITUTE.

**IX   Occupation of father ALWAYS
       REQUIRED, IF UNEMPLOYED
       OR DECEASED, GIVE LAST JOB**

Occup:

Indust:

Self-employed: Yes ......|...... 1
                No   ......|...... 2

X   Whether father is on shift work
Father is on shift work (include if
on permanent night work, or usually away from home overnight
for two nights or more each week)...|...... 1
Father not on shift work ....|...... 2

**XI   Occupation of mother—REQUIRED
       ONLY IF GAINFULLY EM-
       PLOYED NOW**

                    D.N.A. Not employed......... ... 1

Occup:

Indust:

XII   Hours away from home
TOTAL LENGTH OF ABSENCE
FROM HOME ON WEEKDAYS.
(INCLUDE TRAVELLING TIME,
AND LUNCH HOURS,
WHETHER TAKEN AT HOME
OR AT WORK).

	(a) Father	(b) Mother
D.N.A. Not gainfully em- ployed, No Father/Mother...	1	1
Can't say, hours to variable..	2	2
Works on home premises...	3	3
Away under 5 hours per day	4	4
Away 5 but less than 10 hrs.	5	5
Away 10 but less than 12 hrs.	6	6
Away 12 hours or over......	7	7

OFF.

USE

**XIII Income of Father (or H.O.H.) and total income
of family.** In (A) give father's net income, less
deductions, plus overtime, bonuses, etc.
(Exclude Family Allowances, incomes from rent,
etc. from (A)).

(A) Father or   (B) Total income of family,
father substitute   i.e. father's plus mother's net
(otherwise H.O.H.)   incomes, plus any family
                        allowances, income from rent,
                        etc.
**ALWAYS COMPLETE BOTH COLUMNS
EVEN IF (A) & (B) ARE THE SAME**

                                    D.N.A....   A..................

SHOW CARD

Last week	(Per Year)	(A)	(B)
Up to £7.10	(Up to £390)	1	1
Over £7.10 to £10	(Over £390 to £520)	2	2
Over £10 to £12.10 .	(Over £520 to £650)	3	3
Over £12.10 to £15	(Over £650 to £780)	4	4
Over £15 to £20	(Over £780 to £1,040)....	5	5
Over £20 to £25	(Over £1,040 to £1,300)..	6	6
Over £25 to £30	(Over £1,300 to £1,560)..	7	7
Over £30.................	(Over £1,560)............	8	8
D.K.		9	9
Refusal		10	10

OFF.

USE

XIV	Country of birth of parents	(a) Father	(b) Mother
	U.K. (including N. Ireland, Channel Isles, Isle of Man)	1	1
	Eire (Southern Ireland)	2	2
	Europe (including U.S.S.R.)	3	3
	West Indies (including Jamaica, Trinidad)	4	4
	Africa	5	5
	Asia (including India, Pakistan, China)	6	6
	Canada, Australia, New Zealand	7	7
	Other (specify) Father	OFF. USE	
	Mother		

XV	Age at which child's parents completed full time continuous formal education. GAPS OF ANY LENGTH DUE TO ILLNESS AND OF THREE MONTHS OR LESS FOR ANY OTHER REASON SHOULD BE IGNORED.	(a) Father	(b) Mother
	14 and under	1	1
	15 but under 16	2	2
	16 but under 17	3	3
	17 but under 18	4	4
	18 and over	5	5
	D.K.	6	6
		OFF. USE	

XVI Type of school attended for full time formal education

A. Number of brothers plus sisters of the selected child who are now at, *or* last attended each type of school. EXCLUDE SELECTED CHILD.

B. Type of school parents last attended   A. (IF NONE, WRITE IN 'O').

TYPE OF SCHOOL	A. TOTAL NO. OF BROTHERS PLUS SISTERS		B. PARENTS	
	NOW ATTENDING	LAST ATTENDED TYPES OF SCHOOLS GIVEN BELOW	TYPE OF SCHOOL LAST ATTENDED BY:	
			Father	Mother
Not yet started school	i			
Nursery/kindergarten	ii			
State primary schools	iii			
Private preparatory/primary schools	iv			
Secondary modern/elementary/non-grammar denominational schools	v		1	1
Post-1947 Comprehensive schools	vi		2	2
Pre-1947 Central/intermediate/higher grade	vii		3	3
Technical School/Tech. college (up to and incl. age of 18)	viii		4	4
State Grammar/pre-1947 Secondary school	ix		5	5
Private Grammar/public school	x		6	6
Private commercial schools/colleges (up to and incl. age of 18)	xi		7	7
All Foreign schools including Eire (up to and incl. age of 18)	xii		8	8
D.K. type of institution	xiii		9	9
Other (describe fully, making clear whether state or private and whether applies to father or mother)	xiv			
N.B. CHECK ALL BROTHERS AND SISTERS ACCOUNTED FOR WHETHER AT PRESENT IN HOUSEHOLD OR NOT.				

XVII **Further Education of Parents**, i.e. since leaving school (Professional, academic, commercial, trade vocational).
Count only if course pursued for at least one session (i.e. one academic year, or three terms) or longer

	(a) Father	(b) Mother
	CODE ONE ONLY, PRIORITY CODE ONE DOWNWARDS	
No further education	1	1
Full-time course in university, college, other educational institution...	2	2
Full apprenticeship completed (S.R.N. completed)	3	3
Part-time/correspondence course pursued	4	4
D.K.	5	5

OFF. USE

XVIII **Recreational/Leisure Courses**
Any recreational/leisure/interest courses taken
COUNT ONLY IF TAKEN FOR ONE SESSION
(i.e. ONE YEAR OR THREE TERMS) OR LONGER.

		(a) Father	(b) Mother
	Yes	1	1
	No	2	2
	D.K.	3	3

OFF. USE

XIX **Qualifications obtained by parents**
Give highest qualification only, exclude apprenticeships and S.R.N.

	(a) Father	(b) Mother
	CODE ONE ONLY, PRIORITY CODE ONE DOWNWARDS	
No qualifications obtained	1	1
University degree, higher degree (including full medical training)...	2	2
Teachers Certificate, Membership of a professional institute, Full or intermediate professional qualification, G.C.E. 'A' level, Higher School Certificate, Intermediate (Arts/Science) Higher National Certificate/Diploma	3	3
G.C.E. 'O' level, Matriculation, General School Certificate, Ordinary National Certificate/Diploma, City and Guilds, R.S.A., Forces Educational Certificates, Commercial or trade certificates/diplomas	4	4
D.K.	5	5
Other (specify)		

OFF. USE

62. Is there anything else that you would like to say about ....'s school, or about infants or junior schooling in general?

Criticisms of large classes, overcrowding, shortage of teachers	1
Criticisms of school buildings, accommodation, facilities, equipment	2
Criticisms of school meals; food or drink provided at breaks	3
Children should be segregated by sex in infants/junior schools	4
In infants/juniors, problem or unfairness of starting or changing schools by month of birthday (e.g. have to stay extra year or have year less in infants/juniors)	5
Criticism of 11 as age of transfer to/selection for secondary school	6
Other (specify)	

APPENDIX 4

The Regression Analyses of the National Survey

by G. F. Peaker

1. THE BROAD OUTLINE

1. In marshalling the evidence to test conjectures about the reasons why some children make more progress in school than others a prime difficulty is to know what evidence is relevant, and to what extent. There would be no purpose in an inquiry if we knew this at the outset. The difficulty lies mainly in the right application of the phrase "other things being equal". For example, consider the question of the effect of the size of the teacher's class. It is very hard to believe that, if other things are equal, merely adding several more children to the class will improve the average achievement. Yet most surveys, including our own, show mild positive simple correlations between the average size of class in a school and the average test score for that school. Thus for our survey the highest such simple correlation is ·25 for Lower Junior Boys. In other words schools with larger classes tend, on the whole, to do rather better than schools with smaller classes. But this can hardly be the whole story. The result has only to be stated to arouse the conjecture that there must be various favourable circumstances, associated with large classes, to explain a result that would otherwise be incredible. But what can these circumstances be?

2. It is natural to think that the way to explore this question is to replace the simple two-way table, in which schools are grouped according to their average size of class and their average score, by a number of tables, in each of which there is only a small range for the other relevant circumstances. Thus we could classify the schools according to their average parental income, into three grades, and replace the single table by three tables, one for high, one for middling, and one for low average income. In the same way we could make another three-fold classification for the next variable that we think may be relevant. We now have nine tables. Bringing in a third variable will produce 27 tables. Continuing on these lines we should reach 59,049 tables for 10 variables, and more than two hundred billion for 30 variables. If we had more than three grades for each variable the number of tables needed would of course be much larger.

3. But, it may be said, the number of variables that can have any perceptible influence must be far smaller than 30. Long before we reach this point we must reach the point beyond which the influence of further variables is small and altogether uncertain on any evidence we can find. This is quite true. The trouble is that in order to apply it we should have to know in advance which variables were relevant and which were not, and the whole purpose of the inquiry is to find this out. It might be thought that it would be safe to take the variables in the descending order of their simple correlation, but, as is shown later, this is not the case. It is not the case because the relevance of a variable

depends not only upon its simple correlation with the criterion, but also on its correlation with its fellows, and with their correlations among themselves. This makes it impossible to guess the order of importance. All the variables in the picture have to be considered before any of them can be declared irrelevant.

4. These considerations make it clear that a direct attack on the problem is bound to break down, from sheer numerical complication, before it has made any appreciable progress. For a practicable method it is necessary to invoke some rather complicated algebra which, together with electronic computation, enables a solution to be found. The algebra has a long history, going back to the Gaussian method of solving linear equations by successive elimination. In recent years electronic computation has made it possible to apply this to equations with a hundred unknowns or more. This in turn makes it practicable to apply the method of stepwise multiple regression even to cases like ours where there are initially more than a hundred variables in the correlation matrix. It is hardly practicable to describe the process without resort to mathematical language. For the moment it will be enough to say that the computer selects the variables that turn out to be relevant, on the evidence of the sample, and rejects the others. The proviso "on the evidence of the sample" is material. Other samples drawn in the same way would provide somewhat different evidence, and lead to a somewhat different selection of variables. It is therefore important to consider the extent to which the results may be affected by sampling variation. The main point here is that the estimates of the total effects of broad classes of variables are more reliable than the estimates for individual variables. This suggests grouping the variables into three classes representing (1) parental attitudes, (2) home circumstances, (3) schooling. The estimate for the first class shows the effect on the child's progress of hopeful and encouraging interest on the part of the parents. The second class shows the effect of the parents' material circumstances, and of their own education. The third class shows the effect of the variation of various school circumstances. Before the inquiry it was plain, as a matter of common-sense and common observation, that parental encouragement and support could take the child some way. What the inquiry has shown is that "some way" can reasonably be interpreted as "a long way", and that the variation in parental encouragement and support has much greater effect than either the variation in home circumstances or the variation in schools. The reason why the school variables play so small a part is not, of course, that schooling is unimportant. It is that the variation between schools is much less than the variation between parental attitudes. If the least co-operative parents rose to the level of the most co-operative the effect would be much larger than if the worst schools rose to the level of the best or the least prosperous parents to the level of the most prosperous, because the effect of the range in co-operation is much greater than the effect of the range in parental prosperity or that of the range in schooling.

5. This part of the inquiry shows how much could be gained if less co-operative parents became more cooperative. It throws no light on the extent to which this could be brought about by persuasion. On this point we have two kinds of evidence. In the first place we can use regression again to test the firmness of the link between the parents attitudes and their circumstances.

It is reasonable to regard the attitudes as being partly determined by the other circumstances, and if we take the attitudes as criteria and the other circumstances as predictors we can get some light on the interpretation of "partly". We find that up to a quarter of the variation in attitudes can be put down to the variation in circumstances. This leaves three-quarters or more to be accounted for in other ways. It is reasonable to suppose that among these other ways persuasion, from a great variety of sources, must play a large part, and it is therefore reasonable to hope that attempts to change attitudes by persuasion might have some success. On the other hand such direct evidence as we have on this point is not very encouraging. It falls under three heads. In the first place several of our variables (e.g. Is there a parent/teacher association? How many meetings with parents are held?) were intended to measure aspects of persuasion already in use. But these variables often failed to reach significance in the regression analyses. Secondly, a special group of schools where the relations between parents and teachers were thought to be particularly good was selected by H.M. Inspectorate. But although the evidence subsequently collected from these schools vindicated the judgements that led to their selection there was little difference between the average achievement of the children in this group and those in the representative sample. Thus the special group merely confirmed the result from the sample (which was, of course, not yet known when the special group inquiry was planned). In the third place rather more encouraging results were obtained from the experimental attempt to influence parental attitudes that was carried out in one school with the co-operation of the Institute of Community Studies. In this case a small but recognisable improvement in the children's achievement was obtained. The first two results are less encouraging than might have been hoped, though perhaps not surprising when we remember the vast sums spent by the advertising industry in attempts to change attitudes about relatively trivial matters. On the other hand the modest success of the experiment is encouraging, and suggests that we should remember the principle, though not the particular instance, of Mr. Pickwick's views on brandy and water as a prophylactic—that where it failed it was because the sufferer had fallen into the vulgar error of not taking enough of it. On the evidence we may be confident that there is ample scope for persuasion, while recognising that to find the right kind and amount of persuasion will be a matter of difficult and delicate experiment, needing ingenuity and above all tact.

6. *The conclusions reached may be set out as follows:*
   (a) The variation in parental attitudes can account for more of the variation in children's school achievement than either the variation in home circumstances or the variation in schools.
   (b) Among the school variables of which we took notice the most important appeared to be the quality of the teaching. Although we found, as other inquiries have done, an association between better work and larger classes we also found that there were invariably other favourable circumstances, associated with the larger classes, to account for their apparent superiority.
   (c) Although the variation in parental material circumstances and parental education can account for some of the variation in parental attitudes it cannot account for very much, and leaves open the possibility that attitudes may be changed by persuasion.

(d) There is no doubt that attitudes have changed and are changing. Perhaps the strongest evidence of the change in attitudes is the large and continuing rise in the proportion of children who stay at school beyond the statutory leaving age.

(e) Despite the evidence that attitudes are not closely conditioned by material circumstances, and that they have changed with time, our positive evidence on the question of how far they are open to persuasion was rather disappointing. A number of our variables attempted to measure the efforts and persuasion applied by the schools, but these variables were not very conspicuous in their contributions to the children's achievements.

(f) Consequently we may be confident that there is ample scope for persuasion while recognising that to find the right kind and amount of persuasion will be a difficult and delicate experiment, needing much ingenuity and tact.

2. THE ANALYSES IN DETAIL

Analyses Between and Within Schools

7. The allocation of the sample of schools and pupils is set out in some detail at the end of the previous appendix. Here it will be enough to recall a few salient facts. To make the sampling frame schools were stratified by size. Within each size group they were drawn with probability proportionate to size. From each selected school within each size group a constant number of children was drawn. This number was 12, 8, or 4 per age group, according to the size group to which the school belonged. Boys and girls were drawn in equal numbers from mixed schools. Since the junior mixed and infants schools contained children in all six age and sex groups there were about a hundred schools and about five hundred pupils in each group.

8. Two kinds of analysis—between and within schools—were carried out. For the analyses between schools the variables were either attributes of the school, such as the average size of class in that school, or the sample means of pupil variables for that school, such as the mean parental income of the selected boys, or girls, in that school. For the analyses within schools the variables were the deviations from the mean of each school. These are of course zero for the school attributes, which do not therefore figure in the analyses within schools.

9. Since there are about a hundred schools and five hundred pupils in the sample for each of the six age and sex groups it will be seen that the standard errors of the simple correlation coefficients lie in the range from ·10 to ·07, according to the size of the correlation, for the analyses between schools, and in the range of ·05 to ·03 for the analyses between pupils within schools. This sampling variation determines the number of variables subsequently picked up by the stepwise regression process, and the size of the standard errors of the regression coefficients for these variables, which centred round ·08 and ·035 respectively for the two kinds of analysis. The general effect of sampling variation is to make the estimates for broad classes of variables more reliable than those for individual variables, particularly when the number of variables is large. This has a bearing on the selection of a short list from the long list of variables, as described in the next sub section.

The Long and the Short Lists of Variables

10. The original, long list of variables is set out in the two attached tables. Table 1 contains the variables that were derived from the interviews with parents conducted by the Social Survey. In drawing up the long list the general principle was to try to think of variables that might be relevant, and to include them if it seemed likely that reliable information could be obtained. Some variables that failed to satisfy the second condition were excluded after a pilot inquiry. After the field work had been done the Social Survey carried out a factor analysis in order to group some of the original questions into more satisfactory composite variables. This is described in the previous appendix. The first 14 variables in the Social Survey list are such composites.

11. The Social Survey list provides two of the three broad classes into which the variables can be divided. In the first place we have variables that measure parental attitudes. These are marked A in the list. Secondly we have the variables that represent the pupils' home circumstances, such as the parental income, the number of dependent children, the father's occupation, and the physical amenities of the home. These are marked B in the list. The parents' education is included in the second class, since it represents events that have already occurred. On the other hand the literacy of the home, which is perhaps less firmly anchored to the past, has been included in the first category.

12. Table 2, containing the school variables, comprises the third broad category. This information was supplied partly by the schools and partly by the Inspectorate, who provided, for example, the teaching assessment for each member of the staff concerned. In this list the letter P attached to a variable means that for this variable information was obtained for each pupil in the sample. Thus P is attached to the teaching assessment because the latter refers to the pupil's teacher. For the analyses between schools these variables provided a score for each school made by averaging them for the pupils in the sample for that school. For the analyses between pupils within schools the scores were the deviations from each school average. Some variables, originally included for the other purposes, have been deleted from the regression analyses either because they overlapped heavily with others or because they were quasi criterion variables. These are marked D.

13. The school list contains the criterion variables. For the analyses between schools the criterion was the score in a test of reading comprehension appropriate to the pupils' age. (The infants also had a picture intelligence test.) For the analyses between pupils within schools it was the pupils' rank order converted to a normal deviate. The rank order was, of course, based on the teacher's judgement, and since this analysis was within schools the usual difficulty of comparing the judgements of teachers in different schools did not arise.

14. The first set of analyses was run on the long list of variables. After deletions there were 104 variables for the analyses between schools, and 73 for those between pupils within schools. With a rather lenient significance stop (as described in the final section) about a dozen variables emerged from each analysis as making significant contributions to the criterion variation. These contributions were summed over the three broad classes of variable, and the results are set out in Table 3. The complete tables for the long list have not been printed, but they served their purpose in two ways. In the first

place they enabled the long list summary table to be made. Secondly they were a useful guide to the composition of the short list. The long list summary is probably a better guide than the short list summary to the total amount of variation accounted for by each of the three classes of variable. This follows from considerations set out in the final section. The detailed tables for the long list were useful as a guide to the composition of the short list because variables appeared in them with different frequencies. Although these tables are not replications, since each refers to a different sex, age group, or test it seems reasonable to say that a variable that never, or hardly ever, appears in them is unlikely to have much relevance. This enabled a large number of variables to be rejected, of which perhaps the most notable were average size of class and number on the school roll. There were no variables that appeared in every table, so the short list was made up of Aspiration, Literacy, and Interest, which appeared most frequently, and 14 others chosen either because they appeared often, or because, owing to their special interest, it was urged that they should be given another chance of appearing. It could in fact be foreseen, with fairly high probability, that these variables were unlikely to take advantage of their second chance, and in the upshot they did not. This accounts for some of the blanks in the detailed tables for the short list.

15. A variable that was not included in the short list, because it never emerged from the long, was average size of class. Owing to the special interest attaching to this variable its correlations were subsequently included in the matrices for the short list, and the normal equations solved iteratively by hand. The resulting regression coefficients uniformly failed to reach significance, despite the fact that the simple correlation was, in one case (Lower Junior Boys), as high as ·25.

The Results and their Interpretation

16. Reserving further discussion of the stepwise regression process and the effect of sampling variation until the final section let us now turn to the results and their interpretation. The summary of the results derived from the long list is set out in Table 3. The short list is covered by Tables 4.1–4.6 (between schools) and Tables 5.1–5.6 (between pupils within schools) and their attached summaries.

17. All these tables bear a strong family likeness. Two main points emerge. In the first place more of the variation in the children's school achievement is specifically accounted for by the variation in parental attitudes than by either the variation in the material circumstances of parents or by the variation in schools. Secondly, the relative importance of the parental attitudes increases as the children grow older.

18. The new results extend, but are not incompatible with, those derived from the surveys reported in *Early Leaving, Fifteen to Eighteen* and *Half our Future*. Those surveys dealt with parental variations of the second kind. The new survey brings in the first kind (parental attitudes) as well. The effect of bringing in the attitude variables is two-fold. In the first place much more of the variation in the children's achievement is accounted for. Secondly, part of the variation that would be attributable to home circumstances, if attitudes were ignored, is transferred to the account of attitudes when these are brought in. This is analogous to the relations between the

statures of fathers, mothers, and children. Tall fathers tend to have tall sons partly because they tend to marry tall wives. The simple correlations are ·5 between parents and children and ·3 between spouses. If fathers alone are considered they account for 25 per cent of the variations in sons. But when mothers are brought into the picture the total accounted for rises from 25 per cent to 38 per cent, but the father's contribution is reduced from 25 per cent to 19 per cent, because in the earlier assessment he was, so to speak, borrowing from the mother. In this way bringing in the parental attitudes increases the total amount of variation accounted for while reducing somewhat the amount attributed to the other kind of variable before the attitudes were brought in. This point is discussed further in the final section.

19. It will be seen from Table 3 that the long list of variables accounts for about two thirds of the total variation between schools and for about half of the total variation within schools. The remaining third (or half) is attributable to the circumstances that we have not taken into account, such as individual differences between children that are not related to their parents' attitudes or circumstances, or to those aspects of schooling that we have not taken into account, and also to our errors of measurement. To some extent the individual differences are averaged out when the pupil variables are summed over each school for the analyses between schools. This is the main reason why our variables account for two thirds of the variation between schools, and only half the variation between pupils within schools. But in both cases the amount of variation accounted for is remarkably high, and in particular the high contribution from the attitude side indicates the care and skill with which the difficult task of interviewing parents was carried out by the workers of the Social Survey.

20. Qualitatively the results are in no way surprising. Common sense and common observation lead us to expect that a child's school achievement will be determined, to some extent, by the attitudes of his parents, and that these attitudes in turn will partly depend upon their material circumstances. It was indeed this common sense expectation that guided the planning of the inquiry. What could not be foreseen, until the inquiry was complete, was the quantitative aspect. We could foresee that parental attitudes, parental circumstances, and schooling would each make a contribution. What we could not foresee, and what the inquiry has shown, is the relative size of these contributions. The fact that attitudes play so large a part is hopeful, since it is at least possible that attitudes may be open to persuasion. Two kinds of evidence on this point have already been mentioned, in paragraph 5. Let us now consider the first kind of evidence in more detail.

21. In the first part of our inquiry we have used multiple regression with the children's achievement in school as the criterion, and parental attitudes, parental circumstances, and school variables as the predictors. But we can also use it with parental attitudes as the criteria and parental circumstances as the predictors. In this way we can test the firmness of the link between attitudes and material circumstances. Without falling into the error of assuming that correlations are sufficient, as well as necessary, evidence of causal relations we can, at any rate, make an assumption, or set up a model, and work out its consequences. For example, we can assume that causal lines run from parental circumstances to parental attitudes, and thence to the children's achievement, in the way shown in the diagram below (Figure 1),

which is based on the variables used in the short list. On the left of the diagram we have the five variables of the second kind in the short list namely (8) Physical amenities of the home, (12) No. of dependent children, (13) Father's occupational group, (14) Father's education, (15) Mother's education. In the middle column we have the three variables of the first kind, namely, (9) Aspiration for the child, (10) Literacy of the home, (11) Parental interest in school work and progress. On the right we have the final criterion, the child's school achievement. The arrows are the causal lines, and the

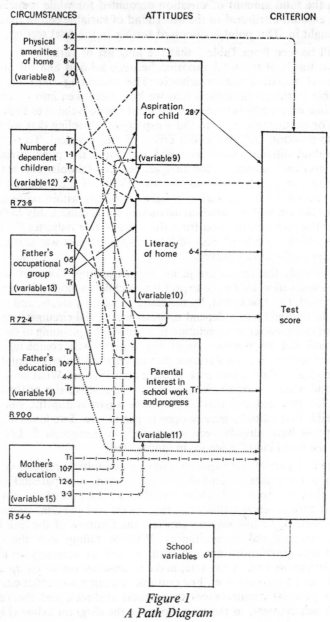

Figure 1
A Path Diagram

number on each arrow is the percentage of the variance, of the variable to which it runs, that it carries. These are determined from the regression equations. Since these contributions always fall short of 100 per cent we also need the arrows coming in out of the blue to carry the residuals. For the final criterion there is also a contribution from the schooling variables.

22. Figure 1 relates to the analysis between schools for the Top Junior Boys. The connections shown in it between parental circumstances and parental attitudes, and the corresponding facts for the Top Junior Girls, can also be exhibited in tabular form as follows. (The variables denoted by numbers in the following tables can be identified by Fig. 1):

Variable	Top Junior Boys						Top Junior Girls				
	9	10	11	Total	Mean		9	10	11	Total	Mean
8	3·2	8·4	4·0	15·6	5·2		1·8	13·6	1·9	17·3	5·8
12	1·1	0·0	2·7	3·8	1·3		0·9	3·6	4·0	8·5	2·8
13	0·5	2·2	0·0	2·7	0·9		2·2	0·9	0·0	3·1	1·0
14	10·7	4·4	0·0	15·1	5·0		7·6	5·3	2·5	15·4	5·1
15	10·7	12·6	3·3	26·6	8·9		5·4	11·8	0·0	17·2	5·7
Total	26·2	27·6	10·0	63·8	21·3		17·9	35·2	8·4	61·5	20·5

For the analyses between pupils within schools the corresponding tables are:—

Variable	Top Junior Boys						Top Junior Girls				
	9	10	11	Total	Mean		9	10	11	Total	Mean
8	3·8	2·1	2·2	8·1	2·7		2·4	0·6	0·7	3·7	1·2
12	3·6	4·0	0·1	7·7	2·6		1·3	0·6	1·8	3·7	1·2
13	1·5	5·0	4·6	11·1	3·7		5·6	1·5	2·2	9·3	3·1
14	1·8	1·3	0·0	3·1	1·0		3·8	3·5	0·7	8·0	2·7
15	3·0	3·2	1·5	7·7	·2·6		1·6	3·3	0·5	5·4	1·8
Total	13·7	15·6	8·4	37·7	12·6		14·7	9·5	5·9	30·1	10·0

23. Among the five variables placed on the left in Figure 1 there are two which stand in a special position. These are (14) Father's education and (15) Mother's education. As we have defined them these are entirely records of past events, and this may be held to give them a better right than the other three to be put first in a causal sequence. If we take them by themselves we obtain:

	Variable	Boys					Variable	Girls				
		9	10	11	Total	Mean		9	10	11	Total	Mean
Top Juniors	14	10·2	8·5	0·0	18·7	6·2	14	9·8	8·7	2·1	20·6	6·9
	15	10·2	10·9	3·6	24·7	8·2	15	6·1	13·0	0·0	19·1	6·4
	Total	20·4	19·2	3·6	43·4	14·5	Total	15·9	21·7	2·1	39·7	13·2

	Variable	Boys					Variable	Girls				
		9	10	11	Total	Mean		9	10	11	Total	Mean
Lower Juniors	14	20·8	9·9	0·9	31·6	10·5	14	10·4	8·8	1·1	20·3	7·8
	15	7·7	19·7	0·0	27·4	9·1	15	5·8	13·0	0·0	18·8	6·3
	Total	28·5	29·6	0·9	59·0	14·6	Total	16·2	21·8	1·1	39·1	13·0

	Variable	Boys					Variable	Girls				
		9	10	11	Total	Mean		9	10	11	Total	Mean
Infants	14	5·7	5·3	2·7	13·7	4·6	14	10·3	22·4	1·7	34·4	11·5
	15	4·7	3·7	−0·2	8·2	2·7	15	10·3	5·2	6·0	15·5	5·2
	Total	10·4	9·0	2·5	21·9	7·3	Total	20·6	27·6	1·7	49·9	16·6

Summary (Average Contributions)

		Boys	Girls	Mean
14	Father's education	7·1	8·4	7·8
15	Mother's education	6·9	5·9	6·4
	Total	14·0	14·3	14·4

It is interesting to note that (11), Parental interest, depends less upon parental education than either (9) or (10). It is easy to see a possible reason for this.

G

It is also interesting to note in the summary that, as usual, fathers are rather more important for daughters and mothers for sons.

24. The main point to be noted in Figure 1, and in the corresponding diagrams for other age and sex groups that could be drawn from the tables above, is the size of the residual terms. It is the arrows coming in out of the blue that carry the weight. The variables representing parental circumstances and past history account for only about a quarter of the variation in attitudes, leaving about three quarters to be accounted for by other variables that we have not brought into the picture. Common sense, common observation, and introspection suggest that among these variables communication and persuasion, from a great variety of sources, must play a considerable part. Or, to put the matter another way, if we were able to see through the eyes of omniscience, and use a measure of parental education that included the whole impact of other minds, far more of the variation in attitudes could be accounted for. And although, like the younger Mr. Weller *on a famous occasion, we have to confess that our vision is more limited we may none the less conclude that it is not unreasonable to hope that parental attitudes can be changed by persuasion in such a way that on the whole parents and teachers become more co-operative. On the one hand the fact that parental circumstances do not account for very much of parental attitudes leaves plenty of room for believing that persuasion may be effective. On the other hand the fact that they account for some of the variation gives grounds for expecting that as circumstances improve so will attitudes. These grounds are strengthened by the fact that our evidence shows direct links between parental circumstances and children's school achievements, in addition to the indirect links through parental attitudes.

Summary

25. Two questions may be asked at the end of any inquiry. They are:
    (*a*) Are the conclusions compatible with earlier evidence?
    (*b*) If so, have we learnt anything that we did not know at the outset?
Here there is no difficulty about the first question. The starting point of the inquiry was the previous evidence that both the attitudes and the home circumstances of parents had a good deal to do with the progress of their offspring in school. What the previous evidence did not indicate was the relative importance of the two sides, and the relation between them. Were attitudes more important than circumstances, or vice versa? And how far were attitudes conditioned by circumstances? Do parental circumstances operate directly on children's school progress, or do they operate indirectly by conditioning attitudes, or do they operate partly in one way and partly in the other? It is on these questions that our inquiry has thrown some new light.

26. The conclusions suggested are that:
    (1) The specific contributions made by the variation in parental attitudes are greater than those made by the variation in home circumstances, while the latter in turn are greater than those made by the variations between schools and teachers that we have taken into account.

---

* See final section

(2) Only about a quarter of the variation in parental attitudes is conditioned by the variation in circumstances. The remainder must be conditioned to a large extent by communication and persuasion, so that it is reasonable to hope that an attempt to improve the co-operation of parents and teachers by persuasion might attain some success.

(3) Although parental attitudes are largely independent of home circumstances they are conditioned by them to some extent. For this reason, and also because parental circumstances operate directly, as well as through parental attitudes, on children's progress it is reasonable to hope that the latter will improve as circumstances improve.

27. The weight to be attached to these conclusions depends on the strength of the evidence supporting them, and this in turn may be considered under four heads. In the first place there is the accuracy of the sampling, of schools, children and parents. Secondly there is the appropriateness of the variables chosen. In the third place there is the accuracy with which the variables have been measured. And finally there is the validity of the inferential arguments used. In the general description of the inquiry given in this section something has been said under all these heads. Some rather more technical considerations follow in the final section.

3. SOME TECHNICALITIES

" *Yes, I have a pair of eyes*", said Sam, "*and that's just it. If they wos a pair o' patent double million magnifyin' microscopes of hextra power, p'raps I might be able to see through a flight o' stairs and a deal door; but bein' only eyes, you see my wision's limited*".

28. Like most of the younger Mr. Weller's remarks this has a wide application. Its bearing upon educational inquiries, of whatever kind, is to remind us of the extent of our ignorance. None of us can know much about the workings of other's minds, though we may reasonably hope to learn a little more. That is to say, we can reasonably hope to obtain new evidence that makes some conjectures rather more probable, and others rather less so. New evidence can only do this if it is both well founded and appropriately analysed. The foundations of our evidence have been discussed above. The least familiar aspect of the analysis is the use of stepwise regression, to which we now turn.

Stepwise Regression

29. In this process successive regression equations, like

$$y = b_i \, x_i \qquad\qquad\qquad (1)$$
$$y = b_i' \, x_i + b_j' \, x_j \qquad\qquad (2)$$
$$y = b_i'' x_i + b_j'' x_j + b_k'' x_k \qquad (3)$$
$$\text{etc.} \qquad\qquad \text{etc.}$$

are produced by adding one variable at a time. At each step the computer selects the variable which, at this stage, will make the largest reduction in the remainder sum of squares. At any step it is possible that a variable previously selected may cease to be significant, and if so it is removed from the equation. When no variable remains that can make a significant reduction the process comes to an end. Thus Table 5.1 was reached by the sequence of seven steps shown below:

Variable	Regression Coefficients, b Step							Simple Correlations, r
	1	2	3	4	5	6	7	r
(11)	·415	·365	·315	·307	·263	·254	·252	·415
(9)		·356	·318	·295	·252	·241	·251	·408
(3)			·236	·204	·197	·190	·200	·370
(7)				·194	·203	·263	·248	·312
(10)					·150	·148	·148	·355
(5)						·144	·150	·067
(2)							·102	·076

30. The first variable to be selected is, of course, the one with the largest simple correlation with the criterion. But the subsequent order of selection is not necessarily the same as the descending order of the simple correlation, as may be seen by looking down the right hand column, which shows (7) selected before (10), although the latter has a larger simple correlation. Furthermore, the last two variables to reach significance, (5) and (2), have much smaller simple correlations than several variables which are not selected at all. For example (13), which is Father's occupational group, has a simple correlation of ·20, and there are simple correlations of ·20 and ·16 for (14) and (15), which are Father's education and Mother's education respectively. A variable with a fairly high simple correlation may fail to enter the regression equation because it is too highly correlated with variables that the equation already contains. This is illustrated below for (13).

31. It will be seen that as the process goes on the coefficients tend to settle down. Thus the changes produced by the first three steps are much greater than those produced by the last three. Variable (11), which is the pioneer, takes some hard knocks to begin with, but is pretty steady after the fifth step, while (10), which only comes in at the fifth step, is steady from the start. This illustrates a general feature of the process.

32. The contributions to the assigned variation can be obtained by multiplying the regression coefficient by the simple correlation, and are as follows (in percentages):

Variable	Assigned Variation, % Step							$100r^2$
	1	2	3	4	5	6	7	
(11)	17·2	15·1	13·1	12·7	10·9	10·5	10·5	17·2
(9)		14·5	13·0	12·0	10·3	9·8	10·2	16·7
(3)			8·7	7·5	7·3	7·0	7·4	13·7
(7)				6·1	6·3	8·2	7·7	9·7
(10)					5·3	5·3	5·3	12·7
(5)						1·0	1·0	0·4
(2)							0·8	0·6
Total	17·2	29·6	34·8	38·3	40·1	41·8	42·9	71·0
$100sr^2$	17·2	33·9	47·6	57·3	70·0	70·4	71·0	

33. Since each row in this table is derived from the corresponding row in the previous table by multiplying by the same quantity the new table shows the same tendency to settle down as the old one. The total of the assignable variation increases as each new variable comes in, but the increase, at first rapid, is very slight for the last three steps. This is partly because the later

variables to be selected have smaller simple correlations, and partly also because they have smaller regression coefficients. The final row in the table shows what the assignable variation would be if the predictors were uncorrelated among themselves. If this were so each regression coefficient would simply be the corresponding simple correlation with the criterion. Since 42·9 is only 60 per cent of 71·0 there is a 40 per cent loss of efficiency owing to the intercorrelation of the seven predictors among themselves.

34. This intercorrelation is shown in the following table, which also contains the correlations with the criterion Y, and three supplementary columns that are explained below:

Correlation Matrix

	Y	(2)	(3)	(5)	(7)	(9)	(10)	(11)	A b	B (13)	C b(13)
Y	1000	076	370	067	312	408	355	415		200	
(2)	076	1000	−081	−125	148	−082	−034	−006	102	154	016
(3)	370	−081	1000	−005	203	189	154	233	200	232	046
(5)	067	−125	−005	1000	−392	029	053	048	150	−039	−006
(7)	312	148	203	−392	1000	157	020	098	248	098	024
(9)	408	−082	189	029	159	1000	325	143	251	143	036
(10)	355	−034	154	053	020	325	1000	340	148	273	040
(11)	415	−006	233	048	098	143	340	1000	252	122	031

[013]
—— [1000] [013]
200

(Decimal points omitted)

35. The first supplementary column, headed A, contains the regression coefficients for the seven variables, taken from the first table above but rearranged in the new order. The sum of the products of each entry in this column and the corresponding entry in any of the predictor columns is the simple correlation at the head of that column, as may be verified. This is the clue to the iterative method of obtaining the regression coefficients, which is an alternative to the process of inverting the intercorrelation matrix. It also enables us to see how it is that variable (13), with a substantial correlation of ·20 with the criterion, does not enter into the regression. The column headed B contains the simple correlations of (13) with the criterion and the other seven variables, the entry [1·000] at the foot being its correlation with itself, like the diagonal entries in the matrix. Each entry in A is multiplied by the entry in B to give the entry in C. The seven entries in C sum to ·187, which is ·013 short of ·200, the simple correlation between (13) and the criterion. If we now enter ·013 at the foot of the A column, and multiply it by 1·000 in the B column, we get ·013 at the foot of the C column, which now sums to ·200, the simple correlation of (13) with the criterion. Consequently ·013 would be the first shot at the regression coefficient for (13) if we were using the iterative solution for the stepwise procedure. It is not the final value because inserting it produces small additions to the sums of products for all the other variables, so that slight adjustments in the other regression coefficients are needed to get rid of these, and this in turn will alter the ·013 somewhat. The reader who is interested can carry out the process for himself by going back a step in the regression, starting with the first six variables, and obtaining by the iterative process the coefficients when (2) is brought in. The iterative method shows both why every coefficient needs adjustment

when a new variable is brought in, and also why the adjustments are small in the later stages.

36. Here however the immediate point is that (13) does not enter the regression equation because the seven regression coefficients already found give it a total entry in the C column which differs from its simple correlation with the criterion by an insignificant amount. It can be seen from the column that all the preceding seven variables, except for (2) and (5), contribute roughly equally to this result. By the same token it can be seen from columns (2) and (5) that the reason why these variables enter into the regression equation, despite their low simple correlations, is the presence of negative intercorrelations in their columns. A variable tends (not) to enter the equation if it has a high (low) simple correlation with the criterion, or if it has a low (high) correlation with the resultant of the previous predictors. As these cases illustrate the two requirements may be in conflict.

37. The iterative solution shows why a variable with a small simple correlation may none the less be important. The computer programme proceeds on different lines. It begins with the complete correlation matrix and transforms it step by step until the regression coefficients and the inverse matrix are obtained for the significant variables. At each step it examines all the variables to find which makes the largest reduction in the outstanding variation at that stage, and puts that variable in the regression if the reduction is significant. At the mth step the test of significance is that F should exceed F_0, where

$$F = \frac{R_m^2 - R_{m-1}^2}{1 - R_m^2} \quad (n - m - 1)$$

R_m is the multiple correlation when m variables are in the regression, and n is the number of schools, or pupils as the case may be, in the sample for this sex and age group. Thus, for the fourth step in the table on page 190, with 498 top junior boys in the sample,

$$F = \frac{\cdot 383 - \cdot 348}{1 - \cdot 383} \times 493$$

$= 28 \cdot 0$, or $28 \cdot 2088$ from the computer, which retains more figures.

For the seventh and final step

$$F = \frac{\cdot 429 - \cdot 418}{1 - \cdot 429} \times 490$$

$= 9$, the more accurate value being $8 \cdot 4780$ from the computer.

F_0 is at choice, in the range from three to six: the higher the value the more severe the test of significance. In this case all choices in the range produce the same result, since the lowest F is nine, which exceeds six. But in general a low choice for F_0 may admit one or two steps that would be excluded by a high choice. For the present work the low choice, three, was fed into the computer throughout. The grounds for this are that one does not know at the outset how the results will come out, and that steps that have been taken can always be excluded by a revised choice of F_0, whereas steps that have not been taken at first cannot subsequently be added without running the whole programme again.

38. It should be noted that while the reduction made by the mth variable in the outstanding variation is, of course, the same as the addition made to the assigned variation it is not the same as the "contribution". Thus at the fourth step in the preceding table the reduction (or addition) is $38\cdot3 - 34\cdot8 = 3\cdot5$ per cent, while the contribution is $6\cdot1$ per cent. The contributions from the earlier steps are changed somewhat at each new step, and the new contribution is made up partly of the addition and partly of the amount transferred from variables chosen earlier. At the second step the addition made by (9) is $29\cdot6 - 17\cdot2 = 12\cdot4$ per cent, but the contribution is $14\cdot5$ per cent. The difference of $2\cdot1$ per cent had, so to speak, been "borrowed" by (11) at the first stage. Comparing the extreme entries in the top row shows that the total "borrowings" of (11) from the other six variables were $17\cdot2 - 10\cdot5 = 6\cdot7$ per cent.

39. With a sample of this size the process for this sex and age group stops at the seventh step, but if the sample were much larger it would go on for one or two more steps, and evidence of further slight borrowings would appear— "slight" because the process is clearly settling down by the seventh step. But if we had a much larger sample it would be better to divide it into inter-penetrating random sub-samples and so obtain replications of the tables. Four replicated sets of tables from four samples of 100 schools each would give a better idea of the stability of the estimates than one set from 400 schools. This is because the stepwise procedure has the defects of its virtues. Its merit is that it excludes variables that fail to make significant addition to the assigned variation, on the evidence of a particular sample. Its demerit is that the evidence of a particular sample may lead to the inclusion of variables that ought, on their population values, to be excluded, and vice versa. The lowest regression coefficients admitted to our between schools and within schools tables are $\cdot11$ and $\cdot06$ respectively, on the long list, and $\cdot13$ and $\cdot07$, on the short list. The standard errors of the coefficients in the "between schools" tables are all close to $\cdot08$. In the "within schools" tables they are all close to $\cdot035$, there being about five times as many boys (or girls) as schools in the sample for each sex and age group.

40. We know that about a sixth of the estimates will be too large by one standard error or more, and another sixth too small. Similarly we know that about one estimate in 40 will be too large by two standard errors, or more, and about one in 40 too small. We know nothing about the actual errors beyond the fact that they are distributed in this way. But this is enough to make us confident that some of the variables with small coefficients that are in the table ought not to be, and that others that are not included ought to be. "Ought to be" means here "would have been included more often than not" if we had had a great many samples instead of only one.

41. The effects are more serious for the "between schools" tables than for the "within schools" tables, because the standard errors are twice as large for the former, and more serious for the long list than the short list, because the tables from the long list contain more variables with small coefficients many of which would be replaced by others if we could afford to replicate.

42. The advantage of a long list is that it gives a very large number of variables a chance of appearing in the evidence. Of this large number there are probably some that are real, but small, contributors. But which of these real but small contributors actually appear in the tables depends very much on the chance of sampling, as has been shown. A short list has the initial, and serious, disadvantage that the variables excluded from it cannot appear in the evidence however much they deserve to do so. On the other hand the evidence about the variables that are included is less at the mercy of chance effects, and no variable that appeared important in the results from the long list has been excluded from the short.

43. What this amounts to is that only the summary tables from the long list are worth interpretation. For the short list interpretation may reasonably be applied to the individual variables that appear, as well as to the summaries. The summary tables for the long list have been made by dividing the variables into the three broad classes, and summing the contributions from each class of variable over each sex and age group. This has also been done for the tables from the short list, but in addition the summaries include the contributions of individual variables. Complete tables, giving the simple correlations and the regression coefficients as well as the contributions, have also been given for the short list.

Bias
44. It should be noted that the estimate of the assignable variation is subject to bias as well as to sampling variation. If we had a large number of samples instead of only one each sample would give a somewhat different value of R^2 and the average of these values would be somewhat greater than the true value. If the true value is R^2 the expected value is

$$R^2 + (1 - R^2)(p-1)/(n-1)$$

where n is the number of sampling units (schools or pupils) in the sample and p the number of variables that emerge as significant. Thus, with 100 schools and 10 variables emerging, and a true R^2 of 50 per cent, the expected estimate would be 54·5 per cent. With 500 boys and girls it would be 50·9 per cent. For the analyses within schools the effect is altogether trifling, but it is less so for the analyses between schools. The reason for the bias is that the addition of any variable, even a purely random one, is bound to make some addition to the multiple correlation, in the absence of a fantastically improbable numerical coincidence, and that since R is essentially positive these small contributions add up. The significance stop in the stepwise regression process prevents much damage being done, but where the number of emerging variables is an appreciable fraction of the number of sampling units the effect is not completely negligible though it is less than that of sampling variation. In the case of the analyses between schools it is like having a gun aimed five degrees off the target with two thirds of the shots falling within seven degrees of the aiming point. Within schools this becomes one degree and three degrees.

Cause and Effect
45. The form of the argument is as follows. The previous evidence makes it initially probable that variations in parental attitudes, parental circumstances, and school circumstances all have some effect on the progress of

children in school. The regression analysis with school achievement as the criterion increases this probability, and also gives us estimates of the relative parts played by the three classes of variable. This first part of the evidence strongly suggests that if parental attitudes could be changed by persuasion there would be a marked rise in the general level of school achievement. The second part of the evidence comes from the regression analyses with parental attitudes as the criteria. This shows that while the variation in circumstances can account for some of the variation in attitudes it cannot account for very much. This part of the evidence leaves the door open, so to speak, for persuasion, and taken in conjunction with the first part suggests that more educational effort could profitably be directed to changing parental attitudes by persuasion. However, when we look for positive evidence on this the results are rather disappointing. On the one hand the "persuasion" variables turned out to have negligible regression coefficients for the most part, and on the other the average performance of the special group of schools with good parent-teacher relations was no better than the general average. The most hopeful feature is that there was an improvement in achievement in the one school where a deliberate experiment in persuasion was made. This result needs replication in other schools before great weight can be attached to it, but so far as it goes it is encouraging.

46. Elderly observers like the writer can have little doubt that the general level of parental attitudes, and with it the general level of school achievement, has risen a great deal during the last half century, so that the question is really whether this progress can be accelerated by persuasion. The general conclusion seems to be that a successful attempt to accelerate the improvement in attitudes by persuasion would be extremely rewarding, but that the attempt is likely to be a difficult and delicate task, demanding both ingenuity and tact in a high degree.

Table 1

Variables from the parental interviews for the multiple regression analysis (Long List)

Variables marked A have been classified as Attitudes.
Variables marked B have been classified as Home Circumstances.
Variables marked F are composites reached through the factor analysis.

A1   *F.1. Responsibility and initiative taken by parents over child's education*

Transform items as follows and then sum the new codes for each parent.

(i)   Whether talked to class teachers
          Code 1. Yes.
          Code 2. No. D.K.

(ii)   Number of talks with head or class teacher
          Code 1. Four or more talks.
          Code 2. Three talks.
          Code 3. Two talks.
          Code 4. One talk or D.K.
          Code 5. No talks.

    (iii)   Whether seen head or class teacher about educational **matters**
            Code 1. Yes.
            Code 2. No. D.K.

    (iv)   Whether had talk about teaching methods used
            Code 1. Had talk.
            Code 2. No talk.

    (v)   Whether talked to head when child started school
            Code 1. Yes.
            Code 2. No. D.K.

    (vi)   Whether husband has been to child's school and talked to head
            Code 1. Husband has been to school and talked to head
            Code 2. Husband has been to school but not talked to head
            Code 3. Husband has *not* been to school.

    (vii)   Whether asked for work for child or how to help child at home
            Code 1. Asked for homework.
            Code 2. Homework already given.
            Code 3. Has not asked for homework.

    (viii)   Number of possible types of school function attended.

A2   *F.2. Relations between parents and teachers.*

    (i)   It's very easy to see the teachers whenever you want to
            Code 1. Agrees.
            Code 2. D.K.
            Code 3. Disagrees.

    (ii)   The teachers seem very pleased when parents go along to see
            them
            Code 1. Agrees.
            Code 2. D.K.
            Code 3. Disagrees.

    (iii)   Whether happy with arrangements for seeing head or class
            teacher
            Code 1. Yes.
            Code 2. D.K.
            Code 3. No.

    (iv)   I feel that teachers would like to keep parents out of the school
            Code 1. Disagrees.
            Code 2. D.K.
            Code 3. Agrees.

    (v)   The teachers definitely seem interested in what you think about
            your child's education
            Code 1. Agrees.
            Code 2. D.K.
            Code 3. Disagrees.

    (vi)   I would feel that I was interfering if I went to the school
            uninvited
            Code 1. Disagrees.
            Code 2. D.K.
            Code 3. Agrees.

(vii)   If you go up to the school they only tell you what you know
          already
          Code 1. Disagrees.
          Code 2. D.K.
          Code 3. Agrees.

(viii) The teachers seem really interested in all the children
          Code 1. Agrees.
          Code 2. D.K.
          Code 3. Disagrees.

A3   *F.3. Paternal interest and support.*

(i)   Whether husband helps with control of children
          Code 1. Husband takes big or equal part.
          Code 2. Husband takes small part.
          Code 3. No husband/wife.

(ii)   Whether husband takes interest in how child is progressing
          school
          Code 1. Husband takes interest.
          Code 2. No interest, or no husband.

(iii)   Whether husband does things with child at weekends
          Code 1. Yes, most weekends.
          Code 2. Yes, occasional weekends.
          Code 3. No, or no husband.

(iv)   Whether husband plays with child in evenings
          Code 1. Yes, most evenings.
          Code 2. Yes, occasional evenings.
          Code 3. No, or no husband.

(v)   Whether husband took interest in school child went to
          Code 1. Husband took interest.
          Code 2. No interest or no husband.

(vi)   Husband's hours away from home at work
          Code 1. Less than 10 hours.
          Code 2. Ten but less than 12 hours.
          Code 3. Twelve hours or over.

(vii)   Whether husband has been to child's school and talked to head
          Code 1. Husband has been to school and talked to head.
          Code 2. Husband has been to school and *not* talked to head
          Code 3. Husband has *not* been to school.

A4   *F.5. Attitude to corporal punishment.*

(i)   Having the cane is very bad for most children
          Code 1. Agrees.
          Code 2. D.K.
          Code 3. Disagrees.

(ii)   I would agree to the school using the cane occasionally
          Code 1. Disagrees.
          Code 2. D.K.
          Code 3. Agrees.

    (iii)   Most children need to be smacked quite often
            Code 1. Disagrees.
            Code 2. D.K.
            Code 3. Agrees.

B5   *F.6. Physical amenities of home.*
    (i)   Whether fixed bath or shower
            Code 1. Yes, own.
            Code 2. Yes, shared.
            Code 3. No.
    (ii)   Whether hot water from a tap
            Code 1. Yes, own.
            Code 2. Yes, shared.
            Code 3. No.
    (iii)   Whether child usually plays in street or not
            Code 1. Does *not* play mainly in street.
            Code 2. Plays mainly in street.
    (iv)   Whether dwelling has garden or yard child can use
            Code 1. Yes.
            Code 2. No garden or yard.

A6   *F.7. Whether parents devote time and attention to child's development*
    (i)   Parents should leave all teaching and helping with school subjects to the teachers
            Code 1. Disagrees.
            Code 2. D.K.
             Code 3. Agrees.
    (ii)   Whether help with school work given to child at home
            Code 1. Yes, by husband and/or wife.
            Code 2. Yes, but *not* by husband or wife.
            Code 3. No.
    (iii)   I have too much to do to spend time on helping with school work
            Code 1. Disagrees.
            Code 2. D.K.
            Code 3. Agrees.
    (iv)   Whether mother plays with child in the evenings
            Code 1. Yes, most evenings.
            Code 2. Yes, occasionally.
            Code 3. No.
    (v)   Teaching children to behave should be mainly the school's job
            Code 1. Disagrees.
            Code 2. D.K.
            Code 3. Agrees.

A7   *F.8. Educational aspirations for child.*
    (i)   Whether particular type of secondary school wanted for child
            Code 1. Yes, particular type wanted.
            Code 2. No, doesn't mind. D.K.

(ii)   Whether grammar school wanted for child
        Code 1. Yes, grammar wanted.
        Code 2. No, doesn't mind.

(iii)   Preferred age of leaving school for child
        Code 1. 18 or over.
        Code 2. 16 or 17.
        Code 3. Can't say, depends on child.

A8   *F.9. Whether parents have taken any recreational or leisure courses.*

(i)   Whether father has taken any recreational/leisure courses
        Code 1. Yes.
        Code 2. No. D.K.

(ii)   Whether mother has taken any recreational/leisure courses
        Code 1. Yes.
        Code 2. No. D.K.

A9   *F.10. Whether parents took steps to find out about school when child was starting there.*

(i)   Whether made inquiries about school before child started
        Code 1. Made inquiries.
        Code 2. No inquiries made, or not needed.

(ii)   Whether knew what school was like before child started
        Code 1. Knew about school.
        Code 2. Did not know about school.

(iii)   Whether parent talked to head when child started school
        Code 1. Yes.
        Code 2. No.

A10 *F.11. Whether active antagonism shown to the school or not.*

(i)   Whether parent has complained to head or class teacher
        Code 1. *Not* complained.
        Code 2. Complained.

(ii)   Whether parent has seen head or class teacher on own initiative
        Code 1. No. D.K.
        Code 2. Yes.

(iii)   Whether teachers treat all children fairly
        Code 1. Children treated fairly.
        Code 2. D.K.
        Code 3. Children *not* treated fairly.

(iv)   The teachers have favourites among the parents
        Code 1. Disagrees.
        Code 2. D.K.

A11 *F.12. Literacy of home.*

(i)   Whether husband or wife belongs to library
        Code 1. One or both belongs.
        Code 2. Neither belongs but one belonged within 10 years.
        Code 3. Neither belonged within last 10 years.

    (ii)   Whether wife reads
             Code 1. Yes, non-fiction.
             Code 2. Yes, newspapers, magazines, or fiction.
             Code 3. No reading, or no wife.

    (iii)   Number of books in home
             Code 1. More than five books.
             Code 2. One to five books.
             Code 3. No books.

    (iv)   Whether husband reads
             Code 2. Yes, non-fiction.
             Code 2. Yes, newspapers, magazines, or fiction.
             Code 3. No reading, or no husband.

    (v)   Whether child has library books at home
             Code 1. Yes.
             Code 2. No. D.K.

    (vi)   Whether child reads at home apart from homework
             Code 1. Yes, four times a week or oftener, books.
             Code 2. Yes, two or three times a week, books.
             Code 3. Yes, less than twice a week, books.
             Code 4. Comics or magazines only.
             Code 5. No reading.

A12 *F.13. Parental interest in and knowledge of work child is doing at school and progress.*

    (i)   Whether child talks to parent about school work
             Code 1. Yes, often.
             Code 2. No, or rarely.

    (ii)   Whether child brings books home from school to read
             Code 1. Yes.
             Code 2. No. D.K.

    (iii)   Whether child reads at home
             Code 1. Yes, four times a week or oftener, books.
             Code 2. Yes, two or three times a week.
             Code 3. Yes, less than twice a week, books.
             Code 4. Comics or magazines only.
             Code 5. No reading.

    (iv)   Whether mother plays with child in evenings
             Code 1. Yes, most evenings.
             Code 2. Yes, occasionally.
             Code 3. No, no answer.

    (v)   Whether parent happy about teaching methods used
             Code 1. Happy.
             Code 2. Worried.

    (vi)   I would like to be told more about how my child is getting on
             Code 1. Disagrees.
             Code 2. D.K.
             Code 3. Agrees.

(vii)   I think that the teachers should ask me more about my child
        Code 1. Disagrees.
        Code 2. D.K.
        Code 3. Agrees.

A13 *F.18. Attitude to starting age.*

(i)   Starting age preferred
        Code 1. 6 or older.
        Code 2. $5\frac{1}{2}$ but less than 6.
        Code 3. 5 but less than $5\frac{1}{2}$.
        Code 4. $4\frac{1}{2}$ but less than 5.
        Code 5. 4 but less than $4\frac{1}{2}$.
        Code 6. Less than 4.

(ii)   Whether better for child to have started morning and afternoons or not
        Code 1. Only mornings or afternoons best.
        Code 2. D.K. Can't say.
        Code 3. Mornings and afternoons best.

A14 *F.19. Whether school should be stricter or less strict.*

(i)   The schools should be stricter with the children
        Code 1. Disagrees.
        Code 2. D.K.
        Code 3. Agrees.

(ii)   Whether teachers should be firmer or less firm with the children
        Code 1. Should be less firm.
        Code 2. Quite happy or D.K.
        Code 3. Should be firmer.

(iii)   The teacher should try to get the children on faster in their work
        Code 1. Disagrees.
        Code 2. D.K.
        Code 3. Agrees.
        (End of factor composites)

A15 I feel that teachers have enough to do already without having to talk to parents
        Code 1. Disagrees.
        Code 2. D.K.
        Code 3. Agrees.

A16 Whether streaming preferred or not
        Code 1. Better for quicker and slower children to be *in one class together.*
        Code 2. D.K. No opinion, depends on child.
        Code 3. Better for quicker and slower children to be *in separate classes.*

A17   Whether child should be given some school work to do at home
            Code 1. Should be given homework.
            Code 2. D.K.
            Code 3. Should *not* have homework.

A18   Whether parents bought copies of school books
            Code 1. Yes.
            Code 2. No. D.K.

A19   There is too much concentration on working for the eleven plus exam
            Code 1. Agrees.
            Code 2. D.K.
            Code 3. Disagrees.

A20   Whether parent finds child easy or difficult to control
            Code 1. Easy to control.
            Code 2. Some ways easy, some difficult.
            Code 3. Difficult to control.

A21   I think schools which give children a lot of freedom are good
            Code 1. Agrees.
            Code 2. D.K.
            Code 3. Disagrees.

A22   Whether grammar school particularly disliked for child
            Code 1. No. D.K.
            Code 2. Yes, grammar school *disliked*.

A23   Whether type of secondary school should be decided by exam or teacher
            Code 1. Mainly by teacher.
            Code 2. Both equally, no opinion.
            Code 3. Mainly by exam.

B24   Number of types of amenity in area
            Code 1. Seven types of amenity.
            Code 2. Six types of amenity.
            Code 3. Five types of amenity.
            Code 4. Four types of amenity.
            Code 5. Three types of amenity.
            Code 6. Two types of amenity.
            Code 7. One type of amenity.
            Code 8. No amenities.

B25   Number of types of amenity in area used
            Code 1. Seven types of amenity used.
            Code 2. Six types of amenity used.
            Code 3. Five types of amenity used.
            Code 4. Four types of amenity used.
            Code 5. Three types of amenity used.
            Code 6. Two types of amenity used.
            Code 7. One type of amenity used.

A26 Whether husband strict or lenient with the children
            Code 1. Husband strict.
            Code 2. Husband moderate, in some ways strict/lenient.
            Code 3. Fairly lenient, no husband.
            Code 4. Very lenient.

A27 Whether family goes on outings together
            Code 1. Yes, Christmas or more recently.
            Code 2. Yes, but before Christmas.
            Code 3. No.

B28 Whether family has a car
            Code 1. Yes.
            Code 2. No.

B29 Whether lives in whole house
            Code 1. Yes, in whole house.
            Code 2. In flat, rooms, caravan.

B30 Whether owns dwelling
            Code 1. Own or buying dwelling.
            Code 2. Dwelling rented or rent free.

B31 Whether father on shift work
            Code 1. Father *not* on shift work.
            Code 2. Father on shift work or away from home.

A32 Whether parent ever asked for permission for child to go to a different
     school
            Code 1. No. D.K.
            Code 2. Yes.

A33 Whether child went to a nursery school or nursery class
            Code 1. Yes.
            Code 2. No. D.K.

A34 Age child started to go to school in morning and afternoon
            Code 1. Under $3\frac{1}{2}$.
            Code 2. $3\frac{1}{2}$ but less than 4.
            Code 3. 4 but less than $4\frac{1}{2}$.
            Code 4. $4\frac{1}{2}$ but less than 5.
            Code 5. 5 but less than $5\frac{1}{2}$
            Code 6. $5\frac{1}{2}$ but less than 6.
            Code 7. 6 or older.

B35 Whether child has changed schools
            Code 1. Not changed schools.
            Code 2. Changed schools once.
            Code 3. Changed schools twice.
            Code 4. Changed schools thrice.
            Code 5. Changed schools four or more times.

B36 Total number of persons in household

B37 Total number of children in household
(i.e. Selected child and brothers and sisters)

B38 Whether natural or substitute parents in family
Code 1. Natural father and natural mother in household.
Code 2. Natural father and/or natural mother missing from household.

B39 Whether mother only in family, no father
Code 1. Natural or substitute father present in household.
Code 2. No father in household, mother only.

B40 Whether selected child is eldest or only child
Code 1. Selected child is eldest or only child.
Code 2. Selected child is *not* eldest or only child.

B41 Total number of dependent children, i.e. those still undergoing or not yet started full-time education

B42 Bedroom deficiency index
Code 1. Three or more bedrooms above standard.
Code 2. Two bedrooms above standard.
Code 3. One bedroom above standard.
Code 4. Equal to standard.
Code 5. One bedroom less than standard.
Code 6. Two bedrooms less than standard.
Code 7. Three or more bedrooms below standard.

B43 Occupation of father
Code 1. Professional S.C. I.
Code 2. Managerial, minor professional S.C. II.
Code 3. Skilled and clerical S.C. III.
Code 4. Semi-skilled S.C. IV.
Code 5. Unskilled, labourers S.C. V.

B44 Mother's hours of work
Code 1. Mother not working.
Code 2. Mother working under five hours per day.
Code 3. Mother working over five hours per day, no mother.

B45 Income of father or head of household
Code 1. Over £30.
Code 2. Over £25 to £30.
Code 3. Over £20 to £25.
Code 4. Over £15 to £20.
Code 5. Over £12 10s. to £15.
Code 6. Over £10 to £12 10s.
Code 7. £10 and under.

B46   Income of family
            Code 1. Over £30.
            Code 2. Over £25 to £30.
            Code 3. Over £20 to £25.
            Code 4. Over £15 to £20.
            Code 5. Over £12 10s. to £15.
            Code 6. Over £10 to £12 10s.
            Code 7. £10 and under.

B47   Whether parents born in U.K. or not
            Code 1. Both parents born in U.K.
            Code 2. One parent only born in U.K.
            Code 3. Neither parent born in U.K.

B48   Age at which *father* completed full-time education
            Code 1. 18 and over.
            Code 2. 17 but under 18.
            Code 3. 16 but under 17.
            Code 4. 15 but under 16.
            Code 5. 14 and under.

B49   Age at which *mother* completed full-time education
            Code 1. 18 and over.
            Code 2. 17 but under 18.
            Code 3. 16 but under 17.
            Code 4. 15 but under 16.
            Code 5. 14 and under.

B50   Whether any member of child's family has been to a selective secondary
       school
            Code 1. At least one member has been to selective secondary
                    school.
            Code 2. Not known whether member has been to selective
                    secondary school.
            Code 3. No member of family has been to selective secondary
                    school.

B51   Whether *father* has had any further education since leaving school
            Code 1. Yes, had some further education.
            Code 2. No further education. D.K.

B52   Whether *mother* has had any further education since leaving school
            Code 1. Yes, had some further education.
            Code 2. No further education. D.K.

B53   Whether any qualifications obtained by *father*
            Code 1. Qualifications above "O" level.
            Code 2. Qualifications "O" level or below.
            Code 3. No qualifications.

B54   Whether any qualifications obtained by *mother*
            Code 1. Qualifications above "O" level.
            Code 2. Qualifications "O" level or below.
            Code 3. No qualifications.

Table 2

School Variables

Variables marked P are those for which information was obtained for each pupil in the sample.

Variables marked D were deleted from the regression analyses (see para 12).

    1. Age range of school (J.M. & I. junior or infants).

    2. Status of school (county, voluntary controlled, voluntary aided.)

    3. Zoning (strict, broad or not).

D.   4. Percentage of parents over whole school in professional or managerial occupations (head's assessments).

D.   5. As above, for semi and unskilled occupations.

    6. Parent/Teacher Association in school.

    7. Parents' meetings arranged on educational matters.

    8. Social functions arranged for parents.

    9. Parental help for school (money, kind, or labour).

  10. Number of social functions for parents, arranged when fathers are probably working.

  11. Number of social functions, arranged when fathers are available.

  12. Total number of parents' meetings arranged when fathers probably working.

  13. Total number of parents' meetings arranged when fathers available.

  14. Number of families seeking interview(s) on their initiative in a year.

  15. Number of children on school roll.

  16. Average size of class.

  17. Classes streamed in the school.

D. 18. Percentage of pupils going on to 100 per cent comprehensive schools (J.M. & I. and junior schools only) over previous three years.

D. 19. Percentage of pupils going on to secondary modern schools without extended courses (as above).

  20. Number of school and class library books per 100 pupils.

  21. Average annual expenditure per pupil on school and class library books (over $3\frac{1}{2}$ years).

  22. Children allowed to take library books home.

  23. Men stayers, on staff Sept. 1 1961 until June 1964 (as percentage of total full-time staff members who have taught in school during period).

  24. Women stayers, on staff Sept. 1961 until June 1964 (percentage expressed as above).

  25. Transient men staff, appointed to school and left between Sept. 1961 and June 1964 (percentage expressed as above).

  26. Transient women staff, appointed to school and left between Sept. 1961 and June 1964 (percentage expressed as above).

P. 27. Teacher's sex.

P.   28. Age of teacher.

P.   29. Marital status of teacher.

P.   30. Teacher's responsibility (status in school).

P.   31. Years of teaching experience since break in service (if any).

P.   32. Total years of teaching experience.

P.   33. Average length of service in each school.

P.   34. Number of days spent since June 1 1961 on short courses of in-service training (each course less than 30 days).

P.   35. Number of long courses of in-service training attended since June 1 1961 (each course lasting 30 days or more).

P.   36. Teaching mark (assessed by H.M.I.; given to teachers of sample children only).

P.   37. Size of class including sample child.

P.   38. Sample child in streamed class.

P.   39. Sample child's sex (later combined into regression group number).

P.   40. Sample child's age (in months).

P.   41. Sample child's height (in centimetres).

P.   42. Number of half-days sample child absent Sept. 1 1963–March 31 1964 (i.e. two terms).

P.   43. Reasons for sample child's absence satisfactory to teacher.

P.   44, 45, 46.
       Sample child's first test score (criterion variable).
       Top juniors Watts–Vernon closed test.
       Bottom juniors N.F.E.R. Sentence Reading Test I (A. F. Watts).
       Top infants N.F.E.R. NS45 Reading Test (E. J. Standish).

P.   46, 47.
       Sample child's second test score (criterion variable).
       Top juniors no second test.
       Bottom juniors NS45 Reading.
       Top infants N.F.E.R. Picture Test I (J. E. Stuart).

P.   48. Sample child's rank order in school sample group (expressed as normal deviate) (criterion variable for within school analysis).

D.P.   49. Marked improvement or deterioration in achievement of sample child over previous three years (top juniors only).

D.P.   50. Linguistic ability markedly different from sample child's normal achievement.

D.P.   51. Mathematical ability markedly different.

D.P.   52. Artistic ability markedly different.

D.P.   53. Skill in physical movement markedly different.

D.P.   54. Sample child's attitude to school (assessed on 3-point scale).

D.P.   55. Sample child's co-operation with other children.
       The next four variables were assessed by H.M.I. on a 5-point scale, with national distribution over the five intervals retained as 5 per cent, 20 per cent, 50 per cent, 20 per cent and 5 per cent.

      56. All-round quality of school.

      57. Head's leadership (taking into account particular needs of school).

      58. Average teaching competence of staff.

59. School's adoption of modern educational trends (permissive discipline; provision for individual rates of progress; opportunities for creative work; readiness to reconsider content of curriculum; awareness of unity of knowledge).

   The next six variables were assessed by H.M.I. on a three-interval scale.

60. Quality of books provided.
61. Backwash of selection procedures on curriculum.
62. L.E.A. public relations, as shown by dealings with parents.
63. Continuity home to school.
64. Continuity from infant to junior school.
65. Continuity within J.M. & I. school.
66. Sex of head teacher.

Table 3

Percentages of the Criterion variation accounted for by the three classes of variable in the long list. See paragraphs 13 and 14.

A. BETWEEN SCHOOLS

	Top Juniors		Lower Juniors		Infants	
	Boys	Girls	Boys	Girls	Boys	Girls
Parental Attitudes	45	32	20	19	26	22
Home Circumstances	10	25	22	29	11	21
School Variables	16	7	20	23	16	23
Total	71	64	62	71	53	66

	Top Juniors	Lower Juniors	Infants	All Boys	All Girls	All Pupils
Parental Attitudes	39	20	24	31	25	28
Home Circumstances	17	25	16	14	25	20
School Variables	12	22	20	17	17	17
Total	68	67	60	62	67	65

B. BETWEEN PUPILS WITHIN SCHOOLS

	Top Juniors		Lower Juniors		Infants	
	Boys	Girls	Boys	Girls	Boys	Girls
Parental Attitudes	24	33	17	12	14	17
Home Circumstances	6	8	4	14	10	10
School Variables	27	18	15	16	16	12
Total	57	59	36	42	40	39

	Top Juniors	Lower Juniors	Infants	All Boys	All Girls	All Pupils
Parental Attitudes	29	15	16	18	21	20
Home Circumstances	7	9	9	7	11	9
School Variables	22	15	14	19	15	17
Total	58	39	39	44	47	46

Table 4.1—Top Junior Boys: Between Schools

(a) Parental Variables

Number (Short list)	Short Description	Simple Correlation r	Standardised Regression Coefficient b	Percentage of Variance 100 rb
9	Aspiration for child	·59	·48	28·7
10	Literacy of home	·39	·17	6·4
11	Parental interest in school work and progress	·21		
	Total			35·1
8	Physical amenities of home	·28	·15	4·2
12	No. of dependent children	−·18		
13	Father's occupational group	·20		
14	Father's education	·25		
15	Mother's education	·38		
	Total			4·2
	Parental Total			39·3

(b) School Variables

Number	Short Description	Simple Correlation r	Standardised Regression Coefficient b	Percentage of Variance 100 rb
11	Meetings (father available)	·10	·18	1·8
1	Teacher's sex	·03		
2	Teacher's marital status	·00		
3	Teacher's degree of responsibility	·05		
4	Teacher's total experience	·04		
5	Teacher's short courses	·12		
6	Teacher's long courses	·00		
7	Teaching mark	·26	·16	4·3
17	Continuity			
	School Total			6·1
	Grand Total			45·4
	R^2			·454
	R			·674

Table 4.2—Top Junior Girls: Between Schools

(a) *Parental Variables*

Number (Short list)	Simple Correlation r	Standardised Regression Coefficient b	Percentage of Variance 100 rb
9	·48	·24	11·6
10	·56	·40	22·6
11	·20		
Total			34·3
8	·37		
12	·20		
13	·38	·21	7·8
14	·34		
15	·40		
Total			7·8
Parental Total			42·0

(b) *School Variables*

16	·16		
1	·04		
2	·13		
3	·12	·19	2·1
4	·16		
5	·16		
6	·09		
7	·08		
17	·20	·23	4·5
School Total			6·6
Grand Total			48·6
R^2			·486
R			·697

Table 4.3—Lower Junior Boys: Between Schools

(a) Parental Variables

Number (Short list)	Simple Correlation r	Standardised Regression Coefficient b	Percentage of Variance 100 rb
9	·51	·42	21·2
10	·40		
11	·22	·18	4·0
Total			25·2
8	·28		
12	—·14		
13	·39	·25	9·9
14	·46		
15	·35		
Total			9·9
Parental Total			35·1

(b) School Variables

16	20		
1	·09		
2	·01		
3	·11		
4	·09		
5	·21		
6	·03		
7	·25		
17	·13		
School Total			0·0
Grand Total			35·1
R^2			·351
R			·593

Table 4.4—Lower Junior Girls: Between Schools

(a) *Parental Variables*

Number (Short list)	Simple Correlation r	Standardised Regression Coefficient b	Percentage of Variance 100 rb
9	·02		
10	·45	·28	12·6
11	·36	·20	7·2
Total			19·8
8	·41	·30	12·3
12	—·03		
13	·29		
14	·21		
15	·22		
Total			12·3
Parental Total			32·1

(b) *School Variables*

16	·20		
1	·32	·28	9·1
2	·00		
3	·08		
4	·04		
5	·04		
6	·03		
7	·11		
17	·07		
School Total			9·1
Grand Total			41·2
R^2			·412
R			·642

Table 4.5—Infant Boys: Between Schools

(a) Parental Variables

Number (Short list)	Simple Correlation r	Standardised Regression Coefficient b	Percentage of Variance 100 rb
9	·27		
10	·38	·32	11·9
11	·33	·24	7·9
Total			19·8
8	·13		
12	−·24		
13	·18		
14	·21		
15	·10		
Total			0·0
Parental Total			19·8

(b) School Variables

16	·15		
1	·15		
2	·07		
3	·12		
4	·29	·29	8·5
5	·15		
6	·17	·15	2·5
7	·04		
17	·06		
School Total			11·0
Grand Total			30·8
R^2			·308
R			·554

APPENDIX 4

Table 4.6—Infant Girls: Between Schools

(a) *Parental Variables*

Number (Short list)	Simple Correlation r	Standardised Regression Coefficient b	Percentage of Variance 100 rb
9	·31		
10	·44	·31	13·8
11	·31	·18	5·5
Total			19·3
8	·16		
12	−·26	−·21	5·6
13	·38	·13	4·9
14	·24		
15	·19		
Total			10·5
Parental Total			29·8

(b) *School Variables*

Number	Simple Correlation r	Standardised Regression Coefficient b	Percentage of Variance 100 rb
16	·13		
1	·21	·14	3·0
2	·14		
3	·07		
4	·01		
5	·07		
6	·17	·13	2·3
7	·04		
17	·00		
School Total			5·3
Grand Total			35·1
R^2			·351
R			·592

Summary of Tables 4.1–4.6 (Between Schools)

Variables		Top Juniors B	Top Juniors G	Lower Juniors B	Lower Juniors G	Infants B	Infants G	All Top Juniors	All Lower Juniors	All Infants	All Pupils
9	Aspiration for child	29	12	21	—	—	—	20	11	—	10
10	Literacy of home	6	12	—	13	12	14	15	6	13	12
11	Parental interest in school work and progress	—	—	4	7	8	5	—	6	7	4
	Parental attitudes total	35	35	25	20	20	19	35	23	20	26
8	Physical amenities of home	4	—	—	12	—	—	2	6	—	3
12	No. of dependent children	—	—	—	—	—	6	—	—	3	1
13	Father's occupational group	—	8	10	—	—	5	4	5	2	3
14	Father's education	—	—	—	—	—	—	—	—	—	—
15	Mother's education	—	—	—	—	—	—	—	—	—	—
	Home circumstances total	4	8	10	12	—	11	6	11	5	7
1	Teacher's sex	—	—	—	9	—	3	—	4	2	3
2	Teacher's marital status	—	—	—	—	—	—	—	—	—	—
3	Teacher's degree of responsibility	—	2	—	—	—	—	1	—	—	—
4	Teacher's total experience	—	—	—	—	9	—	—	—	4	1
5	Teacher's short courses	—	—	—	—	—	—	—	—	—	—
6	Teacher's long courses	—	—	—	—	2	2	—	—	2	—
7	Teaching mark	4	—	—	—	—	—	2	—	—	1
16	Meetings (father available)	2	—	—	—	—	—	1	—	—	—
17	Continuity	—	4	—	—	—	—	2	—	—	1
	School total	6	6	—	9	11	5	6	4	8	6
	Grand total	45	49	35	41	31	35	47	38	33	39

Table 5.1—Top Junior Boys: Within Schools

(a) Parental Variables

Number (Short list)	Short Description	Simple Correlation r	Standardised Regression Coefficient b	Percentage of Variance 100 rb
9	Aspiration for child	·41	·25	10·2
10	Literacy of home	·36	·15	5·3
11	Parental interest in school work and progress	·42	·25	10·5
	Total			26·0
8	Physical amenities of home	·18		
12	No. of dependent children	—·13		
13	Father's occupational group	·20		
14	Father's education	·20		
15	Mother's education	·16		
	Total			0·0
	Parental Total			26·0

Table 5.1 (cont.)—Top Junior Boys: Within Schools

(b) School Variables

Number (Short list)	Short Description	Simple Correlation r	Standardised Regression Coefficient b	Percentage of Variance 100 rb
1	Teacher's sex	·02		
2	Teacher's marital status	·08	·10	0·8
3	Teacher's degree of responsibility	·37	·20	7·4
4	Teacher's total experience	·16		
5	Teacher's short courses	·07	·15	1·0
6	Teacher's long courses	·10		
7	Teaching mark	·31	·25	7·7
	School Total			16·9
	Grand Total			42·9
	R^2			·429
	R			·654

Table 5.2—Top Junior Girls: Within Schools

(a) Parental Variables

Number (Short list)	Simple Correlation r	Standardised Regression Coefficient b	Percentage of Variance 100 rb
9	·57	·38	21·5
10	·37	·14	5·2
11	·43	·20	8·8
Total			35·5
8	·14		
12	—·20	—·09	1·8
13	·25		
14	·27	·08	2·0
15	·18		
Total			3·8
Parental Total			39·3

(b) School Variables

	Simple Correlation r	Standardised Regression Coefficient b	Percentage of Variance 100 rb
1	·05		
2	·07	·11	0·7
3	·31	·17	5·3
4	·18		
5	·12	·10	1·1
6	·16		
7	·06		
School Total			7·1
Grand Total			46·4
R^2			·464
R			·665

Table 5.3—Lower Junior Boys: Within Schools

(a) Parental Variables

Number (Short list)	Simple Correlation r	Standardised Regression Coefficient b	Percentage of Variance 100 rb
9	·27	·20	5·3
10	·34	·21	7·2
11	·22	·11	2·3
Total			14·8
8	·02		
12	—·17	—·11	1·9
13	·17		
14	·18		
15	·16	·10	1·6
Total			3·5
Parental Total			18·3

(b) School Variables

1	·04		
2	·04	·08	0·3
3	·12		
4	·16	·13	2·1
5	·00		
6	·10	·10	0·9
7	·09	·08	0·8
School Total			4·1
Grand Total			22·4
R^2			·224
R			·473

Table 5.4—Lower Junior Girls: Within Schools

(a) *Parental Variables*

Number (Short list)	Simple Correlation r	Standardised Regression Coefficient b	Percentage of Variance 100 rb
9	·25	·14	3·4
10	·26	·14	3·6
11	·24	·20	4·7
Total			11·7
8	·08		
12	—·17	—·13	2·2
13	·21		
14	·17		
15	·25	·16	3·9
Total			6·1
Parental Total			17·8

(b) *School Variables*

1	·06		
2	·10	·11	1·0
3	·01		
4	·08	·07	0·6
5	·11	·10	1·1
6	·16	·18	2·9
7	·16	·09	1·4
School Total			7·0
Grand Total			24·8
R^2			·248
R			·498

Table 5.5—Infant Boys: Within Schools

(a) Parental Variables

Number (Short list)	Simple Correlation r	Standardised Regression Coefficient b	Percentage of Variance 100 rb
9	·20	·10	2·1
10	·31	·21	6·6
11	·23	·17	3·9
Total			12·6
8	·07		
12	—·13	—·10	1·3
13	·17		
14	·18	·13	2·2
15	·14		
Total			3·5
Parental Total			16·1

(b) School Variables

Number	Simple Correlation r	Standardised Regression Coefficient b	Percentage of Variance 100 rb
1	·00		
2	·03		
3	·05		
4	·11	·10	1·1
5	·00		
6	·01		
7	·00		
School Total			1·1
Grand Total			17·2
R^2			·172
R			·415

H

Table 5.6—Infant Girls: Within Schools

(a) *Parental Variables*

Number (Short list)	Simple Correlation r	Standardised Regression Coefficient b	Percentage of Variance 100 rb
9	·22	·12	2·6
10	·29	·16	4·4
11	·37	·30	11·0
Total			18·0
8	·06		
12	—·16	—·11	1·6
13	·15		
14	·10		
15	·12		
Total			1·6
Parental Total			19·6

(b) *School Variables*

1	·05		
2	·05		
3	·07	·07	0·5
4	·07		
5	·05		
6	·02		
7	·01		
School Total			0·5
Grand Total			20·1
R²			·201
P			·449

Summary of Tables 5.1–5.6 (Pupils Within Schools)

Variables		Top Juniors B	Top Juniors G	Lower Juniors B	Lower Juniors G	Infants B	Infants G	All Top Juniors	All Lower Juniors	All Infants	All Pupils
9	Aspirations for child	10	22	5	3	2	3	16	4	2	7
10	Literacy of home	5	5	7	4	6	4	5	6	5	6
11	Parental interest	11	9	3	5	4	11	10	4	8	7
	Parental attitudes total	26	36	15	12	12	18	31	14	15	20
8	Physical amenities of home	—	—	—	—	—	—	—	—	—	—
12	No. of dependent children	—	2	2	2	2	2	1	2	2	2
13	Father's occupational group	—	—	—	—	—	—	—	—	—	—
14	Father's education	—	2	—	—	2	—	1	—	1	1
15	Mother's education	—	—	2	4	—	—	—	3	—	1
	Home circumstances total	—	4	4	6	4	2	2	5	3	3*
1	Teacher's sex	—	—	—	—	—	—	—	—	—	—
2	Teacher's marital status	1	1	—	1	—	—	1	—	—	—
3	Teacher's degree of responsibility	7	5	—	—	—	1	6	—	—	2
4	Teacher's total experience	1	—	2	1	1	—	1	2	1	1
5	Teacher's short courses	—	1	—	1	—	—	—	1	—	—
6	Teacher's long courses	—	—	1	3	—	—	—	2	—	1
7	Teacher's teaching mark	8	—	1	1	—	—	4	1	—	2
	School total	17	7	4	7	1	1	12	5*	1	6
	Grand total	43	47	23	25	17	21	45	24	19	29

Rounding

APPENDIX 5

THE 1964 NATIONAL SURVEY: DATA FROM THE SCHOOLS

Sources of Data

1. Information about the schools, staff and children was supplied by heads, class teachers, and by H.M.Is., who filled in a series of questionnaires which can be found on pages 266 to 287 following Appendix 7. Schedule A, completed by the head teacher, was concerned primarily with school organisation. Supplementary information about the arrangements made for admission of children to infants and junior mixed and infant schools, and transfer to junior schools, was provided by heads. Heads were also responsible for returning details about their staffing both on Schedule A and on a staffing form. H.M.Is. made some assessments of the schools and their staff on Schedule C. They also provided information on the relationships between primary schools and the home, and between infant schools and junior schools. Class teachers filled in questionnaires about individual pupils whose parents were interviewed. (Schedule B.)

2. Much of this information is summarised here in terms of the schools, the staff and the children. Information about staggering of entry to schools, part-time entry, early and late transfer to secondary schools and arrangements for ensuring continuity between schools was also used for the main Report (Volume 1) but is not repeated here.

THE SCHOOLS

The Sample

3. There were 171 schools in the sample, 139 of which were county and controlled (81 per cent) and the rest were aided. Schools were grouped in this way because there seemed likely to be more similarity between county and controlled than between voluntary controlled and aided schools. Of the 171 schools, 49 (29 per cent) were junior mixed and infants, 56 (33 per cent) were junior, and 66 (38 per cent) were infant. The larger number of infant schools is explained by the fact that junior schools, which often contain larger age groups than infant schools, drew into the sample the infant schools which contributed to them. Table 1 shows the status of schools in the various age ranges. Aided schools, whose child population may be geographically scattered, often provide for the whole primary age range.

Table 1
Age Range of School by Status

Age Range of School	Status of School	
	County and Controlled	Aided
Junior mixed and Infants	22	56
Junior	35	22
Infants	43	22
Total number 100%	(139)	(32)

Zoning

4. Over half the schools (58 per cent) were not zoned. A large proportion of aided schools, whose admissions are controlled by their managers, were not zoned. Other schools not zoned officially must have been so placed geographically that parents had little choice of school. Zoned schools were about evenly divided between strict and broad zoning.

Table 2

Zoning Arrangements According to the Status of the School

Zoning	Status of School			
	County %	Controlled %	Aided %	Total %
Strictly zoned with few or no exceptions	28	19	—	22
Broadly zoned with many exceptions	23	19	10	20
Not zoned	49	62	90	58
Total numbers (100%)	(123)	(16)	(32)	(171)

Parent-Teacher Relations

5. A number of questions were asked about parent-teacher relations in the schools. Seventeen per cent of the schools had a P.T.A., a percentage identical with that found in the N.C.D.S. sample (see Appendix 10). Sixty-three per cent arranged meetings for parents on educational matters (arrangement by school or association); 66 per cent arranged social functions for parents—carol concerts, sports days and so forth; and in 62 per cent of schools parents were said to have provided substantial help in money, kind or labour each year. These figures are rather higher than in the N.C.D.S. sample. Table 3 shows the average number of occasions, for the whole sample, when parents could meet various teachers to discuss their child, school policy or both.

Table 3

Opportunities for Parents to Meet Teachers (Figures given are means)

Opportunities for parents to meet	Head teacher	Class teacher	Both Head and class teacher	Total number of occasions	
				when father is probably working	when father is available
To discuss individual child	0·76	0·05	1·02	1·02	0·82
To explain or discuss school policy and practice	0·46	0·01	0·24	0·32	0·40
To discuss both individual child and school policy	0·34	0·02	0·51	0·44	0·44
For general social occasions				1·8	1·21
Totals				3·6	2·9

Points of interest in this table are the relatively few occasions when parents can discuss school policy and practice, and when parents can meet class teachers as contrasted with head teachers. It is also of interest that more opportunities were provided for parents to visit the schools when the father is probably working than when he is available.

6. Opportunities for parents to visit the schools were examined in relation to the age range, status and social composition of the schools. It is noteworthy that infant schools provide substantially fewer occasions when fathers are likely to be available (4·6 occasions when father probably working, 1·8 when father available). There was little variation in the pattern of visits arranged for county and controlled, and aided schools, save that aided schools provided somewhat fewer occasions. The pattern of visits was also examined according to the estimated percentage of parents in professional/managerial and semi-skilled/unskilled occupations. There was one major difference. Schools where more than 16 per cent of fathers belonged to professional/managerial occupations were alone in arranging more occasions for parents to visit when the father was likely to be available than when he was working. The higher the proportion of semi-skilled and unskilled workers, the less likely were parents' meetings to be arranged at times when fathers could visit the school: there was also a slight decline in the total number of meetings arranged as the proportion of semi-skilled and unskilled workers rose. Yet it seems probable that it is particularly important for schools to gain collaboration in children's education of parents in semi-skilled and unskilled occupations. It is of some interest that the Social Survey interviews showed no relationship between social class and the provision of opportunities for parents to visit schools. On social class, the data from the Social Survey is likely to be more reliable: the number of meetings provided by schools is probably more reliably reported by the schools than by parents. The Social Survey interviews showed that manual workers were less likely to attend meetings arranged at the school. Schools with relatively high proportions of semi-skilled and unskilled workers may become discouraged in efforts to gain co-operation from parents.

7. The median scores of parental interest in, and knowledge of, children's work, a variable which was shown to be of importance by the regression analyses, were studied in relation to socio-economic class (divided into three broad bands), and the number of parents' meetings provided by the school at a time when the father was available (according to the school data). Table 4 shows the median scores. A low score means a high level of parental interest.

Table 4

Median Scores of Level of Parental Interest in and Knowledge of Child's Work at School, according to Number of Parents' Meetings Provided at a Time when Fathers are Probably Available

Social Class	Number of Parents' Meetings (father available)						
	0	1–2	3–4	5–6	7–8	9–10	11+
Professional and Managerial	10·8	10·7	10·6	10·4	10·3	9·5	
Clerical and Skilled Manual	11·5	11·3	11·1	10·6	10·4	9·9	10·3
Semi and Unskilled	12·4	11·3	11·4	11·6	10·7	10·5	

Parental interest increases according to the number of parents' meetings arranged by the school, which can be attended by fathers. However the variables deriving from the number of meetings often failed to reach significance in the regression analyses.

Sizes and Organisation of Schools

8. Information was also collected about the size and organisation of schools, and the sizes of schools were related to H.M.I. ratings of all-round quality and of modern trends in the school. As can be seen from Table 5 schools of 201–350 were more often thought average or above average than smaller or larger schools. No clear relationship emerged between the school's acceptance of modern trends and numbers on roll, average size of class or social composition of school. H.M.I., in assessing the overall quality of schools, tended to make little use of the extreme categories. Rather more use was made of them in assessing acceptance of modern trends: the distribution was slightly skewed to the below average.

Table 5

Rating of Schools According to Size of School

Rating of all round Quality	Number on Roll						Total Nos.	Total %
	0–25	26–50	51–200	201–350	351–500	501+		
Very Good				1		10	2	1
Good			22	17	28	40	36	21
Average		50	54	74	47	50	104	61
Below Average		50	22	8	22		27	16
Poor			2		3		2	1
Total numbers (100%)		(6)	(51)	(72)	(32)	(10)	(171)	

Table 6

Rating of Schools' Acceptance of Modern Educational Trends

Assessment of school's acceptance of modern educational trends	%
Very good	3
Good	18
Average	47
Below Average	29
Poor	3
Total numbers (100%)	(171)

9. Schools were asked how children were classified. Forty-five per cent placed children in their classes by age only, 35 per cent by age and achievement, and two per cent used other means. Some heads may have described schools as being classified by age only, when the great majority of children—as distinct from all children—were allocated to classes in this way. Table 7 shows the

percentages of schools in different age ranges which classified children by age only or by age and achievement. Junior schools were much more likely than the others to be streamed; three-fifths of J.M.I. schools were also streamed, however. Table 8 shows that, as might be expected, rather more of the larger schools were streamed.

Table 7

Methods of Classification According to Age Range of School

| Classification | Age Range of School | | | Total |
	J.M.I. %	Juniors %	Infants %	%
Age and achievement	61	82	23	35
Age only	39	18	73	45
Other means	—	—	4	2
Total numbers (100%)	(49)	(56)	(66)	(171)

Table 8

Methods of Classification According to Size of School

| Classification | Size of School | | | | |
	26–50 %	51–200 %	201–350 %	351–500 %	500+ %
Age and achievement	17	47	57	56	70
Age only	83	53	40	41	30
Other means	—	—	3	3	—
Total numbers (100%)	(6)	(51)	(72)	(32)	(10)

Books in Schools

10. Table 9 collates information provided about books, other than text books, in the sample schools.

Table 9

Books in the Schools

Provision of Books	Average over Sample
Number of school and class library books	1800

Average annual expenditure per
  head on such books
  (September 1961–June 1964)
	5·88s.

Are children allowed to take library books home?	
Yes	65
No	35
Total numbers (100%)	(171)

Though the average expenditure per head on books was only 5·88 shillings, one school spent more than 37 shillings per head. The amount spent on books tended to increase as the percentage of fathers in semi-skilled and unskilled occupations increased. Sixty-five per cent of children were allowed to take school library books home, a figure that is compatible with the replies of parents to Social Survey interviewers that 52 per cent of children took books home.

THE TEACHERS

Turnover

11. Heads provided information about staff turnover from September 1961 to June 1964 (for men and women staff separately). This data on staff turnover can be examined in two ways—amount of movement of all teachers in the sample schools during the given period, and average establishment and turnover. Tables 10 and 11 show the proportion of those teachers still on staff and those who have left the staff expressed as percentages of all teachers in the schools during the period. The important cells are the upper left hand, the stayers, and the lower right hand, those who came to and left a school during the period. Only 40 per cent of the women compared to 51 per cent of the men were in the schools to which they had been appointed two years nine months earlier. Six per cent of the men and 13 per cent of the women had joined and left the schools during the period.

Table 10

Turnover of Staff (All Schools: Men Staff)

Staff appointed	Still on staff June 1964	Left school September 2, 1961 onwards	Total %	Total numbers
Up to September 1, 1961	51·31	21·85	73·16	308
September 2, 1961 and after	20·43	6·41	26·84	113
Total	71·73	28·27	100·00	421

Table 11

Turnover of Staff (All Schools: Women Staff)

Staff appointed	Still on staff	Left school September 2, 1961 onwards	Total %	Total numbers
Up to September 1, 1961	40·01	22·82	62·83	1,104
September 2, 1961 and after	23·90	13·26	37·17	653
Total	63·92	36·08	100·00	1,757

When staff turnover was examined in relationship to the age range of schools, it was apparent that the infant schools were worse off. Table 12 shows that teachers appointed up to September 1961 amounted to no more than 34 per cent of the staff who had taught in schools between September 1961 and June 1964.

Table 12

Turnover of Staff (Infant Schools)

Staff appointed	Still on staff	Left school September 2, 1961 onwards	Total %	Total numbers
Up to September 1, 1961	34·88	23·34	58·22	464
September 2, 1961 and after	24·97	16·81	41·78	333
Total	59·85	40·15	100·00	797

The staff of aided schools stayed rather longer than those in county and controlled schools.

12. Tables 13, 14 and 15 are based on the same data, expressed as mean figures per school. Table 13 shows the overall figures for all 171 schools. On average, each school had just over eight teachers in September 1961 and in June 1964. Five teachers stayed on the staff throughout the period. The other three teachers left some time during the period and were replaced. 1·5 of these new teachers also left and were in turn replaced. Tables 14 and 15 give the data for junior mixed and infant and junior schools, and for infants' schools. The establishment for the average junior mixed and infant, and junior school stayed at just over nine teachers at the beginning and end of the period. Six teachers stayed throughout, and three left. Of the new teachers, one place had to be refilled during the period. Infants' schools were different in several respects. On average they had a smaller establishment of teachers, but the size of staff increased slightly over the period, from just under to just over seven. Four teachers stayed and nearly three left. The actual number of staff leaving after September 1, 1961 was the same as for the other schools, but they were a larger proportion of the total establishment, and two out of three places had to be filled twice during the period.

Table 13

Average Staff Turnover (All Schools)

	Still on staff	Left September 2, 1961 and after	Total
On staff before September 1, 1961	5·37	2·88	8·26
Appointed September 2, 1961 and after	2·96	1·52	4·48
Total	8·33	4·4	12·73

Table 14

Average Staff Turnover (J.M.I. and Junior)

	Still on staff	Left September 2, 1961 and after	Total
On staff before September 1, 1961	6·17	2·94	9·11
Appointed September 2, 1961 and after	2·94	1·2	4·14
Total	9·11	4·14	13·25

Table 15

Average Staff Turnover (Infants)

	Still on staff	Left September 2, 1961 and after	Total
On staff before September 1, 1961	4·10	2·78	6·89
Appointed September 2, 1961 and after	2·98	2·03	5·01
Total	7·09	4·81	11·9

Teachers' Qualifications

13. Much additional information about the teachers was available from staffing forms. The particulars of 1,555 teachers were included; 317 (20 per cent) were men and 1,238 (80 per cent) women. Eighty-two per cent of the men and 58 per cent of the women were married. Table 16 shows the qualifications held by men and women. It is noteworthy that more men than women were graduates and that more women than men were unqualified. As can be seen from the following table there were more unqualified teachers in infant schools than in other schools and fewest unqualified teachers in junior schools. There were no differences in qualifications between teachers in county and controlled, and aided schools.

Table 16

Qualifications of Teachers (Men and Women Separately)

Qualification	Men %	Women %
Teacher's certificate	87	88
Post Graduate Teacher's Diploma or Certificate	9	2
Degree only	2	1
Years of experience	0	3
Unqualified	2	6
Total numbers (100%)	(317)	(1,238)

Table 17

Qualifications of Teachers in Schools of Different Age Ranges

Teacher's Qualification	Age Range of School			Total
	J.M. and I.	Junior Only	Infants Only	
Teacher's Certificate	84	90	87	88
Post Graduate Teacher's Diploma or Certificate	5	5	1	4
Degree only	1	1	1	1
Years of experience	5	1	3	2
Unqualified	5	3	8	5
Total numbers (100%)	(373)	(646)	(536)	(1,555)

14. Although only one in five of the staff in the sample were men, more than half held posts of responsibility as head, deputy or a holder of a graded post, whereas less than one-quarter of the women were in similar positions. It is particularly noteworthy that 24 per cent of the men held headships as contrasted with eight per cent of the women.

Table 18

Teachers' Status in School According to Sex

Status in School	Men	Women
Head	24	8
Deputy Head	13	7
Post of responsibility	13	7
All other	20	77
Total numbers (100%)	(317)	(1,238)

In-Service Training

15. A great deal of information was collected on the in-service training taken by teachers in the sample during the previous three years, because there was little information on this extremely important subject other than that deriving from impression. In the period under review 26 per cent of all teachers attended a mathematical course, 21 per cent a physical education course, 17 per cent an English course, 17 per cent an art and craft course and seven per cent a science course. Only nine per cent attended a general primary course, three per cent a junior school course and nine per cent a general infant course.

16. We have reproduced our own data in some detail here. Men and women are grouped together since the proportion of men is too small for useful separate analysis. The estimates of time spent in courses are bound to be generous because the length of courses could not be assessed with precision. Thus two sessions* counted as a day and a three session day as a day and a half. A one hour or two hour session could not be differentiated from three hours: therefore each was assessed as a half day. Table 19 shows the distribution of the 2,504 courses taken by the sample of 1,555 teachers, according to length of course and sponsor of course. More courses were sponsored by

* A session is normally reckoned as half a day

local authorities than by other bodies and most lasted less than a week, nearly a half only one or two days.

17. In Table 20 the courses are divided into those lasting one–seven days, 8–29 days and over 29 days, and distributed according to subject and sponsor. In the largest group, those lasting one–seven days, 21 per cent were on mathematics, 16 per cent on physical education, 13 per cent on English and 11 per cent on arts and crafts. When courses were considered according to sponsor, the proportions changed. Of local authority courses, 21 per cent were on physical education, 19 per cent on mathematics, 13 per cent on arts and crafts and 11 per cent on English. Institutes of education and other bodies provided higher proportions of mathematics courses (22 per cent and 25 per cent respectively) and English courses (21 per cent and 15 per cent). In the small numbers of courses lasting more than eight days, there was a fairly high proportion (nearly a quarter) of arts and crafts courses.

Table 19

Numbers of Courses Attended According to Length and Sponsor of Course

Length of Course (in days)	Sponsor of Course				Total Number of Courses
	L.E.A.	Department of Education (ex. Min. of Education)	Institute of Education	Other Bodies	
1	428	5	72	122	627
2	385	8	61	127	581
3	321	12	47	52	432
4	153	6	49	38	246
5	88	5	39	24	156
6	106	1	18	13	138
7	24	4	5	16	49
8	11	1	5	5	22
9	5	1	4	3	13
10	32	11	13	8	64
11	2	1	0	0	3
12	18	1	9	3	31
13	3	0	0	2	5
14	10	5	0	1	16
15	5	0	2	6	13
16	0	0	3	0	3
17	0	0	0	1	1
18	4	0	8	4	16
19	0	0	0	0	0
20	14	0	0	0	14
21	0	0	0	1	1
22	0	0	0	0	0
23	0	0	0	0	0
24	0	0	0	1	1
25	0	0	1	0	1
26	0	0	0	0	0
27	0	0	0	0	0
28	1	0	1	1	3
29	0	0	0	0	0
Over 29 days	25	6	21	16	68
Total courses	1,635	67	358	444	2,504

Table 20

Number of Courses Attended According to Subject, Sponsor and Length

Subject of Course	Sponsor of Course												Total Number of Courses
	L.E.A.			Department of Education			Institute of Education			Other Bodies			
Length (Days)	1 to 7	8 to 29	29 +	1 to 7	8 to 29	29 +	1 to 7	8 to 29	29 +	1 to 7	8 to 29	29 +	
General— Primary education	74	4	0	1	1		33	7	4	29	6	2	162
General— Infant education	74	7	0	4	1		22	0	0	35	1	1	145
General— Junior education	36	2	0	3	1	0	6	2	3	7	0	0	60
English	168	9	1	3	1	0	60	8	3	6	0	3	316
3Rs (incl. Maths. and English)	48	2	0	0	0	0	11	0	0	13	0	0	74
Environmental study	27	2	0	0	2	0	2	2	1	8	3	0	47
Mathematics	291	3	1	18	6	1	63	2	0	99	3	0	487
Science	70	0	2	3	2	0	21	4	0	20	4	0	126
Arts and Crafts	188	43	6	0	0	0	19	8	1	32	3	5	305
Music	106	5	1	2	0	2	9	1	0	21	2	0	149
Physical education	313	6	4	0	3	0	8	1	0	34	3	0	372
Teachers of handi- capped children	29	0	1	0	1	1	20	2	3	1	2	0	60
Religious education	28	1	1	2	0	0	6	2	0	25	7	1	73
French	8	15	1	5	1	0	2	2	1	1	0	0	36
Russian	0	0	1	0	0	0	0	0	0	0	0	0	1
Spanish	0	1	0	0	0	0	0	0	0	0	0	0	1
Geography	0	0	0	0	0	0	0	2	0	1	1	0	4
History	0	0	0	0	0	0	2	0	0	0	0	0	2
Dip. Ed. (no other information)	0	0	0	0	0	0	0	1	4	0	0	0	5
Other Subjects	45	5	6	0	1	1	7	2	1	6	1	4	79
Total Courses	1,505	105	25	41	20	6	291	46	21	392	36	16	2,504

18. Table 20A is an expansion of the third part of Table 20, that is, courses lasting 29 days and longer. It shows the total number of days spent, distributed according to subject and sponsor of the course. Several interesting points emerge from this table: although the number of courses involved (68) was only 2·7 per cent of the total attended (Table 20) the total of days spent on these courses was over a third (37 per cent) of the total time given. (Table 21.) Department of Education courses and institute of education courses tended to be longer than those of the other sponsoring bodies. Teachers took courses lasting a year (given as 150 days) or longer in teaching of handicapped children (two of 150 days, one 200 days, one 250 days), general primary education (two 150 days, one 180 days), music (one 180 days, one 200 days), Diploma in Education (one 150 days, one 300 days), religious education (one 450 days), and one 150, one 180 and one 200 days on other subjects not individually identified.

Table 20A

Days Spent on Individual Courses Lasting 29 Days and Longer, According to Subject and Sponsor of Course

Subject	Sponsor				Total Days
	L.E.A.	Department of Education	Institute of Education	Other Bodies	
General primary	0	150	420	66	636
General primary —Infants	0	0	0	49	49
General primary —Junior	0	0	166	0	166
English	31	0	137	102	270
Three Rs	0	0	0	0	0
Environmental studies	0	0	32	0	32
Mathematics	35	50	0	0	85
Science	70	0	0	0	70
Arts and Crafts	207	0	36	186	429
Music	45	380	0	0	425
Physical Education	146	0	0	0	146
Teachers of handi- capped children	30	200	550	0	780
Religious Education	35	0	0	450	485
French	35	0	30	0	65
Russian	30	0	0	0	30
Spanish, Geography, History	0	0	0	0	0
Dip. Ed.	0	0	555	0	555
Others	224	200	150	304	878
Total Days	888	980	2,076	1,157	5,101
Number of Courses	26	6	21	15	68

19. Table 21 shows the numbers of teachers attending courses and the numbers of days spent at courses according to subject and sponsor. These tables are so drawn up that each teacher is recorded once only in any "number of staff" cell, even though he may have contributed more than once to the associated "number of days" cell. Thus the contribution to the total of a teacher who went to many short courses on one subject is indistinguishable from that of a teacher who went to one long course. Sixty-six per cent of teachers went to at least one course during the three years previous to the enquiry. On average they spent 13 days on in-service training. The average time spent varied according to the sponsor of the course: teachers who went to courses provided by local education authorities spent an average of eight days at them; on courses provided by other bodies they spent nine days; teachers who went to institute of education courses spent 14 days at them. Those who attended Department of Education courses spent 23 days at them. It must be recalled that this number of days may have been—and in most cases probably was— spent at more than one course.

APPENDIX 5

Table 21

Numbers of Staff Attending Courses According to Sponsor and Subject of
Course, and Number of Days Given to Each Subject

| Subject of Course | Sponsor of Course | | | | | | | | Totals | |
| | L.E.A. | | Department of Education | | Institute of Education | | Other Bodies | | | |
	Number of Staff	Number of Days Spent	Number of Staff	Number of Days Spent	Number of Staff	Number of Days Spent	Number of Staff	Number of Days Spent	Number of Staff	Number of Days Spent
General—Primary	70	214	3	167	39	629	32	227	128	1,237
General—Infant	78	309	5	25	22	69	37	167	136	570
General—Junior	38	147	4	25	10	206	7	20	57	398
English	170	537	4	27	69	423	59	218	277	1,205
3Rs (incl. Maths. and English)	47	140	0	0	11	28	13	33	70	201
Environmental	28	92	2	24	5	63	11	68	46	247
Mathematics	262	762	24	164	62	191	92	264	400	1,381
Science	65	270	5	28	23	125	24	95	116	518
Arts and Crafts	210	1,374	0	0	27	216	36	316	262	1,906
Music	109	349	4	386	10	41	23	82	141	858
Physical education	300	1,063	3	30	9	34	33	144	331	1,271
Teachers of handi-capped children	30	150	2	212	25	640	3	26	59	1,028
Religious education	30	119	2	8	8	28	33	597	69	752
French	24	254	5	33	5	52	1	1	34	340
Russian	1	30	0	0	0	0	0	0	1	30
Spanish	1	10	0	0	0	0	0	0	1	10
Geography	0	0	0	0	2	21	2	12	4	33
History	0	0	0	0	2	4	0	0	2	4
Dip. Ed. (no other information)	0	0	0	0	5	570	0	0	5	570
Others	45	410	2	211	10	194	11	356	66	1,171
Totals	804	6,230	58	1,340	240	3,534	303	2,626	1,021	13,730

Non-Attenders

20. An analysis (Tables 22–25) was made of teachers who did not attend any
courses in the three years 1961–64. It showed proportions very little different
from the main sample. Sixty-five per cent were married as compared with 60
per cent in the sample. Twenty-seven per cent were in the age group 20–29 as
compared with 24 per cent of teachers in the total sample. Thirty-seven per
cent of the group were in infant schools, as compared with 34 per cent in the
main sample. Whereas 32 per cent of the main sample were heads, deputy
heads or holders of graded posts, only 15 per cent of those who did not attend
courses held such posts. It is perhaps disconcerting that even this number
failed to attend any in-service training.

Teachers Who Did Not Attend Courses June 1961–June 1964 (Main Sample
Percentages Given for Comparison)

Table 22
Sex

Sex	%	Main Sample %
Men	18	20
Women	82	80
Total Numbers (100%)	(534)	

Table 23
Marital Status

Marital Status	%	Main Sample %
Single	32	37
Married	65	60
Widow(er)	3	3

Table 24
School Status

Status in School	%	Main Sample %
Head	4	
Deputy Head	4	32
Position of responsibility	7	
No responsibility	85	68

Table 25
Age Range of School

Age Range of School	%	Main Sample %
J.M. and I.	23	24
Junior	40	42
Infants	37	34

Table 26
Age of Teachers

Age	%	Main Sample
17–19	0	0
20–29	27	24
30–39	23	21
40–49	16	21
50–59	23	26
60+	10	7
Others (no age given)	1	1

21. The largest numbers of teachers in the group who attended courses went, as can be seen from Table 21, to mathematics and physical education courses, but the average number of days spent per person were only three and four respectively. The largest total number of days were spent at arts and crafts courses with an average of seven days per person. The next largest totals were for mathematics and physical education which also involved large numbers of teachers and therefore low average lengths of stay. English courses involved a fairly large number of teachers and of days spent; the average per person was four. On average, those teachers who went to courses on general primary education, French, and handicapped children spent more time on them. The

duration of local authority courses was on average three to four days, but that of institute of education courses on the same subjects varied from three to 20 days, probably reflecting the policy of different institutes.

22. Tables 27 and 28 show courses distributed according to the age range of the teachers' schools. The average number of days spent varied from 17 for J.M. and I. teachers, to 15 for junior teachers and nine for infant teachers. In J.M. and I. schools, most time in total was given to arts and crafts, with an average of eight days. Next was general primary education, but with many fewer staff involved, giving on average 13 days. Similarly, a small number of staff attended courses on teaching handicapped children, but the average time spent was 52 days. Most teachers went to courses on mathematics, arts and crafts, physical education and English. In junior schools as well, most days were given to arts and crafts with an average of seven days per teacher, then to physical education, English and mathematics. Infant schools show a rather different pattern. Most time was given to R.E., particularly to courses arranged by bodies other than local education authorities; these courses were attended by few teachers, but for an average of 17 days per teacher. Next came mathematics and general courses on infant teaching, physical education and English: all these involved a large number of teachers, and the average number of days therefore are low (three, four, two and three). It is interesting that in this group more teachers were involved in music courses than in those on arts and crafts.

23. When attendance by teachers at courses was analysed according to status of school, the main difference was that teachers at aided schools spent less time than those at county and controlled schools on general primary courses, as compared with subject courses. When teachers were divided according to their ages, a distinctive pattern appeared. Table 29 shows that the group of teachers aged 30–39 spent much more time, on average, on courses than any others, particularly on courses provided by the Department of Education and by institutes of education on teaching of handicapped children, Diploma of Education courses and general primary school work. Moreover, they spent more days, in total, on a different group of subjects from the overall pattern. They spent more time on general courses on primary teaching, then religious education, then teaching of handicapped children and finally music, with averages respectively of 25, 47, 31 and 15 days per teacher. These teachers are striving to equip themselves for promotion already won or sought. They concentrate on general primary work, and on fields in which the class teacher often needs help.

Comment

24. It is difficult to distinguish between supply of courses and demand for them. Have teachers attended courses because these were the only ones provided for them, or the only ones to which they could gain admission? Have courses been provided on certain subjects because teachers asked for them? The total numbers of courses conceal great variations between localities.

25. Some facts emerging from the survey are satisfactory. Even if the time spent on courses was somewhat inflated by the way it was measured, it is creditable that two-thirds of all teachers had attended a course during the

past three years, and that these teachers spent on average 13 days at courses during the period. Most courses are, however, very short and their impact may on this account be diminished. It is also satisfactory that large numbers in the age group 30–39 attend courses, and that they are concerned both to develop their general understanding of primary education and to study aspects of the curriculum in which there are known weaknesses in the schools. But one-third of all teachers have not attended a course in the past three years.

Table 27

Attendance at Courses: Junior School Teachers

Subject of Course	Sponsor of Course								Totals	
	L.E.A.		Department of Education		Institute of Education		Other Bodies			
	Number of Staff	Number of Days Spent	Number of Staff	Number of Days Spent	Number of Staff	Number of Days Spent	Number of Staff	Number of Days Spent	Number of Staff	Number of Days Spent
General— Primary	32	105	0	0	17	266	12	73	52	444
General— Infant	1	1	0	0	2	10	0	0	3	11
General— Junior	28	106	4	25	8	157	3	5	40	286
English	75	323	1	3	31	139	29	133	123	598
3Rs (incl. Maths. and English)	8	26	0	0	1	1	11	28	19	55
Environmental	14	48	1	10	3	30	7	58	25	146
Mathematics	100	312	9	40	28	95	29	93	148	540
Science	38	198	5	28	19	111	19	73	80	410
Arts and Crafts	115	809	0	0	21	196	21	149	152	1,154
Music	34	111	1	200	5	30	12	53	49	394
Physical education	142	558	2	20	4	22	25	107	162	707
Teachers of handicapped children	13	45	0	0	11	346	2	18	25	409
Religious education	12	31	0	0	1	1	8	41	19	73
French	19	222	2	6	1	30	0	0	22	258
Russian	1	30	0	0	0	0	0	0	1	30
Spanish	1	10	0	0	0	0	0	0	1	10
Geography	0	0	0	0	0	0	1	2	1	2
History	0	0	0	0	2	4	0	0	2	4
Dip. Ed. (no other information)	0	0	0	0	3	360	0	0	3	360
Others	17	148	1	200	10	194	3	52	30	594
Totals	350	3,083	24	532	102	1,992	115	885	435	6,485

Table 28

Attendance at Courses: Infant School Teachers

Subject of Course	Sponsor of Course								Totals	
	L.E.A.		Department of Education		Institute of Education		Other Bodies			
	Number of Staff	Number of Days Spent	Number of Staff	Number of Days Spent	Number of Staff	Number of Days Spent	Number of Staff	Number of Days Spent	Number of Staff	Number of Days Spent
General—Primary	21	71	0	0	8	45	7	105	32	221
General—Infant	59	217	5	25	18	57	30	105	106	404
General—Junior	0	0	0	0	0	0	1	2	1	2
English	52	119	1	3	20	79	17	27	85	228
3Rs (incl. Maths. and English)	18	46	0	0	9	24	2	5	29	75
Environmental	2	11	0	0	1	32	2	7	5	50
Mathematics	90	226	10	49	9	28	42	109	141	412
Science	14	45	0	0	2	2	1	15	17	62
Arts and Crafts	34	148	0	0	0	0	1	36	34	184
Music	53	131	2	6	4	9	5	13	62	159
Physical education	92	207	0	0	5	12	2	9	97	228
Teachers of handicapped children	12	57	1	12	10	26	0	0	23	95
Religious education	13	28	1	1	6	8	12	483	30	520
French	1	12	0	0	0	0	0	0	1	12
Russian	0	0	0	0	0	0	0	0	0	0
Spanish	0	0	0	0	0	0	0	0	0	0
Geography	0	0	0	0	0	0	0	0	0	0
History	0	0	0	0	0	0	0	0	0	0
Dip. Ed. (no other information)	0	0	0	0	1	60	0	0	1	60
Others	16	55	0	0	0	0	3	89	19	144
Totals	260	1,373	17	96	75	3,821	102	1,005	339	2,956

Table 29

Attendance at Courses: Teachers aged 30–39

Subject of Course	L.E.A.		Department of Education		Institute of Education		Other Bodies		Totals	
	Number of Staff	Number of Days Spent	Number of Staff	Number of Days Spent	Number of Staff	Number of Days Spent	Number of Staff	Number of Days Spent	Number of Staff	Number of Days Spent
General— Primary	10	36	2	157	12	431	4	42	26	666
General— Infant	14	59	1	4	3	6	8	20	24	89
General— Junior	4	35	0	0	3	116	0	0	7	151
English	39	115	0	0	18	129	12	26	59	270
3Rs (incl. Maths. and English)	9	31	0	0	0	0	1	1	10	32
Environmental	6	13	0	0	1	18	2	19	9	50
Mathematics	46	132	2	7	9	33	15	46	70	218
Science	11	41	2	12	7	40	5	32	25	125
Arts and Crafts	42	273	0	0	6	56	9	86	54	415
Music	24	62	2	380	1	2	7	23	32	467
Physical education	68	213	0	0	1	2	8	39	76	254
Teachers of handicapped children	7	61	0	0	8	426	1	8	16	495
Religious education	6	15	0	0	1	10	5	491	11	516
French	12	97	1	3	2	11	1	1	15	112
Russian	0	0	0	0	0	0	0	0	0	0
Spanish	0	0	0	0	0	0	0	0	0	0
Geography	0	0	0	0	0	0	2	12	2	12
History	0	0	0	0	0	0	0	0	0	0
Dip. Ed. (no other information)	0	0	0	0	3	465	0	0	3	465
Others	8	84	0	0	4	14	2	47	13	145
Totals	166	1,267	10	563	53	1,759	62	893	212	4,482

26. There is some ground for concern about the distribution of courses. It was to be expected that a large number of teachers would be found to have attended mathematics courses, and the results of this in-service training have been described in Volume 1. The large number of courses—and days spent on courses—on physical education seem to be having rather less impact in the schools. It may be that these courses have become something of a routine and that their content needs to be re-examined. The relatively small amount of time spent on science courses (although it is now probably increasing) and the small amount of time and number of teachers involved in courses in history, geography and environmental study are disturbing. These aspects of the curriculum may appear in general courses on primary education. But the numbers of teachers who attended general courses, whether on the whole primary age range, on infant or on junior education, were less than those attending courses on either mathematics or physical education.

27. From the account given both of the schools and the teachers, the infants fare worst. They have more unqualified teachers and their staffs change more quickly. The teachers are also less experienced, and attend fewer courses than do teachers in other types of primary school.

Teaching Competence

28. Those teachers in charge of the children in the main sample were assessed for teaching competence on a five point scale. The proportion of men and women in these subsamples corresponded to that in the main sample of teachers. Men teachers were rated slightly higher than women as can be seen from Table 30.

Table 30

Assessment of Teaching Competence

Teaching Mark	Men	Women
A	2	1
B+	14	10
B	17	16
B−	7	10
C	1	3
No Mark	59	60
Total numbers (100%)	(317)	(1,238)

Men teachers are on the whole more experienced than women teachers and an analysis of teaching marks according to years of experience showed that no teachers with less than five years experience were rated A, rather fewer were rated B+ and more were rated B− than the average. Of teachers graded A and B+, nearly half held some post of special responsibility; this is well above the overall sample value (32 per cent). No significant differences were found when teachers' marks were analysed according to the status and age range of schools save that J.M. and I. schools had rather more teachers rated B− rather than B, compared with infant and junior schools.

29. Table 31 shows the total time spent on in-service training during the previous three years by teachers given teaching marks. Teachers with a poorer teaching mark were less likely to have had any in-service training, and the courses they did attend generally totalled less than 10 days.

Table 31

Total Days Spent on In-Service Training According to Teaching Mark

Total Days Spent	Teaching Mark				
	A	B+	B	B−	C
0	8	26	29	41	33
1–9	68	39	49	47	46
10–24	16	24	14	8	14
25–49	8	6·5	5	4	5
50–99	0	3·5	2	0	2
100–149	0	0·5	0	0	0
150+	0	0·5	1	0	0
Total numbers (100%)	(26)	(173)	(247)	(144)	(43)

THE CHILDREN

30. For the purposes of the regression analysis, children were assessed by objective tests and, for the analysis within schools, by rank order. Table 32 shows boys' and girls' mean scores. Except for Test 1, the Watts-Vernon reading test, and for Test 4, N.F.E.R. picture intelligence test, the girls did better than the boys within the age group. The differences between boys and girls may be due partly to different rates of development and partly to bias in tests. Teachers were also asked to assess whether boys or girls were "all

Table 32

Mean Scores of Regression Groups for Each Test Taken

Regression Group		Test 1 Watts- Vernon	Test 2 N.F.E.R. S.R.I.	Test 3 N.F.E.R. N.S.45	Test 4 N.F.E.R. Picture Test 1
Top Junior Boys	1.	16·4			
Top Junior Girls	2.	16·1			
Bottom Junior Boys	3.		15.3	19.6	
Bottom Junior Girls	4.		18·1	22·8	
Top Infant Boys	5.			13·7	31·5
Top Infant Girls	6.			15·8	31·9

rounders" or markedly better or worse linguistically, mathematically, in painting or modelling or in physical skill. Table 33 shows that most children were thought to have all-round ability; about the same percentage were markedly better as were markedly worse in linguistic and mathematic ability. In painting and modelling, and in physical skill only two per cent were markedly better and three or four times as many were worse. Perhaps these figures reflect the teachers' difficulties in helping children who are clumsy or lack ability to paint.

Table 33

Ability in Special Field Compared with Overall Ability (Percentages)

Special Field	Markedly better	On level with over-all ability	Markedly worse
Linguistic ability	6	86	8
Mathematical ability	6	88	6
Ability in painting or modelling	2	91	7
Skill in physical movement	2	88	10

31. Teachers of fourth year juniors were asked if children had shown marked improvement during the past three years. About 21 per cent had improved markedly, and they included slightly more girls than boys. Surprisingly only one per cent were thought to have deteriorated.

32. Improvement was examined according to the socio-economic group of the pupils and the sex of teachers and pupils. Tables 34 and 35 show that boys appear to do slightly better with women teachers and girls substantially better. It is difficult to know whether these results reflect a more optimistic view-point on the part of the women teachers than on the part of the men.

33. Finally, absence was examined. Four per cent of primary children in the sample were considered by their teacher to be absent from school for un-satisfactory reasons.

Table 34

Boys' Improvement or Deterioration According to Socio-Economic Class and Sex of Teachers

	Boys' Improvement	Professional and Managerial	Clerical and Skilled Manual	Semi- and Unskilled	Total
Man Teacher	Markedly improved	28	17	24	20
	No change	72	83	75	80
	Markedly deteriorated	0	0	1	0
	Total numbers (100%)	(39)	(184)	(67)	(290)
	No information	1	14	8	23
Woman Teacher	Markedly improved	26	25	22	24
	No change	72	74	78	75
	Markedly deteriorated	2	1	0	1
	Total numbers (100%)	(39)	(97)	(40)	(176)
	No information				

Table 35

Girls' Improvement or Deterioration According to Socio-Economic Class and Sex of Teachers

	Girls' Improvement	Professional and Managerial	Clerical and Skilled Manual	Semi- and Unskilled	Total
Man Teacher	Markedly improved	18	19	9	17
	No change	80	80	90	81
	Markedly deteriorated	2	1	1	2
	Total numbers (100%)	(49)	(171)	(57)	(277)
	No information	2	2	4	8
Woman Teacher	Markedly improved	29	31	26	30
	No change	71	69	72	70
	Markedly deteriorated	0	0	2	0
	Total numbers (100%)	(35)	(126)	(50)	(211)
	No information				

APPENDIX 6

THE 1964 NATIONAL SURVEY: THE INFANT STARTERS

1. A special sample was drawn from children who had started school, at the beginning of the term during which interviewing was carried out, in schools already selected for the main sample.

Sources of Data

2. There were three sources of data about these children in addition to the general school information (from Schedules A, C and Staffing Form) which was available from the main sample. The child's teacher was asked to complete a special Schedule (D) which replaced, for the children in this sample, the main survey Schedule B. Questions were concerned with the arrangements made by the school for the new entrants, and with the child's reactions to school, as seen by the teacher. The parent of the child (generally the mother) was interviewed, using the same Social Survey Interview Schedule as for the main survey, and an extra question, specifically about settling in at school, was included. The third source of information was a medical examination and previous medical history of the child, provided by the school doctor, with information given by the child's mother, on Schedule M.

The Sample

3. The numbers of children for whom these documents are available are not constant over the three sources. There were 255 complete Schedule Ds, 249 completed home interviews and 227 medical schedules. It was difficult to get children, particularly in the rural areas, to attend the school clinics for the examination. Therefore, the base totals in the tables vary considerably, according to the source of the data being analysed.

4. Fifty-two per cent of the sample were boys and 48 per cent girls, compared with 50·7 per cent and 49·3 per cent respectively in the main sample. The social class of the families of beginners at school differed from the main sample in one important respect:—over two-thirds (67 per cent) were classified as Class III, whereas the main sample has 59 per cent in this group, and the general population group of married males used for comparison in the Social Survey Report, had 51 per cent. This large discrepancy was balanced by two smaller differences (in the opposite direction) between the two samples in Classes II and V.

Ease of Control

5. Mothers were asked if they found the child easy or difficult to control. The children in the special sample were considered less easy than those in the main sample; 63 per cent of the mothers as against 73 per cent in the main sample said their child was easy to control; 16 per cent as against 11 per cent considered their child difficult. Probably more difficulty is experienced with five-year-old children than with older children.

243

Table 1
Social Class of Parents

Social Class of Parents (see Social Survey Report)	%
I. Professional	4
II. Managerial (including self-employed)	10
IIIa. Non-Manual clerical (including minor supervisory grades)	14
IIIb. Skilled Manual (including foremen)	53
IV. Semi-Skilled	14.5
V. Unskilled labourers	3
Unclassified	1.5
Total numbers 100%	(249)

Table 2
Age of Children at Entry

Age at entry	%
Under 5 years	66
5 years and over	34
Total numbers 100%	(255)

Table 3
Size of Class on Starting School

Size of Class	%
Up to 30	28
31–40	46
41 and over	26
Total numbers 100%	(255)

Table 4
Prior Visit to School

Did child visit the school before he was admitted?	
Yes	71
No	29
Total numbers 100%	(255)

Table 5
Prior Visit to Class

Did child visit his class before he was admitted?	%
Yes	46
No	54
No answer	0
Total numbers 100%	(255)

Full- or Part-Time Attendance on Entry
6. All the sample children attended school full-time immediately (99 per cent of the main sample did so). Thirty-six per cent of mothers would have preferred their child to have attended only in the mornings or in the afternoons (23 per cent in the main sample). About two-thirds of the children were under five when they first started school.

Size of Class
7. Just over a quarter of the children entered a class of 30 or under; slightly fewer went into a class with more than 40 children. The rest were in classes of 31–40.

Prior Visits
8. Seventy per cent of the children visited the school before they were admitted at the beginning of term, and of these 64 per cent (46 per cent of the total) visited their class.

Settling in
9. According to the teachers' assessments, about a quarter of the children showed some signs of distress at leaving their mothers when they came to school. Distress lasted for under a week in 50 per cent of these cases. About 20 per cent of the group, five per cent of the total, were distressed for a month or more.

10. The mother was asked also how the child settled in his first term at infants' school. On the whole, they were satisfied with the way the teacher helped the child to settle; only eight per cent had any complaints or worries.

11. Mothers were asked whether children showed any worry or disturbance over school. Twenty-seven per cent were disturbed in some way; the main reasons were worry or upset by other children and dislike of certain aspects of school life. A few mentioned that their child disliked leaving them on going into the school. In actual numbers, only half as many mothers as teachers thought that children had shown dislike of school for a month or more. It must be remembered that the numbers involved are small. The difference may be a product of the form of question; the mother may have forgotten an earlier disturbance which had gone by the time of interview; alternatively, the child concealed disturbance from the mother and it was apparent only when he was separated from her.

12. Questions concerning the behaviour and development of the child, as assessed by the teacher, were analysed according to the sex and age of the child starting school. The age groups were five and over, and under five. Conclusions can be tentative only, as the sample groups are small.

13. Table 6 shows that there was practically no difference between the proportions of boys and girls who showed distress at leaving their mother when they first came to school. Older boys were more likely to be distressed than the younger boys, whereas younger girls were more likely to be so. Boys may have been more inclined to conceal distress from their mothers.

Table 6

Distress at Leaving Mother (Boys and Girls)

Did child show signs of distress at leaving mother when he came to school		Age Group 1 (5 and over)	Age Group 2 (under 5)	Total
Boys	Yes	30	22	25
	No	70	78	75
	Total numbers 100%	(46)	(88)	(134)
Girls	Yes	22	28	26
	No	78	72	74
	Total numbers 100%	(41)	(80)	(121)

14. Within the group of children showing distress at leaving their mothers, 30 were distressed for a week or longer. Of these children, seven did not attend for a medical examination. These are one quarter of all those who did not attend for medical examinations, whereas the whole group of distressed children are only one eighth of the total sample. There were therefore medical data for only 23 of these children, a very small group indeed. It is however of some interest that it included a higher proportion of early deliveries, of children weighing less than 5 lb. 8 oz. and of non-normal deliveries than the rest of the sample. According to mothers, the following behavioural characteristics were more typical of the distressed group than others:

Child making little or no attempt to mix with other children, child often disobedient, child often worried, worries about many things, and child fussy or over particular. As might be expected, more mothers of these children also reported crying on arrival at school and refusal to go into school. The proportions were nevertheless very low. A larger proportion of these children also showed some form of feeding difficulty, generally described as being "picky" or "fussy". These children were slightly behind the others in doing up buttons, and much more so at manipulating shoe laces.

Tiredness

15. The child's tiredness at the end of the afternoon was also assessed on a three point scale. Over half the children showed no signs of tiredness, and only four per cent of the total were markedly tired. Table 7 shows the categories used, and the distribution. Girls were more likely to have shown no signs of tiredness (61 per cent as against 48 per cent for boys). The older boys and the younger girls again appeared to be the more vulnerable groups; 65 per cent of older boys were average or markedly tired, as against 44 per cent of the younger group: 32 per cent of older girls as against 42·5 per cent of younger girls for the same category. From the group who started school aged five or over, the girls were more likely to show no signs of tiredness (68 per cent as against 35 per cent); there was a slight difference in the same direction for the younger group (57·5 per cent as against 55 per cent). Although boys

were more often tired than girls, mothers were more likely to consider that girls needed part-time school (40 per cent preferred part-time attendance for girls, as against 32 per cent for boys).

Table 7
Children's Fatigue

To what extent is child overtired, fretful or difficult at the end of the afternoon?	Age Group 1 (5 and over)	Age Group 2 (under 5)	Total
Boys Markedly tired	9	3	5
Average	56	41	46
No signs of tiredness	35	55	48
No answer	0	1	1
Total numbers 100%	(46)	(88)	(134)
Girls Markedly tired	5	2·5	3
Average	27	40	36
No signs of tiredness	68	57·5	61
Total numbers 100%	(41)	(80)	(121)

The difference is marked in the older age group, 46 per cent for part-time for girls and 29 per cent for boys. (See Table 8.)

Table 8
Preference for Part-Time or Full-time School on Entry

Mother preferred child to attend school:	Age Group 1 (5 and over)	Age Group 2 (under 5)	Total
Boys Mornings and afternoons	71	66	68
Only mornings or afternoons	29	34	32
Total numbers 100%	(42)	(86)	(128)
Girls Mornings and afternoons	54	63	60
Only mornings or afternoons	46	37	40
Total numbers 100%	(46)	(75)	(121)

Need of Adult Support

16. Teachers assessed the child's need for support of an adult (Table 9). Boys were slightly more likely to need some support than girls. The difference was particularly marked in the older age group, where well over twice as many boys as girls were assessed as having a marked need for adult support (26 per cent against 10 per cent).

Table 9
Need of Adult Support (Boys and Girls)

Child's need for the support of an adult (three point scale)	Age Group 1 (5 and over)	Age Group 2 (under 5)	Total
Boys			
Marked need	26	14	18
Average need	52	60	57·5
Little need	22	25	24
No answer	0	1	0·5
Total numbers 100%	(46)	(88)	(134)
Girls			
Marked need	10	11	10
Average need	51	64	60
Little need	39	25	30
No answer	0	0	0
Total numbers 100%	(41)	(80)	(121)

Children's Power of Expression

17. Table 10 shows teacher's estimates of the child's power of expressing himself in words. Overall, girls were more advanced than boys (41 per cent were "good", against 30 per cent); within the older age group, nearly twice as many girls as boys were assessed as "good" (46 per cent to 24 per cent); the difference between those within the group assessed as "poor" was only five per cent however; 12 per cent girls, 17 per cent boys.

Table 10
Power of Verbal Expression (Boys and Girls)

What is the child's power of expressing himself in words?	Age Group 1 (5 and over)	Age Group 2 (under 5)	Total
Boys			
Good	24	33	30
Average	59	43	49
Poor	17	22	20
No answer	0	2	1
Total numbers 100%	(46)	(88)	(134)
Girls			
Good	46	39	41
Average	42	50	47
Poor	12	11	12
No answer	0	0	0
Total numbers 100%	(41)	(80)	(121)

Children's Development and Size of Class

18. The possible relationship between size of class, the child's development and the parents' contacts with the school was examined. As Table 11
shows, the younger children were more likely to enter classes with less than 31
children. This may be a result of deliberate policy, or may more likely be a
result of sample distribution.

Table 11
Size of Class Related to Age of Children

Size of class	Age Group 1 (5 and over)	Age Group 2 (under 5)	Total %
Up to 30	22	32	28
31–40	49	44	46
Over 40	29	24	26
Total numbers 100%	(78)	(142)	(220)

19. Table 12 shows the distribution of teacher's estimates of the child's need
for the support of an adult, according to the size of class the child is in. There
were no clear differences between the groups except that a lower proportion
of children in the classes of 30 and under showed a marked need for adult
support (11 per cent as against 16 per cent and 15 per cent).

Table 12
Size of Class Related to Need for Adult Support

Child's need for the support of an adult (three point scale)		Up to 30	31–40	over 40	Total
All children	Marked need	11	16	15	14
	Average need	61	56	60	59
	Little need	28	27	25	27
	No answer	0	1	0	0
Total numbers 100%		(72)	(118)	(65)	(255)

Table 13
Contact Between Parent and Head Related to Size of Class

Whether parent talked to head when child started school or before	Up to 30	31–40	Over 40	Total
Talked to head	66	78	74	74
Did not talk to head	34	22	26	26
Couldn't remember	0	0	0	0
Total numbers 100%	(62)	(101)	(57)	(220)

Table 14
Contact Between Parent and Class Teacher Related to Size of Class

Whether parent has talked with child's class teacher(s) since child started	Size of Class			Total
	Up to 30	31–40	over 40	
Talked to class teacher(s)	66	69	82	72
Did not talk to teacher(s)	34	31	18	28
Total numbers 100%	(62)	(101)	(57)	(220)

20. Tables 13 and 14 analyse the mother's contacts with the head and the child's class teacher, according to the size of class. Unexpectedly, mothers of children in the smaller classes were less likely to have talked to the head before, or when, the child started school, and were less likely to have talked with the child's class teacher since. The most surprising figure is in Table 14; 82 per cent of mothers with children in classes of over 40 had talked with the child's class teacher since the child started school, compared with 66 per cent and 69 per cent for the small and medium classes respectively.

21. The explanation of these figures probably lies in the socio-economic circumstances of schools of different sizes, and in the organisation of the schools. Large classes tend to be in large schools in residential areas where parents are anxious to make contact with the schools. Many of the smaller classes must have been in rural schools where heads were in charge of a class, and some were in contact with parents out of school.

Introduction to School
22. Various factors concerning the child's introduction to school were examined. The mother might have known something about the school already, and the child might have visited the school and perhaps his class before starting. As Table 15 shows, when a child had not visited school before starting, his mother was slightly more likely to know something about the school. This factor apparently had no relation to visiting the class or not. (Table 16.) The questions were so phrased, however, that previous knowledge about the school did not necessarily apply to the child in the sample, whereas visiting school and class did apply to him.

Table 15
Parents' Knowledge Related to Child's Visit to School Before Entry

Whether mother knew about school before *child started	Did child visit school before he was admitted?		Total
	Yes	No	
Mother knew about school	48	52	49
Mother did not know about school	49	46	49
New school	3	2	2
Total numbers 100%	(157)	(63)	(220)

*Not necessarily sample child.

Table 16
Parents' Knowledge Related to Child's Visit to Class Before Entry

Whether mother knew about school before *child started	Did child visit class before he/she started school?			Total
	Yes	No	No answer	
Mother knew about school	50	50	0	49
Mother did not know about school	48	48	100	49
New school	2	2	0	2
No answer	0	0	0	0
Total numbers 100%	(101)	(117)	(2)	(220)

*Not necessarily sample child.

Table 17
Mothers' Contact with Teacher After Entry Related to Visits Before Entry

Whether mother has talked to class teacher since child started school	Did child visit class before he/she started school			Total
	Yes	No	No answer	
Yes	74	69	100	72
No	26	31	0	28
Total numbers 100%	(101)	(117)	(2)	(220)

23. If the child had visited his class before starting, the mother was rather more likely to have talked to the class teacher since then. As Table 17 shows, 74 per cent of mothers renewed the contact, while 69 per cent of those whose children had not visited the class talked to the teacher.

Table 18
Children's Distress Related to Prior Visits

Did child show signs of distress at leaving his mother when he came to school?	Did this child visit the school before he was admitted?		Total
	Yes	No	
Yes	27	21	25
No	73	79	75
Total numbers 100%	(180)	(75)	(255)

24. Finally an analysis was made to see if contacts with the school and the mother's contacts with the head and class teachers had any relation to distress shown by the child when he started school. The proportion showing distress

amongst those children who had visited was six per cent higher than among those who had not visited the school (27 per cent to 21 per cent). Table 19 shows no difference in the proportions showing distress according to whether parents had talked to heads when children started school.

Table 19
Children's Distress Related to Parent and Head Teacher Contacts

Whether child showed signs of distress at leaving mother when he/she started school	Whether parent talked to head when child started school		Total
	Yes	No	
Yes	26	26	26
No	74	74	74
Total numbers 100%	(162)	(58)	(220)

25. A higher percentage of mothers of children showing distress on entering school talked to class teachers than of mothers of children showing no distress (30 per cent compared with 16 per cent where mother had not talked to the teacher (Table 20)). It seems probable that children who have lived happily with their mothers, as well as anxious children, may show distress on entering school, and that prior contact with school may not be substantial enough to alleviate distress.

Table 20
Children's Distress Related to Parent's Contact with Class Teacher

Whether child showed signs of distress at leaving mother when he/she started school	Whether parent has talked with child's class teacher(s)		Total
	Yes	No	
Yes	30	16	26
No	70	84	74
Total numbers 100%	(158)	(62)	(220)

Children's Development and Family Relationships

26. It has often been suggested that a child's development at school and in society depends on his family relationships. Mothers were asked how often they were able to do things with their child in the evenings after school, and this was analysed in relation to the child's power of expressing himself in words. There appeared to be no difference between children whose mothers were free most evenings or only occasionally (Table 21). Unfortunately the group of mothers who did not manage to play with their children is too small for reliable analysis. The teachers' estimates of the child's need for adult support were examined with respect to the children's contacts with their mothers. For both sexes, it seemed that the children whose mothers were available only on occasional evenings were less likely to have need of adult support (Table 22). The groups, however, are small.

Table 21

Children's Expression Related to Play with Mother

Child's power of expressing himself in words (three point scale)	Mother plays with child			Total
	Most evenings	Occasional evenings	No evenings	
Good	38	39	16	37
Average	48	51	42	48
Poor	14	10	42	15
No answer	0	0	0	0
Total numbers 100%	(157)	(51)	(12)	(220)

Table 22

Need for Support Related to Play with Mother

Child's need for adult support (three point scale)		Mother plays with child			Total
		Most evenings	Occasional evenings	No evenings	
Boys	Marked need	22	14	11	19
	Average need	58	46	89	58
	Little need	20	40	0	23
	Total numbers 100%	(77)	(28)	(9)	(114)
Girls	Marked need	9	9	33	9
	Average need	70	39	0	62
	Little need	21	47	67	28
	No answer	0	5	0	1
	Total numbers 100%	(80)	(23)	(3)	(106)

Family Discipline

27. Another parental attitude examined was that of the father to family discipline. The mother was asked about her husband's attitude to the children, whether he tended to strictness, in some things at least, or whether he was lenient. Seventy-four per cent of the boys came from families with fathers tending to strictness as compared with 58 per cent of the girls. The proportions of boys and girls with a marked need for adult support were higher in the groups with lenient fathers than in the groups with strict fathers. Amongst boys, leniency also produced a higher proportion with little need for adult support; for girls there was a slight difference in the opposite direction.

Table 23

Need for Support Related to Family Discipline

	Child's need for adult support (three point scale)	Father tends to		Total
		Strictness	Leniency	
Boys	Marked need	17	27	19
	Average need	63	43	58
	Little need	20	30	23
	Total numbers 100%	(84)	(30)	(114)
Girls	Marked need	3	18	9
	Average need	65	56	62
	Little need	30	26	28
	No answer	2	0	1
	Total numbers 100%	(61)	(45)	(106)

Children's Behaviour

28. During the medical examination mothers were asked about the behaviour of the child. They were asked, for example, whether the statement—"child makes little or no attempt to mix with other children"—applied at all to their own child. As Table 24 shows, this statement was slightly more likely to apply to children whose fathers were rated as lenient.

29. Estimates of the child's behaviour made by his mother and teacher were examined together. As the numbers were so small, the categories which indicated that the child tended not to mix with other children were combined. As Table 25 shows, a tendency not to mix with other children did not necessarily go with an estimate of poor co-operation.

Table 24

Sociability Related to Family Discipline

Child makes little or no attempt to mix with other children (three point scale)	Father tends to		
	Strictness	Leniency	
Does not apply	85	82	84
Applies somewhat	7	9	8
Certainly applies	8	9	8
Total numbers 100%	(133)	(76)	(209)

Table 25
Co-operation Related to Sociability

Child's co-operation with other children (three point scale)	Makes little or no attempt to mix with other children		Total
	Does not apply	Applies "somewhat' or "certainly'	
Good Co-operation	45	33	43
Average co-operation	44	52	45
Poor co-operation	11	12	12
No answer	0	3	0
Total numbers 100%	(176)	(33)	(209)

30. Mothers may have been influenced in their preferences for full or part-time attendance at school by their ease or difficulty in controlling children. As Table 26 shows, if a child was considered difficult to control, the mother was more likely to think full-time attendance preferable (77·5 per cent) than if he was easy (62 per cent).

31. More mothers preferred boys than girls to attend full-time. If the boy was difficult to control, a slightly higher proportion of mothers preferred full-time attendance than if the boy was easy to control (71 per cent to 68 per cent. This difference was much more marked for girls, 84 per cent compared with 57 per cent.) It is interesting that if the mother assessed the child as in some ways difficult, in some ways easy to control, the proportion preferring part-time attendance was higher than for the other two categories. This was particularly noticeable amongst the girls (Table 27).

32. Only 21 per cent of mothers in the special infant starters' sample were working. A number of factors were analysed to see if working mothers held different opinions from non-working mothers or treated their children differently. Overall, working mothers were more likely to prefer part-time attendance at school (42 per cent compared with 35 per cent of non-working mothers). As Table 28 shows, the non-working mothers much preferred full-time school for boys, while slightly more working mothers preferred it for girls.

Table 26
Parents' Estimates of Value of Full and Part-time Attendance Related to Ease of Control (Both Sexes)

Would have been better if child had attended school	Easy or difficult child to control on the whole			Total
	Easy to control %	Some ways easy Some ways difficult %	Difficult to control %	
Mornings and afternoons	62	58	77·5	64
Only mornings or afternoons	38	42	22·5	36
Total numbers 100%	(157)	(52)	(40)	(249)

Table 27

Parents' Estimates of Value of Full and Part-time Attendance Related to Ease of Control (Boys and Girls)

Would have been better if child had attended school		Easy or difficult child to control on the whole			Total
		Easy to control %	Some ways easy Some ways difficult %	Difficult to control %	
Boys	Mornings and afternoons	68	67	71	68
	Only mornings or afternoons	32	33	29	32
	Total numbers 100%	(80)	(27)	(21)	(128)
Girls	Mornings and afternoons	57	48	84	60
	Only mornings or afternoons	43	52	16	40
	Total numbers 100%	(77)	(25)	(19)	(121)

Table 28

Estimates of Value of Full or Part-time Attendance by Working and Non-Working Mothers (Boys and Girls)

Would have been better if child had attended school		Mother not working	Mother working	Total
Boys	Mornings and afternoons	72	55	68
	Only mornings or afternoons	28	45	32
	Total numbers 100%	(99)	(29)	(128)
Girls	Mornings and afternoons	59	61	60
	Only mornings or afternoons	41	39	40
	Total numbers 100%	(98)	(23)	(121)

Table 29
Amount Working and Non-Working Mothers Play with Child

Does the mother play with the child in evenings	Mother not working	Mother working	Total
Yes, does things with child most evenings	75	64	72
Yes, but only an occasional evenings	21	27	23
No	4	9	5
Total numbers 100%	(197)	(52)	(249)

33. A smaller proportion of working than of non-working mothers were free to do things with their children in the evenings. As Table 29 shows, however, even in this group nearly two thirds managed to have some time free most evenings and another quarter were free on occasional evenings. Table 30 shows that although there is no difference according to whether the mother works in the proportions of children estimated by their teachers as having a poor power of expression in words, those with working mothers are more likely to be assessed as average, and less likely to be rated good (56 per cent to 47 per cent, and 30 per cent to 39 per cent respectively).

Table 30
Powers of Expression of Children of Working and Non-Working Mothers

Child's power of expressing himself in words (three point scale)	Mother not working	Mother working	Total
Good	39	30	37
Average	47	56	48
Poor	14	14	15
No answer	0	0	0
Total numbers 100%	(173)	(47)	(220)

Table 31
Distress at Starting School of Children of Working and Non-Working Mothers

Whether child showed signs of distress at leaving mother when he/she started school	Mother not working	Mother working	Total
Yes	27	21	26
No	73	79	74
Total numbers 100%	(173)	(47)	(220)

34. The distributions in Table 31 indicate that the children of working mothers were less likely to show distress at leaving them to start school. This presumably could be expected if the child is already used to separation. A similar trend is found in Table 32. A slightly higher proportion of children with working mothers had little need of adult support (30 per cent as against 25 per cent). This was more marked in the case of boys.

Table 32

Need for Support of Children of Working and Non-Working Mothers

	Child's need for adult support (three point scale)	Mother not working	Mother working	Total
Boys	Marked need	20	15	19
	Average need	60	50	58
	Little need	20	35	23
	Total numbers 100%	(88)	(26)	(114)
Girls	Marked need	10	10	9
	Average need	60	67	62
	Little need	29	23	28
	No answer	1	0	1
	Total numbers 100%	(85)	(21)	(106)
Both Sexes	Marked need	15	13	15
	Average need	60	57	60
	Little need	25	30	25
	No answer	0	0	0
	Total numbers 100%	(173)	(47)	(220)

Medical Data

35. Full medical data were available for 227 children (except for the few adopted children about whom early details were not known). 74 per cent were full term deliveries, 12 per cent were early (ranging from one to eight weeks) and 10 per cent late from one to four weeks. The remainder did not answer the questions. There were 14 per cent non-normal deliveries, mainly instrumental. Six per cent of children were 5 lb. 8 oz. or under at birth. Twenty-three per cent had been admitted to hospital; one per cent had been in a residential nursery, and one child was in the care of the local authority. Fourteen per cent of children had some kind of feeding difficulty and 10 per cent had sleeping difficulties; only two per cent had a severe form of either. The majority of children, at least two-thirds in each case, had never complained of such physical disturbances as headache, stomach ac he,feeling sick

vomiting, nor had wet themselves during day or night for the previous year. Twelve per cent had had stomach ache and 10 per cent had wet their beds at least once a month.

36. The children did not on the whole show many behavioural disturbances (for complete list of categories see Q.25 A–M onSchedule M). Nearly 50 per cent had temper tantrums "at least somewhat", and nearly 50 per cent were said to tend to do things on their own. These large proportions may be due to mis-interpretation of the questions. About a third of the sample, in each case, tended to be fussy, to worry about things, to be fearful of new things, to be disobedient, and to fight with other children. Other disturbances were not found so frequently; the ones least frequently reported by mothers were crying on arrival at school and refusal to go into school. Nearly all children could pick up a pin easily; 86 per cent could do up buttons easily and 74 per cent could dress themselves. Sixty-two per cent could not do up shoe laces and only 15 per cent could do this easily. Mothers may have found this question difficult to answer; five per cent of children were said to wear buckled shoes and there may have been others.

APPENDIX 7

STANDARDS OF READING OF ELEVEN YEAR OLDS, 1948–1964
BY G. F. PEAKER

I. PROGRESS SINCE THE WAR

1. Since the end of the war there has been a remarkable improvement in standards of reading. In 1964 boys and girls aged eleven reached on the average the standard of pupils 17 months older in 1948. If the 17 months is expressed as a percentage of 72 months between the age of beginning school and the age of 11, this improvement can be stated as an increase of 24 per cent in the pace of learning. It is also the case that the standard reached or exceeded by half the boys and girls in 1948 was reached or exceeded by three quarters of their successors in 1964. There has been a corresponding advance among boys and girls aged 15.

II. THE SURVEYS

2. This is a striking record of progress. What is the evidence for it? The evidence is to be found in the results of national surveys (1) (2) that took place in 1948, 1952, 1956, 1961 and 1964. The 1948 survey was carried out by the Inter-departmental Illiteracy Committee, and the subsequent surveys by Her Majesty's Inspectors. In all of them attention has been concentrated on two ages, namely 11 and 15. In 1952 and 1956 each group covered an age range of three months, centred on 15·0 and 11·0. The boys and girls surveyed in 1961 were fourth year pupils whose average age was somewhat below 15, and the juniors surveyed in 1964 were somewhat older than their predecessors. But it is easy to calculate from the results an appropriate age allowance at each age. For juniors it is in fact five months for each point in the test score, and seven for seniors. This enables the scores to be adjusted to a common basis, and this has been done throughout the tables and diagrams that follow. The 1961 survey was carried out for the Newsom Committee and was restricted to comprehensive and modern schools. The 1964 survey was confined to primary schools.

3. The same reading comprehension test has been used for all the surveys in the chain. It was devised by Dr. A. F. Watts, H.M.I., and Professor P. E. Vernon. It occupies both sides of a foolscap sheet, contains 35 questions and has a time limit of 10 minutes. For each question the pupil has to select the right answer from five given words. The questions become progressively harder. The first questions could be read and answered by an intelligent child in the infant school. The later questions need the same sort of vocabulary and understanding as the leading article in a good newspaper. This long range is ample for the juniors but does not completely extend the best seniors. If 10 harder questions were added to the test many of the best seniors, but hardly any of the juniors, would be able to deal with some of them. This is the explanation of what will be noticed in the tables, that for seniors the median score is higher than the mean, and for juniors vice versa.

4. The confidence that can be placed in the results of the surveys clearly depends on the one hand on the appropriateness of the test, and on the other on the accuracy of the sampling. These questions are considered in Sections III and IV.

Table 1 (for Diagram 1)
Percentile Scores for Pupils Aged Eleven

Rank %	1948	1952	1956	1964
90	18·4	19·5	21·1	22·8
80	15·9	16·8	18·8	20·5
70	14·2	15·1	16·7	18·4
60	12·7	13·6	14·7	16·4
50	11·3	12·2	13·0	14·7
40	9·8	10·7	11·3	13·0
30	8·1	9·0	9·6	11·3
20	6·6	7·2	7·9	9·4
10	3·9	4·9	5·6	7·5
MEAN SCORE	11·6	12·4	13·3	15·0

5. Table 1 and Diagram 1 show the mean and percentile scores obtained by juniors in the four years when they were surveyed. The progress from 1948 to 1964 can be most easily seen from the diagram. It is apparent that the curve for 1948 has to be pushed forward by about three and a half points to cover the curve for 1964. The two curves are much the same shape; in other words there has been progress in all parts of the range. By reading the diagram horizontally, the increase in score for any percentile can be seen. By reading it vertically, the percentile ranks corresponding to the same score at different epochs can be seen. Percentile for percentile there has been an advance of about three and a half points, and score for score a fall of about 20 percentile ranks, so that a score that would have gained a good rank in 1948 would by no means suffice to do so in 1964. At the foot of the scale the tenth percentile was 3·9 in 1948, but had risen to 7·5 in 1964. In 1948 five per cent of the juniors were scoring two points or fewer, in 1964 there were hardly any.

6. It is apparent from the diagram that for most of the range a point of score is equivalent to about six percentile ranks. This is one useful figure to keep in mind in considering what is meant by an average gain of three and a half points. Another is that a point of score is equivalent to five months of age, for juniors. This cannot be seen from the diagram; it is the gradient obtained by considering the average scores for different (chronological) ages. As the age increases, the gradient gradually declines, so that for seniors, aged 15, it is not five months to the point, but seven months.

7. It will be seen that the statement in the opening section, so far as it relates to juniors, is simply the result of translating the average gains shown in points of score in Table 2 into gains in reading age, at five months to the point, and gains in percentile ranks, at six ranks to the point.

8. The complete account of the survey shows a considerable overlap between the two age groups. Four per cent of the children of 11 are in advance of 50 per cent of children of 15.

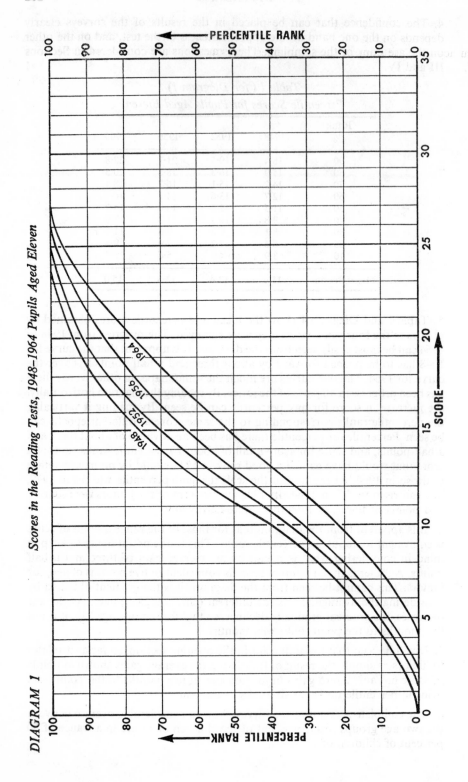

DIAGRAM 1

Scores in the Reading Tests, 1948–1964 Pupils Aged Eleven

III. THE APPROPRIATENESS OF THE TEST

9. The strength of the evidence in favour of the remarkable progress illustrated by Table 1 can be considered under two heads. These are the appropriateness of the test and the accuracy of the sampling. The questions are practically independent. The accuracy of the sampling would need to be demonstrated whatever the test, and the appropriateness of the tests would need to be considered whatever the accuracy of the sampling, and indeed if every child in the whole country had been tested.

10. What grounds are there for thinking the test appropriate? It would be easier to discuss this question if the test could be printed on the opposite page. But to publish the test would be to endanger its usefulness for future surveys, since it would not be clear how much of apparent future improvements was due merely to familiarity with the test itself. The fact that it has already been used for five surveys, and has not been published, constitutes its main claim to usefulness in the future. The first use of a new test can only form a link in a chain of surveys by means of a dubious and difficult process of calibration, unless it has been given to a national sample at the same time as the old test, and this is a strong argument for preserving a well-tried instrument until it begins to show signs of obsolescence.

11. The general nature of the test is that it consists of 35 questions increasing rapidly in difficulty. It is called a test of reading comprehension, and it seems likely that the early questions test mainly reading, and the later ones comprehension. The early questions are so simple that almost any pupil could answer them if they are put to him orally, so that if he fails to answer them it is reasonable to think that this is because he cannot read them. On the other hand a pupil may have mastered the mechanics of reading and still be quite unable to obtain a high score because he lacks the vocabulary, the general knowledge, and the understanding needed to grasp the meaning and give the answer when he is confronted by the later questions. At one end the test answers the question "Can he read at all?", and at the other end the question "Can he read to some purpose, like an educated man?". It would be hard to ask for more in the course of 10 minutes.

12. If the test were to be used as the sole measure of the ability of a particular child it could very properly be objected that however much the authors were guided by previous trial in their choice of questions they must perforce in the last resort select one question and reject another, and that in so doing they are making a random distribution of good and bad fortune among the children who will subsequently take the test. But it is the essence of randomness that it tends to cancel out over large numbers, and the object of the surveys is not to make judgements about individuals, but to assess the progress of populations, by means of samples large enough for the good and bad luck to cancel out. Even where the distribution of good and bad fortune is not random, the effects are eliminated provided that the proportions remain the same. This is strikingly illustrated by the constancy of the bias of the test in favour of boys, which has been very steady at about a point from the beginning. Analysis has shown that this bias lies almost entirely in nine of the questions, with one of them accounting for more than a fifth of the total. This is a case where the distribution of luck implied by the choice of question is known not to be random, but to favour one sex. But because the favour is constant it does not invalidate the comparisons of one year with another.

13. These arguments go some way to suggest that different methods of assessing average progress will lead to much the same conclusions for a moderately long period. They are not, however, demonstrative. Many definitions of reading ability and many methods of assessment have been proposed, and experiment has shown only moderate correlations between them for individual pupils. Although it seems likely that there would be much closer agreement between them over long term changes in averages there is no conclusive evidence of this. Perhaps the strongest arguments in favour of the present test are first that it implies a definition of reading ability that is in accordance with common sense, and secondly that it takes no more than 10 minutes of the pupil's time. This economy in time is valuable, since the business of the school is not to test but to teach. Moreover it is not 10 minutes of every pupil's time that is needed. It is shown in the next section that with careful sampling design reliable estimates of national averages for an age group can be obtained from samples containing only one pupil in 400.

IV. ARE THE SAMPLES FAIR AND ACCURATE?

14. The essence of fairness in sampling is to make the draw by giving each member of the target population a specifiable chance of appearing in the sample. The chances need not be equal, but if they are unequal differential weighting is needed in compensation. Provided that the draw is made in this way the accuracy or representativeness of the sample can be assessed from the internal evidence that it contains. This can be done by working out the standard error of any estimate needed from the sample. In doing this account must be taken of the structure of the sample, and in particular of the number of stages in which it is drawn. In all except the first of the surveys in this series (for which the samples were judgement samples) the draw has been made in either two or three stages. When it was desirable to localise the survey, to enable ancillary work to be more easily done, three stages were used, and two were used where this was not the case. The three stages consisted first of the selection of local education authority areas, secondly of the selection of schools from within selected areas, and finally of pupils from selected schools. Although beginning with the selection of areas is a great convenience it is fairly expensive in terms of increasing the standard errors, or, what amounts to the same thing, increasing the number of schools and children needed for standard errors of a given size. Experience in designing these and other surveys has shown that a good rough preliminary rule, at the design stage, is to assume that when areas and schools are stratified about three per cent of the variation will lie between areas, seven per cent between schools within areas, and the remainder between pupils within schools. In two stage sampling this reduces to 10 per cent between schools and 90 per cent between pupils within schools. These rules enable one to make preliminary estimates, for any allocation of the sample, either of the standard errors or of the simple equivalent sample—that is, a single stage sample of pupils that would give standard errors of the same size. Thus if a sample of 2,000 pupils comes from 100 schools in 20 local authority areas the simple equivalent sample is 380 pupils. If the 100 schools came from only five areas the simple equivalent sample would fall to 140. If it were a two stage sample with the 100 schools selected directly from the whole country the simple equivalent sample would be 690, while if the 2,000 were drawn from 200 schools instead of 100 the simple equivalent

sample would be 1,050. These simple illustrations show the importance of having enough schools, as well as pupils, in the samples, and of having enough areas if the sampling is three stage.

15. The preliminary calculations cannot, of course, be left at that. After the event it is necessary to find out what the standard errors actually are, as distinct from what it was hoped, from the preliminary rule, that they would be. Owing to various complications, such as the fact that even after stratification schools vary a good deal in size, the posterior calculations may be fairly lengthy. But in fact the results have seldom differed much from those forecast by the preliminary rule. Indeed, for two stage sampling the rule of 90 for the pupil and 10 for the school has recently proved useful over a dozen countries.

16. Table 2 gives the standard errors for the mean scores in the various surveys.

Table 2

Mean Scores — Pupils Aged Eleven

1948	1952	1956	1964
11·59±0·59	12·42±0·30	13·30±0·32	15·00±0·21

17. The 1948 sample has been treated as if it were a probability sample, though it was in fact a judgement sample. The reason for its large standard error is that it was a three stage sample with only a small number (four) of local authorities. The 1952 sample was based on 15 local authorities, and the 1956 on 23. The sample of 1964 was a two stage sample with schools drawn direct from the whole country.

18. The simple rule of three per cent for the area, seven per cent for the school, and 90 per cent for the pupil gives an initial estimate of 0·59 for the standard error when applied to the four areas, 80 schools and 2,800 pupils of the 1948 sample. Applied to the 23 areas, 138 schools and 1,374 pupils of the 1956 sample it gives an initial estimate of 0·31. It will be seen that both these initial estimates are remarkably close to the final estimates given in Table 6 above. This illustrates the value of the rough rule for sampling design.

19. Combining the evidence gives the standard error of the gain in mean score as 18 per cent of the gain, if we begin with the rather weak estimate for 1948. Over the probability samples proper from 1952–1964 the standard error of the gain is 14 per cent. The gain itself is 3·4 points over the 16 years, and it is remarkably steady, since it is made up of 0·8 and 0·9 for the first two periods of four years, together with 1·7 for the final period of eight years. This suggests that it is likely to continue at the same rate for some time.

20. If we convert the gain from points to months we get 17±3·0 as the gain in months from 1948. In the opening paragraph the gain in months of reading age was converted to an increase in the pace of learning by dividing it by the preceding length of school life. Taking account of the standard error gives (24±4·2) per cent as the increase in the pace of learning. Allowing two standard errors each way to cover the luck of the draw in sampling would give upper and lower limits of 32 and 16 per cent, but this interval is probably

unduly wide, since the size of the standard error depends mainly on the weak determination of 1948 and the estimates, including the 1948 estimate, are remarkably consistent. This makes it reasonable to believe that the gain is in fact very close to 24 per cent.

References

(1) *Standards of Reading*, 1948–1956, H.M.S.O., 1957.
(2) *Progress in Reading*, 1948–64, H.M.S.O., 1966 (which incorporates this account).

These Annexes contain copies of the forms completed by head teachers, class teachers, H.M.Is. and medical officers concerned with the schools in the Survey.

Serial No.				

SCHEDULE A

In Confidence

CENTRAL ADVISORY COUNCIL FOR EDUCATION (ENGLAND)

Inquiry into children's achievements related to parental attitudes and school characteristics.

(To be filled in by Heads of Schools drawn in sample. Wherever possible, alternative answers have been provided in order to reduce the amount of clerical work and simplify analysis. In these cases, please ring the number opposite the appropriate answer as has already been done for question 2.)

1. School ....

2. Type of school

County	1
Voluntary controlled	2
Voluntary aided	3

3. Name of head...

4. Has the school been zoned by the L.E.A. at any time in past three years?

Strictly zoned, with few or no exceptions	1
Broadly zoned, with many exceptions	2
Not zoned	3

5. Please show on following table the approximate numbers of fathers in each occupation (see note 1):—

	Occupations	Number
(i)	Professional or Managerial	
(ii)	Clerical	
(iii)	Skilled	
(iv)	Semi- and un-skilled ..	
(v)	Unknown	
(vi)	TOTAL	

6. Parent/teacher relations (all questions apply whether or not there is a parent/teacher association).

	Yes	No
(a) Is there a parent/teacher association?	1	2
(b) Are meetings arranged for parents, by school or association, on educational matters?	1	2
(c) Are any social functions organised for parents?	1	2
(d) Have parents provided substantial help for school in money, kind or labour?	1	2

e) Please show on the following table approximately how many occasions are arranged, by school or parent/teacher association, for parents to visit the school during the school year. Any one occasion should appear only once in the columns a, b and c. It should appear on the same line in d or e and in total (see Note 2).

	Opportunities for parents to meet	Head teacher	Class teacher	Both Head and Class teacher	Total number of occasions		
					When father is probably working	When father is available	
		a	b	c	d	e	
(i)	To discuss individual child						(i)
(ii)	To explain or discuss school policy and practice						(ii)
(iii)	To discuss both the individual child and school policy						(iii)
(iv)	For general social occasions*						(iv)
(v)	TOTALS						(v)

*Refers to occasions such as sports days, carol concerts, exhibitions open to all parents.

(f) Please estimate the number of families where parents seek, *at their own initiative*, without arrangement by school, at least one interview in a year .. ..

(g) Please supply on separate sheet any additional information you think relevant if there is a parent/teacher association, a leaflet or programme would be useful.

7. Organisation
   (a) Number of children on roll .. ..

   (b) Number of classes .. ..

   (c) How are children usually placed in classes?
       By age alone   1
       By age combined with achievement   2
       By other means, e.g. vertical grouping   3

Office use
only

8. Arrangements for secondary education (to be filled in only by junior mixed and infant schools, and by junior schools).
   How many children from your school were transferred 1961–63 to comprehensive schools, selective schools or courses, modern schools with and without extended courses? Please complete following table: (See note 3)

	September	Comprehensive schools a	Selective schools and courses b	Modern schools		Total e	
				With extended courses c	Without extended courses d		
(i)	1961						(i)
(ii)	1962						(ii)
(iii)	1963						(iii)
(iv)	Total						(iv)
(v)	*Over-age pupils included in above total						(v)
(vi)	*Under-age pupils included in above total						(vi)

*By over-age pupils is meant those whose transfer to secondary education was delayed because they were thought to be immature; by under-age pupils is meant those who were promoted early on grounds of special ability.

9. Provision of books:

   (a) Total number of school and class library books (*including* books on semi-permanent loan from public library but excluding text books) available to pupils ..   ..

   (b) Average annual expenditure per head on school and class library books (*excluding* text books) September 1961–June 1964 inclusive   ..   ..

   (c) Are children allowed to take library books home?

Yes	.. ..	1
No	.. ..	2

Office use
only

10. Please enter on the tables below the names of the.........................pupils in each age group whose parents are being interviewed by the Social Survey. The name of the pupil who is first in overall achievement should be entered first, then the second and so on. "Ties" are allowed but should be avoided whenever possible. The test scores and rank should correspond with those entered by class teacher on Schedule B, Questions 9 and 10.

(a) *Top Infants*

Rank	Name of Pupil	NFER picture test score	NFER reading test NS45 score	Office use only

(b) *First Year Juniors*

Rank	Name of pupil	NFER reading test NS45 score	NFER sentence reading test 1 score	Office use only

(c) *Fourth Year Juniors*

Rank		Watts-Vernon test score	Office use only

11. The whole of the top junior age group is being assessed on the Watts-Vernon test. Please fill in the following tables:

(a) Number of pupils in top junior age group

	Boys	Girls	Total

(b) Number of top junior age group whose test scores were as follows:

Test score	Boys	Girls	Office use only
0–5			
6–11			
12–17			
18–23			
24–29			
30–35			
Total			

12. Please show turn-over of full-time qualified men and women staff from September 1 1961 to present time on following tables, *including yourself*: do not include part-time staff. (See note 4.)

Men Staff

		Still on staff	Left school September 2 onwards	Total
(i)	School staff September 1, 1961			
(ii)	Appointed September 2 to present time			
(iii)	Total			
		a	b	c

Women Staff

		Still on staff	Left school September 2 onwards	Total
(i)	School staff September 1 1961			
(ii)	Appointed September 2 to present time			
(iii)	Total			
		a	b	c

13. State present number of unfilled vacancies (short of establishment) ....

Signature ....

Date ....

NOTES TO SCHEDULE A

Note 1.—In filling in Schedule A, question 5, you may be helped by the following examples of occupations:

(a) *Professional or managerial*

Lawyers, clergymen, doctors, pharmacists, engineers, surveyors, architects, civil servants (executive and administrative grades), actuaries, accountants, teachers, managers of industrial or commercial concerns, officers of local authorities, army, navy and air force officers, inspectors and other senior police officers.

(b) *Clerical*

Clerks (including Civil Service and Local Government clerical grades), Shorthand-typists, secretaries (not company secretaries), other office machine operators.

(c) *Skilled*

Market gardeners, fitters, electricians, instrument makers, foremen, overlookers, viewers, weavers, furriers, boot and shoe makers, tailors, upholsterers, carpenters, joiners, engine-drivers, compositors, bookbinders, postmen, shop assistants, police constables, hewers, getters, and machinemen in (mining), bus drivers.

(d) *Semi-skilled and unskilled*

Agricultural workers, miners (other than those in (c)), kilnmen, foundry labourers, metal enamellers, solderers and brazers, garment machinists and pressers, maltsters, plate-layers, ticket-collectors, bus conductors, bargemen, barmen, laundry workers, packers, oilers and greasers. Unskilled labourers generally, navvies, porters, dock labourers, lift attendants, costermongers, hawkers, newspaper sellers, watchmen, rag, bone, bottlesorters, kitchen hands.

Note 2.—The following example shows how the table in question 6(e) might be filled in for one school and its interpretation:

	Opportunities for parents to meet	Head teacher	Class teacher	Both head and class teacher	Total number of occasions		
					When father is probably working	When father is available	
		a	b	c	d	e	
(i)	To discuss individual child			1*		1	(i)
(ii)	To explain or discuss school policy	3+				3	(ii)
(iii)	To discuss both the individual child and school policy						(iii)
(iv)	For general social occasions				2×	1⁰	(iv)
(v)	TOTALS				2	5	(v)

This school arranges an open evening for each year group in February when parents have staggered interviews with class teachers and can also see head teacher (1*). It also has a termly evening meeting at which educational matters are discussed (3+). There is usually a carol service and a sports day (both in the afternoon (2×)), and an exhibition of work one evening in July (1⁰).

Note 3.—The following example shows how the table in Schedule A, question 8, might be filled in:

	September	Compre-hensive schools	Selective schools or courses	Modern schools		Total	
				With extended courses	Without extended courses		
		a	b	c	d	e	
(i)	1961	—	20	36	24	80	(i)
(ii)	1962	—	18	40	30	88	(ii)
(iii)	1963	—	24	38	23	85	(iii)
(iv)	Total	—	62	114	77	253	(iv)
(v)	Over-age pupils included above	—	—	—	1	—	(v)
(vi)	Under-age pupils included above in 3 year period	—	6	—	—	—	(vi)

This is a two stream primary school with an age group of about 80 children of whom about 25 per cent go to selective schools and remainder to two secondary modern schools (of which one has no extended course). There are no comprehensive schools in the neighbourhood. In certain conditions children of 10·6 can be transferred to selective education. One boy who had spent a long period in hospital spent an extra year in the primary school.

Note 4.—The following example shows how the table in question 12 might be filled in:

Women Staff

		Still on staff	Left school September 2 onwards	Total
(i)	School staff September 1, 1961	3+	4++	7+++
(ii)	Appointed September 2 to present time	6×	10××	16×××
(iii)	Total	9⁰	14⁰⁰	23⁰⁰⁰
		a	b	c

This table shows the staffing of an infant school with six classes in 1961 and eight classes in 1964. In 1961 the staff consisted of seven teachers including the head (7+++). Of these three (3+) have stayed till present time and four (4++) have left. At the present time there are nine teachers (9⁰), comprising the three original members (3+) and six newcomers (6×). Ten others (10××) joined the staff after September 1961 but have already left. Twenty-three full-time teachers (23⁰⁰⁰) have been on the staff at some time in the period specified.

SCHEDULE B

In Confidence

Serial No. (a) School

(b) Child

Top infants—Blue Form
First year juniors—Green Form
Fourth year juniors—Yellow Form

CENTRAL ADVISORY COUNCIL FOR EDUCATION (ENGLAND)

Inquiry into children's achievement related to parental attitudes and school characteristics

(To be filled in by class teachers of children whose parents are drawn in the sample and returned by July 16 1964. Wherever possible, alternative answers have been provided in order to reduce the amount of clerical work and simplify analysis. In these cases, please ring the number opposite the appropriate answer.)

1. School ....

2. Name of class teacher ....

3. Name of class ....

4. Size of class ....

5. How has this class been formed?
   Mainly on age   1
   As an upper ability stream ..   2
   As a middle ability stream (e.g. of three streams)   3
   As a lower ability stream ..   4
   As a remedial class ..   5

6. Name of child .... Sex: Boy   1
                                                  Girl   2

7. Date of birth ....

8. Height in inches without shoes ....

9. (a) Number of half-days absent September 1 1963–March 31 1964 ....
   (b) Are you satisfied that absence is almost always due to child's illness?
       Yes ..   1
       No   ..   2
   (c) If not, is absence due to
       Sickness in home? ..   3
       Parental indifference?   4
       Truancy or school phobia?   5

10. Child's test score

			Office use
Name of test			a
Score			b
			c
			d

Office Use:

a	b	c	d	e	f	g	h	i	j

11. Four, eight or 12 children in this group age are being studied in this school. Please give this child's rank in order of overall achievement. "Ties" are allowed but are to be avoided if possible. This rank should correspond with that on Schedule A, Question 10.

Rank [ ]

12. Most children are probably "all-rounders" but if this child is markedly better or worse in any of the following abilities than in his general achievement, please ring the number in the appropriate space.

	Markedly better	Markedly worse	Office use	
(i) Linguistic ability	1	2		(i)
(ii) Mathematical ability	1	2		(ii)
(iii) Ability in painting or modelling	1	2		(iii)
(iv) Skill in physical movement	1	2		(iv)

13. *This question alone is to be answered for fourth year junior children only.* It would be helpful to know of children whose achievement has *markedly* improved or deteriorated in past three years. Please ring the appropriate number

Markedly improved .. 1
No change .. 2
Markedly deteriorated .. 3
Unknown .. 4

14. Please estimate on a three point scale this child's attitude to school

Likes school .. 1
Accepts school without showing any very positive like or dislike 2
Dislikes school .. 3

15. Please estimate on a three point scale this child's co-operation with other children.

Good co-operation .. 1
Average co-operation .. 2
Poor co-operation .. 3

16. Please estimate on a three point scale this child's co-operation with his class teacher.

Good co-operation .. 1
Average co-operation .. 2
Poor co-operation .. 3

School Serial No.

SCHEDULE C

In Confidence

CENTRAL ADVISORY COUNCIL FOR EDUCATION (ENGLAND)

Inquiry into children's achievements related to parental attitudes and school characteristics.

Assessment by H.M.I. of schools included in national sample of primary schools

On all occasions on which assessment on a five point scale is asked for, please allow for a national distribution of

$$5\%$$
$$20\%$$
$$50\%$$
$$20\%$$
$$5\%$$

1. How do you assess the all-round quality of this school on a five point scale? Please ring the appropriate rating.

Very good	1
Good	2
Average	3
Below average	4
Poor	5

2. How do you assess the head's leadership, taking into account the particular needs of this school?

Very good	1
Good	2
Average	3
Below average	4
Poor	5

3. How do you assess the average teaching competence of the staff?

Very good	1
Good	2
Average	3
Below average	4
Poor	5

4. How do you rate the extent to which this school is in line with modern educational trends, taking into consideration:

      (i) Permissive discipline?

      (ii) Provision for individual rates of progress?

      (iii) Opportunities for creative work?

      (iv) Readiness to reconsider content of curriculum?

      (v) Awareness of unity of knowledge?

Very good	1
Good	2
Average	3
Below average	4
Poor	5

5. Please assess, *on a three point scale*, the quality of the books provided.

Good	1
Average	2
Poor	3

6. Please assess, *on a three point scale*, the backwash of selection procedures on the curriculum.

Little	1
Average	2
Considerable	3

7. Please assess, *on a three point scale*, L.E.A. public relations, as shown, for example, by the information provided for parents on secondary provision.

Good	1
Average	2
Poor	3

8. Please assess, as A, B or C, the teaching competence of the members of staff responsible for classes in which there are pupils whose individual achievement is being studied; — and + may be used with B but not with A or C. It is important that B rather than B+ should be taken as the average mark.

9. Assessment of Continuity from Home to School.

Good	1
Average	2
Poor	3
Not applicable	4

10. Assessment of Continuity from Infant to Junior School.

Good	1
Average	2
Poor	3
Not applicable	4

11. Assessment of Continuity—within Junior Mixed and Infant School.

Good	1
Average	2
Poor	3
Not applicable	4

SCHEDULE D

In Confidence

Serial No. (a) School

(b) Child

Reception class—Pink Form

CENTRAL ADVISORY COUNCIL FOR EDUCATION (ENGLAND)

Inquiry into the arrangements made for the admission of children to school in the summer term 1964, and into their reactions to school in the first months.

(To be filled in by class teachers of admission class pupils included in the sample. Wherever possible, alternative answers have been provided. In these cases please ring the number opposite the appropriate answer.)

1. School ....

2. Name of class teacher ....

3. Non-teaching help available in school (please express as decimal of full-time teacher).

....

....

....

4. Size of class...

5. Age range of class ....

6. Name of child ....Sex: Boy   1
                                          Girl   2

7. Date of birth ....

8. Height in inches without shoes ....

9. (a) Number of half-days absent—from beginning of term to June 15, 1964 ....

    (b) Are you satisfied that absence is almost always due to child's illness?

           Yes   1
           No   2

    (c) If not, is absence due to
           Sickness in home?   1
           Parental indifference?   2
           Parental over-anxiousness?   3

10. Did this child visit
    (a) The school before he was admitted?

Yes	1
No	2

    (b) His class before he was admitted?

Yes	1
No	2

11. Will this child remain with
    (a) The same class teacher after the holiday?

Yes	1
No	2

    (b) Largely the same pupils after the holiday?

Yes	1
No	2

Office Use										
	a	b	c	d	e	f	g	h	i	j

12. Did the child show signs of distress at leaving his mother when he came to school?

Yes	1
No	2

13. If distress was shown for how long did it persist?

(a) For one week	1
(b) For two weeks	2
(c) For a month or more	3

14. What is the child's power of expressing himself in words?

(a) Good	1
(b) Average	2
(c) Poor	3

15. Please estimate, on a three point scale, this child's co-operation with other children.

Good co-operation	1
Average co-operation	2
Poor co-operation	3

16. Please estimate, on a three point scale, this child's need for the support of an adult.

Marked need for adult support	1
Average need for adult support	2
Little need for adult support	3

17. Does the child attend school?

Full-time	1
Part-time	2

18. If full-time, to what extent is he overtired, fretful or difficult at the end of the afternoon?

Markedly tired	1
Averagely tired	2
No signs of tiredness	3

SCHEDULE M

CENTRAL ADVISORY COUNCIL ON EDUCATION (ENGLAND)

INQUIRY INTO PARENTAL ATTITUDES

Medical Examination of Supplementary Sample of Five-year-old Children, July, 1964

The examining doctor is asked to complete this form with the help of the parent by circling the appropriate figure or letter, or specifying as necessary.

Name ....   School..

Date of birth...............................   L.E.A..

Address ....

....

Serial No.

PRE- AND PERI-NATAL HISTORY

1. Was pregnancy normal?
   No 0
   Yes 1

   If not, was there:
   Toxaemia? 2
   Haemorrhage? 3
   Rubella? 4
   Rh incompatibility? 5
   Any other condition? ....

   ....

2. Was delivery full term?
   No 0
   Yes 1

   If not, how early or late? ....
   ....

3. Was delivery normal?
   No 0
   Yes 1

   If not, was it:
   Instrumental? 2
   Caesarean? 3
   Breech? 4
   Duration of labour ....
   ....

4. Birth weight ....

5. At birth, did the child have:
   Asphyxia? 1
   Jaundice? 2

6. During the first week, did the child have:
   A convulsion? 1
   Difficulty in sucking? .. 2

7. Was the child quite normal to handle during the first week?

    No 0
    Yes 1

If not, was he:
    Stiff or rigid? 2
    Limp or floppy?.. 3

8. Was there any other cause for alarm during the first 10 days?

    No 0
    Yes 1

If yes, specify:
....

9. Had the child been discharged home by the 10th day?

    No 0
    Yes 1
    Does not apply 9

If not, by what day was he discharged?
....

10. Where was the child born?

....

....

DEVELOPMENTAL HISTORY

11. At what age did the child:

Sit without support on a hard surface? ....

Walk unaided? ....

First use single words with meaning? ....
(excluding "mum", "dad", "hullo", "bye-bye")

Have bowel control? ....

Have bladder control during the day? ....

Have bladder control at night? ....

PAST HISTORY

12. Has the child had any of the following immunisations or infections? (Put tick (√) in appropriate column.)

	Immunisation		Infection		
	Yes	No	Yes	No	When
Smallpox	....	....	....	....	....
Whooping cough ..	....	....	....	....	....
Diphtheria	....	....	....	....	....
Poliomyelitis ..	....	....	....	....	....
Measles			....	....	....
Chickenpox			....	....	....
Mumps			....	....	....
Meningitis			....	....	....

13. Has the child had bronchitis? (An illness with cough as the major symptom and moderate or severe constitutional upset.)

No	0
Once	1
More than once	2

If more than once, how often?
....

When was the last time?
....

14. Does the child have more than four colds a year

No	0
Yes	1

If so, how many as a rule?
....

15. Has the child had earache?

No	0
Once	1
More than once	2

If more than once, how often?
....

When was the last time?
....

16. Has the child had a convulsion since the age of two weeks?

No	0
Yes	1

If yes:
  At what age?...
  Did it recur?
    No/Yes—how often? ....
  Has the child had an EEG?
    No/Yes
  Is he on anti-convulsant drugs?
    No/Yes

17. Has the child had any other serious illness or accident?

No	0
Yes	1

If yes: What and when?
....
....

18. Has the child attended his own doctor during the last six months?

No	0
Yes	1

If yes: Why? ....
....

19. Has the child ever been admitted to hospital?

No	0
Yes	1

If yes:
  Which hospital? ....
  When? ....
  Why?..

20. Has the child ever been in a residential nursery?

No	0
Yes	1

If yes:
  When? ....
  For how long? ....
  Why?..

21. Is the child in the care of the local authority now?

No	0
Yes	1

K

PRESENT HEALTH AND BEHAVIOUR

22. Below are a number of health problems which most children have at some time. According to how often the child has each, please put a tick (√) in the appropriate column.

	1 At least once per week	2 At least once per month	3 Less than once per month	4 Never in last year
A. Complains of headache	....	....	....	....
B. Has stomach ache	....	....	....	....
C. Complains of feeling sick ..	....	....	....	....
D. Vomits	....	....	....	....
E. Wets his/her pants during the day	....	....	....	....
F. Wets his/her bed at night ..	....	....	....	....
G. Soils him/herself	....	....	....	....

23. Does the child have any feeding   If yes, specify................................
difficulty?   ....
     No 0   ....
     Yes, mild 1
     Yes, severe 2

24. Does the child have any sleeping   If yes, specify................................
difficulty?   ....
     No 0   ....
     Yes, mild 1
     Yes, severe 2

25. Below are a series of descriptions of behaviour often shown by children. If the child definitely shows the behaviour described, put a circle round "A". If the child is inclined to show the behaviour or does so only occasionally, put a circle round "S". If, as far as you understand from the parent, the child does not show the behaviour, circle "D".

	Does not Apply	Applies Somewhat	Certainly Applies
A. Frequently sucks thumb or finger ..	D	S	A
B. Frequently bites nails or fingers ..	D	S	A
C. Is fussy or over particular	D	S	A
D. Often worried, worries about many things	D	S	A
E. Tends to be fearful or afraid of things or new situations	D	S	A
F. Tends to do things on his own ..	D	S	A
G. Makes little or no attempt to mix with other children	D	S	A
H. Frequently fights with other children	D	S	A
I. Has temper tantrums	D	S	A
J. Is often disobedient	D	S	A
K. Often tells lies	D	S	A
L. Cries on arrival at school	D	S	A
M. Refuses to go into school	D	S	A

MEDICAL EXAMINATION

26. Height .... ins.
     (*without shoes*)

Weight .... lbs.
    (*in underpants or knickers only*)

27. Visual acuity:
    Right eye unaided............................
    Left eye unaided ....

If spectacles worn:
    Both eyes ....
    Why are they worn?................................

28. Squint (Cover Test)
    No   0
    Yes   1

29. Hearing:
    Normal   0
    Poor   1
    Very poor   2

How assessed?
    Clinical test   3
    Pure tone audiometer   4

30. Ears:
    A. Discharge
    Present   1
    Absent   0
    B. Drum

If present, is infection:
    Acute?   2
    Persistent?   3
    Recurrent?   4

	Left	*Right*
Intact ..	0	.. 0
Perforated ..	1	.. 1
Scarred ..	2	.. 2

31. Nose: Is nasal catarrh:
    Absent?   0
    Present?   0

If present, is it:
    Coryzal?..   2
    Chronic?   3

32. Skin and scalp:
Has the child a condition requiring treatment?
    No   0
    Yes   1

If so, specify ....
....

33. Lungs:
Is there any evidence of respiratory disease?
    No   0
    Yes   1

If so, specify ....
....

34. Heart:
Is there any evidence of cardiac abnormality?
    No   0
    Yes   1

If so, specify ....
....

35. Locomotor system:
    Has the child any defect of this?
    No   0
    Yes   1

If yes, specify ....
....

36. Has the child any other defect or disease (including a congenital abnormality)
    No   0
    Yes   1

If so, specify ....
....

HEIGHT OF PARENTS

37. Height of mother .... ins.
            (*without shoes*)

38. If the mother knows the height of her husband, what is it? .... ins.

DEVELOPMENTAL EXAMINATION

39. Speech:
    Has the child normal articulation?
    No   0
    Yes   1
If not, does he show:
Stammer:
    Mildly   2
    Severely   3
Dyslalia:
    Mildly   4
    Markedly   5

Any other defect (specify) ....
....
....

Is speech:
    Muddled (but not due to difficulty in articulation)   ..   6
    Only in single words or short phrases   7
    In sentences   8

40. Manipulation:
    A. Can the child pick up a pin?
        No   0
        With difficulty   1
        Easily   2

    B. Can the child do up buttons?
        No   .. ·   0
        With difficulty   1
        Easily   2

    C. Can the child dress him/herself?
        No   0
        With help   1
        Yes   2

D. Can the child do up shoe laces?
    No   0
    With difficulty   1
    Easily   2

Ask the child to copy this square. (You may show him by outlining the square with your finger.)

Ask the child to draw a picture of a man. (You may repeat the request and say once: "What else does he have?")

Staff list including head; please enter alphabetically men teachers and then women; include part-time teachers, entering a on foot of form in completing column 8.

Name of teacher	Office use	2 Year of Birth	3 Marital status			4 Qualification					5 Status			
			Single	Married	Widower or Widow	Tchrs Cert-ificate	Post-Grad. Tchrs Dip. or Cert-ificate	De-gree only	Years of exper-ience	Un-quali-fied	H.M.	Dep. Head	Post of Re-sponsibility	Other

MEN

1			1	2	3	1	2	3	4	5	1	2	3	4
2			1	2	3	1	2	3	4	5	1	2	3	4
3			1	2	3	1	2	3	4	5	1	2	3	4
4			1	2	3	1	2	3	4	5	1	2	3	4
5			1	2	3	1	2	3	4	5	1	2	3	4
6			1	2	3	1	2	3	4	5	1	2	3	4
7			1	2	3	1	2	3	4	5	1	2	3	4
8			1	2	3	1	2	3	4	5	1	2	3	4
9			1	2	3	1	2	3	4	5	1	2	3	4
10			1	2	3	1	2	3	4	5	1	2	3	4

WOMEN

1			1	2	3	1	2	3	4	5	1	2	3	4
2			1	2	3	1	2	3	4	5	1	2	3	4
3			1	2	3	1	2	3	4	5	1	2	3	4
4			1	2	3	1	2	3	4	5	1	2	3	4
5			1	2	3	1	2	3	4	5	1	2	3	4
6			1	2	3	1	2	3	4	5	1	2	3	4
7			1	2	3	1	2	3	4	5	1	2	3	4
8			1	2	3	1	2	3	4	5	1	2	3	4
9			1	2	3	1	2	3	4	5	1	2	3	4
10			1	2	3	1	2	3	4	5	1	2	3	4
11			1	2	3	1	2	3	4	5	1	2	3	4
12			1	2	3	1	2	3	4	5	1	2	3	4
13			1	2	3	1	2	3	4	5	1	2	3	4
14			1	2	3	1	2	3	4	5	1	2	3	4
15			1	2	3	1	2	3	4	5	1	2	3	4
16			1	2	3	1	2	3	4	5	1	2	3	4
17			1	2	3	1	2	3	4	5	1	2	3	4
18			1	2	3	1	2	3	4	5	1	2	3	4

You are asked to use the following code in filling in the staff form column 8.
(a) Give one of the following letters to show what body sponsored the course:

A = Local Education Authority.
E = Department of Education (formerly Ministry of Education).
I = Institute of Education.
O = Other Bodies, e.g. Froebel Association.

(b) Indicates subject of course by use of following letters:

G = General course in primary education.
Gi = General course in infants education.
Gj = General course in junior education.
Eng. = English and English subjects (reading, written English, drama, poetry and literature, history).
R = 3 Rs (i.e. including Mathematics and English).
Env. = Environmental study.

School Serial Number

decimal fraction of full-time immediately after name; please ring the appropriate number in columns 3, 4 and 5; use code

6 Experience in complete years of service—please use 3 cols. if experience interrupted by 1 year or more			7 No. of schools in which served for one term or more	8 In-service training from June 1, 1961 to present. Please see note on foot of form for code		9 Name of class for which respons- ible	10 Year of appoint- ment to this school	For office use only	
Before break	After break	Total			Total number of days at courses				
									1
									2
									3
									4
									5
									6
									7
									8
									9
									10

									1
									2
									3
									4
									5
									6
									7
									8
									9
									10
									11
									12
									13
									14
									15
									16
									17
									18

M = Mathematics.
S = Science.
A = Arts and Crafts.
Mu = Music.
P = Physical Education.
H = Courses for teachers of handicapped children.
Re = Religious Education.
(c) Show by a figure (and if necessary a decimal fraction) the number of days spent; reckon a single morning, afternoon or evening session as 0·5 of a day.

(p) Examples (i) E M 10 represents a 10 day course on mathematics run by Ministry of Education.
(ii) I S 1 represents two evening sessions at a course on science in primary schools, run by an Institute of Education.

APPENDIX 8

THE SOCIAL SERVICES AND PRIMARY EDUCATION:
A STUDY OF THREE LOCAL AUTHORITY AREAS

FOREWORD

1. At the Council's request, three research workers in social administration, Mr. A. T. Collis (Senior Lecturer in Social Study, Faculty of Commerce and Social Science, Birmingham University), Mrs. J. Parker (Tutor in Social Administration, Department of Social and Administrative Studies, Oxford University) and Mr. G. Miller (Studies Officer in the Centre for the Study of Educational Policies, University of London Institute of Education) undertook studies of the social services available to primary school children and their families in three widely differing areas of England. They completed their studies at great speed and the results were very helpful in the drafting of Chapter 7 of the Council's main report.

2. This Appendix contains a summary of the three surveys, prepared by Mr. A. T. Collis and Dr. Joyce Long (Research Fellow, Institute of Local Government Studies, Birmingham University). The Council join the researchers in thanking the local authorities who permitted these studies, and the chief officers, head teacher and other staff who gave so much help with the inquiries.

CONTENTS

SOCIAL SERVICES AND THE PRIMARY SCHOOLS:
THREE SURVEYS

I. INTRODUCTION

1. *Objectives*

1. The social services available to primary school children and their families in three widely differing types of area—a relatively small county borough, a large city and a rural county—were studied in the Autumn of 1964. It was agreed not to identify the areas which for convenience are referred to in this Report as Smallham, Largeborough and Exshire respectively. The methods by which the information was collected varied slightly in the three areas since shortage of time and lack of research assistance made it necessary to collect the evidence by the quickest available methods and these depended on the particular administrative procedures in each area. Consequently the detailed results of each survey were presented in somewhat different forms and occupy separate sections of this Appendix where differences in methodology and analysis are explained. All three surveys, however, adopted the same basic approach. Each examined a defined category of "welfare cases" which arose during the Autumn term of 1964 in a sample of schools. Information was gathered about any child whose social development, health or educational performance appeared to be suffering because of home circumstances or other environmental factors. These cases included children referred for child guidance and the help of the School Psychological Service. The more serious cases of infestation were included but matters relating simply to medical issues where there was no indication of parental failure were excluded. Thus the School Medical Service which plays a vital rôle in the general welfare of school children figures less fully in these surveys than it would have done if a wider definition of welfare cases had been used. All the surveys were designed :—

(*a*) to examine the local statutory and voluntary services available to primary school children and their families,

(*b*) to ascertain the nature and incidence of welfare problems arising among primary school children and the ways in which they were brought to the attention of, and dealt with by, the services,

(*c*) to determine how often several different agencies were involved with the same case and what arrangements were made to co-ordinate their activities,

(*d*) to ascertain the views of teaching staff on their relations with the welfare services.

2. It was impossible, with the available resources, to attempt an independent assessment of the children attending the schools to determine whether their intellectual, physical or social development was being adversely effected by home circumstances. The surveys included only those cases reported by the schools and associated welfare services. There is no way of knowing to what extent the numbers recorded would correspond with an independent assessment. The attitudes, interests and understanding of the teachers and other officers concerned are likely to influence the number of cases reported.

2. *The Areas Studied*

3. *Smallham* has a population of slightly more than 100,000. It is an important market town and administrative centre which has experienced much industrial growth during the last few decades. In 1963 nearly one

quarter of the working population was classed as professional workers or central and local government officials, a third was in the service industries and about a third was employed in one predominant industry.

4. *Largeborough* is a large industrial and commercial centre. It underwent large-scale unplanned expansion in the nineteenth century followed by continued growth in the twentieth. Four different urban zones can be distinguished. First there is the central commercial and administrative district which is being rapidly redeveloped. Beyond this three irregular concentric zones can be identified. That nearest the centre has the highest density of population and contains the oldest and most dilapidated houses and industrial buildings. It also contains large areas of good amenity and landscape as a result of redevelopment which is being carried out by the corporation on a scale and at a pace comparable to that of any large city in Europe. Nevertheless, this inner zone still accounts for the hard core of the city's slum clearance problem; congested terraces, closely packed courtyards with back-to-back housing, communal lavatories and water piped only to a downstairs sink are still to be found. The intermediate zone consists largely of industrial premises and long terraces of late nineteenth and early twentieth century houses. Industry is more localised and in larger units than near the city centre. The outer ring is of a quite different character. It was largely developed in the twentieth century and consists of private and corporation estates with localised industrial tracts.

5. The population includes many people born outside the United Kingdom, particularly from Ireland, the British Caribbean territories, and from India, Pakistan and Ceylon. Most of the newcomers are accommodated in the poorest housing districts and although they have greatly benefited the area by helping to meet the high demand for labour, their influx has added to the problems of the social services. In 1963 rather more than half of the total number of persons employed were in manufacturing industry and just over a tenth in the distributive trades. The middle classes form a much smaller element in Largeborough's population than in that of Smallham.

6. *Exshire*, with a population of 130,000, is a widely dispersed rural area. The population has been growing quite rapidly, due partly to natural increase, but largely to the planned influx of population from a nearby conurbation. About two thirds of the population live in rural districts and even the towns (the largest with a population of less than 25,000) have a rural atmosphere. Rural areas may well have certain characteristics which tend to lessen local demands on the social services. Primary groups are more important than in urban areas; families see more of each other and the extended family group is stable and cohesive; neighbours have more intimate contacts and there is greater geographical stability. Under these conditions there are strong pressures to conform to rural mores and customs and the needs of families in genuine difficulties are often satisfied by the primary groups in a traditional although not always constructive manner. Thus some real social needs may be masked and some services may develop more slowly than in urban areas. Nevertheless, the survey showed that, as the social services had been extended over the preceding few years, their advantages, when compared with some old customs, had been recognized.

II. A Description of the Statutory and Voluntary Social Services Available to Primary School Children and their Families

7. The departmental structure of the three authorities was found to be much the same. The Education Department in each case had a number of separate sections among which the School Attendance and Welfare Department or the Special Services Department (the actual name varied) was the one which most concerned the surveys. The Public Health and the Education Departments were linked in the School Health Service which in Largeborough included the School Psychological Service. In Exshire this latter service was administered as part of the Education Department. The other local authority service most closely involved was the Children's Department. Voluntary organizations helping with the care of primary school children and their families varied in number and activity between the areas.

1. *The Education Welfare Service*

8. This service goes under different names in different areas. It is responsible for children whose education is liable to suffer because their parents (due to illness, unemployment, inadequacy, social attitudes, or low motivation) do not ensure their regular attendance at school or do not provide for them adequately in other ways.

In all three areas none of the educational welfare officers had any formal social work or social science qualification although some had attended short courses of various kinds. In Largeborough all officers attended lectures given by the Superintendent of the Department and 20 had been given time off to attend courses for the new certificate in education welfare. All three departments reported staffing difficulties. Largeborough had been experiencing a high turnover of staff which was particularly harmful since it was the best officers who tended to move on, taking with them a fund of knowledge about their districts, families and schools. Education welfare officers' salaries at the time were £770–£980 p.a. Table 1 shows that the number of school children per officer was highest in the county area and lowest in the large city.

Table 1

Establishment of Educational Welfare Officers in Relation to the Number of School Children (1964)

	Number of educational welfare officers and superintendents	Ratio
Largeborough	74( )	1:2,500
Smallham	5([2])	1:3,800
Exshire	4([3])	1:5,000

([1]) In 1964 there were periods when establishment was two or three officers below strength.
([2]) An additional officer was engaged in 1965.
([3]) One post was vacant in 1964 and one officer was part-time. Since then all posts have been made full-time and filled.

Duties of the Education Welfare Officers

9. The work of education welfare departments goes back to the introduction of compulsory school attendance in the 1870's. Originally they were concerned almost exclusively to ensure regular school attendance. In 1964 this responsibility remains but there were notable differences between the three areas in the extent and conduct of this part of their work. Further duties included the enforcement of Street Trading and Child Employment laws; the completion of application and assessment forms for free school meals and clothing; the maintenance of a census of the child population; helping in the transport of children to special schools. In Smallham the welfare officers helped in arranging holidays for handicapped children and in Exshire and Smallham they helped to arrange tuition for children in hospital. In Largeborough home visits were carried out for other departments dealing with such matters as the issuing of vermin notices and checking the whereabouts of families or responsibility for inter-authority education payments. In all areas officers were expected to have regard for the welfare of school children, to provide a liaison between the school, families and other local services and to refer social problems or other matters with which they were not competent to deal to the appropriate agency.

10. In their work of preventing absenteeism the welfare officers tried to alleviate hindrances to regular attendance and rely on persuasion, but if this failed verbal and then written warnings would be issued. In the last resort a local education authority may proceed against parents under Section 39 of the Education Act, 1944, or it may, under Section 40 of the Act, bring the child before the juvenile court. In Largeborough, where warnings were by far the most numerous, there was an extra procedure before prosecution was considered. Parents were invited to attend a sub-committee of the Education Committee at which each case would be reviewed and further warnings or suggestions for help given. Table 2 shows that in spite of this prosecutions were much more common in Largeborough than in Smallham and Exshire; the total number of school children in Largeborough was roughly ten times as large as in the other two areas but proceedings against parents and in the juvenile court were proportionately much greater. Thirty per cent of the 269 children appearing before the magistrates in the Largeborough Juvenile Court were at primary schools.

Table 2

Proceedings against Parents and in the Juvenile Court (1964)

	Legal proceedings against parents	Juvenile Court proceedings
Largeborough	336(1)	269(2)
Smallham	6	1
Exshire	—	4(3)

(1) Fines of between 10 shillings and £10 were imposed in 227 cases.
(2) In some cases there were also proceedings against the parents. These are included in previous column.
(3) In 1964 there were only four prosecutions but in some years there were as many as 16.

The Organization of Education Welfare Services

11. In Smallham and Exshire there was far less routine visiting of the homes of children absent from school than in Largeborough. Since 1955 attendance work in Smallham had been based on an "agreed" list of irregular attenders drawn up as a result of consultation between head teachers and welfare officers. A weekly report was made by the schools on the attendance of each of these children and head teachers could notify the Special Services Department immediately if one were absent without plausible excuse. In 1964, there were 430 children on the "agreed" list, 190 of them being of primary school age. In 1964 only two of the five education welfare officers were engaged in the field on attendance work. Each of the others had special responsibilities for such matters as handicapped children, applications for free meals and clothing, etc. In Exshire each officer had responsibility for the full range of duties in his own area and was notified by head teachers when they thought cases of absenteeism needed investigation.

12. In Largeborough, on the other hand, 60 of the 74 officers employed in 1964 were engaged in the field on attendance work, amongst other duties. They were each allocated a district for which they were expected to maintain the census schedule and to carry out all other duties. All the officers worked from a single office in the centre of the city. At the beginning of each week an officer collected the absence slips from the schools in his area. These slips were made out by the class teachers and were in the form of a small register. The slip for any child absent during the week was passed to the head teacher for transmission to the visiting officer. Children did not necessarily live in the district covered by the welfare officer calling at their school, so the slips were taken back to the central office for re-distribution. Not all absences resulted in a home visit. It was up to each officer to decide on the basis of the child's attendance record and his knowledge of the family whether a call on the parents was required. Towards the end of the week the slips were collected and re-distributed for return to the schools. The reason for absence and any special action taken was recorded on the slip but again the officer returning the slip to the school was not necessarily the one who had made the visit and knew the child's home.

13. In all three areas the work of the Education Welfare Departments brought them into contact with the School Psychological Service, the School Health Service, the Children's Department, the National Assistance Board and, occasionally, with voluntary societies.

14. In Largeborough the individual officers had very limited personal contact with other agencies as most matters calling for such contacts were referred to the central office and dealt with there. These contacts tended to be more formal than in the other areas for the department had an office of its own. In Exshire the welfare section of the Education Department was served by three administrative and clerical staff who also did the clerical work for the school psychological service. This office served as a kind of clearing house for all welfare problems. Problems were referred to appropriate departments and agencies by official letters and the workers concerned were often able to discuss cases informally with each other. The work of the Smallham department was divided amongst officers who specialized in different

branches of the work and they had closer and more continuous contacts with other agencies than those in Largeborough.

2. *The School Health Service* (including the School Psychological and Child Guidance Service)

15. In Largeborough the School Health Service was found to be a largely autonomous and distinct part of the education and health services. The full-time school medical officers and the school nurses were engaged exclusively on work for school children. The medical officer of health for the city was the principal school medical officer but a senior school medical officer was in charge of the day to day administration of the service. The medical and nursing staff worked from 15 school medical clinics each of which dealt exclusively with a school population of between 10,000 and 16,000 children.

16. In Smallham and Exshire medical and nursing staff did not specialize in work for the schools. In Smallham some school medical officers were also general practitioners; in Exshire they were sometimes medical officers of health for district councils. In both areas the nursing staff acted as school nurses and as general health visitors and were sometimes attached to group practices. They worked with people of all ages including the mentally sub-normal, old people, problem families and handicapped children and the emphasis in their job was on health visiting rather than on school nursing. In 1964 Smallham had four multi-purpose clinics whilst Exshire had two such clinics and others were planned. As a result of this multiplicity of functions in Smallham and Exshire, co-ordination of work with families might be expected to present less of a problem than in Largeborough.

17. Despite these differences in structure the School Health Services of the three areas had the same functions and, apart from the medical inspections and treatment which they carry out, school doctors can play an important part in advising head teachers about difficulties in the behaviour of children and their parents.

18. One problem was far greater in Largeborough than in the other two areas. In Exshire and Smallham infestation was negligible and in Exshire the frequency of examinations for cleanliness was left to the discretion of the nursing staff. But in Largeborough there were, on the average, two inspections per annum for each school child and verminous cases amounted to 4·7 per cent of the number inspected. During 1963, cleansing notices were issued in respect of 2,420 pupils (under Section 54 (2), Education Act, 1944) and cleansing orders in respect of 2,113 pupils (under Section 54 (3) of the same Act). These figures were slightly lower than those for 1962, but 307 cases of scabies were treated at clinics thus continuing the annual increase in this type of infestation which had been going on since 1958.

19. Another problem facing the School Medical Service in Largeborough was the shortage of speech therapists. There was no appreciable waiting list for speech therapy in the other two areas but in Largeborough the number on the waiting list increased from 375 in 1961 to 500 in 1963.

The School Psychological Service and Child Guidance

20. All three areas had suffered and were still suffering in 1964 from a shortage of qualified professional staff especially in the Child Guidance

Service. Exshire had been unable to obtain the services of a consultant psychiatrist and psychiatric cases were referred to two part-time clinics run by the Regional Hospital Board. There were vacancies in Smallham and Largeborough for educational psychologists. Lack of staff, especially psychiatric social workers, was holding up a comprehensive plan for the development of child guidance in Largeborough where the waiting list was lengthy and waiting periods of nine to ten months were common. Table 3 shows the staff employed in the Autumn of 1964 in the three areas. It will be remembered that the school population of Largeborough was nearly ten times that of the other two areas.

Table 3

School Psychological Service Staff (*Autumn Term*, **1964**)

Medical staff	Educational Psychologists	Psychiatric Social Workers	Other Social Workers	Remedial Teachers
Largeborough				
Three child guidance clinics manned by consultant psychiatrists	6 (Establishment =8)	3 (1 part-time)	2 (both part-time)	19
		(Establishment=6)		
Smallham				
One psychiatrist (part-time) Two registrars (provided by Regional Hospital Board)	1 (Establishment =2)	1(1)	—	3
Exshire				
Nil. Psychiatric cases referred to clinics run by Regional Hospital Board	2	1	Nil (1 employed by R.H. Bd.)	5

(1) This member of staff was on leave of absence during the survey period.

The Functions of the School Psychological Service

21. In all three areas the work of the service fell into two broad categories. Firstly, it dealt with behaviour problems and, secondly, with problems of a more strictly educational type where children were having learning difficulties. Cases were referred largely by school medical officers, head teachers and general practitioners but parents, probation officers, hospitals and other agencies could also ask for advice. In all areas the number of children who failed to keep appointments at clinics was causing concern but the shortage of social workers prevented a personal follow-up of these cases.

3. The Children's Department and Family Casework

22. Children's Departments were set up under the Children Act, 1948, with the function of providing for children deprived of a normal home life.

Deprivation arises through the death, illness or desertion of parents or because parents have been unable for any other reason to care for their children properly. The departments are also responsible for children committed to the care of local authorities by juvenile courts because they have been neglected or ill-treated, or are beyond control, irregular attenders at school, in moral danger or offenders.

23. Children's Departments try, in the first instance, to provide support for families in danger of breaking up and, if this fails, they try and see that relatives or friends take over care of the children. If children have to be taken into care efforts are made to find a suitable substitute home with foster parents or in a children's home. Work to prevent the disintegration of the natural family had gone on for many years but it was not until the Children and Young Persons Act, 1963, that children's committees were given the specific duty to take action to prevent children being removed from home or from appearing before the juvenile court. Children's Departments also have responsibilities for the supervision of children placed for adoption or in private foster homes. They provide approved schools, remand home accommodation and 'places of safety' for children removed from their own homes on magistrates' orders and they have certain responsibilities for providing reports to the juvenile courts. At any one time a Children's Department will be working on behalf of many more children than are in its care under the 1948 Act.

24. The Children's Departments required regular reports from the schools on the progress of children in care and from time to time were in contact with schools over children appearing before the juvenile courts or children of families with whom the Departments were concerned. School reports were usually obtained by formal written notes and the feeling in the schools, particularly in one area, was that more information about the children in care and more contact with the staff of the Children's Department would be useful.

Family Casework

25. The three areas varied in their arrangements for family casework. Small-ham had established in 1963 a family casework unit within its Children's Department. In Exshire the senior child care officer had general responsibility for preventive work. In Largeborough no specialized unit had been set up under the 1963 Act, each child care officer carrying his own load of preventive work. A family care unit for dealing with problem families had, however, been established as early as 1954 within the Mental Health Service of the Public Health Department. In December, 1964, 90 families were receiving help from this unit although out of an establishment of fifteen social workers it had only seven. Since the survey was carried out in Largeborough family case workers in the family care section have been split up among the mental health teams covering the city. More mental health officers are also acquiring the training required and undertaking such work. A Family Service Unit supported by a grant from the City Council also operated in the northern part of the city and the Council of Social Service provided a personal and family casework service.

Table 4

Children in Care Under Children Act, 1948, and the Staff of Children's Departments

| | Number in care of local authority | Number received into care during year | | | | Number going out of care annually | Child care staff of Children's Dept. [1] 1964 |
| | | Under fit person orders | | Under Section 1 of Children Act | Total | | |
		Offenders	Non-offenders				
Largeborough	1,722 (March, 1964)	25	55	1,704	1,784[2]	1,666[2]	59
		80					
Smallham	242 (December, 1964)	38		239	277[3]	134[3]	15
Exshire	155 (December, 1964)	1	8	88	97[2]	111[2]	9
		9					

[1] Includes Children's Officer, Deputy and Assistant Children's Officer, all child care officers, trainee workers and supervisors.
[2] Year ending 31st March 1964.
[3] Year ending 31st December 1964.

4. The Probation Service

26. Since the age of criminal responsibility was raised to ten years under the Children and Young Persons Act, 1963, probation officers' contacts with primary school children have been considerably reduced although they are still concerned with primary school children subject to supervision orders made as a result of children having appeared before the juvenile court as in need of care, protection or control. A negligible proportion of primary school children are affected by such orders but in Largeborough 219 school children were under statutory supervision for school attendance in December, 1964—a relatively high figure reflecting the large number of bad attenders taken before the juvenile courts by the Education Welfare Department. Probation officers are expected to maintain contact with the school while a child is under supervision, although they are not allowed to interview the child on school premises.

27. In all three areas probation officers did much work which indirectly benefited primary school children in giving advice about matrimonial, housing, financial, legal and family problems.

5. Other Statutory Agencies

28. Other statutory agencies were only concerned with primary school children indirectly. The National Assistance Board was sometimes asked by Education Welfare Departments to certify income in respect of free school meal applications and occasional inquiries made of them to see if special

grants could be paid to a family on National Assistance. Mental welfare officers in Health Departments occasionally dealt with the parents of primary school children and local authority housing departments though decisions to rehouse or evict could make a big difference to the environment and welfare of children.

6. *Voluntary Organizations*

29. In all three areas the N.S.P.C.C. was the only voluntary society concerned specifically with the welfare of children and their families but there were other organizations whose interests, although more general, brought them into contact with primary school children. Largeborough had a particularly varied selection of such organizations as shown in the list below.

Largeborough	*Smallham*	*Exshire*
N.S.P.C.C.	N.S.P.C.C.	N.S.P.C.C.
W.V.S.	W.V.S.	W.V.S.
Red Cross and St. Johns	Red Cross and St. Johns	Red Cross
Council of Social Service	Council of Social Service	Diocesan Board of Moral Welfare
Diocesan Council for Family and Social Welfare	Moral Welfare Association	Dr. Barnardo's
Marriage Guidance Council	Marriage Guidance Council	
Various specialist bodies such as Institute for the Deaf, National Institute for the Blind, Spastics Association, etc.	Deaf Welfare Association	
Family Service Unit		
Residential Settlement		
A Training Centre for Neglectful Parents		
Religious organizations such as Jewish United Benevolent Board, Society of St. Vincent de Paul, Salvation Army		

N.S.P.C.C. inspectors helped over 3,000 children in Largeborough during 1964 and in Exshire 67 children were helped during the Autumn term, 1964. In Smallham 25 families were under supervision in December, 1964. The *Red Cross* occasionally provided transport to special schools. The *W.V.S.* did the same and also provided clothing and arranged holidays for children in need. The Council of Social Service in Largeborough provided a casework service and sought to co-ordinate the work of statutory and voluntary agencies. In both Largeborough and Smallham the main work of the moral welfare associations was with unmarried mothers but they also dealt with family problems such as marital trouble, eviction notices, debts, etc. In Smallham, the New Centre for the Deaf co-operated with the development of partial hearing units in certain schools and, during school holidays, classes were held in the Centre. Mothers came to the Training Centre for mothers in Largeborough from all over the country, accompanied by their younger children, and were shown how to look after their families. Whole families from the city could also spend periods in some flats under the guidance of the warden and her staff. The Largeborough Family Service Unit operated from headquarters in one of the worst slum areas and confined itself to working with families in the neighbourhood needing intensive long term support. In March, 1964, the Unit had seven caseworkers (including the organizer); 101 cases were active. The turnover of cases was small—only about 25 a year.

7. Co-ordination of Services

30. In view of the highly specialized structure of English statutory and voluntary social services it is inevitable that from time to time several services become involved in the problems of a single family. Co-ordination of effort to avoid conflicting policies and to ensure a co-operative and mutually supportive approach is obviously necessary.

Local Committees

31. In 1950 the Ministry of Health, the Home Office and the Ministry of Education issued a joint circular asking local authorities to consider appointing a designated officer to co-ordinate the work of statutory and voluntary services dealing with children who were in danger of being neglected or ill-treated in their own homes. It was suggested that this officer would be helped in his work by the setting up of a co-ordinating committee composed of representatives of the local services.

32. By 1964, the co-ordinating conference in Smallham, presided over by the children's officer and composed of heads of sections, was meeting eight times a year to review, on average, thirteen families on each occasion. Information was exchanged and decisions reached as to which officers should visit particular families. This committee also discussed broad policy issues. Separate case conferences of field workers met to deal with specific families and were convened by the children's officer.

33. Largeborough had never designated an officer for this work but the medical officer of health had called into being a 'Conference of Social Workers' to review families presenting complex urgent problems. This met six times in 1964 and discussed four to five cases at each meeting.

34. Exshire had two formal methods of co-ordinating departments. One was a 'Children at Risk' Committee which met monthly. About 40 children and their families had been discussed, many several times, in the two years since its inception. In addition there were problem family conferences called by district medical officers of health. Table 5 shows the composition of the committees for co-ordinating the social services in the different areas.

Table 5

Composition of Co-ordinating Committees

Largeborough	Smallham	Exshire	
The Conference of Social Workers	The Co-ordinating Conference	Children at Risk Committee and Co-ordinating Case Committee	Problem Families Conference
Public Health Dept.	Children's Dept.	Children's Dept.	Health Dept.
School Health Service	Health Dept.	Health Dept.	District medical
Children's Dept.	Welfare Services	School Psycho-	officer of health
Probation Service	Dept.	logical Service	Health visitors plus
School Attendance	Education Dept.	Welfare Dept.	other agencies
and Welfare Dept.	Probation Service	Probation Service	involved in the
Housing Management	N.A.B.	Education Dept.	cases such as
Dept.	Housing Dept.		Housing Dept.,
N.S.P.C.C.	N.S.P.C.C.		N.S.P.C.C.
Family Service Unit	Moral welfare		
Council of Social	worker		
Service (Personal	A policewoman		
Service Committee)			
The Warden of			
Training Flats			
N.A.B.			

Other Means of Securing Co-ordination

35. As might be expected in Smallham—a smaller and more compact area than Largeborough with far fewer social welfare workers—there was considerable informal co-operation between workers both by telephone and in personal discussion. Moreover, both in Smallham and Exshire, workers in the School Health Service had other functions and worked from multi-purpose clinics.

36. In Largeborough additional aids to co-ordination existed in the Council of Social Service. The Council's Personal Service Committee Case Panel brought together social workers from statutory and voluntary agencies to discuss cases of common concern. The Children's Department's Central Index of Cases recorded details of cases sent by local agencies where the children of the family were thought to be "at risk". The Largeborough City Council, aware of problems such as the multi-visiting of families and the need for more effective co-ordination between services, had set on foot a study of the welfare work of its various departments. At the time the study of primary schools was made the committee had not reported but since then the Council has received a report and important new measures are in hand. Departments have been asked to rationalize the areas into which they divide their work. The medical officer of health has been asked to set up a welfare centre in each of the areas planned and together with other chief officers will try to co-ordinate field work. Regular case conferences will be held and the active co-operation of voluntary organizations is being sought.

III. THE SURVEYS

1. *Educational Provision in the Three Areas*

37. Largeborough had long been struggling with a shortage of teachers and this was reflected in that city's staffing ratio. An interesting point illustrating the different social composition of the two cities was that in Largeborough less than three per cent of all school children were receiving private education whereas in Smallham the figure was 24 per cent.

2. *The Sample of Schools Chosen*

38. In each area the schools selected for study varied in size, were representative of different social and economic conditions and included, as well as maintained schools, some which were voluntary aided and run by religious bodies. In Exshire the small size of many rural schools made it necessary to include a larger number than in either of the other areas. Within each area there was a wide range in the size of classes in the selected schools. Table 6 gives details of the schools included in the samples.

Table 6

Size of Schools and Their Religious Affiliations (If Any)
(Autumn Term, 1964)

Area	Total No. of schools selected	County schools	Roman Catholic voluntary schools	Church of England voluntary schools	Total No. of children in selected schools	As % of all Primary school children in area	Average size of school	No. of children in smallest school	No. of children in largest school
Largeborough	12	8	2	2	3,946	3·9	329	134	668
(a) Inner area	5	3	1	1	2,083	—	417	238	668
(b) Outer area	7(¹)	5	1	1	1,863	—	266	134	438
Smallham	10	5(²)	1	4	2,667	32·8	267	63(³)	608
Exshire	21	5	1	15	3,083	26·6	147	25	338

(¹) In two instances where there were separate head teachers and buildings for infant and junior sections of the primary school these have been counted as separate schools.
(²) Includes one special school for E.S.N. children.
(³) Includes 26 in nursery class.

In each area the schools were situated in contrasting types of districts:—

Largeborough

39. Shortage of time and the need to use scarce research assistance in limited areas of the city within easy reach of the research centre precluded any attempt to develop a sample of schools which was fully representative of all the primary schools in the city. It was therefore decided to take two convenient districts which, in their distinctive ways, were typical of many other parts of the city. Five schools were in the inner ring where much of the housing was 19th century terraced tunnel-back artisan dwellings. The population consisted largely of manual workers and their families living in rented accommodation. According to the 1961 Census, housing densities, the movement of population, the percentage of the population under 21 and of married women at work were all higher in this catchment area than in the city as a whole. There were small localized pockets of immigrants. The

catchment area of the other seven schools was part of the outer urban zone and consisted predominantly of a municipal housing estate built during the 1930s. The 1961 Census showed that 14 per cent of the families were in owner-occupied property, three per cent in private rented accommodation and 83 per cent in municipal property. There was little overcrowding, the population was relatively stable and the 1961 Census showed only 0·64 per cent of the population born outside the United Kingdom. As with the inner area the population consisted predominantly of manual workers and their families but there were fewer unskilled manual workers and more non-manual workers and managers. The percentage of married women at work was lower than the city average.

Smallham

40. The position in Smallham can be briefly summarized:—

	No. of schools
Predominantly professional middle class district	2
New working class estate	2
Central area rapidly becoming depopulated	1
Areas developed in the 1930s	5

Exshire

41. The 21 schools studied in Exshire were situated in four widely separated parts of the county but were chosen as representative of the whole county. In spite of the rural surroundings of the schools, only 20 per cent of the pupils' fathers were in agricultural occupations. The biggest group (45 per cent) was employed on unskilled manual work. The schools were situated as follows:—

Predominantly rural districts	14
Urban and semi-urban district	7

3. *The Methods Adopted in Each Area to Locate and Study Welfare Cases*

42. Welfare cases were defined as any instance where a child's health, social adjustment or educational performance appeared to be suffering because of adverse home or other social factors.

43. In all three areas "welfare case" was interpreted so as to include children whose behaviour, clothing or cleanliness gave cause for concern and failure on the part of parents to obtain medical treatment when required or to ensure that spectacles and other medical appliances recommended for their children were used. Children referred for examination with a view to special educational provision were included as were applicants for free school meals or other material aid although it was appreciated that such cases are not necessarily associated with family failure.

44. In each area welfare cases were found by asking head teachers to report on children who came within the category of welfare cases as defined. The heads were particularly requested to interpret welfare case in a broad sense and in some instances matters referred to the investigators were disregarded as not falling within the definition. Beyond this point the methods used for collecting further information and for recording data diverged and are dealt with in separate accounts of the surveys.

4. The Largeborough Survey

45. In Largeborough the schools were visited each week and details of the welfare cases furnished by head teachers entered on schedules—one for each child involved in each separate welfare matter. Because of the system previously described for dealing with absences details of these cases were collected each week from the education welfare officers (E.W.Os.). These officers were also asked to record all other welfare matters with which they dealt whether arising from referrals by other agencies or otherwise picked up in the course of their work. As the school clinics played an important part in the general welfare of school children especially in the inner area where some parents were in the habit of taking health and behaviour problems direct to the school medical officer, the clinics were asked to record welfare cases coming to their notice as well as contacts they had with other agencies on such cases. When the schedules for the term had been completed contact was made with the Children's Department, Probation Service, N.S.P.C.C., the Family Care Section of the Public Health Department, the Family Service Unit and the Largeborough Council of Social Service to ascertain whether they had had dealings with the families of the welfare cases during the Autumn term or at any time during the previous two years.

The summary and tables which follow show the results of the survey.

(i) Education Welfare and Attendance Service

46. Taking the attendance work of the E.W.Os., the most significant points arising from Table 7A, which analyses the amount of work and number of children involved, were the enormous volume of absence slips, the large number of home visits and the high percentage of children in respect of whom home visits were made—37 per cent in the inner area and 22 per cent in the outer area. There was nothing like this in the other two authorities. In all the above respects the aggregate figures for the inner area were much higher than those for the outer area. There were, however, marked differences which are difficult to explain between schools in the same area so that the highest percentage of children from one school whose homes were visited in the outer area (41 per cent) was almost as high as the highest in the inner area (43 per cent).

Table 7A
The Number of Children whose Homes were Visited
INNER AREA

	Schools					Total
	A	B	C	D	E	
No. of slips passed out to E.W.O.	1,517	368	624	855	1,858	5,222
No. of slips where home visit followed	472	76	149	313	598	1,608
Percentage visited	31	21	24	37	32	31
No. of children involved in visits	209	53	84	164	256	766
No. of children on school register	489	262	238	426	668	2,083
Percentage of children on register involved in visits to home	43	20	35	39	38	37
No. of children visited where E.W.O. knew other agencies dealing with family	31	3	3	40	14	91

OUTER AREA

	Schools							Total
	A	B	C	D	E	F	G	
No. of slips passed out to E.W.O.	554	474	385	344	263	738	527	3,285
No. of slips where home visit followed	180	132	83	73	59	83	84	694
Percentage visited	33	28	22	21	22	11	16	21
No. of children involved in visits	89	79	43	51	39	59	53	413
No. of children on school register	219	296	134	217	245	438	314	1,863
Percentage of children on register involved in visits to home	41	27	32	24	16	14	17	22
No. of children visited where E.W.O. knew other agencies dealing with family	1	6	1	—	2	6	2	17

47. Table 7B deals solely with those children whose homes were visited during the term. In the inner area 50 per cent of the children were visited only once and 23 per cent had two visits compared with 62 per cent and 22 per cent respectively, in the outer area. Twice as many children (15 per cent) were visited four or more times in the inner area as in the outer (seven per cent).

Table 7B
Number of Visits to Each Child's Home

Number of visits to each child's home	The number of children visited at each school							Total number of children visited
INNER AREA								
	A	B	C	D	E			
1	93	39	46	90	115			383 (50%)
2	54	9	25	34	51			173 (23%)
3	28	2	5	23	35			93 (12%)
4	9	2	4	6	24			45 (6%)
5	9	1	2	6	18			36 (5%)
6	11	—	2	3	8			24 (3%)
7	2	—	—	2	2			6 (1%)
8	1	—	—	—	1			2
9	2	—	—	—	—			2
10	—	—	—	—	2			2
Total number of children visited	209	53	84	164	256			766 (100%)
OUTER AREA								
	A	B	C	D	E	F	G	
1	47	53	18	35	27	42	34	256 (62%)
2	18	15	14	11	6	14	12	90 (22%)
3	11	5	8	4	4	1	4	37 (9%)
4	5	2	2	1	2	1	1	14 (3%)
5	6	1	1	—	—	—	2	10 (2%)
6	1	—	—	—	—	1	—	2
7	—	3	—	—	—	—	—	3 (1%)
8	1	—	—	—	—	—	—	1
9	—	—	—	—	—	—	—	—
10	—	—	—	—	—	—	—	—
Total number of children visited	89	79	43	51	39	59	53	413 (100%)

48. In the outer area 87 per cent of all homes visited resulted in no reply or a reply to the effect that the child was ill or receiving medical attention. The percentage in the inner area was 74 per cent (Table 7C). The incidence of all other reasons—most of which would serve as a possible warning light for a preventive social work service—was roughly twice as high for the inner area as for the outer. The percentage of home visits on which further action was taken by the E.W.Os. was in fact almost twice as high in the inner area (13 per cent) as in the outer (seven per cent) but bearing in mind the enormous number of cases originating from absence slips the proportion in which further action was taken by the department was exceedingly small (Table 7D).

Table 7C

Results of Visits to Homes

Result of visit	The number of visits to children enrolled in each school							*Total number of visits*
INNER AREA								
	A	B	C	D	E			
No reply/wrong address	137	21	48	72	168			446 (28%)
Child ill	208	40	61	147	231			687 (43%)
Child attending Dr., hospital, clinic	18	4	3	13	15			53 (3%)
Mother ill	8	1	—	10	26			45 (3%)
Child/family moved	17	1	21	19	19			77 (5%)
On holiday or child temporarily elsewhere	12	5	7	14	59			97 (6%)
Late—missed mark	3	—	3	1	8			15 (1%)
Overslept	10	—	3	10	17			40 (2%)
Truanting	12	—	2	1	4			19 (1%)
Child refused to go	4	1	—	1	3			9 (1%)
Lack of clothing, footwear	9	—	1	5	3			18 (1%)
Kept at home to shop/look after house, etc.	13	2	—	7	24			46 (3%)
Other reasons	21	1	—	13	21			56 (3%)
TOTALS	472	76	149	313	598			1,608 (100%)
OUTER AREA								
	A	B	C	D	E	F	G	
No reply/wrong address	53	41	15	19	24	35	31	218 (31%)
Child ill	106	66	55	39	26	37	44	373 (54%)
Child attending Dr., hospital, clinic	2	2	1	2	3	3	1	14 (2%)
Mother ill	1	1	2	1	1	—	—	6 (1%)
Child/family moved	5	9	2	1	2	3	—	22 (3%)
On holiday or child temporarily elsewhere	4	5	3	5	2	—	4	23 (3%)
Late—missed mark	—	—	—	1	—	—	—	1
Overslept	5	—	1	1	—	2	1	10 (1%)
Truanting	—	—	—	—	1	—	—	1
Child refused to go	1	—	—	1	—	—	—	2
Lack of clothing, footwear	—	—	—	—	—	—	—	—
Kept at home to shop/look after home, etc.	3	6	3	2	—	2	—	16 (2%)
Other reasons	—	2	1	1	—	1	3	8 (1%)
TOTALS	180	132	83	73	59	83	84	694 (100%)

Table 7D
Visits after which Further Action was Taken

	Schools					Total
INNER AREA	A	B	C	D	E	
No. of visits after which further action taken	63	10	7	65	65	210
Percentage of total visits (on which further action taken)	13	13	5	21	11	13%
Nature of further action taken (more than one type of action may follow one visit):						
Discussed with head teacher	38	14	5	43	23	123
Referred to senior officer for contact with other agency	4	—	—	5	7	16
Referred to senior officer for possible prosecution	3	2	—	1	—	6[1]
Referred to senior officer for information of S.O.	—	—	—	1	—	1
Referred to senior officer for advice	—	—	—	—	4	4
Direct contact with another agency	—	1	—	2	—	3
Further home visit made	7	1	—	4	1	13
Warning letter sent	6	—	3	18	20	47
Verbal warning given	13	1	—	5	19	38
Parents called to attend Appeals Committee	5	—	—	2	6	13[2]
Visit to another school	1	—	—	—	—	1
TOTALS	77	19	8	81	80	265

								Total
OUTER AREA	A	B	C	D	E	F	G	
No. of visits after which further action taken	12	9	9	3	3	2	14	52
Percentage of total visits (on which further action taken)	7	7	11	4	5	2	17	7%
Nature of further action taken (more than one type of action may follow one visit):								
Discussion with head teacher	4	3	4	2	1	—	2	16
Referred senior officer for contact with another agency	—	—	—	—	1	—	—	1
Referred to senior officer for possible prosecution	—	—	—	—	—	—	1	1[3]
Referred to senior officer for information of S.O.	—	—	—	—	—	—	1	1
Referred to senior officer for advice	—	—	—	—	—	—	—	—
Direct contact with another agency	—	2	—	—	—	—	2	4
Further home visit made	—	1	—	—	1	2	—	4
Warning letter sent	—	2	1	—	—	—	1	4
Verbal warning given	8	1	3	1	—	—	4	17
Parents called to attend Appeals Committee	—	—	—	—	1	2	3	6[4]
Visit to another school	—	—	1	—	—	—	—	1
TOTALS	12	9	9	3	4	4	14	55

see notes on page 310

49. Most of the work arising from home visits related to the warning of parents. The greater number of verbal and written warnings in the inner area, 85, as compared with 21 for the outer area, indicated the more serious view taken of the absences from those schools. One might, however, ask whether a warning was always the best method of dealing with some of these cases and whether closer investigation and a fuller knowledge of all relevant details might not have indicated the need for social work help. The E.W.Os. were not trained social workers and had not the skills for making a scientific diagnosis nor had they the time or responsibility to probe into the affairs of the families. A close linking of services might, however, show up cases where unsatisfactorily explained absence from school was one of the several indications of possible parental failure and when this occurred a social work agency with the appropriate workers could be alerted and asked to investigate more fully. In very few cases did E.W.Os. have any direct contact with other agencies and in both areas together only 17 cases were referred to a senior officer for contact with other agencies. In the seven cases referred for possible prosecution, legal proceedings followed in five—all in the inner area. In all 13 cases where parents from the inner area were invited to attend the Appeals Committee (the special sub-committee to interview parents and assess absence cases) warnings that the parents would be summoned unless the children attended regularly in the future were issued. The parents of two families (involving six school children) were called in from the outer area and in these cases the sub-committee recommended further action to try to help the parents with their problems.

50. E.W.Os. dealt with 159 cases other than those arising from absence slips: 127 in the inner area and 32 in the outer area. Most cases were referred by the School Meals Department (51), the School Health Service (42) and, to a lesser extent, by parents (17), school staff (15), voluntary bodies (four) and miscellaneous agencies (eight). The remaining 22 cases, mostly concerned with lack of footwear, were picked up by the E.W.Os. in the course of their work. The two most important reasons for referral were (a) infestation, where the E.W.O. was required to serve personally on the parents a copy of the statutory notice issued by the School Medical Service requiring the parents to see that the child was cleansed, and (b) the assessment of parents whose children had free school dinners. The next largest category concerned lack of shoes and clothing. Most of these were referred by the schools or were raised by parents to see whether the officers were prepared to grant any of the "boot tickets" which they dispensed on behalf of a local charity. In ten cases officers were asked to help with family problems relating to the care of a child, but four of these only involved visiting a family on behalf of a voluntary agency to deliver goods and obtain information.

51. Table 8 shows the action taken by the E.W.Os. to deal with matters other than absence slips. Contacts with parents were mostly in connection

(1) In five cases legal proceedings were taken: parents prosecuted in two cases (the child being directed to Juvenile Court in one case): child taken direct to Juvenile Court in three cases.

(2) Parents warned in all 13 cases (i.e. 'regular attendance or summons').

(3) No legal proceedings were taken.

(4) These cases involved two families (three children from each). In both instances the Committee recommended what they thought would be more positive action to help.

with school meals and vermin notices (94 cases), collecting information or giving advice on other matters (24 cases)—and clothing or footwear needs (23 cases).

Table 8

The Action taken by Educational Welfare Officers in other than Absence Slip Cases (Total Number of Cases=159)

Action taken by E.W.O. (More than one action may be taken on a single case)	Inner Area	Outer Area	Total for both areas
Home visit to serve vermin notice or deal with vermin case	41	1	42
Home visit to deal with school meals	41	11	52
Home visit for inquiries, give advice, etc.	14	10	24
Provision of clothing/shoes/material aid	15	8	23
Discussion of matter with head teacher	9	6	15
Matter referred to another agency to deal with	7	—	7
Discussion with another agency	—	4	4
Referred to Senior Officer	4	—	4
Information noted—no action	6	—	6
Attendance at Court for vermin case	1	—	1
Other	—	2	2
TOTALS	138	42	180

52. If the number of home visits made by the E.W.Os. on account of absence is added to all other welfare cases with which they dealt the total comes to 1,735 for the inner area and 726 for the outer area. This works out at an average of 27 per week per school in the inner area and in the outer area (counting the separate infant and junior schools as one school) of 11 per week. An E.W.O's case load (the number of school children for whom he is responsible) in the inner area is just over two thousand so his weekly number of cases in term time would be about 120. In the outer area, where an average case load is 4,000 children, the weekly number of cases requiring attention would be about 110. With this number of cases plus the census of school-age children and other duties it seems clear there would be little time for work in depth with families or for contacts with other local workers.

(ii) *The Schools*

53. Head teachers were asked to report each week on (a) contacts which outside agencies had with the schools on welfare matters involving their pupils, (b) welfare cases arising within the schools which required referral to another service, (c) welfare cases which arose out of parents contacting the schools or which necessitated the schools contacting parents, and (d) welfare cases arising within the schools which were dealt with by the schools without the help of an outside agency.

54. Table 9 shows the extent to which other agencies referred to the schools during the term. It should be remembered that the table deals solely with cases (other than those arising from absence slips) which fall into the definition of welfare case used for this study. Although a wide range of services were in touch with the schools the total of 95 contacts from outside covered 10 complete primary schools over a period of 14 weeks so the weekly average per school was less than one. There were many more outside contacts with schools in the inner area than in the outer area where over a third of the referrals were by Children's Department residential staff about children in nearby grouped cottage and family homes.

Table 9—Agencies which referred Welfare Matters to Schools

Referring Agencies	INNER AREA				OUTER AREA			
	Mode of Contact			Total	Mode of Contact			Total
	Tel.	Letter	Personal		Tel.	Letter	Personal	
Education Welfare Office	—	—	3	3	—	—	5	5
School Nurse/Health Visitor	—	—	—	—	—	—	3	3
School Psychological Service	—	—	2	2	—	1	—	1
Child Guidance Clinic	3	—	2	5	1	1	1	3
Special Schools Section	—	9	—	9	—	3	—	3
Speech Therapy Service	—	5	—	5	—	—	—	—
School Meals Department	—	5	—	5	4	1	5	10
Children's Dept. Residential Staff	—	—	—	—	—	—	—	—
Children's Dept. other staff	4	—	—	4	—	—	—	—
Probation Dept.	2	—	1	3	—	—	—	—
Other Schools	4	—	1	5	1	—	—	1
Other voluntary agencies	7	—	1	8	—	—	—	—
Police	—	—	4	4	—	—	—	—
National Assistance Board	—	—	6	6	—	—	—	—
Hospitals	—	—	1	1	1	—	—	1
Member of public	1	—	5	6	—	—	—	—
Others	—	—	2	2	—	—	—	—
TOTALS	21	19	28	68	7	6	14	27

55. Among the more numerous reasons for referral to the schools were the need to obtain information about a child (16 cases), to report or discuss behaviour problems or truancy (15 cases), the need for free school meals, clothing or footwear (15 cases), matters relating to children in the care of the local authority (10 cases), backwardness or speech defects (seven cases) and family problems (six cases).

56. Many of the matters brought to the attention of the schools by outside agencies could be dealt with on the telephone or by correspondence but in 10 cases in the inner area head teachers felt it necessary to ask parents to come to see them, although three failed to attend. Two other parents were written to by head teachers in the inner area, who also had to take matters up with the children involved in seven cases. In the outer area no case led to head teachers meeting parents although parents were written to or contacted by telephone in two cases. In three cases clothing was provided for children by the schools.

57. Table 10 shows that 93 welfare matters arising within the schools were referred to other agencies by the schools (apart from the absence slips). If matters referred to the school attendance officer, school nurse or health visitor and school medical officer were removed there would be only 50 matters left and almost a half (23) were to the Speech Therapy Service.

Table 10—Cases Referred to Other Agencies by the Schools

Agency to which referred	INNER AREA				OUTER AREA			
	Mode of Contact				Mode of Contact			
	Tel.	Letter	Personal	Total	Tel.	Letter	Personal	Total
Education Welfare Officer	2	—	9	11	—	—	13	13
School Nurse/Health Visitor	—	—	3	3	—	—	8	8
School Medical Officer	1	—	5	6	—	2	—	2
School Psychological Services	—	—	—	—	—	2	—	2
Child Guidance Clinic	1	—	1	2	—	—	—	—
Special School Section	—	2	—	2	—	3	—	3
Speech Therapy Service	—	19	3	22	—	1	—	1
School Meals Department	4	1	—	5	—	—	—	—
Children's Dept. (Residential)	—	1	—	1	2	1	—	3
Children's Dept. (C.C.O.)	—	—	—	—	1	—	—	1
Other schools	—	—	—	—	—	—	—	—
Vicar/Priest	—	—	1	1	—	—	—	—
Religious Welfare Agencies	—	—	1	1	2	—	—	2
Other voluntary agencies	—	—	—	—	—	—	—	—
National Assistance Board	—	—	3	3	—	—	—	—
Hospitals	1	—	—	1	—	—	—	—
TOTALS	9	23	26	58	5	9	21	35

58. The problems giving rise to referrals to other agencies were:—

	Inner Area	Outer Area
Speech impediments	23	2
Free school meals/clothing/footwear	10	4
Truanting and other absence queries	7	3
Family problems/failure over appointments	6	9
Behaviour problems	6	—
Enuresis/Encopresis	2	2
Dirty clothing/body/vermin	1	6
Backwardness	1	6
Matters relating to child in care of local authority	—	3
Others	2	—
	88	35

59. Table 11 shows the nature of contacts on welfare matters between the schools and the parents. In each category the contacts have been divided into those initiated by the parents and those by the school. They are further broken down according to the mode of contact. Over twice as many welfare matters gave rise to contacts with parents in inner area compared with the outer zone. But even so the total of welfare incidents giving rise to contact between parents and school in the inner area was 187, which is an average of only just over 2·5 per week per school. In that total of 187 the same child has also been involved on more than one occasion. Free school meals, need for footwear or clothing, truanting and behaviour problems presented—in that order of size—the major reasons for the head teacher seeing parents in the inner area. Family problems (which included problems of marital relationships, financial problems, difficulties in providing for the proper care of children, illness in family) provided the next largest group together with incidents where children were subject to assault, interference or bullying by other children or by outside persons. The differences in the outer area were that truanting problems were negligible and the need for clothing, footwear and free school meals much less.

Table 11—Contacts between Schools and Parents on Welfare Matters

Nature of Concern	INNER AREA									OUTER AREA								
	Approach by Parents				Approach by School				Grand Total	Approach by Parents				Approach by School				Grand Total
	Tel.	Letter	Personal	Total	Tel.	Letter	Personal	Total		Tel.	Letter	Personal	Total	Tel.	Letter	Personal	Total	
Truanting	—	1	12	13	—	9	3	12	25	—	—	1	1	—	—	—	—	1
Other absence queries	—	—	1	1	—	—	—	—	1	—	—	—	—	—	—	—	—	—
Behaviour problems	2	—	13	15	—	4	4	8	23	1	2	7	10	—	—	5	5	15
Victim of assault, interference, bullying	1	2	12	15	—	—	1	1	16	—	—	5	5	1	—	—	1	6
Enuresis/Encopresis	—	—	2	2	—	2	—	2	4*	—	—	2	2	—	—	—	—	2
Dirty clothing/body/vermin	—	—	2	2	—	2	1	3	5	—	—	1	1	—	—	—	—	1
Need for clothing, footwear, etc.	—	13	16	29	—	1	1	2	31	1	2	2	5	—	—	—	—	5
Family problems	2	1	13	16	—	—	—	—	16	—	3	2	5	—	1	4	5	10
E.S.N./Backwardness	—	—	3	3	—	—	—	—	3	1	2	12	15	—	—	—	—	15
Child's whereabouts	—	—	2	2	—	—	—	—	2	—	—	—	—	—	—	—	—	—
Free school meals	—	20	33	53	—	—	—	—	53	—	1	—	1	—	—	—	—	1
Special admission to school	1	—	—	1	—	—	—	—	1	—	1	14	15	—	—	—	—	15
Information required on child	—	—	1	1	—	—	—	—	1	—	—	—	—	—	—	—	—	—
Others	1	—	4	5	—	1	—	1	6	—	—	2	2	—	2	—	2	4
TOTALS	7	37	114	158	—	19	10	29	187	3	11	48	62	1	3	9	13	75

60. Following contacts with parents 66 children (51 in the inner area and 15 in the outer) were put on free school meals or referred for the attention of the School Meals Service. Sixty-three cases in the inner area and 19 in the outer area were either discussed with or referred to other agencies—mostly the Education Welfare and Attendance Department. Parents were advised to contact other agencies in 12 cases in the inner area. In the church schools use was made of religious welfare agencies, ministers and sisters of churches where this was thought appropriate. In nine cases clothing was provided by school staff.

61. Head teachers recorded only 28 cases (12 in the inner area and 16 in the outer) which were noted and dealt with in the schools without parents or an outside service being involved. Behaviour problems (11 cases), the need for free meals, clothing or footwear (eight cases) and minor family problems (five cases) constituted the bulk of these. In five cases the schools supplied shoes or clothing to help the children.

(iii) *The School Medical Service*

62. Each set of schools in the sample was dealt with—among many others— by one school clinic, so research contacts were restricted to one clinic in each area. The School Medical Officers and the school nursing staff see a great deal of children and parents. In the inner area, for example, the School Medical Officer carried out over 250 medical examinations during the term and over 2,000 children were seen by nursing staff at school surveys. In 345 instances in the inner area children were found to be verminous and 222 initial warning notices with an accompanying offer of help in cleansing were sent to parents during the term. In the outer area 37 initial warnings were sent and no further action was called for during the term. A second more severe stricture giving the parent 48 hours in which to get the child's head clean and which is served by hand by the E.W.O. was served in just over fifty cases in the inner area. It was at this stage that a verminous condition was counted as a "welfare case" from the point of view of this research.

63. The school medical officers and nursing staff co-operated in recording welfare matters falling within the scope of the inquiry although, from their point of view this naturally involved a very narrow definition of welfare. The number recorded amounted to 146 in the two areas. Ninety-two cases arose in the course of the work of the clinics mainly through verminous conditions and failure of parents to keep appointments for their children's medical examination or treatment. These cases usually led to a home visit by the school nurse. Fifty-four cases were referred to the clinics from schools (22 cases), parents (17 cases), other sections of the School Health Service (eight cases) and outside agencies (seven cases). More parents went with their problems to the clinic in the inner area which was easily accessible and where the same S.M.O. had worked for fifteen years. The more numerous reasons for referral to the clinics were behaviour problems (12), family problems (10), parental failure over appointments (10), enuresis/encopresis (seven) and speech impediments (five). In 12 cases the matters were referred by the clinics to another agency.

Table 12—Children and Families involved in Welfare Incidents and in Welfare Cases

	INNER AREA—No. on Register=2,083				OUTER AREA—No. on Register=1,863			
	Welfare Incidents Recorded	No. of Children Involved	Percentage of Children on Registers	No. of Families Involved	Welfare Incidents Recorded	No. of Children Involved	Percentage of Children on Registers	No. of Families Involved
Schools Education Welfare and Attendance	325	204	9·8	138	153	110	6·0	90
Attendance cases (home visits)	1,608	766	36·8	618	694	420	22·5	369
Other cases	127	111	5·3	66	32	31	1·7	29
Total	1,735	877	42·1		726	451	24·2	25
School Clinics	115	107	5·1	90	31	30	1·6	
TOTAL WELFARE INCIDENTS	2,175	969	46·2	736	910	483	25·9	421
WELFARE CASES	—	438	21·0	293	—	148	7·9	113

(Residue of children involved after absence cases where 'no reply' or 'ill' was recorded have been excluded)

(iv) *The Overall Pattern of Welfare Activities*

64. In Table 12 the welfare activities of the schools, E.W.Os. and school clinics have been brought together. Only those absence slip cases where a home visit was made are included.

65. It will be seen that the schools in the inner area were involved in some way—apart from absence cases—with nearly 10 per cent of their children whereas in the outer area it was six per cent. The E.W.Os. had dealings with 42 per cent of the children in the inner area and 24 per cent in the outer.

66. The accumulated total of incidents recorded was 2,175 for the inner area and 910 for the outer, an average of approximately 30 per week and 13 per week per complete primary school respectively. There is, of course, an element of double counting in this total as incidents recorded as referrals out by the school, E.W.O. or clinic to one of the others were referrals in to the receiving body. But the actual *net* number of children involved in all these incidents was 969, or 46 per cent of the children on the registers in the inner area and 483, or 26 per cent, of children in the outer. The net number of families was 736 and 421 respectively. There was no record obtained of the number of families with children at the schools but it seems safe to assume that the percentage of families concerned in the welfare incidents would be similar to that of the children.

67. In the analysis so far, many children have been included simply because an E.W.O. had made a home visit in respect of absence from school, although there was no reason to doubt parental capacity to provide properly for their care and education. If all cases are eliminated where the attendance officer either had no reply or found the child was ill, 438 children in 293 families are left in the inner area and 148 children in 113 families in the outer. It is these children and their families that must be regarded as the welfare cases. The children formed 21 per cent of the children on the registers in the inner area and 7·9 per cent of those in the outer area (14·9 per cent for the two areas combined).

(v) *The Extent to which Welfare Case Families were also known to Other Agencies*

68. The welfare cases described above were checked against the records of the Children's Department, Probation Service, N.S.P.C.C., Family Care Section of Public Health Department, Family Service Unit and the Personal Service Committee of the Council of Social Service to see whether the families were known to these agencies. It was found (Table 13) that almost a quarter of the families had been dealt with by one or more of these agencies during the Autumn term, 1964, and 30 per cent during the two years, 1963/64. Thirty per cent were on the Children's Department Central Index. The contribution of the Conference of Social Workers to the co-ordination of services—at least in terms of coverage—was, for this particular sample of families, negligible. Only one case in each area had been discussed despite the fact that, as Table 14 shows, 15 families were known to three or more of the six agencies checked and 120 were on the Children's Department Index of "children at risk".

Table 13

Families known to Other Agencies

	Inner Area	Outer Area	Total	Percentage of total No. of welfare families
Number of families involved in welfare cases	293	113	406	100
Families known to one or more of six other agencies checked (Sept.—Dec. 1964)	69	27	96	24
Families known to one or more of six other agencies checked (1963/64)	88	33	121	30
Families on Central Index of Children's Department	82	38	120	30
Families discussed by Conference of Social Workers	1	1	2	—

69. Table 14 analyses the families known to other agencies at any time during 1963/64. The highest number was known to the Children's Department with the Probation Service, N.S.P.C.C., Council of Social Service, Family Service Unit and Family Care Section following in that order. (The last two did not accept cases from the outer area.) The second part of Table 14 shows the number of agencies to which each family was known. As would be expected there was a greater number of families known to several agencies in the inner area than in the outer. Fifteen out of the 406 families checked—roughly four per cent—were known to three or more of the six agencies.

Table 14

The Other Agencies to which Welfare Case Families were Known
(covering the two years, 1963/64)

Agency	Inner Area (No. of Welfare Case Families =293)	Outer Area (No. of Welfare Case Families =113)	Total (Total of Welfare Case Families =406)
Children's Department	51	23	74
Probation Department	43	15	58
N.S.P.C.C.	19	11	30
F.S.U.	10	—	10
Family Care Section	1	—	1
Council of Social Service	18	5	23
No. of Families			
Known to one agency	48	17	65
Known to two agencies	30	11	41
Known to three agencies	6	5	11
Known to four agencies	4	—	4
Total known to other agencies	88	33	121

5. The Smallham Survey

70. During the Autumn term the schools were visited weekly to collect and sift information about the welfare cases. The head teachers provided the data but there were opportunities for talking to class teachers and in this way information was gained about their attitudes and their knowledge of the social services. Further information about the teachers' attitudes to the social services was collected by a questionnaire. Cases referred by the schools to other agencies were followed up to see what transpired. This entailed weekly visits to the Special Services Department and the list of welfare cases collected was checked against records of the Children's Department, N.S.P.C.C., Moral Welfare Association, Probation Department, School Psychological Service, School Medical Service, and the Co-ordinating Conference records for 1964 to see how far these agencies were involved in the same cases.

71. Out of the 2,667 children in the sample of schools, 84 were finally selected as welfare cases from those reported by head teachers because their behaviour, health or educational performance appeared to be unsatisfactory. The 84 cases fell roughly into five groups according to where the emphasis of the problem lay. (1) Attendance cases where failure to attend school gave rise to concern. (2) Behaviour cases such as stealing, unruly behaviour, bullying or withdrawal. (3) Medical cases involving failure to keep clinic appointments where there seemed to be no good reason and verminous conditions. (4) Education cases which included retarded development, queries about mental incapacity or the need for remedial teaching. (5) Social cases consisting of such matters as application for investigation of the need for free school meals or other forms of material help. Some children had several problems but the majority fitted naturally into one or other category and it is therefore helpful to analyse the cases on this basis, taking the groups in order according to the number of cases in each.

(i) Attendance Cases

72. A total of 25 children were recorded as attendance cases. Twenty-four were reported to the Special Services Department of the Education Authority and of these:

—Twenty children were dealt with by that department without calling in or consulting any other agency. (Eighteen were on the agreed list of irregular attenders).

—Nine children received only one visit; seven had an acceptable excuse, one child was reprimanded by the head teacher, and an official warning letter was sent to the parents of another.

—Eleven children received more than one visit (eight received two visits; two received three visits; one received four visits). Most of the absences were due to minor illnesses or holidays with parents but three children, who came from problem families, had no valid excuse.

73. In four cases the head teacher or special services officer consulted other departments. Of these:

—Two children were referred to the School Psychological Service. One was a non-urgent case. The other, an adopted boy, aged nine, who refused to go to school, presented a more complicated problem. The head teacher consulted the Special Services Department and the School Psychological Service, which referred the boy to the Child Guidance Clinic.

—Two children were referred to the Children's Department. In one case the head teacher telephoned the Special Services Department because a child was absent; the family had been evicted, its whereabouts were unknown, and the mother had attempted suicide. A telephone call to the Special Services Department from the Children's Department, which was supervising the family, revealed that they were in the homeless families unit. This information was passed to the school. In general, the children of this family attended school regularly. In the second case, the special services officer consulted the Children's Department about the family background of a girl aged eight. He already knew that the father had attempted to commit suicide and, subsequently the mother had suffered a near nervous breakdown. However, the family were unknown at the time to the Children's Department although it came to their attention later when problems of illegitimacy and rent arrears developed.

74. Head teachers discussed only two of the 25 attendance cases with parents. Children were often not discussed with the social service departments to which they or their families were already known. In 15 cases the child or his family was known to either the School Psychological Service or the Children's Department, and in nine cases the Special Services Department knew about this, but no discussion appeared to have taken place. Other agencies which knew about these families were the N.S.P.C.C. (two families), the Probation Service (one family), the Moral Welfare Association (two families). The co-ordinating committee had discussed two of the 25 children during the previous year. Only nine families of the 25 children noted for attendance problems appeared to be unknown to one or more agencies other than the school and Special Services Department.

(ii) *Behaviour Cases*

75. Nineteen children, including five who had been found stealing, were recorded in this category. They were referred as follows:

No. of Children	Department to which referred (*or person*)
16	School Psychological Service
5	Special Services Department
5	Children's Department
7	School Medical Service
4	Discussed with other head teachers
7	Discussed with parents.

Of the 16 cases referred to the School Psychological Service
—Ten were reported directly to the educational psychologist;
—Six were referred to remedial advisory teacher for testing; of these five were subsequently referred to the educational psychologist and, of these, three were recommended for remedial reading lessons.

76. Of the 15 cases referred to the educational psychologist, three had not been seen at the end of term (two were waiting for appointments and one had

failed to keep four appointments) and five were referred to the child guidance clinic. Of these five, two became in-patients and one an out-patient at the children's psychiatric hospital, whilst one transferred to the day school for maladjusted children.

77. In three cases only the School Psychological Service was not involved.

—One boy, aged seven, was found stealing. As it was a trifling amount the head teacher intended to ignore it but the health visitor reported it to the Children's Department, the boy was admitted to the hospital where day teaching is provided for maladjusted children;

—One boy, aged 11, was difficult and unruly at school. The head teacher and school medical officer suggested to the mother that she should take the boy to the Child Guidance Clinic. She refused. The health visitor reported that, in a material sense, the home was good. The child's behaviour improved and no further action was contemplated;

—One boy was difficult and unruly and refused to eat at school, he was living with his mother but his parents were separated and he had spent a period in an L.C.C. children's home. The Children's Department was supervising the case.

78. The following list shows the number of agencies dealing with the children in this category.

No. of children   *The number of services to which children were referred*

9   1. In seven cases this was School Psychological Service and in one case each, the Children's Department and the School Medical Service.

7   2. School Psychological Service was involved with six children, the School Medical Service with five, the Special Services Department with two, the Children's Department with one.

2   4. These were brothers aged seven and eight who were discovered wandering by the police three times in one month. Neither had caused trouble at school. They appeared before the juvenile court and were committed to the care of the local authority. The police, the Children's Department, the Special Services Department, and the School Psychological Service were all involved.

1   5. This was a girl aged five who caused concern in school by her generally disturbed behaviour and by running away. The police, the Children's Department, the Special Services Department, the School Psychological Service, and the School Medical Service were all concerned.

79. The families of 17 of the 19 children were already known to at least one agency and five families had been discussed by the co-ordinating committee during 1964. Thus the school was by no means the only organization to notice that some families had problems but class teachers were the first to notice the behaviour of 12 children. There were a number of cases where children or their families were known to agencies, other than those to which they were referred, without the latter apparently being aware that these other agencies were or had been in touch with the families.

(iii) *Medical Cases*

80. Eighteen children were classified as medical cases. Of these, 16 were attended by the School Health Service and in only two cases did this service consult anybody else, except perhaps the family doctor. The other two cases were dealt with by the Special Services Department on being approached directly by the parents. In one case it called in the School Health Service, the Children's Department, and the N.S.P.C.C. In the second case it called in the Housing Department.

81. The great majority of problems were not of a serious nature, being mainly to do with failure to keep appointments, listlessness in school for which some kind of special care or treatment was recommended, or advice on how to deal with a dirty head. Usually, after a little persuasion, the advice was observed.

82. One or two cases however, required more attention. In one case where a child continually lost or broke his spectacles and where appointments were disregarded a prosecution was being considered. Another child, aged five, appeared in school with face injuries. The head teacher called in the school nurse who telephoned to the Children's Department and the N.S.P.C.C. The general practitioner was also called and the child was sent to hospital; the child care officer visited the child's home. In another case a parent complained that the ill-health of her child was caused by poor housing conditions. At the suggestion of the general practitioner the school nurse had a lengthy talk with both parents and, after deciding that the mother was suffering from extreme anxiety, advised her to seek medical help; the general practitioner and psychiatrist visited the home and advised a move; the Housing Department offered the family another house. The head teacher was unaware of the child's illness although he was known to be backward in reading.

83. The extent to which children or their families in cases classified as medical were already known to other departments is shown by the following list.

No. of Families	Agency to which known
8	Children's Department. The school nurse knew of this in five cases but in only one case did she find it necessary to consult the child care officer.
3	N.S.P.C.C. The school nurse was only aware of this in one case when she telephoned the inspector.
2	Probation Service. The School Medical Service was unaware of this.
1	Moral Welfare Association.
2	Discussed during 1964 by co-ordinating committee.
1	School Psychological Service.

Nine of these families were apparently known only to the School Medical Service. Teachers were the first to notice ten of the medical cases. One child was reported by a play group supervisor. Other cases were noticed by the doctor, school nurse or parent.

(iv) *Education Cases*

84. There were 13 children in this category all of whom were referred to the School Psychological Service. Three children were referred directly to the

educational psychologist. Ten children were referred to remedial advisory teachers for testing, who, subsequently, referred eight of them to the educational psychologist. Out of the total of 11 children referred to the educational psychologist two did not keep their appointments; remedial teaching was recommended for three children and four were referred to the Child Guidance Clinic. The parents of one child referred to the clinic refused to co-operate. The parents of a second child would not agree to its being transferred to a training centre. One child became an out-patient at the children's hospital.

85. There were few instances of other departments being called in. Two or three cases were referred to the school medical officer, generally for hearing tests, and the school medical officer referred one child to the hospital for a thorough medical examination. In one case, where lack of progress at school was combined with very bad attendance, the head teacher contacted the Special Services Department. In two cases head teachers discussed the problem with parents although all parents were, of course, notified formally by the head teacher or through the School Medical Service if their children were recommended to visit the educational psychologist or the Child Guidance Clinic.

86. The extent to which children or their families were known to other agencies is shown below.

No. of children	Agency to which known
8	Children's Department
4	N.S.P.C.C.
1	Probation Service
1	Moral Welfare Association
1	Discussed by co-ordinating committee during 1964.

87. Only four cases were not already known to an agency other than the School Psychological Service which itself had already had dealings with five of these children or their families.

88. As was to be expected poor progress was largely a matter for the schools. Class teachers reported nine children and, during a survey of eight-year-old children, remedial teachers confirmed that the progress of four others was unsatisfactory. On only one occasion was a school approached by a parent who was worried about his child's progress.

(v) *Social Cases*

89. Social problems ranged from applications for financial and material help to difficulties about getting children to school. There were nine children in this category.

90. Eight children were referred to the Special Services Department either by the parents or by the school. Three were dealt with solely by this Department, three referred to one other department, and two referred to two other departments. The other services and persons involved were the Children's Department, the School Psychological Service, the school medical officer, the health visitor and the domestic help service. In the ninth case the School Medical Service was approached directly by a parent.

91. In one of the more serious social cases two children were found wandering by the police at 5 a.m. This was reported to the head teacher who

informed the Special Services Department which, in turn, contacted the Children's Department. A child care officer visited the family. A health visitor was already visiting the family frequently.

92. Most of the children came from homes where standards were poor. In seven out of the nine cases the families were known to the Children's Department and the special services officer who dealt with the cases was aware of this in four instances. The N.S.P.C.C. had been in touch with two families though the Inspector was not consulted by the Special Services Department. The School Psychological Service knew of three of the families and Probation one. The co-ordinating conference had discussed three of the families in 1964. Here again, it was clear that these were not new social problems discovered by the schools. The school noticed and brought forward two of the nine cases recorded during the term but both families were already well known to other agencies.

(vi) *The Overall Pattern of Welfare Cases*

93. In the sample of schools, three per cent of the children were recognized as presenting some sort of welfare problem. During the survey no instances were mentioned of problems which the schools had been able to deal with without the help of any outside department. A number of children were under observation in the schools but, apparently, this meant simply that they would be watched for a term or two before a final decision was taken to refer them to outside departments. There was no evidence of home visiting by any of the teachers. The School Psychological Service specifically discouraged children under the age of seven being referred for treatment, since it was held that any behavioural difficulties might well disappear as they grew older. Head teachers only discussed children's problems with parents on 13 occasions.

94. All the welfare cases, then, were referred to some outside department. A summary is given in Table 15. In nearly half the cases this was the Special Services Department, in 39 per cent some branch of the School Psychological Service and a similar proportion was referred to some part of the School Medical Service. The Children's Department was contacted in 11 cases, and the Housing Department and the N.S.P.C.C. were each brought in on one case. Two-thirds of the cases were dealt with solely by the department to which they were initially referred but 26 children were referred to, or discussed by more than one department. No cases were referred to the Probation Service, perhaps partly because of its agreement that the Children's Department should undertake voluntary supervision.

95. Nearly three-quarters of the children or their families were already known to outside welfare departments. Forty-eight were known to the Children's Department, 34 to the School Psychological Service, 12 to the N.S.P.C.C., five to the Probation Service and four to the Moral Welfare Association. During 1964, the co-ordinating conference had discussed 13 of the families included in the sample. Altogether 60 of the 84 children in the sample were already known to an outside welfare agency and in 17 instances the department to which the child was referred during the survey period knew about this. In only 24 or just over one-quarter of the cases reported by the schools was this the first time that the child or its family had been in touch with a welfare department apart from the Special Services Department.

Table 15—Summary of Welfare Cases

1 Type	2 No.	Person or Agency discovering case			Depts. or Persons Informed or Consulted						Cases referred to more than one Dept.	Depts. already knowing Child or Family						Children not already known to outside Dept.
		3 School	4 Parent	5 Other	6 SSD	7 SMS	8 SPS	9 Ch	10 Parent	11 Other	12	13 SPS	14 Ch	15 CC	16 NSPCC	17 Probation	18 MWA	19
Attendance	25	25	—	—	24	—	2	2	2	1	4	9	13	2	2	1	2	9
Behaviour	19	15	4	4	5	7	16	5	7	4	10	16	12	5	1	—	—	2
Medical	18	10	2	6	2	16	—	1	—	2	2	1	8	2	3	2	1	9
Education	13	13	1	4	1	5	13	—	4	—	5	5	8	1	4	1	1	3
Social	9	2	6	1	8	3	1	3	—	1	5	3	7	3	2	1	—	1
Totals	84	65	13	15	40	31	32	11	13	8	26	34	48	13	12	5	4	24

SSD—Special Services Department   CC—Co-ordinating Committee.
SMS—School Medical Service   MWA—Moral Welfare Association.
SPS—School Psychological Service.
Ch—Children's Department.
Columns 3, 4 and 5 do not necessarily add up to the figure in column 2, since several persons were sometimes aware of a particular case.

Table 16

Cases Not Previously Known to Outside Welfare Agency

| Type of Case | Person or agency first noticing case | | | Total |
	Teachers	Parents	School Medical Service	
Attendance	9	—	—	9
Behaviour	2	—	—	2
Medical	5	2	2	9
Education	3	—	—	3
Social	—	1	—	1
TOTAL	19	3	2	24

96. The great majority of children reported by the schools were noticed to be in difficulties by their teachers. In 13 cases parents made the first move, although in three instances the teacher was also aware of a child's difficulties; in four cases the police took action, although one child's behaviour had already attracted the teacher's attention; five children were first reported by the School Medical Service and one by a play group supervisor. Of the 24 cases not previously known to outside welfare departments, 19 were first noticed by teachers, three by parents and two by the School Medical Service (see Table 16).

6. *The Exshire Survey*

97. As in the other areas the sample of schools was visited regularly to gather from head teachers details of the children and the nature of problems arising. Contacts between the schools and welfare agencies were noted as were those between teaching staff and parents. Officers in local authority services and other agencies were contacted during the term for further information.

(i) *The Welfare Cases*

98. There were 220 welfare cases involving children who required attention which fell outside the immediate scope of primary education or the more straight-forward forms of medical treatment. The welfare cases were classified under a number of heads. (1) Backwardness, in which was included all cases of suspected retardation or mental incapacity which required investigation. (2) Attendance, covering cases of failure to attend school. (3) Material welfare, which covered applications or inquiries for free school dinners, help with clothing or shoes and other material needs. (4) Inadequate/ irregular families, in which the general welfare of children gave rise to concern because the family situation presented grave difficulties for the children or where one or other of the parents was absent. (5) Behaviour, which covered such things as stealing, bullying and other forms of overt aggression or marked withdrawal. (6) Medical, where parents were not apparently taking necessary steps to safeguard the health, sight, hearing, etc., of their children. The numbers of cases falling into each category are shown in Table 19.

99. Of the total sample of 3,083 children only seven per cent were ascertained as welfare cases and about a third of these were cases of backwardness only.

Some schools referred far more welfare cases than others (see Table 17). This reflected differences in the attitude of head teachers to referring problems outside the school to other agencies and their awareness of the existence of problems as well as in the actual incidence of problems.

Table 17

Distribution of Welfare Cases between Schools

Welfare cases as percentage of number enrolled in each school	Number of Schools
%	
0—4	4
5—9	10
10—14	4
15—19	1
20—24	2

100. Table 19 shows the extent to which different agencies were involved with the welfare cases. The weight falling on the School Psychological Service reflects the relatively high proportion of educational problems.

Table 18*

Services Involved

(Several agencies were often dealing with a single case)

Agency or Department	Number of cases (N=220)
Schools	215
School Psychological Service in Psychologists and peripatetic remedial teachers	102 ⎱ 115
Psychiatric social worker	13 ⎰
Education Welfare Office	60
Children's Department	39
Health Visitors	20
Red Cross or W.V.S.	7
N.S.P.C.C.	6

101. Table 20 shows that in 57 per cent of the 220 welfare cases backwardness was a matter of concern whereas poor attendance, behaviour problems and the need for material aid each accounted for only 17 per cent. Nearly half the children with problems came from families which were either inadequate in the sense that the children were neglected, or suffered emotional and social deprivation or disturbance, or irregular in that at least one parent was missing. Many of these children with problems would therefore seem to require intensive social treatment. Backwardness which occurs so frequently in the welfare cases is often looked upon as a problem in itself but may well be a symptom of environmental difficulties.

---

* For purposes of analysis cases are broken down here between agencies. As the Chief Education Officer pointed out, however, the working arrangements are such that divisions between agencies on individual cases often do not exist.

Table 19

Frequency of Problems

(Some children had more than one problem)

Problem	Number of children	Percentage of 220 welfare cases
Backwardness	126	57%
Attendance	39	17%
Behaviour	38	17%
Material Welfare	37	17%
Inadequate/irregular families	97	44%
Medical	8	4%
Other	4	2%
From families where more than one child had problems	82	36%

(ii) *The Incidence of Welfare Cases according to the Characteristics of Children, Their Families and Their Schools*

102. Table 20 shows the incidence of welfare problems according to sex. There were equal numbers of boys and girls in the whole school sample but boys presented welfare problems far more often than girls and boys had more than one problem more often than girls. Behaviour problems were commoner amongst boys than amongst girls. On the other hand there were more irregular attenders amongst the girls than amongst the boys. Backwardness was the most common problem amongst both sexes.

Table 20

Incidence of Problems amongst Boys and Girls

(Percentages refer to totals in boys' and girls' sub-groups)

Problem	Sex		Total (220)
	Boys (133)	Girls (87)	
Backwardness	90 (67%)	36 (41%)	126
Attendance	15 (11%)	24 (28%)	39
Behaviour	29 (22%)	9 (11%)	38
Material Welfare	19 (13%)	18 (20%)	37

103. In the following tables of welfare cases by age of children (Table 21) and father's occupation (Table 22) no accurate comparison was possible with the population of the county as a whole, since the 1961 census statistics were not available at the time. For example, it was not possible to assess properly whether any occupational grouping was over-or under-represented. It was found, however, that non-manual workers' families provided only 10 per cent of the children with problems and manual groups provided 77 per cent, with 13 per cent not known.

Table 21

Frequency of Problems according to Age

(Figures in brackets show distribution of welfare cases by age)

Problem				Age				Totals
	5 (25)	6 (27)	7 (22)	8 (44)	9 (53)	10 (37)	11 (12)	(220)
Backwardness	3	8	9	32	36	29	9	126
Behaviour	5	5	5	6	10	6	1	38
Attendance	7	9	5	6	7	3	2	39
Material Welfare	10	6	2	6	6	6	1	37

104. Backward children were fairly evenly distributed over the years eight to ten. The Table reflects a consistent coverage over the junior years on the part of psychologists and remedial teachers, with some attention already being paid to backward children in infant schools.

Table 22

Type of Problem According to Father's Occupation

	Non-Manual		Manual				
	Higher clerical and pro-fessional	Clerical routine	Manual skilled	Manual unskilled	Agri-cultural	Not known	Total
Total number of welfare cases	1	20	43	86	41	29	220
		10%		77%		13%	
Problem							
Backwardness	—	14	20	47	30	15	126
Attendance	—	2	9	22	4	2	39
Behaviour	—	6	5	19	4	4	38
Material Welfare	—	1	5	11	7	13	37

105. Amongst problem children whose fathers were in clerical and manual occupations backwardness was the most common difficulty, but amongst the children of agricultural workers material welfare in the sense of free meals and clothing relief were also important. Behaviour and attendance problems were most prominent amongst the children of unskilled workers and probably disproportionate to their percentage in the school population of the county.

Table 23

Type of Welfare Problem According to School Stream (if any)

	Stream					
	Un-streamed	A Stream	B Stream	C Stream	Remedial or Special Class	Total
Total number of welfare cases	61	8	18	23	110	220
Problem						
Attendance	17 (28%)	1 (12%)	5 (28%)	4 (22%)	12 (11%)	39
Behaviour	11 (18%)	1 (12%)	4 (22%)	5 (17%)	17 (15%)	38
Material Welfare	12 (20%)	6 (75%)	2 (11%)	6 (26%)	11 (10%)	37
Inadequate or irregular homes	32 (50%)	6 (75%)	13 (72%)	14 (61%)	32 (29%)	97

106. Table 23 showing the frequency of the more important problems apart from backwardness according to school stream indicates that among the B and C stream children there was a higher proportion of behaviour problems than amongst other children. Cases of backwardness have been excluded from this Table as the vast majority would obviously be found in remedial or special classes or in C streams.

Only 29 per cent of the children in remedial and special classes came from inadequate or irregular families, although these families accounted for 44 per cent of the welfare cases. Thus 71 per cent of the low achieving children must have come from the 56 per cent of normal homes in the sub-sample.

Table 24
Size of Family and Type of Problem

	Number of Children in Family									Not Known	Total
	1	2	3	4	5	6	7	8	9		
Number of welfare cases	19	39	46	38	28	20	6	4	17	3	220
		104				113					
Problem											
Backwardness	10	20	26	20	18	14	2	2	11	3	126
Attendance	1	4	11	4	8	5	2	—	4	—	39
Behaviour	3	9	4	5	4	7	2	1	1	2	38
Material welfare	—	3	5	9	4	6	3	—	7	—	37
Families where more than one child had problems	—	16	17	6	13	11	3	—	16	—	82

107. Table 24 relating size of family to type of problem shows that amongst children coming from large families the problem of backwardness accounted for a slightly larger proportion of welfare cases than amongst those coming from smaller families. Behaviour problems did not account for a dispro-portionately large proportion of the welfare cases in large families. As might be expected, however, children from families with four or more children needed more help in the form of free meals and other material aid.

Table 25
Backwardness and Behaviour Problems According to Number of Schools Attended

	Number of Schools attended						Total
	1	2	3	4	5	6	
Total Welfare Cases	118	76	20	4	1	1	220
Backwardness	71	42	9	3	—	1	126
Behaviour	16	13	8	1	—	—	38

108. Table 25 shows that backwardness was roughly as common amongst those who had attended only one school (60 per cent of the welfare cases) as amongst those who had attended two or more schools (54 per cent). On the other hand behaviour problems increased with the number of schools

attended. Of the children who attended three or more schools 34 per cent had behaviour problems compared with 13 per cent of those who attended only one school. Some Service families included in the survey seem to have had a number of moves as had families of some of the less well settled farm workers.

Table 26

Inadequate/Irregular Homes and Types of Problems

Problem	Cases from inadequate/irregular homes		Cases from 'normal' families		Total
	(a)	(a) as % (c)	(b)	(b) as % (c)	(c)
Backwardness	43	34	83	66	126
Attendance	17	44	22	56	39
Behaviour	25	65	13	35	38
Material Welfare	27	73	10	27	37
All welfare cases	97	44	123	56	220

109. The 97 children from inadequate and irregular families comprised 44 per cent of all the welfare cases. Yet, as Table 26 shows, these children contributed only 34 per cent of the total number of cases of backwardness and retardation—as well as only 29 per cent of those in remedial or special classes. (See Table 23.) But children from these same families contributed more than their quota of behaviour problems (i.e. they accounted for 65 per cent of all behaviour cases but for only 44 per cent of all the welfare cases). Their need for material welfare was also, as would be expected, disproportionate; 73 per cent of those needing free meals or other forms of aid came from inadequate/irregular families.

(iii) *Multi-Problem and Single Problem Children*

(a) *Multi-problem Children*

110. There were 98 children reported for two or more problems. They constituted 3·1 per cent of the children enrolled in the sample schools. Table 27 analyses the kinds of problems they presented and shows that 72 per cent came from inadequate or irregular families. Over half the multi-problem children were backward.

Table 27

The Relative Importance of the Different Types of Problem Affecting 'Multi-Problem' Children

Problem	Number	As percentage of 98 multi-problem children in sample %
Backwardness	56	57
Attendance	29	29
Behaviour	35	36
Material Welfare	30	30
Inadequate/irregular home	71	72
Medical	6	6

Table 28

Attention Received by ' Multi-Problem' Cases (98 children)

Attention Received	Number
Head teacher's contact with parents	61
Casework by Psychiatric Social Worker	9
Home visit by Educational Welfare Officer	34
Home visit by Psychologist	9
Home visit by Remedial Teacher	—
Remedial Teaching in School	54
Home visits by School Nurse/Health Visitor	2

111. Table 28 shows the attention given to the multi-problem children. Head teachers' contacts with parents were not always interviews in the head's office but sometimes they were made through a health visitor or welfare officer. Only nine children were being seen by the psychiatric social worker. Although all multi-problem children do not require intensive casework, this number of referrals is very small when it is remembered that 71 children came from inadequate or irregular homes and that 35 had behaviour problems. Psychologists visited only nine children, and remedial teachers none. Although officially home visiting is encouraged there is little time left after the primary tasks of remedial teaching and assessment have been fulfilled. Educational welfare officers visited the parents of 28 children, mostly to check for absence or to arrange relief and school meals. Social casework was not expected from the E.W.Os. for they had neither the training nor the time to do such work.

(b) *Single Problem Children*

112. One hundred and twenty-two children were reported as having only one problem (see Table 29) but they may have had other problems which went unrecognized by the workers who reported them because of pressure of time and the well known tendency for workers to view problems largely in terms of their own professional orientation. The parents of only 18 of the 122 single problem children had been contacted by head teachers.

Table 29

The Nature of Single Problems (122 children)

Problem	Number	%
Backwardness	70	57
Attendance	10	8
Behaviour	3	2
Material Welfare	7	6
Inadequate/Irregular home	26	22
Medical	2	2
Other	4	3
TOTAL	122	100

113. The most likely group to have the full implications of their problems incompletely dealt with would be the backward children who presented no other apparent problem. Most would be regarded by heads and remedial teachers as having educational problems only. Of the single problem children, 70 were backward, 68 of whom were having remedial teaching. Table 30 shows that there were no visits to the homes of single problem backward children by remedial teachers, welfare officers or psychologists. Only four of the backward children's parents were contacted by head teachers; the psychiatric social worker was engaged with only five of the families. Children who were very withdrawn or aggressive were generally given treatment but the academic performance of some of the more quiet inoffensive children might also have been improved by sustained casework with their parents. Some of these children give no trouble but are disturbed nevertheless and their difficulties are not so easily detected as those in children who exhibit more spectacular behaviour.

Table 30

Treatment of 70 'Single Problem' Backward Children

Attention given	Number of children
Remedial teaching	68
Head teachers' contact with parents	4
Social casework by Psychiatric Social Worker	5
Psychological treatment	2
Home visit by Remedial Teacher	—
Home visit by Psychologist	—
Home visit by Educational Welfare Officer	—

114. Only 11 single problem backward children received any attention other than remedial teaching. Moreover, not all the children who qualified for remedial teaching were receiving it. Testing of children in the eight plus and nine plus age ranges was undertaken in 1964 and showed that approximately 20 per cent had a reading quotient of less than 85. Not all of the 20 per cent would need remedial teaching. Six hundred and sixteen out of a total sample of 3,083 children would have a reading quotient of less than 85 and one might expect that head teachers would refer more than 126 for special attention.

(iv) *The Welfare Cases of the Various Departments*

(a) *Schools*

115. As expected, head teachers were aware of most of the welfare cases which emerged during the survey (215 out of 220 cases). As Table 31 shows, backwardness was their main concern (58 per cent of cases). Head teachers had contact with parents in over a third of the cases; in particular, with parents whose children were irregular attenders or had behaviour problems. However, not all such contacts were with the parents in person; some visits were made by health visitors or welfare officers on the head's behalf. It seems likely that some problems went unrecognized because, for example, only seven per cent of the children in the sample schools were reported to provide

welfare problems of any kind. But if reading difficulties can go undetected (see para. 114) it is likely that non-educational problems will be less often noted. Tables 31 and 32 are based on data supplied by head teachers. There is no provision for meticulous records of such cases to be kept in the schools, and hence these Tables show a little variance with other Tables originated in the various welfare departments.

Table 31

Problems of Concern to Head Teachers and Contacts with Parents
(Some children had more than one problem and therefore appear in more than one category)

	Welfare cases with which Headteachers concerned (215)	Headteachers' contacts with parents of 79 children (37% of welfare cases)	
Nature of Concern	Number of Children	Number of Children	(b) as % (a)
	(a)	(b)	
Backwardness	126	38	30
Attendance	39	28	71
Behaviour	38	23	61
Material Welfare	37	21	56
Inadequate home	73	38	52
Irregular home	48	21	43
Medical	37	18	49

Table 32

Action Taken by Head Teachers

Action taken by heads on 215 welfare cases	Number of Children
Remedial teaching (mostly referrals to Remedial Teacher)	113
Referrals to Psychologist	66
Referrals to Psychiatric Social Worker	5
Referral to Education Welfare Officer (absence, free meals)	39
Contact with parents	79
Action within school only	28
Discussions with Health Visitors (hygiene, health, deafness, sight)	30
Referral to Children's Dept.	3
Relief from W.V.S. and Red Cross	5

116. Table 32 shows how the head teachers dealt with the cases with which they were concerned. As was to be expected from the nature of the problems, referrals were mainly to remedial teachers, the School Psychological Service or Education Welfare Department.

(b) *The School Psychological Service*

117. Since this service was established in Exshire only in 1962 with very small staff it was decided to concentrate on primary school children during the early years to ensure the fullest possible coverage for the future.

Psychologists

118. Of 75 children who were referred to the educational psychologists (see Table 33) 66 were referred by the schools, eight by a psychiatrist, two by parents and one by a speech therapist. They were all referred for testing and diagnosis and, beyond this, most were of no further direct concern to the psychologists but were referred to remedial teachers. Psychologists were giving intensive treatment and teaching to a small number of the more serious and complicated cases of backwardness and behaviour.

Table 33

Problems of Concern to Psychologists (75 children)

Problem	Number of Children
Backwardness	50
Attendance	6
Behaviour (including five cases of cruelty)	19
Inadequate home	11
Medical	8

Table 34

Action taken by Psychologists (75 children)
(Some children appear under more than one heading)

Action by Psychologists	Number of Children
Remedial teaching by Psychologist	9
Allocation to special or E.S.N. class	7
Referral to Peripatetic (remedial) Teachers	41
Psychological treatment and continuing diagnosis	12
Referral to Psychiatric Social Worker	7
Home visit by Psychologist	9
Other contact with parents	1
Referral to Children's Dept.	3
Referral to Health Dept.	5
Relief from Red Cross or W.V.S.	2

119. Most problems referred to the School Psychological Service were of an educational nature and Table 34 shows the action taken. It was the official policy to bring parents into the treatment process but, of 75 cases, only seven were referred to the psychiatric social worker and the psychologists met only 10 parents. It is possible that more children's difficulties could be mitigated if

there could be greater consultation between home and educational services, so that some integration of these two major segments of the child's world might be achieved. At the time of the survey this could be attempted only in the most extreme cases.

Psychiatric Social Worker

120. As Table 35 shows only 13 of the 220 welfare cases in the sample were referred to the one psychiatric social worker employed. Several of the children were siblings from one family.

Table 35

The Psychiatric Social Worker: Problems of the 13 Children Referred and Action Taken

(Some children appear in more than one classification)

Problem	Number of Children
Backwardness	8
Attendance	1
Behaviour	7
Inadequate/Irregular home	4
Medical	2
ACTION TAKEN	
Casework with family	13
Referral to Psychologist	1
Referral to Remedial Teacher	1
Relief from Red Cross or W.V.S.	2

Although eight children were backward this was probably incidental to the primary reasons for referral which were likely to be behaviour, poverty and gross parental inadequacy. Table 35 shows that the psychiatric social worker was largely concerned with multi-problem children; the 13 cases between them had 23 problems. Most of the psychiatric social worker's cases were referred by the psychologists, peripatetic teachers or schools, although she sometimes worked with the Children's Department on cases where there was some emotional disturbance. The small proportion of welfare cases referred to the psychiatric social worker suggests that psychologists, peripatetic teachers and head teachers viewed children's problems largely in terms of school and the education of the child, rather than of "the whole child" in his global setting. It seemed that psychiatric social workers, as members of the School Psychological Service, were often regarded as workers who specialized in "abnormal" children. Thus many "normal" children who may be experiencing marked social difficulties may not be referred to them. It appeared to the researcher that generically trained social workers with a sound orientation in education and child development might be more appropriate for the task of treating "normal" children having difficulties and would more often attract direct referrals from head teachers. These workers could deal with problems that were not of direct concern to educational psychologists and would relieve educational welfare officers of an unreasonable load for which few have the time or qualifications to deal.

Peripatetic Remedial Teachers

121. All the 89 children dealt with by these teachers were backward and 12, in addition, presented behaviour problems. Although remedial teachers were officially encouraged to make home visits and to have other contacts with parents, none was reported (see Table 36). No doubt large case-loads were the reason for this, and it is doubtful whether the remedial teachers' orientation and training would fit them for the more complicated and continual contacts with the children's families. It was recognized that case-loads for remedial work alone at the time of the survey were too large and shortly afterwards three more peripatetic teachers were recruited.

Table 36

The Action taken by Peripatetic Teachers (89 children)

Action taken	Number of Children
Remedial teaching in school	86
Remedial teaching in clinic	3
Referred to Psychologist	6
Referred to Psychiatric Social Worker	4
Home visits	—
Other contact with parents	—

Most remedial teaching took place in schools but, as the new clinics are developed, more will probably be done in them. This will provide greater opportunities for parents to be interviewed when they bring their children. Any problems which were seen to fall outside the remedial teachers' primary function were usually reported to the psychologist, psychiatric social worker or child care officer and home visits are a feature of their work.

Education Welfare Officers

122. The work of the E.W.Os. took them mostly to secondary modern schools. They devoted only about ten per cent of their time to primary school children and a negligible amount of time to grammar school pupils. Amongst the study sample of 3,083 children, E.W.Os. investigated 39 cases of irregular attendance, 15 of which required some simple form of welfare such as school meals or clothing relief, four were referred to the children's officer and two to the educational psychologist.

123. School meals and clothing relief were often arranged by direct contact between the head teachers and the administrative officers of the Education Welfare Department. E.W.Os. therefore spent most of their time on attendance inquiries but, as their referrals to the children's officer and psychologist indicate, they were in a key position to notice difficulties and inadequacies in pupils' homes. Reports were always made to head teachers and when this had been done the officers' function was apparently fulfilled.

124. Secondary modern school children required three times as many visits from E.W.Os. as did primary school children, although there were only about 8,000 children in secondary schools compared with 11,611 in primary schools. This means that secondary modern schools have an absentee rate of over

four times that of the primary schools. There are, however, difficulties over transport in some country districts where special school buses collect secondary school children. If a child misses the school bus he has no other way of getting to school apart from private car.

125. Work with children and parents at the primary school stage to bridge the gap between home and school is of the utmost importance and more promising than attempted rescue operation at the secondary modern level by which time the motivations of absenteeism and early leaving have already developed and probably become established.

(d) *School Nurse/Health Visitors*

126. Health visitors who in Exshire also undertake school nursing duties were not often concerned directly with primary school children. Routine visits have been abandoned since there has been so much improvement in public health. During the survey, health visitors noted only eight primary school children with whom they were directly concerned (for details see Table 37) although head teachers claimed to have consulted them about 37. Health visitors work closely with general practitioners rather than with schools, and there is probably some overlap of school cases and general practitioner cases.

Table 37

Problems dealt with by Health Visitors (eight children)

Nature of concern	Number of Children
Emergency (mother away, children in need of care)	3
Inadequate home, dirtiness, neglect, etc.	6
School behaviour	7
Action taken by health visitors	
Arrange housekeeper help	2
Advise mother	8
Contact Children's Officer re hostel accommodation	2

Few cases of head infestation were noted. The behaviour cases were reported by a small number of head teachers who saw the health visitor as a general social worker. Health visitors did, in fact, play a kind of social worker rôle and had influence with mothers, though this centred chiefly around the health of pre-school children.

(e) *The Children's Department*

127. The Children's Department was primarily geared to the care of children in emergencies and other difficulties, and its connections with schools were incidental to the care of children. Tables 38 and 39 show the frequencies of problems and the action taken; 21 of the 39 cases were emergencies resulting from the mother's desertion or admission to hospital. The Children's Department had many contacts with other agencies. Ten children with difficult and complex problems were discussed with head teachers to acquaint heads with the children's general situation where this was considered to be in the interests of the children.

Table 38

Children's Department Cases (39 children)

Problem	Number of Children
Emergency (mother in hospital or left family)	21
Inadequacy of home (dirt, neglect)	6
Irregular home (parent missing, step-parent, etc.)	6
Housing problem	4
Backwardness	—
Behaviour	6
Attendance	4
Cruelty	3
Medical	1

Cases referred by: Police (8).
                      Other Social Worker (7).
                      Health Visitor or Doctor (6).
                      Parents, Relatives (14).
                      Welfare Officer (4).

Table 39

Action taken by Children's Department (39 children)

Action taken	Number of Children
Taken into care	24
Casework	25
Placed in home	12
Foster placement	15
Referral to Psychologist, P.S.W. (or consultation)	4
Consultation with School Teacher	10
Consultation with Probation Officer	7
Consultant with/referral to Psychiatrist	5
Referred to Health Visitor	8
Housing Department negotiations	4
Tracing parents	9
Referred to N.S.P.C.C.	6
Fit Person Orders	2

(f) N.S.P.C.C. and Other Voluntary Agencies

128. The N.S.P.C.C. was dealing with five cases from three families in the 21 sample schools; four were cases of neglect following desertion by parents and one was a case of violence. Most referrals to the Inspector came from the general public but most cases were already known to the Probation Service, the Police, the National Assistance Board or the Children's Department.

129. The only other voluntary organizations known to help primary school children in Exshire were the Red Cross (which over the whole County provided transport for five children) and the W.V.S. (which over the whole County provided clothing for 96 primary school children).

(v) *Co-ordination between Departments and Agencies*

130. There was much evidence of efforts to secure co-ordination. Workers met regularly for joint discussions in the School Psychological Service about the most serious cases. In addition formal and informal exchange took place daily between workers of the various departments. Table 41 shows that 67 of the 220 welfare cases included in the survey were the subject of active consultation between two or more agencies. Most would be children with severe problems. Only two of the primary school children's families were discussed at Families at Risk meetings but it should be remembered that the focus at these meetings was mostly on the total family situation and primary school children and their problems were by no means the main issue.

Table 40

The Co-ordination of the Social Services (220 children)

Degree of co-ordination	Number of Children
Some evidence of agency's knowledge of role of other agencies in case, e.g. cross referral	143
Active consultation between agencies	67
Case discussed at Families at Risk meetings	2
Only one agency concerned	8

7. Teaching Staff and the Social Services

131. The rôles of head teachers and of class teachers are rather different. The class teacher is in the better position to notice any problems of behaviour or learning but dealings with outside agencies on welfare matters are normally conducted by head teachers. The Education Department and other agencies get in touch with head teachers and it is the head teacher's responsibility to decide whether a child should be referred to an outside agency.

Head Teachers

132. *Largeborough.* The 12 head teachers in the sample schools all said that during their training they had no separate course on the social services but remembered references in hygiene or other lectures to clinics, special schools and children's homes. As students they had no discussion of the rôle of teachers in relation to the social services and their only contacts with these services were odd visits to special schools, clinics and children's homes. They had been forced to pick up knowledge of the different services as they went along, mostly since appointment to headships, and some were clearly perplexed at the number and variety of statutory and voluntary services. All relied on picking up knowledge from the E.W.Os., school medical officers and nurses. A suggestion that newly appointed head teachers and their deputies should be invited to attend a course on the administrative and welfare responsibilities of head teachers received unanimous support from head teachers. All the heads had to acquire information about individual pupils (apart from formal reports on educational attainment) in their personal contacts with class teachers. The welfare problems and social background of individual children were never discussed at staff meetings; all the schools

relied on informal communication between the head and other teachers. The head teachers were asked what they considered to be the welfare problem causing them the greatest concern and, as Table 41 shows, family failure predominated.

Table 41

Welfare Problem Causing the Greatest Concern to Largeborough Head Teachers

(Some of the 12 head teachers named more than one problem)

Problem	Number of head teachers mentioning each category
Lack of co-operation between parents and school	1
Family failure*	10
Problem children (stealing, difficult behaviour in school)	3
Lack of information about children in care of local authority	2

* Including ' problem families ', ' broken homes ', ' matrimonial problems ', ' mental and physical neglect of children ', ' mental cruelty ', and ' mothers out working '.

133. *Exshire.* Attitudes amongst head teachers to the social services varied widely. A very small minority were out-spokenly unfavourable to them, others seemed sceptical or unaware of problems; one maintained that there were no welfare problems amongst his 300 pupils in spite of the fact that 30 were in a special class for backward children. Other heads were well aware of problems, but some seemed hesitant to call in other agencies saying cases should be referred only if treatment within the school failed. In Exshire, as in many rural districts, most heads of small schools are also class teachers.

Teachers

134. Questionnaires circulated to teachers in the sample schools, and interviews with teachers, showed that their training contained little systematic teaching or discussion about the welfare services, but some had clearly received more instruction in this subject than had the head teachers in Largeborough. Some specific instruction during training was mentioned by just over half the teachers in Smallham, less than a half in Largeborough, and about a quarter of those in Exshire. The courses appeared to have been concentrated largely on school health services and provisions for handicapped children. Some of the younger teachers had studied the question of when a child should be referred to some outside agency.

135. In all three areas teachers had little contact with outside agencies. For information about the social background of their children they relied very much on their colleagues within the schools (school records were usually very meagre or non-existent in this respect) and what they could glean from parents, children, and the school nurse. Most teachers said they would welcome closer contact with social workers. In both Largeborough and Smallham opinion was sought and found to be strongly against teachers

visiting the homes of children and even those in favour had reservations such as "limiting it to special cases and problems". When asked which welfare problems were causing them the most concern, most of the teachers in Exshire replied "broken homes" with a smaller number specifying "health and hygiene". In the inner area of Largeborough, adverse home conditions, inadequate care of children, working mothers and maladjusted and backward children were frequently mentioned. But in the outer area there were no serious welfare problems bothering the teachers. Similarly in Smallham most of the teachers said that the problems connected with their pupils causing them most anxiety were conditions within the school such as old buildings, large numbers in classes and overcrowded time-tables.

IV. CONCLUSIONS

136. Table 42 shows how the incidence of welfare cases varied between the three areas. The figures are affected by differences between the surveys in the precise interpretation of the term "welfare case" and in the methods by which data were collected and analysed but there was sufficient similarity to justify comparisons.

Table 42

The Incidence of Welfare Cases (Autumn, 1964)

Area	Number of welfare cases (a)	Number of children in school sample (b)	(a) as % (b)
Largeborough	586	3,946	14·9
Inner Area	438	2,083	21·0
Outer Area	148	1,863	7·9
Smallham	84	2,667	3·2
Exshire	220	3,083	7·1

137. In Smallham, welfare cases formed only 3·2 per cent of the children in the selected schools as compared with 7·1 per cent in Exshire and 14·9 per cent in Largeborough. In the outer area of Largeborough, however, the incidence of welfare cases was only just over a third of that in the inner area and close to that in Exshire. Since pupils in the outer area schools lived predominantly in houses on corporation estates where families from inner areas had been rehoused, this marked difference in the incidence of welfare cases appears to be a pertinent reflection on the influence of housing conditions and general environment. Before definite conclusions could be drawn a careful study of the selection process and the social character of the population moved to the new estate would have to be made. In Exshire the School Psychological Service had made a particular effort to tackle the problem of backwardness with the result that 32 per cent of the children reported as being welfare cases were cases of educational backwardness: the incidence of other types of problem was quite low.

138. In each area a substantial proportion of the welfare cases consisted of children who were either already known to the welfare agencies or whose

families had, on some previous occasion, required the attention of these agencies. In Smallham two-thirds of the children in the sample, or their families, were already known to those outside welfare departments contacted by the researchers, compared with nearly one-third in Largeborough. Had the School Psychological Service been included as one of the outside bodies for this purpose in Largeborough, as it was in Smallham, there is no doubt that the percentage known to outside bodies would have been higher. This confirms the findings of other inquiries that a relatively small group of families is responsible for the hard core of multiple social problems. It means that many families with problems are likely to come to the notice of, and be dealt with, first by agencies outside the schools, but it still leaves the primary schools with an important rôle in co-operation with other social services in preventive work.

139. When head teachers were doubtful as to what to do about children who were causing concern they found the E.W.Os. a useful first line of approach but none of the E.W.Os. had a social work training and few had the time for intensive social work. The character of their work varied according to the organization of particular departments. In Largeborough the department was highly centralized and the E.W.Os. carried their heavy loads of routine attendance and census work in relative isolation from workers in other departments, cases being referred to other departments through senior officers. In Smallham and Exshire, on the other hand, the E.W.Os. had more time to give some closer attention to a small number of the more complex cases since visits to ordinary cases of absenteeism had been reduced to a minimum; in addition, they had frequent informal contacts with members of other departments. The place of E.W.Os. in the social welfare services requires close attention.

140. The task of co-ordinating the different services was much greater in Largeborough than in Smallham and Exshire, partly because of Largeborough's larger population and consequently greater number of officers but also because of the highly specialized nature of some of its services. Nevertheless even in Smallham where there was close proximity between the offices of various departments and more contact between officers at field work level officers were sometimes unaware that other departments had already been concerned with particular cases and might well have useful information about them. Even when they knew of another department's interest there was sometimes no consultation although this may have been because the immediate problems were quite straightforward and it was not thought necessary to exchange information. In Exshire there was evidence of quite effective co-ordination and of considerable consultation; only eight of the 220 welfare cases were dealt with quite independently by a single agency without consultation or any exchange of information. Nevertheless even in that area educational problems tended to be treated in isolation. Educational psychologists had contact with the parents of only about a seventh of the children in the sample referred to them and remedial teachers recorded no contact with any of the parents in the sample. In Largeborough no analysis was made of the work of the School Psychological Service but with the severe shortage of psychiatric social workers and long waiting lists for child guidance clinics it appeared that problems of backwardness and retardation were largely dealt with in an

educational setting. Closer links between School Psychological Services and the social workers with knowledge of the home and school situation and time to undertake casework with the family seems to be needed for the sake of the children.

141. As far as co-ordination by formal committees was concerned, a negligible number of the families involved in welfare cases recorded during the surveys had been discussed by the Conference of Social Workers in Largeborough or the Families at Risk Committee in Exshire. It must be remembered that these meetings focused on the total family situation, and the time available allowed only the most serious and immediately critical cases to be considered. In Smallham the proportion of families which had been discussed by the Co-ordinating Conference was considerably larger.

142. In all three areas there was a shortage of social workers, especially of psychiatric social workers, which resulted in staff being below establishment in many cases. Moreover, the most acute shortages were in Largeborough where social problems were most severe. The effects on primary school children of this shortage are particularly important since the early diagnosis and treatment of problems may well prevent more serious trouble at a later stage. Comparing the inner area of Largeborough with the outer, not only were welfare cases nearly three times as numerous but, during the term in which the survey was carried out, the staff/pupil ratio and the number of graduate teachers was lower, whilst the turnover of teaching staff and of pupils and the number of unqualified teachers were higher.

143. Head teachers were responsible for deciding what to do about welfare cases, although class teachers were often the first to notice a child's problems. The teachers' training, however, included virtually no systematic instruction about the social services. Teaching staff, particularly head teachers whose experience had made them realize their inadequate knowledge, said they would welcome more information. School records about the social background of children were generally either meagre or non-existent. There was no guarantee that a teacher wanting to know about the home background of a child in order to be able to meet more adequately that child's needs would know where to find an objective, skilled assessment of the situation.

144. Ideally teachers should know: (a) the importance of the social background of the children they are teaching, (b) where information about this background could be readily obtained, and (c) the precise agency to which any welfare case should be referred. They would want each case to be dealt with promptly and expect information about treatment and disposal to be passed on to them without delay. This involves a ready flow of communication between the social services and schools and within the schools. These are the ends to which collaboration between social services and schools should be directed. They would require social workers to have a proper understanding of the schools and as great an understanding of child development as the teachers. Without that it will be difficult for teachers and social workers to work effectively together.

APPENDIX 9

THE MANCHESTER SURVEY:

FOREWORD

1. The survey contained in this appendix was made by a team from the School of Education, University of Manchester directed by Professor Stephen Wiseman, and is concerned with ten-year-old children in the Manchester area.

2. The note contained in the rest of this Foreword has been written jointly by the authors of this survey and of Appendix 4.

3. The attentive reader is bound to notice some striking differences between the tables of Appendix 4 and those of Appendix 9. For example, in Table 8 of the latter "Size of Class" stands out. In Table 4 of the former it does not appear at all. Since this can hardly mean that "Size of Class" is peculiarly important in Manchester some other explanation must be sought.

4. In fact the explanation is to be found in the difference between the methods used for summarising the evidence. In both cases the evidence before it is summarised consists of a large number of correlation coefficients. Thus for the analyses between schools in Appendix 4 there were 104 variables and six age and sex groups, giving 33,072 coefficients in all. For the Manchester evidence there were 87 variables, giving 3,741 coefficients. These numbers remind us of the bishops in the Gondoliers, who were in point of fact too many. They must be reduced to put the evidence into a more comprehensible form.

5. In both cases the reduction is made by replacing the original variables by composite variables which are weighted sums of the originals. But different principles are used to obtain the weights. In the factor analysis used to reduce the Manchester data the principle is to choose the weights so that the 87 original variables, which are correlated, are replaced by 87 composites which are not. At first sight this seems little improvement, but the advance lies in the fact that nearly all the variation is concentrated in the first six composites (and about three-quarters of it in the first one) so that the rest may reasonably be discarded as unimportant. This is not quite the whole story. There is in fact an infinite number of sets of uncorrelated composites that contain the same information as the original variables, so that further principles of choice are needed. After the factor analysis has been done, the factors are "rotated" by the computer so as to achieve what is known as "simple structure": i.e. a set which maximizes the number of zero or near-zero loadings in each factor. This produces a simplification of the 87 composites, so that each one now covers only a proportion of the original variables; its effect is concentrated over only part of the total field. It so happens in this analysis that nearly three-quarters of the total variation in the educational tests is concentrated in the first factor. A consequence of this is that the weights (or loadings) of the other variables in the first composite (or factor) are roughly proportional to, but rather greater than, the average correlations of these variables with the educa-

M

tional tests, as may be seen by comparing Table 3 with Table 8 in Appendix 9. For example, for "Size of Class" the average correlation is ·32, and the loading is ·36.

6. In regression analysis, which was used to summarise the evidence from the English sample, the principle is to select one variable as the criterion and reduce the others to a single composite, namely that composite which has the highest correlation with the criterion. In this process, which is described at some length in Section 4 of Appendix 3, the weights (regression coefficients) are not proportional to the simple correlations, because allowance is made for the extent to which the variables in the composite are correlated among themselves. A variable that has a substantial correlation with the criterion may have a negligibly small partial correlation, when the other variables are held constant, and if so it will have no weight in the composite. Because of this only about a dozen of the original 104 appeared in the composite for each age and sex group.

7. Each mode of analysis brings out important facts. For example in the factor analysis the substantial weight given in the first factor to "Average Size of Class" brings out the fact that on the whole schools with large classes make somewhat higher scores in the tests than those with smaller classes. But "Average Size of Class" has no weight in the regression composite for any age and sex group. This brings out the fact that when the other variables are held constant it is no longer the case that schools with large classes make higher scores in the tests. This applies generally.

8. There are three stages in inquiries of this kind. First the evidence must be collected. Then it must be reduced to a more manageable form. Finally it must be interpreted. The second stage consists first of the choice of the principles to be used for the reduction, and secondly of straightforward though lengthy computations. The choice of the principles for the reduction is a matter of judgement. This choice determines the nature of the computations, which then automatically give the results. The interpretation of the results is again a matter of judgement.

9. Association, though necessary, is not sufficient evidence of causality. For example, a factor loading—or a first order correlation coefficient—showing a positive relationship between size of class and school attainment does not justify the corollary that increasing class size will improve scholastic ability. A similar association with number of books in the home does not mean that if one made a present of a dozen books to a family, this would improve the child's school work. Winning the pools, and thus dramatically raising the family income, is unlikely to have any advantageous educational effects on the children, despite the correlation between income level and attainment. If the school nurse disinfests the hair of one or two children, this is irrelevant to their results on the next arithmetic test, in spite of the Manchester results on "cleanliness".

10. What both analyses show is that adverse factors tend to go together; and that of these adverse factors, the most important are those concerned with parental attitude (encouragement, interest and aspiration) which are clearly more important than social class, occupation or income. School variables are further down the list, and here the adverse factors—like those in the home—hang together, as might be expected.

11. It is when the interested reader looks at individual variables (such as size of class, or streaming) hoping to find support for his own beliefs or ammunition against his opponent, that the greatest care must be exercised in interpretation, and where our warnings against the assumption of causality are most needed. An appropriate approach here is the Bayesian one: to accept that the weight of the evidence needed depends upon the nature of the conclusion. If a conclusion is no more than a quantification of a general proposition acceptable to the common sense of those who know something about the matter in hand comparatively little weight is needed to support the quantification. If, on the other hand, any result appears to fly in the face of such common sense then very heavy weight is needed. Thus a result that 30 per cent of the school achievement was owing to (caused by) their parents' attitudes, and 20 per cent to their parents' material circumstances, is a mere quantification of the view, which most sensible men would accept, that part must be owing to the one and part to the other. On the other hand, a result that, other things being equal, the achievement would be improved (a statement of causality) by giving the teachers more pupils to cope with is contrary to the common sense of sensible men, and therefore needs very heavy weight and much more supporting evidence before such a jump from association to causality can be made. One naturally looks to alternative explanations of the association. Bayes' point that the posterior probability is the product of the prior probability and the likelihood is a most important one, particularly since readers of educational research are often prone to seize on isolated results and either accept them as evidence of propositions that are very hard to believe, or alternatively as evidence that the whole effort is completely worthless.

The Manchester Survey

by Stephen Wiseman[1]

12. Our brief for this inquiry was to investigate the relationship between the educational attainment of primary school children and environmental factors, with particular reference to the environment within the school. The design of the experiment was controlled by two major considerations: (a) the experience gained in our secondary school surveys in Manchester and Salford in 1951 and 1957[2], and (b) the necessity for a strict timetable, with the autumn of 1965 as a deadline for the completed Report. This limitation in time affected both the size of the sample, and the type of criterion measure adopted. It was clear that in the time available it would be impossible to construct specially designed measures for our purpose, and we had to rely on existing measures—measures which must, of course, be directly comparable, school with school. We de-

[1] I must acknowledge my indebtedness to Professor Frank Warburton, who was concerned with the project from the start; to Mr. Tom Derrick, the Research Officer, who was responsible for collecting the data; to Miss Anne Sutherland and Mr. Brian Start, who monitored the computer work; and to the officers of the Manchester L.E.A., in particular Mr. Elliot, the Chief Education Officer, and Dr. Laybourne, his deputy, for their willing and whole-hearted co-operation. But most of all my gratitude must go to the head teachers and teachers in the sampled schools for their interest, their patience and their invaluable help. Without their full support this inquiry would have been impossible.
[2] Reported in Wiseman, 1964, *Education and Environment*, Manchester University Press.

cided to study ten year old children, because these children had received the
full impact of primary school education. The ten year olds in 1964 had taken
standardised tests at 7+, 8+, 9+ and 10+, and the results of these tests were
accepted as our criterion measures. There were 12 such measures:

7+	MH Picture Intelligence
	NFER Mechanical Arithmetic
8+	NFER Sentence Reading
	Manchester Mechanical Arithmetic
	Manchester Problem Arithmetic
9+	MH Junior Reasoning
	MH Junior English
10+	MH Verbal Reasoning
	MH English
	MH Mathematics I
	MH Mathematics II
	Manchester Composition

13. The limitations of criterion measures of this kind must be stressed. They
consist of tests of the tool subjects only, and, with the exception of composition, they are all objective tests. Such measures are a necessary *part* of any
criterion of primary school attainment, but they are far from giving a balanced
picture. No account is taken of the many other activities which go on in the
average primary school, the work in art and craft, in music, in science and
geography and history, and in the many other pursuits which can often not be
classified under the traditional "subject" labels, but which, nevertheless, are
of very great significance educationally. Our choice of criterion measures must
not be taken to indicate a belief that the 3 R's are all that matter, nor should
the limitations of our tests be forgotten in interpreting the results of our
inquiry.

14. Our experience in earlier researches, and the fact that we were particularly interested in the environment within the school, led us to plan the
research as a *school based* one, with the schools as the units. We were anxious,
however, to support this main inquiry with a more intensive study of individual children, and we were glad to discover that we could draw on the services
of the Social Survey to interview the parents of such a sub-sample. Our
inquiry, therefore—and this Report—covers first, the main research comparing schools, and second, a sub-sample research comparing pupils.

Sample of Schools

15. In 1964 there were 176 primary schools in Manchester with children of
10+. Ninety-two of these were county schools, 40 Church of England, 43
Roman Catholic and one Jewish. It was decided to take a 25 per cent sample
of these schools, stratified by school type. The two other factors which it was
desirable to control in the sample were socio-economic level and school size.
Our previous surveys had given us a good deal of information about the distribution of social factors over the city, and it seemed that these could best be
controlled by stratifying the sample on a geographical basis. The central area
of the city contains the blackest region from the point of view of housing,
crime, disease and poverty. The northern extremity—hardly to be called

suburban, since in this direction there is no break in the conurbation—shows a significant improvement over the central area in all social variables, while the southern wards (Didsbury, Withington and Burnage, etc.) contain the "best" areas within the city boundary. These three divisions of the city could well form the basis of a socio-economic stratification. There remained the extreme southern section formed by the Wythenshawe wards of Northenden, Baguley, Benchill and Woodhouse Park. Our 1951 and 1957 results showed this area to be "white" on such variables as *J-index*, *Persons per acre* and *Death-rate*, but as "black" as Moss Side on *Birth-rate*, *Committals to Care*, *Cruelty and Neglect*, and *Children on Probation*. A high proportion of residents are from slum clearance areas, and the region is clearly an atypical one and deserving of separation from the rest of the city. As a result of considerations such as this, we stratified geographically as follows:

7 Northern wards

18 Central wards

9 Southern wards

4 Wythenshawe wards

When the 176 primary schools are classified under school type and social district the picture is as shown in Table 1:

Table I

All Manchester Primary Schools

	County	C.E.	R.C.	Other	Total
Northern	18	5	8	1	32
Central	42	28	22	—	92
Southern	18	6	8	—	32
Wythenshawe	14	1	5	—	20
TOTAL	92	40	43	1	176

16. In order to control *size of school* we decided to draw a 50 per cent sample of schools in the first instance, to arrange the schools within each cell in the table in order of size, and to take alternate schools for final 25 per cent sample. This yielded the final sample of 44 schools, shown in Table II, which provide about 2,000 ten-year-old children:

Table II

Sample of Tested Schools

	County	C.E.	R.C.	Total
Northern	5	1	2	8
Central	10	7	6	23
Southern	5	1	2	8
Wythenshawe	4	—	1	5
TOTAL	24	9	11	44

17. Three additional schools were chosen, one County, one C.E. and one R.C., to form pilot schools for Mr. Derrick to visit first, to try out his interviewing and recording methods before starting on the sample proper.

Social Survey Sub-Sample

18. Interview load limited the size of the sub-sample of children whose parents were to be interviewed by the Social Survey to 200: i.e. a one-tenth sample. Two plans were discussed:

(a) a one-tenth sample of all the 2,300 children in the main sample,

(b) a sample of 230 children taken from 10 schools of the 44 in the sample.

Plan (a) covered all the schools, but at the cost of providing, on average, only five pupils per school, and entailing a wider geographical spread for the social survey interviewers. Plan (b) concentrated the interviews, but inadequately covered the schools. And since our inquiry was to be, in the main, school based, this was a serious disadvantage. Finally, and with some degree of hesitation, we settled on the following design:

(a) a randomly selected 50 per cent sample of the 44 schools, stratified as in Table II,

(b) 10 children, randomly selected from each of the 22 schools, irrespective of school size.

I THE SCHOOLS ANALYSIS

Criterion measures

19. Our previous surveys of secondary schools were all school-based, and we had then discovered the value of employing measures of attainment which covered intensity of "backwardness" and "brightness" as well as the average level of ability in a school. As I have said elsewhere, "this gives a richer and more meaningful result than using a single average score. Certainly from the teacher's point of view these two percentages mean much more than an average score, since they demonstrate so clearly the teaching problem by indicating the spread of ability. Two schools may have identical average scores, but if one has 10 per cent backward children and 10 per cent bright, while the other has one per cent and one per cent, they are very different schools to the teacher".* We used the same—arbitrary—measures of "backwardness" and "brightness" as we had used earlier: the percentage of pupils with a standard score of 85 and below, and of 115 and above.

We thus had twelve tests, with three measures from each test: a total of 36 criterion scores.

School Environment

20. Professor Warburton's 1951 inquiry in Salford has shown that subjective estimates of "progressiveness", socio-economic status and quality of school buildings could be more valuable than the objective measures of attendance, class size and date of school building. This finding led us to search for ratings that might reasonably be expected to pinpoint some of the elusive components of "school atmosphere". As a result of preliminary meetings with the Head Teachers of the primary schools involved, and discussions with representatives of the L.E.A. and with colleagues in the University, we finally decided upon 34 school environmental variables of which 16 were at least partly subjective.

---

* *Education and Environment*, p. 78.

21. Most of the information on the straightforward, objective variables was supplied by the Head Teachers in reply to questionnaires. *Size of Class, Size of School*, and *Percentage Attendance*, which had proved useful enough in Salford, were obvious first priorities.

22. So many schools are experiencing staffing difficulties these days that we decided to include some variables that might reflect particular aspects of this problem. Articles in educational journals and letters to the press constantly comment on the damage to our children's schooling caused by too many staff changes, and by the need to recruit large numbers of married women whose first loyalties may be to their own families. One reads, too, of the trials facing newly qualified young teachers, especially in "tough" areas. There is discussion, too, about the balance of the sexes in teacher training, and the desirability of training more men than previously for primary work. Despite the fervour of many writers on these problems, very little is actually known about the influence of different categories of teachers on primary schooling. We therefore included the following variables in our survey to see if they linked up in any way with measures of academic achievement or school atmosphere: *Proportion of Teachers under 30 years of Age, Proportion of Teachers over 50 years of Age, Turnover Rate, Percentage of Graduates on the Staff, Sex of the Head Teacher* and *Proportion of Men on the Staff*. From the information supplied by the questionnaire, it was possible to work out the Teacher/pupil ratio. From the Heads we also learned how many pupils in each school had qualified for some form of *Special Schooling* since September, 1962. We asked for the various types of special schooling to be detailed in the hope of having additional checks on any areas where physical handicap appeared unduly heavy; in practice, however, the great majority of children involved were the educationally subnormal, and the numbers were in any case low, so that it was not practicable to separate out the different categories. In addition, we obtained the number of incidents of *Breaking and entering school* since January 1960 (strictly speaking, a "neighbourhood" rather than a "school" variable) and, at the suggestion of the Head Teachers, the number of pupils whose *mother tongue was not English*. These children are causing a growing teaching problem in many of our larger cities, although perhaps it is not in its most acute form in Manchester.

23. From information supplied by the L.E.A., we calculated the *average ratio* of grammar: secondary modern places gained by pupils in each school over a period of four years.

24. The ratings on variables associated with "school atmosphere" were made by the Research Officer, who spent a day in each of the 44 schools of the sample, after trying out his procedure of interviews and ratings on the three pilot schools. In each school he discussed the home backgrounds of the children with the Head and with the Staff as a body, but perhaps the most valuable information was gleaned during 15–20 minute visits to nearly every classroom. Naturally, the children's own class teachers tended to know more than did the Heads about which children's backgrounds, physically or psychologically, were poor or atypical. Our Observer then chatted to several of the children, either individually or in groups of two or three, as unobtrusively as possible, while the normal classwork continued around them. Some of these

children had been pointed out by their teachers; others he chose at random. Our Observer's talks with the pupils, of course, appeared to them quite informal, but many of the topics he raised were chosen to provide information, directly or indirectly, on the home backgrounds, the leisure opportunities of the neighbourhood and the school atmosphere. For instance, he frequently asked the children what they liked best out of school and where they went to play, who helped them to read, and whether they chose their neighbour in class (to provide a lead on the degree of formality in the classroom organisation). While in each school he also visited the library, the gymnasium, and the art room.

25. After each visit, he rated the school, usually on a five point scale, on the following variables:

(a) *First impression of the school:* influenced by cleanliness, decoration and any indications of the general atmosphere;

(b) *Quality of the building:* taking into account the adequacy and attractiveness of classroom, staffroom, playground and toilet facilities, the noise from traffic and the general outlook;

(c) *Quality of Equipment:* including P.E. equipment, Art and Craft materials, Mathematical apparatus, and the types of pupils' desks and chairs;

(d) *Library:* its structure and use. Primary school "libraries" ranged from a couple of shelves to some of high standard;

(e) *Classroom space:* an objective rating of the floor space per child in the 10+ classroom(s).

Some variables reflected school organisation and policy:

(f) *Recently re-organised* from all-age. It seemed possible that in some recently re-organised schools, the ethos of the secondary school might tend to continue in the primary school;

(g) *Streaming.* Schools with only one stream entry were classified as "unstreamed" except for seven schools who grouped to some extent on ability and mixed age groups;

(h) *Corporal Punishment.* The Head Teachers were not asked directly about its use, but sometimes evidence was gained either from incidents witnessed or in the course of conversation. Thus, the only possible ratings on this variable were "used" and "not in evidence", although presumably schools in which no teacher or pupil mentioned corporal punishment would tend to resort to it rarely, if at all;

(i) *Homework.* From conversations with the children, the Observer gathered how early in the primary course homework was set (if at all) and how much stress was laid upon doing it;

(j) *Out-of-School Activities.* Again using the children's information, our Observer estimated what opportunities they had for sport, day trips, camping, museum classes and so on.

The other Observer ratings were all planned to capture aspects of the "school atmosphere".

(k) *Appearance and Sociability* of the children. In this purely subjective rating, the most important factors were the attitudes towards, and verbal skills of the children in conversation with, the Observer. "Appearance" was reckoned only in terms of neatness and cleanliness—no school in the central area was rated low if the children had worn, but clean, clothing;

(l) *Attitude of the Staff to the Inquiry:* a rather coarse three point rating;

(m) *Quality of the Head* and *Quality of the Staff*;

(n) *Examination Technique:* a somewhat tentative rating of how well the school seemed geared to obtaining the best test results from the pupils;

(o) *Progressiveness.* Since our earlier work had found a more convincing association between progressiveness and school success than had any previous inquiry, we were anxious to investigate this concept further. In Salford, only one rating was made of this quality, that of the L.E.A.; Kemp had two independent ratings, made by himself and by school inspectors, although these assessments were later combined. Our Observer rated each school on progressiveness, basing his estimate on the evidence he saw, during his visits, of modern trends in school work, other than examination techniques. Several of our other subjective variables, however, noticeably "*Appearance and Sociability*" and "*Quality of Head and Staff*" were undoubtedly connected with progressiveness. In order to reduce the chances of a "halo" effect distorting our findings, we asked the L.E.A. for certain independent assessments of the schools. The estimate by the Local Authority was almost identical in basis with the Observer's "Progressiveness"; they rated the schools on a five point scale from "Informal, free progressive" to "Formal, rigid, orthodox".

26. We had planned to include a few variables about Parent-Teacher Associations since this seemed an obvious way of assessing objectively one aspect of parental interest in the school. To our surprise, not one school in the sample had such an organisation.

Home and Neighbourhood Environment

27. In our previous Manchester surveys, social variables were calculated on a ward basis; in 1957, for instance, we allocated each child to the ward of his home address and his "score" on each social variable was the rating of his ward. This time, however, we concerned ourselves only with the children and families represented in the schools of the sample. Naturally, this approach limited the environmental variables we could use. *Birth-rate, Illegitimacy, Deaths under one year,* useful though they had been in 1957, had, of course, to be dropped. Fortunately, however, many of the variables that had been most closely linked with educational success in 1957 could be calculated on a school, as well as on a ward, basis, and so were used in the present research: *Children taken into care, Verminous Conditions, Distribution of Shoes and Clothing* either *Free,* at *Part-payment,* or at *Full Cost* (the last category applying to families on National Assistance who still save money as the clothing is cheaper than it would be retail). Head Teachers, Medical Officers and Welfare Officers, as seemed most appropriate in each case, informed us of the numbers of children in each school to whom these variables applied. Each Head Teacher also gave us the number of pupils in his school receiving *free meals,* another variable clearly related to the economic level.

28. Independent assessments of the Standard of Housing in the school neighbourhood were made by the School Health Department and by the Observer during his visits. The school nurses had the advantage of some knowledge of the interior state of the houses while our Observer could view them only

externally. These two ratings were pooled. They were very similar to the rating of "*School Neighbourhood*" which proved valuable in Salford.

29. To obtain some social data for individual pupils we supplied both the Medical and Welfare departments with a list of the names of the children in the sample and asked them to mark those whose homes, in their confidential opinion, were suffering from any of the following conditions:

(a) *Shortage of material needs:* the food, clothing, living space that an average home provides;

(b) *Clearly classifiable as dirty:* this variable is comparable to the "Cleansing Notices" obtained on a ward basis in 1957;

(c) *Disrupted homes,* based on information under the following heads:

    A   parents divorced;
    B   one parent deceased;
    C   child illegitimate;
    D   a foster parent;
    E   child adopted;
    F   a history of incapacitating illness in one parent;
    G   grave emotional tension in the home.

We were especially interested in the correlates of such *disrupted homes* since Fraser (1959) had shown this factor to be particularly detrimental to school achievement.

30. Four other pieces of individual data were related to the socio-economic level: *Father's occupation* (rated on the Registrar General's five point scale); whether the child's *mother worked*, and whether the family lived in a *Corporation House*. One physical variable, the child's *height* was also included.

31. The Manchester police, too, were most co-operative in allowing us access to their records. From these, we found out which children in the sample had already been *Convicted* or *Officially Cautioned*, and those cases in which another member of the *family*, or someone living in the *same house* had a police record. Difficulties arose when someone of a different surname, but with the same address as a child in the sample, had a record, especially a recent record. There was no way of distinguishing between members of the child's immediate family circle (e.g. a foster-brother, a step-father or maternal cousin), lodgers, co-tenants and previous tenants. Hence our variable *Criminal record of House Address* probably contains a pretty heterogeneous sample. Carter and Jephcott (1954) in Radby, and research being at present carried out in Wythenshawe, have shown how there can be "black" and "white" patches, or even streets, lying cheek by jowl in the same district. As an additional neighbourhood measure we therefore calculated the number of families, in which at least one member had a conviction, living within 50 houses of the home address of each child in our sample (*Neighbourhood Crime*). A full list of all variables, with their bases of classification, is given in the appendix.

RESULTS

A. CORRELATION ANALYSIS

32. It will be seen that our research had grown to a formidable size by this time. Including the test results (remembering that there are three separate scores for each school for each of the 12 tests) we now had 87 variables. The

first job was to calculate intercorrelations for the whole matrix. This showed us which of the environmental variables had a significant association with the results of the educational measures. Perhaps the easiest way of summarizing the data is to calculate the average correlation of each variable with all the 36 test variables. (This was done ignoring the signs of the correlations, since the signs for backwardness and brightness are in opposite directions.)

Mean correlations

33. The highest correlation (·622), as might have been expected, was with the four year average of 11+ success, but this might reasonably be regarded as a criterion variable rather than an environmental variable. Of the remaining mean correlations, 17 are found to be over 0·3. Ten of these are with neighbourhood variables, seven with school variables. This stronger connection with the social factors in the home and neighbourhood is brought out even more clearly if we average the correlations of all the 18 social variables with the total tests. The result, ·295, contrasts with a similar average for the 34 school variables, ·212. And if the quasi-criterion variable of 11+ success is omitted, the average school variable correlation drops to ·199. It seems as if the forces operating outside the school walls are more pervasive and more powerful than those within.

The table below lists the 17 correlations over 0·3:

Table III

Average correlations of particular environmental variables with the 36 test variables

Home and Neighbourhood		School	
Verminous children	—·476		
Cleanliness of home	·475		
Free meals	—·471		
Material needs	—·440	Appearance and sociability	·422
Parental occupation	—·417	Attendance	·414
Crime (family)	—·378	Streaming	·385
Free clothing	—·369	Children qualified for special school	—·360
Children's height	·322	Class size	·316
Housing standard	·311	School size	·315
Crime (neighbourhood)	—·303	Homework	·303

34. The emphasis on measures of *dirt* and of *poverty* support the results we found in our earlier surveys of secondary school pupils. The inclusion of two *crime* variables emphasises the importance of the moral and psychological atmosphere of the home and neighbourhood, even at the primary school stage.

35. Our interest, however, is particularly in the school environment. The entries in the right-hand column are headed by *Appearance and Sociability*, a rating made by our Observer, and one which attempted to disregard socioeconomic level. It is, perhaps, a measure which should be thought of as straddling the "school" and "neighbourhood" columns: no doubt the school may have some effect here, but the home is almost certainly the major influence.

This variable is closely followed by *Attendance* (·414)—a logical result, though perhaps some might have expected a higher correlation. Another logical association is that with *Children qualified for special schools* (·360).

36. The third most powerful association in the school list is one of particular interest, that of *Streaming* (·385). The direction of the association should be noted: streamed schools have *better* records of attainment. An average of ·385 means that some individual tests have much higher correlations with streaming than this: for example, brightness, 10+ composition, ·659, brightness, 10+ Arithmetic I, ·604; brightness, 9+ English ·597. A study of the individual correlations shows that the effect of streaming lies mainly in increasing the proportion of bright children in a school. Of the 10 highest correlations (all over 0·5) seven are with measures of brightness, and three with average score. There is only one correlation greater than 0·4 with the measures of backwardness: 10+ Arithmetic I (−·457). But there is no suggestion that streaming has an *adverse* effect on the children of low ability: streamed schools tend to have fewer backward children than unstreamed schools at all ages and in all tests. The 12 measures of backwardness have an average correlation of −·237 with streaming, compared with ·471 for the measures of brightness.

37. The positive correlations between attainment and *class size* (·316) and *school size* (·315) indicate that large schools and large classes are associated with *good* attainment: a result which supports other researches in this field (e.g. Kemp, and Morris). Many schools were unstreamed merely because of small size. A one-form entry school is almost certain to be an unstreamed school. And in view of the positive correlation between school size and educational attainment, it may well be that the relationship between streaming and attainment is caused by this third factor. A correlation of ·655 between streaming and school size is found, emphasizing the relationship already mentioned. The size of this coefficient makes it all the more necessary to check on the possibility that our streaming/attainment association is an artifact. We therefore calculated the partial correlation between streaming and the mean results of all the tests at the 10+ age level, holding size of school constant. This analysis reduced the correlation from ·464 to ·326, but it is still significant, even when the effect of school size is removed.

38. The positive association between educational attainment and *size of class* is one unlikely to carry conviction with the practising teacher, and may well be that this is an example of the effect, already noted, that bedevils all research of this kind—an artifact of correlation arising from the association of each variable (class size, and educational attainment) with a third more pervasive variable (the socio-economic level of the school neighbourhood). The central area of the city is the area affected by slum clearance, and many of the (small) schools still existing there produce class-size figures much lower than those of the new and larger primary schools in the well-to-do suburbs. In order to investigate this possibility, we calculated some partial correlations, by which means it is possible to eliminate the effect of a third factor. We took the average correlation between all the 10+ tests and class size (·372) and calculated what this would be if the variables of *parental occupation* were held constant. The correlation dropped, but only slightly, to ·317. We then tried again with *housing standard* partialled out. This produced a slightly greater fall, to ·301. Finally we tried *free meals*, which produced a partial correlation

of ·296. It looks, therefore, as though there *is* a small, but positive, association between size of class and educational attainment. What is abundantly clear is that this variable is much less important than the quality of the home and the standard of the neighbourhood.

39. The final correlation listed in the right hand column of the tables is that of ·303 for *homework*. Schools which give homework (at the 10+ level) tend to produce higher scores in the tests. The pressures for homework in the final school year often come from the middle class parents in the outer suburbs, and it may be that the ·303 correlation is merely reflecting the more pervasive social factors. This is unlikely, however, since the *r* between occupation and homework is only ·107. Nor does the partial correlation, holding parental occupation constant, give any support to this theory; no reduction is produced in the correlation between homework and 10+ attainment.

Age-trends

40. So far we have looked at the relationships revealed by a study of the mean correlations over the whole of the 36 educational measures. But these measures cover four age-groups (7, 8, 9 and 10) three types of test (intelligence, English and arithmetic) and three methods of assessment (school mean score, per cent of "bright" children, and per cent of "backward" children). These breakdowns enable us to look a little more closely at the effect of environment on attainment. First, let us consider *age*: what differences appear here? The average correlations rise as the children get older, as will be seen from Table IV. The same trend is shown for both neighbourhood variables and school variables.

Table IV

Average correlations for each year of age

	7+	8+	9+	10+
All variables	·204	·231	·261	·252
Home and neighbourhood variables	·261	·275	·329	·306
School variables	·174	·208	·225	·224

41. Over and above the general trend shown in the table, there are interesting results from some of the individual variables. The greatest increase with age is found with *streaming* (·17, ·39, ·39, ·46), with *school size* (·14, ·35, ·33, ·36), with *class size* (·18, ·32, ·30, ·37) and with *homework* (·14, ·28, ·39, ·35). What are even more interesting are those school variables which show no increase with age, or even a decrease—such as *teacher turnover* (·14, ·15, ·06, ·03), *school equipment* (·21, ·20, ·14, ·13), and proportion of *teachers over 50 years of age* (·13, ·09, ·13, ·06). Although these correlations are low, the absence of the prevailing age trend might be suggestive.

42. When we turn to the home and neighbourhood variables, those showing a steeper rise than the average are free clothing (·22, ·34, ·41, ·43), *per cent of verminous children* (·34, ·49, ·55, ·49), and *material needs* (·34, ·40, ·51, ·48). Thus the effects of poverty and dirt appear to be cumulative. Those variables showing no rise with age are—curiously enough—*disrupted homes* (·26, ·10, ·20, ·18) and *crime—house address* (·14, ·08, ·14, ·07).

43. The general tendency for the correlations to rise with age merits a closer examination. There is some doubt as to whether this represents a true picture. It must be remembered that these correlations are between the test results of children who were 10 years of age when the environmental variables were measured, so that the 10+ test results and the other measures are coincident in time. But the 7+ test results are those of these same children three years ago, the 8+ two years ago, and so on. It would not be surprising, therefore, if these correlations have been subject to some degree of shrinkage. If so, the possibility exists that the level of correlation between attainment and environment does *not* rise with age. It may even *fall*: our results cannot be used to disprove such a hypothesis. A comparison of our results from primary school with those from secondary schools in 1957, studying pupils of 14+, suggests that this might well be the case. The correlations of attainment with environmental variables all tend to be higher at 10+ than at 14+. Only two of the social variables were identical in the two surveys: per cent of verminous children and per cent in receipt of free shoes and clothing. The average correlations of the former with attainment are ·483 at 10+, ·383 at 14+. For the latter the figures are ·237 and ·173. The fall from 10+ to 14+ is apparent for all three types of test, with the change for arithmetic being greater than for English, the smallest change being with the intelligence test.

44. The suggestion that the impact of environmental factors on attainment gets progressively weaker as we go up the age range is supported by other evidence. Furneaux's study of university selection* finds that "the proportion of those wishing to have a university education who are actually able to apply is much the same for pupils in all occupational groups", and again, "among pupils who have already reached the upper-sixth form, differences of home background are only associated to a very small degree with the strength of the desire for a university education". Much the same was found by the Robbins Committee. Their Table 7 (Appendix I, Robbins Report) shows that "within each ability group at 11+, there is no significant difference in performance [at A-level] between children from the different [social] classes who stay on".

Types of test
45. Let us now look at average correlations for the three types of test. Table V shows these for all variables, and also separately for home and neighbourhood variables and school variables.

Table V

Average correlation for each type of test

	Intelligence	English	Arithmetic
All variables	·233	·244	·210
Home and neighbourhood variables	·314	·299	·262
School variables	·190	·215	·182

46. Over-all, the English tests show a higher mean correlation with the environmental variables than do the intelligence tests or the arithmetic tests.

* *The Chosen Few* (1961)

When we consider "home" and "school" variables separately, however, it is seen that intelligence has a stronger relation with the "home" variables than the two measures of attainment, and this is in marked contrast to the results for the "school" variables. The differences shown in the last two lines of Table V may be considered small, but it should be remembered that these are average coefficients (taking due regard of sign) and are based on a considerable number of single correlations. The figure of ·190, for example (the mean correlation of IQ with school variables) is derived from 306 separate correlations, while the entry ·215 for English is based on 408 coefficients. The mean correlation for IQ with home and neighbourhood variables may be regarded as the least stable of these figures, but even this is derived from 162 separate coefficients, while the "school" and "arithmetic" figure is based on no fewer than 510.

47. It is interesting to speculate on the possible reasons for the different emphasis found for the measures of intelligence. Why should IQ be more closely connected with the home and neighbourhood environment? A possible explanation lies in the stronger genetic element in the results from such tests, and the correlation between the intelligence of children and that of their parents. The factors in the environment which affect parents (and which are affected by them) are likely to show more association with children's IQ (correlated with parental IQ) than are those factors which affect children only (i.e. most of the school factors). In other words, the adverse social environment tends to contain more parents with low IQs, whose children tend to have low IQs. When we look at the individual correlations, there is some support for this. The strongest gradient on the IQ, English, Arithmetic line is found for poverty and crime: *Neighbourhood crime:* ·401, ·275, ·266; *Free meals:* ·544, ·491, ·410, *Family crime:* ·456, ·388, ·325. A reversal of this trend is found with the highly individual variable of *mother working:* ·197, ·262, ·253. Turning to the school variables, the strongest gradiant here—in the opposite direction, of course—is found with *Streaming:* ·293, ·468, ·351, *class space:* ·245, ·315, ·252 and *class size:* ·272, ·363, ·305; while a reverse effect is found with *Appearance and Sociability:* ·480, ·432, ·380—surely a variable which is closely connected with parental care and upbringing.

Backwardness and Brightness

48. We might look now at the differences revealed between average correlations for *Backwardness* and *Brightness*. It will be remembered that some of the most interesting results from our secondary school survey were related to differences between these measures. Table VI shows the average correlations.

Table VI
Average correlations: Backwardness and Brightness

	Backwardness	Brightness
All variables	·195	·241
Home and neighbourhood variables	·258	·293
School variables	·161	·214

49. It will be seen that the environment appears to have more effect on brightness than on backwardness, and that this differential is rather more marked with the school variables than with the home and neighbourhood variables.

There are, however, some interesting exceptions to this general trend. *Neighbourhood crime* correlates ·326 with backwardness, only ·243 with brightness; *Family crime* shows the same trend, ·394 and ·315. Among the school variables five can be noticed which correlate more highly with backwardness than brightness: *Appearance and sociability*, ·424, ·383; *Progressiveness* (LEA rating), ·233, ·157; *Teachers under 30*, ·185, ·084; *Teachers over 50*, ·108, ·021; and *Corporal Punishment*, ·100, ·000. Only four variables however (excluding *11+ success*) show mean correlations greater than ·4 with the measures of backwardness: *cleanliness* (·443), *appearance and sociability* (·424), *verminous children:* ·419) and *free meals* (·415).

In contrast with this there are 10 correlations over ·4 with brightness:

Verminous children	−·497	Streaming	·471
Mother working	−·481	Attendance	·423
Material needs	−·479	School size	·413
Free meals	−·475	Qual. for spec. school	·411
Cleanliness	+·458		
Free clothing	−·413		

50. The strong connection with *poverty* and *dirt* is clear, as it was in our 1957 survey.

51. It should be emphasised that these results have been obtained from an investigation of schools and not of individual children. Nevertheless, the association between brightness and environmental factors is a particularly important one. The consistency of the findings from three separate surveys in Manchester, together with supporting evidence from Burt and Fraser, point to the virtual certainty that an adverse environment has its greatest educational effects on children of above average ability. If we can discover how to counteract such effects—even partially—then the educational profit will be very large.

B FACTOR ANALYSIS

52. So far we have been looking at correlation coefficients. We have tried, by means of averaging, to see what general trends are discernible. In this research, with 87 variables, there are 3,741 individual correlations to be related to each other. This calls for the drawing of many millions of comparison between pairs of coefficients. Moreover, as we have already become aware in the foregoing section, the degree of correlation between two variables A and B is by no means the only information contained in a correlation table, since A and B may also agree in that they both correlate highly with certain other variables, C, D, E and F, moderately highly with G, H, I and J, not at all with K, L, M and N, and negatively with O, P, Q and R. There are untold millions of complex comparisons to be made, a task beyond human competence. This can be performed, however, by the process of factor analysis, which replaces scores on the 88 variables, which are partly dependent on one another, which are of relatively small statistical importance (variance), and which have low powers of implication and prediction, by scores on a small number of *factors*, which are completely independent and which have far greater predictive and implicative powers than any of the individual variables. Although other

methods of analysis can be used (and will be used in the later phases of this research) such as the comparison of the mean scores of certain subgroups (analysis of variance), such techniques are much weaker for explanatory purposes, since the investigator himself decides on the crucial "factors" and no tests of the relative weight (as opposed to the "significance") of variance factors can be obtained. Nevertheless, in following up results for the more interesting individual variables, the technique of variance analysis and regression analysis should be of considerable value. Its application to scores for the major factors revealed in the factor analysis is an obvious example for its application. To begin with, however, an ordering of such a complex (and relatively unexplored) field by factorial techniques is essential.

53. The Atlas computer produced for us a Principal Components analysis, followed by a Varimax rotation of the first 10 factors. A scrutiny of this showed that six of the 10 factors covered 93·6 per cent of the total variance on the educational tests: the following analysis deals only with these six factors.

Table VII

Percentage variance on the 12 tests contributed by 6 factors

Factor	I	VII	V	IX	III	X	Total
% Variance	71·8	7·9	6·6	2·6	2·5	2·2	93·6

54. As will be seen from Table VII, the first factor is overwhelming in its importance. It covers 72 per cent of the total educational variance, leaving only 22 per cent for the remaining five factors. From a practical point of view, therefore, its effect is all important. From the standpoint of a research worker, however, the patterns revealed in the other five factors are of particular interest, and we must certainly not ignore them. In the remaining sections of this report, however, it must be kept in mind that factor I carries more than three times the weight of all the rest put together.

55. A table giving the full Varimax analysis is given in the Appendix. Table VIII* summarizes the major loadings on the six factors listed above, and also shows, at the bottom of the table, the way the total "educational" variance is distributed over age, type of test, and level of performance. One of the interesting things about Table VIII is the absence of some 12 of the environmental variables: absent because they have no sizeable loadings on the six factors which are associated with educational attainment. The absence of some of these may be viewed with some degree of equanimity: variable 6, for example, *Mother tongue not English*. The maximum incidence of such children in our 44 schools (see Appendix—List of Variables) was 13·6 per cent: a clear indication that this is, as yet, far from a major problem in this city. And the factor analysis shows that this level of incidence has little or no degree of association with level of attainment. It is more surprising, however, to find that 22 *Quality of Head Teacher* and 23 *Quality of Staff* have insignificant loadings on the "attainment" factors. A study of the full varimax analysis shows these variables with heavy loadings in Factor II: but this contributes only 1·35 per cent to the test variance. Our two measures of *Progressiveness*

---

* Variable 32, 11+*success*, has been omitted from this table, since we regard this as a criterion variable rather than an environmental one.

Table VIII

Summary of Factor Loadings

		I	VII	V	IX	III	X
1.	**SCHOOL VARIABLES**						
(a)	*Physical*						
38	School equipment			—46			
36	Age of building			40		—62	
37	Quality of building			—32		42	
1	Size of school			32		76	
2	Size of class	36				64	
3	Pupil/teacher ratio					73	
39	Classroom space				45		
(b)	*Teachers*						
14	Teachers under 30 years of age						—33
15	Teachers over 50 years of age						39
18	Male teachers						—30
20	Married women teachers with children						76
16	Graduate teachers			31			50
17	Teacher turnover			—64			
21	Teachers' attitude to enquiry		41				
(c)	*Organization and Policy*						
27	Examination technique		36				
35	Recently re-organized		69				
29	Homework	37	49				
33	Streaming	42	45			42	
4	Attendance	43				42	
5	Children qualified for special school	—43			47		
34	Corporal punishment				38	—53	
2.	**NEIGHBOURHOOD VARIABLES**						
41	Housing standard			33		56	
49	Corporation housing			37		44	
42	School breaking and entering					60	
44	Play areas					63	
52	Crime—house address					33	
43	Crime—neighbourhood	—36					
3.	**HOME VARIABLES**						
51	Crime—family	—55					
13	Crime—Child				—59		
9	Free clothing	—40	—45		—43		
8	Free meals	—54					
12	Children's height	39					
45	Parental occupation	—48					
47	Material needs inadequate	—47					
11	Verminous children	—56					—39
48	Cleanliness of home inadequate	—59					
7	Appearance and sociability	51					
46	Mother working					—45	

Percentage variance on educational tests:

	I	VII	V	IX	III	X
Total Variance	72	8	7	3	3	2
7+	52	8	[14	[7]	1	[5
8+	60	10	16]	3	3	4]
9+	[76	9	2	2	3	0
10+	84]	6	0	1	3	1

continued on next page

TABLE VIII continued

I.Q.	[78	6	1	2	1	3
English	79]	9	2	2	3	0
Arithmetic	62	8	[14]	4	3	3
Backwardness	73	5	8	3	1	3
Brightness	63	[16]	6	3	[4]	2
Average score	79	4	6	2	2	2

(24 and 25) are also missing—and here we have a contrast with our secondary school survey, where Professor Warburton found a significant association between Progressiveness and both reading and arithmetic. The loading of ·26 on Factor I is in the right direction, but is disappointingly low.

Factor I

56. Let us now look more closely at the major attainment factor. A glance at Table VIII reveals that the major loadings are concentrated among the *Home* variables, with the School and the Neighbourhood much less involved. Indeed, if we calculate the amount of "environmental" variance contributed by each of these categories to Factor I (making appropriate adjustments to take into account the fact that there are different numbers of individual variables in each category) we find that *School* effects contribute 18 per cent, *Neighbourhood* effects 20 per cent, and *Home* effects no less than 62 per cent. This is a finding of the greatest significance, and underlines with considerable emphasis the problem facing the primary school. The adverse forces in the home are, at this stage of education, the overwhelming ones, and the lower loadings (and the fewer loadings) on the school variables suggest that in the present circumstances we are doing little to counteract them by forces within the school. It is surprising to find that none of the *teacher* variables have loadings over ·3 on this factor: the major effect seems to lie in the direction of *organisation and policy*, with *streaming* and *homework* as two of the outstanding variables. *Size of class*, too, bears out the association already noted in our correlational analysis, with schools with large classes tending to have better standards of attainment than those with small classes.

57. When we focus our attention on the crucial sector of *Home*, we get again the close connection between attainment and both *poverty* and *maternal care*. This is seen very clearly if we list the major loadings in order of size:

Cleanliness of home	—·59
Verminous children	—·56
Family crime	—·55
Free meals	—·54
Appearance and sociability of children ..	·51
Parental occupation	—·48
Material needs inadequate	—·47

58. These figures, together with the likelihood (already noted) that the early years bear the heaviest impact of adverse environmental forces, suggest two obvious lines of attack in our efforts to rescue the under-privileged and socially handicapped child from the worst effects of his adverse environment. First there is the provision of nursery schools, so that some educational countermeasures may be applied before the age of five. And such provision is seen not so much to counteract the poor *physical* environment of the home as to

begin the process of adaptation to the school and the teacher, and with the hope that it might affect the child's attitude towards education. The continued appearance of the *maternal care* factor suggests that the underlying mechanism may lie in the formation of what McDougall called the "self-regarding sentiment", with all that this implies for the formation of attitudes towards education and towards authority. If this is so, therapeutic action before the age of five is essential.

59. The second line of attack is to support and encourage a recent new development in the field of teacher training. A few colleges of education have begun to offer courses which include some element of training in social work. The results of this research underline the desirability of increasing the number of such courses. The aim should not be that of trying to produce fully-trained social workers, but rather the training of a proportion of teachers with some knowledge of (and first-hand experience in) adverse environments, with some appreciation of the problems and techniques of social work, and with the attitudes necessary to achieve effective co-operation with social workers and social agencies. If local authorities possessed a teaching force which included, say five per cent of teachers trained in this way, they could expect them to become familiar with the home backgrounds of the children in the most difficult areas, and to engage in liaison work between home and school. The most difficult cases would, of course, be beyond them, but part of their function would be important one of early referral to more expert and more capable agencies. It may be argued, with some justification, that as yet we do not know enough about the adverse forces and their method of operation to be able to mount such training courses with any degree of certainty about the validity of method and content. But this is being too timid and too conservative. The development of more courses of this kind will assist in the development of new knowledge and new insights, and if they tend to show differences in approach and in organisation this may be all to the good at this developmental stage.

Minor factors

60. As we have emphasized, Factor I is by far the most important, carrying nearly three-quarters of the total variance on the educational measures. The other five factors are, however, of considerable theoretical interest, and, as we shall see, the effect of some of them to particular directions is far from negligible.

61. Let us look first at the partitioning of the "educational" variance shown at the foot of Table VIII. Factor VII is clearly one which is important for *Brightness*, and Factor III supports this in a smaller degree. Between them they account for 20 per cent of the *Brightness* variance. Factors V and X (and IX to some extent) have their greatest effect at the 7+ and 8+ ages, with Factor V concentrating very heavily on *Arithmetic*.

62. The age-pattern is of particular interest. Quite clearly the pattern of abilities changes radically between the age of 7 and 10. Notice how only 52 per cent of the 7+ variance is covered by the major Factor I. Environmental forces appear to be much more complicated at the earlier ages.

63. The summary at the foot of Table VIII shows the way the educational variance is spread over the six factors. We can do an equivalent analysis on the environmental variance. It is a little more complicated because of the difference in the number of individual variables in the categories School, Neighbourhood and Home. But if we adjust for this, and if we take the total environmental variance on these six factors only as being 100 per cent, we arrive at Table IX. A comparison of this with the breakdown of educational variance shown in Table VIII is most interesting. Notice how Factor I, with its lion's share of educational variance, is now overshadowed by Factor III. The other four factors are all about the same level of weighting, nine per cent or 10 per cent each. The side totals show roughly equal contributions by school, neighbourhood and home (but notice that that the school is lowest of the three) although individual factors show very obvious differences here.

Table IX

Percentage allocation of environmental variance among six factors

	I	VII	V	IX	III	X	Total
School variables	4·9	4·1	4·4	2·8	10·3	4·4	30·9
Neighbourhood variables	5·4	1·6	4·2	1·4	20·9	2·5	35·9
Home variables	16·8	3·0	1·4	5·7	2·7	3·5	33·2
TOTAL	27·1	8·7	10·0	9·9	33·9	10·4	100·0

64. If we consider the top line of the table, we may analyse a little further, by breaking down the variance on the School variables into the three divisions already employed in the upper part of Table VIII. This breakdown is shown in Table X.

Table X

Percentage allocation of variance on the School Variables among six factors

	I	VII	V	IX	III	X	Total
(a) Physical	7	2	6	4	27	1	47
(b) Teachers	3	2	5	2	1	12	25
(c) Organization and policy	6	9	3	4	6	1	29
TOTAL	16	13	14	10	34	14	101

65. We see from the right hand totals that the physical aspects of the school environment have a much greater importance than either the teachers or the organisation and policy, and that this effect is concentrated very heavily in Factor III. Factor X is the one which is almost entirely concerned with *teachers*—and this, it will be remembered, contributes only two per cent of the variance on the educational tests, although it is significant that its effects are concentrated on the *younger* children.

Factors associated with age

66. Table VIII shows us that Factors V, IX and X have much stronger effects at 7+ and 8+ than at the upper end of the primary school. Factor V has its

heaviest loading in 17 *teacher turnover* rate. Indeed, this is the only factor out of the 10 which shows any connection with this variable. And it is logically sensible that high rates of teacher turnover are particularly deleterious to the younger children (and particularly important for attainment in *arithmetic*). It is, however, a little surprising that the ten-year-olds seem almost completely unaffected by this. Other "school" loadings on Factor V are for 38 *School equipment*, 36 *Age of building* (both in the "wrong" direction, curiously enough), 37 *Quality of building* and 16 proportion of *Graduate Teachers*. This last is particularly interesting, since it is supported by Factor X (also "young children" factor) and is in contrast to Factor I where a lowish loading on this variable is negative. Why should graduate teachers in primary schools have a positive effect at the lower end of the age range, and a negative effect at the upper? Many people would believe that, if any such differential existed, it would be in the reverse direction. The presence of married women graduates, with young children of their own, may have a bearing on this.

67. Factor X is almost entirely a "teacher" factor, and from this it will be seen that attainment at the 7+ and 8+ levels is associated with older rather than younger teachers, with women teachers rather than with men teachers, and that the heaviest loading of all is for the proportion of married women teachers with children of their own. It is heartening to find reasons additional to mere teacher shortage for this return to the profession. The third factor associated with young children (Factor IX) has only one loading of particular note, that of 39, *Classroom space*. It is interesting to find this associated positively with test attainment.

Factors associated with "brightness"

68. Factors VII and III show particular associations with high scores on the tests. A study of the major loadings show that newer schools, larger schools and larger classes tend to have higher proportions of bright children, while *streaming* and the existence of homework are also positive factors. Neighbourhood variables involved include *housing standard* and *play areas*, with oddly perverse signs for *crime* (house address) and *school breaking and entering*. Of the "home" variables the only sizeable loadings are *free meals* ($-\cdot45$) and mother working ($-\cdot45$).

SUMMARY

69. This report has been concerned with the statistics related to 44 schools, their environment, and the environment of their children. The unit of analysis has been the school, and not the individual child, and it is necessary to keep this in mind when we survey the results of our labours.

70. We have analyzed the inter-correlations of 87 separate variables, 36 of them scores on tests, at four stages, and 51 of them measures of the children's environment, school, neighbourhood and home. Our analysis has first been done by means of average correlations, and then, more comprehensively, by factor analysis.

71. The most important of our findings, perhaps, is the demonstration that the major forces associated with educational attainment are to be found

within the home circumstances of the children. These "home" variables have, *pro rata*, nearly twice the weight of "neighbourhood" and "school" variables put together. That this may—at least partially—be caused by our choice of variables, and that a different selection might upset this order of influence, is a valid argument. But a scrutiny of the categories of measurement would suggest that our results might *under*estimate the power of the home. We endeavoured to cover all aspects of the school environment in our survey, taking account of not only those matters which are capable of objective measurement such as school size, pupil/teacher ratio, and the age-distribution of teachers, but also of those aspects of school life which are matters of judgement rather than matters of counting: variables such as progressiveness, social atmosphere, quality of building, of equipment and of staff. Estimates of such matters are subject to error and are far from the level of reliability that can be attached to measures such as the age of the school building, or the proportion of men teachers on the staff. The factor analysis demonstrates, however, that the element of unreliability was not so great as to swamp the element of valid judgement. Our school variables, therefore, are many and varied, covering children, teachers, equipment and structure and it is difficult to believe that we have omitted any set of variables that would show a significantly stronger relationship with attainment. Our measures of the home and of the neighbourhood, on the other hand, are relatively few in number and limited in scope. It is not impossible that a more comprehensive coverage would have the effect of increasing the average effect of "home" as against "school".

72. The aspects of home background that have the strongest associations with attainment on the tests seem to be those measures of *maternal care* which we have previously found so powerful in their association with the attainment of children in secondary schools. Such variables, together with those associated with *material need*, make up most of the "home" effect. But dirt and crime seem more important than poverty in this context.

73. The second fundamental result of our researches, and one of the utmost significance, is the demonstration that the effects of environment seem to press more heavily on the brightest of the children. The adverse elements in home, neighbourhood and school conditions are shown to reduce the proportion of able children in the schools. This finding, which has some support from other inquiries, is of the greatest significance for educationists, for politicians, and for society as a whole. When we think of the problem of material and cultural deprivation, we see it as a problem affecting the "submerged tenth" the slum dwellers, the poverty-stricken. We tend to assume that it affects only the tail-end of the ability-range as well as the tail-end of the income-range. Both of these views are wrong, and the second is even more radically wrong than the first. Educational deprivation is *not* mainly the effect of poverty: parental attitude and maternal care are more important than the level of material needs. The child from a home with an income of £20 per week may be more at risk than one from a much poorer home. The assumption that educational deprivation breeds educational backwardness is true but misleading. What is more in accord with the facts is the dictum that educational deprivation *prevents* the flowering of latent abilities, and that the higher the potential, the more potent and the more catastrophic is its effects.

74. It seems possible that environmental effects are strongest at the lower end of the school, and tend to fall off in their impact on educational attainment as the children get older. We cannot be categorical about this, since the design of this research is incapable of demonstrating it unequivocally. But our results provide some support for such an hypothesis. This would suggest that the provision of nursery schools ought to be seen as a way of counteracting adverse home conditions at the earliest possible moment—and counteracting adverse intellectual and attitudinal factors rather than the merely physical. This is the point at which the battle should first be joined: and the battle for the bright as well as for the dull.

75. When we survey the results of our investigations of the school environment we find the surprising result that organisational and physical aspects have stronger associations with the criterion tests than have the teacher variables and those associated with school atmosphere. The major factor, covering nearly three-quarters of the total test variance, contains only five "school" variables with loadings over 0·3—and of these, *attendance* can clearly be regarded as one at least partially (and perhaps mainly) mediated by the home and the parents. A second one—the proportion of children qualified for special school—can hardly be regarded as a measure over which the primary school has much control: it is mainly a measure of one aspect of the quality of the school's intake. These leave us with only three significant variables; streaming, homework and size of class.

76. Little emphasis ought to be placed on the positive relationship between streamed schools and test performance, for two reasons. First, we are dealing with a relatively small sample of schools—44 only, of which 28 are one-form entry. An unstreamed school in this survey is not unstreamed because of a policy-decision on the part of the head teacher, but because it cannot be anything else! It is true that seven of these 28 were categorized as "streamed" by our Observer, on the grounds that the age-groups were mixed and the children were grouped on ability, but there was no evidence that the remaining 21 were possessed of a "non-streaming ethos". Secondly, it is necessary to emphasize again the limitations of our criterion measures. The tests given at 10+ were those used by the authority for secondary school selection: those at the earlier ages were of a similar type. These objective measures of the tool subjects are those which might be expected to benefit most from the formal methods of teaching which tend to accompany streaming. But this should not blind us to the possibility that other kinds of assessment might produce the reverse effect. "Progressive" methods and "activity" methods are designed to do more than produce skill and competence in the three R's: the advocates of non-streaming tend to be those who argue for less formal teaching and a wider curriculum. The fact that we perforce had to use objective tests of English, Arithmetic and Verbal Intelligence as our criteria means that we have left untapped wide areas of primary school achievement, and have loaded the scales against more progressive methods of teaching and organisation. It is unfortunate that the controversy about streaming has become a major politico-educational issue. It is an extremely complex matter to investigate, and it would be folly to suggest that the results from 44 schools in a single authority can throw any but the most feeble gleam of light on this problem. It is suggested that the only fact of any significance in our results may well be

the demonstration that, even using objectives tests of limited coverage, streaming does not produce adverse effects at the lower end of the ability range. As we said earlier, streamed schools tend to have fewer backward children than unstreamed schools at all ages and in all tests.

77. The positive association of *homework* with attainment must also be related to the nature of our criterion measures. We have shown, by using the technique of partial correlation, that this is unlikely to be the result of parental pressures from the middle-class homes: it would seem more likely to be a school reaction to the pressures of 11+ selection.

78. The factor loading of ·36 with *size of class* brings this research into line with many others which have shown a similar relationship. Our data show that this is partly—but only partly—a function of school size and quality of neighbourhood (in a city where many of the smallest primary schools are in the worst areas, awaiting demolition).

79. The less important factors thrown up in the factor analysis provide some interesting results, particularly for the younger children of 7+ and 8+. *Teacher turnover rate* is shown to be particularly important here, as well as the presence of *older* teachers, of *women* teachers, and of *married women teachers with children*.

80. All in all, it is clear that our schools analysis has raised a number of questions rather than produced solutions to problems. This is to be expected in a field which has been so neglected in research. The limitations of correlational analysis are many, and it must be remembered that the figures we have presented here are measures of association: they are not (necessarily) indications of causality. And the special nature of a research using schools as units must be remembered: correlations between schools cannot be used as substitutes for—or assumed to be equal to—correlations between individual pupils. The second stage of our inquiry becomes important, therefore, not only for the intrinsic value of its results, but for the relationship shown (if any) between the school analysis and the pupil analysis.

II THE PUPIL ANALYSIS

81. The sub-sample of individual pupils for this part of the inquiry was drawn from 22 schools. From each of the sampled schools 10 children were chosen, using a table of random numbers. By the same method, two children were chosen as reserves. The parents of 191 children in the original sample were interviewed. Three children had left the school, and in 12 further cases no contact could be established, either because the family had moved (sometimes because of slum clearance), or were on holiday, or because the parents were reported by neighbours to be always out, or (in one case only) because the address given was non-existent. Thirteen parents refused to be interviewed. Three of these "had no time to spare", and a fourth was ill. Of the rest, only four refused outright, the other six made appointments but later broke them. In addition, one interview was abandoned because of the Pakistani parents' lack of English. Nineteen of the non-respondents were replaced by reserves, so that there were in all 210 interviews.

82. Further wastage occurred because of lack of complete data on the criterion tests. If a child in the sample had missed only one or, at the most, two of the twelve tests used as criterion measures, or if the school specifically stated that he had not taken one or more of the 10+ (selection) tests for reasons of backwardness (and provided that he had taken all the earlier tests), the missing scores were inserted by calculating the child's average score for the appropriate type of test (English, Arithmetic, Intelligence). For 24 children the omissions were more frequent and they were excluded from the analysis. This report is thus concerned with the results from 186 children and their parents.

Variables

83. The criterion variables were, of course, the results of the 12 tests of intelligence, English and arithmetic given at 7+, 8+, 9+ and 10+. There were also a number of the home and school variables used in the schools analysis that were applicable to individual children: *Head teachers' rating, Material needs inadequate, Cleanliness of home, Disrupted homes, Family crime, Neighbourhood crime.*

84. In selecting those responses to the C.O.I. questionnaire which should be quantified and used in the analysis, we had the benefit of a factor analysis of the questionnaire items. Using this as a guide, a first selection was made of 53 items. Some of these were closely related, e.g. *Type of house* and *Council house; Talks with teacher* and *Whether discussed child's progress with teacher; Complained at school* and *Dissatisfaction with teachers.* These were included in the correlation matrix, and exclusion decided upon in the light of the size of the correlation coefficients. This scrutiny led to the dropping of 13 variables, most because of overlap (as above) but some because of lack of correlation with the criterion variables. For example, *Sex of child* had an average correlation of ·041 with the educational tests, *Availability of children's clubs* ·034, *Mother working* −·051, *No garden* −·091, *Husband lenient with child* −·062, *Parents' belief in corporal punishment* ·038, *Age child started school* ·048.

85. Since we had obtained interesting results on backwardness and brightness in the school analysis, we were anxious to include similar measures for the individual study. This is not so simple, however. For a school, the percentage of children scoring over 115 or under 85 is a statistic which produces a graduated scale of measurement over a sample of schools: for an individual child his score on any particular test either is or is not outside one or other of these arbitrary limits. There are a number of ways in which the association between brightness or backwardness and social factors may be assessed in a sample of children: we finally decided to use a simple dichotomy (bright, not bright; backward, not backward) as a scoring device for each child on each test. Since the correlations between these measures themselves, and between them and the actual test score will inevitably be high, it was judged safest to perform three separate factor analyses: the first using actual test scores as criterion variables, the second using the bright: not bright dichotomies as the criteria, the third using backward: not backward. For each analysis we thus had 52 variables, 12 criterion measures and 40 "family" measures. The results of the three factor analyses are treated separately below. The annex contains a list of the variables involved, together with a description of their bases and a note of distribution or range.

A. TEST SCORE ANALYSIS

Average correlations

86. Table XI shows, in the upper half, all the variables having an average correlation with the 12 tests of over ·2. The lower half of the table includes a *selection* of the remaining variables: it is not comprehensive, and it must not be assumed that because a variable is not included here its average correlation is lower than that of the bottom entry.

87. The highest correlation of all is given by *62 Preferred age of leaving*, a six-point scale ranging from "under 15 if possible" up to "18+". This is perhaps the sharpest and quickest way of indicating parental attitude towards education. The superiority of the I.Q. correlation (·422) over that of English (·409) and Arithmetic (·392) tends to support the view put forward in the earlier part of this Report of the importance of the genetic element. The second variable in the list (*70 Homework given*) is the response to the question "Have the teachers at ——— school given the child any work to do at home?" This should not be regarded as necessarily a *school* variable. A negative response may indicate parental ignorance and lack of interest—or, indeed, the child's refusal to conform.

88. What is very significant is the presence in the "top seven" of the four variables dealing with *reading*, with average correlations with all tests ranging from ·272 to ·341, and an overall average of ·312. Compare this with the bottom line of Table II: *Father's occupation* ·098. Although there is some slight association with social class, what matters is the *degree of literacy* within the home, and the attitude of parents towards books and towards school. These correlations emphasize the existence of many "good" homes in the working class, and many "bad" homes in the middle class. The differences between the three kinds of test are also interesting for the *reading* variables. The *child's reading* understandably shows the highest correlation with the English tests: if we average the correlations of the other three reading variables we get I.Q. ·325, English ·307 and Arithmetic ·283. It is not unreasonable to assume that the standard of literacy in the home, and the interest the parents show in reading, are—like their readiness to keep the child at school beyond the statutory leaving age—correlated with the parents' level of intelligence. Indeed, one would expect a strong association here. It is not surprising therefore, to find a high correlation of these variables with the level of intelligence of the child. As in the schools analysis, variables which are parent-determined, or which are likely to be affected by parental action or attitude, tend to show higher correlations with the child's I.Q. than with the measure of attainment.

Age trends

89. There is a general tendency, as in the schools analysis, for coefficients to rise with age; but, as we pointed out, this may not be significant. There are indications, however, of variables which seem to have stronger associations with the attainment of the younger children. The easiest way to pick these out is to run the eye down the 7+ column, noticing any figures which breaks the order of size. Four variables stand out in this respect: *Disrupted home, Neighbourhood crime, Mother plays with children in the evening* and—rather oddly

Table XI—Average Correlations

		All Tests	7+	8+	9+	10+	IQ	English	Arithmetic
62	Preferred age of leaving	405	389	400	429	405	422	409	392
70	Homework given	357	353	324	386	367	402	337	346
59	Child's reading	341	320	316	366	355	352	366	315
56	Parents members of library	339	311	322	358	352	366	334	326
61	Prefer grammar school	309	269	286	313	338	335	306	297
57	Whether parents read	294	267	302	345	280	298	319	272
58	Number of books in home	272	245	252	305	281	310	268	251
76	Complaints against teacher	−242	−206	−202	−258	−275	−247	−252	−232
72	Worried about child's school work	−223	−176	−239	−209	−238	−197	−227	−235
50	Disrupted home	−217	−216	−210	−219	−220	−249	−203	−208
60	Expressed desire for particular school	211	173	194	221	232	202	239	194
46	Cleanliness of home	188	141	149	207	222	199	216	158
45	Material needs inadequate	−166	−126	−167	−173	−179	−173	−177	−154
41	Neighbourhood crime	−162	−175	−140	−190	−160	−205	−146	−150
55	Age parents completed education	154	125	139	190	161	164	174	132
63	Talks with teacher or head	141	106	109	161	168	173	155	112
51	Non-natural family	−136	−113	−185	−134	−117	−141	−129	−139
68	Husband's interest in school work	129	112	111	143	141	166	113	119
53	Mother plays with children in evening	116	122	100	098	131	116	082	144
52	Family crime	−107	−069	−094	−116	−128	−099	−119	−103
75	Number of schools attended	−106	−090	−096	−098	−123	−101	−098	−116
43	Father's occupation	098	120	102	079	095	088	087	113

—*Father's occupation. Disrupted home* and *Mother's play* are logically enough the kinds of factors very likely to have major impact on the youngest children but it is puzzling to see why *Neighbourhood crime* should show this tendency when *Family crime* does not. The result for *Father's occupation* seems to have little relation to economic factors, since *Material needs inadequate* shows no similar trend $(7+, -\cdot126; 8+, -\cdot167; 9+, -\cdot173; 10+, -\cdot179)$.

Factor Analysis

90. A principal components analysis was carried out followed by a Varimax rotation of 17 factors. When the variance contributed by the educational tests to these factors was calculated, it was found that 94·2 per cent of this variance lay in the first factor: none of the other factors contributed more than 0·7 per cent. We have, therefore. a simple and uncomplicated solution.

91. The major loadings on the only (educationally) significant factor are given on Table XII. It will be seen that—as we would expect from a mono-factor solution—it bears a close resemblance to the average correlation data in Table XI. The heaviest loadings are for those variables indicating parental *attitude towards education* and the *literacy of the home.* Good attainment is achieved by pupils with parents who want them to stay on at school beyond 16, who prefer a grammar school education, who are members of a public library, who possess books themselves, and who tend to read both fiction and non-fiction. Poor attainment is shown by children whose parents are worried about teaching methods or the child's school progress, who are critical of the

Table XII

Major loadings on Factor I—Test Score analysis

62	Preferred age of leaving		·437
59	Child's reading		·433
70	Homework given		·379
61	Parents prefer grammar school		·356
56	Parents members of library		·343
57	Whether parents read		·325
58	No. of books in home		·282
72	Worried about child's school work		−·273
76	Complaints against teacher		−·247
50	Disrupted home		−·205
40	Discussed problem behaviour at school		−·204
60	Expressed desire for particular school		·201
42	Facilities for neighbourhood play		−·197
41	Neighbourhood crime		−·181
73	Children should be brought on faster		−·157
39	Difficult to control at home		−·155
48	Bedroom deficiency		−·151
46	Cleanliness of home		·145
49	No fixed bath		−·141
47	Type of house		−·132
55	Age parents completed education		·129

Average test variance on Factor I:

7+	·688	IQ	·814	Total	·778
8+	·783	Eng.	·765		
9+	·819	Arith.	·766		
10+	·794				

child's teachers, who have visited the school to discuss the child's behavioural problems, and who believe that teachers should try to get children on faster in their work. The psychological aspects of the home (e.g. disruption, child difficult to control) tend to be more important than the physical environment (e.g. bedroom deficiency, no fixed bath, cleanliness, type of house). It is, perhaps, surprising to find a relatively low loading on *55 Age parents completed education:* this, perhaps, does not argue a great deal of success for the educational system. Those of us who chafe at what often seems the impossibility of achieving radical change quickly—and this is undoubtedly the case for the problem of environmental handicap—sometimes try to comfort ourselves with the belief that, with succeeding generations, education itself will provide the remedy. We get small comfort from this analysis. Education beyond the statutory leaving age seems, in this sample, to have comparatively little effect on attitude towards the education of their own children. It correlates only ·210 with *Preferred age of leaving* and ·123 with *Grammar school preferred.* Even with the literacy variables the correlations are low: *Parent's reading* ·215, *Membership of library* ·208 and *Books in home* ·129. On the other hand, our sample of parents is probably less than fully representative here. The distribution of ratings on variables 55 shows that, of 186 families, in 132 both mother and father left school at 14 (or earlier) and in 28 further cases one parent left at 14 and one at 15. This perhaps may serve to underline one of the problems of interpretation of inquiries such as this: the possibility that certain results reflect the circumstances of a particular *region,* and cannot be generalized to the country as a whole. The hazards of applying results obtained in large cities to country towns or villages are obvious: there may be equal hazards in generalizing from the North to the South, in view of what we know of the social and educational gradient existing in Britain.

92. Age-trends and test-trends are shown at the bottom of Table XII, from which it can be seen that this factor has its strongest loadings on the educational measures at the age of 9+, and that its connection with general ability is clearly stronger than with English or Arithmetic.

B. BRIGHTNESS ANALYSIS

93. The computer programme identified 17 factors from the principal components analysis for Varimax rotation. Of the total educational variance contributed by these factors, 76 per cent came from Factor I. The next highest fraction was from Factor 12, but since this was only 5·1 per cent, its influence is of little account. We are therefore left with another single factor analysis. The major loadings on this first factor are given in Table XIII.

94. There are considerable similarities in this pattern and the one for the score analysis. The four measures of home literacy are again found among the top seven variables, for example. But the primacy of *62 Preferred age of leaving* yields place to *61 Grammar school preference.* This is perhaps a sharper measure of parental attitude for the above-average child than the wider-ranging 62. What is of most interest perhaps is the collection of variables which appear in this table but which were not included in the 21 measures having the strongest loadings in the score analysis: *68 Husband's interest, 75 Changes of school, 45 Material needs inadequate,* and *63 Talks with head or*

Table XIII

Major loadings on Factor I—Brightness analysis

61	Grammar school preference	·407
56	Membership of library	·360
59	Child's reading	·283
57	Parent's reading	·279
62	Preferred age of leaving	·258
68	Husband's interest	·223
58	Books in house	·219
72	Child below standard	−·208
75	Changes of school	−·200
70	Homework given	·184
76	Dissatisfaction with teacher	−·182
42	Facilities for play	−·167
60	Secondary school preference	·163
41	Neighbourhood crime	−·153
45	Material needs inadequate	−·153
63	Talks with head or class teacher	·146
73	Children should be brought on faster	−·145
50	Disrupted home	−·138
46	Cleanliness of home below standard	−·128
39	Difficult to control at home	−·123

Average test variance on Factor:

7+	·286	IQ	·587	Total	·539
8+	·529	Eng.	·619		
9+	·635	Arith.	·448		
10+	·608				

class teacher. In contrast to these, there are five variables included in the previous list which find no place here: *40 Discussed problem behaviour at school, 55 Age parents completed education, 47 Type of house, 48 Bedroom deficiency,* and *49 No fixed bath.* It seems, therefore, that although poverty might exercise an inhibiting effect on the emergence of brightness, the purely physical aspects of the home environment are relatively unimportant. The interest of the child's father in school work, however, is markedly associated with brightness, as well as evidence of parental interest as shown by discussions with the school staff—provided, however, that these are sharply distinguished from those visits made to discuss unsatisfactory progress. The low loading on *55 Age parents completed education* remarked on in the discussion of the score analysis is paralleled by an even lower loading on the brightness factor (·061 as compared with ·129).

95. The bottom of Table XIII shows the age-trends and test-trends for the factor. As in the score analysis, 9+ shows the highest proportion of variance, but is not markedly higher than 10+. The major difference lies in the much lower contribution from the 7+ tests in the brightness analysis. This is made even clearer if the figures are expressed as ratios. Taking the 9+ variance as 100 in each case, the 7+, 8+ and 10+ contributions are, for the test score analysis, respectively 84, 96 and 97. For brightness, they are 45, 83 and 95. This indicates, perhaps, more radical changes in level of attainment over the years for those children at the upper end of the ability range, thus emphasizing again the greater environmental risk for the bright child.

96. For test score, I.Q. contributed more to Factor I than either English or Arithmetic. Expressed as ratios, the variances are 100: 94: 94. The picture for brightness is different, with English showing up strongly, and Arithmetic much lower: 100: 105: 76. Other investigators have stressed the importance of verbal ability and its susceptibility to environmental influences. These results suggest that they may be rather more important at the upper end of the ability range than with the average child.

C. BACKWARDNESS ANALYSIS

97. The backwardness analysis was a replication of that done for brightness. The computer rotated 18 factors to a Varimax solution. The first factor covered 73 per cent of the test variance, but on this occasion a second factor proved to have a sizeable weighting: Factor 16, contributing 11·7 per cent of the variance on the educational tests. It has only one sixth of the power of Factor I, but its influence is obviously not negligible.

The first factor

98. Loadings of ·100 and over on this factor are shown in Table XIV. A fuller comparison of this table with the corresponding tables for the other analysis is made later, but certain obvious points may be noted. First, the four "home literacy" variables again appear in the top half of the table, but with slightly less importance. The average rank order of these four measures are four for brightness, five for score, and six for backwardness. *70 Homework given* goes to the top here, in contrast to its rank of 3rd for score and 10th for

Table XIV

Major loadings on Factor I—Backwardness analysis

70	Homework given	·320
62	Preferred age of leaving	·292
59	Child's reading	·289
40	Discussed problem behaviour at school	—·226
57	Parents' reading	·219
72	Child below standard	—·218
58	Books in house	·209
50	Disrupted home	—·159
56	Membership of library	·144
41	Neighbourhood crime	·143
76	Dissatisfaction with teacher	—·143
60	Secondary school preference	·123
67	Child talks about school work	·120
46	Cleanliness of home inadequate	—·116
66	Mother not too busy to help with school work	·109
49	No fixed bath	—·107
61	Grammar school preference	·102
55	Age parents completed education	·100

Average test variance on Factor:

7+	·285	IQ	·456	Total	·540
8+	·631	Eng.	·655		
9+	·650	Arith.	·498		
10+	·542				

brightness. Of the direct parental attitude measures, *62 Preferred age of leaving* parallels the score analysis as being the most important, *61 Grammar school preference* coming 17th here as compared with first for the brightness analysis.

Only two variables appear in this table and not in the other two: *67 Child talks about school work* and *66 Mother not too busy to help with school work.* Thus it seems that parental attitude towards the child, and support for him in his educational difficulties, are of some importance in the prevention of backwardness. But note that this falls well below home literacy and attitude towards education in the order of importance.

Factor 16

Table XV

Major loadings on Factor 16—Backwardness analysis

53	Mother spends time with child in evenings	·512	
43	Father's occupation	−·238	
65	All teaching matters not to be left to the teacher	·180	
75	Changes of school	−·163	
59	Child's reading	·147	
67	Child talks about school work	·136	
54	Parents' further education	·113	
46	Cleanliness of home inadequate	·113	
45	Material needs inadequate	·103	

Average test variance on Factor:

7	+ ·251	IQ	·086	Total	·086
8	+ ·054	Eng.	·020		
9	+ ·006	Arith.	·138		
10	+ ·070				

99. A glance at the bottom section of Table XV makes it clear that this factor reflects associations *only* at 7+, and *only* with Arithmetic. Notice, however, that the average 7+ variance of ·251 is commensurate with the 7+ variance of ·285 on Factor 1: for these young children, both factors are of equal importance.

The variables represented in Table XV tend to support the last comment made about the first factor, and to underline the importance of *parental attitude to the child*. Variable 53 has a loading more than twice as great as any other measure, and is clearly the "marker variable" for this factor. It plays no part in the constellation of variables making up the first factors in our three analyses: the loadings on *53 Mother spends time with the child in the evenings* are ·120 (score), ·046 (brightness) and ·073 (backwardness). We now see, however, that this aspect of maternal attitude and behaviour *has* some relevance to backwardness, but only with reference to the youngest age group.

100. The second variable, *43 Father's occupation*, also appears for the first time as a significant variable. Its loadings on the three first factors are −·077 (score), −·104 (brightness) and ·078 (backwardness). The perverse sign in the last entry is probably of no significance, since the loading is not significantly different from zero. The uniformly low loadings in this variable, so often used by sociologists, re-emphasizes the importance of *intra*-class differences in background and parental attitude as compared with *inter*-class differences.

101. Of the other measures included in Table XV, 65 and 67 tend to support the *maternal attitude* aspect of this variable, while the deleterious effect on the young pupil of *changes of school* is again drawn to our notice. That this factor is concerned almost entirely with backwardness in *arithmetic* will not escape notice: the effect of changes of school is very likely to show itself in performance in such a logical subject as this.

D. THE THREE ANALYSES COMPARED

102. We have here three separate analyses, each yielding a single factor contributing three quarters or more to the total test variance. What are the similarities and differences in the factor patterns? Does this investigation of 186 children show differences between backwardness and brightness similar to those yielded by the investigation of 44 schools?

Similarities

103. Let us begin by considering the common elements in all three analyses. In order to avoid making what might be misleading comparisons between the actual size of loadings, we shall pay most attention to *rank order of importance* of variables. If we take—arbitrarily—the "top ten" loadings in each of the first factors, what are the variables which appear in all three analyses? The variables are these, the major common elements:

    56   Membership of library
    57   Parents' reading
    58   Books in house
    59   Child's reading
    62   Preferred age of leaving
    70   Homework given
    72   Child below standard

104. Here we have a clear indication of the importance of *home literacy* (56–59) and *parental attitude towards education* (62, 72). *The homework* variable, as suggested earlier in this report, is perhaps to be regarded as a blend of school policy, parental interest and child's attitude.

105. Two other variables appear in the "top ten" in two of the analyses only. *61 Grammar school preference* is important in the brightness and the score analyses, but much less so for backwardness. This is not an illogical result: for the average and above-average pupil this is a good measure of parental attitude, but is obviously less so for the backward child, when ambition is tempered with realism. Variable *50, Disrupted home*, appears in the top half of the tables for backwardness and score, but it is less potent for brightness.

Differences

106. As a simple way of measuring differences, and to ensure that none was overlooked, the first factor loadings of all variables were ranked in order of numerical size for all three analyses. Rank differences were then found for each variable. Those with differences of 10 ranks or more* were then listed. These are given in Table XVI.

---

* (Out of 38 environmental variables: 37 *Head teacher's rating of pupil*, and 38 *Result of* 11+ *selection tests* were omitted—as they are in the table of loadings given previously—as belonging to the criterion category rather than the environmental.)

Table XVI

Variables with 10 or more ranks difference between analyses

	Variable	Rank placing		
		Bright	Score	Backward
68	Husband's interest	6	25	37
75	Changes of school	9	29	36
63	Talks with head or class teacher	16	27	34
61	Grammar school preference	1	4	18
45	Material needs inadequate	15	26	29
40	Discussed problem behaviour at school	24	11	4
67	Child talks about school work	29	30	13
66	Mother not too busy to help with school work	30	31	15
50	Disrupted family	18	10	9
55	Age parents completed education	29	21	18

107. The top half of the table shows those measures whose effect is stronger for *brightness*, the bottom half those which affect *backwardness* most. This brings out very clearly the difference already noted, that the factors affecting backwardness tend to be those denoting maternal attitude to the *child*, while for brightness the parents' attitude to *education* seems the more important. The backward child is a pupil beset with problems. Support, affection and understanding at home help him to surmount these. The potentially bright child, on the other hand, needs not so much help in overcoming difficulties as encouragement to take full advantage of the opportunities offered. The parents' view of schooling, the value they put on education, are the factors that are likely to affect the progress of the able child.

108. Nevertheless, there still remain some puzzles in Table XVI. Who would have hypothesized that *75 Changes of school* would have the strongest effect on brightness, and the least on backwardness? It is true that the additional Factor 16 brings this in as a variable associated with backwardness at 7+, but even here its loading is low. This is a differential we find unable to understand. Similarly, the inadequacy of *material needs*, as a variable having a stronger association with brightness than with backwardness, is, at our present level of insight, inexplicable. Finally, *55 Age parents completed education* adds a third element to our puzzlement. We have already commented on the pessimistic results for this particular variable, and it will be noted that its highest rank is 19th. But why should even this tenuous measure of association be confined to backwardness? A rank of 29 for brightness (corresponding to a loading of only ·061) is, in our view, a wholly unexpected result.

SUMMARY

109. The schools analysis underlined the importance of the home background as a determinant of the educational progress and attainment of primary school children. This second phase of our inquiry, in which we look more closely at 186 individual pupils and their parents, begins to unravel some of the strands in this backcloth. It supports the schools analysis in finding that economic level and social class are much less important than aspects of parental atti-

tude, attitude to education, and attitude to books and reading. A high wage-packet and a middle-class home does not guarantee a favourable background for educational progress, and literate homes with good parental attitude to school may be found in the slums as well as in the suburbs. *Family literacy*, as evinced by measures of reading and library membership, proves to be a highly significant measure in all three analyses of individual pupils. Parental attitude to education is an equally strong indicator of educational attainment. As a single measure of this, *Preferred age of leaving* is pre-eminent for the average and the backward child; *Grammar school preference* supersedes it for the bright child.

110. The factor of parental care which has manifested itself in all our school-based surveys begins to be more clearly delineated in the pupil-analysis. Maternal attitude to the child and to his educational problems is shown as an important factor in the backwardness analysis. The problems associated with educational failure are likely to be eased with maternal support in a stable home, and so permit better school progress. On the other hand, the variable in this context which has most association with brightness is the *father's interest in school work*, which seems to act as a spur to (or a release of) ambition. A father's support and encouragement might well counteract the more adverse attitudinal forces of the neighbourhood and the peer group. The role of the mother defending and protecting the weak child and that of the father stimulating and encouraging the strong emerges surprisingly clearly from our analysis: but one suspects that the situation may not be quite so simple as it looks.

111. The pupil analysis is surprising in that it fails to support the emphasis given in the wider survey to factors of *cleanliness* and *crime*.The commanding position of these in the schools analysis is not paralleled in the analysis of individual pupils. This may be an accident of sampling—186 pupils as against 2,000, and drawn from only 22 schools—or it may be that we need a more thorough investigation of the "cleanliness" variable for individual homes. Only 23 out of 186 homes were rated by the Medical and Welfare departments as falling below an "adequate" level: such a dichotomy is a very crude measure. Similarly only 17 of our families had any criminal record.

CONCLUSION

112. Our survey was necessarily a limited one, limited in time and in coverage. We have already commented on the narrowness of our criterion measures, and on the smallness of the sample of 44 schools drawn from only one, urban, region. Nevertheless, some significant results have emerged, as well as a score or more of questions which must lead on to further research. For our part, we regard two of our findings as being of the first importance: that environmental forces bear most heavily on the brightest of our children; and that factors in the home are overwhelmingly more powerful than those of the neighbourhood and the school—and of these, factors of parental attitude to education, to the school and to books are of far greater significance than social class and occupational level. There is strong reason to believe that adverse forces of this nature operate from the earliest ages, and we see the provision of nursery schools as an important way cf attempting to counteract

them as early as possible. It seems patently obvious to us, too, that much more attention to environmental effects on education needs to be given in the training of our teachers, and we see the necessity to encourage, by every means, the institution of special courses within colleges of education. These should provide, for those students who so wish, a training in educational sociology and social work which will enable them to view these problems with a wider perspective, recognising that experiences outside the classroom are important not only for children but for teachers. In addition to such options in initial training courses, what is also needed are training courses for experienced teachers, so that they may be equipped to co-operate with the officers of the other social agencies within local authorities. Their task would be, not only to recognise cases of deprivation and to refer them to the appropriate experts, but also to bring home and school, parents and teachers, into closer relationship, to their mutual understanding and benefit. Such teachers are as necessary as remedial teachers, careers masters, or guidance counsellors, and would—like them—spend only part of their time within the classroom. The existence of a small corps of such teachers—social workers within an authority (and particularly the large urban authorities) would be of the greatest benefit in increasing our knowledge of the complex interactions between environment and educational attainment, and in developing new strategies in our efforts to provide the conditions for the full flowering of every child's potentiality.

ANNEX

Annex I

LIST OF VARIABLES—SCHOOL ANALYSIS

	Variable	Source	Basis	Distribution (actual distribution for 3-and 5-point scales: range only for remainder)
1.	Size of school	H.T.	No. of children on roll	41 – 545
2.	Size of class	H.T.	(1)÷No. of classes	22 – 43
3.	Pupil/teacher ratio	H.T.	(1)÷No. of teachers (including H.T.)	12 – 35
4.	Attendance	H.T.	% for Junior Dept. 1962/63	82·6 – 94·2
5.	Children qualified for special school	H.T.	% of school roll, Sept. 1962—April 1964	0 – 10·1
6.	Mother tongue not English	H.T.	% of school roll	0 – 13·6
7.	Appearance and sociability	Observer	5-point rating on (a) general liveliness, (b) appearance (no penalty for worn but clean clothing), (c) attitude towards Observer	2:17:19:5:1
8.	Free meals	H.T.	% of school roll, Spring Term 1964	2·6 – 31
9.	Free clothing	H.T.	% of school roll, Spring Term 1964	0 – 10
10.	Footwear: full payment (N.A.B.)	H.T.	% of school roll, Spring Term 1964	0 – 7·6
11.	Verminous	Medical Dept.	% of school roll found verminous by school nurse	2·8 – 37·3
12.	Children's height	Medical Dept.	Average height of 10+ children	3·5 – 10·5 (deviations from 4 ft. 6 in.)
13.	Criminal record: children	Criminal Record Office	% of 10+ children with court conviction or police caution	0 – 12·5
14.	Teachers < 30 years of age	H.T.	% of staff, including H.T.	0 – 100
15.	Teachers > 50 years of age	H.T.	% of staff, including H.T.	0 – 66·7
16.	Graduate teachers	H.T.	% of staff, including H.T.	0 – 50·0
17.	Teacher turnover	H.T.	No. of teachers appointed within last 2 years as % of staff in March 1964	0 – 150
18.	Male teachers	H.T.	% of staff, excluding H.T.	0 – 75
19.	"Sex" of school	H.T.	4-point scale: Girls only: Mixed, female H.T.: Mixed, male H.T.: Boys only	2:16:24:2
20.	Married women teachers with children	H.T.	Married women teachers with children as % of staff, excluding H.T.	0 – 50

continued on next page

LIST OF VARIABLES—SCHOOL ANALYSIS—*continued*

Annex I—continued

	Variable	Source	Basis	Distribution (actual distribution for 3-and 5-point scales: range only for remainder)
21.	Attitude to enquiry	Observer	3-point scale	22:13:9
22.	Quality of H.T.	Observer	5-point scale: sympathy with modern methods; efficiency; relations with staff and children	1:15:16:10:2
23.	Quality of staff	Observer	5-point scale: sympathy with modern methods; efficiency; relations with staff and children	2:6:24:10:2
24.	Progressiveness (L.E.A.)	L.E.A. Inspector	5-point scale	1:14:21:5:3
25.	Progressiveness (Observer)	Observer	5-point scale: "formal-free" scale, ranging from extremely formal and orthodox to most informal, free and progressive	0:13:8:15:8
27.	Examination technique	Observer	5-point scale: rating of emphasis on and efficiency in, preparation for exams and objective tests	2:19:15:6:2
28.	Social atmosphere of school	Observer	5-point scale: general social atmosphere of school, with emphasis on staff-children relationship	3:10:11:13:7
29.	Homework	Observer	3-point scale, based on interviews with children	18:17:9
30.	Out-of-school activities	Observer	5-point scale, based on interviews with children and covering sports, day-trips, camping, music, museum classes, etc.	1:7:14:14:8
31.	First impression of school	Observer	5-point scale: cleanliness, neatness and decoration of building and general atmosphere	1:7:14:14:8
32.	11+ success	L.E.A.	4-year average, % places obtained in selective schools	0 – 39
33.	Streaming	Observer	2-point scale. One-form entry counted as un-streamed, except for seven schools which grouped on ability and mixed the age-groups	23:21
34.	Corporal punishment	Observer	2-point scale: present—not in evidence	19:24

continued on next page

LIST OF VARIABLES—SCHOOL ANALYSIS—*continued*

Annex I—continued

	Variable	Source	Basis	Distribution (actual distribution for 3- and 5-point scales: range only for remainder)
35.	Recently re-organized	H.T.	2-point scale: whether reorganized within last 4 years	9:35
36.	Age of building	H.T.	Date of building of main structure	1 – 130 years
37.	Quality of building	Observer	5-point scale: provision and size of hall, toilets, spare classrooms, traffic noise, field or garden, staff rooms and medical rooms, general outlook	5:12:11:11:5
38.	School equipment	Observer	5-point scale: amount and quality of P.E. equipment, art and craft materials, maths apparatus, desks and chairs	5:18:12:6:3
39.	Classroom space	Observer	Floor-space per child in 10+ classes	11 – 24 sq. ft.
40.	Library	Observer	5-point scale: space and equipment available, and use to which it was put	10:11:8:10:5
41.	Housing standard	School nurses and Observer	9/5-point scales: pooled independent assessments by nurse and Observer of housing standards of school catchment area	22 to 80
42.	School breaking and entering	H.T.	No. of breaking and entering incidents January 1960—Spring 1964	0 – 13
43.	Crime: neighbourhood	C.R.O.	No. of criminal families living within 50 houses of the child's home address: average per child.	1·55 – 22·02
44.	Play areas	Observer	5-point scale: areas available near children's homes, access undisturbed by major traffic arteries	13:9:11:4:7
45.	Parental occupation	Medical Dept.	Mean of 10+ children's parents' occupations on Registrar-General's Scale	2·95 – 4·00
46.	Mother working	H.T.	% of 10+ mothers in regular employment, part- or full-time	19 – 100

continued on next page

LIST OF VARIABLES—SCHOOL ANALYSIS—continued

Annex I—continued

	Variable	Source	Basis	Distribution (actual distribution for 3- and 5-point scales: range only for remainder)
47.	Material needs	Medical Dept. and Welfare Dept.	Pooled independent assessments of 10+ homes where reasonable material needs of children were not being met	0 – 33
48.	Cleanliness of home	Medical and Welfare Depts.	Pooled independent assessments of 10+ homes falling below adequate levels of cleanliness	0 – 37
49.	Corporation housing	Welfare Dept. and Housing Dept.	% of 10+ children living in corporation houses	0 – 100
50.	Disrupted homes	Medical and Welfare Depts.	Pooled independent assessments of homes affected by: drink and drugs, incapacitatory illness of parent, divorce, one parent deceased, child illegitimate, foster parent, adoption, parental disharmony	1 – 42
51.	Crime: family	C.R.O.	% of 10+ children's families with criminal record	1·23 – 30
52.	Crime: house address	C.R.O.	% of 10+ children's houses with inhabitants with criminal record	0 – 72·2
53.	7+ Picture Intelligence Test (M.H.)	Test	Mean score	82·91 – 121·93
54.		Test	% 10+ children < 85 standard score	0 – 45·6
55.		Test	% 10+ children > 115 standard score	0 – 69·0
56.	7+ Arithmetic (NFER)	Test	Mean score	80·82 – 115·64
57.		Test	% < 85	0 – 54·5
58.		Test	% > 115	0 – 50·0
59.	8+ Sentence Reading Test (NFER)	Test	Mean score	77·73 – 110·56
60.		Test	% < 85	1·9 – 81·8
61.		Test	% > 115	0 – 54·2

continued on next page

List of Variables—School Analysis—continued

Annex I—continued

	Variable	Source	Basis	Distribution (actual distribution for 3- and 5-point scales: range only for remainder)
62.	8+ Mechanical Arithmetic Test (Manchester)	Test	Mean score	84·90 – 108·93
63.		Test	% < 85	0 – 38·8
64.		Test	% > 115	0 – 42·2
65.	8+ Problem Arithmetic Test (Manchester)	Test	Mean score	74·73 – 108·17
66.		Test	% < 85	0 – 90·9
67.		Test	% > 115	0 – 40·4
68.	9+ M.H. Junior Reasoning Test	Test	Mean score	85·58 – 115·22
69.		Test	% < 85	0 – 36·0
70.		Test	% > 115	0 – 53·9
71.	9+ M.H. Junior English Test	Test	Mean score	80·42 – 112·96
72.		Test	% < 85	0 – 83·3
73.		Test	% > 115	0 – 49·1
74.	10+ M.H. Verbal Reasoning Test	Test	Mean score	79·4 – 107·12
75.		Test	% < 85	0 – 60·0
76.		Test	% > 115	0 – 37·5
77.	10+ M.H. English Test	Test	Mean score	80·20 – 113·83
78.		Test	% < 85	0 – 90·0
79.		Test	% > 115	0 – 44·4
80.	10+ Composition Test (Manchester)	Test	Mean score	77·30 – 110·94
81.		Test	% < 85	0 – 100·0
82.		Test	% > 115	0 – 33·3

continued on next page

LIST OF VARIABLES—SCHOOL ANALYSIS—*continued*

Annex I—continued

	Variable	Source	Basis	Distribution (actual distribution for 3- and 5-point scales: range only for remainder)
83.	10+ M.H. Mathematics	Test	Mean score	75·20 – 110·74
84.	Test I	Test	% < 85	0 – 90·0
85.		Test	% > 115	0 – 42·9
86.	10+ M.H. Mathematics	Test	Mean score	81·67 – 111·59
87.	Test II	Test	% < 85	0 – 60·0
88.		Test	% > 115	0 – 44·4

VARIMAX ANALYSIS

Variables	1	2	3	4	5	6	7	8	9	10	h²
CHILDREN											
No. of children in the school	295	056	757	039	-110	-143	318	157	-192	004	86
Average number of children in a class	362	-202	644	-056	-037	-102	003	059	-042	-030	61
Pupil/Teacher ratio	297	-211	728	-022	008	-173	062	-092	-142	-094	74
Attendance	425	170	422	126	175	139	160	-242	174	105	58
Percentage qualifying for special schools	-430	-074	-212	-054	238	-011	-214	197	472	-101	61
Percentage non-English	155	196	018	-700	198	-184	279	298	-040	035	80
Appearance and sociability	510	260	-074	-024	088	137	-015	-481	005	157	62
Percentage free meals in school	-536	-072	-133	-298	126	126	-127	568	-123	-225	84
Percentage free clothing	-399	084	-033	015	-112	082	-445	269	-426	-087	65
N.A.B. footwear	-220	221	-096	-402	-173	235	-091	248	-280	-132	52
Verminous	-557	-092	-165	014	-047	-121	-287	130	-152	-387	64
Height	386	086	003	185	-147	-393	-011	-059	-311	228	52
Criminal	-011	-080	-007	-165	-058	-001	003	045	-588	020	39
TEACHERS											
Age < 30	-185	155	020	-203	-064	-618	028	-082	-110	-326	61
Age > 50	128	-369	-125	188	-105	495	-102	-055	-020	394	63
Graduate trained	-233	036	-021	-003	311	-173	-025	-046	-189	503	47
Turnover rate	002	089	040	-027	-640	-029	004	042	-092	090	44
No. of male teachers	-196	180	-130	-002	015	644	-064	064	167	-304	63
"Sex" of school	-141	-066	032	-106	-025	793	075	-137	-232	-081	75
Proportion of married women with children (-H.T.)	277	127	094	073	-093	-029	017	-056	095	762	71

continued on next page

VARIMAX ANALYSIS—continued

Annex II—continued

Variables	1	2	3	4	5	6	7	8	9	10	h²
TEACHING											
Attitude to inquiry	-026	417	-046	054	004	-102	406	-033	-119	-105	38
Quality of head teacher	-166	687	-041	212	-024	072	082	004	031	-024	56
Quality of staff	121	741	108	-144	-018	-139	165	-307	053	-077	75
Progressiveness (L.E.A. rating)	255	510	-271	332	088	-033	093	098	177	161	59
Progressiveness (Observer rating)	000	773	-124	-027	-272	-002	-084	-018	008	041	70
Examination technique	160	658	-056	-054	124	-006	363	-260	-022	124	70
Social—adults with children	-006	496	-157	219	252	-123	-060	-083	105	-224	47
Homework	-365	-215	-021	286	142	-016	-493	042	151	045	55
Out of school activities	-291	387	105	354	064	327	-012	168	-150	-036	53
First impression of school	-013	830	149	-067	-084	-033	039	098	073	118	75
11+ success over past four years	715	153	387	061	-017	029	216	-259	016	212	85
Streaming	-420	252	-421	173	092	116	-446	-065	000	-032	67
Corporal punishment	091	235	-534	360	-007	-063	182	007	380	001	66
Reorganized	152	291	064	-055	-111	108	685	-056	202	-001	65
BUILDING											
Age	-310	-222	-621	142	402	-048	-084	055	108	060	74
Quality	188	579	422	146	-316	089	-165	062	050	126	73
Equipment	-116	565	-223	332	-459	-040	050	184	-083	175	78
Class space	-299	231	-194	-271	-142	-052	-097	085	448	154	52
Library	062	420	056	686	014	091	-131	096	-045	122	71
NEIGHBOURHOOD											
Housing (Health and Observer combined)	236	111	557	373	332	020	111	-366	096	-128	80
Breaking and entering	-218	-098	597	014	054	069	-099	296	100	187	56
Crime rate of child's neighbourhood	-360	-121	007	-537	051	-096	104	484	-258	-206	80
Play areas	257	222	633	224	100	090	149	-008	059	141	63

continued on next page

VARIMAX ANALYSIS—*continued*

Annex II—continued

Variables	1	2	3	4	5	6	7	8	9	10	h²
HOME											
Father's occupation	-476	-079	-024	-266	045	397	-207	146	-075	-177	56
Mother working	-251	070	-452	106	-252	121	055	-160	-184	-158	45
Material needs (Medical and Welfare combined)	-465	-132	-235	015	029	-038	-258	439	042	-278	63
Cleanliness (Medical and Welfare combined)	-594	011	-108	142	-062	023	-062	218	032	-249	50
Corporation housing	-219	174	439	059	373	076	-226	-224	033	-278	60
Psychological (Medical and Welfare combined)	-128	-084	059	-034	-111	158	-015	805	082	-035	72
Crime of family	-546	117	232	-262	173	207	046	071	133	-022	53
Crime of house	-081	235	327	-150	-097	-293	-028	657	-013	217	77
CRITERIA											
7+ I.Q. M	795	106	057	076	087	-133	-202	-212	-012	220	81
−	-417	-348	051	034	-169	044	360	346	-212	-349	75
+	821	034	026	018	-045	053	-072	096	-060	085	71
7+ A M	640	-127	020	-104	431	-045	-269	-170	-384	134	89
−	581	-016	125	058	-398	-149	-362	150	145	-194	75
+	471	-137	063	-233	517	-183	-128	300	-331	-006	81
8+ E M	829	-086	236	-006	184	-011	225	054	-096	-012	85
−	-833	-043	-060	081	-089	-003	-026	-108	040	-075	73
+	751	-093	190	044	216	053	335	-065	-188	020	81
A(M) M	570	-095	157	073	583	042	233	018	-175	252	85
−	-420	059	-061	-067	-665	-072	002	011	-180	-229	72
+	484	168	119	-024	361	-075	473	141	-218	293	79
A(P) M	773	004	187	211	230	-128	075	028	-090	231	81
−	-793	-040	-129	-163	-157	008	139	057	-070	-018	73
+	552	084	038	223	246	-162	464	129	-148	221	75

continued on next page

Annex II—continued

VARIMAX ANALYSIS—continued

Variables	1	2	3	4	5	6	7	8	9	10	h²
CRITERIA *continued*											
9+ I.Q. M	897	019	−047	201	152	011	140	−096	−104	114	92
−	−712	−206	101	−303	−078	−221	−143	121	160	005	77
+	809	−153	058	134	077	−024	301	−074	−158	088	83
E M	874	−059	149	096	138	078	308	−045	−107	−011	93
−	−825	−019	047	−063	−207	−178	−143	−008	−020	063	79
+	688	−081	339	046	167	−059	433	−090	−101	002	83
10+ I.Q. M	916	−022	124	026	−061	−034	−011	−154	058	033	89
−	−885	060	014	034	006	017	−121	025	−124	022	82
+	792	031	174	103	−039	−082	−359	−046	009	023	81
10+ E M	924	−056	137	−036	022	−118	−071	−135	−049	−015	92
−	−893	−003	058	036	035	111	−149	−003	010	022	84
+	773	007	079	024	084	−124	−467	−118	−146	−029	88
10+ E(C) M	826	−098	160	−049	−016	−253	−200	−011	128	065	84
−	−777	114	−127	102	084	226	023	−030	−239	013	76
+	703	−062	161	−033	036	−276	−345	−149	062	−059	75
10+ A(i) M	939	091	121	−002	−035	−020	−077	−127	064	−019	93
−	−877	−008	061	−024	023	072	−167	028	−187	158	87
+	791	157	286	014	−019	−012	−281	−060	019	097	82
10+ A(ii) M	921	096	160	−052	007	037	−045	−132	040	074	91
−	−821	−070	−066	164	116	−058	−249	−060	−127	−045	81
+	744	064	310	004	−051	−112	−309	−148	004	126	80
COMMON FACTOR VARIANCE	26·17	6·06	5·72	3·73	3·84	3·24	4·58	3·76	2·68	2·88	

    395

Annex III

LIST OF VARIABLES—PUPIL ANALYSIS

Variable	Source	Basis (In distributions, the highest coding given to the category on the right)	Distribution or Range
1. 7+ Picture Intelligence (M.H.)	Test	Raw score	70 – 140
2. 7+ Arithmetic (NFER)	Test	Raw score	65 – 136
3. 8+ Sentence Reading Test (NFER)	Test	Raw score	65 – 137
4. 8+ Mechanical Arithmetic Test (Manchester)	Test	Raw score	65 – 126
5. 8+ Problem Arithmetic Test (Manchester)	Test	Raw score	65 – 126
6. 9+ M.H. Junior Reasoning Test	Test	Raw score	70 – 139
7. 9+ M.H. Junior English Test	Test	Raw score	65 – 135
8. 10+ M.H. Verbal Reasoning Test	Test	Raw score	68 – 130
9. 10+ M.H. English Test	Test	Raw score	68 – 140
10. 10+ Composition Test (Manchester)	Test	Raw score	68 – 148
11. 10+ M.H. Mathematics Test I	Test	Raw score	64 – 134
12. 10+ M.H. Mathematics Test II	Test	Raw score	62 – 136
13. 7+ Picture Intelligence (M.H.)	Test	Whether < 85	164:22
14.	Test	Whether > 115	135:51
15. 7+ Arithmetic (NFER)	Test	Whether < 85	148:38
16.	Test	Whether > 115	166:20
17. 8+ Sentence Reading Test (NFER)	Test	Whether < 85	138:48
18.	Test	Whether > 115	156:30
19. 8+ Mechanical Arithmetic Test (Manchester)	Test	Whether < 85	154:32
20.	Test	Whether > 115	163:23

continued on next page

LIST OF VARIABLES—PUPIL ANALYSIS—continued

Annex III—continued

	Variable	Source	Basis (In distributions, the highest coding given to the category on the right)	Distribution or Range
21.	8+ Problem Arithmetic	Test	Whether < 85	146:40
22.	Test (Manchester)	Test	Whether > 115	162:24
23.	9+ M.H. Junior Reasoning	Test	Whether < 85	159:27
24.	Test	Test	Whether > 115	131:55
25.	9+ M.H. Junior English	Test	Whether < 85	143:43
26.	Test	Test	Whether > 115	147:39
27.	10+ M.H. Verbal	Test	Whether < 85	141:45
28.	Reasoning Test	Test	Whether > 115	162:24
29.	10+ English Test	Test	Whether < 85	138:48
30.		Test	Whether > 115	157:29
31.	10+ Composition	Test	Whether < 85	134:52
32.	Test (Manchester)	Test	Whether > 115	158:28
33.	10+ M.H. Mathematics	Test	Whether < 85	136:50
34.	Test I	Test	Whether > 115	162:24
35.	10+ M.H. Mathematics	Test	Whether < 85	134:52
36.	Test II	Test	Whether > 115	163:23
37.	Head teacher's rating of pupil	H.T.	5-point rating on overall benefit gained from primary school education, after making allowances for differences in general scholastic ability	8:39:75:49:15

continued on next page

LIST OF VARIABLES—PUPIL ANALYSIS—continued

Annex III—continued

	Variable	Source	Basis (In distributions, the highest coding given to the category on the right)	Distribution or Range
38.	Type of secondary school to which child will go	C.O.I.	4-point rating on basis of selectivity: Secondary modern: Comprehensive: Technical: Grammar	128:10:22:26
39.	Whether child is difficult to control at home	C.O.I.	3-point scale. Answer to "Do you find......is an easy or difficult child to control on the whole?"	148:23:15
40.	Whether parent has discussed child's problem behaviour at school	C.O.I.	Whether parent mentioned behavioural problems "e.g. nervousness, worry, bad behaviour" as a topic discussed with the head or class teacher	130 No, 56 Yes
41.	Crime rating of neighbourhood	C.R.O.	No. of criminal families living within 50 houses of the child's home address	0 – 17
42.	Facilities for play	C.O.I.	5-point scale. How many of the following were checked as accessible for the child: parks or fields, playgrounds; swimming baths; indoor play-centres	4:16:53:79:34
43.	Father's occupation	C.O.I.	3-point scale. Modified Registrar General's scale dividing manual and non-manual workers in Classes III and IV	2:13:88:19:37:6:19 :2
44.	Number of children in the household	C.O.I.	Number of siblings of all ages, plus any other children living in the household	Range 1 – 11 25:45:40:27:13:20: 9:4:1:1:1
45.	Material needs	Medical Dept. and Welfare Dept.	Pooled independent assessments of homes where reasonable material needs of children were not being met	161 No, 25 Yes
46.	Cleanliness	Medical Dept. and Welfare Dept.	Pooled independent assessments of homes falling below adequate levels of cleanliness	163 No, 23 Yes
47.	Type of house	C.O.I.	5-point scale, measuring detachment of house: detached: semi-detached: terraced: flat: rooms	2:55:107:21:1
48.	Bedroom deficiency	C.O.I.	Number of bedrooms above or below standard minimum. 8-point scale	1:1:20:74:63:21:5:1

continued on next page

LIST OF VARIABLES—PUPIL ANALYSIS—continued

Annex III—continued

	Variable	Source	Basis (In distributions, the highest coding given to the category on the right)	Distribution or Range
49.	No fixed bath	C.O.I.	3-point scale. Whether there was a fixed bath or shower for family's own use: shared: none	135:1:50
50.	Psychological disruption	Medical Dept. and Welfare Dept.	Pooled independent assessments of homes affected by:—drink and drugs, incapacitatory illness of parent, divorce, one parent deceased, child illegitimate, foster parent, adoption, parental disharmony. 3-point scale: none of these: one of these: two of these	160:19:7
51.	Non-natural family	C.O.I.	7-point scale. Child living with natural father and mother: natural mother, father substitute: natural father, mother substitute: natural mother, no father or substitute: natural father, no mother or substitute: living with relatives other than natural parents: living with people to whom he/she is not related	159:7:0:16:4:0:0:
52.	Family crime	C.R.O.	Whether any member of the family had a criminal record	169 No, 17 Yes
53.	Mother does things with child in the evening	C.O.I.	Whether mother spends time with child in the evenings, playing or reading with him/her, taking him/her out. 3-point scale: No: occasional evenings only: most evenings	28:95:63
54.	Parents' further education	C.O.I.	7-point scale. Pooling ratings of father's and mother's further education (if any), each parent's F.E. assessed on a 4-point scale: none: part-time or correspondence course: full-time apprenticeship: full-time course in college or university	117:18:33:12:3:1:2
55.	Age when parents completed education	C.O.I.	7-point scale, pooling the coded ages at which child's father and mother completed full-time education	132:28:17:4:1:3:1
56.	Membership of library	C.O.I.	Parent's membership of a library. 3-point scale: neither parent a member within previous 10 years: at least one parent a member within 10 years: at least one parent a present member	81:46:59

continued on next page

LIST OF VARIABLES—PUPIL ANALYSIS—*continued*

Annex III—continued

Variable	Source	Basis (In distributions, the highest coding given to the category on the right	Distribution or Range
57. Parents' reading	C.O.I.	7-point scale, pooling parents' reading scores, each parent's reading assessed on a 4-point scale: none: periodicals only: fiction with or without periodicals: some non-fiction books included	27:6:39:28:33:18:35
58. Books in house	C.O.I.	Presence of books in the house, excluding magazines and children's books. 3-point scale: none: 1–5 books: over 5 books	47:20:119
59. Child's reading	C.O.I.	Child's reading at home, apart from homework. 5-point scale: no reading: comics only: reads books less than twice a week: reads books two or three times a week: reads books most days	12:10:30:42:92
60. Secondary school preference	C.O.I.	Whether parent expressed a wish for any particular type of secondary school, e.g. grammar, secondary modern, when asked "What type of secondary school did you hope he/she would go to?	59 No, 127 Yes
61. Grammar school preference	C.O.I.	Whether, in reply to above question, parent expressed a wish for a grammar school education for the child	130 No, 56 Yes
62. Preferred age of leaving	C.O.I.	6-point scale: under 15 were it possible: as soon as possible: 16: 17: 18+	20:7:26:31:42
63. Talks with head or class teacher	C.O.I.	Number of talks with head or class teachers of present school: 6-point scale: none: one talk: two talks: three talks: four to six talks: over six talks	11:9:15:16:44:91
64. Inquiries before starting present school	C.O.I.	6-point scale, source, if any, from whom parents obtained information about the scale in advance: no inquiries: neighbours without children at the school: neighbours whose children attended the school: religious adviser: teachers at previous school: inquiries made at the school	98:0:22:1:1:64

continued on next page

LIST OF VARIABLES—PUPIL ANALYSIS—*continued*   *Annex III—continued*

Variable	Source	Basis (In distributions, the highest coding given to the category on the right)	Distribution or Range
65. All teaching matters not to be left to the teachers	C.O.I.	Asked to indicate agreement with statement "Parents should leave all teaching and helping with school subjects to the teachers". 3-point scale. Agree: uncertain: disagrees	96:4:86
66. Not too busy to help with school work	C.O.I.	Asked to indicate agreement with statement "I have too much to do to spend time on helping with school work". 3-point scale: agree: uncertain: disagree	45:4:137
67. Child talks about school work	C.O.I.	Dichotomy: no, or only occasionally: yes, often	58:128
68. Husband's interest	C.O.I.	3-point scale: all left to wife: no husband: husband interested	31:20:135
69. Against stricter schools	C.O.I.	5-point scale, pooling answers to two questions on whether (a) the schools should be stricter, (b) the teachers should be firmer or less firm	39:48:15:82:2
70. Homework given	C.O.I.	Whether child is given homework at this present school	42 No, 144 Yes
71. Should be homework	C.O.I.	Parents asked whether they thought the child should have homework. 3-point scale: No: ?: Yes	27:7:152
72. Child below standard	C.O.I.	Parents mentioned child was below standard in reply to open question about any worries about the child's progress	144 No, 40 Yes
73. Children should be brought on faster	C.O.I.	Asked to indicate agreement with statement "Children should be brought on faster". 3-point scale: No: ?: Yes	122:15:49
74. Believes there are faults in the child	C.O.I.	Parents referred to a fault in the child, e.g. not paying attention/lazy, in reply to the open question about worries about the child's progress	175:11

APPENDIX 10

FIRST REPORT OF THE NATIONAL CHILD DEVELOPMENT STUDY
(1958 COHORT)

1. In this Appendix we reproduce an abbreviated version of the First Report of the National Child Development Study (1958 Cohort). This multi-disciplinary study of children born in 1958 has been financed, at the Council's suggestion, by the Department of Education and Science and other interested Government Departments in the belief that the data in the 1958 Perinatal Mortality Survey provided an opportunity for follow-up which should not be missed. It was hoped that a preliminary report would throw light on several of the major issues on which the Central Advisory Council were asked to report to the Secretary of State.

2. By any standards, the N.C.D.S. research team, directed by Dr. M. Kellmer Pringle and Professor Neville Butler, and led by Mr. Ronald Davie, have succeeded well in providing us with an all-round picture of children at seven. Their success is all the more remarkable in view of the shortness of time in which they have produced their study. Unfortunately, there have been some disappointments—in the time available it was not possible, for example, to assess the effects of nursery education on children's subsequent performance at school. Other difficulties, particularly in the study of children settling in at school for the first time, have arisen from the fact that the study lay fallow for the seven years after the children were born—a reflection, perhaps, on the difficulty of getting funds for research. The risk of using data necessarily derived from parents' and teachers' recollection was bound to be present and was fully appreciated from the outset. This has been taken into account in interpreting the relevant results which, despite this inevitable shortcoming are, nevertheless, significant and valuable.

3. In the selection from the whole Report which is published here, two major excisions have been made. The full Report contains many tables of medical data. Some in the main text and most in the Appendix have been omitted for reasons of space. Secondly, the correlations between the data reported here and those in the 1958 Perinatal Mortality Survey had not been worked out at the time of publication and we are, therefore, unable to publish an interim report of them. We have also omitted the copies of the Questionnaires used by the Study. Our reasons for these omissions, apart from those of space, are that the whole of this First Report is to be published by Messrs. Longmans, Green & Company in January 1967, and those who wish to follow up medical data will find full details in that publication.

4. It will be clear to readers of this Appendix that the National Child Development Study promises to produce information of major importance to all who are interested in the educational, health and welfare services for children. We have already made use of their findings in our own Report. The N.C.D.S. research team will be the first to point out that these findings are preliminary, but they give a powerful indication at least of what more is to

follow. The sponsoring bodies, the University of London Institute of Child Health, the National Birthday Trust Fund, the National Bureau for Co-operation in Child Care, the National Foundation for Educational Research in England and Wales, are to be congratulated on encouraging the production of what promises to be a valuable contribution to our knowledge.

FIRST REPORT

of the

NATIONAL CHILD DEVELOPMENT STUDY
(1958 Cohort)

submitted to

THE CENTRAL ADVISORY COUNCIL FOR EDUCATION
(ENGLAND)

APRIL, 1966

Sponsored by:

Institute of Child Health, University of London
National Birthday Trust Fund
National Bureau for Co-operation in Child Care
National Foundation for Educational Research in England and Wales

in collaboration with:

Association of Chief Education Officers (in England and Wales)
Society of Medical Officers of Health
Association of Directors of Education (in Scotland)

CONTENTS OF FULL REPORT (INCLUDING THOSE SECTIONS OMITTED IN THIS VERSION. REFERENCES TO SECTIONS AND TABLES FOLLOW THE FULL REPORT)

Section VI: Inter-relationship of the Variables

Section VII: Interim Findings—Summary and Discussion of Main Findings

APPENDIX 1

APPENDIX 2

RESEARCH TEAM

Co-Directors: Professor N. R. Butler, M.D., F.R.C.P., D.C.H.[1]
                  Mrs. M. L. Kellmer Pringle, B.A., Ph.D., Dip.Ed.Psych.[2]

Principal Research Officer: R. Davie, B.A., Dip.Ed.Psych.

Senior Medical Research Officer: M. J. Ball, B.Sc., M.B., B.S., D.P.H.

Research Officers: Miss M. J. A. Moncrieff, M.A. (October 1964 to
                       November 1965).
                       Miss M. Levius, B.A. (from November 1965).

Statistician: H. Goldstein, B.Sc.[3]

Administrative Secretary: Miss V. Shenton.

[1] Professor of Child Health, University of Bristol.
[2] Director, National Bureau for Co-operation in Child Care.
  Lecturer in Statistics, Institute of Child Health, University of London.

ACKNOWLEDGEMENTS

A project, such as the National Child Development Study, would not be possible without the help and co-operation of a large number of individuals and organizations. The sponsoring bodies of the Study, the Co-Directors and the research team gratefully acknowledge and thank all those who have contributed to this enormous task.

The Study has been carried out with the collaboration of the Association of Chief Education Officers (in England and Wales), the Society of Medical Officers of Health and the Association of Directors of Education (in Scotland), who have throughout given their advice and support.

Acknowledgement and thanks are due to the Central Advisory Council for Education (England) and the then Welsh Department, Department of Education and Science, and to the Scottish Education Department, who wrote to all the Local Education Authorities; and to the Ministry of Health for circularising the Local N.H.S. Executive Councils.

Assistance was kindly given by the Senior Administrative Medical Officers of the Regional Hospital Boards, the staff of the Local N.H.S. Executive Councils and also by many Children's Officers.

The staffs of The Government Social Survey (Central Office of Information), the General Register Office and the M.R.C. Medical Sociology Research Unit in Aberdeen have given valuable advice and assistance.

The generous co-operation of the Chief Education Officers, Principal School Medical Officers and their staffs who were concerned with the administration of the Study in each local authority is gratefully acknowledged. They are warmly thanked for all the time and attention they have given to ensure the success of the Study.

Special appreciation must also be expressed to the teachers, school medical officers and health visitors and school welfare officers in every part of England, Scotland and Wales, who undertook all the interviewing, testing and examining. Without their help, indeed, the Study could not have been carried out. The parents of the children are most warmly thanked for their co-operation and support. It is the second time that most of them have given valuable information about their children.

The sponsoring bodies, the Co-Directors and the research team are glad to be able to take this opportunity of thanking the members of the Steering Committee, both collectively and individually, for their invaluable and unfailing help and support; and to acknowledge and thank the organizations and their representatives on the Consultative Committee.

Acknowledgement and thanks for the interest and specialist help are due to many people, all of whom cannot be named, but among whom must be mentioned: Mr. W. B. Barrett, Dr. D. E. Cullington, Mrs. J. Davey, Dr. J. J. B. Dempster, Dr. P. A. Gardiner, Professor M. Healy, Professor R. Illsley, Miss H. J. Lewin, Miss M. Manning, Dr. I. C. Monro, Dr. J. Morris, Dr. R. C. Pearson, Mr. T. V. Pretty, Mr. A. P. Round, Professor M. Quenouille, and Dr. M. Sheridan.

Mrs. V. Booth and Dr. D. H. Stott generously waived royalties on their test material, and the latter also gave further help.

Special thanks are due to the staffs of the four sponsoring bodies for all they have contributed and for their patience and competence in the face of the frequent and very heavy demands made on them.

Mention must also be made of all those temporary staff who for varying times have so enthusiastically helped with the vast amount of clerical and administrative work involved.

The University of London Press kindly supplied the Bristol Social-Adjustment Guides and the Southgate Tests at cost; and the Ames Company gave Urine Test material for all the children concerned.

o

FOREWORD

This Report, prepared for the Central Advisory Council for Education (England), is inevitably very much of an interim nature.

The follow-through Study of the 1958 Cohort of children was not begun until October 1964, and the task of tracing the whereabouts of 17,000 children nearly seven years after their birth was itself immense and had to be completed substantially before the field work could begin in 1965. Not unexpectedly, the analysis of the data for this Report had to commence before information on all the children had come in. Hence, the work reported here bears upon only 11,000 of the children in England and consists of relatively straightforward analyses.

It does, however, represent a considerable feat. The reader will be surprised at the width and richness of this harvest of facts—many of them barely surmised before—which have been obtained, analysed and presented in a total period of 19 months. The deadline for this Report could not have been met in this way without the fullest and most rapid co-operation of the schools, the parents, the medical and social services, without the organizing skill and drive of the Co-Directors and, above all, without the devotion and competence of the very small research and clerical staff assigned to the project. Particular mention should be made of the Principal Research Officer, Mr. R. Davie, and the Statistician, Mr. H. Goldstein.

The Steering Committee wishes to place on record its awareness of certain inevitable shortcomings—the absence of the more complex and powerful analyses, the fact that the references to previous literature have not all been followed up, and the marks of haste which will be apparent to the attentive reader. It also wishes to underline the achievement of the team in carrying through what to many of us experienced in these things would appear an impossible task in the time.

W. D. WALL,
Chairman of the Steering Committee.

I—INTRODUCTION

The group of seven-year-old children featured in this Report are part of a larger national cohort in England, Scotland and Wales. The children were the subjects of a survey at the time of their birth; and information has now been gathered on many aspects of their growth and development. It is hoped that this study of the children can be continued at intervals throughout their childhood and, perhaps, into adult life.

A. BACKGROUND TO THE STUDY

1. *The 1958 Perinatal Mortality Survey*

In 1958 information was gathered on some 17,000 babies born during the week 3rd to 9th March in England, Scotland and Wales. This Survey (Butler and Bonham, 1963), sponsored by the National Birthday Trust Fund, reviewed the administration of British maternity services and the causes of perinatal death (still births and deaths in the first week).

During the course of the investigation a vast amount of sociological and medical data were collected about the children and their families, including details of the parents' education and occupations; ante-natal care; any obstetrical medical complications; the duration of the pregnancy; and the condition and weight of the babies at birth.

This cohort of children can be considered unique for a number of reasons: it was a truly national series, selected only by date of birth; the very high proportion of returns (an estimated 98 per cent of all babies born during the week in question) reduced the possibility of any bias; and the comprehensive nature of the perinatal data was unparalleled in the world for any national cohort.

2. *The National Child Development Study (1958 Cohort)*

In 1964 the opportunity arose to trace and study these children again, and the National Child Development Study (1958 Cohort) was set up for this purpose. The Study is financially supported by a grant from the Department of Education and Science, the Home Office and the Scottish Education Department, and is sponsored by the four bodies detailed at the beginning of this Report; one of these bodies, the National Bureau for Co-operation in Child Care, is responsible for its administration.

The investigation is at present a three year project, but it is hoped that it will constitute the second stage of a longitudinal study of the original 1958 cohort of children throughout their childhood and into adult life. Thus, the aims of the Study can be divided into: short-term goals relating to the present three year investigation; and long-term aims which depend upon continued follow-up of the children. The former may be summarised as follows:

(*a*) To study the educational, behavioural, emotional, social and physical development of a large and representative group of British children in order to gather normative data; to investigate the complex inter-relationships between the many facets, both normal and deviant, of children's development; and to report the incidence of handicaps and the provision currently being made.

(*b*) To utilize the uniquely comprehensive perinatal data, already available, in an evaluation of the relationships between conditions during pregnancy and at birth, both medical and social, and the development of children in all its aspects at the age of seven years. From this investigation it is hoped amongst other things to determine some of the factors at birth which place children "at risk" of developing handicapping conditions. Such information should permit early identification of "vulnerable" children so that earlier diagnosis and treatment, or provision, will be possible. The kinds of disability about which this sort of information is needed are not only the grosser forms, but also the more numerous "minimal" handicaps which, if undetected, at best prevent children from realizing their full potential and, at worst, cause grave psychological damage due to the covert nature of the difficulties.

The long-term aims of the Study are:

(a) To explore the constancy and change in the pattern of children's development, longitudinally, and to investigate the associated educational, environmental and physical factors.

(b) To follow the progress—over a longer period—of those children who at birth might be considered "at risk" in order to evaluate possible latent effects; and also to examine any post-natal factors, environmental, educational or medical, which may minimise a handicap.

(c) To identify and follow the progress of children who at seven years of age are already handicapped or showing signs of difficulty; those who because of adverse social or other circumstances might be considered "at risk" of becoming educationally backward or socially deviant; and those who display exceptional talent or aptitude.

(d) To evaluate the efficacy of medical and educational provision for handicapped, deviant and exceptional children.

(e) To identify groups of children of special interest, including many of those enumerated under (c) and (d) above, so that intensive studies may be mounted by expert teams. This would permit much more detailed and comprehensive investigations of the factors involved against a "backcloth" of the necessarily cruder data gathered in the follow-up of the whole cohort.

These aims demand an inter-disciplinary research team and an integrated approach. The Co-Directors are an educational psychologist and a paediatrician: the former is also the Director of the National Bureau for Co-operation in Child Care, providing a direct link with the body responsible for the administration of the Study; and the latter, having directed the 1958 Perinatal Survey, establishes a link with the earlier work. An educational psychologist has overall charge of the research, and the staff further consists of a Senior Medical Research Officer—for a period of 18 months—a Sociological Research Officer and an Administrative Secretary. In addition, a statistician was seconded part-time to the Study and has been concerned with all aspects of the research.

3. The Structure of the Research

The research team for the present three year project started their work in October 1964, with the exception of the Senior Medical Research Officer, who commenced three months later.

The children in the cohort were at this time about $6\frac{1}{2}$ years old and it was decided to complete as much of the field work as possible by the end of July

1965 for a number of reasons. First, the majority of the children would be leaving infant schools and classes at this date and it was obviously desirable, where a change of school was involved, to gather educational information from teachers who, in many cases, had had the opportunity of observing the children's development over a number of years. Secondly, a change of school would involve further administrative work in tracing new schools. Thirdly, the Study had undertaken to present an interim report to the Central Advisory Council by the spring of 1966, so that time was extremely short.

Tracing the children was the first major exercise, and it would not have been practicable without the generous assistance of every local educational authority in the country. In response to a request from the Central Advisory Council for Education (England) and the then Welsh Department, Department of Education and Science, and from the Scottish Education Department, the authorities circularized schools, scrutinized their records and returned details of every child known to them born in the "Survey week". However, a sizeable minority of children were still untraced and a great deal of time and effort has been spent in reducing the size of this residual group in order to obtain a maximum possible return.

Even more administrative work was involved in the task of identifying the perinatal records of the 15,300 children whose names were returned so that the data gathered in the Perinatal Survey could be "linked" with current data. The invaluable help of the General Register Office must be acknowledged here.

The Study was mounted in collaboration with the Association of Chief Education Officers (in England and Wales), the Association of Directors of Education (in Scotland) and the Society of Medical Officers of Health. With their support and advice, active co-operation was obtained from every local authority in gathering data on the children. The Chief Education Officers and Principal School Medical Officers kindly undertook to arrange for the completion and return of the questionnaires and tests used; and for the prior distribution of letters to schools and parents.

The material consisted of an "Educational Assessment" booklet and five tests (for schools); a "Parental Questionnaire" to be completed usually by a health visitor, in an interview with the mother; and a "Medical Questionnaire" for completion by a school medical officer on examination of the child. Further details about this material and the processing of the data is contained in Section III: "Methodology of Data Collection". Copies of the three questionnaires are in Appendix 2.

The educational material was distributed to local authorities in March 1965, shortly after the children's seventh birthday, and the Parental and Medical Questionnaires were sent in the following month.

B. THE PRESENT REPORT

This Report, then, is of an interim nature, being produced about half-way through the span of the three year project. Further, it had in general to be confined to a consideration of the results for children in England because of the terms of reference of the Central Advisory Council. The data for the Scottish and Welsh children will, of course, feature in subsequent analyses.

Most of the first 18 months was, of course, devoted to tracing the children and then identifying their perinatal records; deciding what kinds of information would be gathered and from whom; formulating hypotheses to be tested;

designing the various questionnaires and selecting the most appropriate tests to be used; distributing material to all the local authorities; checking it for accuracy and completeness as it was returned; and transferring the data on to punched cards and then on to magnetic tape for computer analysis. More detailed accounts of some of these aspects of the project are given elsewhere in this Report.

In order to produce a report for the Central Advisory Council to consider, it was necessary to impose a "deadline" after which no material could be included for analysis. Thus, material received after the middle of August 1965 has not been utilised, but will subsequently be added to the earlier material which forms the basis of the present Report; all the data, including the information on children in Wales and Scotland, will then be analysed afresh for the final Report of the three-year project.

The present Report, therefore, is based upon a sub-sample of the cohort of children. There is evidence of some bias in this sample of "early returns", and this is fully discussed in Section IIB: "Description of the Sample". However, such bias as there is has been taken into account, where appropriate, in any interpretations made or conclusions drawn.

The terms of reference of the Central Advisory Council and the great speed with which the present Report had to be prepared have both played their part in shaping it. In addition, tentative interpretations of the results have been made where more elaborate or more sensitive statistical treatment is indicated but has not yet been possible.

Information obtained from this Study falls broadly into two categories. First there is a "descriptive" element. A large amount of data has been gathered on a national sample of seven-year-old children. This information is of considerable interest and value in itself, providing as it does a picture of many facets of the children's education, growth, behaviour, health and environment. The results are presented and discussed in Section V: "Descriptive Statistics". Strictly speaking, however, this section is not of a purely "descriptive" nature since, where appropriate, comparisons are made between the results for boys and for girls, so that hypotheses are being tested about possible sex differences.

The second category of information is contained in Section VI: "Interrelationship of the Variables", which deals with a few of the relationships between the many factors likely to affect children's development. Of course, the most interesting relationships are causal ones because these are most likely to have practical implications. If, for example, it can be shown that a particular circumstance, or combination of circumstances, is likely to lead to certain adverse effects, the way may be open for preventive measures. Even where prevention is impossible, a knowledge of causation may permit some amelioration of the effects.

However, to demonstrate an association between factors is not necessarily to show a cause-effect relationship. For example, it is known that there is a relationship between children's height and their measured intelligence. But this does not mean that on the whole taller children are more intelligent than shorter ones *because* of their height. It seems probable that both of these factors are linked to others which form part of a complex web of predisposing conditions favouring both physical growth (in terms of height) and mental growth (in terms of intelligence).

Great care must therefore be taken in interpreting demonstrable relationships. The factors involved are often complex and subtle, and it is extremely unlikely that simple answers will be found to those questions we most want answered.

The analyses carried out and discussed in this Report are, then, in the nature of first steps along a difficult but challenging path towards a greater understanding of children's growth and development. Some of the results presented confirm those obtained by other workers in this field; some produce interesting new evidence; some point the way to further investigation; and some results have not been presented at all at this stage because of the danger of oversimplification or because it was considered advisable to await a more comprehensive analysis of all the material. Finally, there are, of course, many aspects of the Study which have not yet been examined for lack of time.

References

BUTLER, N. R. and BONHAM, D. G., *Perinatal Mortality*. (E. & S. Livingstone Ltd.) (1963.)

II—DESCRIPTION OF THE SAMPLE

A. THE POPULATION

The population selected for the present Report consists of all children who were singleton births, living in England at the time of the survey, who were born between 3rd and 9th March, 1958, inclusive. (See Section III for a description of data collection.)

This Study was designed so as to include the surviving children of the Perinatal Mortality Survey (Butler & Bonham, 1963) who were currently living in England. In addition, the population includes immigrants and some children who were born in Britain during 3rd–9th March but who were, for various reasons, not included in the Perinatal Survey.

Where the population of interest is different from the above (e.g., children in local authority schools only), this is indicated in the body of the text.

B. THE PRESENT SAMPLE

The children included in the present sample are those for whom information had been received by the middle of August 1965.

Since more "Educational Assessment" booklets had been completed by this date, and since punched cards—containing most of this information—were available at an early stage, some of the analyses were completed using this data before all the information on each child was available for analysis. The total number of children for whom most of the educational data were available was 10,963; of these, 10,833 were known to be in maintained infant, junior with infants or all-age schools, or in independent schools catering wholly or mainly for children who are not handicapped; and this latter figure is the total involved in "counter sorter" analyses using these cards. The number of completed Parental and Medical Questionnaires received by the middle of August was 7,985; in general, therefore, where tabulations were produced from these questionnaires using the counter sorter, this latter is the total involved. Where computer analyses were done, the totals for tables will vary according to the number of cases where particular information was unanswered. (See Section IIIF for the details of the data processing.)

In addition to the above, 1,896 "late returns" had come in by the beginning of January 1966. Although it was not possible to include these "late returns" in the main analyses, the Social Class distribution has been compared with that of the present sample. An overall test of significance indicates a difference in the distributions, although a test for trend of the proportions of "late returns" in each Social Class category (Registrar General's classification) from Class I to Class V was not significant (see Table 1). Thus, although there does appear to be a difference between the two groups occurring in Social Classes II and V, there is no evidence that it involves a shift towards one end of the (nominal) scale.

In most analyses, however, comparisons have been made within occupational group classifications, thus allowing for any bias arising in this way.

The 1961 census figures on occupational classification are also presented in Table 1. It should be noted that the present survey is of seven-year-old children, whereas the census figures relate to a sample of households.

Table 1

Occupational Group Distributions

Registrar General (1960) Social Class Classification	PRESENT SAMPLE		LATE RETURNS		1961 CENSUS
	N	Per cent	N	Per cent	Per cent
1	443	5·7	96	5·1	3·8
2	1,131	14·6	338	17·8	17·0
3	4,387	56·8	1,025	54·1	51·3
4	1,322	17·1	292	15·4	20·3
5	440	5·7	145	7·6	7·6
TOTAL	7,723	100*	1,896	100*	100*

Test present sample against late returns

Chi-squared (Trend) = 0·02; not significant

Chi-squared (Departure from linear trend) = 25·5 (3 d.f.); $p < 0.001$

Total chi-squared = 25·5 (4 d.f.); $p < 0.001$

*Throughout the Report percentages in tables are quoted to one decimal place and the total percentage is always given as 100.

A further comparison has been made using sex, reading and adjustment scores, comparing the children for whom there are educational data but no parental and medical information with those for whom this latter information is also available. Significantly worse adjustment and reading scores were found among those children with the missing parental and medical information, but no significant difference was found in the proportion of the two sexes (see Table 2).

Table 2

(a)

Southgate Reading Test Score	Without Parental and Medical information		With Parental and Medical information	
	N	Per cent	N	Per cent
0– 3	29	0·8	40	0·6
4– 6	96	2·6	115	1·7
7– 9	193	5·3	269	4·0
10–12	219	6·0	227	3·4
13–15	235	6·4	389	5·9
16–18	253	6·9	437	6·6
19–21	304	8·3	570	8·6
22–24	363	9·9	755	11·4
25–27	614	16·8	1,047	15·8
28–30	1,348	36·9	2,785	42·0
TOTAL	3,654	100	6,634	100

Chi-squared (Trend) $= 50\cdot2$; $p < 0.001$

(b)

Bristol Social-Adjustment Guide Total Score	Without Parental and Medical information		With Parental and Medical information	
	N	Per cent	N	Per cent
0– 9	1,975	59·0	4,305	66·6
10–19	828	24·7	1,395	21·6
20–29	402	12·0	591	9·1
30–39	116	3·5	152	2·3
40–49	24	0·7	19	0·3
50+	5	0·1	5	0·1
TOTAL	3,350	100	6,467	100

Chi-squared (Trend) $= 65\cdot2$; $p < 0.001$

C. INFERENCES MADE FROM THE SAMPLE

Inferences from the present sample are strictly applicable only to the (one week) population as defined above. However, it may reasonably be assumed that this population is a representative, although strictly speaking non-random, sample from a larger population consisting of children aged between 7 and 7½ years (the ages when the data were obtained) who were born during an (unspecified) period of time which includes 3rd to 9th March, 1958. Thus, interest centres on inferences made about all children aged between 7 and 7½. Therefore, the assumptions have been made that secular trends have not taken place—or were negligible—during such a period and that the period is long compared to the one week of the sample; and for the purpose of testing hypotheses the sample has been treated as if it were a random sample from a population which, for practical purposes, can be considered infinite. Where it is felt that these assumptions are inadmissible, especially with regard to estimation of population means, this is indicated in the main text.

It must also be emphasized that the basic sampling unit is the child. It is not possible, therefore, to use the data directly to estimate population parameters of distributions where the basic units are not individual children but, for example, households or schools. Thus, an estimate of the mean size of infant schools, calculated in the usual way from the sample, would yield an estimate too large since the larger schools contribute more children to the sample.

All estimates which are given are therefore applicable only to the population of school children.

D. SOURCES OF BIAS IN THE PRESENT SAMPLE DUE TO NON-RESPONSE

In the present sample this matter has been investigated quantitatively in the comparison of "early" with "late" returns for Occupational Group, Reading and Social-Adjustment. Some of the possible sources of bias might, with advantage, be outlined.

Four categories of children who will not be included can be distinguished. First, there were those whose parents decided not to participate. This category is small—a little more than one per cent at present. Secondly, there were the children whose home circumstances made it impossible for a parental interview or medical examination to be made; or whose parents simply failed to keep appointments. This group will contain a disproportionate number of children from large families, socially underprivileged homes; or parents who for any reason have little time to devote to their children. Thirdly, there were the children in the cohort who have not as yet been traced or, having been traced, moved to another area and have not yet been re-traced. It is likely that in the majority of these cases incorrectly recorded dates of birth or other clerical error is responsible. However, this category will contain a disproportionate number of children whose families move home frequently. The fourth category includes children who have emigrated since the 1958 Perinatal Study. This will be relevant only to associations with retrospective data, including the perinatal material.

References

BUTLER, N. R. and BONHAM, D. G. *Perinatal Mortality*. (E. & S. Livingstone Ltd.) (1963.)

III—METHODOLOGY OF DATA COLLECTION

A. DESIGN OF THE STRUCTURED QUESTIONNAIRES

It was decided to gather the information from three main sources: from schools, by means of a questionnaire (the "Educational Assessment" booklet), specific tests and other assessments; from mothers, who would be interviewed by an officer of the local authority, usually a health visitor, using a structured questionnaire (the "Parental Questionnaire"); and from School

Health Services, who would undertake a medical examination, some special tests and complete a questionnaire (the "Medical Questionnaire").

In considering the data to be collected, the following factors were particularly important:

1. The relative priorities to be given to contemporary and to retrospective data, having in mind that no information was gathered on the children during a seven-year period.

2. The extent to which comparable information could be obtained from many different field workers; and also the difficulty of interpreting data of a subjective nature.

3. The need to limit the burden of work and time for local authorities, schools and parents.

4. The time available for reviewing what others had done in the field, for drafting and "piloting" the questionnaires.

5. The amount of time which would be available later for processing and analysing the material.

It became apparent at an early stage that the material would have to be designed so that the data could be transferred to punched cards. Furthermore, it was decided to structure the questionnaires so that the answers were, wherever possible, in pre-coded form; i.e., the field workers in response to the questions were asked to ring a code rather than write in an answer. This reduced the need for coding the material when it was returned. Such a structure, of course, imposed limitations upon the kinds of questions that could be included and determined to some extent the way in which they were asked.

It was further decided that the questionnaires should require no transcription sheets, so that the data could be punched direct on to cards from the forms themselves. Before the general layout was finalised, advice was sought both from the printers and from the commercial bureau who were to do the card punching. Amongst other factors which had to be decided were the size of print and paper, the spacing of the questions and hence the overall size of the documents. Important considerations here were general "readability" and attractiveness of layout and, not least, the cost involved in terms of the weight and quality of paper.

By and large, the individual experience, skills and qualifications of the members of the research team determined who did the actual drafting of particular items or questionnaires. However, since the approach throughout was inter-disciplinary, regular and detailed discussions on all the questionnaires took place, involving the Co-Directors and the whole research team. Advice and comment was sought from all members of the Steering Committee and some members of the Consultative Committee, as well as from countless other individuals—doctors, teachers, health visitors, school welfare officers, research workers—all experts or practitioners in their respective fields. It was possible to do some piloting on all the questionnaires, but pressure of time meant that we were unable to do as much of this as would have been desirable. For the most part the material took shape and was finalised as a result of exhaustive discussion and consultation.

It was thought essential to ensure that anyone who was to use the material should know something about the Study. Each of the questionnaires, therefore, contained a brief summary of the background to the Study and its present aims.

B. THE EDUCATIONAL ASSESSMENT

A questionnaire was needed which would establish certain basic facts about the children's school environment, such as the type and size of school and size of class. It was thought desirable, too, to obtain some information about less tangible aspects of the environment, such as the contact between the school and the home, the "social class" of the parents whose children attended the school and the basis on which children were allocated to classes. Finally, a fairly comprehensive picture was needed of the individual child: his abilities, his adjustment and behaviour and the interest and support given by his parents.

Finally, six different forms of assessment were decided upon:

1. *The "Educational Assessment" booklet* which established facts about the school and its organization, the relationship between the school and parents, and which required assessments by the teacher of the child's ability and certain aspects of his behaviour.

2. *The Bristol Social Adjustment Guide* (Stott, 1963) to obtain a picture of the child's behaviour in the school setting. The Guide is a four-page booklet containing some 250 descriptions of behaviour. The teacher is asked to underline the descriptions which best fit the child. Items of behaviour which are, in varying degrees, deviant or which may be symptomatic of emotional disturbance or social maladjustment are later identified by means of a system of coding and transferred to a separate form. It is thus possible, by summing the number of coded items, to obtain a quantitative assessment of the child's adjustment in school: the higher the score, the more indications there are of deviant behaviour. In addition, it is possible, by summing groups of coded items, to obtain a quantitative indication of the way in which any maladjustment is manifesting itself. Stott has suggested that certain "syndromes" of behaviour disturbance are meaningful, and separate scores can be obtained for each (e.g., unforthcomingness, withdrawal, anxiety for acceptance by adults, hostility towards adults, "inconsequential" behaviour).

3. *The Southgate Reading Test* (Southgate, 1962) for an objective assessment of the child's reading ability. This is essentially a test of word recognition. The child is asked to select from a number of words the one which corresponds to a picture in the test booklet; in other items the teacher reads out a word and, again, the child is asked to identify the word from a number which he has before him. There are 30 items in all in this test. A graded word reading test was considered, but it was felt that the Southgate Test was less likely to be known or used already by teachers in infant schools; that it would save time where there was more than one child in a school; that it would, possibly, be less formal and therefore less stressful for seven-year-olds. While this test was unable to extend the above average reader at this age, it did differentiate very clearly the backward readers. For the aims of the Study, this advantage outweighed the disadvantage of a rather low "ceiling".

4. *The "Copying Designs" Test* to obtain some assessment of the child's perceptuo-motor ability. Although this test has been scored, it has not been possible as yet to use it for any analyses.

5. *The "Drawing a Man" Test* as an indication of the child's general mental and perceptual ability as well as other maturational aspects. Although there has not been time or money available at this stage to mark and process this test, it is very cheap as well as quick and easy for teachers to administer; moreover, it was felt that it would provide them with a useful "sandwich" between the formal tests. It is hoped eventually to use a more sophisticated marking procedure than that suggested by Goodenough (1926). When analysis does become possible, it is intended to correlate the results with other factors.

6. *The Problem Arithmetic Test* (copy excluded from this version) to assess the child's ability in this field. The individual items were chosen in the main from a large number previously used by the National Foundation for Educational Research, so that information was available on their facility values and it was possible to select those items which on a seven-year-old population would produce a normal distribution of scores. We are indebted to the N.F.E.R. for their help on this.

Piloting of the educational assessment indicated that completion for one child would take from one to one-and-a-half hours. For more than one child an additional half to three-quarters-of-an-hour per child would be needed. However, most teachers would have only one child in their class who was taking part in the Study.

C. THE PARENTAL QUESTIONNAIRE

A questionnaire had to be designed which would be suitable for completion by an officer of the local authority, usually a health visitor, by means of an interview, where possible, with the child's mother or permanent mother substitute. Specially trained interviewers would obviously have been preferable, but this was too costly even to consider.

It was soon realised that the problem of achieving a satisfactory compromise in terms of items which would be included was going to be most acute in this particular document. The chief difficulty lay in reconciling the need to obtain information about the child's present environment and development with the desirability of obtaining retrospective data over a seven-year-period without over-burdening the informant and interviewer in terms of the time needed to complete the questionnaire.

It thus became essential to establish some priorities in respect of items to be included. It was felt that basic contemporary data should have first priority since in general these would normally be more reliable (i.e., less subject to distortion or simple inadequacy of memory) than retrospective details. However, some kinds of contemporary data, such as the parents' religion, could equally well be ascertained in future studies of the children and was therefore given lower priority.

With regard to retrospective information, a balance had to be achieved between the assumed importance of particular aspects in relation to the child's development and the extent to which any reliability could be attached to the mother's present report. Information about developmental milestones or pre-school difficulties are good illustrations of this difficulty. On the one hand, it was felt that such information would be valuable whilst on the other hand it seemed likely that mothers' memory of these events might not only be faulty—particularly if she had a large family—but, more important, might actively be influenced or distorted by the child's subsequent development.

Information about the emotional and intellectual climate in the home, the parents' aspirations for the child and their general attitudes towards bringing up children would have been most valuable. Reluctantly, it was decided, however, either to omit or cover only sketchily these particular areas because of the limitations of time, the varying circumstances under which the interviews would take place and the varying experience of the interviewers.

The Parental Questionnaire was considered to be the most suitable means of obtaining a full medical history from the mother. Not only would this save the doctor's time during the medical examination, but in many cases the health visitor might be acquainted with the health of the child, both in its pre-school and school days. It was advised, and proved possible in the great majority of cases, that the completed Parental Questionnaire be made available to the doctor in time for his examination of the child. For those instances in which this was not possible, part of the medical history, the systemically classified section, was reproduced in the Medical Questionnaire for completion or amendment at the time of the examination if this was thought necessary. Piloting of the questionnaires indicated that they would take an hour to an hour-and-a-quarter to complete for an "average" child.

D. THE MEDICAL QUESTIONNAIRE

A comprehensive medical examination of each child was considered to be an essential part of the follow-up of this cohort. Since the examinations were to involve large numbers of full-time and part-time medical officers of the local authorities, it was important to ensure as far as possible a uniform pattern of examination, as well as a standardised method of recording the findings. To give full clinical freedom in taking the medical history or in conducting the examination would create an impossible task in the classification and analysis of the data; at the other extreme, over-simplification leads not only to loss of information but also to a sense of frustration in professional field workers whose skills are not fully utilised.

It is hoped that the method by which medical data were gathered for this Study avoided these two extremes by careful questionnaire design. The spectrum of information was wide, whilst individual bands within that spectrum were sharply defined.

The pre-coded form of question was adopted to this end, and a questionnaire designed with sections classified in such a way that they matched the corresponding sections of the medical history in the Parental Questionnaire. To overcome the limitations imposed by the form of question used, the opportunity for written amplification of each answer was provided with each question.

In the case of tests of function and the examination of the special senses, the conditions for the examination were set out in detail in order to ensure that the results would be as comparable as possible.

The questionnaire included measurements of height, weight and head circumference; tests and assessments of vision, speech and hearing, including an audiogram; a urine test; tests of motor co-ordination and laterality; as well as a full clinical examination. Piloting indicated that, with the help of a school nurse, the whole examination, without the audiogram, would take 30–45 minutes.

E. THE COMPLETION AND RETURN OF THE MATERIAL

The material was sent in bulk to each local authority, which then made arrangements for its distribution, completion and return. In most cases, too, the authorities were able to give further help by checking the material for completeness before returning it.

F. DATA PROCESSING

The returned questionnaires and test forms were double checked by hand for completeness, coding errors, certain logical inconsistencies and accuracy of scoring. Where errors had occurred it was sometimes possible to rectify them by reference to other parts of the questionnaires.

The data for each child were punched on to seven 80-column cards, the last of which also contained information from the 1958 Perinatal Mortality Survey for those children whose records had been linked. These latter data were reproduced from the 1958 Survey punched cards.

The punching and verifying of the cards was carried out by a commercial bureau because of the size of this operation.

The first card containing most of the educational data for each child was punched by the end of August 1965 and used for "counter sorter" analysis. When all seven cards for each child were available in January 1966, they were loaded on to magnetic tapes using the IBM.1401 computer at Imperial College, London, and the data were edited on the IBM.7090 computer at Imperial College for incorrectly coded and mis-punched information.

The edited magnetic tapes were then used for computer analysis on the 7090. This work was carried out using an adaptation of a program lent to the Study by the Government Social Survey (Central Office of Information).

Due to technical difficulties which could not be resolved in the time available, data for some 300 children could not be loaded from the cards on to the magnetic tapes. Thus, where comparable analyses were carried out on the computer and also on the counter sorter, the totals differ somewhat.

For the latter analyses, the cards (1 to 7) were divided into seven separate packs and straight counts and two-way tabulations produced from each pack.

References
GOODENOUGH, F. *Measurement of Intelligence by Drawings* (World Book Co.) (1926).
SOUTHGATE, V. *Southgate Group Reading Tests: Manual of Instructions* (University of London Press Ltd.) (1962).
STOTT, D. H. *The Social-Adjustment of Children: Manual to the Bristol Social-Adjustment Guides* (University of London Press Ltd.) (1963).

IV—STATISTICAL ANALYSIS

Due largely to the shortage of time, the statistical analysis has been restricted to providing estimates for means and testing hypotheses of a straightforward nature, using the methods of analysis detailed below.

Since most of the hypotheses were concerned with associations in contingency tables, the basic method of analysis has been to apply an overall test of association. Although in some cases more detailed hypotheses have been formulated, it has not always been possible to use a more powerful procedure than the overall chi-square test.

In other cases, however, particularly where sex differences are concerned and a natural ordering exists in the levels of the other classification, a test for a linear trend of the proportion in the resulting $2 \times K$ table has been carried out, with integers 1 to K used as scores. This also furnishes a valid test of no difference between the mean scores of the two levels of the dichotomous classification (Armitage, 1955). This test is referred to as the Trend Test.

It is also possible to obtain a test for departure from a linear trend. If no such departure exists, it may be inferred that the trend persists throughout the whole table and that the mean proportions in any two levels of the K-level classification are different.

In relation to sex differences, one may reasonably assume in most cases that the sexes are randomised over other factors and that any contrast between the sexes is orthogonal with respect to the other factors.

One limitation of the present analyses is the absence of powerful tests for partial association in multi-dimensional tables, except in the special case of a $2 \times 2 \times K$ table (Birch, 1964) where the hypothesis concerns the partial association of two factors at fixed levels of a further factor and where the assumption of no second order interaction has been made; that is to say, the degree of association is the same in each constituent 2×2 table. Tests for second order interaction have been made (Plackett, 1962), and in no case has a significant interaction been found.

In any set of analyses on one sample, the statistical tests of hypotheses will not generally be independent. This fact must be taken into account in the interpretation of any results.

Furthermore, in a large group of independent tests, some are to be expected to show significance at the nominal level, even if the null hypotheses are true —purely by chance—and this has led to regarding the one per cent level rather than the five per cent level as the more appropriate one at which to begin rejecting null hypotheses, although significance values are shown at the five per cent as well as the one per cent and 0·1 per cent levels. Thus, the tendency has been towards a conservative interpretation of the results, which is also desirable in an interim report of this nature.

The hypotheses to be tested had all been formulated in advance. This was done on the basis of past evidence with a view to confirming the results of previous research studies and experience and to answer certain basic but relatively straightforward questions.

References

ARMITAGE, P. "Tests for linear trends in proportions and frequencies". *Biometrics II*, pp. 375–386 (1955).

BIRCH, M. W. "The Detection of Partial Association, 1: The 2×2 case". *Journal of the Royal Statistical Society*, Series B 26, pp. 313–324 (1964).

PLACKETT. "A Note on Interactions in Contingency Tables". *Journal of the Royal Statistical Society*, Series B 24, pp. 162–166 (1962).

V—DESCRIPTIVE STATISTICS

A. EDUCATIONAL FACTORS

1. *Introduction*

The data included and discussed in this section were gathered from schools. The topics dealt with centre on children's abilities and the question of backwardness and difficulties in school; the results for boys and girls are compared.

It will be seen that the total number of children for whom results are given differs in various sub-sections. The reasons for this are outlined in Section IIB: "Description of the Sample".

However, they might with advantage be re-stated in so far as they relate to the educational data presented here. Most of these data were recorded on one 80-column punched card. This card was available at an earlier date than the other six cards and it was therefore possible by sorting the cards (using a "counter sorter") to obtain information and produce simple tables. The number of children in English schools for whom this card was available was 10,963.

A breakdown of this number by the type of school attended is given in Table 3. It will be seen that 10,833 of the children were known to be in "ordinary" maintained and independent schools, i.e., infant, junior with infants, and all-age schools and independent schools catering wholly or mainly for children who are not handicapped; 48 children were in special schools for handicapped pupils; and there were 73 children in schools which apparently did not fall into any of the categories listed. At a later stage, a re-scrutiny of the individual Educational Assessment booklets may make it possible to classify these schools.

Table 3

Type of School Attended

	No. of children
Maintained schools	
Infant School	5,981
Junior with Infants School (or Primary with Infants)	4,529
All-age	34
Day Special School	32
Residential Special School	6
Other	40
No data	9
Independent Schools	
Independent School (to include grant-aided schools) catering wholly or mainly for children who are not handicapped	289
Special School for handicapped children	10
Other	33
TOTAL	10,963

In this sub-section, results are presented largely for children in "ordinary" schools; thus, if the results were obtained by means of sorting punched cards, the total number of children involved is 10,833.

At a later stage in the data processing, the information was transferred to magnetic tape for computer analysis. There were one or two minor difficulties at that stage which could not be resolved in the time available, so the data for some 300 children had to be excluded. Where the results are presented from computer analysis, therefore, the total number of children involved in "ordinary" schools is 10,596.

There is one further total which appears frequently in tables in this section where there is a comparison between the sexes. When the comparisons are one facet of more detailed computer analyses involving the Occupational Groups of the fathers, the figures for boys and for girls have been abstracted from larger tables. Where the Occupational Group of the father was not known at the time, it was not possible to separate the boys from the girls in these larger tables (not presented in this Report). Thus, it has only been possible to compare the sexes, if the figures were abstracted from larger tables, when the Occupational Group was known. For these tables, then, the results are presented for a sub-sample of 6,878 children in "ordinary" schools. There is evidence that this sub-sample is biased in certain respects: better reading ability; better social-adjustment in school. However, there is no reason to believe that this bias will affect the validity of the comparison between the boys and the girls in that group.

2. *Reading Ability*
(a) *Southgate Group Reading Test Results*
This test is one which is primarily an assessment of word recognition. The results have been abstracted from a more detailed table, not presented in this Report, and are for children in "ordinary" maintained and independent schools. They are given in Table 4 and in graph form in Figure 1.

The superiority of the girls when compared with the boys is very clear. The difference in the distribution of the scores between the sexes is highly significant statistically. It will be seen that of the boys tested in this sub-sample only 1,202 (35 per cent) achieved a score of 28 or more, whereas 1,583 (approximately 47 per cent) of the girls did so. Further, the results of the statistical analysis confirm what inspection of the table suggest, namely, that there is a difference between the sexes at every level of reading ability, as assessed by this test.

The overall superiority of the girls was not unexpected and confirmed the hypothesis which was postulated in advance.

Table 4

Southgate Reading Test Score

$N=6,878$

Reading Scores	Boys		Girls	
	N	Per cent	N	Per cent
0– 3	26	0·8	14	0·4
4– 6	68	2·0	47	1·4
7– 9	170	4·9	99	2·9
10–12	205	6·0	122	3·6
13–15	250	7·3	139	4·1
16–18	256	7·4	181	5·3
19–21	317	9·2	253	7·4
22–24	380	11·1	375	11·0
25–27	564	16·4	583	17·2
28–30	1,202	35·0	1,583	46·6
Total tested	3,438	100	3,396	100
No data	24		20	
GRAND TOTAL	3,462		3,416	

Chi-squared (Trend) $=137·4$; $p< 0·001$
Chi-squared (Departure) $=13·8$ (8 d.f.); $p >0·05$ not significant

Table A1 of Appendix 1 gives a more representative picture when the results for boys and girls are combined and is based upon a larger sample of 10,596 children. One point is worthy of note in relation to the distribution of scores. The test clearly did not contain sufficient difficult items to "extend" the more able readers. Thus, 47 per cent of the girls and about 35 per cent of the boys achieved a score of 28 or more out of a possible 30. This was expected and, as is explained elsewhere, this test was chosen partly because it was known that it would give good discrimination among the poorer readers.

Figure 1

Southgate Group Reading Test Scores by Sex
Children in Ordinary Maintained and Independent Schools

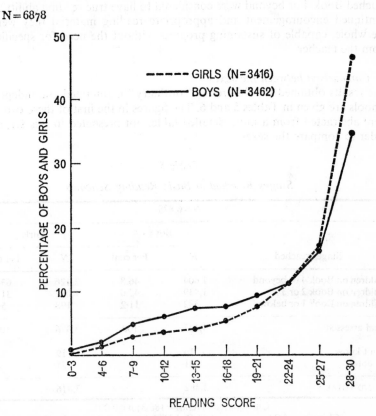

(b) *Stage Reached in Basic Reading Scheme*
In addition to the Southgate Test, information was obtained about the "primer" or reading book in the basic reading scheme which the children were currently using.
This item of information was gathered to supplement the results of the reading test and a rating of the children's reading ability by their teachers. Secondly, it was considered that the results obtained would be of particular interest to teachers, since the assessment of a child's reading ability in terms of the primer he is reading is a familiar frame of reference. Thirdly, the results

would have possible implications for reading provision not only in infant but also in junior classes. Fourthly, it was felt that a comparison of the present findings with those of Morris (1959) in Kent schools would be valuable.

It is recognised that there will be some variability in the level of difficulty of books in the most widely used reading schemes. Nevertheless, Morris found—on questioning experienced teachers—that, despite the variability, meaningful distinctions could be made between children who had reached different stages. Thus, "it was customary for infant teachers to consider a first primer as dividing the poor and non-readers from the rest at the age of seven". Children who by this age were reading Book 2 or Book 3 were at this stage where their reading was mainly mechanical; such children still needed a great deal of skilled help and encouragement for optimal progress. Pupils who had reached Book 4 or beyond were considered to have true reading ability; given continued encouragement and appropriate reading material they were, on the whole, capable of sustaining progress without the need for specific help from the teacher.

(i) Comparison between the sexes

The results obtained for children in "ordinary" maintained and independent schools are given in Tables 5 and 6. The figures in the first of these two tables were abstracted from a more detailed table, not presented in this Report, in order to compare the sexes.

Table 5

Stages Reached in Basic Reading Schemes

		$N=6,878$		
	Boys		Girls	
Stages reached	N	Per cent	N	Per cent
Children on Book 4 or beyond	1,604	46.8	2,126	63·0
Children on Book 2 or 3	1,439	42·0	1,052	31·2
Children on Book 1 or below	382	11·2	198	5·9
Total assessed	3,425	100	3,376	100
Don't know	16		19	
No data	21		21	
GRAND TOTAL	3,462		3,416	

Chi-squared (Trend) $=186\cdot3$; $p < 0\cdot001$
Chi-squared (Departure) $=4\cdot95$ (1 d.f.); $0\cdot05 > p > 0\cdot01$ not significant

The superior reading ability of the girls on this criterion is again very clear and highly significant statistically. This adds to the findings discussed in the previous sub-section in that the ability to read Book 4 or beyond will require not only word recognition but will, in the main, be accompanied by good comprehension of what is read.

The statistical evidence also indicates that there is no departure from this overall tendency. Thus, the difference between the sexes is consistent at all levels of reading ability, as assessed by this "primer criterion".

(ii) *The present findings*

The figures for the sexes are not totalled in Table 5 to give overall results because of possible bias. However, figures based on a larger sample of 10,596 children are given in Table 6 and there is no expectation of bias here. They are presented together with results achieved by Morris in her Kent sample.

Table 6

Stages Reached in Basic Reading Schemes

	Present Sample		Kent Sample (Morris)	
Stage reached	*N*	Per cent	*N*	Per cent
Children on Book 4 or beyond	5,519	52·8	1,644	54·4
Children on Book 2 or Book 3	3,899	37·3	797	26·4
Children on Book 1 or below	1,028	9·8	581	19·2
Total assessed	10,446	100	3,022	100
Don't know	55			
No data	95			
GRAND TOTAL	10,596		3,022	

Chi-squared (Trend) = 29·8; $p < 0.001$
Chi-squared (Departure) = 224·7 (1 d.f.); $p < 0.001$

The present findings, in so far as they represent the national situation in 1965, indicate that some 10 per cent of seven-year-olds in the final term of their infant schooling had still barely made a start with reading. A further 37 per cent had progressed beyond this stage but continued to need specific help.

It has been acknowledged that this criterion of reading ability is relatively crude. Furthermore, the interim nature of the present report dictates a need for care in using precise figures. However, it is clear that a substantial proportion of children transferring to junior schools or classes has not reached a stage in reading where they can make optimal progress without continued teaching of the basic reading skills. Given the present age of transfer, it follows that teachers in charge of first-year junior classes should have a thorough knowledge of methods of teaching reading. Clearly this has practical implications for teacher training as well as for the staffing of junior schools and departments.

(iii) *Comparison with Morris's results*

It will be seen in Table 6 that there is virtually no difference in the proportion of children in the two samples who were on Book 4 or beyond. There may have been differences between the children of above average reading ability, but since this criterion gives no differentiation among this group, no conclusions can be drawn. The most striking difference between the samples is that whereas about 19 per cent of the Kent pupils had not progressed beyond a first primer, only 10 per cent of the children in the present sample were in this category.

Interpretation of the difference between the present 1965 findings and those of Morris, obtained in 1954, in terms of a national trend, is not straight-forward, although the difference between the samples is, statistically, highly significant.

A number of factors must be considered. First, the average age of the Kent children when the assessment was made—at the beginning of their junior school course—would have been approximately $7\frac{1}{2}$ years, slightly higher than that of the present sample. Secondly, it is very likely that the reading standard of these Kent children was above the national average, not only because of the generally higher socio-economic level in Kent, but also because Morris found on testing a sample of 10–11-year-olds in that county "that the reading attainment of Kent children at the end of their primary school course was above average for the country as a whole".

Against this, the present sample included a proportion (less than three per cent) of children in independent schools whose reading standard as a group is likely to have been higher than for the rest of the sample, whereas the Kent pupils were all in maintained schools.

Thirdly, a small proportion of the present sample would no doubt have been using the "initial teaching alphabet" (Downing, 1964) in learning to read, whilst none of Morris's sample would have done so. It is possible that this medium might alter the level of difficulty of primers and so change the nature of the criterion. Lastly, there were differences in the sampling technique used in the two studies.

These complicating factors impose a need for caution in interpretation. Further, if the difference between the two samples does reflect a national trend, it provides no evidence for an increase in the proportion of good readers. This is not to say that such a change has not taken place; unfortunately, this "primer criterion" does not discriminate amongst the children of average reading ability and above, i.e., those who are reading Book 4 or beyond. Nevertheless, the difference between the proportion of children in the two samples who had not progressed beyond Book 1 is very marked. The tentative conclusion seems warranted that in the country as a whole the number of poor and non-readers transferring to junior schools and classes has dropped in the interval from 1954 to 1965.

(c) Teachers' Ratings of Reading Ability

A third assessment of the children's reading ability was obtained in the form of a rating by the teacher on a five-point scale.

In an attempt to increase the comparability of ratings made by several thousand different teachers, three steps were taken. A distribution of ratings was suggested which the teachers were told might be expected in a represen-tative cross-section of children of this age; the teachers were asked to rate the child "in relation to all children of his age (i.e., not just his present class or, even, school)"; verbal descriptions were given for each of the five possible ratings.

These verbal descriptions are detailed in Table 7, together with the results for boys and girls. Once again the figures are abstracted from a more detailed table, not presented in this Report, but the combined results for the sexes on a sample of 10,833 children in "ordinary" maintained and independent schools are given in Appendix 1, Table A3.

Table 7

Teachers' Ratings of Reading Ability

N=6878

Descriptions of Ratings	Boys		Girls	
	N	Per cent	N	Per cent
Avid reader. Reads fluently and widely in relation to his age	176	5·1	296	8·7
Above average ability. Comprehends well what he reads	716	20·8	1,016	29·8
Average reader	1,493	43·3	1,512	44·3
Poor reader. Limited comprehension	958	27·8	540	15·8
Non-reader, or recognizes very few words	105	3·1	48	1·4
Total tested	3,448	100	3,412	100
No data	14		4	
GRAND TOTAL	3,462		3,416	

Chi-squared (Trend) $=206\cdot3$; $p<0\cdot01$
Chi-squared (Departure) $=14\cdot0$ (3 d.f.); $0\cdot01>p>0\cdot001$

Once again the superior reading ability of the girls in this sample can be clearly seen and is statistically highly significant. There were more girls (approximately 39 per cent) than boys (about 26 per cent) rated as of above average ability; also, there were fewer girls (approximately 17 per cent) than boys (approximately 31 per cent) below average.

The difference between the sexes is so marked, and confirmed by the results of the other two assessments of reading ability, that the firm conclusion is warranted that at this age girls are superior to boys in all aspects of reading ability.

3. Ability in Number Work

(a) Problem Arithmetic Test Results

There was some difficulty in deciding upon an appropriate objective assessment of the children's ability in number work. A test of mechanical arithmetic could have been devised or selected; but this, it was thought, would hardly do justice to the wider range of activities to be found in many infant classes. On the other hand, a test of mathematical concepts might have been time-consuming or difficult to administer. It was finally decided to devise a short test of problem arithmetic, thus avoiding some of the restrictions of purely mechanical calculation and assessing to some extent the ability to apply arithmetical knowledge to problems appropriate to this age group.

The test was devised especially for use in this Study. There were ten problems in all and they were presented in the estimated order of difficulty. Six of the problems had been used before by the National Foundation for Educational Research on a large sample of seven-year-old children. Information was therefore available on the probable level of difficulty for these questions.

The original intention had been to make this an oral test to avoid penalizing those children who could not read fluently. However, in doing this it was possible that some children would be put at a disadvantage because of difficulty in remembering questions accurately whilst calculating the answers. Thus, it was decided to present the problems in printed form but also to ask teachers to read the questions one at a time to the children (repeating where necessary) and allowing as much time as was needed for answering. If a child because of some disability was unable to write his answers, the teachers were asked to record them for him.

The results for a sub-sample of boys and girls in "ordinary" schools are given in Table 8. They were abstracted from a larger table not presented in this Report. The combined results for the sexes taken from this same table on a sample of 10,596 children are given in Appendix 1, Table A2.

Table 8

Problem Arithmetic Results

$N = 6878$

Arithmetic Scores	Boys		Girls	
	N	Per cent	N	Per cent
0	76	2·2	68	2·0
1	145	4·2	147	4·3
2	290	8·4	325	9·6
3	384	11·2	478	14·1
4	479	14·0	493	14·5
5	502	14·6	476	14·0
6	470	13·7	443	13·1
7	374	10·9	399	11·8
8	332	9·7	268	7·9
9	237	6·9	181	5·3
10	143	4·2	114	3·4
Total tested	3,432	100	3,392	100
No data	30		24	
GRAND TOTAL	3,462		3,416	

Chi-squared (Trend) = 16·1; $p < 0·001$
Chi-squared (Departure) = 16·5 (9 d.f.); $p > 0·05$ not significant

There was a highly significant difference between the distribution of scores for the sexes, strongly indicating that boys are superior to girls in the particular aspect of arithmetic ability assessed by this test. The statistical analysis provided no evidence of any departure from linear trend, indicating that this difference between the sexes persists over the whole range of test scores.

(b) Teachers' Ratings of Number Work
As with reading ability, a subjective rating was obtained from the teachers of the children's ability in number work. The introduction to all the ratings was the same and has been outlined in sub-section 2(c) of this section.
Once again, verbal descriptions were given for the five points on the rating

scale. It will be seen from these descriptions shown, together with the results in Table 8, that stress was laid upon an assessment of the children's insight and grasp of new processes rather than their ability to calculate accurately. These results were obtained from sorting the punched cards so that the total number of children involved is 10,833 (see Introduction to present section).

Table 9

Teachers' Ratings of Number Work

Descriptions of Ratings	Boys		Girls		Total	
	N	Per cent	N	Per cent	N	Per cent
Extremely good facility with number and/or other mathematical concepts. Grasps new processes very quickly. Shows insight and understanding	205	3·7	120	2·3	325	3·0
Understanding of number work well developed. Grasps new processes without difficulty	1,008	18·2	856	16·2	1,864	17·2
Average ability in this sphere	2,332	42·1	2,385	45·1	4,717	43·6
Rather slow to understand new processes. Rather poor facility with numbers, although able to do some things by rote	1,780	32·2	1,757	33·2	3,537	32·7
Little, if any, ability in this sphere. Shows virtually no understanding at all	208	3·8	176	3·3	384	3·6
Total rated	5,533	100	5,294	100	10,827	100
No data	3		3		6	
GRAND TOTAL	5,536		5,297		10,833	

Chi-squared (Trend) $=9·5$; $0·01>p>0·001$
Chi-squared (Departure) $=23·3$ (3 d.f.); $p<0·001$

The statistical test used rejects the hypothesis that there is no difference between boys and girls in their number ability as rated by their teachers. There was a significant overall tendency for the boys to receive higher ratings. However, the highly significant departure from linear trend shows that this tendency was not consistent at all levels of number ability.

Inspection of the table suggests that the reason for this departure from linear trend is that the proportion of boys and girls rated below average is virtually the same, approximately 36 per cent; on the other hand, about 22 per cent of the boys were rated above average, whilst only 18·5 per cent of the girls were placed in this category.

The conclusion seems warranted that within the framework of ratings which lay stress upon insight and understanding in number work, teachers feel that boys of this age show more evidence of above average ability, whereas there is little or no difference between the sexes in the proportions which are below average.

The difference between this finding and the analysis of the Problem Arithmetic testing, which produced no evidence of any differential results above and below average for boys and girls, may be due to the different nature of the two assessments or to different aspects of number ability being assessed. Further research should throw more light on this matter.

However, the results of both assessments indicate that there are more boys than girls of above average arithmetic ability.

4. Other Abilities

(a) Introduction

In addition to assessments of number ability and reading, it was important to obtain a more complete and rounded picture of the children's abilities for a number of reasons. Thus, it is hoped at a later date to combine the assessments of other abilities in order to obtain a measure of the children's general level of intellectual functioning. Such a measure will make it possible, for example, to contrast those who are making slower progress in school than would be predicted from a knowledge of their general level of ability with those who are making better progress. Further, it will make possible analyses of the children's attainment when some allowance or correction has been made for those abilities less directly influenced by teaching in school.

An additional reason was that, although there is little published information about children's progress in reading and arithmetic in infant schools, there is even less available about other abilities.

It would have been possible, by adding an intelligence test to the range of objective tests included in the assessment of the children's development, to obtain a measure which might have fulfilled some of the functions outlined. However, intelligence tests which could readily have been administered by the teachers tend to have limited reliability at this age; further, it was felt that to add another test would have been an unreasonable imposition upon the teachers' time in the context of an educational assessment which was already to take more than an hour for an individual child.

It was decided, therefore, to obtain ratings by the teachers of each child's "oral ability", "awareness of the world around" and "creativity". These areas of functioning, it was felt, were very relevant to children's progress in school; they were aspects of development which schools would be attempting to foster; at the same time, they were likely to be influenced by factors outside the school to a greater extent than were reading or arithmetic.

The shortcomings of ratings were fully appreciated; and the attempts made to reduce subjectivity have been briefly outlined already (see sub-section 2(c) of the present section). Time has not yet permitted any "pooling" of the ratings to obtain some more general measure; moreover, particular care will be needed in devising a system of weighting to take account of the different distributions of the three ratings.

In the following three sub-sections, the results for boys and girls are compared. The hypothesis tested in each case was that there would be no difference between the sexes.

(b) Oral Ability

The ability to express thought and meaning orally is of obvious relevance to educational progress. It cannot be equated with verbal ability, which embraces the capacity for understanding and dealing with verbal material of all kinds; nevertheless, these two abilities will be highly correlated. Since a rating of verbal ability would be influenced to some extent by a child's performance in reading, it was decided to obtain an assessment of the children's oral ability, as it manifested itself in conversation and in the normal verbal inter-play of the classroom.

Table 10

Teachers' Ratings of Oral Ability

Descriptions of Ratings	Boys		Girls		Total	
	N	Per cent	N	Per cent	N	Per cent
In conversation expresses himself well	572	10·3	665	12·6	1,237	11·4
In conversation, or oral lessons, has good vocabulary and variety of phrases in relation to his age	749	13·5	805	15·2	1,554	14·4
Average oral ability for his age	2,810	50·8	2,910	54·9	5,720	52·8
Below average oral ability, tends to use simple word groupings	1,153	20·9	796	15·0	1,949	18·0
Markedly poor oral ability	247	4·5	120	2·3	367	3·4
Total rated	5,531	100	5,296	100	10,827	100
No data	5		1		6	
GRAND TOTAL	5,536		5,297		10,833	

Chi-squared (Trend) $=79·8$; $p < 0·001$

Chi-squared (Departure) $=35·2$ (3 d.f.); $p < 0·001$

There is a highly significant difference between the sexes, the girls receiving more favourable ratings than the boys. However, there was a highly significant departure from linear trend, indicating that the "gap" between the sexes is not consistent at all levels of oral ability. The results suggest that there is a greater difference between the sexes below average than above. It will be seen that about 24 per cent of the boys were rated above average compared with 28 per cent of the girls; on the other hand, approximately 25 per cent of boys were rated below average, against 17 per cent of the girls.

It is likely that the superiority of the girls in this context is to some extent a reflection of their tendency to be more forthcoming, orally, at this age.

(c) Awareness of the World Around

Some may question the inclusion of this rating in a consideration of abilities on the grounds that what was being assessed was knowledge rather than ability. It could be argued that the acquisition of knowledge is dependent upon this knowledge being made available to a child and therefore it is not a "true" ability. However, if "awareness of the world around" is regarded as a child's ability to comprehend a complex world, the distinction is surely a fine one. It may be that this comprehension and the background of general knowledge which accompanies it is more dependent upon environmental factors than are many other facets of intellectual functioning; but this is a

matter of degree rather than kind. In any event, there can be little doubt
about its relevance to and association with educational progress.

The results for children in "ordinary" maintained and independent schools
are given in Table 11.

Table 11

Awareness of the World Around

	Boys		Girls		Total	
	N	Per cent	*N*	Per cent	*N*	Per cent
Exceptionally well-informed for his age	189	3·4	112	2·1	301	2·8
Good background of general knowledge	1,246	22·5	893	16·9	2,139	19·8
Average in this respect	2,471	44·7	2,818	53·3	5,289	48·9
Rather limited knowledge	1,374	24·8	1,275	24·1	2,649	24·5
Largely ignorant of the world around him. Lack of general knowledge is a substantial handicap in school	251	4·5	191	3·6	442	4·1
Total rated	5,531	100	5,289	100	10,820	100
No data	5		8		13	
GRAND TOTAL	5,536		5,297		10,833	

Chi-squared (Trend) = 12·1; $p < 0.001$
Chi-squared (Departure) = 95·1 (3 d.f.); $p < 0.001$

The statistical test for linear trend shows a highly significant tendency for
boys to be given higher ratings for this factor. Again, however, there was a
highly significant departure from the linear trend.

The results indicate that whereas a higher proportion of boys than girls are
felt by their teachers to have above average "awareness of the world around"
—the proportions were about 26 per cent and 19 per cent respectively—there
is little or no difference in the proportions below average. In fact, what small
difference there was in this latter category in the present sample was in the
girls' favour.

(d) Creativity

There has been increased interest in recent years in the assessment of creativity,
particularly at the secondary school level. It has been claimed that it is possible
to measure and distinguish creative thought processes from the kinds of
ability assessed by conventional tests of intelligence. No attempt is made in
the present Report to produce any fresh evidence on this topic; indeed, it is
open to question whether such relatively crude measures as ratings could do
so. Nevertheless, within the context of the assessments made, it was felt that
such a rating might prove a useful and interesting addition.

One of the principal difficulties in assessing creativity is its multi-dimensional
character, and it can operate in many different spheres. One can opt for a
clearly defined area of creativity as, for example, in free written expression.
However, to do so is to penalise those children with reading difficulties as well

as to exclude those whose creativity manifests itself in other activities. To ask for a more global assessment carries the risk of reduced reliability and validity, since the verbal descriptions of each point in the rating scale must be rather more general in nature. One way to escape from this dilemma is to ask for ratings of creativity in a number of well-defined fields. However, this would have been a further imposition upon the teachers' time, which was not felt to be justified.

It was finally decided to obtain a global assessment, but to stress the generality of the rating by giving examples of the activities in which it was anticipated that creativity would be shown. In the Educational Assessment booklet, therefore, the heading "Creativity" was followed by: "(e.g., in free writing, telling a story, handwork, painting, drawing, dramatic work)".

The results are shown in Table 12.

The difference between the distribution of rating was statistically highly significant. The result indicates that, as assessed by this rating scale, girls of this age are felt by their teachers to show more evidence of creativity in school. It will be noted that there was no statistically significant departure from this tendency, suggesting that the difference between the sexes is consistent at all levels of "creative" ability.

Table 12

Teachers' Ratings of Creativity

	Boys		Girls		Total	
Description of Ratings	N	Per cent	N	Per cent	N	Per cent
Shows marked originality or creativity in most areas	154	2·8	152	2·9	306	2·8
Usually produces good, original work	806	14·6	983	18·6	1,789	16·5
Shows some imagination or originality in most areas	2,608	47·2	2,565	48·5	5,173	47·8
Little originality or creativity in all areas	1,765	32·0	1,456	27·5	3,221	29·8
Never shows a trace of originality or creativity in any of his work	190	3·4	136	2.6	326	3·0
Total rated	5,523	100	5,292	100	10,815	100
No data	13		5		18	
GRAND TOTAL	5,536		5,297		10,833	

Chi-squared (Trend) $=42·5$; $p < 0·001$
Chi-squared (Departure) $=9·0$ (3 d.f.); $p > 0·05$ not significant

5. Backwardness and Difficulties in School

(a) Children Receiving Special Educational Help in Ordinary Schools

Within the framework of the "ordinary" school, the term "special educational help" is here preferred to the more widely used "special educational treatment".

Children needing such help come within the broad definition of handicapped pupils categorized as "educationally subnormal" (H.M.S.O., 1953), namely:

"pupils who, by reason of limited ability or other conditions resulting in educational retardation, require some specialized form of education, wholly or partly in substitution for the education normally given in ordinary schools".

This definition and its implications were further elaborated in "Special Educational Treatment" and in "Slow Learners at School" (H.M.S.O., 1946 and 1964). It was made clear that the definition is interpreted broadly and covers every kind of educational provision for children who "need special help", even if this is only "in certain parts of their work". It was estimated in the former publication that about 10 per cent of the school population would fall into this category; of these, some eight or nine per cent would be catered for in ordinary schools. These estimates related to "registered pupils over the age of seven" but, in fact, excluded children of this age who were in infant classes; indeed, in a footnote it was indicated "that special educational treatment is not normally required for infants unless they are so seriously retarded that they should attend a special school". The statement is not in line with some more recent thought on this question; thus, "a crucial time for getting to grips with backwardness is the last year of the infant school and the beginning of the junior school" (Tansley and Gulliford, 1960).

In order to identify children with learning difficulties and to throw some light on the current situation in infant classes, it was decided to ask the head teachers of the children in the present cohort whether the children were currently receiving any special educational help in school; and, if they were not receiving it, whether they would benefit from such help.

The first question was phrased: "Apart from anything which the class teacher may be able to do in the normal way, is the child receiving any help within the school because of educational or mental backwardness?" Of the 10,833 children in ordinary schools for whom the information is available, approximately seven per cent of the boys (379) and four per cent of the girls (205) were receiving this help. The total proportion of children was thus over five per cent (584). The difference between the sexes in this respect was highly significant ($p < \cdot 001$).

Of those who were not receiving any help, the head teachers were asked if they considered that the children "would benefit from such help within the school at the present time". A further 879 children (eight per cent) the head teachers considered would benefit. Of these, 541 (10 per cent) were boys and 338 (six per cent) were girls. The difference between the sexes was again highly significant ($p < \cdot 001$).

It is particularly important that the figures relating to the second question be viewed in relation to its precise wording. The term "would benefit" (i.e., from special help) was used; the corresponding term in the definition of educational subnormality, quoted above, was "require". The former term was considered to be more acceptable to head teachers in the context of the present study: it would minimize their natural reluctance to "label" a child prematurely; and it would afford them greater freedom to express an opinion which had regard above all else for the needs of the individual child. Substitution of the term "require" would, it is felt, have reduced the number of children thus classified by schools.

In summary, more than five per cent of the children were already receiving special educational help in infant classes and there was a further eight per cent who, it was considered, would benefit from such help. The fact that more than 13 per cent of this sample could, with advantage, have been given such help stands in such marked contrast to the opinion expressed in the publication mentioned above (H.M.S.O., 1946) that there is clearly an urgent need to re-examine this issue.

The question of provision at the junior stage is discussed in sub-section (c) of the present section.

(b) Children in Need of Special Schooling

The figures given at the beginning of this main section show that 48 (0·4 per cent) of the children were in special schools. It is likely that some of the 73 children in "unclassified" schools were also receiving special schooling, but it is not possible to determine this at present since time does not permit individual re-scrutiny of the Educational Assessment booklets.

Of the children in ordinary schools, the head teachers were asked: "Do you consider, irrespective of the facilities in your area, that the child would benefit *now* from attendance at a special school?" In their view, two per cent (219) of the children would have benefited; 2·6 per cent of the boys (144) and 1·4 per cent of the girls (75) were included in this category. The difference between the sexes was highly significant ($p < ·001$).

In terms of the total number of children who might have benefited from special schooling at the infant stage, the above must be considered as minimum figures; for a further 190 children (1·8 per cent) the head teachers felt unable to give a definite answer. This latter group would obviously have contained a proportion of "borderline" cases.

In interpreting the situation, one must again weigh the effect of the term "would benefit" used in this question. Nevertheless, it is felt that an affirmative answer about the need for transfer to a special school would not have been made by head teachers in respect of children still in infant classes without considerable forethought. The results would appear to reflect a need felt by the head teachers for earlier transfer to special schools than is currently the practice.

(c) Children Likely to Need Special Educational Treatment in Future

The term "special educational treatment" is here used to denote special schooling as well as special educational help within an ordinary school.

As a separate question, the head teachers of all the children currently in ordinary schools were asked: "Do you consider, irrespective of the facilities in your area, that the child is likely to need some form of special schooling or other special educational help within the next two years?" The number of children thus classified was 530 (approximately five per cent); 348 (6·3 per cent) of the boys were included in this total and 182 (3·4 per cent) of the girls. Once again, the difference between the sexes was highly significant ($p < ·001$). There were a further 381 children (3·5 per cent) whose head teachers were not able to express a definite opinion as to their future needs. Again there were more boys than girls: 243 (4·4 per cent) and 138 (2·6 per cent) respectively. This difference, too, was highly significant ($p < ·001$). It seems likely that the majority of these children would be "borderline" cases.

The overall position is thus as follows:

 (i) 48 children (0·4 per cent of the sample) were already in special schools.

(ii) 73 children (0·7 per cent) were in "unclassified" schools, some of whom may have been ascertained as handicapped and have been receiving "special educational treatment". Inspection of documents at a later stage will enable this situation to be clarified.

(iii) 533 children (approximately five per cent) of the children in ordinary schools were said by their head teachers to be "likely to need some form of special schooling or other special educational help within the next two years". It must be made clear that this five per cent of children included the two per cent, mentioned in the previous sub-section, said to be currently in need of special schooling.

(iv) There were an additional 381 children (3·5 per cent) whose head teachers were not able to commit themselves on the question of future needs.

If one totals the proportions of children in items (i) and (iii), and makes the assumption that the majority of the children in item (iv) were "borderline" cases and approximately half of them would in fact need help, then one would conclude that about seven per cent of the present sample were likely to need some form of "special educational treatment" between the ages of seven and nine years. The assumption that the 3·5 per cent in item (iv) were "borderline" cases is supported by the fact that three-quarters of these children were rated as poor or non-readers by their teachers. A detailed scrutiny of the questionnaires at a later stage should enable a more precise estimate to be made.

However, at present there are three factors which prompt one to feel that the above estimate of seven per cent should be regarded as a minimum figure. First, the fact that head teachers were asked in this question to predict the children's likely needs over a period of two years may have led to some reservations and a cautious approach which gave the child the benefit of any doubt.

Secondly, the possibility must be considered that the answers may have been influenced by the presentation of the question. The head teachers were asked: "Do you consider, irrespective of the facilities in your area, that the child (a) would benefit now from attendance at a special school" (already discussed in sub-section (b)); and "(b) is likely to need some form of special schooling or other special educational help within the next two years?" It will be seen that the juxtaposition of the two questions, the order in which they were asked and the order of the two alternatives in the second question may have predisposed head teachers to have the possibility of special schooling uppermost in their minds. Further, the nature of the "other special educational help" was not made explicit, which may have led some head teachers to have in mind a narrower concept of possible provision than is now embraced by the term "special educational treatment".

Thirdly, the evidence from the head teachers' replies to the question relating to the children's current educational needs—discussed in sub-section (a)— suggests that the above estimate of seven per cent should be seen as a minimum figure. It will be recalled that some 13 per cent of the children in the head teachers' opinions could, with advantage, have been given special educational help in ordinary schools. Although it is no doubt true that some of these children's need for help might have diminished or even disappeared by the time they transferred to junior classes, it is hardly credible that the proportion would have dropped so markedly—from 13 per cent to seven per cent. One reason for this changed picture is likely to be the use of the term "benefit from" (special help) in the earlier question and "need" (special educational treatment) in the later one. It is arguable which of these terms best reflects the actual needs of children.

To summarise, then, it is estimated that at least seven per cent of the children in the present sample were likely to "need" some form of special educational treatment whilst they were from seven to nine years old. It is difficult to compare this figure with the estimates of the incidence of children requiring "special educational treatment", made by the Ministry of Education (H.M.S.O., 1946), since these estimates give no indication of the incidence of multiple handicap. In particular, the definition of educationally subnormal pupils, quoted earlier, if strictly interpreted could include many of the children with other handicaps. In view of these complicating factors, all that can be said at the present stage is that our findings do not provide evidence on whether the figures given by the Ministry under- or over-estimate the position. There is strong evidence from the present Study to suggest that the phraseology used in defining children in need of special educational treatment is more crucial than may be realized.

(d) Children Referred to Outside Agencies

The original reasons for including a question about referral to outside agencies were fourfold: to discover which children had been referred so that a more detailed study of the causes of referral could be made; to study the extent to which various agencies had been used; to discover the overall proportion of children who had been referred; and to test the hypothesis that more boys than girls would have been referred.

Although identification of the children concerned is straightforward, a detailed study of the causes of referral and the use made of various agencies necessitates perusal and analysis of the individual "Educational Assessment" booklets, and there has not yet been time for this. However, results are presented on the second two points.

The question was put to head teachers as follows:

"Has the child, *because of difficulties which have affected his progress or behaviour in school*, been referred to your knowledge to any agency? (e.g., School Health Service, Child Guidance Clinic, School Psychological Service, Education Welfare Service or School Attendance Officer, Children's Department, General Practitioner, Private Specialist.)

(Include referrals made at a routine medical examination, and any made by another school or by the parents, if known.)"

Where the answer was "Yes", the head teachers were asked to state the agency/agencies involved and, briefly, the reasons for referral.

The number of children in the sample reported to have been referred was 1,127 (9·5 per cent). It will be evident that this should be seen as a minimum figure since there would have been a number of children falling into this category where the information was not available to the head teachers for various reasons.

Approximately 11 per cent of the boys (604) and eight per cent of the girls (423) had been referred. The difference between the sexes in this respect was highly significant ($p < ·001$). This result, then, confirmed the hypothesis previously postulated.

P

6. *Summary*

(*a*) Three criteria were used in assessing the children's reading ability: performance on a standardized test of word recognition (the Southgate Group Reading Test); the stage reached in the reading scheme used by the school; and the teacher's rating of reading ability on a five point scale.

Judged by all three criteria, the girls were better readers than the boys. The differences were so marked and consistent that the generalization is warranted that at this stage in their schooling, shortly before transferring to junior schools and departments, girls are superior to boys in all respects of reading ability.

A comparison was made between the results of the present Study and a study conducted in 1954 (Morris, 1959). The tentative conclusion was reached that in the country as a whole, the number of poor and non-readers transferring to junior classes has dropped in the interval from 1954 to 1965.

Approximately 47 per cent of the present sample had in the final stage of infant schooling not reached a stage where they could make optimal progress without further specific help in the acquisition of basic reading skills. About a fifth of these children (10 per cent of the present sample) had barely made a start with reading. It was clear that given the present age of transfer, junior schools and departments have to be prepared and equipped to continue the specific teaching of reading skills to a substantial proportion of their first year children.

(*b*) Two assessments were made of ability in number work: performance in a Problem Arithmetic Test designed for the present Study; and a teacher's rating of number work on a five-point scale which stressed insight and understanding rather than mechanical or rote ability.

There was evidence that in problem arithmetic ability, as assessed by this test, boys of this age are superior to girls. There was evidence from the analysis of the teachers' ratings, too, of superior ability amongst boys; but here the indications were that there are more boys of above average ability and no difference between the sexes in the proportions below average.

This variation in the results obtained may have been due to the nature of the two assessments or to the different aspects of arithmetical ability assessed.

(*c*) Ratings were also obtained from the teachers of the children's "oral ability", "awareness of the world around" and "creativity".

As rated by teachers, girls manifest better "oral ability" than boys, and there were indications that this tendency is more marked in the children of below average "oral ability" than those above average.

Boys are felt by their teachers to have more "awareness of the world around" than girls, but this difference between the sexes appears to be confined to the children rated above average.

Compared with boys, girls show evidence at this age of superior "creativity" as rated by their teachers.

(*d*) More than five per cent of the present sample in ordinary schools were receiving special educational help because of educational or mental backwardness. The head teachers considered that a further eight per cent would have benefited from such help.

In view of the statement (H.M.S.O., 1946) that "special educational treatment is not normally required for infants unless they are so seriously retarded that they should attend a special school", the present findings indicate a need to re-examine this matter.

(e) Approximately 0·4 per cent of the sample were known to be in special schools. Of the children in ordinary schools, head teachers considered that about two per cent would currently have benefited from special schooling. For a further 1·8 per cent the head teachers did not feel able to express a definite opinion. These results appeared to reflect a need felt by the head teachers for earlier transfer to special schools than is the practice at the present time.

(f) It was estimated on the basis of head teachers' opinions that at least seven per cent of the present sample were likely to need special educational treatment whilst they were between the ages of seven and nine years. However, there were a number of complicating factors and it was not possible to draw any conclusions about the accuracy of estimates previously made (H.M.S.O., 1946).

There was evidence that when head teachers' opinions are sought on the question of special educational treatment, the precise terminology used is of more importance than may be realized. If it is asked whether children "would benefit" from such provision, the proportion of children included is likely to be higher than if the term "need" (and, probably, "require") is used. It is arguable which of these terms is most appropriate.

References

DEPARTMENT OF EDUCATION AND SCIENCE. *Slow Learners at School.* Pamphlet No. 46 (H.M.S.O.) (1964).

MINISTRY OF EDUCATION. *School Health Service and Handicapped Pupils Regulations* (H.M.S.O.) (1953).

MINISTRY OF EDUCATION. *Special Educational Treatment.* Pamphlet No. 5 (H.M.S.O.) (1946).

DOWNING, J. *The i.t.a. Reading Experiment* (Evans Bros.) (1964).

MORRIS, J. M. *Reading in the Primary School* (National Foundation for Educational Research) (1959).

TANSLEY, A. E. and GULLIFORD, R. *The Education of Slow Learning Children* (Routledge and Kegan Paul) (1960).

B. SCHOOL VARIABLES

1. *Introduction*

All the information gathered in this project was judged to have possible relevance to the development of individual children. Some of the data describes characteristics of the schools, and it is intended at a later stage to test certain hypotheses concerning associations between these characteristics and the development of the children.

In this section descriptive statistics are presented for those school variables upon which little or no information is available from other sources. It must be emphasized here that the Study is concerned essentially with a representative sample of children and not of schools. Thus, the data cannot be used to answer this kind of question: "What proportion of schools catering for seven-year-olds have parent/teacher associations?" However, the data can answer the question: "What proportion of seven-year-olds are in schools which have a parent/teacher association?" There may, in fact, be little or no difference between the answers to the two kinds of question; but where the characteristic being considered is related to the size of the school there will be a difference, since larger schools contribute more children to the cohort than smaller ones.

The 10,833 children for whom information is given in this section were all in maintained infant, junior with infants or all-age schools, or in independent schools catering wholly or mainly for children who are not handicapped. The actual numbers in each type of school are detailed in the Introduction to Section VA: "Educational Factors". In one sub-section (5) the results for a smaller sample of children had to be used for reasons which are mentioned in this sub-section.

2. Contact Between Schools and Parents

Of course, the most important contacts made are those in which parents discuss their children with the teacher or head teacher. This topic is specifically dealt with in Section VF: "Environmental Factors".

In this sub-section the emphasis is upon organized and relatively more formal contacts between the school and the parents. Nevertheless, these also create opportunities for informal discussion. There is a wide range of school activities and occasions in which parents may participate. An attempt was made to seek information about those contacts which might best reflect the general tenor of the relationship between the school and the home; also those which at a later stage of analysis might afford some measure of discrimination between schools which chose—or were able—to foster actively the interest and involvement of the parents in the school's work. Even within this general area a rigorous selection of questions had to be made to achieve a reasonable balance between the various educational aspects to be studied.

Four questions were put to schools and the results are detailed in Table 13.

Table 13

Contact Between Schools and Parents

$N = 10,833$

	N	Per cent
The number of children at schools which had a parent/teacher association	1,861	17·2
The number of children at schools where meetings were arranged for parents, by school or association, on educational matters	6,668	61·6
The number of children at schools where any social functions were organized for parents	5,628	52·0
The number of children at schools where parents provided substantial help for the school in money, kind or labour	5,788	53·4

Although these results are given in one table, it will be appreciated that the questions were not mutually exclusive. The numbers in each category are expressed as a percentage of 10,833.

It is clear that the majority of the schools in this sample preferred to establish contacts with parents without the more formal framework of a parent/teacher association.

3. *Introduction to School*

It is the practice of some head teachers to allow pre-school children to spend some time in the school before they actually start. Many people consider that this has much to commend it. It goes some way towards lessening any anxiety felt by children as they approach what is for them a new world.

Whether the practice is adopted will depend upon a number of factors, amongst which the staff/pupil ratio is likely to be very important. In this sample, the schools of 3,443 children (approximately 32 per cent) were in fact, using some form of "introductory attendance".

4. *Allocation of Children to Classes*

The question of the allocation of children to classes is more complex than would at first appear. It might seem that children are either "streamed" by ability—however this is assessed—or they are not. Instead, one is not faced with two possibilities but with a continuum. At one end of this continuum would lie those schools in which the head teacher feels that the best class grouping is one which achieves the greatest heterogeneity in terms of the children's ages and abilities. Infant school head teachers who adopt this approach place children from five to seven years old in the same class, deliberately setting out to achieve a wide ability and age range. Such a practice is sometimes referred to as "family grouping".

At the other end of the continuum are head teachers who feel that the more homogeneous the class, the better is the teacher able to meet the needs of the children. Such a head teacher would "stream" by ability, where possible. In between these two positions are a large variety of situations: for example, all the infants may be in one class, so that a heterogeneous group is inevitable; or children may be allocated to classes by age, in which case a measure of homogeneity is sought. Even between classes formed in the same overt way there will be differences in approach on the part of the teachers which will reflect in some measure their attitudes—or those of the head teachers— towards this question.

Enough has been said to outline some of the difficulties in assessing what is basically an educational approach or an attitude. All that was possible in the present Study was to obtain relatively crude information on the method of allocation to classes. It was felt, nevertheless, that this data, despite their limitations, would be valuable since no other information appears to have been published in this country on pupils' allocation to classes at the infant stage.

Table 14
Formation of Class

	N	Per cent
One class only for all "infants"	531	4·9
A deliberate cross-section by age and ability of more than one year group of children—sometimes called 'family grouping'	576	5·3
By age in year groups (e.g., one class per year, or parallel classes)	4,122	38·1
Selected by age within the year group (e.g. children born in the first half of the year in one class, and the remainder in another)	3,738	34·6
"Streamed" by ability or attainment — An upper ability (or attainment) class within the school	402	3·7
A middle ability (or attainment) class within the school (e.g. of three classes)	171	1·6
A lower ability (or attainment) class within the school	220	2·0
Other arrangements	1,057	9·8
Total answered	10,817	100
No data	16	
GRAND TOTAL	10,833	

It will be seen that the majority of the children (about 73 per cent) were allocated to classes by age: in year groups, or selected by age within the year group. Approximately seven per cent were overtly "streamed" by ability or attainment. However, there was a further 10 per cent of children in classes formed by "other arrangements". It seems likely that in the majority of these classes an attempt was being made to achieve some kind of homogeneous grouping; for example, by promoting brighter children to a higher class or holding back the less able.

The nature of these "other arrangements" has been detailed by the schools, but at this stage time does not permit an analysis of the replies.

5. *Age of Starting Full-time Infant Schooling*

There has been increasing interest of late in the association between date of birth and educational performance. Younger children in any school year group appear to be at a disadvantage compared with the older ones (Pidgeon, 1965).

There is clearly more than one factor operating here, but an important one would seem to be the length of schooling obtained. The age at which children are admitted to infant schools in England varies between education authorities and also within authorities from year to year depending upon the provision available in relation to the numbers of children approaching the age of five. Two years is the minimum period normally spent in an infant school or department, but children are in some areas admitted at four years of age, provided that they will become five before the start of the next term, whilst in others an earlier start than this is possible. In some cases, therefore, a much longer period than two years is spent in school before transfer to a junior school or department.

Thus, although the children in the present sample are virtually all of the same age, it was known that there would be differences in the length of schooling received prior to the present educational assessment. In Section VIB the relationship between the age of starting full-time infant schooling, educational performance and social adjustment at seven years of age is examined.

Here, the numbers of children starting full-time infant schooling at different ages is presented. It will be noted that the total number of children (5,805) is much smaller than elsewhere in this section.

There are a number of reasons for this. First, it was only possible to include children for whom a Parental Questionnaire had been received when the data processing was commenced, because the information about the age of starting school was obtained from the mothers. Secondly, children are included only where it was known that they had not attended a nursery school or class, since it was felt that children who had had nursery schooling might as a group be atypical in this context; furthermore, it would in some cases be difficult to determine when nursery schooling ceased and infant schooling commenced. Another fact to be noted is that the figures detailed below are abstracted from a larger table, not included in this Report, which includes a breakdown of the figures in relation to the Occupational Group of the father. Thus, children for whom this information was not available, including those in families where there was no male head of the household, are grouped together with those who started school outside the limits of the three age groupings for which numbers are detailed.

Table 15

Age of Starting Full-time Infant Schooling

	N	Per cent
4 years to 4 years 5 months	75	1·3
4 years 6 months to 4 years 11 months	2,772	47·8
5 years to 5 years 5 months	2,505	43·2
Started school outside these limits or Occupational Group of father not known	448	7·7
Total information	5,800	100
No data	5	
GRAND TOTAL	5,805	

The results indicate that nearly half of this sub-sample started school when they were between 4 years 6 months to 4 years 11 months old. The great majority of these would have started school in January 1963, since they were five years old in March of that year. Over 43 per cent would have started school at the beginning of the following term.

In assessing the reliability of these figures and the extent to which they may be representative of the situation in the country as a whole, a number of factors should be borne in mind.

First, the fact that those children who could not be classified by the Occupational Group of their fathers are included with those who started school outside the three specified age groupings will depress the percentage figures for these groupings. However, the effect of this has been checked; it is minimal and does not alter the overall position.

Secondly, the information was obtained from the mothers, and some may have had difficulty in recalling an event which occurred two years earlier in terms of the age categories detailed above. As against this, the question was put by health visitors—or another officer of the local authority—who would have helped mothers, where necessary, with this "calculation". Of course, health visitors are likely to be familiar with local practice.

Thirdly, the school year 1962–63 was a difficult one for schools and authorities because of the effect of increasing the training college courses for teachers from two to three years at this time. The consequent acute shortage of staff may have forced some schools to take children later than was their usual practice.

For these reasons, then, the figures should be viewed with some caution. However, despite these reservations, the suggestion by Pidgeon and Dodds (1961) that "There is a general, but not universal, rule in this country that children start formal schooling at the beginning of the term in which they will become five years old" clearly needs re-examination in the light of our findings.

6. *Age of Commencing Phonics in Reading*

There is a wide variety of possible approaches to the introduction and subsequent teaching of reading. In this Study one particular aspect was selected for closer investigation; namely the stage at which a systematic attempt is made to introduce children to the sounds of individual letters or phonemes. The introduction of "phonics"—as this is customarily termed—is made much earlier in the reading programme in some schools than in others.

There has been—and still is—considerable debate amongst schools, and in educational circles generally, about the age at which phonics should be systematically taught. To say that the right time is when the individual child is "ready" is to avoid the issue in the absence of any universally agreed or well validated criteria as to what constitutes readiness.

This Study cannot claim to throw any new light of an experimental nature upon this question. However, it can give information, hitherto not available, about the age at which this systematic introduction is in fact commenced in schools. Although this Report is concerned with children in England, it was felt that comparative figures for Wales and Scotland would be of interest in this particular context. The results are given in Table 16 and reproduced in graph form in Figure 2.

It will be seen that there are a substantial number of "Don't knows" in this table. This was expected, since the data for most of the children were retrospective and staff changes, as well as changes of school by the children, will have meant that information on this question was sometimes unobtainable. However, there is no reason to believe that if the information for these children had been available it would have differed in overall pattern from that obtained for the rest of the children. Thus, it was felt appropriate to exclude "Don't know" replies from the percentaging.

The differences between the three countries are marked and interesting. The English pupils were introduced to phonics at a later age: the peak age for its introduction in the English schools was from 5 years 6 months to 5 years 11 months, whilst in Wales and Scotland the corresponding age was from 5 years to 5 years 5 months. The differences in the distribution, both between England and Wales and between England and Scotland, are highly significant statistically. Phonics had been taught to about 54 per cent of the children for whom this information was available in Scottish schools before the age of 5½ and to 46 per cent of the children in Welsh schools; the corresponding percentage for the children in England was about 29 per cent.

Since no teacher would commence teaching phonics before she considered a child was ready for this step, it would appear that the teachers in Wales and Scotland considered their pupils to be ready at an earlier age than their colleagues in England. It is interesting to speculate whether there are any real differences in the children's degree of readiness or whether tradition or teacher training courses are responsible. Or perhaps a combination of these? Additionally, some of the Welsh children were Welsh-speaking and would have been taught to read in that language, which may lend itself to a more phonic approach than English.

Apart from the difference between the children in English schools and those in Wales and Scotland in relation to the age at which phonics were introduced, there is also evidence of more variability in the English and Welsh samples than in the Scottish. Both of these findings may be a reflection of more uniformity in Scotland, if this is the case, in the age of starting school.

Table 16

Age at which the Systematic Teaching of Phonics (i.e., Letter Sounds) was Commenced in School

$N=13,018$

	England		Wales		Scotland	
	N	Per cent	N	Per cent	N	Per cent
Under 5 years of age	357	3·7	78	11·6	26	1·9
From 5 years to 5 years 5 months	2,438	25·6	232	34·4	697	52·2
From 5 years 6 months to 5 years 11 months	3,134	32·9	153	22·7	541	40·6
From 6 years to 6 years 5 mths.	1,980	20·8	110	16·3	56	4·2
From 6 years 6 months to 6 years 11 months	1,069	11·2	63	9·3	9	0·7
From 7 years to 7 years 5 months	128	1·3	8	1·2	1	0·1
Not commenced	425	4·5	30	4·5	4	0·3
Total information	9,531	100	674	100	1,334	100
Don't know	1,293		67		108	
No data	9		1		1	
GRAND TOTAL	10,833		742		1,443	

Chi-squared (Trend) England and Wales $=38·0$; $p < 0·001$

Chi-squared (Trend) England and Scotland $=452·6$; $p < 0·001$

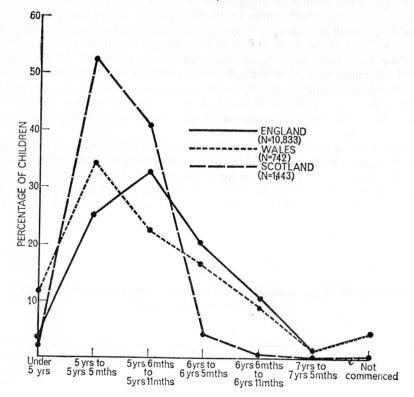

Figure 2

*Age at which the Systematic Teaching of Phonics (i.e., Letter Sounds)
was Commenced in School*

(English, Welsh and Scottish children in 'ordinary' maintained and independent schools)

$N=13,018$

7. *Age of Commencing "Formal" Written Arithmetic*

There have been considerable changes in many infant schools during recent years in the approach to number work. An increasing use of the term "number work" or even "mathematics" in place of "arithmetic" or "sums" is symptomatic of this change and the wider approach adopted in some schools. One accompaniment of the change has often been the introduction of "formal" written arithmetic at a later stage.

Again, a comparison of the practice in England, Scotland and Wales is made. The results are presented in Table 17 and in graph form in Figure 3.

Table 17

Age at which "Sums" (i.e., "Formal" Written Arithmetic) was Introduced in School

$N = 13,018$

	England		Wales		Scotland	
	N	Per cent	N	Per cent	N	Per cent
Under 5 years of age	78	0·8	24	3·5	4	0·3
From 5 years to 5 years 5 months	1,525	15·9	192	28·2	182	13·7
From 5 years 6 months to 5 years 11 months	4,073	42.5	245	36·0	825	61·9
From 6 years to 6 years 5 months	2,340	24·4	137	20·1	250	18·8
From 6 years 6 months to 6 years 11 months	1,007	10·5	57	8·4	62	4·7
From 7 years to 7 years 5 months	136	1·4	14	2·1	1	0·1
Not commenced	426	4·4	12	1·8	8	0·6
Total information	9,585	100	681	100	1,332	100
Don't know	1,239		60		110	
No data	9		1		1	
GRAND TOTAL	10,833		742		1,443	

Chi-squared (Trend) England and Wales $= 54·0$; $p < 0·001$

Chi-squared (Trend) England and Scotland $= 96·8$; $p < 0·001$

As in Table 16, there are a substantial number of "Don't knows" and, for the same reason, discussed in the previous sub-section, they have been excluded from the percentaging.

In English schools pupils were introduced to "sums" at a later age than their peers in Wales and in Scotland. The difference between the practice in the English and Welsh schools seems to centre on the fact that more of the children (approximately 32 per cent) in the latter schools had reached this stage before 5½ years of age than in England (approximately 17 per cent).

Figure 3

Age at which Children were Introduced to "Sums" (i.e., "Formal" Written Arithmetic) in School

(English, Welsh and Scottish children in 'ordinary' maintained and independent schools)

$N = 13,018$

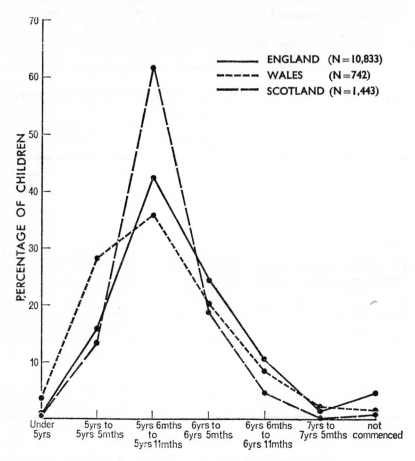

One apparent difference in practice among the Scottish schools as reflected in this sample of children is in their greater uniformity. Thus, although the peak period for the commencement of "formal" written arithmetic was between 5 years 6 months and 5 years 11 months in all three countries, well over half (about 62 per cent) of the Scottish sample reached this stage during this six-month period, whereas in England and Wales the corresponding percentages were about 43 per cent and 36 per cent. This may be a reflection of more uniformity in Scotland, if this is the case, in the age of starting school.

8. *Summary*

(*a*) Whilst the majority of the children were at schools in which there was some form of organized contact between the school and the parents, most schools established these contacts without the framework of a parent/teacher association.

(*b*) About one-third of the children attended schools in which the head teachers adopted the practice of allowing pre-school children to spend some time in the school before actually starting.

(*c*) The allocation of children to classes was done mainly on an age basis. It appeared that about half of the children were in classes where an attempt had been made to achieve a degree of homogeneity by some form of selective grouping, based on age within the year group, on ability or by some other arrangement. Only seven per cent of the children were in "streamed" classes.

(*d*) The results indicated that of those children who had had no nursery schooling nearly half started school when they were aged 4 years 6 months to 4 years 11 months; the great majority of these would have commenced at the beginning of the term in which they attained the age of five. The mothers' reports showed that over 43 per cent of the children commenced school at the beginning of the following term. The school year 1962–63 may have been untypical because of the particularly acute shortage of teachers due to the lengthening of the teacher training college courses at that time.

(*e*) A comparison was made between the practice in England and that in Wales and in Scotland in relation to the age at which the systematic teaching of "phonics" was commenced with these children and also the age at which "sums" or "formal" written arithmetic was introduced. The evidence was that pupils in English schools are introduced to both these aspects of their school work at a later age than those in Wales and Scotland. In all three countries a majority of the children had commenced "formal" written arithmetic and were receiving some systematic teaching of "phonics" before the age of six. There was also evidence of more uniformity of practice in Scotland than in Wales or England in both these spheres.

(*f*) In varying degrees all the questions here discussed have relevance to the educational development of children; it is therefore somewhat surprising that there is an almost complete lack of comparable information from other sources, particularly on a national basis. Such information is relatively straightforward to collect; moreover, if gathered at regular intervals it would be valuable to individual schools and teachers, to administrators and to those with responsibility for the training of teachers; also it would reflect changing practice and act as a stimulus to further change.

References

PIDGEON, D. A. Date of Birth and Scholastic Performance, *Educational Research*, Vol. VIII, No. 1 (National Foundation for Educational Research) (1965).

PIDGEON, D. A. and DODDS, E. M. Length of Schooling and its Effect on Performance in the Junior School, *Educational Research*, Vol. III, No. 3 (1961).

C. MEDICAL AND PHYSICAL FACTORS

NOTE.—Most of the tables from which the summary tables in this and the
   following sections are derived are excluded from this version. They
   are given in full in Appendix 1 to the full version.

1. *Introduction*

This part of the Study is concerned with some aspects of the physical and
medical status of the sample children. The information contained in this and
in the following section (VD) is based upon data from approximately 8,000
Parental and Medical Questionnaires received by the middle of August 1965.
The total number of children for whom information is available differs
slightly in different tables. This is due to certain minor technical considerations, including the fact that the data in this and the following two sections
were divided among four different punched cards. The data were derived
from a general and systemic medical history gathered from the mother and
from the results of examinations by school medical officers.

(a) *Medical History*

The design of this part of the enquiry is discussed in Section III D. Information was sought on a wide variety of conditions and recorded on a pre-
coded form. A positive reply to a question on whether the child suffered from
a given condition led the interviewer to ask about age of onset, recent history
or other specified details. These data are sometimes retrospective and with
attendant possibility of bias. These considerations are discussed in more
detail in the Introduction to Section V E: "Medical and Developmental Sex
Comparisons".

(b) *Medical Examination*

A special problem was posed in the design of the Medical Questionnaire on
which the results of the medical examination were to be recorded. It is known
that analysis of school medical records yields gross fluctuations in incidence,
suggesting very wide variations in interpretation. The pattern of the questionnaire, therefore, differed from that used for routine school records, though
every effort was made to avoid complicated format. The medical practitioners
who conducted the examinations consisted almost entirely of school medical
officers, who are probably more experienced in technique of routine examination of children than any other section of the medical profession. With the
exception of certain tests of special senses, it was therefore unnecessary to
specify the *manner* in which the clinical examination should be carried out.
The specially framed questions provided an objective determination of the
current physical and medical status of the children. Any enquiry asking only
for defects or abnormal findings to be noted would have allowed preconceived
notions of normality to govern the decision whether or not an observation
should be recorded. Therefore, within each system the medical examiner was
asked to indicate a positive or negative response to the presence of specified
conditions. Care was taken as far as possible to avoid questions inviting
varying interpretations or subjective responses. For many specified conditions
further details were enquired for special analysis. The doctor was also asked
to comment upon any residual abnormality in each system examined.
In the main, therefore, facts rather than opinions were sought. However,
clinical assessments were also included in certain fields, notably the special

senses, to allow subsequent comparison with test results. Specific tests of special senses, laterality or co-ordination were mostly derived from existing tests of proven value in clinical practice. In order to maximize comparability of results among a large number of examiners it was necessary to define the conditions of special tests in detail on the questionnaire.

(c) Interpretations

The medical and physical data on this incomplete sub-sample justify only tentative conclusions. For instance, it is known that the children involved in these "early returns" are biased in family Occupational Group compared with "late returns". Moreover, those "early returns" with Parental and Medical assessments show better reading and social adjustment than children for whom only educational information was available (see Section II: "Description of the Sample"). Although the overall bias is not marked, it may become relevant when individual incidences or distributions in this sub-sample of "early returns" are considered. Bias would be particularly important if a given physical factor is not associated with normal social circumstances, educational progress or behaviour and adjustment. Time has not permitted a comparison of the sub-sample of "early returns" with the "late returns" for any medical or physical factors. The possibility exists, for example, that the sub-sample does not contain a representative proportion of physically handicapped children. The present Report, therefore, deals with tests of special senses and with incidences of minor physical abnormality rather than with severe handicaps or major conditions requiring special treatment or education. A later report will present physical data, including height and weight, correlations between current physical status and perinatal information obtained on the children at birth from the Perinatal Survey of the National Birthday Trust Fund, and also relationships between current educational and medical status of the cohort.

2. Speech

(a) Introduction

Information was sought from the mother on a number of speech difficulties to which the child might have been subject; and the medical examiner used a speech test, noted any stammer and assessed the intelligibility of the child's speech.

(b) History and Examination

The results of the history and examination are summarized in Table 18.

Table 18
Speech: Summary of History and Examination
Number of boys = 4,053; Number of Girls = 3,933; Total = 7,986

	Incidence per cent			Sex difference	
				Chi-squared	
	Boys	Girls	Total	(1 d.f.)	P value
History of stammer or stutter	7·9	4·5	6·2	40·2	< 0·001
History of any other speech difficulty	11·5	8·5	10·0	20·0	< 0·001
Any stammer observed on examination	1·3	0·8	1·1	4·9	$0·05 > p > 0·01$ not sig.
Speech not fully intelligible on testing	16·2	11·4	14·0	39·5	< 0·001

The superiority of girls over boys in speech function is amply demonstrated in the above table. Three of the sex differences are highly significant and the fourth is in the same direction, although it fails to reach the one per cent level of significance.

Fewer girls than boys were reported to have attended Speech Therapy Clinics (Table A33: Appendix 1), again suggesting superior speech function. However, both this sex difference and that in "history of other speech difficulty" (Table 18) may simply have resulted from later speech development in boys, since more girls were reported by their mothers to have been talking (i.e., "joining two words") by the age of two years (Boys 92·4 per cent; Girls 95·2 per cent).

The *overall incidence* as opposed to sex comparisons of speech difficulty in Table 18 should be regarded with particular caution in view of the retrospective nature of the information and any bias in this sub-sample.

It should also be noted that in the great majority of children in whom some stammer was observed, the handicap was slight; and likewise for any lack of intelligibility on testing of speech.

(c) Speech Test

The sentences used in this speech test were composed of words chosen to demonstrate the commonest defects of speech in children (Sheridan, 1945, 1965). When applied by a large number of medical examiners the test can be expected to produce somewhat less reliable results than it would in the hands of those with specialized knowledge of speech development.

Table 19

Speech Test Results

Mispronounced words	11	10	9	8	7	6	5	4	3	2	1	0
Cumulative frequencies:												
Boys	78	109	136	174	242	314	448	643	942	1467	2175	4008
Girls	43	65	87	117	153	224	305	442	684	1148	1906	3868
Cumulative percentages:												
Boys	1·9	2·7	3·4	4·3	6·0	7·8	11·2	16·0	23·5	36·6	54·0	100
Girls	1·1	1·7	2·2	3·0	4·0	5·8	7·9	11·4	17·7	29·7	49·3	100

Chi-squared (Trend) $=30·6$; $p < 0·001$

Six sentences were used in the test. The child was asked to repeat each one after the examiner, who noted any mis-pronounced words and recorded the total number of errors.

Cumulative percentages are shown in Table 19 and presented in graph form in Figure 4. Both the table and the figure are based upon the children ($N = 7,876$) for whom this information was available when the data were processed.

A trend test for sex difference in the proportion of mis-pronounced words in Table 19 confirms a superior performance in girls.

Figure 4
Speech Test

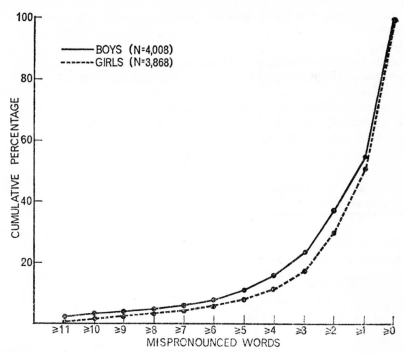

BOYS (N=4,008)
GIRLS (N=3,868)

CUMULATIVE PERCENTAGE

MISPRONOUNCED WORDS
≥11 ≥10 ≥9 ≥8 ≥7 ≥6 ≥5 ≥4 ≥3 ≥2 ≥1 ≥0

3. Vision
(a) Introduction
Information presented here on the children's vision includes the results of visual acuity testing, of a reported history of squint, of evidence of squint on examination and of a clinical assessment by the examining doctor of the severity and educational implications of any observed visual defects.

One objective of the present Study was to obtain representative national figures using defined procedures, although it was an inevitable drawback that many examiners had to be used. Later it is hoped to present fresh methods of classification, as published figures suggest gross variability in the way visual defect is assessed and reported. Thus, the incidences quoted by individual local authorities for visual defects in school children of all ages ranged in 1963 from 1·38 per cent to 25·2 per cent (H.M.S.O., 1964). In 1961 (H.M.S.O., 1962) the reported incidence of squint varied from 0·045 per cent to 10·6 per cent.

(b) Visual Acuity
A standard Snellen test chart of block capitals was specified for the vision test and instructions were given in the Questionnaire on the conditions of the test as well as for the procedure to be adopted when a child did not know the letters in the chart. Each eye was tested separately without glasses and also with glasses if these were worn.

Table 20 shows the visual acuity in each eye of all the children in this sample for whom this information was available when tested without glasses. The number of children for whom results are presented differs very slightly for the right eye and the left in Table 20 and in the following two tables due to difficulties in processing the data.

A sex difference was tested for each eye separately and the results were as follows:

Left eye
Chi-squared (Trend)=0·5; $p>0·05$ not significant
Chi-squared (Departure)=7·5 (6 d.f.); $p>0·05$ not significant

Right eye
Chi-squared (Trend)=0·0; $p>0·05$ not significant
Chi-squared (Departure)=6·2 (6 d.f.); $p>0·05$ not significant

As will be seen, no significant sex differences were found.

Table 20

Uncorrected Vision (i.e., without glasses)

(All children)

	Right eye		Left eye	
	Cumulative Frequencies	Cumulative Percentages	Cumulative Frequencies	Cumulative Percentages
Less than 6/60 or blind	13	0·2	8	0·1
6/60 and less	34	0·4	27	0·3
6/36 and less	78	1·0	67	0·8
6/24 and less	139	1·8	135	1·7
6/18 and less	236	3·0	246	3·1
6/12 and less	440	5·6	454	5·7
6/9 and less	1,319	16·7	1,333	16·9
6/6 and less	7,916	100	7,897	100
	Percentage with 6/6 vision = 83·4		Percentage with 6/6 vision = 83·2	

Table 21

Vision of Children who never wear glasses

	Right eye		Left eye	
	Cumulative Frequencies	Cumulative Percentages	Cumulative Frequencies	Cumulative Percentages
Less than 6/60 or blind	6	0·1	3	0·04
6/60 and less	11	0·2	8	0·1
6/36 and less	28	0·4	18	0·2
6/24 and less	55	0·7	45	0·6
6/18 and less	105	1·4	94	1·3
6/12 and less	248	3·3	250	3·4
6/9 and less	1,018	13·7	979	13·3
6/6 and less	7,434	100	7,368	100

Table 20 shows that 17 per cent of all the children tested had sub-optimal visual acuity in the right eye, taking 6/6 as perfect vision. A similar proportion had sub-optimal vision in the left eye, but the degree of overlap is not yet known.

However, Table 20 does not distinguish between those children who already had glasses prescribed and those who had never worn glasses. The test results of the children who had never worn glasses are therefore shown in Table 21.

Table 21 shows that over 13 per cent of children who did not wear glasses had at least one eye with visual acuity below the optimum, taking 6/6 as perfect vision.

If 6/9 vision is considered acceptable, only three per cent of these children are shown to have imperfect vision in at least one eye, but some authorities would not be prepared to accept 6/9 vision as normal in a child until an examination by an ophthalmologist or ophthalmic optician had shown that an eye defect had been excluded.

Table 22

Corrected Vision of Children wearing glasses

	Right eye		Left eye	
	Cumulative Frequencies	Cumulative Percentages	Cumulative Frequencies	Cumulative Percentages
Less than 6/60 or blind	4	1·1	0	0
6/60 and less	5	1·4	0	0
6/36 and less	10	2·8	12	3·3
6/24 and less	19	5·3	23	6·3
6/18 and less	39	10·8	55	15·1
6/12 and less	91	25·2	95	26·1
6/9 and less	182	50·4	193	53·0
6/6 and less	361	100	364	100

In those children tested wearing their glasses, the testing of the right eye showed sub-optimal vision in just over 50 per cent, and results for the left eye were similar. It may be that some children were tested wearing glasses which were intended for close work or reading, but the figures suggest that it would be a wise precaution for teachers to consider any child wearing glasses in a primary school to have defective vision and to place that child near the front of the class.

(c) Squint

A history of squint or of suspected squint obtained from the mother was recorded in the Parental Questionnaire. A *manifest* squint observed by the examining doctor was recorded and two tests were specified to enable him to detect the presence of a *latent* squint, i.e., a tendency to squint which is, in normal circumstances, kept under control. The type of squint (divergent or convergent) and the eye affected were also recorded for later analysis.

The teacher and school medical officer are favourably placed to pick out a child with this condition at school, but squint may derive from a number of causes dating from before birth to any time thereafter. Early detection of squint and other visual defects in the pre-school child is dependent upon the powers of observation of the mother and the use she might make of her general practitioner and the child welfare facilities. Neglect of a severe squint, or other visual defect, may result in the sight of an affected eye becoming permanently impaired.

The results of the history and examination are shown in Table 23 in summary.

Table 23

Squint

Number of boys = 4,058; Number of girls = 3,927; Total = 7,985

	Incidence per cent			Sex difference	
				Chi-squared (1 d.f.)	P value
	Boys	Girls	Total		
History of squint or suspected squint	6·4	6·1	6·3	0·3	>0·05 not sig.
Squint found on examination	3·2	3·0	3·1	0·3	>0·05 not sig.
Latent squint on examination	2·4	3·4	2·9	6·8	0·01 > p > 0·001

It will be seen from Table 23 that approximately six per cent of the children had either a latent or manifest squint on examination. The significantly greater percentage of latent squints in girls is an unexpected finding. There was no difference between the sexes for manifest squint or for a history of squint or suspected squint.

(d) Visual Assessment

On completing the examination of the eyes and after the eye test, the medical officers were asked to rate the educational implications of any visual defect. This was done on a five-point scale, but in Table 24 all children who received any one of the lowest three ratings are aggregated. The numbers with these ratings were very small and it was felt unwise to consider them as separate groups until time permits individual scrutiny of the questionnaires.

This crude breakdown was also considered advisable because many of the medical examinations were undertaken in clinics and the medical officers may have had no opportunity to discuss detailed educational difficulties arising out of any visual defect with school staffs.

Table 24

Visual Assessment

	Boys	Girls	Total	Total incidence per cent
Normal vision	3,453	3,325	6,778	86·2
Visual defect, but judged to be no handicap to normal schooling and everyday activities	541	522	1,063	13·5
Visual defect judged to be a handicap in school in some degree (including blindness)	10	8	18	0·3
Total assessed	4,004	3,855	7,859	100
Don't know	38	47	85	
No data	11	15	26	
GRAND TOTAL	4,053	3,917	7,970	

Sex difference—Chi-squared (Normal vision: Any visual defect) = 0·0 (1 d.f.) not significant

It will be seen that there is no significant sex difference.

This assessment serves to identify the 14 per cent of children judged to have some visual handicap. Thus, it is an assessment of function and it cannot fully take into account all the degrees of visual acuity shown in Tables 20, 21 and 22.

4. Hearing
(a) Introduction
The testing and assessment of the children's hearing included a pure-tone audiogram; a functional assessment of hearing by the examining doctor; a clinical hearing test; and any reported history of hearing difficulty or attendance at an audiology clinic. Time has not yet permitted any analysis of the audiograms.

(b) Assessment of Hearing
A functional assessment of hearing was carried out by the school doctor after he had completed the examination and hearing test. The assessment was made on a four-point scale and the definitions at each point on the scale were framed to correspond approximately to the statutory definitions of deaf and partially hearing children.

In view of the small number of children who were assessed as having some degree of auditory handicap and the impossibility of scrutinizing the questionnaires individually to confirm the appropriate category, it was decided to group together all such children. The purpose was to compare them with those judged to have "normal hearing". The results are shown in Table 25, in which children with "some degree of hearing impairment" include those with hearing loss which had been corrected by a hearing aid; those whose understanding of speech was impaired (even with a hearing aid); and those whose hearing disability was so severe that they could not understand speech at all. The proportion of children in the present sub-sample who fell into the latter two categories was 0·1 per cent.

Table 25
Assessment of Hearing

	Boys		Girls		Total	
	N	Per cent	N	Per cent	N	Per cent
Normal hearing	3,810	95·1	3,684	95·2	7,494	95·1
Some degree of hearing impairment	199	4·9	185	4·8	384	4·9
Total assessed	4,009	100	3,869	100	7,878	100
Don't know	33		34		67	
No data	11		14		25	
GRAND TOTAL	4,053		3,917		7,970	

Chi-squared $=0·1$ (1 d.f.); $p>0·05$ not significant

The difference between the sexes on this assessment is not significant. A little under five per cent of the children in this sub-sample were judged by the medical officers to have some degree of hearing impairment.

(c) Hearing Test

The hearing test consisted of twelve test words which the child was required to repeat one by one after the examiner. The test conditions were specified in detail in the questionnaire. The twelve words were selected to test the auditory acuity over the speech frequency range (Sheridan, 1958 and 1965). A preliminary analysis of the results is presented in the following table.

Table 26

Hearing Test

Number of boys = 4,053; Number of girls = 3,917; Total = 7,970

Test words Score of errors	Right ear Cumulative Percentages		Left ear Cumulative Percentages	
	Boys	Girls	Boys	Girls
9 or more	0·6	1·0	0·8	0·9
8 or more	0·8	1·1	0·9	1·1
7 or more	1·0	1·1	1·1	1·3
6 or more	1·3	1·3	1·3	1·6
5 or more	1·7	1·6	1·8	2·1
4 or more	2·4	2·6	2·8	3·0
3 or more	3·9	3·9	5·1	4·6
2 or more	10·7	9·7	11·2	9·9
1 or more	28·9	25·4	28·4	26·3
0 or more	100	100	100	100
Percentage with no errors	71·1	74·6	71·6	73·7

Sex differences: Chi-squared (Trend): left ear = 0·8; $p > 0·05$ not significant

Chi-squared (Trend): right ear = 1·9; $p > 0·05$ not significant

There were no significant sex differences on the results of this hearing test for each ear separately.

It will be seen that some four to five per cent of the children, for each ear separately, failed to repeat three or more words of the twelve used. A functional assessment by the examining doctor (Table 25) indicated also that five per cent of the children had some degree of hearing impairment. Some further analysis will be necessary to determine any correlation between the two, test and assessment, and their relationship to audiometry results.

In the hearing test a poor understanding of the meaning of words or an inability to concentrate may adversely affect the score of a child with a minor degree of hearing loss. Conversely, a bright child will be at an advantage in coping with a loss of auditory acuity. The audiogram and the clinical hearing test are therefore complementary in the assessment of hearing.

The test was developed from one which was originally designed for individual specialist use. Its application to the children in this Study may, after further analysis, establish its value as an additional screening test for use in conjunction with existing pure-tone audiometric screening methods.

(d) *History of Hearing Difficulty and Clinic Attendance*

Table 27

History of Hearing Difficulty and Clinic Attendance

Number of boys =4,059; Number of girls =3,926; Total =7,985

	Incidence per cent			Sex difference	
	Boys	Girls	Total	Chi-squared (1 d.f.)	P value
Hearing difficulty suspected or confirmed	10·9	9·5	10·3	4·3	$0·05 > p > 0·01$ not sig.
Attendance at a hearing or audiology clinic	8·1	7·8	7·9	0·2	$> 0·05$ not sig.

The results of the analysis showed no significant sex differences.

Some 10 per cent of the children in this sub-sample were reported by their mothers to have had a suspected or confirmed hearing difficulty at any time in the first seven years of life. Numbered amongst these will be children who had a temporary catarrhal deafness following a cold; those whose lack of attention or responsiveness had led to a suspicion of hearing difficulty; and those whose hearing might have been shown with certainty to be impaired. Approximately eight per cent of the children were reported to have attended hearing or audiology clinics. These children would include a considerable number who had been sent for routine audiometry as a result of doubtful screening tests of hearing at school. On re-testing, the majority of the children are found to be normal. The figure of eight per cent does, however, give some indication of the amount of work undertaken by audiology clinics.

5. Laterality

(a) *Introduction*

The school child who is left-handed differs from the majority of his fellows. In the past, attempts were made by parents and teachers to correct left-handed tendencies in what was then thought to be the best interests of the child. The modern attitude is more permissive. The large number of theories on handedness merely reflect the uncertainty about its origins and its implications. Hereafter in this section, the term "handedness" is confined to the mother's opinion on the child, and "laterality" is used to describe the results of the tests.

Results on handedness and tests of laterality will be analysed in the Study for three main purposes:

(i) to determine the pattern of right or left dominance and mixed laterality in this cohort;
(ii) to investigate whether any of these tendencies are associated with educational, emotional or other handicap;
(iii) to establish any relationship with events occurring in pregnancy or the perinatal period.

Preliminary results are presented here on the first of these items.

(b) Handedness—Mothers' Information

The mothers were asked whether their child was right-handed, left-handed or mixed right-handed and left-handed. The results are shown in Table 28.

Table 28

Handedness (Mothers' Information)

Number of boys =4,058; Number of girls =3,927; Total =7,985

	Right-handed	Left-handed	Mixed-handedness	Total	Don't know	No data
Boys						
Number	3,227	455	351	4,033	5	20
Per cent	80·0	11·3	8·7	100		
Girls						
Number	3,337	344	230	3,911	6	10
Per cent	85·3	8·8	5·9	100		
TOTAL						
Number	6,564	799	581	7,944	11	30
Per cent	82·7	10·1	7·3	100		

Sex differences:
Chi-squared (Left-handed: Right-handed and Mixed-handed) =13·6 (1 d.f.); $p < 0·001$
Chi-squared (Mixed-handed: Right and Left-handed) =23·3 (1 d.f.); $p < 0·001$

The evidence from the analysis is that, as reported by mothers, more boys than girls are left-handed and also more boys are mixed-handed.

(c) Tests of Laterality

The pattern of limb-dominance or eye-dominance is not necessarily invariable for any one person but may depend upon the activity or task which is undertaken. Thus, "mixed-handedness" reported by the mother (Table 28) will in most cases refer to the child's ability or preference to use different hands for different purposes.

During the medical examination tests were used to determine the hand, foot and eye which was used by each child in specific tasks. The examiner was asked to record for the two tasks involving the use of the hand and arm whether only the right hand was used; only the left hand; or, both right and left hands. Similarly, a record was made of the preferred foot and eye.

In Table 29 the results of these tests are presented separately for hand, foot and eye. On the basis of their performance in the tests, the children were allocated to one of three groups: "Right" (when only the right hand, foot or eye was used); "Left"; or "Mixed" laterality. The categories to which the children have been allocated should be seen in terms of the type and number of tasks set. For example, had more tests been used, the number of "mixed-laterals" may have been somewhat higher. In testing for sex differences, therefore, "mixed-laterals" were excluded.

The results show that more boys than girls show a preference for using the left hand, left foot or left eye in terms of the tasks specified. The percentage figures relate only to these particular tests and, in any case, should be regarded as provisional at the present stage. Approximately one third of the

Table 29

Laterality Tests

Number of boys = 4,053; Number of girls = 3,917; Total = 7,970

	Right	Left	Mixed Laterality	Total	Don't know	No data
HAND						
Boys						
Number	3,202	353	485	4,040	9	4
Per cent	79·3	8·7	12·0	100		
Girls						
Number	3,143	237	527	3,907	8	2
Per cent	80·0	6·1	13·5	100		
TOTAL						
Number	6,345	590	1,012	7,947	17	6
Per cent	79·8	7·4	12·7	100		
FOOT						
Boys						
Number	2,235	329	1,464	4,028	12	13
Per cent	55·5	8·2	36·3	100		
Girls						
Number	2,330	234	1,333	3,897	13	7
Per cent	59·8	6·0	34·2	100		
TOTAL						
Number	4,565	563	2,797	7,925	25	20
Per cent	57·6	7·1	35·3	100		
EYE						
Boys						
Number	2,303	1,418	314	4,035	13	5
Per cent	57·1	35·1	7·8	100		
Girls						
Number	2,343	1,259	301	3,903	12	2
Per cent	60·0	32·3	7·7	100		
TOTAL						
Number	4,646	2,677	615	7,938	25	6
Per cent	58·5	33·7	7·7	100		

Sex differences:
Hand
Chi-squared Right: Left (excluding "Mixed laterals") = 18.9 (1 d.f.) $p < 0.001$
Foot
Chi-squared Right: Left (excluding "Mixed laterals") = 18.0 (1 d.f.) $p < 0.001$
Eye
Chi-squared Right: Left (excluding "Mixed laterals") = 7.9 (1 d.f.) $0.01 > p > 0.001$

children showed no clear foot preference and 58 per cent were right-footed. One third showed left eye dominance. Although the incidence of left-hand laterality shown by testing was not as high as left-handedness reported by mothers, it remains higher than that shown by many other workers.

6. Dental Examination

(a) Introduction

The medical examination of the 1958 cohort provided the opportunity to assess the state of children's teeth at the stage of transition from infant school to junior school on a national scale, though it was realized that such an inspection carried out by doctors could not achieve the same degree of accuracy as that undertaken by dental officers.

The index of dental caries used—the total number of decayed, missing and filled teeth—provides a basis for comparison with existing figures and allows possible associations with other factors to be sought at a future date.

A record of the number of decayed, missing or filled teeth has the added advantage that it allows some assessment of the amount of dental decay more or less independent of the dental treatment. However, this index does not make separate allowance for naturally shed teeth which, at the age of seven years, is a relevant factor.

For the purpose of comparison, figures for Nottinghamshire in 1963 (H.M.S.O., 1964) are reproduced in Table 30, since they show the sexes separately.

Table 30

Dental Decay (Nottinghamshire, 1963)

$N=1,435$

	Percentage of children showing no D.M.F.* teeth		Average number of D.M.F.* teeth per child examined	
	Boys	Girls	Boys	Girls
5 year age group	28·0	22·8	4·1	4·0
12 year age group	6·8	5·4	4·0	4·1

*Decayed, missing and filled.

(b) Dental Decay

The results of the dental examination of the present sub-sample are shown in Table 31 for those children for whom this information is available.

Table 31

Dental Decay

$N=7,928$

	Percentage of children showing no D.M.F. teeth		Average number of D.M.F. teeth per child examined	
	Boys	Girls	Boys	Girls
7 year age group	12·7	12·3	4·7	4·6

It will be seen that the percentage of children with no decayed, missing or filled teeth in the present sub-sample lies between the figures quoted for five-year-olds and 12-year-olds in Nottinghamshire (Table 30). Inspection of Table 31 suggests no sex difference, and there is further evidence of this when analysis is carried out on the full distribution of D.M.F. teeth in the sample (Table 32). These results are shown in graph form in Figure 5.

The provisional figures shown in Appendix 1, Table A33, show that some three-quarters of the sub-sample were reported to have attended, at some time in the past, a dental clinic, dental surgeon or orthodontist. A more significant point, perhaps, might be that nearly a quarter of the children were reported as not having made use of these facilities in spite of the availability of a school dental service and a free personal dental service. Both these services are already over-worked, and if the needs indicated by the present findings are to be met, clearly a reappraisal of dental establishment is required.

Table 32

Dental Decay

Number of boys = 4,029; Number of girls = 3,899; Total = 7,928

Number of decayed, missing and filled teeth	13+	12+	11+	10+	9+	8+	7+	6+	5+	4+	3+	2+	1+	0+
Cumulative percentages:														
Boys	2·8	4·4	6·4	9·9	14	21	29	38	48	60	69	79	87	100
Girls	1·8	3·3	5·2	8·2	13	20	27	37	47	59	69	80	88	100

Sex differences:
Chi-squared (Trend) = 0·06; $p > 0.05$ not significant
Chi-squared (Departure) = 18·0 (11 d.f.); $p > 0.05$ not significant

Figure 5

Dental Decay

$N = 7,928$

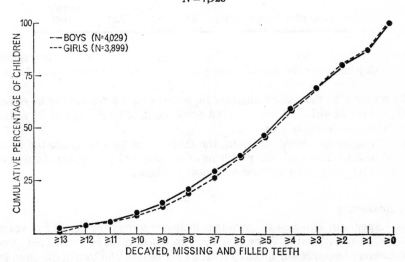

7. Micturition and Bowel Control

(a) Introduction

In obtaining information about micturition and bowel control, as for other developmental milestones, retrospective inquiry from each mother as to the age at which these milestones were reached would have very limited value.

Instead, an age was chosen at which it was known that the great majority of children would have achieved bladder or bowel control and the mothers were asked whether their child had achieved control by this time. Though answers obtained would still not be without a measure of unreliability, the major aim was not to establish norms for these facets of development. It was rather to identify those children who had reached these milestones later than the majority of their peers so that these facets could be related to other aspects of health and development; and also so that a comparison could be made between the sexes in these respects.

(*b*) *Micturition and Bowel Control by Day*

Two questions were put to mothers about micturition and bowel control by day. The results are summarized in Table 33.

Table 33

Micturition and Bowel Control by Day

Number of boys =4,059; Number of girls =3,926; Total =7,985

	Incidence per cent			Sex difference	
	Boys	Girls	Total	Chi-squared (1 d.f.)	P value
Wet by day after 3 years	4·4	4·3	4·4	0·1	>0·05 not sig.
Soiled by day after 4 years	1·8	0·6	1·2	22·1	<0·001

The percentage of boys and girls who were reported to have wet themselves in the daytime over the age of three years is similar; approximately 4·4 per cent.

The response to the second question suggested that 1·8 per cent of boys and 0·6 per cent of girls had not achieved bowel control by the age of four. The sex difference is highly significant.

In replying to the above questions, the mother was told to ignore the occasional mishap. However, the problems of wetting and soiling are clearly not likely to be great, even in nursery schools or classes.

(*c*) *Bedwetting*

The response in Table 34 suggests that bedwetting over the age of five years, even when occasional mishaps have been excluded, must be considered quite a common phenomenon, affecting some 11 per cent of children in this sample. As this question related to events occurring within two years of the Study, it is less likely to evoke unreliable replies than those concerning the earlier milestones.

More boys were reported to be wet at night after five years of age than were girls (12·1 per cent boys and 9·7 per cent girls). The difference between the sexes is highly significant.

Table 34

Bedwetting

Number of boys = 4,059; Number of girls = 3,926; Total = 7,985

	Incidence per cent			Sex difference	
	Boys	Girls	Total	Chi-squared (1 d.f.)	P value
Wet by night after 5 years	12·1	9·7	10·9	11·4	< 0·001

The figure of 11 per cent is high enough to merit further investigation. It may be that the age at which bladder control is normally attained extends over a greater range than is generally accepted.

References

DEPARTMENT OF EDUCATION AND SCIENCE. *The Health of the School Child 1962 and 1963* (H.M.S.O.) (1964).

MINISTRY OF EDUCATION. *The Health of the School Child 1960 and 1961* (H.M.S.O.) (1962).

SHERIDAN, M. D. The Child's Acquisition of Speech, *Brit. Med. J.* i, p. 707 (1945).

SHERIDAN, M. D. Simple Clinical Hearing Tests for Very Young or Mentally Retarded Children, *Brit. Med. J.* ii, pp. 999–1,004 (1958).

SHERIDAN, M. D. *Personal Communication*. Paediatric Research Unit, Guy's Hospital, London (1965).

D. MEDICAL AND DEVELOPMENTAL SEX COMPARISONS

1. *Introduction*

In this section comparisons are made between boys and girls for incidence of some past illnesses, accidents, hospital admissions, attendance at specialist clinics; and for some data from the medical examination of the children at seven years of age.

The totals from which these comparisons are made should not be seen as more than estimates of incidence of illnesses or other factors in the whole cohort for a number of reasons. First, the cohort was not studied between birth and the present time; the historical data are thus retrospective. Secondly, it was gathered from parents and not from hospital or other records, although it is intended to obtain corroborative data from hospitals or clinics.

The possibility exists of differential parental recall on some items favouring one or other sex, but this is not likely to be an important source of bias. In this section the results of sex comparisons are summarized from tables which are contained occasionally in Section VC or in Appendix 1, Table A33. However, the majority of the tables on which sex comparisons are based have been omitted. These are published elsewhere.* Where comment is made on a sex difference in the text this is significant at a level of at least one per cent unless otherwise specified.

*PRINGLE, M. L. K., BUTLER, N. R., and DAVIE, R., *11,000 Seven-Year-Olds* (Longmans, Green & Co. Ltd.), (1966).

Mortality rates are known to be higher in boys than in girls; a greater male perinatal death rate was also found for the present cohort in the Perinatal Mortality Survey. It is therefore reasonable to expect that there should be greater childhood morbidity in males than in females, and these hypotheses can be tested for many illnesses and childhood conditions.

2. Accidents

The results on this sub-sample of children confirm the view that, in general, boys are more accident-prone than girls. Thus, a higher proportion of boys had had one or more hospital admissions for road accidents (Boys 3·0 per cent; Girls 1·7 per cent) and for all other accidents or injuries which had not occurred within the home (Boys 9·7 per cent; Girls 6·9 per cent). More boys, too, were reported as having had in the past a head injury with loss of consciousness (Boys 3·5 per cent; Girls 2·6 per cent). For home accidents, however, there was no significant difference between the sexes (Boys 9·9 per cent; Girls 8·8 per cent).

From these provisional figures it would appear that about three per cent of the boys had been admitted to hospital on one or more occasions for a road accident; as many as about 10 per cent had had an accident in the home severe enough to require hospital admission; and a similar proportion were reported to have been admitted to hospital for other accidents or injuries sustained outside the home. The corresponding figures for girls were still disconcertingly high, emphasizing the need for increased concentration upon accident prevention in childhood.

3. Upper Respiratory Infections

Past upper respiratory infections showed no sex difference, as judged by a history of three or more ear infections during the year preceding the medical examination (Boys 12·8 per cent; Girls 13·9 per cent) or by a history of admission to hospital for tonsils and/or adenoids (Boys 15·3 per cent; Girls 15·7 per cent). On the other hand, current upper respiratory conditions did show a male preponderance in that the medical examinations revealed a higher proportion of boys with nasal obstruction (Boys 10·2 per cent; Girls 7·9 per cent) and some evidence of $(0·05 > p > 0·01)$ more nasal or postnasal discharge (Boys 10·7 per cent; Girls 9·0 per cent) and enlarged glands in the neck (Boys 25·9 per cent; Girls 22·6 per cent); the mothers also reported that boys were more often habitual snorers and mouth breathers (Boys 26·0 per cent; Girls 22·0 per cent).

4. Psychosomatic and Behaviour Problems

A history of travel sickness was reported more frequently in girls than boys (Boys 18·3 per cent; Girls 29·2 per cent). There was also some evidence $(0·05 > p > 0·01)$ of more frequent periodic abdominal pain in girls (Boys 14·0 per cent; Girls 15·7 per cent).

Boys more frequently showed a history of tics or habit spasms (Boys 5·9 per cent; Girls 4·4 per cent); breath holding, head banging or "rocking" (Boys 9·7 per cent; Girls 7·3 per cent); and were more frequently reported to have attended child guidance clinics (Table A33).

No sex difference emerged in the history of frequent headaches or migraine (Boys 8·2 per cent; Girls 7·9 per cent), or in that of periodic vomiting or bilious attacks (Boys 17·0 per cent; Girls 17·5 per cent).

5. Convulsions

There was some evidence ($0.05 > p > 0.01$) that boys had had more fits in the first year of life (Boys 2·2 per cent; Girls 1·6 per cent), but there was not an excess of males with fits after one year (Boys 2·9 per cent; Girls 2·2 per cent) or with petit mal (Boys 0·5 per cent; Girls 0·8 per cent).

6. Allergic States

The objectivity of a history of asthma or eczema given by the mother is difficult to assess without confirmation. More boys were reported to have had asthma (Boys 3·6 per cent; Girls 2·3 per cent) or bronchitis with wheezing (Boys 19·4 per cent; Girls 15·9 per cent). There was no sex difference in history of eczema after one year of age (Boys 5·5 per cent; Girls 5·7 per cent), or of eczema on examination (Boys 2·8 per cent; Girls 2·7 per cent), or of a history of hay fever (Boys 5·9 per cent; Girls 5·2 per cent).

7. Speech

A history of stammer and of other speech difficulty was reported more often in boys; on examination, more boys were assessed as being not fully intelligible during speech testing and there was also some evidence ($0.05 > p > 0.01$) of a higher incidence of observed stammer (see VC, Table 18). Fewer boys were reported to have been "talking" (i.e., joining two words) by the age of two years (Boys 92·4 per cent; Girls 95·2 per cent). It is not therefore surprising that more boys of seven years had already attended for speech therapy (Table A33).

8. Ophthalmological Conditions·

There were no significant sex differences in a history of squint or suspected squint, nor of manifest squint on examination (Section VC, Table 23); further, no sex difference was found in those assessed by the medical officer to have a visual defect (Table 24). However, more girls than boys were found to have latent squint on examination (Table 23).

9. Auditory Conditions

A comparison of the sexes revealed no difference in the results of a clinical hearing test, in an assessment of hearing impairment by the medical examiners or in the proportion of boys and girls who had attended hearing or audiology clinics (Section VC, Tables 25, 26, 27). On examination there was no difference between boys and girls in the frequency with which signs of past or present otitis media were present.

A higher proportion of girls were reported by their mothers as having had earache in the first seven years of life (Boys 29·7 per cent; Girls 33·4 per cent).

10. Dental Status

At seven years of age, as judged by the number of decayed, missing or filled teeth, there was no sex difference (Section VC, Table 32) and no sex differential in past utilization of dental services (Table A33). A minor finding was that a history of recurrent mouth ulcers was more frequent in girls (Boys 7·5 per cent; Girls 11·6 per cent).

11. Congenital Malformations

Sex differences were tested on a few congenital anomalies in this sub-sample. A history of "port-wine stains" of the skin was commoner in girls (Boys

4·4 per cent; Girls 6·4 per cent) and there was some evidence of a similar sex difference ($0·05 > p > 0·01$) in the history of "strawberry naevi" (Boys 4·4 per cent; Girls 5·4 per cent). On examination, "birth marks" were reported more frequently in girls (Boys 11·2 per cent; Girls 13·8 per cent). There was also a preponderance of girls (Boys 0·05 per cent; Girls 0·3 per cent) with a history of congenital dislocation of the hip—although actual numbers were small—and some evidence ($0·05 > p > 0·01$) of a similar difference in the history of talipes (Boys 0·6 per cent; Girls 1·1 per cent). More boys were reported to show deformities of chest (Boys 3·3 per cent; Girls 1·7 per cent) and external ear (Boys 2·3 per cent; Girls 0·7 per cent).

12. *Hernia*
More boys than girls had a reported history of this condition and more had been admitted to hospital for hernia repair (Boys 2·7 per cent; Girls 1·0 per cent). This difference between the sexes was apparent, too, at the medical examinations, where more boys were reported by the medical officers to have inguinal hernia (Boys 0·8 per cent; Girls 0·1 per cent).

E. ENVIRONMENTAL FACTORS

1. *Introduction*
A comprehensive study of children's growth and development must include a study of home background. There is mounting evidence from investigations into the complex processes involved in a child's response to school (for example, Fraser, 1959; Floud, Halsey and Martin, 1957; Douglas, 1964; Wiseman, 1964) to indicate the vital importance of social factors in educational achievement and progress.

In this section some of the data which were collected about the home background of the children in the present sample are presented and discussed. Most of the information was obtained in interviews with mothers, but questions relating to school attendance and parents' interest in the child's education were answered by head teachers.

Only a fraction of the relevant information could be included in this section. A choice had to be made among the original factors selected for study, and it does not necessarily follow that because a topic is included here there are not others which may prove to be of equal, or possibly greater, importance that have been omitted. Within the limits of availability, items were chosen according to two criteria: first, their assumed importance and relevance to children's development; and, secondly, the likelihood of their being of special interest to the Central Advisory Council.

The material presented in this section is essentially of a descriptive nature. Time has not permitted many comparisons with other studies, but not infrequently other data were not available or were not strictly comparable. Within the sample, sex differences have been considered where relevant.

The numbers of children included in the different tables will vary as follows:

    10,833—All children in "ordinary" maintained and independent schools for whom data from the Educational Assessment booklet were available for sorting on punched cards. (See Introduction to Section V A: "Educational Factors".)

     7,985—All children with data from completed Parental Questionnaires available for sorting on punched cards, irrespective of their schooling.

In addition, some of the figures were abstracted from computer tables and totals will vary according to the number of cases where particular information was available. It should be noted that all totals from computer tables in this section include children known to be either in "ordinary" or "special" schools. These children whose type of school was not known, and the very few resident in hospital, are not included.

Much of the information contained in this section was derived from Parental Questionnaires; that is, for a sub-sample of 7,985 children.

The question of the representative nature of this sub-sample has been discussed elsewhere (Section II: "Description of the Sample") and may be summarized as follows: first, there were no very marked differences between the social class distribution of the sub-sample and that of the national sample; such differences, as there were, are difficult to interpret. Secondly, a comparison of the social class distribution of the sub-sample with that of "late returns" showed an overall significant difference, but did not indicate a consistent change in the social class distribution. Thirdly, the reading ability and social adjustment at school of the sub-sample was compared with that of the children for whom a Parental Questionnaire had not been received. Here there was statistically significant evidence that the children in the sub-sample were better readers and better adjusted than the children whose Parental Questionnaires had not been received.

The implications of this statistically significant but not marked bias in the sub-sample are that when information is derived from the Parental Question-naires, any findings relating to adverse conditions are likely to under-estimate the incidence of such circumstances in the total cohort.

2. Socio-Economic Status

Information was available about the occupations of the children's fathers or the male heads of households, both from the Perinatal Survey and from the present Study. This allowed the possibility of a choice between using current or past information for classification into socio-economic groups.

The value of using current information about the father's occupation lay in the nature of the material to be presented in the Report. Where perinatal data were to be linked with current data about the children, the arguments for and against using present or past information seemed fairly evenly balanced. But for much of the Report the educational, medical and social information presented and discussed was concerned directly with the children's development at the age of seven. For this, the use of father's present occu-pation was considered most relevant.

It was finally decided, therefore, to use the father's present occupation in all analyses of this Report which use the socio-economic status of the family as a variable.

Information about the occupation of each child's father, or the male head of household, was obtained from 7,723 of the 7,985 Parental Questionnaires which were completed and returned in time for analysis. Of the remaining 262 questionnaires, information about the father's occupation was incomplete or not available in 60 cases, and in 202 cases the children were living in households without a father or male head.

Each occupation was grouped initially in the five Social Class categories of the General Register Office's "Classification of Occupations 1960". The

Q

proportions in each Social Class for the present sub-sample are shown in Table 38.

Table 38

Social Class Distribution

(Children for whom Parental Questionnaires had been returned by August, 1965)

		Present sample	
Social class categories		N	Per cent
I	Professional, etc., occupations	443	5·7
II	Intermediate occupations	1,131	14·6
III	Skilled occupations	4,387	56·8
IV	Partly skilled occupations	1,322	17·1
V	Unskilled occupations	440	5·7
Total information		7,723	100
No male head of household		202	
No data		60	
GRAND TOTAL		7,985	

A comparison has been made (see Section II B: "Description of the Sample") between the above distribution and that of a 10 per cent sample of married women in England and Wales, classified by their husbands' occupations (H.M.S.O., 1966). The differences between the two distributions are not marked and may be due to the following factors: the present sample is of children and not of households; the data were gathered four years later; the present sample is only part of the 1958 cohort and does not include the data from Welsh children.

In order to check further on the representative nature of this sub-sample of "early returns", a comparison was made between the Social Class distribution of this group and that of the "late returns". These two groups were also compared for reading ability and social adjustment in school (see Section II B: "Description of the Sample").

Some modification of the General Register Office's five Social Class categories was considered advisable for the purpose of socio-economic classification in this Report. Social Class I and II are grouped together, as it was considered that the distinctions between the two categories are minimal in this kind of analysis. On the other hand, in relation to many factors in social analysis including children's development, it has been found that many of the characteristics of workers in clerical and other non-manual occupations are not similar to skilled manual workers, but lie between professional workers and skilled manual workers. As the Registrar General's Social Class III includes both non-manual and the skilled manual occupations, it was decided to separate the skilled manual workers from the non-manual workers in Social Class III. It was not considered meaningful to separate the small proportion of non-manual from manual workers in Social Class IV. The resulting regrouping and nomenclature are shown in Table 68.

Table 39

Occupational Groupings Used in this Study

N.C.D.S. Descriptive category	N.C.D.S. Occupational groups	Corresponding R.G.'s social class groups	No. of Children	Per cent
Professional and technical	Occupational group 1	I and II	1,574	20·4
Other non-manual	Occupational group 2	III Non-manual	830	10·7
Skilled manual	Occupational group 3	III Skilled manual	3,557	46·1
Partly skilled manual	Occupational group 4	IV Partly skilled	1,322	17·1
Unskilled manual	Occupational group 5	V Unskilled	440	5·7
Total			7,723	100
No male head of household			202	
No data			60	
GRAND TOTAL			7,985	

The above five Occupational Groups are the basis of the main socio-economic classifications used in this interim report. Although the father's occupation on its own must be considered a relatively crude index of a family's social, economic and cultural environment, nevertheless, there are meaningful distinctions in this kind of grouping which are highly relevant to children's development. Further information from the questionnaires is available on the social and economic circumstances of the children's families, both at the time of birth and at the age of seven. It is intended at a later stage to combine some or all of this data to provide a basis for a more sophisticated socio-economic classification.

The data from the questionnaires containing information about children with no male head of household are included in all tables in the Descriptive Statistics Section and in other sections of the Report where there is no Occupational Group breakdown. When there is an Occupational Group classification, this data had to be excluded and is shown on tables under the "No data" columns; thus, it does not appear in the percentaged totals.

3. *Family Structure*

(a) *Parental Situation*

Table 40

Parental Situation

	N	Per cent
Living with both natural parents	6,808	93·8
Not living with both natural parents	452	6·2
TOTAL INFORMATION	7,260	100

The second category in the above table covers all known situations where children were not being cared for by their own mothers and fathers. It includes those living with only one parent because of illegitimacy, desertion, divorce, separation or death; those with one step-parent as well as children who were adopted, fostered or in care. The very small number who live more or less permanently in hospitals, or similar institutions, are excluded.

At the time when the information was obtained, six per cent of the present sub-sample was living in a family or group situation which was different in one or more respects from the majority. It is, of course, difficult to assess the influence and weight of abnormal factors in a child's family situation. For example, a child living with his own parents, one of whom may be mentally or physically seriously ill, may well be growing up in an atmosphere of much greater stress than another child who has been successfully adopted or fostered. Nevertheless, a child not living with both his natural parents will, in many cases, have experienced a period of separation which may have been prolonged; in others, for example, one-parent families, the child may be permanently deprived of a normal home life. Thus, at some time or another he will probably have undergone an upsetting, if not seriously traumatic, experience.

There is considerable evidence from research findings (Lewis, 1954; Fraser, 1959; Wynn, 1964; Pringle, 1965; Roe, 1965) to show that in our society the lives of children from incomplete or broken families are adversely affected by a combination of circumstances; these extend not only to emotional but also to social and educational development. Findings relating to the reading ability of this group of children compared with the total sample are discussed in Section VI C of this Report.

(b) Number of Children in the Household

The relationship between family size and measures of ability and attainment has been shown in a number of studies. Douglas (1964), for example, found that children of families of four or more in each of the socio-economic groups he examined were at a disadvantage educationally when compared with their peers in smaller families; the differences were most marked for children of manual workers. Of course, there are large families at all economic levels; however, there are proportionately more among unskilled workers, so that being a member of a large family may sometimes be another factor in an interacting set of unfavourable circumstances which have an adverse effect on a child's development.

Family size can be defined in various ways. The number of children in the "normal" family will usually be the same under any meaningful definition, but for some family situations different definitions will affect the number of children to be included. Thus, different indices may be relevant in considering different aspects of children's development.

Here it was considered that, as an index of the social climate of the child's home life, the total number of children in the household under the age of 21 would be most meaningful. All children under 21 years belonging to one household were included, irrespective of whether or not they were related to the sample child (e.g., foster children, cousins, etc.). Also included were those living at home only during school holidays or for other short periods. The results presented in Table 41 show the distribution of children by the size of household.

Table 41

Number of Children in Household Under the Age of 21 Years
(including sample child)

	N	Per cent
One	665	9·2
Two	2,629	36·2
Three	1,879	25·9
Four	1,068	14·7
Five	498	6·9
Six or more	519	7·1
TOTAL INFORMATION	7,258	100

In this sample of seven-year-olds, nine per cent were only children and seven per cent came from households of six or more. Since the sample was of children and not of households, the figures cannot, of course, be taken as an estimate of the distribution in the general population of numbers of children in households.

It is hoped at a later stage to compare these figures with other classifications of family size which can be obtained from the data.

4. Overcrowding

In accordance with the definition of maximum occupation density used by the 1961 census, the children in the sample were considered to be living in overcrowded homes whenever there were more than $1\frac{1}{2}$ persons to a room. By this criterion, a family of three living in two rooms is not considered overcrowded, whereas a family of four people or more in the same accommodation is judged to be so. This official definition employs quite a severe standard (H.M.S.O., 1965) and one that many people—even in average income sections of the community—would not regard as acceptable.

Data are available from the questionnaires on other main indices of poor housing conditions, such as multiple occupation and lack of basic domestic facilities. However, as this information could not be included at this stage, the present results cover only one aspect of unsatisfactory housing.

Table 42

Proportion of Children Living in Overcrowded Conditions

	N	Per cent
Not overcrowded	6,391	88·8
Overcrowded	805	11·2
TOTAL INFORMATION	7,196	100

It can be seen from Table 42 that 11·2 per cent of this sub-sample were living in overcrowded conditions, as defined above.

It has been suggested that there is an association between various aspects of children's development and housing conditions (Douglas, 1964; Fraser, 1959), with poor housing being adversely related to children's general progress and school performance. This association, however, is an extremely complex one. Other factors must be taken into consideration, even when family difficulties appear at first to be primarily related to unsatisfactory housing.

Conditions of housing vary, of course, in different regions and neighbour-hoods, with respect to factors such as age, size and state of repair, as well as sheer availability. Poor accommodation in a slum area may be differently associated with a child's progress than overcrowded accommodation in a better neighbourhood; similarly, much will depend on whether overcrowding is a temporary or permanent situation. The size and composition of the household, as well as the ages of its members, are further important con-siderations, and the personalities of the parents—particularly the mother—can greatly lessen or increase the strain of bad housing. Studies of problems associated with the establishment of new housing estates have shown the relevance of some of these factors, together with the pitfalls of making generalizations based solely or mainly on housing conditions (Taylor and Chave, 1964).

5. Mobility

(a) Moving Home

Data on this question were obtained from mothers of children who had lived with their parents since birth. The moves reported could be of any distance. Table 43 shows how often the family had moved since the child in our sample was born.

Table 43

Number of Times Family has Moved Since Child's Birth

Number of moves	N	Per cent
None	2,866	36·4
One	2,892	36·7
Two	1,064	13·5
Three	512	6·5
Four	262	3·3
Five	102	1·3
Six	82	1·0
More than six	103	1·3
Total information	7,883	100
No data	102	
TOTAL	7,985	

About a third of the children have not moved at all in comparison with 64 per cent who have moved once or more. Thirteen per cent have moved twice and 13 per cent of the children have done so three or more times. These totals may well be an under-estimate of the amount of moving in the total cohort, since the untraced children who are not, of course, included, are more likely to belong to families who move frequently.

Not a great deal is known about the effects of frequent moves on the growth and development of young children. Available data will make it possible to analyse at a later stage some of the factors that may be related to what seems to be a not uncommon experience for about a quarter of the present sample.

(b) Changing School

The number of schools which the mothers reported the child to have attended since the age of five is shown in Table 44.

Table 44

Number of Schools Attended Since the Age of Five

	N	Per cent
One	6,424	82·1
Two	1,209	15·4
Three	165	2·1
Four	20	0·3
Five and over	7	0·1
Total information	7,825	100
No data	160	
TOTAL	7,985	

By the time the children were at the end of their infant schooling, 15·4 per cent had changed school once and 2·5 per cent two or more times. This presents a somewhat different picture from the previous table and may indicate that more frequent moves of home take place before the child goes to school, or that the moves are in the same locality so that no school change is involved.

Reasons for changes of school vary, as will the effect of the changes on children's educational progress. School factors, as well as those in the child's personality and home background, may play an important part. Further analysis of different factors in this group of children's development and home background will be possible at a future stage in relation to the possible influence of changing school and moving house.

6. *School Attendance*

Information was gathered from the schools about the children's attendance from the beginning of the Autumn Term 1964 to the Summer Term 1965, the latter being the time when the educational questionnaires were completed for the majority of the children. Teachers were also asked to give a rating of children's attendance on the Bristol Social Adjustment Guide but, at present, only the objective data are presented.

In the present sample 70 per cent of the children were recorded as having an attendance rate of 90 per cent or higher. This is equivalent approximately to 18 days' absence, or less, in a school year. About nine per cent of children had an attendance record of below 80 per cent. Children who have been admitted to a particular school only recently and thus attended for a short period are included; the results for these children will obviously be less reliable. It was noted in checking the completed material that this particular question was not well answered due, perhaps, in some measure to the way in which it was asked. Although it was felt that this was unlikely to have affected the overall results seriously, these should be regarded as tentative in view of this proviso.

Table 45

Percentage Attendances

Percentage of possible attendances	N	Per cent
95–100	4,854	45·7
90–94	2,505	23·6
85–89	1,517	14·3
80–84	804	7·6
75–79	428	4·0
70–74	202	1·9
Under 70	319	3·0
Total information	10,629	100
No data	16	
GRAND TOTAL	10,645	

Many circumstances in the children's home background may influence their records of attendance. Health is an important aspect and is, itself, associated with other factors in the home background, such as standards of parental care and parents' interest in their children's education. On the other hand, the influence of the school is also very important. It seems likely that just as poor school attendance may adversely affect children's progress in school, so poor progress and adjustment in school may in some cases lead to poor attendance.

Further, there is some evidence (Douglas and Ross, 1965) that schools differ in the extent to which they succeed in helping children whose educational progress has been adversely affected by absence.

7. *Parental Interest*

There is considerable evidence from research that parents' attitudes to and interest in their children's education are closely associated with school performance (Fraser, 1959; Douglas, 1964; Wiseman, 1964). These attitudes and interest are themselves often associated with a number of other factors of general care which are related to children's development. For example, a mother realistically concerned with her child's education is also more likely to take advantage of other available services for his welfare. However, in this section the discussion is confined to the interest that parents show in their children's educational progress.

Two assessments were made of parental interest. The first was a subjective assessment by the teachers who were asked to rate the mother's and father's interest with regard to their child's educational progress. This had the limitations of any subjective estimate. On the other hand, the teacher could take into account a number of factual indications of parental interest besides personal contact, such as the children's comments and parents' attendances at school meetings.

The second assessment was of a more objective nature. Head teachers were asked if, since September 1964, the parents had taken the initiative to discuss the child, even briefly, with any member of the teaching staff. Despite the advantage of greater objectivity, this question also had its limitation because certain parents, however much they were interested in their child's educational progress, might have been unable to visit the school. The results for the subjective assessment of the teachers are presented in Tables 46 and 47.

Table 46

Teachers' Ratings of Maternal Interest

	Maternal interest					
	Boys	Per cent	Girls	Per cent	Total	Per cent
Over-concerned	179	3·2	132	2·5	311	2·9
Very interested	1,811	32·7	1,989	37·6	3,800	35·1
Shows some interest	2,283	41·2	2,077	39·2	4,360	40·3
Shows little or no interest	901	16·3	743	14·0	1,644	15·2
Can't say or inapplicable	360	6·5	354	6·7	714	6·6
Total information	5,534	100	5,295	100	10,829	100
No data	2		2		4	
TOTAL	5,536		5,297		10,833	

Chi-squared (Trend) $= 15·8$; $p < 0·001$

Table 47

Teachers' Rating of Paternal Interest

	Paternal interest					
	Boys	Per cent	Girls	Per cent	Total	Per cent
Over-concerned	83	1·5	59	1·1	142	1·3
Very interested	1,269	23·0	1,283	24·3	2,552	23·6
Shows some interest	1,259	22·8	1,117	21·1	2,376	22·0
Shows little or no interest	960	17·4	793	15·0	1,753	16·2
Can't say or inapplicable	1,949	35·3	2,036	38·5	3,985	36·9
Total information	5,520	100	5,288	100	10,808	100
No data	16		9		25	
TOTAL	5,536		5,297		10,833	

Chi-squared (Trend) $= 7·2$; $0·01 > p > 0·001$

The difference between the assessments of the mothers' reported interest and the fathers' in the "can't say" category would be expected as so many fathers cannot—even if they wish—visit their children's school during the day because of working hours. Even so, teachers felt able to comment on the interest of 63 per cent of the children's fathers. Approximately 75 per cent of the mothers and 46 per cent of the fathers were rated as showing some interest or being very interested in their child's educational progress.

It is worth noting that the proportion of mothers (15·2 per cent) and of fathers (16·2 per cent) reported as showing little or no interest was almost the same. This seems to indicate that teachers were able to give an equally definite rating for each parent in this category despite fathers' greater difficulty in making daytime visits.

The teachers' ratings show a significantly different tendency for parents to take a greater interest in the girls' educational progress than in the boys'. This is rather unexpected, as it contrasts with parental attitudes towards the education of older children; then the reverse is the case, with boys' scholastic progress being considered of much greater importance and greater numbers of boys staying on at school beyond the compulsory school leaving age

Although such trends as do appear tend to favour the girls, the difference in the parents' interest shows rather a complex pattern with no clear-cut results. It is also possible that this finding is due to some bias in the teachers' ratings. Since girls' school performance is better than boys', the teachers' ratings of parental interest may be influenced by a knowledge of the child's performance; i.e., if a child is doing well at school, the teachers may make an assumption of parents' interest in the child's educational progress.

With regard to the second more objective criterion used to assess parental interest, it can be seen (Table 48) that during the current school year 57 per cent of parents took the initiative to discuss their children with one of the teaching staff.

Table 48

Parental Approach to School Staff

	Boys		Girls		Total	
	N	Per cent	N	Per cent	N	Per cent
Have approaehed school staff	3,183	57·5	2,972	56·1	6,155	56·9
Haven't approached school staff	2,348	42·4	2,321	43·8	4,669	43·1
Total information	5,531	100	5,293	100	10,824	100
No data	5		4		9	
TOTAL	5,536		5,297		10,833	

Chi-squared $=1·2$ (1 d.f.); $p>0·05$ not significant

It would be expected that contact between staff and parents would be easier at the infant school stage, when it is more likely that parents will accompany their children to and from school and the general atmosphere is more informal. Even so, it seems that 43 per cent of the parents of this sample had not initiated any contact with school staff during the period in question.

It can be considered that parental interest in their children's education will to some extent be a reflection of the school's own attitudes and interest in the children's families. A further question was asked to find out more about the amount of personal contact between staff and parents, initiated by the staff. Head teachers were asked if there had been any discussion with the parents about the child "at the instigation of you or your teaching staff". The replies to this question are shown in Table 78.

Table 49

School Instigation of Discussion

	Boys		Girls		Total	
	N	Per cent	*N*	Per cent	*N*	Per cent
School has instigated discussion with parents	1,531	27·7	1,231	23·2	2,762	25·5
School has not instigated discussion with parents	3,996	72·3	4,065	76·8	8,061	74·5
Total information	5,527	100	5,296	100	10,823	100
No data	9		1		10	
TOTAL	5,536		5,297		10,833	

Chi-squared $= 28·3$ (1 d.f.); $p < 0·001$

The staff had instigated discussion with 25·5 per cent of the children's parents. There is a difference of four per cent in the proportion of boys and girls discussed. This difference was highly significant statistically. It may, in part at least, be due to the fact that boys in the sample made less satisfactory progress in reading and were less well-adjusted in school (see Section V6). Hence, teachers would feel greater concern about their progress and thus be more anxious to talk to parents about it.

There will be some parents who, as well as having initiated a discussion themselves, will also have discussed their child at the teacher's instigation. After allowance had been made for the overlap between these two groups, a final total was estimated of the number of children whose parents and teachers were reported as having had some discussion about them. This total amounted to 65 per cent of the children in this sample; thus, from September to near the end of the school year, about two thirds of the seven year olds in the Study had been jointly considered by their teachers and parents. Further analysis of parents' interest in their children's educational progress and its relationship to other factors will be made at a later stage. However, an analysis of reading ability and parental interest is made in Section VIC.

8. *Parental Aspiration*

As an indication of a more general attitude to education, mothers were asked if they would like their child to be able to stay on at secondary school after the minimum school leaving age.

Table 50

Parents Wanting Children to Stay on at Secondary School After Minimum School Leaving Age

	Boys		Girls		Total	
	N	Per cent	N	Per cent	N	Per cent
Yes	3,345	82·4	3,132	79·8	6,477	81·2
No	176	4·3	169	4·3	345	4·3
Other	154	3·8	174	4·4	328	4·1
Don't know	382	9·4	449	11·4	831	10·4
Total information	4,057	100	3,924	100	7,981	100
No data	2		2		4	
GRAND TOTAL					7,985	

Chi-squared = 11·6 (3 d.f.); $0·01 > p > 0·001$

The statistical evidence shows that there is a difference between the answers given by parents of boys and by parents of girls. More parents of the boys than of the girls wanted them to stay on at school after the minimum school leaving age. It will be noted that of the criteria of parental interest so far examined, this is the only indication of more interest being taken in boys' education than in girls'.

This question was answered in the affirmative by 81 per cent of the mothers. Of the remainder, only four per cent gave an unqualified "No".

Of course, at this early age when the actual decision is many years ahead and less realistic, a socially more acceptable answer is likely to be given. Very probably, parental attitudes will undergo changes during the years until this question confronts them as an immediate issue. Nevertheless, the present result would seem to indicate a favourable climate of opinion towards continued secondary education beyond the statutory leaving age.

9. *Summary*

(a) Most of the data in this section were obtained from 7,985 completed Parental Questionnaires. The statistically significant but not marked bias in this sub-sample suggests that findings relating to adverse conditions are likely to under-estimate the incidence of such circumstances in the total cohort.

(b) The present occupations of the children's fathers were grouped according to the Registrar General's five Social Class divisions, and the distribution was compared with those of the "late returns" and of a national sample. The Social Class divisions formed the basis of a regrouping of the fathers' occupation into the five Occupational Groups which are used for the main socio-economic classifications in this Report.

(c) Approximately six per cent of the children were not living with both of their natural parents.

(d) Approximately nine per cent were living in households in which they were the only child, 77 per cent in households of two, three or four children, and 14 per cent in households where there were five or more children.

(e) Approximately 11 per cent of the children were living in "overcrowded" conditions.

(f) About two-thirds of the children had moved home once or more since they were born. Approximately 13 per cent had moved twice and a further 13 per cent three or more times.

(g) Since the age of five, 15·4 per cent of the children had changed school once and 2·5 per cent two or more times.

(h) Of 10,645 children for whom this information was available, 70 per cent were recorded as having an attendance rate of 90 per cent or higher. About nine per cent of the sample had a record of below 80 per cent attendance.

(i) Some 57 per cent of parents had approached a member of the school staff in the current academic year in order to discuss their children. There was no significant difference between the parents of boys and girls in this respect. Teachers' ratings of parental interest on the other hand seemed to show that the girls' parents were more interested in their children's educational progress than the boys'. However, it is possible that the teachers' ratings may have been influenced to an extent by the better progress of the girls. Of the 26 per cent of children whose teachers had instigated discussion with parents, there were significantly more boys than girls.

(j) About 81 per cent of the parents said they would like their children to stay on at school after the minimum school leaving age.

References

DOUGLAS, J. W. B. *The Home and the School* (McGibbon and Kee) (1964).
DOUGLAS, J. W. B. and ROSS, J. M. "The Effects of Absence on Primary School Performance". *Brit. J. Educ. Psychol.* **35**, pp. 28–40 (1965).
FLOUD, J. E., HALSEY, A. H. and MARTIN, F. M. *Social Class and Educational Opportunity* (London: Heinemann) (1957).
FRASER, E. D. *Home Environment and the School* (University of London Press) (1959).
GENERAL REGISTER OFFICE. *Classification of Occupations* (H.M.S.O.) (1960).
GENERAL REGISTER OFFICE. *Census 1961: Occupation Tables, England and Wales* (H.M.S.O.) (1966).
LEWIS, H. *Deprived Children, the Mersham Experiment* (Oxford University Press) (1954).
MINISTRY OF HOUSING AND LOCAL GOVERNMENT. *Report of the Committee on Housing in Greater London* (H.M.S.O.) (1965).
PRINGLE, M. L. KELLMER. *Deprivation and Education* (Longmans) (1965).
ROE, M. C. *Survey into Progress of Maladjusted Pupils* (I.L.E.A.) (1965).
TAYLOR, Lord, and CHAVE, S. *Mental Health and Environment* (Longmans) (1964).
WISEMAN, S. *Education and Environment* (Manchester University Press) (1964).
WYNN, M. *Fatherless Families* (Michael Joseph) (1964).

F. BEHAVIOUR AND ADJUSTMENT

1. *Introduction*

This section is concerned with aspects of the children's behaviour and adjustment in school and home as reported by their teachers and mothers. Here, as in other sections of this interim report, the total number of children included in different tables varies. The reasons for this have already been explained.

The evidence (see Section II B: "Description of the Sample") that the children for whom Parental Questionnaires had been received in time for inclusion in the present Report were better adjusted in school than those for whom a Parental Questionnaire had not been received, is particularly relevant to any interpretation of results in this section. It is reasonable to assume that the former group would also be better adjusted at home. Thus, where results are presented here which are derived from mothers' reports of children's behaviour, the figures may under-estimate to some extent the incidence in the total sample, when the behaviour in question is indicative of difficulties.

However, there is no expectation that any such bias will affect comparisons between the sexes.

There is one other general factor which should be stressed. Although all figures presented in this Report should be seen in relation to the circumstances in which the information was collected and the way in which questions were put, it is particularly important to have this in mind when assessing the validity of data about behaviour and adjustment. An attempt has been made to reduce reporting error or bias by gathering, wherever possible, current rather than retrospective data. Nevertheless, in many questions what is being assessed is essentially a facet of a relationship between two people (a mother and a child, a teacher and a child) rather than simply an objective fact about a child. In the case of the mothers' reports of the children's behaviour, these were given to a third person, usually a health visitor.

This factor does not invalidate the results, but it does mean, particularly when statistics are seen as incidences, that the total framework must be borne in mind. Thus, for the sake of convenience and brevity, a sub-section is here entitled "Children's Happiness at School"; in essence, however, the figures tell what the mothers *reported* about their children's happiness at school when posed a particular question on one occasion by a health visitor. It is possible that if the enquiry had been carried out by post, if the mothers had had time to consult their husbands, or if the question had been put by or to teachers, by psychologists or by a trained team of interviewers, then the results obtained may have been somewhat different. On the other hand, it would be foolish to disregard the results on this account unless there was evidence that a question on this topic, and posed under these circumstances, produced a very distorted picture. No method of enquiry is faultless, but each has limitations. Where there is possibility of distortion or bias, the implications are considered.

Information was obtained about the children's behaviour and adjustment in order, first, to test certain hypotheses about general adjustment, as well as particular facets of it, in relation to other factors; to examine, if comparable information can be collected on these children as they mature, the ways in which patterns of behaviour shown at seven years of age change or remain constant at later ages; to provide some data on the behaviour of a representative group of seven-year-olds; and to compare the sexes at this age. Although the last point is here mentioned separately, it should, strictly, be included with the first since a relationship is examined between two variables, namely behaviour and the sex of the children.

In the present section only the last two points are covered: descriptive data are given and the sexes are compared. Sub-section 2 deals with the children's behaviour and adjustment as assessed by their teachers; and in sub-section 3 results are presented for different aspects of behaviour as reported by mothers.

2. Behaviour and Adjustment—Teachers' Assessments

(a) Settling Down Period on Starting School

The head teachers were asked whether on starting school the children settled down within a month; within 1–3 months: or remained unsettled after three months. Since the children's present schools will not always have been their first ones, the results do not relate to the settling down period on first starting school; nevertheless, over 82 per cent of the children had been to one school only (see Section V F: "Environmental Factors").

There will be some loss of reliability due to the fact that the data are retrospective by some two years in the majority of cases. There is also the possibility of some distortion of the results for individual children. Thus, if a child is now quite "normal" and well-adjusted, there is perhaps less likelihood of an unsettled period two years ago being remembered.

The results are presented in Table 80 and relate to children in "ordinary" maintained and independent schools. The large number of children listed as "Can't say" is most likely to be a reflection of the difficulty of obtaining retrospective information from schools because of staff changes. It will be seen that the figures for these children have not been percentaged, since there is no reason to believe that if the information had been available, they would not have been distributed proportionately in the other categories. Where a child had been at a school less than three months, the full range of possible answers was not open to the head teachers. These children were therefore coded as "Inapplicable".

It will be seen that, as judged by this criterion, the great majority of the children (94 per cent) had settled down on starting at a first or a new school within three months.

The difference between the sexes was highly significant statistically. The trend, furthermore, persisted through the three categories. The girls were reported to have settled down in school more quickly than the boys.

Table 51
Settling Down Period on Starting School

	Boys		Girls		Total	
Settling down period	N	Per cent	N	Per cent	N	Per cent
Within 1 month	3,783	74·3	3,883	78·6	7,666	76·4
1–3 months	949	18·6	817	16·5	1,766	17·6
Unsettled after 3 months	358	7·0	241	4·9	599	6·0
Total assessed	5,090	100	4,941	100	10,031	100
Can't say	348		287		635	
Inapplicable	86		64		150	
No data	12		5		17	
GRAND TOTAL	5,536		5,297		10,833	

Chi-squared (Trend)=31·6; $p < 0·01$
Chi-squared (Departure)=0·3 (1 d.f.); $p > 0·05$ not significant

The possibility of some distortion of the results for individual children has already been discussed. It was suggested that a child's present behaviour may influence a teacher's memory of a facet of his behaviour two years before. It may be that such retrospective distortion is partly or wholly responsible for the present findings. Thus, there is evidence that the boys in the sample were less well-adjusted in school (see sub-section 2(b) of the present section). The difference between the sexes demonstrated above may, then, reflect their present behaviour.

However, the fact that the same difference between the sexes is evident when the mothers' reports of the children's settling-down period on first starting school are examined (see sub-section 3(b)) makes it less likely that the present findings are spurious. Nevertheless, the possibility cannot be ruled out that the same factors were operating in the mothers' retrospective reporting.

Under the circumstances, the evidence of a sex difference here must be regarded as tentative at the present stage. Further research is needed to confirm the results.

(b) Bristol Social-Adjustment Guide Scores

The difficulties of obtaining a reliable and valid measure of adjustment are very considerable; much less progress has been made by psychologists in this field than, for example, in measuring intellectual abilities and attainments. Furthermore, in a study of this magnitude of seven-year-olds, one is confined to an assessment of the children's adjustment by some other person. As has been mentioned earlier, one is essentially obtaining a measure of a relationship between two persons; in this case a child and his teacher. This is not irrelevant since social adjustment cannot be viewed in isolation, but in individual cases there will be differences between a child's adjustment as seen by different teachers.

Such differences, however, are less likely to be marked if, instead of obtaining global assessments, one asks specific questions about particular aspects of behaviour. The Bristol Social-Adjustment Guide (Stott, 1963) in effect does this. The Guide consists of a large number of descriptions of behaviour and the teacher is asked to underline those descriptions which best fit the child. Aspects of behaviour which appear to be deviant are specially coded and it is therefore possible, by summing these items for an individual child, to obtain a quantitative assessment of social adjustment in school; the higher the score, the more manifestations of deviant behaviour have been noted by the teacher. It is obvious that a child's behaviour can be deviant in many ways. Thus, he may be unforthcoming, aggressive or over-demanding. A total score masks all these different facets and therefore its use is only warranted as a relatively crude assessment which may be useful in certain kinds of analyses or as a first step before a more detailed and sophisticated analysis.

At the present stage in this Study, there has been time only to examine total scores. For convenience, and as a first step, it has been decided to classify the children as proposed by Stott: children with a score from 0 to 9 are grouped and called "stable"; those with a score from 10 to 19 are called "unsettled"; and the children with a score of 20 or more are called "maladjusted". The groups are therefore operationally defined in these terms. Thus, no assumption is made that children with a score of 20 or more are maladjusted in any sense other than that defined above.

The results are presented in Tables 52 and 53. A word of explanation is needed about these figures. In both tables, the numbers involved are several hundred less than the number of Guide scores available. This reduction is due to technical difficulties arising from the data processing; there is no reason to believe that the children excluded are different from the ones included in any specific way.

In Table 52 the figures for children in all categories of school have been extracted from a more detailed table not presented in this Report, in which there was a breakdown by Occupational Group and Sex. Where there were no data on either the sex of the child (very few) or the occupation of the father, the children were excluded. This sub-sample is known to be biased in that they are better adjusted in school than those where the Occupational Group was not known (see Introduction to present section). Although this bias is not expected to affect a comparison of the sexes, the combined figures would be biased. However, the figures given in Table 53 include all the children in schools (including special schools) in the present sample for whom a score was available, and there is no evidence of bias in this group.

Table 52

Bristol Social-Adjustment Guide Scores—Boys and Girls

Scores	Boys		Girls	
	N	Per cent	N	Per cent
'Stable' (Score 0–9)	1,929	59·5	2,376	73·7
'Unsettled' (Score 10–19)	808	24·9	587	18·2
'Maladjusted' (Score 20+)	507	15·6	260	8·1
TOTAL ASSESSED	3,244	100	3,223	100

Chi-squared (Trend) = 158·7; $p < 0·001$
Chi-squared (Departure) = 2·2 (1 d.f.); $p > 0·05$ not significant

Table 53

Bristol Social-Adjustment Guide Scores—Combined Sexes

Scores	N	Per cent
'Stable' (Score 0–9)	6,280	64·0
'Unsettled' (Score 10–19)	2,223	22·6
'Maladjusted' (Score 20+)	1,314	13·4
TOTAL ASSESSED	9,817	100

The comparison between the sexes in Table 52 shows a highly significant difference; the girls were better adjusted in school. Approximately 60 per cent of the boys were "stable" as against 74 per cent of the girls; on the other hand, nearly 16 per cent of the boys were "maladjusted" compared with eight per cent of the girls. The results, strictly interpreted, apply only to this form of assessment. Nevertheless, in view of the very marked differences shown, the firm conclusion is warranted that at this age boys show more indications of poor adjustment in school than girls.

These results confirm those found by Crawford (1966), who used the Guides in a Liverpool study on 773 boys and girls aged seven and eight years.

Two points should be borne in mind. First, the results derived from total scores may mask other factors. Thus, despite an overall difference between the sexes, it may be that detailed examination of the data will show no differences between the sexes in particular facets of adjustment; or, even, that girls show more deviant behaviour in some ways. For example, boys may be more aggressive or over-demanding and girls may be more timid or withdrawn. This further detailed study of the data will be undertaken later.

Secondly, since this sub-sample is known to be biased in relation to adjustment in school, the percentages shown in Table 52 should not be taken as representative figures for the sexes.

In Table 53 the results are presented for a larger sample of children, since no other results are available for this test on a national sample of this size. There is no expectation of bias in these results.

It was stressed earlier that the definitions of "stable", "unsettled" and "maladjusted" are operational ones and refer only to scores on the Guides. The grouping used by Stott and others has been adopted as a first step and to permit comparison with other studies. To say, therefore, that the present findings indicate that over 13 per cent of seven-year-olds are maladjusted is to say no more than that over 13 per cent of seven-year-olds are likely to obtain a total score of 20 or more on the Social-Adjustment Guides.

It would be taking too extreme a view to say that the term "maladjusted" means all things to all men. Nevertheless, the difficulties of establishing some reliable criterion of maladjustment against which to validate an objective score such as is derived from the Guide are considerable.

From a practical viewpoint there is an obvious need to establish the proportion of school children who would benefit from some form of psychological help or from psychiatric treatment. The need for such information was underlined by the Underwood Committee (H.M.S.O., 1955) and the Scottish Education Department (H.M.S.O., 1964). It is hoped at a later stage to throw some light on this matter with the data available on this cohort of children; and also to examine in some detail the factors which are associated with maladjustment.

3. Behaviour and Adjustment—Mothers' Reports

(a) Happiness at School

The mothers were asked: "Is the child happy at his/her present school?" The answers were pre-coded by the interviewers into the categories shown in Table 54. The results are for children in all types of school.

Table 54

Happiness at School

	Boys		Girls		Total	
	N	Per cent	N	Per cent	N	Per cent
Happy	3,708	92·1	3,694	94·5	7,402	93·2
Not altogether happy	302	7·5	205	5·2	507	6·4
Unhappy	18	0·4	12	0·3	30	0·4
Total information	4,028	100	3,911	100	7,939	100
Don't know	30		15		45	
No data	—		1		1	
GRAND TOTAL	4,058		3,927		7,985	

Chi-squared (Trend) = 17·3; $p < 0.001$
Chi-squared (Departure) = 0.8; (1 d.f.); $p > 0.05$ not significant

The difference between the sexes is highly significant. A strict interpretation of the results would be that girls at this age are reported by their mothers to be happier at school than boys. However, there is some indirect evidence from the present Study to indicate that this may be interpreted as a meaningful difference between the sexes in the extent to which they are in fact happy at school. Thus, the independent assessments of the teachers showed that girls are markedly better adjusted at school, and it is reasonable to assume that this would be reflected in their "happiness".

Nevertheless, the subjectivity of this question imposes a need for caution, particularly in viewing the percentage figures in the three categories. One must consider the possibility that the mothers may have seen their answers as a reflection upon the school, although there is no reason to believe that any such tendency would have acted in one direction only. Further, it had to be left to the interviewer to make a reasoned judgement about which category to code in the light of the mother's answer.

However, within the limitations of this type of question, the overall results are extremely encouraging from an educational standpoint and do credit to the teachers and schools concerned.

(b) Settling Down Period on First Starting School

Information about the length of the settling down period on first starting school was obtained from the mothers. The same question was also put to the head teachers (see sub-section 2(a) of the present section), although their replies would relate to the children's settling down in their present school, which would not necessarily have been their first one.

Some of the children attended a private or a local authority nursery class or school, and the results for these are presented in Table 55; and relate to the settling down period on commencing nursery schooling. In Table 56 the results are given for children who did not attend a nursery class or school. Although these results were obtained by sorting punched cards, it was possible to include a few (52) additional children so that the total for Tables 55 and 56 are slightly higher than for tables in the remainder of this section. The children involved were in all categories of school.

Table 55

Settling Down Period on First Starting School
(*Nursery Class/Nursery School Attenders*)

	Boys		Girls		Total	
	N	Per cent	N	Per cent	N	Per cent
Within a month	506	83·0	502	88·7	1,008	85·7
Within 1–3 months	56	9·2	39	6·9	95	8·1
Still unsettled after 3 months	48	7·9	25	4·4	73	6·2
Total information	610	100	566	100	1,176	100
Don't know	2		5		7	
GRAND TOTAL	612		571		1,183	

Chi-squared (Trend) = 8·6; $0·01 > p > 0·001$
Chi-squared (Departure) = 0·03 (1 d.f.); $p > 0·05$ not significant

Table 56

Settling Down Period on First Starting School
(*Non-Nursery Class/Nursery School Attenders*)

	Boys		Girls		Total	
	N	Per cent	N	Per cent	N	Per cent
Within a month	2,804	82·1	2,814	84·4	5,618	83·2
Within 1–3 months	322	9·4	293	8·8	615	9·1
Still unsettled after 3 months	289	8·5	228	6·8	517	7·7
Total information	3,415	100	3,357	100	6,802	100
Don't know	29		21		50	
No data	1		1		2	
GRAND TOTAL	3,475		3,379		6,854	

Chi-squared (Trend) = 7·6; $0·01 > p > 0·001$
Chi-squared (Departure) = 0·1 (1 d.f.); $p > 0·05$ not significant

It has not been possible at the present time to examine statistically any differences between the settling down period for those who attended a nursery class or school and those who did not. Inspection of the tables suggests no very marked overall differences, but a straightforward comparison of these tables is likely to be misleading; a more sophisticated analysis is needed which takes into account other factors which may be associated with nursery school attendance.

In both tables, however, the results indicate that girls are considered by their mothers to settle down more quickly than boys on first starting school. Although confirming the results obtained in a comparison of the sexes on the teachers' assessments (see sub-section 2(*a*) of this section), the same reservations expressed there apply to the above results.

The overall figures are not strictly comparable with the teachers' assessments given in Table 51, both because of the bias in the present sub-sample and also because the teachers were not necessarily assessing the children's settling down period on first starting school. Furthermore, any differences between Tables 51 and 56 may be due to the fact that mothers and teachers see the situation from different standpoints.

(c) Developmental Difficulties
It was decided to seek information from mothers about developmental difficulties which occurred largely in the home. Three steps were taken to increase the reliability of the data. First, mothers were asked to say whether any of the difficulties had occurred over a prescribed period; namely, "during the last three months". Secondly, specific aspects of behaviour were selected so that it was reasonable to ask for a straightforward "Yes" or "No", although a "Don't know" reply was included in the coding. Thirdly, if the behaviour had occurred only during a period of acute infection, the interviewers were asked to code the answer as "Inapplicable".

The results are presented in Table 57 and relate to all children in the present sample for whom information was available, whether they were in school or not. Percentage figures only are given here and they refer to children whose mothers reported that the behaviour in question occurred during the three months prior to the interview. The small numbers of children where "Don't know" or "Inapplicable" was coded have been excluded from the percentaging. Although the results are presented in one table, the categories are, of course, not mutually exclusive and a child may appear under more than one category.

Table 57
(Percentaged)
Developmental Difficulties Occurring Over a Three-Month Period
Number of boys =4,058; Number of girls =3,927; Total =7,985

Developmental difficulties	Boys Per cent	Girls Per cent	Total Per cent	Chi-squared (2 d.f.)	P value
Has complained of headaches (more than once)	20·3	20·9	20·6	0·4	>0·05*
Has had temper tantrum	29·8	27·1	28·5	7·1	0·01 >p >0·001
Has been reluctant to go to school	12·2	9·6	11·0	13·9	< 0·001
Has had bad dreams or night terrors	17·2	16·1	16·6	1·6	>0·05*
Has had difficulty in getting off to sleep	18·1	20·2	19·1	5·8	0·05 >p >0·01*
Has sleepwalked	3·1	3·4	3·2	0·8	>0·05*
Has been faddy—many dislikes over food	27·8	30·4	29·1	6·2	0·05 >p >0·01*
Has had poor appetite	15·4	17·7	16·5	7·5	0·01 >p >0·001
Has over-eaten for more than the occasional meal	7·1	6·0	6·5	3·7	>0·05*

In examining the table, one must take account of two main factors. First, the bias in this sub-sample, discussed in the introduction to this section, may mean that some of the figures quoted under-estimate the incidence in the total population of seven year olds in the country. Nevertheless, it would be unwise to over-stress the effect or the importance of this bias in considering the value of the results. Its effect is unlikely to be marked and it should be

* Not significant.

viewed within the framework of the limitations inevitably imposed upon data of this kind collected in a large survey. One is dependent upon the mothers' reports, which may be influenced by such factors as their own personalities, education, tolerance level and the attitude of the interviewer; further, the behaviour was reported to have occurred over a particular period of time which, if changed, may have produced somewhat different figures.

Thus, the results in relation to many other kinds of data are of a crude nature. The fact that figures are given to one decimal place must not be taken as implying that exact information is being obtained. On the other hand, no clinician, no teacher, no social worker would claim that information he obtained is without its own limitations. The value of data gathered on a large group of children is that it provides workers in this field with a frame of reference, a "backcloth" against which to view the normality or deviance of behaviour manifested by an individual child, or a group of children, of this age. It will also permit the changing pattern of behaviour to be studied as the children grow towards maturity, if—as is hoped—further information can be gathered upon them. Neither the limitations discussed, nor the bias, are likely to affect the overall pattern of the results, the relative incidence of different difficulties. Thus, it will be seen that the reported occurrence of a temper tantrum or of faddiness is not uncommon; about 30 per cent of the children were reported to have shown these aspects of behaviour. Sleepwalking, on the other hand, is reported as occurring only in a small minority of children of this age.

The second main factor which must be borne in mind is that the figures apply to behaviour in the home as seen by mothers. For some aspects of behaviour, such as difficulties in sleeping, this is the only appropriate framework within which to view the data. However, other behaviour, such as food-faddiness or temper tantrums, manifests itself in other situations—in school, for example. It is highly likely that if information on these aspects of behaviour had been obtained from teachers, different results would have been obtained because children behave differently in different circumstances.

None of these aspects of behaviour in isolation should be seen as an indication of poor adjustment. Nevertheless, it is likely that some are more symptomatic of emotional disturbance than others. In addition, a number of workers have shown that a simple summation of reported behavioural difficulties for individual children provides some measure of adjustment which is associated with poor educational performance and other factors. It is intended to investigate this further at a later stage and to see which difficulties and which combination of difficulties are most closely related to other factors, both in the home and in the school.

With regard to a comparison between the sexes in the reported occurrence of the "developmental difficulties" set out in Table 57, it will be seen that for only three items was there a significant difference. The "P" values are given, and for reasons which are explained in Section IV: "Statistical Analysis", the level of 0·01 has been selected as the one which in this Report is used as the criterion of statistical significance.

There is clear evidence from the present findings that, as reported by mothers, more boys than girls show reluctance to go to school; that more boys have temper tantrums at this age; and that more girls are considered to have poor appetites.

(d) Other Aspects of Children's Behaviour

In addition to the behaviour reported by mothers which has been discussed in the previous sub-section, the mothers were asked about other aspects of behaviour. Although in the Parental Questionnaire and in this Report the two groups of items are presented separately, there is no clear-cut distinction between them from a psychological viewpoint. The developmental difficulties already discussed were so described because this seemed an appropriate term. Nevertheless, some of the aspects of behaviour discussed in this section might equally well have been described as difficulties.

One major reason for separating these two groups of items in the questionnaire was that for some aspects of behaviour it seemed appropriate to ask for a straightforward answer as to whether or not the behaviour had occurred during a prescribed period; for the behaviour discussed here it seemed more appropriate to enquire whether "at the present time" it happened "frequently", "sometimes" or "never".

The results are presented in Table 58 and relate to all children in the sample for whom the information was available, whether they were in school or not. The figures are given in percentage form and where an answer was coded "Don't know" or "Inapplicable", it has been excluded from the percentaging and also from the table.

Table 58
(Percentaged)
Other Aspects of Children's Behaviour

Number of boys = 4,058; Number of girls = 3,927; Total = 7,985

Behavioural descriptions		Boys Per cent	Girls Per cent	Total Per cent	Chi-squared (Trend) (1 d.f.)	P value
Has difficulty in settling to anything for more than a few moments	Frequently	8·4	6·0	7·2		
	Sometimes	26·1	21·9	24·0	41·2	< 0·001
	Never	65·5	72·0	68·7		
Prefers to do things on his/her own rather than with others	Frequently	22·9	21·9	22·4		
	Sometimes	45·9	44·7	45·3	3·8	> 0·05 (not sig.)
	Never	31·1	33·3	32·2		
Is bullied by other children	Frequently	5·3	4·4	4·9		
	Sometimes	32·5	27·8	30·2	24·1	< 0·001
	Never	62·2	67·8	65·0		
Destroys own or others belongings (e.g. tears or breaks)	Frequently	4·3	1·6	3·0		
	Sometimes	16·2	8·4	12·4	168·1	< 0·001
	Never	79·5	90·0	84·7		

Table 58 (Continued)

Behavioural descriptions		Boys Per cent	Girls Per cent	Total Per cent	Chi-squared (Trend) (1 d.f.)	P value
Is miserable or tearful	Frequently	4·4	4·8	4·6		
	Sometimes	36·8	42·1	39·4	21·6	< 0·001
	Never	58·8	53·1	56·0		
Is squirmy or fidgety	Frequently	12·9	10·3	11·6		
	Sometimes	33·3	31·4	32·4	20·3	< 0·001
	Never	53·8	58·3	56·0		
Worries about many things	Frequently	11·5	12·3	11·9		
	Sometimes	36·0	37·1	36·6	3·0	>0·05 (not sig.)
	Never	52·5	50·6	51·6		
Is irritable, quick to fly off the handle	Frequently	11·9	10·9	11·4		
	Sometimes	38·0	36·0	37·0	6·9	$0·01 > p > 0·001$
	Never	50·1	53·1	51·6		
Sucks thumb or finger during day	Frequently	4·8	7·9	6·4		
	Sometimes	5·4	8·3	6·8	58·5	< 0·001
	Never	89·8	83·7	86·8		
Is upset by new situation, by things happening for first time	Frequently	5·8	5·2	5·5		
	Sometimes	22·4	24·9	23·6	1·2	>0·05 (not sig.)
	Never	71·8	69·9	70·9		
Has twitches or mannerisms of the face, eyes or body	Frequently	2·6	1·5	2·0		
	Sometimes	6·5	4·8	5·6	21·7	< 0·001
	Never	91·0	93·7	92·3		
Fights with other children	Frequently	7·7	2·9	5·3		
	Sometimes	61·4	41·0	51·4	526·2	< 0·001
	Never	30·8	56·1	43·3		
Bites nails	Frequently	10·5	12·6	11·5		
	Sometimes	12·0	16·1	14·0	29·7	< 0·001
	Never	77·5	71·3	74·5		
Is disobedient at home	Frequently	4·6	3·4	4·0		
	Sometimes	60·0	52·7	56·4	60·9	< 0·001
	Never	35·4	43·9	39·6		

Of course, the same factors as were discussed in the previous sub-section should be considered in taking account of the above results.

A number of aspects of behaviour appear to be common at this age: disobedience and fighting with other children were reported to occur frequently or sometimes in about 60 per cent of the children. In contrast, twitches or mannerisms were reported in less than eight per cent. The reported incidence of nail-biting (26 per cent) was about half that obtained by Birch (1955) in a local study utilizing teachers' reports and more objective criteria. Preferring to do things alone rather than with others stands out as an aspect of behaviour which was reported to occur frequently in a substantial minority of the children (over 22 per cent).

In all but three items, the difference between the sexes was statistically significant or highly significant when tested for trend. The two most marked differences were both in aggressive behaviour; twice as many boys as girls were reported as destroying their own or others' belongings; and about 70 per cent of the boys fought with other children, whilst only 44 per cent of the girls did so. In general, it was the boys who more often showed deviant behaviour, but more of the girls were nail-biters and sucked their thumb or finger during the day.

As with the behaviour difficulties described in the previous sub-section, it is intended to examine the aspects of behaviour discussed here in more detail at a later stage.

4. *Summary*

(a) On starting at their present school, 94 per cent of the children in "ordinary" maintained and independent schools in the sample were judged by their teachers to have settled down in school within three months.

There was evidence that girls settled down more quickly than boys in infant classes, but in view of the fact that the data were retrospective and may have been influenced by present behaviour, this conclusion was regarded as tentative.

(b) The evidence was very clear that girls at this age in all categories of school are markedly better adjusted than boys when a relatively crude overall assessment is made in terms of the total score of the Bristol Social-Adjustment Guide.

It was noted that this overall assessment may mask other differences between boys and girls when more specific aspects of behaviour are examined. This more detailed analysis will be done at a later stage.

(c) Approximately 93 per cent of a sub-sample of 7,985 children in all categories of school were reported by their mothers to be happy in school. There was also a highly significant tendency for more girls to be reported as happy at school than boys.

(d) Of the children who had attended a private or local authority nursery class or nursery school, some 94 per cent were reported by their mothers to have settled down within three months of first starting nursery schooling.

Of the children who had not attended a nursery class or nursery school, about 91 per cent were reported by their mothers to have settled down within three months of first starting school.

No statistical analysis was made to test any difference between these two groups of children in relation to the settling down period because a straightforward comparison might have been misleading. No conclusions were therefore drawn.

The evidence from a comparison of the sexes in both groups, however, suggested that girls settled down more quickly than boys.

(e) Percentage figures were given for the reported incidence of nine "developmental difficulties" for boys and for girls. In only three was there a significant difference between the sexes: there was evidence that more boys than girls are reluctant to go to school; more boys than girls have temper tantrums; and more girls are felt to have poor appetites.

(f) Information was gathered from mothers about 14 other aspects of children's behaviour.

In all but three items there was a significant difference between the sexes in reported incidence. In general, boys at this age are more often reported to show deviant behaviour at home.

References

BIRCH, L. B. The Incidence of Nail-Biting Amongst School Children. *Brit. J. Educ. Psychol.*, Vol. XXV (1955).

CRAWFORD, A. Department of Psychology, Liverpool University (unpublished communication) (1966).

MINISTRY OF EDUCATION. *Report of the Committee on Maladjusted Children* (H.M.S.O.) (1955).

SCOTTISH EDUCATION DEPARTMENT. *Ascertainment of Maladjusted Children* (H.M.S.O.) (1964).

STOTT, D. H. *The Social Adjustment of Children;* Manual to the Bristol Social-Adjustment Guides (University of London Press Ltd.) (1963).

VI—INTER-RELATIONSHIP OF THE VARIABLES

A. EDUCATIONAL FACTORS

1. Reading and Arithmetic in Relation to Occupational Group

(a) Introduction

There is overwhelming evidence for a relationship between general socio-economic factors and general educational progress. What are therefore now needed are more investigations of particular aspects of the environment in relation to particular facets of educational progress and, indeed, to child development in general.

At the present stage in this Study there has not been time to examine many aspects of the environment in relation to educational factors; and such statistical analyses as have been carried out have been relatively straightforward. More elaborate analyses will be carried out later.

In this section two facets of educational performance—in reading and in arithmetic—are analysed in relation to the Occupational Group of the children's fathers or the male head of the household.

(b) Occupational Group and Attainment in Reading

The ability to read is of central importance to children's progress in school. Once mastered, it is a skill which opens many doors. Whilst most schools now lay more stress upon activities, upon learning through experience and upon oral work in the classroom than was once the case, it remains true that a child who finds reading difficult is gravely handicapped in almost all spheres of his school work.

Other investigations have shown a relationship between the socio-economic level of a child's family and his reading ability, although few studies have been made of this relationship for children in infant schools. It is not difficult to think of reasons for this strong relationship. In general, parents in higher socio-economic groups are more intelligent than those in the other socio-economic groups; thus, their children will tend to be more intelligent and, as a result, better readers. Although no general consensus of opinion exists about the precise contribution which heredity makes towards intellectual functioning, there can be no reasonable doubt that it does play a part (Burt, 1960).

In addition to heredity, and interacting with it, is the influence of the environment in which a child grows. A home in which books and reading material of all kinds are an integral and valued part of daily life is one which is most likely to lay the foundation for the rapid acquisition of reading skill by a child. Reading for him is seen as something which gives his parents enjoyment and which has a purpose. He comes to school, then, wanting to read and may already have made a start.

Motivation is a potent factor, but the influence of the home environment does not rest there. The written word is a symbol which enables the author to convey his thoughts, his ideas and concepts to the reader. If the reader finds difficulty in understanding these thoughts, then any ability to articulate the words will be of little value. True reading ability, then, is more than merely a skill in decoding written symbols; it is an ability to use this skill in understanding what the author is trying to convey. It follows that a home which fosters this true reading ability best is one in which the level of verbal expression is at its highest; where there is a feeling for the spoken word as a tool for conveying precise meaning; where the vocabulary is rich and varied; and where children are stimulated by questions about the world around them and by explanations appropriate to their age.

The factors which have been discussed are complex and extremely difficult to quantify, particularly in large scale investigations such as the present one. Nevertheless, it is reasonable to assume that in general the socio-economic level of the home, much easier to categorize, will be related to these factors. A great deal of information is known about the occupation and education of the parents and the grandparents of the children in the present Study. It is hoped to use this information to arrive at some measure of the social-educational-economic background of the children in order to investigate at a later stage the relationships between this and other factors in the children's development.

Further, it is hoped within the limitations set by the relative crudity of some of the data—virtually inescapable in any large survey—to examine the relationship between particular aspects in the environment and particular facets of children's development. This, however, needs a far more elaborate statistical analysis than there has yet been time to carry out.

As a first step, the relationship is here examined between the Occupational Groups of the children's fathers—as an index of the socio-economic level of the family—and one aspect of children's development, namely reading ability. In sub-section (c) of this section the same analysis is made of arithmetical ability.

The results are given in Table 59 for all the children in the present sample in "ordinary" maintained and independent schools for whom all the requisite information was available. As the index of reading ability, the children's scores on the Southgate Reading Test are used because of their objectivity. Children with a score of 28 or more out of a possible 30 are grouped and operationally defined as "good readers"; those with a score less than 28 are grouped and called "medium and poor readers". Percentage figures only are given in the table below.

Table 59

Southgate Test Score and Occupational Group of the Father

$N=6,834$

	Occupational Group					
Reading groups	1	2	3	4	5	Total
'Good readers' (Score 28–30)	56·2	54·9	36·3	31·2	23·3	40·7
'Poor and medium readers' (Score < 28)	43·8	45·1	63·7	68·8	76·7	59·2
TOTAL	100	100	100	100	100	100

Chi-squared (Trend) $=289$; $p < 0.001$
Chi-squared (Departure) $=25.7$ (3 d.f.); $p < 0.001$

The difference between the two reading groups in relation to Occupational Group is highly significant. There is thus clear evidence that in children of this age the lower the "status" of the fathers' occupations, the poorer the reading attainment of the children. However, there is statistical evidence that this "falling off" of reading attainment through the Occupational Groups is not uniform.

An inspection of the table and Figure 8 suggests that this is because there is little difference between the reading performance of children whose fathers have non-manual occupations (Occupational Groups 1 and 2), but that these children are sharply differentiated from the children whose fathers are skilled, semi-skilled or unskilled workers (Occupational Groups 3, 4 and 5). Nevertheless, the figures indicate that reading performance continues to "fall away" through the three manual groups.

Although the overall tendency is clear and statistically highly significant, and the fact of some departure from this general tendency has also been shown, more sophisticated analysis is needed to establish the validity of the speculations advanced in the above paragraph. This analysis will be done at a later stage.

It will be recalled that the Southgate Test is a measure of word recognition and not of reading comprehension. It may be that the relationship between

Occupational Group and reading for comprehension is stronger than that between Occupational Group and word recognition. Later analysis of the results for the two other assessments of reading ability obtained in this Study should throw some light on this question.

Figure 6

Southgate Test Performance and Occupational Group of Father

$N=6,834$

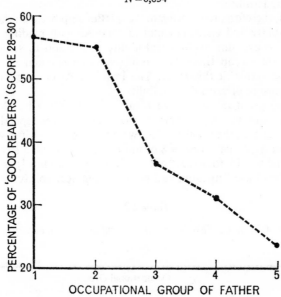

Figure 7

Problem Arithmetic Test Performance and Occupational Group of Father

$N=6,824$

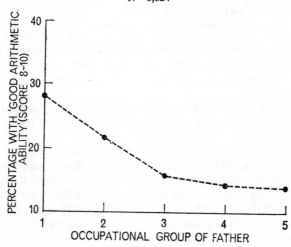

(c) Occupational Group and Attainment in Arithmetic

Much less attention has been given by research workers to the relationship
between arithmetic ability and environmental factors, compared with the
number of studies of reading. This is understandable since reading plays a
more important part in determining children's general progress in school
than does arithmetic. Nevertheless, arithmetical ability does impinge upon
many other school subjects and it is probably true to say that its importance
both in school and in later life will grow along with the rapid technological
advances of modern life.

It was decided, therefore, to investigate the relationship between the children's
arithmetical ability and environmental factors. As with reading ability, the
first step was to examine arithmetical ability in relation to socio-economic
status. Again, the Occupational Group of the father is taken as the index of
socio-economic status at this stage. The Problem Arithmetic Test score is
used as the measure of arithmetical ability.

The results are given in percentage form in Table 60. All children in the
present sample who were in "ordinary" maintained and independent schools
are included where all the requisite data were available. Children with a score
on the Problem Arithmetic Test of 8 or more out of a possible 10 are grouped
and operationally said to have "good arithmetical ability"; those with a
score of 7 or less have "medium and poor arithmetical ability".

Table 60

Problem Arithmetic Test Score and Occupational Group of Father

$N=6,824$

	Occupational Group					
Arithmetic groups	1	2	3	4	5	Total
'Good arithmetical ability' (Score 8–10)	28·1	21·9	15·9	14·5	14·1	18·7
'Medium and poor arithmetical ability' (Score 0–7)	71·9	78·1	84·1	85·5	85·9	81·3
TOTAL	100	100	100	100	100	100

Chi-squared (Trend) $=103; p<0.001$
Chi-squared (Departure) $=16.6$ (3 d.f.); $p<0.001$

As the table shows, the proportion of children with "good arithmetical
ability" in the present sample fell from about 28 per cent in Occupational
Group 1 to about 14 per cent in Occupational Group 5.

The evidence from the statistical tests is that this tendency is highly significant
and one may conclude that in children of this age performance on a test of
problem arithmetic is related to the socio-economic status of the family: the
lower the status of the fathers' Occupational Group, the lower the scores of
the children. However, as with the corresponding analysis of reading ability,
this overall tendency for performance to "fall away" through the Occupational
Groups is not uniform.

An inspection of Table 60 and of Figure 7 showing the pattern of results for children of "good arithmetical ability" in graph form, suggests that there is a differentiation between children in Occupational Groups 1, 2 and 3 (children of non-manual workers and skilled manual workers) but little, if any, difference between the performance of children in Occupational Groups 3, 4 and 5 (children of manual workers) in terms of the criteria adopted.

However, the comments in the preceding paragraph must remain speculative at this stage. Further statistical analysis must be carried out to clarify the position.

(d) *Summary*

The evidence from the two preceding sub-sections points clearly to a relationship between the Occupational Group of children's fathers and children's attainment both in reading and in arithmetic at the age of seven. In both analyses there was evidence that this general relationship is not uniform from one Occupational Group to another.

These should be seen, however, as two separate analyses; it is not valid to make direct comparisons between the two, even at the speculative level. It will be recalled that the criterion of "good" reading ability included about 40 per cent of the children, whereas the children with "good arithmetical ability" were the top 19 per cent of children, as assessed by their scores on the Problem Arithmetic Test.

At a later stage comparisons will be made between reading and arithmetic ability in relation to socio-economic factors, but this will necessitate different and more elaborate statistical techniques.

References

Burt, C. Interaction of Heredity and Environment in Regard to "Measured Intelligence". *Brit. J. of Educ. Psychol.*, Vol. XXX, Part 3 (1960).

B. SCHOOL VARIABLES

1. *Length of Schooling, Educational Attainment and Adjustment in School*

(a) *Introduction*

There is evidence from other investigations, reviewed by Pidgeon (1965), that younger children in an age group are at a disadvantage educationally. Thus, summer-born children have been shown to predominate over autumn-born children in the lower streams of schools; in special schools for educationally subnormal children; and in remedial groups for backward readers. It has been suggested that one of the important factors in this situation is the length of schooling received.

Within a given administrative situation most children start their schooling at specified times in the school year, usually at the beginning of a term, according to their dates of birth. In some areas children commence at the beginning of the term in which they attain the age of five or, even, at the beginning of the school year in which they become five; in others they start school at the beginning of the term following their fifth birthday.

However, whatever the procedure, except for one intake of children per year, older children start school first and the younger children follow at intervals during the school year. This means that the older ones have the advantage not only of greater maturity by reason of their age but also of a longer period in school.

Under most circumstances the assessment of the relationship between the length of schooling and subsequent educational performance presents some difficulties because the children who spend the most time in school are also the older ones. Due allowance must therefore be made for the age of the children and, ideally, allowance must also be made for any possible inter-action between the age of the children and the length of schooling they have received.

In the present Study, however, the children are all of the same age. An opportunity presented itself, therefore, for examining the educational attain-ment and social-adjustment of children nearing the end of their infant schooling who were of the same age but had had varying lengths of schooling. It was decided to restrict the analysis to two major groups: those who had started school when aged between 4 years 6 months and 4 years 11 months, and those who started school between the ages of 5 years and 5 years 6 months, as reported by their mothers. Since all of the children in the cohort had their fifth birthday in early March 1963, the latter group would have started school in the summer term 1963, and it is known that the majority of the former children started the term before, in January 1963. These two groups are here referred to as "early starters" and "late starters". Children who had attended a nursery class or a nursery school were excluded from the groups.

In addition, it was decided to take into account the occupations of the children's fathers since this may be an important variable. The Occupational Group of the father is an indication of the socio-economic status of the family; further, since in general parents of higher socio-economic status are also more intelligent, their children will in general be more intelligent than children of parents in lower Occupational Groups.

Thus, it is important to ascertain not only whether children with the advantage of an early start in their schooling are doing better in school some two years later, but whether any such relationship exists independent of the socio-economic status of the children's families.

It may be, for example, that the children of professional parents, because of their higher intelligence and the intellectual stimulation in the home, are able to make good the deficit of later starting when compared with children of the same socio-economic status who start school earlier. On the other hand, such children may, because of these same characteristics, be able to maintain an advantage over children of the same socio-economic status who have started later.

Another reason why allowance should be made for the Occupational Group is that children whose fathers are in, say, Occupational Groups 4 and 5 are more likely to live in areas where schools are crowded and where there is a particularly acute teacher shortage. In such areas, schools may more often admit children later rather than earlier because of staffing difficulties. If this were the case then a simple comparison between "early starters" and "late starters" might produce a spurious result since the latter group might contain a larger proportion of children from lower socio-economic groups. Thus, any difference between the two groups might be associated with socio-economic factors rather than the length of schooling received.

In this section, then, the "early starters" and the "late starters" are compared for reading ability as measured by the Southgate Reading Test; for arithmetical ability, as measured by the Problem Arithmetic Test; and for social-adjustment, as assessed by the total score on the Bristol Social-Adjustment Guide.

Children included are those in the sample in maintained infant, junior with infants or all-age schools, or in independent schools catering wholly or mainly for children who are not handicapped. Children excluded are those who had attended nursery schools and those for whom all the appropriate information was not available when the data were processed (e.g., age of starting school, Occupational Group of the father).

(b) *Length of Schooling and Reading Attainment*
(i) *Analysis ignoring socio-economic factors*
The most straightforward way of examining the relationship between "early" and "late" starting in school and reading attainment in the present sample is simply to compare the reading performance of the two groups when they were tested near the end of their infant schooling.

Thus, the children were divided into three categories on the basis of their scores on the Southgate Reading Test: the "good readers" with a score of 28 to 30; the "medium readers" with a score from 16 to 27; and the "poor readers". The results are given in Table 61.

Table 61
(Percentaged)
Length of Schooling and Southgate Reading Test Score
N=5,251

Ages of commencing school	Southgate Reading Test score			
	'Good readers' (Score 28–30)	'Medium readers' (Score 16–27)	'Poor readers' (Score 0–15)	Total
'Early starters' 4 years 6 months to 4 years 11 months	43·4	43·4	13·2	100
'Late starters' 5 years to 5 years 6 months	36·2	43·6	20·3	100
TOTAL	40·0	43·5	16·5	100

Chi-squared (Trend) = 52·3; $p < 0.001$

It will be seen that the "early starters" were better readers than the "late starters" when this criterion of reading performance was used. The difference between the groups in reading ability is highly significant.

Thus, one may conclude that children of the same age who make an earlier start with their schooling (aged 4 years 6 months to 4 years 11 months) are better readers, as measured by a test of word recognition, near the end of their infant schooling than those who make a later start (aged 5 years to 5 years 6 months). In the present sample the difference in the length of schooling between the two groups compared was, for the majority of the children, only one term.

(ii) *Analysis allowing for socio-economic factors*
Although the overall relationship between length of schooling and reading ability at seven years of age has been demonstrated, this relationship may not be the same for children from all socio-economic backgrounds.

R

In Table 62 the "early starters" and "late starters" are grouped according to the Occupational Group of their fathers. Further, the particular statistical analysis used necessitated dividing the children into two groups according to their reading ability. It was decided that it would be most appropriate to compare the "good readers" with the "medium and poor" readers.

Table 62
(Percentaged)

Occupational Group of the Father, Length of Schooling and Southgate Reading Test Score

N=5,251

Occupational Groups	Ages of commencing school	Southgate Reading Test Score 'Good' readers (Score 28–30)	'Medium and Poor' readers (Score 0–27)	Total
1	'Early starters' 4 yrs. 6 mths. to 4 yrs. 11 mths.	58·0	42·0	100
1	'Late starters' 5 yrs. to 5 yrs. 5 mths.	47·8	52·3	100
2	'Early starters' 4 yrs. 6 mths. to 4 yrs. 11 mths.	61·9	38·1	100
2	'Late starters' 5 yrs. to 5 yrs. 5 mths.	51·2	48·8	100
3	'Early starters' 4 yrs. 6 mths. to 4 yrs. 11 mths.	39·2	60·8	100
3	'Late starters' 5 yrs. to 5 yrs. 5 mths.	36·7	67·3	100
4	'Early starters' 4 yrs. 6 mths. to 4 yrs. 11 mths.	33·1	66·9	100
4	'Late starters' 5 yrs. to 5 yrs. 5 mths.	28·2	71·8	100
5	'Early starters' 4 yrs. 6 mths. to 4 yrs. 11 mths.	25·7	74·3	100
5	'Late starters' 5 yrs. to 5 yrs. 5 mths.	22·5	77·5	100
TOTAL		40·0	60·0	100

Chi-squared (partial association) $=29\cdot1$; $p<0\cdot001$
Chi-squared (2nd order interaction) $=1\cdot94$ (4 d.f.); $p>0\cdot05$ not significant

It will be seen that in each Occupational Group the "early starters" had a higher proportion than the "late starters" of "good readers" and a smaller proportion of children of "medium and poor" reading ability.

The evidence from the two statistical tests carried out (see Section IV: "Statistical Analysis") is that there is a highly significant difference between the "early starters" and the "late starters", independent of Occupational Group.

Thus, the conclusion is warranted that children of the same age who start school "early" (aged 4 years to 4 years 11 months) are better readers near the end of their infant schooling—irrespective of the Occupational Groups of their fathers—than children who start school "late" (aged 5 years to 5 years 5 months).

(c) Length of Schooling and Arithmetic Attainment
(i) Analysis ignoring socio-economic factors
Once again the most straightforward analysis is presented first.

The "early starters" and "late starters" were divided into three categories according to their score on the Problem Arithmetic Test. Those with a score of 8 to 10 were defined as having "good arithmetical ability"; those scoring from 3 to 7 had "medium arithmetical ability"; and the children scoring 2 or below were defined as having "poor arithmetical ability".

The percentaged results are given in Table 63.

Table 63

(Percentaged)
Length of Schooling and Problem Arithmetic Test Score

$N = 5,242$

	Problem Arithmetic Test Score			
Ages of commencing school	'Good arithmetical ability' (Score 8–10)	'Medium arithmetical ability' (Score 3–7)	'Poor arithmetical ability' (Score 0–2)	Total
'Early starters' 4 yrs. 6 mths. to 4 yrs. 11 mths.	19·9	66·3	13·8	100
'Late starters' (5 yrs. to 5 yrs. 5 mths.	16·1	66·1	17·8	100
TOTAL	18·1	66·2	15·7	100

Chi-squared (Trend) $= 23·7$; $p < 0·001$

The difference between the "early starters" and "late starters" in arithmetical ability, as measured by this test, is highly significant.

Thus, if no account is taken of socio-economic factors, the conclusion is warranted that children of the same age who start school "early" (aged 4 years 6 months to 4 years 11 months) achieve better scores on a problem arithmetic test near the end of their infant schooling than children who start school "late" (aged 5 years to 5 years 5 months).

(ii) *Analysis allowing for socio-economic factors*
As with reading ability, a more detailed analysis was carried out which
allowed for socio-economic factors in so far as these are assessed by the
Occupational Groups of the fathers.

Table 64
(Percentaged)

Occupational Group of the Father, Length of Schooling and
Problem Arithmetic Test Score

$N = 5,242$

		Problem Arithmetic Test Score		
Occupational groups	Ages of commencing school	'Good arithmetical ability' (Score 8–10)	'Medium and poor arithmetical ability' (Score 0–7)	Total
1	'Early starters' 4 yrs. 6 mths. to 4 yrs. 11 mths.	28·2	71·8	100
	'Late starters' 5 yrs. to 5 yrs. 5 mths.	22·7	77·3	100
2	'Early starters' 4 yrs. 6 mths. to 4 yrs. 11 mths.	24·8	75·3	100
	'Late starters' 5 yrs. to 5 yrs. 5 mths.	21·0	79·0	100
3	'Early starters' 4 yrs. 6 mths. to 4 yrs. 11 mths.	17·6	82·4	100
	'Late starters' 5 yrs. to 5 yrs. 5 mths.	14·0	86·1	100
4	'Early starters' 4 yrs. 6 mths. to 4 yrs. 11 mths.	15·2	84·9	100
	'Late starters' 5 yrs. to 5 yrs. 5 mths.	13·6	86·4	100
5	'Early starters' 4 yrs. 6 mths. to 4 yrs. 11 mths.	17·1	82·9	100
	'Late starters' 5 yrs. to 5 yrs. 5 mths.	10·6	89·4	100
TOTAL		18·1	81·9	100

Chi-squared (partial association) $= 12·8$; $p < 0·001$
Chi-squared (2nd order interaction) $= 1·4$ (4 d.f.); $p > 0·05$ not significant

For this statistical analysis it was necessary to place the children into two groups on the basis of their scores on the Problem Arithmetic Test. It was decided, as with the corresponding analysis of reading ability, to place the children with "good arithmetic ability" (with a score of 8 to 10) in one group; and those with "medium and poor arithmetic ability" (with a score below 8) in the other.

The percentage figures are given opposite in Table 64.

There was a higher proportion of "early starters" than "late starters" in each Occupational Group with "good arithmetical ability" and a smaller proportion with "medium and poor" arithmetical ability.

The evidence from the two statistical tests carried out (see Section IV: "Statistical Analysis") is that there is a highly significant difference between the "early starters" and the "late starters", independent of Occupational Group.

The conclusion is warranted that, in terms of performance on a test of problem arithmetic, children of the same age who start school "early" are as a group more advanced near the end of their infant schooling than children who start school "late", irrespective of the Occupational Group of their fathers.

(d) Length of Schooling and Adjustment in School
(i) Analysis ignoring socio-economic factors

As in the previous two sub-sections, the simplest analysis is presented first; "early starters" and "late starters" are compared in terms of their adjustment in school without regard for any factors except for the length of their schooling.

The two groups were divided into three categories on the basis of total scores on the Bristol Social-Adjustment Guides. Those with a score from 0 to 9 were called "stable"; those with a score between 10 and 19 were operationally defined as "unsettled"; and those with a score of 20 or more were called "maladjusted".

The results in percentage form are given in Table 65. It will be noted that the total number of children involved in this analysis is some 300 less than in

Table 65
(Percentaged)
Length of Schooling and Adjustment in School
N=4,917

Ages of commencing school	Adjustment in School			
	'Stable' Total Score 0–9	'Unsettled' Total Score 10–19	'Maladjusted' Total Score 20+	Total
'Early starters' 4 yrs. 6 mths. to 4 yrs. 11 mths.	69·5	19·7	10·8	100
'Late starters' 5 yrs. to 5 yrs. 5 mths.	64·9	22·6	12·4	100
TOTAL	67·4	21·1	11·6	100

Chi-squared (Trend) $= 9\cdot9$; $0\cdot01 > p > 0\cdot001$

the corresponding analyses for reading and arithmetic. This is because fewer
Bristol Social-Adjustment Guides were available for data processing when
this was carried out.

As the above table shows, there was a higher proportion of "stable" children
amongst the "early starters" and a smaller proportion of "unsettled" and
"maladjusted" children. The difference between the "early starters" and the
"late starters" is statistically significant, in percentage form.

There is thus evidence that in terms of the criteria adopted, children of the
same age who start school "early" are better adjusted in school near the end
of their infant schooling than children who start school "late".

(ii) *Analysis allowing for socio-economic factors*

In Table 66 results are given, separately, for "early starters" and "late
starters" in the five Occupational Groups.

The difference between the adjustment in school of "early starters" and "late
starters" was analysed independent of the Occupational Group of their
fathers. In order to carry out this particular statistical analysis, "unsettled"
and "maladjusted" children were grouped together to contrast with "stable"
children.

Table 66
(Percentaged)

Occupation of the Father, Length of Schooling and Adjustment in School

$N=4,917$

Occupational groups	Ages of commencing school	Adjustment in School		Total
		'Stable' Total Score 0–9	'Unsettled and Maladjusted' Total Score 10+	
1	'Early starters' 4 yrs. 6 mths. to 4 yrs. 11 mths.	75·0	25·0	100
	'Late starters' 5 yrs. to 5 yrs. 5 mths.	72·7	27·3	100
2	'Early starters' 4 yrs. 6 mths. to 4 yrs. 11 mths.	78·1	21·9	100
	'Late starters' 5 yrs. to 5 yrs. 5 mths.	76·2	23·8	100
3	'Early starters' 4 yrs. 6 mths. to 4 yrs. 11 mths.	68·6	31·4	100
	'Late starters' 5 yrs. to 5 yrs. 5 mths.	63·9	36·1	100
4	'Early starters' 4 yrs. 6 mths. to 4 yrs. 11 mths.	64·0	36·0	100
	'Late starters' 5 yrs. to 5 yrs. 5 mths.	58·5	41·5	100
5	'Early starters' 4 yrs. 6 mths. to 4 yrs. 11 mths.	59·3	40·7	100
	'Late starters' 5 yrs. to 5 yrs. 5 mths.	46·9	53·1	100
TOTAL		67·4	32·6	100

Chi-squared (partial association) $=11·3$; $p< 0·001$
Chi-squared (2nd order interaction) $=2·06$ (4 d.f.); $p >0·05$ not significant

It will be seen that in each Occupational Group there was a higher proportion of "stable" children amongst the "early starters" and a smaller proportion of "unsettled and maladjusted" children.

The evidence from the two statistical tests (see Section IV: "Statistical Analysis") is that there is a highly significant difference between the adjust-

ment in school of the "early starters" when compared on this criterion with
that of the "late starters".

One may conclude that children of the same age who start school "early"
are better adjusted in school near the end of their infant schooling than those
who start school "late", irrespective of the Occupational Group of their
fathers.

(e) Summary

The highly significant results obtained in the three previous sub-sections only
permit one, strictly, to make inferences in terms of the assessments used.
Nevertheless, the conclusion is warranted that children of the same age who
commence full-time infant schooling before the age of five are, as they
approach the transfer to junior schools or classes some two years later, more
advanced educationally and better adjusted in school than those who commence school after the age of five, irrespective of the socio-economic status
of their families.

It must be borne in mind that this relationship is not necessarily a causal one;
one cannot conclude without further evidence that the relatively poorer
performance of later starters is the direct effect of less time spent in school.
It may be that both the age of commencing school and educational attainment
at seven years of age are related to another factor or factors. For example, if
it were true that earlier starting in school were more common in the south of
England than in the north and also that educational standards were higher
in the south, this may account wholly, or partly, for the demonstrated relationship. This regional factor, and others, will be investigated at a later stage.

It may be thought that even if a causal relationship could be demonstrated,
the topic is of academic interest and has few practical implications since in a
given area it is normal for children of the same age to start school at the
same time. Further, any effect of length of schooling might be assumed to
diminish and even to disappear as children grow older.

Nevertheless, despite the fact that children of the same age in a particular
area generally start school at the same time, some borderline has to be drawn
and children whose ages differ by only a few days or weeks have different
lengths of time in school.

Furthermore, since there is evidence (Pidgeon, 1965) that younger children
in an age group are at a disadvantage, educationally, compared with older
ones, it is important to investigate the factors which contribute to this situation. If the length of schooling is one of these factors, then it may be possible
to take practical steps to ameliorate the position.

Finally, although it appears to be a reasonable assumption that any effects of
length of schooling may diminish with time, the assumption would need to
be verified. It may not be true for all children under all circumstances. For
example, the importance of the children's level of intelligence may be an
important factor, as may the size of organization of the junior schools or
departments which they transfer.

References

PIDGEON, D. A. Date of Birth and Scholastic Performance. *Educational
Research*, Vol. 8, No. 1 (National Foundation for Educational Research)
(1965).

C. ENVIRONMENTAL FACTORS

1. *Parental Situation*

(*a*) *Introduction*

Research evidence supports the thesis that the general progress of children who are not living with both their own natural parents is likely to be less satisfactory than that of children who are. The greater part of research in this country is based on findings from children who have shown difficulties which have required special action. The present Study provides an opportunity to compare children living in "atypical" family circumstances, irrespective of whether or not they are receiving any specialized help, with a large group of children of the same age and otherwise similar background. For the sake of brevity the group of children living with their own parents will be described as "normal" and those not living with both natural parents will be described as "atypical".

It might be expected that a comparison of the children from "normal" family settings with those from "atypical" ones would show certain differences in growth and development. Children not living with both natural parents are more likely to have been subject to adverse experiences which may play an important part in their emotional development or their general progress. Both the total set of circumstances that lead to children living in an "atypical" parental situation and the children's growth and development within the "atypical" setting are likely to be associated with socio-economic status.

Comparisons were made, therefore, between children from "normal" and "atypical" home backgrounds for reading ability as a major indication of progress at school. The comparison between the two groups was made for boys and girls and within Occupational Group. The proportions of the children living in "normal" and "atypical" parental situations within each Occupational Group are given in part (*b*) of this section.

The "normal" group included those children reported by their mothers to be living with or cared for by both natural parents. The "atypical" group covered children reported as having only one natural parent because of illegitimacy, desertion, divorce, separation or death; those with one step-parent; as well as children who were adopted, fostered or in care. Children whose parental situation was not known have been excluded from this second group, although it is likely that a number of them will eventually be found to belong to it. An analysis of the different types of parental situation within the "atypical" group in relation to other factors will be possible at a future stage.

Information about the children's families was gathered on the Parental Questionnaires. In the totals from the punched card analysis (see Section V: "Environmental Factors") six per cent of the children for whom there was information were living in an "atypical" situation. This is likely to be an under-estimate of the proportion in the total cohort because mothers of children with no male head of household are more likely to be in full-time work, so that in consequence their completed Parental Questionnaires would have a greater chance of being among the "late" returns not included in the present sample.

In this section the totals were all derived from computer analysis and will vary according to the number of children within the two groups for whom there was appropriate information. All the analyses were of children both in "ordinary" maintained and independent schools and of children in "special" schools. The 82 children whose schools could not be classified and the very few who were resident in hospital were not included.

The two groups of children were compared wherever possible for three variables: sex; Occupational Groups of the fathers; and Southgate Reading Test Scores. Two-way tables showing the position in the sample as a whole are given before tables showing three way breakdowns.

(b) Parental Situation and Occupational Groups

About a third of the children living in an "atypical" family situation were those without a father or a male head of household and so could not be included in the results presented in Table 67. (It is realized that this group of children in households without fathers may have some special characteristics.)

Table 67

Occupational Group of Fathers by Parental Situation
(Boys and girls combined)

$N = 6,896$

Occupational Groups	Parental Situation	N	Per cent
1	'Normal'	1,355	97·3
	'Atypical'	37	2·7
2	'Normal'	719	96·1
	'Atypical'	29	3·9
3	'Normal'	3,068	95·8
	'Atypical'	136	4·2
4	'Normal'	1,109	94·8
	'Atypical'	61	5·2
5	'Normal'	356	93·2
	'Atypical'	26	6·8
All Occupational Groups	'Normal'	6,607	95·8
	'Atypical'	289	4·2

Chi-squared (Trend) $= 17 \cdot 1$; $p < 0 \cdot 001$
Chi-squared (Departure) $= 0 \cdot 8$ (3 d.f.); $p > 0 \cdot 05$ not significant

The proportion of children living in an "atypical" family situation showed a highly significant and consistent increase from Occupational Group 1 through to Occupational Group 5. Of the children in Occupational Group 1, 2·7 per cent were not living with their own parents, compared with 6·8 per cent of children in Occupational Group 5.

(c) Parental Situation and Southgate Reading Test Score

The association between Reading Score and Parental Situation was tested for boys and girls separately. The children's scores on the Southgate Reading Test (for detailed description see Section III: B.3) were classified into three groups:

"Poor readers" with a score from 0 to 15
"Medium readers" with a score from 16 to 27
and "Good readers" with a score from 28 to 30

Table 68

Parental Situation and Southgate Reading Test for Boys

$N = 3,448$

Parental Situation	'Poor readers' Score 0–15		'Medium readers' Score 16–27		'Good readers' Score 28–30		Total	
	N	Per cent	N	Per cent	N	Per cent	N	Per cent
'Normal'	684	20·7	1,446	43·8	1,170	35·4	3,300	100
'Atypical'	43	29·0	71	48·0	34	23·0	148	100

Chi-squared (Trend) $= 11\cdot3$; $p < 0\cdot001$
Chi-squared (Departure) $= 0\cdot2$ (1 d.f.); $p > 0\cdot05$ not significant

There was a highly significant association between the two parental situation groups and the three reading groups. More boys in the "normal" group had high reading scores (35·4 per cent) than those in the "atypical" group (23 per cent) and, conversely, among the latter the proportion of "poor readers" was higher; 29 per cent compared with 20·7 per cent.

Table 69

Parental Situation and Southgate Reading Test for Girls

$N = 3,404$

Parental Situation	'Poor readers' Score 0–15		'Medium readers' Score 16–27		'Good readers' Score 28–30		Total	
	N	Per cent	N	Per cent	N	Per cent	N	Per cent
'Normal'	403	12·3	1,326	40·6	1,537	47·1	3,266	100
'Atypical'	22	15·9	69	50·0	47	34·1	138	100

Chi-squared (Trend) $= 7\cdot7$; $0\cdot01 > p > 0\cdot001$
Chi-squared (Departure) $= 1\cdot3$ (1 d.f.); $p > 0\cdot05$ not significant

For girls, the same overall pattern was found; there is a significant association with reading in the two groups with a higher proportion of girls who were "good readers" (47·1 per cent) in the "normal" group than in the "atypical" group (34·1 per cent).

(d) *Parental Situation, Occupational Group and Southgate Reading Test Score*
Three Occupational Groups were formed for this analysis, as at this stage in the Study the numbers of children in the "atypical" group were too small for a five-fold classification. The two non-manual Occupational Groups (1 and 2) formed the first new grouping and the partly skilled and unskilled workers in Occupational Groups 4 and 5 formed the second new grouping.

Table 70

Occupational Group, Parental Situation and Southgate Test Score
(Boys and girls combined)

$N = 6,851$

Occupational Groups	Parental Situation	Southgate Test Score						Total	
		'Poor readers' Score 0–15		'Medium readers' Score 16–27		'Good readers' Score 28–30			
		N	Per cent	N	Per cent	N	Per cent	N	Per cent
1 and 2	'Normal'	147	7·1	749	36·4	1,162	56·5	2,058	100
	'Atypical'	8	12·5	36	56·2	20	31·2	64	100

Chi-squared (Trend) = 14·7; $p < 0·001$
Chi-squared (Departure) = 1·5 (1 d.f.); $p > 0·05$ not significant

3	'Normal'	549	18·0	1,383	45·2	1,125	36·8	3,057	100
	'Atypical'	35	26·1	66	49·3	33	24·6	134	100

Chi-squared (Trend) = 10·3; $0·01 > p > 0·001$
Chi-squared (Departure) = 0·0 (1 d.f.); $p > 0·05$ not significant

4 and 5	'Normal'	391	26·9	640	44·1	420	28·9	1,451	100
	'Atypical'	21	24·1	38	43·7	28	32·2	87	100

Chi-squared (Trend) = 0·5; $p > 0·05$ not significant
Chi-squared (Departure) = 0·0 (1 d.f.); $p > 0·05$ not significant

For Occupational Groups 1 and 2 combined, as well as for Occupational Group 3, the difference in the children's reading scores in the two parental situations was highly significant or significant; children in the "normal" group had consistently higher reading scores than those in the "atypical" group. However, in Occupational Groups 4 and 5 this was not the case, there being no significant difference in the reading scores of the "atypical" and "normal" groups.

Two possible interpretations of this result are, first, that an "atypical" parental situation may be only one of a number of potentially adverse environmental factors which occur relatively more often in Occupational Groups 4 and 5 and so is less discernible as a factor in isolation in relation to the children's reading progress. Secondly, it is possible that the patterns of family and neighbourhood life in these two Occupational Groups mitigate some of the possible difficulties of children in an "atypical" situation.

(e) Summary
(i) There was evidence from the present Study of an association between parental situation and socio-economic status; there being a consistent tendency for the number of "atypical" parental situations to increase from Occupational Group 1 through to Occupational Group 5.

(ii) An association was demonstrated between poor reading ability and "atypical" parental situation which was highly significant for boys and significant for girls.

(iii) There was a highly significant association between reading ability and parental situation for Occupational Groups 1 and 2 combined and a significant association with Occupational Group 3; the "normal" group showing better reading ability. However, there was no such association within Occupational Groups 4 and 5 combined.

2. *Parental Approach*

(a) *Introduction*

Parental attitudes to their children's education are related to children's progress in school (for example, Fraser, 1959; Douglas, 1964). Douglas gives evidence that this relationship is highly correlated with his index of socio-economic status; further, the relationship still holds good within the different social classes, irrespective "of standards of living, size of family and academic record of the school".

The children in the present Study are somewhat younger than those in the majority of studies on this subject. Only one criterion of parental interest could be used at this stage of the Study. The objective fact, as reported by head teachers, of whether or not parents had initiated discussion about their children was preferred to the more subjective assessment of the parents' interest made by the teachers. Initiating discussion with their children's teachers is only one indication of parents' concern, and there will be some parents who find it more difficult to visit the school than others; for example, mothers with other children who are very young. The over-anxious or over-concerned mother who tends to make too frequent enquiries cannot be differentiated under this criterion either.

Head teachers were asked: "Since September 1964 have the parents taken the initiative to discuss the child, even briefly, with you or any member of your teaching staff?"

For the sake of brevity, children whose parents had initiated discussion will be described as the "Approached" group and those whose parents had not initiated discussion will be described as the "Not Approached" group.

The replies analysed in the tables in this section concern children both in "ordinary" maintained and independent schools and in "special schools." The children whose schools could not be classified or who were resident in hospitals were not included.

The association between parental approach and the children's progress has been tested in relation to one major factor in educational progress, namely reading ability. The reading ability of children in the two groups ("Approached"/"Not Approached") was considered in relation to sex and Occupational Group.

(b) *Parental Approach and Occupational Group*

The results in Table 72 show that about 70 per cent of parents in Occupational Group 1 initiated discussion with teachers, compared with some 46 per cent in Occupational Group 5. In all Occupational Groups, except Occupational Group 5, a higher proportion of parents had initiated discussion than had not.

Table 71

Occupational Group of Father and Parental Approach
(Boys and girls combined)

$N = 6,896$

Occupational Group	Parental Approach	N	Per cent
1	'Approached'	984	70·7
	'Not approached'	408	29·3
2	'Approached'	494	65·9
	'Not approached'	255	34·0
3	'Approached'	1,727	54·0
	'Not approached'	1,473	46·0
4	'Approached,	644	54·9
	'Not approached'	529	45·1
5	'Approached'	177	46·3
	'Not approached'	205	53·7
TOTAL	'Approached'	4,026	58·4
	'Not approached'	2,870	41·6

Chi-squared (Trend) $= 134·8$; $p < 0·001$
Chi-squared (Departure) $= 24·0$ (3 d.f.); $p < 0·001$

The results of the statistical test (trend) showed that there is a highly significant tendency for the proportion of parents who have approached the school to decrease from Occupational Group 1 through to Occupational Group 5. However, the statistical test for departure from a linear relationship showed that this overall tendency is not consistent through all the paternal Occupational Groups and, thus, that the decrease from one Occupational Group to another in the proportion of parents who have approached the school is not uniform.

An inspection of the table indicates that this departure from the overall tendency for "parental approach" to fall through the Occupational Groups is because the proportions in the "Approached" and "Not Approached" groups in Occupational Group 3 and Occupational Group 4 are virtually the same.

(c) Parental Approach and Southgate Reading Test Score

The children included in the following tables were those with Parental Questionnaires returned completed in time for analysis for this Report.

The association between reading score and Parental Approach was tested for the total sub-sample and then for boys and girls separately. The children's scores on the Southgate Reading Test (for detailed description see Section III B.3) were classified into three groups: "Poor readers"—scoring 0 to 15 on this test; "Medium readers"—scoring 16 to 27; and "Good readers"—scoring 28 to 30.

Table 72

Parental Approach and Southgate Reading Test Score
(Boys and girls combined)

N=6,803

Parental approach	'Poor readers' Score 0–15		'Medium readers' Score 16–27		'Good readers' Score 28–30		Total	
	N	Per cent	N	Per cent	N	Per cent	N	Per cent
'Approached'	551	13·8	1,632	40·8	1,815	45·4	3,998	100
'Not approached'	599	21·3	1,265	45·1	941	33·5	2,805	100

Chi-squared (Trend) $=110·7$; $p<0·001$
Chi-squared (Departure) $=0·2$ (1 d.f.); $p>0·05$ not significant

There were significantly more "good readers" and fewer "poor readers" and "medium readers" in the "Approached" group than in the "Not Approached" group for all the children in this sub-sample.

Table 73

Parental Approach and Southgate Reading Test Score
(Boys only)

N=3,402

Parental Approach	'Poor readers' Score 0–15		'Medium readers' Score 16–27		'Good readers' Score 28–30		Total	
	N	Per cent	N	Per cent	N	Per cent	N	Per cent
'Approached'	351	17·2	881	43·1	811	39·7	2,043	100
'Not approached'	375	27·6	622	45·8	362	26·6	1,359	100

Chi-squared (Trend) $=83·1$; $p<0·001$
Chi-squared (Departure) $=0·0$ (1 d.f.); $p>0·05$ not significant

Table 74

Parental Approach and Southgate Reading Test Score
(Girls only)

N=3,301

Parental approach	'Poor readers' Score 0–15		'Medium readers' Score 16–27		'Good readers' Score 28–30		Total	
	N	Per cent	N	Per cent	N	Per cent	N	Per cent
'Approached'	200	10·2	751	38·4	1,004	51·4	1,955	100
'Not approached'	224	15·5	643	44·5	579	40·0	1,446	100

Chi-squared (Trend) $=48·2$; $p<0·001$
Chi-squared (Departure) $=0·6$ (1 d.f.); $p>0·05$ not significant

The results in Tables 73 and 74 show that both for boys and for girls there is a highly significant association between reading ability and parental interest, as assessed by these criteria. In the "Approached" group about 40 per cent of boys and 51·4 per cent of girls were "good readers", compared with 26·6 per cent of boys and 40 per cent of girls who are "good readers" in the "Not Approached" group.

(d) *Parental Approach and Southgate Reading Test Score within Occupational Groups*

As can be seen in Table 75, for the boys in each Occupational Group the proportion of "good readers" in the "Approached" group was higher than

Table 75

Occupational Groups, Parental Approach and Southgate Reading Test Score
(Boys only)

$N = 3,402$

		Southgate Reading Test Score							
		'Poor readers' Score 0–15		'Medium readers' Score 16–27		'Good readers' Score 28–30		Total	
Occup. groups	Parental approach	N	Per cent	N	Per cent	N	Per cent	N	Per cent
1	'Approached'	40	8·0	200	40·2	258	51·8	498	100
	'Not approached'	31	21·7	61	42·7	51	35·7	143	100

Chi-squared (Trend) = 21·7; $p < 0·001$
Chi-squared (Departure) = 3·2 (1 d.f.); $p > 0·05$ not significant

2	'Approached'	22	9·0	99	40·7	122	50·2	243	100
	'Not approached'	13	11·4	50	43·9	51	44·7	114	100

Chi-squared (Trend) = 1·1; $p > 0·05$ not significant
Chi-squared (Departure) = 0·0 (1 d.f.); $p > 0·05$ not significant

3	'Approached'	174	19·6	404	45·6	308	34·8	886	100
	'Not approached'	194	26·1	353	47·4	197	26·5	744	100

Chi-squared (Trend) = 16·6; $p < 0·001$
Chi-squared (Departure) = 0·1 (1 d.f.); $p > 0·05$ not significant

4	'Approached'	80	24·5	146	44·8	100	30·7	326	100
	'Not approached'	91	36·7	113	45·6	44	17·7	248	100

Chi-squared (Trend) = 16·2; $p < 0·001$
Chi-squared (Departure) = 0·2 (1 d.f.); $p > 0·05$ not significant

5	'Approached'	35	38·9	32	35·6	23	25·6	90	100
	'Not approached'	46	41·8	45	40·9	19	17·3	110	100

Chi-squared (Trend) = 1·1; $p > 0·05$ not significant
Chi-squared (Departure) = 1·0 (1 d.f.); $p > 0·05$ not significant

the proportion of "good readers" in the "Not Approached" group. Conversely, the proportion of "poor readers" is lower in the "Approached" group than in the "Not Approached" group in each Occupational Group. For example, in Occupational Group 1, about 52 per cent in the "Approached" group were "good readers", compared with 36 per cent in the "Not Approached" group; and only eight per cent were "poor readers" in the "Approached" group, compared with 21 per cent in the "Not Approached" group.

For each Occupational Group a statistical test was carried out to determine whether the difference between the reading performance of the two groups was significant. The difference was highly significant for Occupational Groups 1, 3 and 4. Thus, in these three Occupational Groups, and in terms of the criteria adopted, children whose parents initiated discussion with teachers are better readers than those whose parents did not.

In Occupational Groups 2 and 5 the results of the statistical testing were not significant, although the differences were in the same direction as in the other three Occupational Groups. These results may be due to the relatively smaller number of boys in Occupational Groups 2 and 5. Further interpretation of these results must await more detailed statistical treatment.

Inspection of Table 75 also suggests a difference in "parental approach" between the parents of "poor readers" in the manual and non-manual Occupational Groups.

In Occupational Groups 1 and 2 more (numerically) of the parents whose children were "poor readers" were in the "Approached" group than in the "Not Approached" group. In Occupational Groups 3, 4 and 5, however, the reverse was the case, with fewer parents of "poor readers" in the "Approached" group than in the "Not Approached" group.

Table 76

Occupational Groups, Parental Approach and Southgate Reading Test Score
(Girls only)

$N=3,401$

Occup. groups	Parental approach	'Poor readers' Score 0–15		'Medium readers' Score 16–27		'Good readers' Score 28–30		Total	
		N	Per cent	N	Per cent	N	Per cent	N	Per cent
1	'Approached'	17	3·6	147	30·9	311	65·5	475	100
	'Not approached'	17	7·9	76	35·3	122	56·7	215	100

Chi-squared (Trend) $=7·4$; $0·01 > p > 0·001$
Chi-squared (Departure) $=0·9$ (1 d.f.); $p > 0·05$ not significant

2	'Approached'	12	4·8	80	31·9	159	63·3	251	100
	'Not approached'	3	2·2	58	42·3	76	55·5	137	100

Chi-squared (Trend) $=0.8$; $p > 0·05$ not significant
Chi-squared (Departure) $=4·4$ (1 d.f.); $0·05 > p > 0·01$ not significant

3	'Approached'	101	12·1	354	42·3	382	45·6	837	100
	'Not approached'	115	16·0	336	46·6	270	37·4	721	100

Chi-squared (Trend) = 11·8; $p < 0·001$
Chi-squared (Departure) = 0·3 (1 d.f.); $p > 0·05$ not significant

4	'Approached'	47	15·3	133	43·3	127	41·4	307	100
	'Not approached'	57	20·4	132	47·3	90	32·3	279	100

Chi-squared (Trend) = 5·8; $0·05 > p > 0·01$ not significant
Chi-squared (Departure) = 0·2 (1 d.f.); $p > 0·05$ not significant

5	'Approached'	23	27·1	37	43·5	25	29·4	85	100
	'Not approached'	32	34·0	41	43·6	21	22·3	94	100

Chi-squared (Trend) = 1·6; $p > 0·05$ not significant
Chi-squared (Departure) = 0·0 (1 d.f.); $p > 0·05$ not significant

As will be seen in Table 76, the overall pattern of results was similar to that of the boys. In each Occupational Group a higher proportion of girls in the "Approached" group were "good readers", compared with the proportion of "good readers" in the "Not Approached" group. There was a lower proportion of "poor readers" in four of the Occupational Groups among the children whose parents had approached the school than among the children of parents who had not initiated discussion.

Statistical evidence showed the differences between the two groups, "Approached" and "Not Approached", to be highly significant in Occupational Group 3 and to be significant in Occupational Group 1. The difference between the two groups approached the level of statistical significance in Occupational Group 4.

As with the boys, the differences in reading ability were not significant between the two groups of "parental approach" in Occupational Groups 2 and 5.

The results presented in Tables 75 and 76 above indicate that the criterion of "parental approach" as an index of parental interest is associated with reading ability and that this association both for boys and for girls is to some extent independent of socio-economic factors. However, the association justifies a more elaborate statistical approach, which should also take account of the other data on parental interest which are available.

(e) *Summary*

  (i) There is a highly significant tendency for the proportion of parents who have approached the school to decrease from Occupational Group 1 through to Occupational Group 5, although this trend is not wholly consistent.

 (ii) The differences between the "Approached" group and the "Not Approached" group are highly significant in relation to reading scores for the boys and for the girls. Boys and girls in the "Approached" group have better reading ability than in the "Not Approached" group.

(iii) The differences tended to be in a similar direction within Occupational
Groups for boys and girls in relation to reading scores. The differences
between the "Approached" group and the "Not Approached" group
were significant in relation to reading scores for boys and girls separately
in Occupational Groups 1 and 3 and for boys in Occupational Group 4.

References

DOUGLAS, J. W. B. *The Home and the School* (McGibbon and Kee) (1964).
FRASER, E. D. *Home Environment and the School* (University of London
Press) (1959).

D. BEHAVIOUR AND ADJUSTMENT

Adjustment in School in Relation to Occupational Group

The relationship between children's emotional and social adjustment and
other factors is one of the most important yet complex aspects of child
development. It is important because of its practical implications, not only
for children's progress in school and general happiness in childhood, but also
for their later integration into adult society, for their careers and their own
adequacy as parents; it is complex not only because there are many factors
involved which interact with each other, but also because most of these
factors are difficult to "measure" in a meaningful way.

In this section the children's adjustment in school, as assessed by the total
score on the Bristol Social-Adjustment Guides, is related to the Occupational
Group of their fathers. As has been explained elsewhere in this Report, the
Occupational Group is seen as a crude index of the socio-economic status of
the family. This variable might seem to be less relevant to a consideration of
children's adjustment than, say, to their reading attainment. Certainly, the
possibility of a close relationship with attainment in school seems more
predictable. The general level of verbal skills, the intellectual stimulation and
professional and leisure interests of parents in non-manual occupations
contrast sharply with the general pattern to be found in many homes of
unskilled manual workers. But what of emotional and social adjustment?
It seems likely, as was indicated in the opening paragraph, that any relationship between adjustment and socio-economic factors will be more complex.
A number of studies have shown that patterns of child rearing differ between
"social classes". It is unlikely, however, that any comparison between
children from different socio-economic backgrounds will merely reflect this.
It is known, for example, that many of the circumstances most likely to have
an adverse effect upon children's adjustment occur more frequently in homes
of lower socio-economic status.

However, in any study of complex variables, the most straightforward
relationships have first to be examined so that allowance can be made for
these in subsequent analyses. In view of the marked difference between the
sexes in adjustment, as assessed by the total score on the Social-Adjustment
Guides (see Section V G), it was decided to study the association between
adjustment and Occupational Group separately for boys and girls.

The children were divided for the purpose of this analysis into two groups
on the basis of their scores on the Guides: those with a score of 0 to 9
("stable") and those with a score of 10 or more ("unsettled and maladjusted").

In Tables 77 and 78 the results are given in percentage form for all children in the present sample in any category of school for whom all the appropriate information was available.

Table 77

(Percentaged)

Social Adjustment and Occupational Group of the Father for Boys

$N = 3,244$

Social Adjustment Scores	Occupational Groups					Total
	1	2	3	4	5	
'Stable' (Total score 0–9)	68·5	67·5	58·7	51·4	42·5	59·5
'Unsettled and maladjusted' (Total score 10+)	31·5	32·4	41·3	48·5	57·6	40·5
TOTAL	100	100	100	100	100	100

Chi-squared (Trend) $= 64·2$; $p < 0·001$
Chi-squared (Departure) $= 3·6$ (3 d.f.); $p > 0·05$ not significant

Table 78

(Percentaged)

Social Adjustment and Occupational Group of the Father for Girls

$N = 3,223$

Social adjustment scores	Occupational Groups					Total
	1	2	3	4	5	
'Stable' (Total score 0–9)	79·4	82·7	71·3	71·4	61·8	73·7
'Unsettled or maladjusted' (Total score 10+)	20·6	17·3	28·7	28·6	38·1	26·3
TOTAL	100	100	100	100	100	100

Chi-squared (Trend) $= 32·8$; $p < 0·001$
Chi-squared (Departure) $= 11·6$ (3 d.f.); $0·01 > p > 0·001$

It will be seen in both tables and in Figure 8 that the proportion of "stable" children shows a tendency to fall from Occupational Group 1 to Occupational Group 5. In both cases the statistical tests are highly significant, indicating that for both boys and girls of this age there is an overall tendency for adjustment in school to be poorer in children from homes of lower socio-economic status.

Figure 8

Social Adjustment and Occupational Group of Father

$N = 6,467$

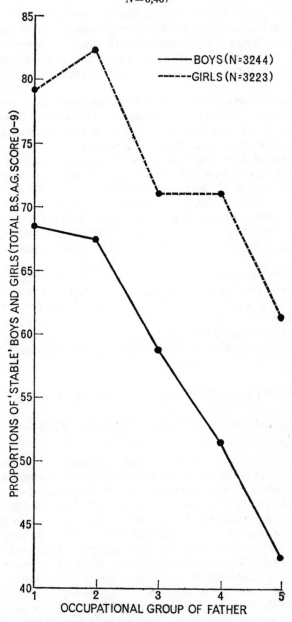

However, there was an interesting difference between the results for the two sexes. In the case of boys of this age there is strong evidence for a decrease in "stable" behaviour the lower the status of the paternal Occupational Group and no evidence that this "decline" is not consistent through the Occupational

Groups. For girls of this age there is the same evidence of a decrease in "stable" behaviour through the Occupational Groups, but there is also evidence that the "drop" from one Occupational Group to another is not uniform.

It will be seen in Table 78 and Figure 8 that the proportion of "stable" girls in Occupational Group 2 in this particular sub-sample was higher than that in Occupational Group 1. In Occupational Group 3 the proportion dropped considerably, but there was virtually no difference between the picture there and in Occupational Group 4. There was then another drop to Occupational Group 5.

In the absence of further statistical analysis no conclusions can be drawn about the patterns of results in this sub-sample. The fact that there were more "stable" girls in Occupational Group 2 than Occupational Group 1 is unexpected and may be due to chance fluctuations.

What does emerge from the analyses of the total scores from the Bristol Social-Adjustment Guides is, first, that girls at the age of seven are markedly better adjusted in school than boys (see Section VG). Secondly, for both sexes there is a strong tendency for the least well-adjusted children to be in lower socio-economic groups. Thirdly, it appears that for boys the relationship between socio-economic factors and adjustment in school is consistent, whereas for girls the relationship is not uniform and appears to be more complex.

It is highly likely that socio-economic factors, as assessed by the Occupational Group of the father, are related to children's adjustment in school because these factors are themselves associated with other circumstances in the social and physical environment of the family and neighbourhood; and also with the physical and mental health of the parents. A more detailed analysis of some of these circumstances in relation to children's adjustment is planned.

VII—FIRST FINDINGS: SUMMARY AND DISCUSSION

A. EDUCATIONAL, BEHAVIOURAL AND SOCIAL ASPECTS

1. *Introduction*

Undoubtedly there were many disadvantages in having to produce an early report, not least of which lay in the need to hedge conclusions around with repeated reminders of the preliminary and incomplete nature of both the sample and the analysis. However, there accrued at least one advantage.

In the past, the delay between the completion of studies, especially large scale ones, and their findings being published has tended to be very long. This enables practitioners and administrators to assert that events may have in the meantime brought about such changes that the need for action had been lessened if not eliminated; or that a new investigation would have to be mounted to take account of changed conditions—thus postponing action. In the case of the National Child Development Study, the interim findings presented in this Report have become available 18 months from the beginning of the project and about 12 months after the data on the children began to be collected. Thus, the information is so recent in origin that even in a period of comparatively rapid social and educational change the findings describe the situation as it actually is at present.

In recent years there has been increasing interest in the complexity of all the influences which affect children's development, and research techniques have grown more subtle, more comprehensive and more rigorous. "The time has certainly come for some co-operative scheme of research into the innumerable questions that arise. A single investigator can do little, except make a few limited and tentative experiments and sketch what appears to be the most valid methods of inquiry. The teacher, the medical officer, the social worker, the psychologist, the statistician—all need to lend their expert knowledge". These prophetic words are from Burt's (1937) classic survey which has never been paralleled, in this country or anywhere else. Yet 27 years later, Wiseman (1964), discussing the relationship between environment and educational progress, has to state that "research is still largely a matter of preliminary survey and exploration, seeking new insights to form the bases of more productive hypotheses. We know very little about the mechanisms underlying the variations of a multitude of environmental factors: with no firm grasp of these, too many research workers attack a small and ill-defined sector of the field, armed with little but a hunch or a prejudice and using whatever variables may come conveniently to hand".

The National Child Development Study has taken account of both Burt's and Wiseman's strictures: conceived as an inter-disciplinary project, it is sponsored jointly by four bodies; financed by a number of Government departments, it depends on the co-operation, indeed active collaboration, of all local authorities in England, Scotland and Wales, which was granted to a most generous extent; and the composition of the research team itself was also multi-disciplinary. Moreover, hypotheses were formulated before any of the material was available for analysis.

The Study has also largely overcome another common difficulty, that of sampling. It is well known that there are strong regional differences because various parts of the country differ widely economically, culturally and socially (Floud, Halsey and Martin, 1957; Derrick, 1961); and one study (Ferrez, 1961) suggests that—at least in France—"geographical factors are even more important than the social ones". Fortunately, sufficient financial support was given to this Study to make it possible to follow-up the entire cohort. It could, of course, be argued that there may still be some sampling bias since all the children were born in one week in March; they could conceivably have certain characteristics which differentiate them from children born in any one or all of the remaining 51 weeks of 1958. Whether and to what extent this is the case will have to await the time when the formidable financial and organizational difficulties involved in mounting more than one national perinatal mortality survey in any one year have been overcome.

The fact that inter-disciplinary research is still largely in an early, almost preliminary, phase means that one of the main productive results of large-scale studies such as ours is the posing of questions to form the stimuli for further investigations. In particular, there are two kinds of study which should follow from it: first, surveys comparable in scope and methodology should be mounted every 10 years or so; this would make possible the observation on a national scale of changes in child development in relation to changes in the economic, social, medical and educational sphere. Secondly, such large-scale studies should prepare the way for smaller but much more detailed and intensive inquiries into individual differences in the development of children's personality, mental and physical growth, health and educational progress. In fact, plans for both these types of investigation have already been prepared (together with financial estimates), and it must now be hoped that the necessary funds will become available.

2. Over-view

This interim report has two aims: the first and main aim was to give as detailed a picture as possible of a large national sample of seven-year-old boys and girls. This is presented in Section IV: "Descriptive Statistics". Of course, data of this kind are normative and no value judgements are made as to what is desirable or undesirable, but attention is focused on what is taking place. When the material for the total sample has been analysed, the picture will then become more reliable and meaningful. The second aim was to make at least a beginning with the much more complex task of unravelling the influence of and relationship between a wide range of factors (including pre- and post-natal conditions) and children's physical and psychological development, educational progress, adjustment and behaviour at home and school. What, then, are the more salient findings thus far?

(a) Settling at School

It would seem that the majority of children settle down within the first month of starting school. However, a sizeable proportion (some 25 per cent) remain unsettled up to three months or longer; there is a very significant difference between the sexes, boys taking longer to settle down than girls. The results indicate that the schools of about one-third of the children use some form of introductory attendance prior to the commencement of full-time schooling. Our data do not readily lend themselves to an exploration of the extent to which such schemes have any effect in shortening the subsequent settling-down process; but at least theoretically one would expect this to be the case.

(b) Parental Interest

The parents' interest in their children's education and their contact with the school was assessed in three ways: first, teachers' ratings of parental interest; these indicated that parents showing little or no interest are in a minority (some 16 per cent), there being no difference between mothers and fathers in this respect. Secondly, teachers were asked whether during the current school year parents had taken the initiative in discussing their child with a member of the staff; a rather high proportion had not done so (43 per cent); when this question was explored in relation to fathers' Occupational Group, it was found that the higher the socio-economic status the greater the proportion of parents who had spontaneously sought an opportunity to discuss their child with a member of staff. Thirdly, asked whether they would wish their child to remain at school beyond the minimum school leaving age, the great majority of mothers replied in the affirmative (over 80 per cent).

Of course, these three criteria are not only rather broad and crude but also involve different degrees of subjectivity. But it looks as if the parents of about half the sample showed an active interest and involvement in their child's schooling, while a minority appear to be lacking such interest.

A first exploration of the relationship between one of the indices of parental interest in the child's education and tested attainment in reading showed there to be a significant association: the proportion of good readers was higher among those children whose parents had themselves initiated some contact with the school, and this was true also for boys and girls separately. Then the relationship was examined between parental interest and reading attainment within each of the five Occupational Groups separately; the same association was found within Occupational Groups for boys in Occupational Groups 1, 3 and 4 and for girls in Occupational Groups 1 and 3.

(c) Educational Attainment

Even at the early age of seven years, girls were found to be significantly better at reading than boys; this held true whether the yardstick was an objective test or the level of the reading book the child was able to manage or the teacher's judgement of the child's reading ability. When this was examined in relation to socio-economic level—assessed in terms of the Occupational Group of the children's fathers—there was a highly significant difference in the direction predicted on the evidence of previous studies: the lower the occupational status of the fathers, the poorer the reading attainment of the children.

Though the children in this Study are all the same age, they have experienced varying length of schooling because administrative arrangements for starting school differ in different parts of the country. This provided an opportunity to compare those who had been admitted to infant schools before the age of five ("early starters") with those whose attendance commenced after their fifth birthday ("late starters"). Looking at the reading attainment of these two groups, a significant difference in favour of the "early starters" was found, even though for the majority the difference in length of schooling had only been one term. This difference between "early" and "late" starters was found to be independent of Occupational Group.

One other environmental variable was explored in relation to reading attainment; namely, whether the child lived with both his natural parents or not, the former being referred to as the "normal" and the latter as the "atypical" family situation. The "atypical" situation included not only "one-parent" families but also children who had one step-parent or who were adopted, fostered or in residential care. It was found that reading attainment was significantly lower for those whose family situation was "atypical", and this was equally true for boys and girls. When the same question was examined in relation to socio-economic status, a rather more complex pattern emerged: for the higher Occupational Groups (1, 2 and 3) the result was the same, namely, reading attainment being higher for children living with both their natural parents; but in Occupational Groups 4 and 5, the proportion of poor readers did not differ whether the children had a "normal" or "atypical" family background.

Now to turn to attainment in arithmetic. Here, boys were found to be superior to girls on a test of problem arithmetic. Again, there was a relationship between attainment in this subject and paternal Occupational Group; the lower the latter, the lower the children's score on the test. Length of schooling was also significantly associated; higher arithmetic scores were attained by "early" than "late" starters. When fathers' socio-economic status was taken into account, the same relationship between starting school "early" and good arithmetic attainment was found to exist independent of Occupational Group.

The few researches that have considered the differences between reading and arithmetic in their response to environmental effects have produced somewhat conflicting results; some showed that reading is more prone to this than is arithmetic (Thorndike, 1951; Burt, 1955; Davis and Kent, 1955; Lynn, 1958), while others do not find this to be the case (Wiseman, 1952; Kemp, 1955). At this stage there has been no analysis of possible differential effects; the present results do, however, indicate that at the age of seven both reading and arithmetic are related to environmental aspects. Further, an "early" start in the infant school is associated with higher attainment in both subjects some two years later, irrespective of parental socio-economic status.

Three other, more general abilities were explored by means of teachers' ratings. For both "oral ability" and "creativity" girls were rated higher by their teachers than boys, while the position was reversed regarding "awareness of the world around". At this stage time did not permit any more detailed examination of these abilities or their relationship to other variables.

(d) Behaviour and Adjustment

These were assessed in two ways: by asking mothers about the behaviour and developmental difficulties of their children; and by obtaining information from teachers by means of the Bristol Social-Adjustment Guides, which were completed for each child. So far, only some preliminary analysis of this material has been possible.

For most aspects of behaviour, there was evidence that a greater proportion of boys, as reported by their mothers, show difficulties at home. However, there are some exceptions; for example, more girls than boys suck their thumb or fingers during the day and bite their nails. The differences between the sexes appeared to be most marked for aggressive types of behaviour. It is worth noting that a sizeable proportion of seven-year-olds are reported to be faddy over food; and to throw the occasional temper tantrum (a little under 30 per cent in each case). In these two aspects of behaviour there were no significant differences between boys and girls. However, more boys are reluctant to go to school than girls.

Deviations from normal behaviour which many clinicians would consider as likely indications of some degree of emotional disturbance occurred only among a small minority. Thus, between one and eight per cent of children were reported to show the following behaviour frequently: difficulty in settling to anything for more than a few moments; destroying their belongings or those of others; frequently disobeying parents; being upset by new situations; and bodily twitches or mannerisms. In this context it is interesting to recall a recent study by Glueck (1966) dealing with the "Identification of potential delinquents at 2–3 years of age". The three behaviour traits which, when manifested at an early age, markedly distinguished later delinquents from non-delinquents were "extreme restlessness, destructiveness and non-submissiveness to parental authority". Thus, these traits are considered by Glueck to have high predictive value, not only for distinguishing future delinquents but also for diagnosing maladjusted or "malfunctioning" children.

When the children's behaviour in school was assessed by means of the Bristol Social-Adjustment Guides, there was again a highly significant difference between the sexes: the proportion of boys being rated as "maladjusted" was twice as great as that of the girls; the converse was also true, namely, significantly more girls were being rated as "stable" than boys. At a later stage qualitative differences in the type of deviant behaviour shown by boys and girls respectively will be explored. However, using the criterion of the Guides, it looks as if about 13 per cent of seven-year-olds show behaviour indicative of "maladjustment".

When adjustment was examined in relation to socio-economic status, it was found that the proportion of "stable" children decreased the lower the Occupational Group of the fathers. Though this was the case for both sexes, the "decline" from one Occupational Group to the next was uniform for boys but not for girls.

"Social-adjustment" was then examined in relation to length of schooling. A significant difference was found between "early" and "late" starters, the latter showing more indications of poor adjustment than the former. This relationship between "early starting" and better adjustment was also found to hold independent of Occupational Group.

(e) Need for Special Provision

This term is used here in the widest sense to include facilities within and outside the ordinary school, as well as provision for all kinds of difficulties, be they educational, emotional or physical.

First, to consider backwardness in reading. There is some evidence from our results that there has been a decrease in the proportion of poor readers during the past ten years (Morris, 1959). Nevertheless, a considerable number of children in this sample of seven-year-olds were described by their teachers as being either non-readers (about three per cent) or poor readers (about 24 per cent). An even larger proportion (almost half the sample) had not achieved a sufficient mastery of this subject near the end of their infant schooling to use it as an effective tool for further learning; rather, reading must continue to be specifically taught, because full mastery of the skill has not yet been attained. Thus, on the evidence of the children's present reading abilities about a quarter will need a continuation of "infant methods" if they are to progress with this basic subject; moreover, a proportion of them will probably be unable to succeed unless given general educational help of one kind or another, not merely help with reading.

To ascertain the likely size of this group, teachers were asked two questions: how many of the children were at present receiving special help because of educational or mental backwardness and how many would benefit from such help if it were available. The answer to the first question was five per cent and to the second question eight per cent; in each case the proportion of boys being significantly greater than that of the girls. Thus, in the teachers' judgement some 13 per cent of the children would derive benefit from educational help additional to what could be provided by class teachers themselves.

With regard to special educational help, including special schooling, teachers were of the opinion that within the next two years this would be a likely requirement for some five per cent; this was in addition to the half per cent already attending special schools. However, for a number of reasons, this figure of five per cent is likely to be an under-estimate.

One other direct method was used to arrive at some estimate of the need for special provision; this was by finding out from teachers how many children had been referred to outside agencies because of behaviour difficulties or lack of progress. The figure reported, 9·5 per cent, is again likely to be an underestimate: some children will have been referred to an outside agency unbeknown to their teachers; and, perhaps much more important, a lack of diagnostic and treatment facilities has a curtailing effect on the number of referrals. Such a lack exists in many areas with a consequent shortage of places in special schools and long waiting lists for an examination in school psychological services and child guidance clinics, where these exist. Conversely, it is a well-known phenomenon that if a new special school or child guidance clinic is opened, there is a steep rise in the number of referrals.

Lastly, there is one indirect way of trying to assess the need for psychological consultation and possibly treatment. The extent of the developmental and behaviour difficulties reported by the mothers and the proportion of children assessed on the Social-Adjustment Guides to be "maladjusted" at school would indicate that a minimum of five per cent have quite serious adjustment problems, while at least a further 10 per cent show stress symptoms of various kinds.

Only further analysis will provide evidence on the degree of overlap between educational and emotional problems as well as on their relation to the whole range of physical handicaps. What seems already beyond doubt is the fact that there is a need for special provision during the second year in the infant school if educational and emotional problems are to be dealt with as soon as they are recognized by teachers and parents.

3. Some Pointers to Policy and Practice

Starting school presents for most children a major step forward in independence, but also a major departure from their previous pattern of life. Might not a more widespread adoption by infant schools of the practice of "introductory attendance" both ease and speed up the process of settling down? It is now widely recognized that parental interest in the child's education plays a vital part in satisfactory progress. Are not infant schools the most natural and logical starting point for fostering such interest on a much wider scale? This would involve giving some priority to them in terms of staff and money. Perhaps increasing responsibility for enlisting parental interest should also be undertaken by school welfare officers and health visitors? Or should teachers who have taken one of the newly established courses for joint social work/teacher training be encouraged to work in infant schools? Could voluntary workers include in their service to the community the task of freeing parents of large families to visit their children's school by looking after those who remain at home?

"Early starters" have higher attainment and better adjustment than children who start school about a term later. Perhaps this advantage is comparatively short-term; only subsequent examinations of the same children will tell. But if the advantages turn out to be long-term, should attempts be made to ensure an earlier start, especially for the culturally and socially underprivileged?

Low socio-economic status is associated, even by the age of seven, with low educational attainment and high "maladjustment". If equal educational opportunity is to become a reality, ought not pre-school education, specially geared to the needs of culturally deprived children, to be given high priority?

The well-known pattern of boys being more backward in reading and showing a higher incidence of behaviour difficulties was found to exist already by the age of seven years. Is there a continuum of vulnerability stretching right back to pre-natal and perinatal days? If later work does establish such a link, would boys' greater vulnerability indicate a need for differential child-rearing and educational practices? Or is their relatively inferior performance a result of current child-rearing and educational practices? For example, could it be related to the fact that it is largely women who care for and educate boys during the early years? Would more male teachers in infant schools have a beneficial result on boys' educational progress and adjustment?

About 45 per cent of children appear not to reach full mastery of reading skills by the time they are due to leave infant schools. This means that the teaching of reading needs to be continued at the junior level; also there should be some continuity in teaching methods and reading schemes. This clearly has implications for both policy and practice. Is the present age of transfer the most appropriate? Must there be a uniform transfer age? Is there effective practical recognition, both in teacher training and in appointing junior school staff, of the need for infant school reading methods beyond the age of seven?

The proportion of educationally backward and emotionally maladjusted children appears to be high enough by the second year in the infant school to warrant greatly increased provision for their needs. Such early provision, including diagnosis and treatment of various kinds, would be in line with the increasing emphasis which is being placed on early detection and prevention. The focus of such early preventive work should be on socially and culturally underprivileged children, especially boys, since by the age of seven their needs are clearly the greatest, at least numerically. Hitherto, a much greater proportion of children from the higher socio-economic groups find their way into child guidance clinics, while a much higher proportion of boys from the lower socio-economic groups eventually appear in Juvenile Courts. Of course, poverty, broken or disrupted family life, housing difficulties, especially of large families, all contribute to this pattern of backwardness and maladjustment. At the same time, early remedial and psychological treatment has much to offer, particularly if it could be part of a more comprehensive scheme for family-centred, preventive and rehabilitative work. What kind of diagnostic and treatment centres would be most appropriate for dealing with those in greatest need? How can parental co-operation be obtained? And is it essential? What should be the relationship between preventive social, educational and psychological services? Need there be better integration of policies, services and practices?

References

BURT, Sir C. *The Backward Child* (University of London Press) (1937).
BURT, Sir C. "The evidence for the concept of intelligence". *Brit. J. Educ. Psychol.* **25**, pp. 158–77 (1955).
DAVIS, D. R. and KENT, N. "Intellectual development in school children, with special reference to family background". *Proc. Roy. Soc. Med.* **48**, pp. 993–5 (1955).
DOUGLAS, J. W. B. *The Home and the School* (MacGibbon and Kee) (1964)

FERREZ, J. "Regional inequalities in educational opportunity". In HALSEY, A. H. (Ed.) *Ability and Educational Opportunity, Organization for Economic Co-operation and Development* (1961).

FLOUD, J. E., HALSEY, A. H. and MARTIN, F. M. *Social Class and Educational Opportunity* (London: Heinemann) (1957).

FRASER, E. D. *Home Environment and the School* (University of London Press) (1959).

GLUECK, E. T. "Identification of potential delinquents at 2–3 years of age". *International J. Soc. Psychiatry*, **12**, pp. 5–16 (1966).

KEMP, L. C. D. "Environment and other characteristics determining attainments in primary schools". *Brit. J. Educ. Psychol.* **25**, pp. 67–77 (1955).

LYNN, R. "Disparity of attainment in reading and arithmetic". *Brit. J. Educ. Psychol.* **28**, pp. 277–80 (1958).

MORRIS, J. M. *Reading in the Primary School* (National Foundation for Educational Research) (1959).

THORNDIKE, R. L. "Community variables as predictors of intelligence and academic achievement". *J. Educ. Psychol.* **42**, pp. 321–38 (1951).

WISEMAN, S. *Education and Environment* (Manchester University Press) (1964).

B. PHYSICAL AND MEDICAL ASPECTS

1. *Scope and Value of the Preliminary Analysis*

New methods of surveillance and investigation of school children's health should be constantly evolving. Easier adaptation to changing circumstances occurs where a large national cohort is used to monitor the proportion of children requiring treatment for physical ill-health. Where this reveals previously undetected or untreated cases, action is indicated—either towards *prevention* through health education or towards *earlier diagnosis* of major and minor handicaps by more screening tests and increased surveillance from infancy onwards.

Follow-up of such a national group of children throughout their childhood can also throw some light upon new ways of establishing an optimum procedure for assessing health and growth. As no interim study of the children had been undertaken since birth, the seven-year-old follow-up included a detailed developmental and medical history as well as a full physical and medical examination. This must not, of course, be taken to imply that a complete medical history and examination is felt to be ideal, or even practicable, as a routine procedure for British school children at seven years of age. Procedures at this age might include selective screening tests; a questionnaire or personal enquiry of parents and teachers; or a medical examination of vulnerable groups. Emphasis on high-risk children is typical of a growing number of school health services.

The present preliminary results also indicate a need for increased medical staff trained in child development; closer contact between parents and educational and school health services; more screening procedures; and added efficiency in early diagnostic procedures to "identify" major and minor handicaps in pre-school and infant school children.

Pre-school records of the present sample show that only in infancy was observation optimal for early diagnosis. Over 80 per cent had attended infant welfare clinics. Between one and five years considerably fewer (38 per cent) had been taken to a pre-school or toddler clinic; an unknown number would have been seen by their general practitioner.

No attempt has been made on this incomplete sample to examine the nature of previously undiagnosed disabilities. At a later stage it is hoped to investigate these cases as well as the age at diagnosis of known handicaps and the educational and medical facilities provided. However, it is doubtful whether even a follow-up of more than 15,000 children will yield a sufficient number of major handicaps to evaluate the efficacy of "treatment" for separate conditions. Interest in the handicapped children will centre mainly on their perinatal correlates.

The present Report covers mainly the field of minor disabilities and deviations and the assessment and testing of special senses. In many spheres the results may be seen as an adjunct to the statistics assembled in the reports of local authority school health services and summarized in the biennial reports of the Chief Medical Officer of the Department of Education and Science. The results are more valuable where national figures are otherwise unavailable and also where gross regional or local variations in reported incidences indicate ambiguities of definition or interpretation.

The present Report, thought to be regarded as provisional, does demonstrate the feasibility of gathering national data on the health of children through the school health services. By using a standard format and modern data-processing techniques, it has been possible to present interim results in a very short period.

The pre-coded answers both for the history obtained from the mother and for the medical examination covered relevant aspects of every system which could readily be reproduced. The medical examinations were carried out without special apparatus or conditions by school medical officers. The information gathered was more comprehensive than would normally be considered necessary or possible at routine examinations, but regular shortened inquiries, pre-coded and rapidly data-processed, would allow decisions to be taken from a consideration of results while still current. The present Study, then, may in part be of value as a pilot for a national system of recording and retrieving data on the health of school children.

2. Descriptive Statistics

Information was obtained on *past development and illnesses*. This was retrospective as the children were not followed between birth and seven years. For this Report careful selection was made in view of its potential unreliability. Most of such data are used only in sex comparisons. However the retrospective data were gathered very much as any routine medical history. Data in Appendix 1* allow the reader to calculate past incidences if he wishes. He may be surprised at the reported frequency of certain conditions of which a history is often considered abnormal. One such condition is nocturnal enuresis; about one in nine of the children were reported as being wet by night more than occasionally between five and seven years. A much smaller proportion (4·4 per cent) had daytime incontinence after three years and only 1·2 per cent were reported to have soiled by day after four years.

Much is written currently on the ill-effect of periods of separation due to hospital admission and the present policy is moving towards unrestricted visiting of children in hospital. The wide importance of this subject is shown

---

* Not included in this version.

by the high proportion of children who had been admitted to hospital by seven years of age for various conditions. Any effect on social adjustment will be investigated later. Strikingly high among causes for admission were accidents and other injuries both at home and elsewhere. This underlines the need for better education in accident prevention.

Sex differences in Section VE ("Medical and Developmental Sex Comparisons") confirm for many morbidity factors what is already known for perinatal, infant and childhood mortality, namely the greater vulnerability of boys. For example, boys attended more often at child guidance clinics and speech clinics and showed more facial tics, stammers and other speech defects, as well as being more accident-prone and, historically, later in developmental "milestones", including walking, talking and bladder control. *Disorders of special function* such as hearing, vision and speech are among the most important educational considerations at the age of seven. Section VC, therefore, summarizes the results of investigations into these functions. The extent to which defects of hearing and speech had impinged upon parental consciousness was indicated by a past history of hearing difficulty in 10 per cent and some speech abnormality in 16 per cent. The work load carried by the corresponding medical services was considerable, though it could only be estimated retrospectively. Apart from school visual or auditory tests, 12 per cent of mothers reported that the children had attended for special visual examination and eight per cent at hearing or audiology clinics.

The strain placed upon the *childhood dental services* was underlined by the fact that three-quarters of the children were reported as having already come under the school or general dental services by seven years of age. Many would feel, however, that *all* children should have dental assessment, and the importance of this is emphasized by the fact that one in five were found on examination to have a minimum of eight or more decayed, missing or filled teeth.

Minor *visual* impairment was also reported to be quite frequent. Approximately one in seven of the children were assessed by the medical examiners to have a visual defect, but only 0·3 per cent were judged as handicapped for normal schooling and everyday activities; some six per cent of the sample were found on examination to have a squint (manifest or latent); over five per cent had uncorrected visual acuity of 6/12th or less in the right eye, and a similar proportion in the left eye. And what of treatment? Six per cent of children wore or had already required glasses, 25 per cent of whom had corrected vision of 6/12th or less in one or other eye. Should more children be regarded as potentially visually handicapped and put near the front of the class?

About five per cent of seven-year-olds were judged by the medical examiners to have a minor degree of *hearing impairment*. Analysis of the clinical hearing test of these children and of their audiograms should throw further light upon this.

Speech difficulties clearly gave concern to parents. One in six of the children were reported as having had current or past stammer or stutter (6·2 per cent), or other speech difficulty (10 per cent). Over two per cent had received speech therapy by the age of seven. A stammer or stutter was observed on examination in about one per cent. In a rating of the children's speech intelligibility by the medical examiners, about 14 per cent were judged to be not fully intelligible, but only 1·4 per cent were assessed as having a moderate or severe impairment of speech.

At the present stage, time has permitted the analysis and presentation of only a part of the medical information which has been gathered. In addition, some results have been withheld until data on the "late returns" can be processed because of particular danger of bias or misleading conclusions. In a later report it is intended not only to fill these gaps but also to examine the correlations between current medical, physical, educational, psychological and social factors and also, of course, to utilize the very comprehensive perinatal data in an investigation of the relationship between factors at or before birth and subsequent health and development.

S

THE TABLES

For reasons of space, most of the tables and all of the questionnaires appearing in the text of the main Report have been omitted in this version. The tables reprinted here are:

A1   SOUTHGATE READING TEST SCORES

A2   PROBLEM ARITHMETIC TEST SCORES

A3   TEACHERS' RATINGS OF READING ABILITY

A33 PAST HISTORY OF SPECIALIST CLINICS AND SERVICES

A40 ASSESSMENT OF SPEECH INTELLIGIBILITY

Table A1

Southgate Reading Test Scores

Reading Scores	N	Per cent
0– 3	69	0·7
4– 6	211	2·0
7– 9	462	4·4
10–12	546	5·2
13–15	624	5·9
16–18	690	6·6
19–21	874	8·3
22–24	1,118	10·7
25–27	1,761	16·8
28–30	4,133	39·4
Total tested	10,488	100
No data	108	
GRAND TOTAL	10,596	

Table A2

Problem Arithmetic Test Scores

Arithmetic Scores	N	Per cent
0	230	2·2
1	486	4·6
2	998	9·5
3	1,317	12·6
4	1,480	14·1
5	1,493	14·2
6	1,375	13·1
7	1,153	11·0
8	919	8·8
9	641	6·1
10	388	3·7
Total tested	10,480	100
No data	116	
GRAND TOTAL	10,596	

Table A3
Teachers' Ratings of Reading Ability

Descriptions of Ratings	N	Per cent
Avid reader. Reads fluently and widely in relation to his age	710	6·6
Above average ability. Comprehends well what he reads	2,569	23·8
Average reader	4,685	43·3
Poor reader. Limited comprehension	2,539	23·5
Non-reader, or recognizes very few words	305	2·8
Total tested	10,808	100
No data	25	
GRAND TOTAL	10,833	

Table A33
Past History of Specialist Clinics and Services

Number of boys =4,059; Number of girls =3,926; Total =7,985

		Attendance			Don't know	No data	Incidence per cent
		Yes	No	Total			
(a) Eye department or clinic, optician or orthoptist	Boys	534	3,500	4,034	18	7	13·2
	Girls	473	3,429	3,902	19	5	12·1
Sex difference—Chi-squared =2·2 (1 d.f.); $p>0·05$ not significant							
(b) Hearing or audiology	Boys	327	3,696	4,023	27	9	8.1
	Girls	305	3,590	3,895	26	5	7·8
Sex difference—Chi-squared =0.2 (1 d.f.); $p>0·05$ not significant							
(c) Dental services	Boys	3,062	975	4,037	12	10	75·8
	Girls	2,986	905	3,891	17	18	76·7
Sex difference—Chi-squared =0·9 (1 d.f.); $p>0·05$ not significant							
(d) Physiotherapy or remedial exercises	Boys	166	3,868	4,034	21	4	4·1
	Girls	152	3,750	3,902	20	4	3·9
Sex difference—Chi-squared =0·2 (1 d.f.); $p>0·05$ not significant							
(e) Child guidance clinics	Boys	48	3,987	4,035	20	4	1·2
	Girls	15	3,891	3,906	19	1	0·4
Sex difference—Chi-squared =16·4 (1 d.f.); $p<0·001$							
(f) Speech therapy	Boys	120	3,913	4,033	21	5	3·0
	Girls	52	3,853	3,905	19	2	1·3
Sex difference—Chi-squared =25·3 (1 d.f.); $p<0·001$							

Table A40

Assessment of Speech Intelligibility

Number of boys = 4,053; Number of girls = 3,917; Total = 7,970

	Boys	Girls	Total
Speech fully intelligible	3,361	3,433	6,794
Almost all words are intelligible	581	406	987
Many words are unintelligible	66	34	100
All or almost all words are unintelligible	10	4	14
Don't know or unable to test	33	38	71
No data	2	2	4

APPENDIX 11

THE ORGANIZATION OF JUNIOR SCHOOLS AND
EFFECTS OF STREAMING:
NATIONAL FOUNDATION FOR EDUCATIONAL RESEARCH:
A PRELIMINARY REPORT

This Appendix is an abridged version of the two reports submitted to the Council by the National Foundation for Educational Research. A fuller version was published in November 1966 as part of a Supplement to *Educational Research*. The reports were written by Mrs. Joan Barker Lunn, assisted by C. J. Tuppen and Mrs. J. Bouri.

The research project on which the material is based was commissioned by the Department of Education and Science in the expectation that its preliminary findings would be of help to the Central Advisory Councils. We are grateful to the Department for this foresight as well as to the Foundation who have so helpfully provided preliminary reports in advance of their own publication. The present report relates to children in different years of junior courses. The Foundation are following up those children who were at the beginning of the junior course when the study was made and this will continue until they are in their final year of the junior school. The whole report will probably be published at the end of 1968.

PART I

Junior Schools and their Type of Organization

INTRODUCTION

The National Foundation for Educational Research was asked by the Department of Education and Science to investigate the effects of "streaming" and "non-streaming" in junior schools.

The inquiry involved three main parts. Firstly, a general survey of current practices was conducted; secondly, a study of 100 junior schools (50 streamed and 50 unstreamed) was undertaken, to enable some assessment to be made of the effects of "streaming" and "non-streaming" on the intellectual and social development of pupils; and, finally, a more intensive study was made of 10 schools to supplement the evidence yielded by the larger scale investigations.

The survey of general practices, which is discussed in the present report, had two aims. The first was to discover the incidence of streaming and the methods of organization practised in junior schools; the second was to obtain the information required to select a suitable sample of schools for the second stage of the study.

A fact-finding questionnaire was constructed to obtain information about the ways in which classes are formed; the criteria used in deciding the correct stream for each child; and the opportunities for transfer between streams. Questions were also asked about the general circumstances of the school and its pupils, e.g. number of teachers and classrooms, parental occupations, etc.

In the early summer of 1963, the questionnaires were sent to a stratified random sample of 2,290 primary schools in England and Wales, and the heads in each of these schools were asked to complete them.

The sample was selected from the population of all primary schools in England and Wales, with the exception of schools which had less than 26 pupils on the school roll. The latter were omitted because the survey was concerned mainly with larger schools in which each year group had to be divided into a number of classes. All local education authorities except one agreed to co-operate.

The sample was stratified by type of school and by number of pupils on the school roll.   There were six categories for type of school: junior urban; junior rural; junior and infant urban; junior and infant rural; all-age urban; all-age rural; and four categories for school-roll number.

Different sampling fractions were used for the different types of school and size categories (see details of the sample in Annex 1), and the sample was drawn from the lists made available by the Department of Education and Science.

One thousand eight hundred and sixty-nine schools returned a completed questionnaire, an overall completion rate of 82 per cent.

Of the 18 per cent that failed to return the questionnaires some schools had closed or had become infants' schools. In others, staff illness, or a recent change in staff, or reconstruction work in progress made it impossible for the questionnaires to be completed. It would therefore seem justifiable to assume that the sample returns were adequately representative, and they have been weighted according to the total junior school population (see Annex 1 for details).

In addition to the stratified random sample discussed above, a special sample of non-streamed schools was obtained by asking all local authorities for lists of their non-streamed junior schools or departments. These were supplied by the majority, and a sample of 50 non-streamed schools was selected, in addition to those which had occurred by chance in the random sample. The 50 schools completed a questionnaire.

These additional schools were not included in the analysis of the random sample but were analysed separately in cases where it was felt that the results obtained from the rather small non-streamed random sample required confirmation. In these instances, reference has been made to the "special L.E.A. Sample".

All-age schools were included in the random sample but since the number of these is steadily diminishing and the total number of returns was only 113, they were discarded.

The discussion of the results relates to the situation in junior and junior mixed with infants' schools in 1963. Throughout the Report, the percentages in the tables are based on the weighted sample returns and are representative of the junior school population. The actual number of schools supplying information is also shown in each table (for details of the sample see Annex 1).

1. TYPES OF JUNIOR SCHOOL ORGANIZATION

1.0 *Introduction*

Many schools, both large and small, are faced with the problem of finding an appropriate method of grouping their pupils into classes. In large schools, the number of pupils in each age-intake is high. The intake has to be divided into several classes, and a decision has to be made as to what should be the basis or criteria for their formation. Sometimes children of one year group are allocated to classes according to their performance in standardized or school-made tests and/or teachers' the judgements, the more able pupils to the upper streams and the less able to lower streams. Less frequently, the children of one year group are assigned at random to different classes. In small schools, the problem may be how best to divide the pupils into classes, when the number of available teachers or classrooms is fewer than the number of year groups. A common method of coping with this problem is to divide the children according to age, with, in certain instances, allowance for some subsequent demotion or promotion according to ability.

One of the aims of this study was to categorize the methods used for allocating *junior pupils* to classes. The method adopted by a school in this respect has been designated in this Report as —*the type of junior school organization.*

The different types of organization found in junior schools or departments present a pattern so varied and complex that no simple classification would be adequate; and indeed, only those schools which follow a consistent pattern throughout the year groups in the formation of their classes can be categorized at all satisfactorily.

The type of junior school organization chosen would seem to depend upon two major factors. The first of these is the number of classes in the school, itself largely determined by the number of pupils and of available staff. The second factor is what might loosely be called the head's social and educational philosophy which is likely to express itself in his attitudes to homogeneous or heterogeneous grouping.

1.1 *Number of Classes and Type of Organization*

The forms that homogeneous or heterogeneous ability grouping can take depend upon the number of classes and the number of children on roll. For this reason the schools have been divided into three main sizes representing various degrees of limitation on the possible forms of organization. This has been done in the following way:

1. *Large schools*—Those with two or more classes within each year group of pupils. For example a junior school taking pupils over the four year span 7–11 is classified as large if it has eight or more classes. These schools are large enough to stream consistently if they wish to do so.

2. *Middle-sized Schools*—Those with more classes than year groups but fewer than twice as many. An example would be a four year junior school with five, six, or seven classes. Some streaming is possible in these circumstances but not throughout the school.

3. *Small Schools*—Those in which the number of classes is equal to fewer than the number of year groups in the school.

1.2 *The Social and Educational Views of the Head*

The educational or social philosophies of heads are not easy to determine or to classify. Nevertheless two contrasting tendencies can be distinguished. If a head thinks that he can best allow for individual differences among his pupils and facilitate teaching by grouping children of like ability or attainment together, he tends to form classes on the basis of the results of a general ability test or some measure of attainment in reading and/or arithmetic. If on the other hand he believes that such practices are educationally harmful, he will assign children to classes by some other, possibly random, procedure.

Some heads do not pursue a consistent policy in this respect. For example in some of the larger schools the youngest two or three year groups were unstreamed and the fourth year streamed. The reasons for adopting this mixed type of organization are not explicitly stated. It may be that some heads believe that an arrangement that is suitable for one age group is not necessarily so for another. Alternatively, a head who favours non-streaming may feel constrained, because of the number of pupils involved or as a result of outside pressures or the demands of the eleven-plus examination, to introduce streaming into the fourth year.

1.3 The Main Types of Organization

Five main types of organization can be distinguished, and these are listed below. A sixth, miscellaneous, category has been added and in this group are included those schools which were inconsistent in their methods of grouping. The seventh category is the one-class junior school, which has, of course, no choice in this respect.

Type 1. Homogeneous Streaming

This form of ability grouping is found only in large schools. The children are assigned to classes within each year group, on the basis of ability and/or attainment. Thus the most able pupils are placed in the top (usually the A) stream, the less able are assigned to other streams.

Type 2. Non-Streaming

This is a form of heterogeneous ability grouping, occurring only in large schools and found in two forms:

(a) Parallel Classes

Within the year group, the children are divided into classes each containing pupils from all ability levels. For example, pupils of similar ability are matched and then divided equally into parallel classes, thus giving within each class a complete cross-section of the ability range. Or, more rarely, children are allocated to classes, within the year group, according to the initial letter of the surname, leading to effective randomization of ability within each class.

(b) According to Age

The children are divided, within each year group, according to their age, thus producing classes having a narrow age range but a complete cross-section of ability. This form of grouping has been categorized as Type 4 in all schools except large schools, where it is, in effect, a type of "non-streaming"

Type 3. Vertical Streaming

This is a form of homogeneous ability grouping across year groups, found mainly in middle-sized schools. The most common method is to have a class for the bright children of one year group, and another for the duller children of two year groups. Alternatively all classes may be drawn from two year groups; for example, the brightest nine and 10 year olds may be allocated to one class, and the remainder to another. Other combinations are also possible. This type of organization results in classes with a wide age range but which are more or less homogeneous in terms of ability.

Type 4. *According to Age*
This type of organization, found in middle-sized and small schools, is a form of heterogeneous ability grouping. It involves pupils being assigned to classes on the basis of age, without reference to their attainment or ability.

Type 5. *"Traditional Standard"*
This form of homogeneous ability grouping is found mostly in small schools and seems to be a partial survival of the old system of "standards". It usually involves the retention or accelerated promotion of a number of pupils each year and its effect is to produce a wide age range but a more or less homogeneous level of attainment within classes.

Type 6. *Other Methods* (Miscellaneous)
These, found in large, middle-sized and small schools, are for the most part combinations and variations of the methods already described, although some schools use other criteria (e.g. sex, Welsh language) for grouping pupils. This category includes both homogeneous and heterogeneous ability grouping.

Type 7. *One Class Junior Schools*
The relationship between the type of junior school organization chosen and the number of classes in the school is illustrated in Table I.

Table I

Relationship between type of school organization and number of junior classes

Number of junior classes		Schools using Homogeneous Streaming	Schools using Non-Streaming	Schools using Vertical Streaming	Schools using According to Age[1]	Schools using Traditional Standard	Schools using Other Methods
Small schools	1						41%
	2				40%	34%	1%
	3			1%	17%	37%	6%
	4			1%	27%	15%	13%
Middle sized schools	5			5%	14%	9%	10%
	6			40%	1%	5%	9%
	7	1%		31%	1%		7%
Large schools	8	36%	42%	8%			3%
	9	16%	22%	7%			2%
	10	15%	12%	3%			2%
	11	8%	9%	3%			2%
	12	12%	11%	1%			1%
	13	3%					1%
	14	4%					1%
	15	1%	2%				1%
	16	3%	2%				
	17	1%					
Percentage[2]		100%	100%	100%	100%	100%	100%
Number of schools giving information		275	43	141	420	439	438

[1] See p. 548, Type 2 (b).
[2] Percentages based on the weighted sample returns and are therefore representative of the junior school population.

1.4 *The number of junior pupils involved in and the proportion of schools using each type of organization*

Table II below shows the approximate number of junior pupils affected by each type of organization and the percentage of schools using each. From these figures it will be seen that a junior school pupil in 1963 was much more likely to be in a school using a form of homogeneous rather than heterogeneous ability grouping—in fact at least 56 per cent[1] of all pupils were in schools using homogeneous ability grouping.

Table II

The approximate number of junior pupils involved in and the proportion of schools using each type of organization

			Approximate % of junior pupils involved	% of junior departments of schools using method
Homogeneous	Type 1	Homogeneous Streaming	31	14
Ability	Type 3	Vertical Streaming	11	7
Grouping	Type 5	Traditional Standard	14	24
Heterogeneous	Type 2	Non-Streaming	5	2
Ability	Type 4	According to Age	16	25
	Type 6	Other Methods	21	16
	Type 7	One Junior Class only	2	12
			100	100

Number of schools giving information = 1,756

SUMMARY OF MAIN CONCLUSIONS

The following provides a summary of the main findings of each section of Part I; for a full discussion see NFER publication *New Research in Education,* November 1966.

2. LARGE SCHOOLS AND THEIR TYPE OF ORGANIZATION
1. In large schools (i.e. eight or more classes) the predominant type of organization was *Homogeneous Streaming*—used by 65 per cent of large schools. Six per cent of large schools only were entirely unstreamed, and five per cent were unstreamed except for one year group. Four per cent kept the two younger year groups unstreamed but used *Homogeneous Streaming* in the two older year groups. Twenty per cent of large schools used other mixed methods.

2. The average size of classes in all large schools was equal, namely 36 pupils. However, class sizes in schools using *Homogeneous Streaming* were more varied than those in non-streamed schools. Higher ability streams tended to have more pupils than lower ability streams, whereas all classes in non-streamed schools had approximately the same number of pupils.

---

[1] The figure is probably nearer 70 per cent since many children in schools classified under Type 6 were in fact in homogeneous groups.

3. There were proportionally more girls than boys in the higher ability streams and conversely more boys than girls in the lower ability streams.

4. There was a difference in the average ages of A, B and C streams in all year groups. The A streams had the highest average age and the lowest ability streams were the youngest.

The most important findings are points three and four above. These indicate that the practice of *Homogeneous Streaming* may penalize boys and younger children of a year group.

Some of the disadvantages of being a "younger" child in a school year group might be removed if all children were allowed to start school at the same point in the year, thus removing the advantage of longer schooling, which the "older" child now has. It seems logical for children to start school together at the beginning of the school year, since at every stage of the education system children born within a school year are treated as a group (e.g. they move up the school together, take 11-plus at the same time, etc.).

3. METHODS OF ALLOCATION TO 'STREAMS' AND CLASSES IN LARGE SCHOOLS AND THE PUPIL'S CHANCES OF TRANSFER

1. Schools using homogeneous ability grouping commonly assigned children to classes in their first year at junior school on the basis of their infant school record. After the first year, an internal examination became the most common criterion.

2. Schools using *Non-Streaming* paid more attention to age and relatively little to infant school record as a criterion for assigning children to classes.

3. After the initial assignment to a class or stream in the first year of the junior school, the chances of a pupil being transferred are very slight.

Taking the school year 1961–62 as a typical year, it appears that movement between streams was relatively small. Once children had been assigned to their streams at seven-plus most of them would remain in the same stream throughout the four years of the junior school. Against this we should put Vernon's estimate, based on the known correlations of the measures used, that about 10 per cent of all children should be upgraded or downgraded each year if relative homogeneity is to be preserved.

Thus reliability and validity of the methods used for grading children to A, B or C streams when they first enter the junior school appear to be of the utmost importance; it is surprising to find that so many junior schools graded their pupils without the help of standardized tests and without making allowance for age.

Since the same largely unscientific criteria as are used to grade the children initially are also used to assess whether second, third or fourth year children should be regraded, it is hardly likely that grading errors will be recognized and rectified at these later stages. Lack of transfers could, of course, be due to an accurate assessment at seven plus, or could be a result of a self-fulfilling prophecy in that membership of a stream tends to condition learning.

4. MIDDLE-SIZED SCHOOLS AND THEIR TYPE OF ORGANIZATION

1. The major type of organization in middle-sized schools (five, six or seven junior classes) was *Vertical Streaming* (28 per cent). Thirty-six per cent used *Other Methods*, 19 per cent *According to Age*, and 17 per cent *Traditional Standard*.

2. Thirty-eight per cent of the classes in schools using *Vertical Streaming* were composed of children from two or more year groups. These classes tended to consist of average and slow pupils, while brighter pupils were more often in classes of one year group only. *Vertical Streaming* was found mainly in six and seven class schools.

3. In schools grouping *According to Age*, 70 per cent of classes were composed of one year group only, while 30 per cent had two or more year groups. *According to Age* was found mainly in five class schools, and nearly half of these had a remedial class, thus leaving one class each for the four year groups.

4. *Traditional Standard* Method was found mainly in five and six class schools.

5. The *average* number of pupils in the class in middle-sized schools was 34·5 although the *actual* numbers in any class varied more than in large schools; there was little difference in class size between the various types of organization.

5. SMALL SCHOOLS AND THEIR TYPES OF ORGANIZATIONS

1. It was found that the major types of organization in small schools (four class or less) were *Traditional Standard* Method (used by 35 per cent) and grouping *According to Age* (also used by 35 per cent).

2. In schools using the *Traditional Standard* Method, the most frequent type of class was that composed mainly of average children but with a few bright younger pupils who had been promoted. Next most frequent were classes in which a few slow pupils had been "kept down".

3. Very often small schools were forced to form classes of more than one year group either because of unequal numbers in the different year groups or through having to allocate four year groups into three classes. The head teacher may, in such circumstances, form classes on the basis of the *Traditional Standard* Method, or he may group *According to Age*.

4. Seventy-six per cent of classes in small schools were composed of two or more year groups.

5. Some head teachers used the *Traditional Standard* Method—i.e. kept slow pupils down and promoted bright pupils—when they were *not* forced by circumstances to mix year groups.

6. The average number of pupils in the class was 28 in schools using *Traditional Standard* and 29 in those grouping *According to Age*.

6. INTRA AND INTER-CLASS GROUPING

A—Intra-class grouping

1. Class teaching (30 per cent of all classes) was used less frequently than group teaching for the 3R's. The least common intra-class practice was for children to remain in the same group for reading, mathematics and English (nine per cent of all classes).

2. There was a tendency for more attainment grouping in schools using heterogeneous ability grouping (i.e. schools using *Non-Streaming* or *According to Age*).

3. Some schools appeared to teach the class as a whole and there was no grouping for the 3R's even though the class was heterogeneous with respect to ability (28 per cent using *Non-Streaming*, 22 per cent in middle-sized schools grouping *According to Age*). This may include schools using individual teaching methods.

4. Some classes were divided into sub-classes on the basis of attainment/ability and pupils were taught the 3R's in these groups.

5. The smaller the school, the more use made of group rather than class teaching.

6. Grouping was used equally frequently for reading and mathematics, but less frequently for English.

B—Inter-class grouping

1. Setting between classes was extremely rare. Four per cent of all schools "set" for English and six per cent for both mathematics and reading.

2. Twenty-one per cent of schools using *Non-Streaming*, 47 per cent of middle-sized schools using *According to Age* and 27 per cent using *Traditional Standard* had a remedial class.

3. The most common form of remedial group in large schools was the one which met irregularly or for part only of the school day.

4. Remedial help of any kind was much rarer in smaller than large schools.

5. A high percentage of large (81 per cent) and middle-sized schools (53 per cent) segregated their slower pupils in a special class. One in five of schools using *Non-Streaming* and a half of those grouping *According to Age* (middle-sized schools) formed remedial classes, even though they did not separate their other ability levels.

6. Slower pupils in small schools were not segregated, although some were "kept down" with a class of younger pupils (35 per cent of small schools used this method).

7. NEW TRENDS IN JUNIOR SCHOOL ORGANIZATION

1. The major types of organization being introduced in junior schools were non-streaming (19 per cent), grouping by age (12 per cent), group teaching (15 per cent), and individual teaching (10 per cent).

2. Nineteen per cent of schools at present using *Homogeneous Streaming* intended to introduce *Non-Streaming* or to extend it beyond the first year.

3. Thirty-six per cent of schools using non-streaming "streamed" their fourth year pupils, but 24 per cent intended to change this and unstream them.

4. The main advantages claimed for non-streaming were: pupils more socially adjusted (51 per cent); pupils not labelled A, B, C (27 per cent); wide ability range (22 per cent); contented staff/easier for staff (23 per cent).

5. The main advantages claimed for *Homogeneous Streaming* were: easier for the staff/contented staff (23 per cent); smaller ability range in the class (19 per cent); more attention to the backward (22 per cent); meets the needs of the child (19 per cent); and higher standard of attainment (18 per cent).

6. Advantages claimed by schools using *Vertical Streaming* were similar to those of schools using *Homogeneous Streaming*.

7. Advantages claimed for grouping *According to Age* in middle-sized schools were similar to those claimed for non-streaming (see above).

8. Advantages given by/for small schools represent advantages resulting from being in a small school, rather than from particular types of organization. The main advantages claimed were: more individual attention; child's needs met; happy family atmosphere.

9. Special difficulties encountered by head teachers were: mainly inadequate number of staff; large classes; inadequate accommodation; too wide ability range and age-range within the class.

Over 50 per cent of head teachers mentioned some special difficulty. Middle-sized schools mentioned the shortage of staff more often than other schools.

8. SOME GENERAL FINDINGS OF THE SURVEY

1. *Qualified and unqualified staff*
Seventy-one per cent of all schools were entirely staffed by qualified teachers. The larger schools were more likely to have an unqualified teacher. Schools using *Homogeneous Streaming* and *Non-Streaming* were equally well staffed.

2. *Staff Turnover*
This was related to the size of the school but not to the type of school organization.

3. *Accommodation*
Large schools had better facilities; they were more likely to have a room for the head, a staff room and a school hall. Schools using *Vertical Streaming* were more likely to have a spare classroom than schools using any other type of organization.

4. *Schools of Different Socio-Economic Categories*
Schools classified as *middle class* or *upper working class* were compared with those classified as *middle or lower working class*.

It was found that the latter group tended to be worse off in terms of number of unqualified staff and turnover of staff. Their heads spent more time teaching. Also they were less well provided with accommodation—however, these schools tended to be small in size, which would explain this finding.

The socio-economic categories were based upon the head's subjective estimate and the above findings must be interpreted with caution.

PART II

The Effects of Streaming and Non-Streaming in Junior Schools

SECTION 1

INTRODUCTION

1.1 *The aims of the investigation*
The inquiry was initiated at the request of the Department of Education and Science and was designed to study the effects of streaming and non-streaming in junior schools.

The aim of the project is to provide evidence concerning the ways in which children are assigned to different classes, and grouped within their classes, in both streamed and non-streamed schools; the attitudes of teachers towards these various forms of organization, the methods of teaching they employ and the facilities with which they are provided; and, finally, the effects of different methods of grouping and treatment on the attainments, personalties and social adjustment of the pupils concerned.

To this end, the inquiry has been undertaken at three levels:

1. A broad survey of grouping practices in a nationally representative sample of junior schools.
2. A comparative study of 50 matched pairs of streamed and non-streamed junior schools.
3. An intensive study carried out in 10 junior schools.

1.2 *Caution*

A report of the survey of practices in junior schools was completed and sub-mitted to the Plowden Committee earlier in the year.[1] The study of 100 schools (50 matched pairs of streamed and non-streamed junior schools) falls into two parts: a longitudinal study of pupils over four years and a cross-sectional study which enables certain preliminary comparisons to be made between the two types of organization based upon samples of children, at present in different years of their course. It is this cross-sectional study with which this Report is concerned. The longitudinal inquiry, which should yield more reliable information concerning the effects of the contrasting forms of organization, cannot, of course, be completed until the four years, planned for the follow-through, have elapsed.

In interpreting what follows, it should be remembered that all the findings are based upon cross-sectional data and that this kind of information has certain disadvantages. The most notable of these is that inferences about the growth of children based upon two groups, tested at the same time, but differing in age, are less reliable than inferences about the same group of children tested or examined at intervals. One cannot, in fact, legitimately generalize from one year-group to another and assume that, because the 10-year-olds of the present sample behaved in certain ways, the seven-year-olds will resemble them closely three years from now. Nor, in cross-sectional samples can conclusions be drawn about the direct effects of a change in organization or in placement, particularly as this may affect children of initially different levels of ability. It is hoped that the follow-through studies will enable firmer conclusions to be drawn in these respects.

A further limitation should be noted. Not all the data from the cross-sectional study could be analysed in time and a number of important questions—the answers to which might well qualify some of the statements made—have had to be left aside for the present. Where this is so, and where it is reasonable to suppose that subsequent analysis may throw a new or different light upon the interpretation of the factual data given, this is pointed out in the text.

Finally, it should be emphasized that the question—to stream or not to stream?—reveals itself, as the research continues—to require a far more complex and nuanced answer than the propagandists on both sides would have one believe.

1.3 *The sample of 100 schools*

As a result of the major survey, details of a large number of streamed schools and of 43 non-streamed schools were available. To increase the size of the non-streamed sample of schools, the Foundation wrote to all local education authorities in England and Wales, asking for addresses of all non-streamed schools. These schools were invited to complete a questionnaire and on the basis of the information thus provided, a further 55 non-streamed schools were selected.

Each of the non-streamed schools was then matched with the most similar streamed school which could be found, using the following criteria for match-ing:

(a) Type of school: junior or junior-with-infants; urban or rural.

(b) Number of classes in the school.

---

[1] Part I pp. 544-554

(c) Average number of pupils per class.

(d) Geographical region.

(e) Percentage of children in L.E.A. attending non-selective schools.

(f) Predominant socio-economic class of parents.

(g) Approximate matching of percentage of parents in professional, clerical and skilled occupations.

All the schools were non-denominational and all were situated in England. In this way, a sample of 100 schools was obtained. Further details of the procedure employed for matching the pairs can be found in Annex 1.

1.4 *Exploratory Research*

One aim of the inquiry is to discover whether children tend to reach higher levels of achievement in the basic school subjects under one system than under the other. For this purpose, tests of attainment are, of course, appropriate. Another stated aim is to examine the effects of streaming and non-streaming on children's personality characteristics and social adjustment. In these areas, however, the choice of suitable measuring instruments depends on the identification of modes of behaviour that are both relevant and susceptible to reasonably objective appraisal. For example, there are references in the literature to concepts such as "the atmosphere of the school". Clearly such a concept needs to be defined in operational terms before any meaningful assessment could be undertaken. Furthermore, it is reasonable to suppose that some of the outcomes of streaming or non-streaming depend not so much on the forms of organization *per se* as on the attitudes and practices of the teachers who operate within them.

For these reasons it was felt essential to carry out exploratory research, in order to discover which aspects of the school, teacher, and pupil could and should be given particular attention in the 100 schools study.

The exploratory research involved six streamed and six non-streamed schools (not included in the 100 schools sample) and consisted of interviews with the heads and staff, and visits to classes. The staff who were interviewed were selected so that the sample included both men and women, with varying amounts of experience and teachers of different year-groups and different streams. Thirty-one interviews were carried out—each lasting about one hour. These interviews were unstructured, so that the teachers could express their views freely, as well as explain their methods of teaching. Each interview was taped and later transcribed.

1.5 *The significance of "traditional" and "progressive" teaching methods and attitudes*

The interviews and the visits to schools suggested that teachers in streamed schools differed from those in non-streamed schools, both in their teaching methods and in their attitudes.

It also became clear that these differences between teachers in their methods and attitudes might possibly outweigh the effects of streaming or non-streaming *per se.* A good deal of attention was therefore given to the construction of questionnaires to assess the method of teaching and the attitudes of the teachers. These questionnaires were based upon the activities described and the opinions offered in the interviews. (See Section 2 for further details of Questionnaires S.1 and S.3.)

1.6 *Hypotheses*
On the basis of the interviews and visits, a number of hypotheses were formulated, some for testing in the cross-sectional study and others in the longitudinal study. Outlined below, are those hypotheses tested in the cross-sectional study and discussed in this Report. Indicated beside each hypothesis is the number of the section in which it is discussed.

(*a*) Streaming and non-streaming may have different effects on children's attainments. (Section 3.)

(*b*) Pupils' attainments may be affected by the methods of teaching used, irrespective of the type of organization chosen by the school. (Section 3.)

(*c*) Pupils' attainments and social behaviour may be influenced by teachers' attitudes. (Section 4.)

1.7 *Number of schools/teachers/pupils involved in the cross-sectional study*
Although the project started with 100 schools, for various reasons certain schools had to be excluded, so that data from only 84 schools, 42 streamed, 42 non-streamed, were analysed in the cross-sectional study. Details of the 42 matched pairs of schools can be found in Annex 1.

Eight hundred and seventy-one teachers and approximately 30,000 junior pupils were involved in the cross-sectional study.

SECTION 2

THE CHARACTERISTICS AND ATTITUDES OF TEACHERS IN STREAMED AND NON-STREAMED SCHOOLS

2.1 *Introduction*
It will be recalled that the two samples of 50 schools were matched as far as possible for their principal characteristics—size, socio-economic status, geographical location, and so on—and were differentiated by their choice of internal organization, into streamed and non-streamed schools. The interviews and visits carried out, as exploratory research, suggested that this difference in organization was reflected in, or arose from, very different views held by the teaching staff which in turn affected the choice of teaching methods.

From the material recorded at the interviews therefore, three questionnaires were devised to enable this hypothesis to be tested in some depth.

2.2 *Information supplied by class teachers*
The first of these questionnaires was concerned with biographical information, sex, age, experience and training.

The second was concerned with more or less objective information about the methods of teaching used and the ways in which children were organized for learning. It fell into three sections:

(*a*) A section dealing with the classroom facilities as perceived by the teachers. This yielded a composite "facilities" score.

(b) A section in which teachers were asked to indicate how often they used various types of lesson, for example—"formal sums". From the responses made, two scores were derived: a "traditional lessons" score, indicating how often the teacher used lessons of the more "traditional" type and a complementary "progressive lessons" score. Each of these scores was studied by the method of item analysis, in order to eliminate items (i.e. types of lesson) which were not correlated with the total score. The final versions contained the following items:

"Traditional"—writing class-prepared compositions; learning lists of spellings; formal grammar—understanding parts of speech; saying and learning tables by rote.

"Progressive"—projects—in which the child does his own "research"; pupils working or helping each other in groups; practical arithmetic, e.g. measuring, apparatus work; free activities.

(c) A section on the use of class teaching, mixed ability group teaching and ability grouping within the class.

The third questionnaire was used to study teachers' attitudes. It took the form of a number of statements of opinion, which had actually been made by other teachers in interviews. Each teacher was asked to indicate his degree of agreement or disagreement with each statement, using a five-point scale ranging from "strongly agree" to "strongly disagree". The questionnaire contained six sub-sections, and each teacher's responses could be scored separately on each section. (The items which were included in the attitude scales had been selected by Guttman's method of scalogram analysis. A table of reproducibility coefficients is given in Annex 3.[1]) These six sub-sections were: "Permissive"/"Obsessional"; attitude towards physical punishment: attitude towards eleven-plus selection; attitude towards noise in the classroom; attitude towards streaming; attitude towards A-stream children.

2.3 *A comparison of Streamed and Non-streamed schools*

Although, of course, few teachers or schools conformed to a clear-cut average, the analysis of the data revealed a considerable degree of polarity between the two types in terms of the age and experience of the teachers, the methods they chose to use and their perception of the facilities available to them. Table I on the following page brings this out clearly, indicating that, with one exception, all the differences found are statistically significant and (where this is appropriate) point in the same direction. The climate in the unstreamed school—if we are to judge by what its teachers say about themselves, their methods and their attitudes—is more permissive and tolerant, less structured and places less emphasis on the more traditional methods of class-teaching than its streamed counterpart. Since, moreover, all the traits studied proved to be intercorrelated positively, this suggests that they are something more than an arbitrary collection of more or less discreet and separate characteristics; that they do represent a coherent pair of opposing syndromes, likely, if they are at all intense in any one school, profoundly to affect the pupils exposed to them.

---

[1] For further details, see STOUFFER, S. A., GUTTMAN, L., *et al. Measurement and Prediction*, Princeton, N.J., 1950.

Table I
Differences Between Streamed and Non-Streamed Schools

	Teachers in streamed schools	Teachers in non-streamed schools	
Age of teacher	Teachers older (Mean = 39·94)	Teachers younger (Mean = 35·55)	$\chi^2 = 37·16$ df = 8 $p < 0·001$ Difference significant
Class facilities: Scores range from 4 (good) to 20 (poor)	Class facilities poorer (Mean = 9·62)	Class facilities better (Mean = 8·67)	$\chi^2 = 49·76$ df = 8 $p < 0·001$ Difference significant
Frequency of formal sums	More frequent	Less frequent	$\chi^2 = 22·12$ df = 5 $p < 0·001$ Difference significant
Frequency of problem sums	More frequent	Less frequent	Not significant
Frequency of practical arithmetic	Less frequent	More frequent	$\chi^2 = 69·52$ df = 5 $p < 0·001$ Difference significant
Frequency of tests in arithmetic or any other subject	More frequent	Less frequent	$\chi^2 = 34·16$ df = 5 $p < 0·001$ Difference significant
Traditional scale: Scores range from 24 (traditional) to 4 (non-traditional)	Traditional	Non-traditional	$\chi^2 = 75·08$ df = 9 $p < 0·001$ Difference significant
Progressive scale: Scores from 4 (progressive) to 24 (non-progressive)	Non-progressive	Progressive	$\chi^2 = 105·72$ df = 8 $p < 0·001$ Difference significant
"Permissive" versus "obsessional" attitude to children's behaviour: Six-point Guttman scale	"Obsessional" attitude	"Permissive" attitude	$\chi^2 = 28·20$ df = 5 $p < 0·001$ Difference significant
Attitude to physical punishment: Seven-point Guttman scale	Pro physical	Anti physical	$\chi^2 = 31·32$ df = 6 $p < 0·001$ Difference significant

continued on next page

Table I — Differences Between Streamed and Non-Streamed Schools — continued

	Teachers in streamed schools	Teachers in non-streamed schools	
Attitude to talking and noise in the classroom:			
Six-point Guttman scale	Low tolerance of noise	High tolerance of noise	$\chi^2 = 49.56$ df $= 5$ $p < 0.001$ Difference significant
Attitude to A-stream/A-children:			
Six-point Guttman scale	Pro A-stream children	Anti A-stream children	$\chi^2 = 89.04$ df $= 5$ $p < 0.001$ Difference significant
Attitude to eleven-plus selection:			
Six-point Guttman scale	Pro 11-plus	Anti 11-plus	$\chi^2 = 64.16$ df $= 6$ $p < 0.001$ Difference significant
Attitude to streaming:			
Eight-point Guttman scale	Believe in streaming	Do not believe in streaming	$\chi^2 = 255.16$ df $= 5$ $p < 0.001$ Difference significant

It must be emphasized, however, that these (Table I) are central tendencies and some elucidatory comment is perhaps required.

2.4 *Age and Experience of Teachers in the Two Types of School*

In general, a higher proportion of the teachers in non-streamed schools tend to be younger and to have less experience than those in streamed schools.

Table II

Age Distribution of Teachers in Streamed and Non-Streamed Schools

	Streamed			Non-Streamed		
	Top quartile	Median	Bottom quartile	Top quartile	Median	Bottom quartile
Age of teacher	49·6	39·3	29·2	44·4	32·7	26·0

Table II shows that a quarter of the teachers in non-streamed schools are aged 26 or below, whilst a quarter of those in streamed schools are verging on their fifties or are older. However, the overlap in age and experience is in fact greater than the difference.

As a group, younger teachers tended to have more "progressive" opinions, particularly in their rejection of eleven-plus selection, their "permissiveness" and their "tolerance of noise". Those with two years' experience or less were the most hostile to 11-plus.

2.5 *Class Facilities*

According to the teachers, the facilities (good lighting, new desks, little outside distraction, plenty of space, etc.) in the unstreamed schools were better. It should be emphasized that this reflects what the teachers thought about what they had, and is not derived from a strictly objective comparison; but there is no reason to suppose that the non-streamed schools were not in fact superior in this respect.

2.6 *Teaching Methods*

Teachers in streamed schools, on average, tended to make more frequent use of "traditional lessons" and less frequent use of "progressive lessons" than teachers in non-streamed schools. But the greater frequency of "traditional lessons" (streamed schools) was in fact more true for teachers of seven-plus children than for teachers of the 10-year-olds, not surprisingly when one considers the meaning of "traditional lessons" at the different ages.

"Traditional lessons" could be defined as learning the basic skills in a formal way—an activity considered important for seven-year-olds even by "permissive" teachers (there was no correlation between use of "traditional lessons" and attitudes for the teachers of seven-year-olds). But by the time a child reaches the fourth year of the junior school, fewer teachers believe in the necessity for daily recitation of tables or practice in formal sums. The teacher who did use "traditional lessons" at 10-plus, tended also to be "obsessional" in outlook[1] (the correlation between the use of "traditional lessons" and the "permissive"/"obsessional" scale was 0·327).

[1] For the meaning of this, see Section 2.7 and Annex 3.

The greater frequency of "progressive lessons"[1] in non-streamed schools was in fact more striking in the case of teachers of 10 year old children than in that of teachers of seven-year-olds. The use of "progressive lessons" also was found to be correlated with the teacher's "permissiveness" in fourth year classes, but less so in the earlier years. One possible explanation for the low correlation between teacher attitude and use of "progressive lessons" at seven-plus is that use of apparatus (e.g. Dienes, Cuisenaire) and consequent group work is becoming increasingly common with these year groups and is introduced by the school rather than being chosen by the individual class teacher. Lessons in formal sums (i.e. mechanical computation) and arithmetic tests and other tests were more frequent in streamed schools whereas practical arithmetic, in general, and the use of apparatus, were more common in non-streamed schools.

In the streamed schools, perhaps in accordance with their greater emphasis on structuring experiences, on teaching children in specific ways and upon the more traditionally systematic and formal approach, significantly more use was made of tests of various kinds to check progress and diagnose difficulties. The only aspect of method studied which did not yield a statistically significant difference was that concerning the use of sums in problem arithmetic. It is possible that differently organized schools are in fact similar in this respect; alternatively the test itself may not have been sufficiently discriminative to detect any difference which might exist.

Table I has shown the difference between schools over all year groups; while Table III, on the next page, shows the frequency of different types of arithmetic lessons at *seven-plus* and at *10-plus*. Note that there are no significant differences in the frequency of problem sums at seven-plus or formal sums at 10-plus.

---

[1] For the "progressive lessons" scale, see paragraph 2.2.

Table III

Frequency of Tests and of Different Types of Arithmetic Lesson in Streamed and Non-Streamed Schools

At seven-plus	Formal sums		Problem sums		Practical arithmetic		Tests in arithmetic or any other subject	
	Streamed	Non-streamed	Streamed	Non-streamed	Streamed	Non-streamed	Streamed	Non-streamed
Every day	54%	46%	27%	31%	10%	28%	—	1%
Every two–three days	36%	28%	38%	35%	22%	20%	2%	1%
Once a week	8%	12%	26%	18%	31%	25%	32%	29%
Less than once a week, but at least once a month	2%	6%	8%	6%	24%	19%	35%	27%
Less than once a month, but at least once a term	—	3%	≠	5%	8%	6%	26%	31%
Less than once a term—or never	—	5%	≠	5%	4%	1%	5%	11%
	100%	100%	100%	100%	100%	100%	100%	100%
Base	107	102	106	103	107	103	106	103
Chi-square test	$\chi^2 = 12 \cdot 66$ df = 5 $p < 0 \cdot 05$		$\chi^2 = 7 \cdot 32$ df = 5 p lies between 0·20 and 0·10		$\chi^2 = 12 \cdot 24$ df = 5 $p < \cdot 05$		$\chi^2 = 51 \cdot 04$ df = 5 $p < \cdot 001$	
Inference	Significant at 5% level. Non-streamed schools have formal sums less frequently.		Not significant. No difference in the frequency of problem sums.		Significant at 5% level. Non-streamed schools have practical arithmetic more frequently.		Significant at 0·01% level. Non-streamed schools have tests less frequently.	

continued on next page

Table III—Frequency of Tests and of Different Types of Arithmetic Lesson in Streamed and Non-Streamed Schools—continued

At ten-plus	Formal sums		Problem sums		Practical arithmetic		Tests in arithmetic or any other subject	
	Streamed	Non-streamed	Streamed	Non-streamed	Streamed	Non-streamed	Streamed	Non-streamed
Every day	46%	30%	37%	36%	2%	10%	2%	3%
Every two–three days	33%	51%	42%	54%	12%	28%	3%	2%
Once a week	11%	12%	17%	4%	35%	24%	39%	32%
Less than once a week, but at least once a month	6%	4%	2%	4%	28%	26%	36%	22%
Less than once a month, but at least once a term	2%	2%	—	—	12%	8%	17%	35%
Less than once a term—or never	3%	1%	2%	2%	10%	4%	3%	6%
	100%	100%	100%	100%	100%	100%	100%	100%
Base	107	107	108	106	108	103	107	108
Chi-square test	$\chi^2 = 9.45$ df = 5 p lies between 0·10 and 0·05		$\chi^2 = 12.12$ df = 5 p < 0·05		$\chi^2 = 19.27$ df = 5 p < 0·01		$\chi^2 = 24.67$ df = 5 p < 0·001	
Inference	Not significant. No difference in the frequency of formal sums.		Significant at 5% level. Non-streamed schools have problem sums more frequently.		Significant at 1% level. Non-streamed schools have practical arithmetic more frequently.		Significant at ·01% level. Non-streamed schools have tests less frequently.	

Note: ≠ Less than 0·5 per cent

The general differences between the two types of school are summed up in the composite score on the two complementary "traditional" and "progressive" scales. How these are distributed is shown in Table IV which sets out the medians and quartiles of the two groups.

Table IV

Traditional and Progressive Scores of Teachers in Streamed and Non-Streamed Schools

	Streamed			Non-streamed		
	Top quartile	Median	Bottom quartile	Top quartile	Median	Bottom quartile
Traditional	17·4	15·4	12·8	15·6	13·3	10·6
Progressive	17·3	14·9	12·5	15·3	12·4	9·5

It should be noted that, on both scales, scores range from four to 24 and that the medians are considerably nearer the "traditional" and "non-progressive" ends of the scale. In terms, therefore, of the views expressed, teachers in both types of school are fairly "traditional"; the difficulties between them would seem to be nuances rather than marked divergences of opinion.

2.7 *Attitudes of Teachers in Streamed and Non-Streamed Schools*

The exploratory research indicated a number of fundamental attitude areas that are relevant in this inquiry. Each area could be represented as a dimension along which teachers could be placed according to the degree to which they manifest the attitude. Six attitude areas were investigated, namely:
(a) "Permissive"/"Obsessional"
(b) Attitude towards physical punishment
(c) Attitude towards noise in the classroom
(d) Attitude towards A-stream children
(e) Attitude towards 11-plus selection
(f) Attitude towards streaming.
The titles of the scales are self-explanatory, with the possible exceptions of (a) and (d); of which more details are given below. It will be noticed, too, that three of these attitudes are of a fairly specific kind and may give some indication of the way in which teachers are likely to react to their pupils and of the kind of climate they will create in the classroom (a, b, and c scales). The remaining three concern views of a socio-political nature and may be said to form a part of a more general system of values.

(a) *"Permissive" versus "Obsessional"*

This scale was intended to rank teachers in terms of the "permissiveness" of their attitudes towards junior school children. The labels "permissive" and "obsessional" must not, of course, be interpreted literally. It is convenient to use some title to describe those teachers who were most prone to object to children fidgeting, to demand clean hands and good manners; the teachers who rated the three Rs more highly than "self-expression" and vice-versa.

There was a tendency (highly significant statistically) for teachers in non-streamed schools to be more "permissive" in this sense than those in streamed schools. For the content of this scale, see Annex 3, Items 6, 14, 17, 20, 23.

Graph No. 1

Permissiveness

Item 20. Naturalness is more important than good manners. (Extreme group.)
31·33 per cent N.S. agree
82·4 per cent S. disagree

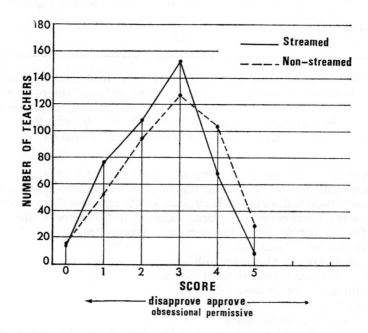

It will be seen from the graphs that the distribution of the scores for the two groups of teachers is very similar, and in fact, the modal statement was the same. The difference arises from a group of teachers in non-streamed schools who hold firm views towards the extreme of the scale. The statement which most clearly differentiates the streamers from the non-streamers is quoted above the graph.

(b) *Attitudes towards physical punishment*

There was, too, a similar tendency ($p < 0.001$) for teachers in non-streamed schools to show disapproval of physical punishment and in streamed schools to show approval. The items forming this scale can be found in Annex 3 (items: 4, 11, 13, 22, 25, 30).

Graph No. 2

Attitude to Physical Punishment

Item 11. Physical punishment does no good at all to any child. (Extreme group)
24 per cent N.S. agree
88 per cent S. disagree (i.e. 12 per cent agree)

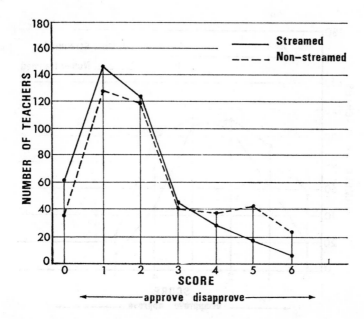

It will be seen from the graph that, as with "permissiveness", the difference arises principally from a small group in the non-streamed schools who have extreme scores on the scale. The statement most clearly differentiating the two groups is that concerning physical punishment in general.

(c) *Attitudes towards noise in the classroom*

The differences between teachers in streamed and non-streamed schools were highly significant ($p < 0.001$). Teachers in non-streamed schools were tolerant of noise (Annex 3 Items: 2, 7, 18, 27, 31) and in streamed schools less tolerant.

Graph No. 3

Attitude to Noise

Item 31. A quiet atmosphere is the one best suited to all school work.
56 per cent N.S. disagree
62 per cent S. agree (i.e. 38 per cent disagree)

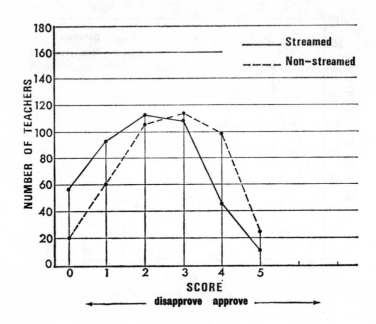

Graph No. 3 shows a clear displacement of scores of the teachers in non-streamed schools towards one end of the scale with differences on most of the statements.

The three more general attitude scales also differentiate between teachers in the two types of school, and if indeed they reflect strongly held views, may deeply influence pupil-teacher relationships.

(d) *Attitude towards A-stream children*

On this scale individuals rank themselves in terms of attitudes towards children in A-streams. It contained items suggesting that A-stream children worry about marks, tend to become conceited, etc. (see Annex 3, Items: 3, 5, 8, 10, 26). Teachers in streamed schools had a more favourable attitude to A-stream children—presumably believing in the value of A-streams for bright children—than teachers in non-streamed schools. The difference was significant ($p < 0.001$).

Graph No. 4

Attitudes to A-stream Children

Item 5. Children in A-streams tend to become conceited about their abilities. (Most discriminating statement.)
69 per cent N.S. agree
59 per cent S. disagree

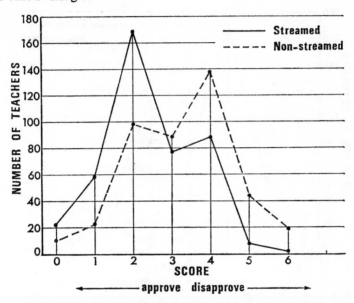

Here the graph shows a rather different distribution with a clearer division of opinion—certainly among substantial groups of teachers in the two types of school. The most discriminating statement is, it will be noted, concerned with the attitude attributed to children.

(e) *Attitudes towards 11-plus selection*

Teachers in non-streamed schools tended to disapprove of selection, while teachers in streamed schools tended to approve. The difference was highly significant statistically ($p < 0.001$). (See Annex 3, Items: 9, 12, 16, 21, 29).

Graph No. 5

Attitude to the 11-plus

Item 11. The 11-plus examination is an entirely fair method of assessing a child's abilities. (Most discriminative statement.)

69 per cent N.S. disagree

56 per cent S. agree

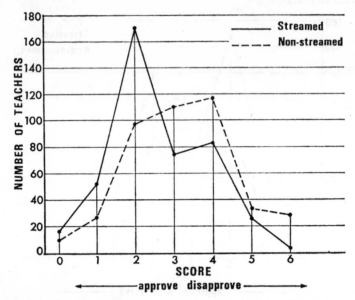

There seems to be a considerable spread of opinion in both groups about this with, however, the bulk of teachers in non-streamed schools further towards one extreme than their colleagues. Two points are worthy of note: that the most discriminating statement concerns the justice of the 11-plus; and that substantial proportions of teachers in both groups are opposed to the system.

(f) *Attitudes towards Streaming*

In many ways this attitude scale is the most important for this research project. If a class teacher does not share the beliefs of his head teacher about the advantages of streaming or non-streaming, it is possible that these advantages will not be realized. This scale can be used as a means of identifying teachers who are committed to one point of view or the other. It has been found that in streamed schools there are some teachers who favour non-streaming, and in non-streamed schools there are some teachers who favour streaming, and in both types of school there are teachers who are uncommitted either way. However, the average differences between teachers in streamed and non-streamed schools were highly significant ($p < 0.001$).

The attitudes of teachers towards streaming were studied in greater detail in order to discover the extent of teachers' agreement with their school's policy. As a first step the attitude scores were used to categorize the teachers into three groups ("pro-streaming", "neutral" and "anti-streaming") according to Guttman's method of intensity analysis.[1]

---

[1] GUTTMAN, L. and SUCHMAN, E. A., Intensity and a zero point for attitude analysis, *American Social Review*, **12**, 57. 1947.

Table V, below, shows the proportion of teachers in each attitude category.

Table V
Attitudes of teachers according to type of school organization

	Pro-streaming	Neutral	Anti-streaming	Total	Base
In streamed schools	45%	45%	10%	100%	422
In non-streamed schools	13%	35%	52%	100%	420

The first point to be noted is that substantial proportions of teachers are in favour of streaming. Since of all junior schools in the country which are large enough to do so, at least 65 per cent stream and only 11 per cent clearly do not,[1] it seems reasonable to suppose that the majority of junior school teachers in England and Wales are in favour of the practice, that a substantial proportion are undecided, and that only relatively few are firmly committed to the opposing view. This finding must be stressed at a time when some writers suggest that the death knell of streaming has already sounded. Coupled with the finding concerning parents' views, reported later in this report (Section 6), it suggests that any universal change recommended may meet with considerable opposition—particularly since the attitudes for or against streaming seem to form part of a whole syndrome of views, practices and beliefs.

An examination of Table V also suggests that on the average, there appears to be one teacher in each school whose views are in conflict with the policy of the school. This, however, is rather misleading. A more detailed analysis revealed that in a few schools less than half the staff were in agreement with the head's policy, while in others all were in accord. Similarly, there were differences (discussed in Section 5) in the views of A, B, C and D-stream teachers.

[1] See Part I, page 550.

T

Graph No. 6

Attitudes to Streaming

Item 24. The bright child will be neglected in non-streamed classes.
74 per cent N.S. disagree
79 per cent S. agree

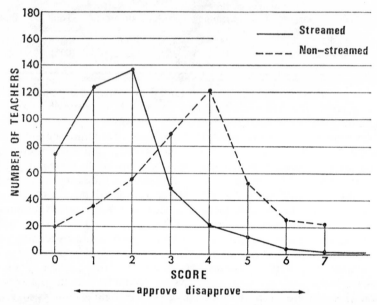

This graph reveals a pattern of response most clearly differentiating the two groups of teachers. Whereas in both groups (as Table V showed more clearly) there are those whose opinions are contrary to the practice of their school, in each the majority seem to adhere to the appropriate norm. The most discriminating statement, significantly, is the one which touches on the fate of the bright child in a non-streamed school. A clear majority of teachers in streamed schools agree that such a child will be neglected; a comparable majority in non-streamed schools oppose this view.

2.8 *Streamed and Non-streamed schools embody different philosophies*

It seems apparent from the foregoing that schools using streaming or non-streaming do not merely differ in their organization: and indeed that the strictly organizational aspects may be the least important in their bearing upon the development of the pupils. The streamed school seems to be more systematic in its approach, concentrates more on conventional lessons, gives more attention to the 3 Rs and is likely to be more "traditional" and at least overtly more authoritarian. Its staff is likely to be somewhat more experienced and older, to approve of bright children, of 11-plus selection and of streaming as a means of adapting to individual differences. The unstreamed school presents an apparent contrast. Its younger teachers hold more "permissive" views on such things as noise, cleanliness and manners; they disapprove of physical punishment and of the differentiation implicit in streaming and in the 11-plus procedures. Their teaching tends to place more emphasis on self-expression, learning by discovery and practical experience. In short, the aims and practices of the two kinds of school seem to embody different views about children and different philosophies of education.

In practice, however, the contrast is probably not so marked as this dichotomy may seem to imply, although, of course, specific schools, where staff and head share very firm convictions, may represent quite thorough-going, even doctrinaire, embodiments of these contrasting approaches. In view, however, of the frequency of streaming in junior schools, it is clear that it is the non-streamed school which, in the statistical sense at least, is deviant. It would also appear that the staffs of non-streamed schools are slightly more in agreement with each other than with the rest of their colleagues. How far this is due to teachers choosing non-streamed schools on account of their views and how far it is due to the influence of the school and the head, it is difficult to say. It seems possible that some of the heads of non-streamed schools, because they are using a new and fashionable method, have been accorded special treatment by their L.E.A. and allowed to select teachers in accordance with their own viewpoint.

Many of the questions raised by this part of the study can be answered only by further analysis and the collection of additional data. One thing is, however, clear and should be kept in mind with regard to Section 3. Any effect which may be shown to be associated with streaming or non-streaming is unlikely to be purely and simply due to the form of organization used. Teaching method, the ideas which underly disciplinary systems, the views about children held by their teachers—in short the whole climate of relationships built up by what teachers say and do and what they appear to their pupils to imply, may well be the critical factors. The comparisons which follow will show the broad differences associated with contrasting types of general attitude and consequent organization. In many schools of both types, however, there are teachers whose views and at least some of whose practices, are in conflict with those of their colleagues. One might expect the influence of such teachers to attenuate any differences that might result from the differences in organization. The extent and nature of this it will only be possible to elucidate in the later comparisons.

SECTION 3

COMPARISON OF ATTAINMENTS IN STREAMED AND NON-STREAMED SCHOOLS

3.1 *The difficulty of finding tests which favour neither type of organization*
Tests of reading, English, mechanical arithmetic and problem arithmetic were given to the pupils in all four junior years in the cross-sectional study. Each test was devised to be suitable for all ages from seven-plus to 10-plus, so that in the longitudinal study, measures of gain in achievement could be made. These tests were specially produced for this project by the test service of the NFER, and their content was of the kind usually demanded for juniors by teachers and education authorities. As was pointed out earlier, however (paragraph 2.7), the teaching methods and the aims of the streamed schools are typical of the majority, whereas non-streamed schools in which teachers held different views are in the minority: hence, the tests used in the cross-

sectional study probably reflect the majority view of teachers. In this sense, they can legitimately be held to be biased against the non-streamed schools, in that they favour outcomes of methods of teaching to which less attention is paid in these schools, and do not include measures of some of the objectives which many non-streamed schools consider to be of great importance. On the other hand, it might reasonably be argued that the bias implicit in the tests is a correct one. On this we hold no views, the important point to make here being that the comparison, *at this stage*, is in terms of the norms and objectives of the majority of teachers. Comparisons have yet to be made on the basis of how far other aims and objectives proposed by the non-streamers are attained.

3.2 *The tests*

Of the four attainment tests used, the most impartial was probably the reading test. Both types of school share the aim of teaching children to read with understanding and, within its limitations, the test gives an accurate measure of how far this has been achieved. The test does not, of course, give a measure of the use and enjoyment of reading, nor can the inquiry furnish evidence of this at the present stage.

The test of English is rather more "biased". It consists principally of tests of comprehension, probably important in themselves for both groups, but on which children who have had some formal practice and teaching are likely to have at least a marginal advantage. Also included in the test are some items based on formal grammar (parts of speech, punctuation) which would favour those pupils whose teachers scored highly on the "traditional lessons" scale— and such teachers were more common in streamed schools.

The two tests of arithmetic are somewhat different from each other. One was concerned with problem arithmetic and since this was that aspect of teaching which did not differentiate between the two kinds of school and teacher, it is reasonable to assume that any bias was probably slight. The test of mechanical arithmetic is another matter. Table I indicates that, over all year groups, daily practice in formal sums was more common in the streamed schools, and one would expect that this would result in a greater facility in this test. Any differences found here then might perhaps be ascribed to the teaching method used rather than to the form of organization as such. (See Footnote on following page.)

In addition to the attainment tests, two measures of ability were used: the NFER Primary Verbal Test I was given to children in the second, third and fourth years; and a Verbal/Non-verbal test, yielding two separate scores was given to fourth year children.[1] This latter test was the one used in 1957 in the Population Investigation Committee Follow-up Study (Douglas, J. W. B., *The Home and the School*.)

Finally, it should be stated that two parallel versions of the attainment tests were used. A random half of the schools worked the A version and the other half the B ones. This has the advantage that, in effect, two independent studies were carried out simultaneously and each acted as a check upon the other.

3.3 *The results of the Attainment testing*

The overall results of the attainment testing suggest that, on the various outcomes measured, pupils in streamed schools performed better than their

---

[1] Budgetary considerations forbade the use of this test for the younger age groups.

counterparts in non-streamed schools. Most of the differences found were statistically significant.

Few of the differences, however, were large; most amounted to less than one-third of a standard deviation and only those derived from the mechanical arithmetic score approached or surpassed half a standard deviation. In effect, what these differences mean is that, on the average, the streamed group got two or three more answers right in tests having 30 or 40 items in them. Some would consider this a small price to pay for non-streaming, if other educational and personal advantages were obtained.

Attention should also be drawn to another feature of the score distributions. In attempting to interpret, in educational terms, statistically significant differences in mean scores, one must ask whether the higher or lower marks were spread similarly in the compared groups or whether the difference is due mainly to a larger proportion in one or other group, obtaining higher or lower marks. The standard deviation of the test scores showed that in streamed schools there was less homogeneity in performance and that more children in these schools were getting higher marks. There was little difference in the percentage of children scoring low marks in the two groups of schools. The most likely interpretation of this seems to be that the most able children in the streamed schools, score more highly than do their counterparts in the un-streamed ones. This may or may not be true, however, the longitudinal study should provide more reliable evidence.

The table which follows below illustrates two other points. It shows the correlations, at the beginning and at the end of the junior school, between the type of organization used by the schools and the results of the four tests of attainment. It will be noticed that, whereas in every case except one the correlations reflect the superiority of the streamed schools in the aspects of attainment measured, there are two gradients of what might be called the intensity of association.

Table VI

Correlation between type of school and test

	Mechanical arithmetic	English	Problem arithmetic	Reading
At seven-plus	0·256	0·139	0·104	0·097
Inference	Significant at 1%. Streamed schools better.	Significant at 1%. Streamed schools better.	Significant at 1%. Streamed schools better.	Significant at 1%. Streamed schools better.
At 10-plus	0·168	0·062	0·081	0·038
Inference	Significant at 1%. Streamed schools better.	Significant at 5%. Streamed schools better.	Significant at 1%. Streamed schools better.	Non-significant. No difference.

[1] The cross-sectional study had to be mounted rapidly and there was not time to devise measures of the less conventional and traditional objectives of primary education. For the longitudinal study, the tests described above are being supplemented by others devised to be more in accord with the aims and philosophy expressed by the non-streamed schools. In particular, a new arithmetic test has been devised to assess children's understanding of mathematical principles and another concerned with creativity, is being constructed to redress somewhat the balance in the measures of attainment in English.

The more the test reflects "traditional" educational practices and emphases, differentiating the two kinds of school, the closer the association is found to be. It is at its highest for mechanical arithmetic and at its lowest for reading. English and problem arithmetic occupy intermediate positions. Secondly, it is apparent that the associations are strongest at seven-plus and weakest at 10-plus. Other workers have found that children taught by "progressive" or "active" methods tend to make a slower start, but catch up with those taught by more "traditional" methods by the end of the primary school.[1], [2]

3.4 Conclusion

In concluding this section, it is necessary to remind ourselves that this Report is concerned with cross-sectional data and that therefore comparisons between successive age groups are of dubious validity. It should be noted that although the two groups of schools were matched as far as possible, one slight difference did emerge. The streamed schools had slightly more pupils from somewhat higher social backgrounds (see Annex 1). Further, the test of verbal ability given to the second, third and fourth year pupils revealed a small superiority in the eight and nine year old children in the streamed schools, though neither this test, nor the verbal/non-verbal test showed any marked difference in the 10-plus groups. The superiority of second and third year children on the verbal ability test in streamed schools could be a result of the school organization, and is not necessarily a cause of the attainment differences found in the two types of school.

Finally, we would draw attention to something which is a feature of the streamed schools and which might have a bearing upon the test results—at least in a marginal way. Table I (Section 2) shows that children in streamed schools were more frequently tested, though not necessarily with standardized tests of the kind used in this study. It is thus possible that they were more "test wise" or at least more habituated to test situations.

These cautions are reiterated to guard against too much emphasis being placed on the results of this part of the inquiry. As they stand they lend small support to the controversialists on either side. They indicate that organizational factors may well mask more important and pervasive influences and that these are perhaps less obscurely to be discerned in the facts reported in Section 2. They also indicate that the effects of teachers' beliefs and attitudes are to be looked for not so much perhaps in differences in formal attainments as in children's beliefs and feelings about themselves and their under-lying attitudes to school and what it stands for.[3] It is not in the nature of cross-sectional evidence to throw much light upon questions such as this, though we may hope that something will emerge from the follow-through study. One point does, however, seem to be clear. A mere change in organization—the abandonment of streaming, for example—unaccompanied by a serious attempt to change teachers' attitudes, beliefs and methods of teaching, is unlikely to make much difference either to attainments or—though this is less certainly based on the present evidence—to the quality of teacher-pupil relationships.

---

[1] MORRIS, J., *Standards and Progress in Reading*, NFER publication (to be published in 1966).

[2] GARDNER, D. E. M., *Testing Results in the Infant School*; *Long term Results of the Infant School*.

[3] Attitudes of children will be measured in the longitudinal study.

The Influence of Teachers' Methods and Attitudes

4.1 Introduction

It has often been suggested that a teacher's effectiveness depends upon his attitudes more than upon his qualifications or even his length of experience. Thus, the individual teacher's attitudes towards streaming may be predicted to have some effect upon his pupils, modifying to some extent the effect of the school's policy of streaming or non-streaming.

This, it would appear from earlier sections, is probably one of the most crucial problems of the whole streaming research. Unfortunately, in the time at our disposal, it has not been possible to go into it as thoroughly as even this cross-sectional data warrants. What follows in this section is a partial examination of the problem. We have been able to examine certain sub-groups of teachers in non-streamed schools and to show some relationship between the teachers' attitudes and their pupils' performances. This section must be regarded as exploratory and is only a "first look" at the data.

Two probes have been made, both based upon contrasting groups of teachers in non-streamed schools. The unstreamed schools were chosen simply because any effects which the views and practices of teachers might have upon the performance and personality variables of their pupils, would not be complicated or concealed by the differences in status of A, B and C-streams. From among the 226 teachers of nine and 10 year old children, in the non-streamed schools, the 28 most convinced supporters of streaming and the 24 most convinced supporters of non-streaming were chosen. Certain of the comparisons which follow (Table VII) are based upon these two groups. It was also possible, since the "obsessive"/"permissive" scale tended to correlate with the streaming/anti-streaming scale, to distinguish two sub-groups within the supporters and opponents of streaming. Eight teachers who strongly favoured streaming were also at the "obsessional" extreme on the appropriate scale, while 13 of the teachers who favoured non-streaming were at the extreme "permissive" end. The comparisons which could be made between the pupils taught by these teachers are shown in Table VII.

Time has not permitted, even with these limited samples, the examination of all the possibly worthwhile questions and what follows is a somewhat arbitrary selection from among those variables which showed statistically significant correlations with teacher attitudes.

It should also be remembered that any relationships found would in any case be small and not very clear-cut, simply because each class had been with its teacher for less than one year. This is not very long for that teacher's influence to modify the effects of home background and previous teaching.

4.2 Some of the effects of teachers' attitudes to streaming

Table VII, on page 579, is based upon the two contrasting groups of teachers of third and fourth year children and upon the results of the attainment tests, a scale of "test anxiety", a sociometric scale dealing with the number of friendless or isolated children in the class and one of the ratings made by the teacher concerned of the number of children considered a pleasure to have in the class. The data dealing with attainments are for the third year only (nine-year-olds) since two analyses could not be done in the time and it would have been meaningless to study nine-and 10-year-olds together on this particular variable. All the other analyses are based upon the nine-and 10-year-olds considered as one group.

So far as attainments are concerned, the results sustain and even reinforce the findings of the broad survey: The scores achieved by the pupils whose teachers are in favour of streaming on mechanical arithmetic and on English are higher than those of the anti-streamers—this is strikingly so in mechanical arithmetic. The pro-streamers in the non-streamed schools made frequent use of "traditional lessons" in contrast to the convinced non-streamers, which suggests that attitudes to streaming are closely related to teachers' preferred types of lesson, rather perhaps than to the particular ethos of the school in which they find themselves. Their use of more formal methods resulted in higher mechanical arithmetic scores although, in fact, their pupils tended to come, on the average, from homes slightly lower on the socio-economic scale, than those in the classes of the non-streamers. The differences in the scores on the English test—which is somewhat less open to the influence of traditional types of teaching—are much smaller and not statistically significant.

In the rest of the table there is the suggestion that the views and methods of the teacher have—in an educational system where differences between the "progressives" and the "traditionalists" may be ideologically considerable without resulting in more than marginal modifications in actual practice—a more marked effect upon the pupils' attitudes to themselves and to their work. The additional analyses of anxiety scores seem to point to this. It was found that the two samples did not match perfectly for socio-economic status and to check whether this might have influenced the results, the scores of girls from socio-economic group 3 (parents in the skilled category) were analysed separately. This confirmed the tendency for girls in classes under a pro-streaming teacher to display more anxiety about being tested than similar girls under an anti-streaming teacher. Girls of below average ability seem to have reacted in a similar fashion under either kind of teacher whereas their more able sisters showed considerably more anxiety under pro-streamers.

We might tentatively sum up this part of the table by saying that it confirms the common view that girls are more anxious than boys (which may account for their higher scores on mechanical arithmetic) and more responsive to nuances in the views and practices of their teachers. The less able girls probably find any kind of test a source of anxiety, but the brighter ones find them more anxiety-provoking with a teacher who believes in competition as a spur. What as yet we do not know from this data is how higher or lower scores on the test anxiety scale are related to higher or lower performances on the various kinds of test—that is whether the anxiety (rather crudely displayed and measured) acts as a spur or an inhibitor.

The last four lines of the table show some apparently slight differences. There seem to be a few more children perceived as "isolates" in the classes of the pro-streamers, a difference of about four per cent in the aggregate. This, however, only seems small until we consider the possibly serious distress which might be felt by the friendless, isolated child. The final line probably reflects a combination of two factors: the rather sterner view of discipline taken by the pro-streamers and perhaps the greater tolerance of those who generally dislike drawing too many distinctions.

Table VII

The effects of teachers' attitudes to streaming—a study of teachers of third and fourth year juniors in non-streamed schools

There were 28 teachers pro-streaming; there were 24 teachers anti-streaming

	Teachers pro-streaming			Teachers anti-streaming			CR	Significance level	Inference
	Mean	SD	N	Mean	SD	N			
Nine-plus boys: Mechanical arithmetic scores	17·82	7·74	182	15·51	7·00	154	9·24	1%	Pro-streamers had higher arithmetic scores
Nine-plus girls: Mechanical arithmetic scores	19·42	—	189	15·89	—	134	By inspection		No difference
Nine-plus boys: English scores	30·12	—	186	29·83	—	156	NS*	NS*	No difference
Nine-plus girls: English scores	35·2	10·22	187	33·4	10·18	136	1·57	NS	No difference
Test anxiety scores: Boys	8·04	—	454	7·84	—	414	NS	NS	No difference
Test anxiety scores: Girls	8·82	3·13	430	8·07	3·42	378	3·28	1%	More anxious with pro-streamers
Test anxiety scores: Girls from Social class III only	9·16	—	152	7·88	—	135	By inspection		More anxious with pro-streamers
Test anxiety scores: Girls below average ability	9·38	—	77	9·40	—	83	NS	NS	No difference
Test anxiety scores: Girls average and above in ability	8·75	—	353	7·70	—	295	By inspection		More anxious with pro-streamers
	%		N	%		N	χ^2 test		Inference
% isolates among boys	21·8		535	18·6		451	1·61	NS	No difference
% isolates among girls	19·0		430	14·5		378	2·88	NS	No difference
% isolates among boys and girls	20·6		965	16·7		829	5·69	5%	Pro-streamers had more isolates
% boys rated "a pleasure to have in the class"	79·0		535	84·5		451	4·96	5%	Pro-streamers rated fewer as pleasure

*NS = Not statistically significant

4.3 *"Permissive" and "Obsessional" Teachers*

On the basis of extreme scores on the "permissive"/"obsessional" scale, two very contrasting groups of teachers were selected from the pro- and anti-streaming groups. Thirteen highly "permissive" anti-streamers were found and eight markedly "obsessional" pro-streamers: between them they taught classes containing 326 children of nine and ten. The numbers are small and any differences have to be considerable to reach statistical significance. Table VIII summarizes the results of the analyses which were made.

Table VIII

Teachers pro-streaming and also holding "obsessional" attitudes, compared with teachers anti-streaming and "permissive"

There were eight "obsessional" teachers and thirteen "permissive" teachers

	Obsessional, pro-streaming			Permissive, anti-streaming			CR	Significance level	Inference
	Mean	SD	N	Mean	SD	N			
Test anxiety scores— boys	8·40	3·58	129	7·84	3·33	231	1·48	NS	No difference
Test anxiety scores— girls	9·59	2·85	128	8·29	3·54	198	3·65	1%	More anxious with obsessionals
Number anxiety scores—boys	7·20	—	129	7·39	—	231	—	NS	No difference
	%		N	%		N	χ^2 test		
% of isolates among boys	26%		140	16%		252	5·07	5%	Obsessionals had more isolates
% of isolates among girls	15·6%		128	14·6%		198	—	NS	No difference
% of boys rated as disobedient	28%		140	17%		252	5·88	2%	Obsessionals perceived more dis-obedience

From this table, the generally greater test anxiety shown by girls again emerges and this time is even more clearly shown to have a relationship to the teacher's views and methods. More striking is the fact that the "obsessionals" disapprove of "bad manners"—aspects of behaviour more common among boys—which is reflected in their tendency to rate proportionally more boys as difficult than do their "permissive" colleagues. This in turn may go at least part way to explain why there are significantly more isolates among boys in their classes. It seems not unreasonable to suggest that the teachers probably manifest disapproval of certain boys and that this induces the class to reject them also.

One final, highly tentative hypothesis might be put forward. The "permissive" teachers' classes did not achieve lower anxiety scores than those achieved in the anti-streaming teachers' classes generally—in fact the mean is slightly higher. This suggests that there may be a non-linear relationship between "permissiveness" and anxiety, and that beyond a certain point of "permissiveness", anxiety may in fact mount.

4.4 Conclusion

It must again be emphasized that in the nature of the data available, no very striking distinctions could be expected from the analyses of this section. It is the more interesting, therefore, that—particularly in the number of "isolates" and in the test anxiety scores of girls—some fairly reliable differences have been found. The nature of these underlines the complexities of the problem under review and suggests that the more important and far reaching effects of streaming or non-streaming lie much less in formal attainments than in the human and personal aims of education. The emphasis, too, is shifted from the forms of organization—the effects of which may be counteracted consciously or unconsciously by the teacher—to the teacher himself, his personality, views and attitudes, and consequent choice of methods. Organization may perhaps facilitate or hinder the attainment of particular ends; the really important factor is undoubtedly the teacher who passes the whole day with an impressionable group of young children.

The following tables show the allocation to each stream o fchildren having had six, seven, eight and nine terms of infant schooling.

Table IX

The length of infant schooling of children in different streams

	Two-stream schools (23 schools, 6,390 children)		
	A-stream	B-stream	Total
Six terms in infants'	24·5%	31·1%	27·6%
Seven terms in infants'	21·1%	28·0%	24·3%
Eight terms in infants'	25·6%	21·5%	23·7%
Nine terms in infants'	28·7%	19·4%	24·4%
TOTAL	100%	100%	100%
Base	3,422	2,968	6,390

Three and Four-stream schools
(19 schools, 7,778 children)

	A-stream	B-stream	C/D-stream	Total
Six terms in infants'	18·4%	25·6%	30·7%	24·5%
Seven terms in infants'	22·5%	25·1%	26·3%	24·5%
Eight terms in infants'	25·6%	23·4%	23·0%	24·1%
Nine terms in infants'	33·5%	25·9%	20·0%	26·9%
TOTAL	100%	100%	100%	100%
Base	2,865	2,569	2,344	7,778

There is a consistent trend for the A-streams to have more children with nine terms infant schooling than would be expected by chance, and relatively fewer of those children who had spent a short time in the infants' school. For the lower streams, the trend is reversed. This tendency was found to persist even in the final school year: this accords with the low rate of transfer between streams that was noted in the survey report. The length of infants' schooling would appear to have had a lasting effect on the child's educational career, at least to the age of 10-plus.

The differences between streams with regard to the length of infants' schooling are statistically highly significant ($p < 0.01$) in both sizes of schools. It will be seen that the trend was more marked in the three and four-stream schools. The remedial classes in the 100 school study defined as "the lowest stream combining two or more year groups and the E-stream of the largest schools", showed the same tendency to a startling degree. Almost two-fifths of the children in these classes had had only six terms infants' schooling. On the other hand, only 12 per cent with nine terms in the infants' school were found in a remedial class.

Table X

The length of infant schooling of children in remedial classes

	Six terms	Seven terms	Eight terms	Nine terms	Total	Base
Remedial classes	39%	30%	19%	12%	100%	564

These results are in line with the findings of previous similar investigations.[1,2,3]

Some of the disadvantages of being a "younger" child in a school year group might be removed if all children were allowed to start school at the same point in the year, thus removing the advantage of longer schooling which the "older" child now has. It would be more logical for children to start school together at the beginning of the school year, since at every stage of the edu-

[1] JACKSON, B. (1964) *Streaming: an Education System in Miniature.* London: Routledge and Kegan Paul.

[2] JINKS, P. C. (1964) An Investigation into the Effect of Date of Birth on Subsequent School Performance. *Educational Research*, Vol. VI, No. 3.

[3] FREYMAN, R. (1965) Further Evidence on the Effect of Date of Birth on Subsequent School Performance. *Educational Research*, Vol. VIII, No. 1.

cation system children born within the same year are treated as a unit (i.e. they move up the school together, take 11-plus at the same time, etc.). The fact that a quarter of the children in the sample had missed a full year's schooling as compared with their older classmates, does not seem compatible with the policy of treating them as one age group. A review of current practice may well be thought necessary.

5.5 *Experience and Age of the Teacher*
The teachers of the A-streams tended to have more experience—and consequently were older—than the teachers of other streams.

Table XI

Experience and age of the teacher

	Age of teacher					Years of experience				
	Two streams		Three or four streams			Two streams		Three or four streams		
	A	B	A	B	C/D	A	B	A	B	C/D
Bottom quartile	35·0	27·2	30·9	29·3	27·2	10·9	5·2	9·8	6·5	4·8
Median	43·5	34·9	40·9	40·5	37·8	17·1	10·0	16·6	14·3	10·7
Top quartile	51·4	47·4	50·9	49·6	48·0	28·4	17·9	27·7	24·5	18·2

This tendency is in line with the observations made by Jackson[1] in the 10 streamed schools that he studied. There is also a tendency throughout the schools for younger children to be taught by younger and less experienced teachers.

5.6 *Facilities in the classroom*
The data available to us were analysed to see if there were any tendencies for any one stream to be given classrooms with better facilities than the others (desks, lighting, noise, space). For the most part, any differences were not significant statistically. There were, however, two exceptions. In the three-stream-schools, the lower streams were significantly favoured with regard to floor space ($p < 0.01$). This accords with the observed tendency for lower-stream classes to be smaller. It was also found that, in the three-streamed schools, the lower streams were placed in significantly less well-lit classrooms ($p < 0.05$). There seems to be no more plausible explanation for this difference than that, where differential conditions exist, these tend to be allocated to the detriment of the lower streams. Most schools would have fairly uniform facilities, but enough schools would have relatively ill-lit classrooms facing north for their allocation to constitute a measurable tendency.

5.7 *Changes of teachers*
Taking all the year-groups together, there was no significant tendency for some streams to have suffered more than others from changes of teacher during the year. When the total variables affecting the fourth year, however, were subjected to a complete analysis, a small but significant correlation ($r = 0.247$) was found between type of class and the number of changes of teacher. There was in fact a slight but positive association between low ability stream and change of teachers. The correlation for the first year children was not significant. More detailed work must be done before this point is completely clear.

1 JACKSON, B. (1964) *Streaming: an Education System in Miniature*. London: Routledge and Kegan Paul.

5.8 *Teachers' Attitudes*

In two-streamed schools, some tendencies were found which might indicate differences of attitude among teachers of different streams. Greater differences were found in schools with three or more streams, where there is probably a greater awareness of the fact that the school is streamed.

(1) In two-streamed schools, there were relatively more highly "permissive" teachers in B-streams than in A-streams. No such differences were found in the larger streamed schools.

(2) In the larger streamed schools, there was a consistent trend for teachers of higher streams to favour 11-plus selection more than teachers of lower streams. In the two-stream school there was a less pronounced tendency for relatively more B-stream than A-stream teachers to disapprove of selection.

(3) Teachers of A-streams in large schools were the group who disapproved most strongly of noise; there were no consistent differences between teachers of middle and lower streams.

(4) In two-streamed schools, a slightly higher proportion of B-stream teachers favoured streaming than A-stream teachers (45 per cent and 40 per cent). In larger schools, more A-stream teachers were favourable (58 per cent) than middle-stream teachers (42 per cent) or lowest stream teachers (32 per cent). This may suggest that the status-hierarchy of children and teachers is much more apparent in large streamed schools than in two-streamed schools.

(5) In all streamed schools there was a definite tendency for A-stream teachers to be the most favourable towards A-streams. Teachers of the lowest streams were the least favourable (but not nearly as unfavourable as the teachers in non-streamed schools).

Results (4) and (5) both show the same trends among teachers of different ability streams. Teachers of A-streams tend to favour streaming and to perceive favourable qualities in A-stream classes. Teachers of the lowest streams tend to be neutral in attitudes to streaming and less favourable towards A-stream children.

SECTION 6

ATTITUDES OF PARENTS
(In co-operation with the Government Social Survey)

6.1 *Introduction*

In the course of a more extensive survey of parental opinion 224 parents of children in the schools included in the present study were interviewed in autumn 1964. They were the parents of selected children in their second year at four large junior schools, situated in Chester, Leicester, Wellingborough and Manchester. The children had been selected from the sample in such a way that a range of social classes and all levels of ability were represented. Two socio-economic categories were distinguished—UPPER (non-manual and skilled manual occupations) and LOWER (semi-skilled and non-skilled manual occupations). Five categories of pupils' ability were distinguished, as measured by the NFER Primary Verbal Test.

Two of these schools were streamed and two were entirely non-streamed.

The parents were interviewed in their homes by staff of the C.O.I., using an extensive pre-coded interview schedule. The C.O.I. had included a number of questions which were relevant to the streaming project. These have been analysed at the NFER, making use of our special information on the pupils, i.e. their streams, measured ability and parental occupation.

The findings which follow are tentative, since they are based on small samples, particularly when broken down into smaller sub-groups. Statistical tests have been applied where possible. These results should be interpreted with caution and regarded as providing suggestive rather than conclusive evidence.

6.2 *Parents' knowledge of school organization*

Parents were asked: "Do you know how the children of . . . . . .'s age are put into classes at (present school)? Are they put into classes by age, or do they put the quicker ones into one class and the slower ones into another?"

It was found that 85 per cent of parents of children in streamed schools could correctly identify the school organization (i.e. streamed or non-streamed). In non-streamed schools, only 69 per cent of parents knew that streaming was not used; 17 per cent imagined that streaming by ability was used.

Table XII
Parents' knowledge of school organization

Percentage of parents believing that:	Streamed schools	Non-streamed schools
Children put in classes by age	11%	59%
Children put in classes by ability	85%	17%
Don't know	4%	14%
Some other method specified	—	10%
Number giving information	111	113

6.3 *Parents' attitudes to streaming and non-streaming*

Parents were then asked: "For children of . . .'s age, could you tell me which of these you think is better? For the quicker and slower children to be mixed together in one class, or for the quicker children to be put in one class and the slower in another?" The first alternative, of course, refers to non-streaming and the second to streaming.

Streaming was the more commonly chosen alternative. In the streamed schools it was chosen by 79 per cent of parents; in the non-streamed schools by 65 per cent. (Streamed and non-streamed schools differed significantly, $\chi^2 = 6.70$, $p < .01$.) There were six per cent of "Don't knows" in each case. Less than one-third of the parents of children in non-streamed schools approved of non-streaming.

Table XIII
Percentages of parents preferring streaming and non-streaming

	Streamed schools	Non-streamed schools
Prefer non-streaming	15%	29%
Prefer streaming	79%	65%
Don't know	6%	6%
TOTAL	100%	100%
Number giving information	111	113

It seemed possible that parents in different social categories would differ in their attitudes. It was found, however, that this was not the case. The percentages preferring each method were almost identical.

Parents of B-stream children appeared to be less favourable to streaming than either A-stream or C-stream parents; although this difference was not statistically significant ($\chi^2=5.67$ $p<.06$). Table XIV shows that 28 per cent of B-stream parents preferred non-streaming, as compared with an overall 15 per cent. The sample is rather small, however.

Table XIV

Percentages of parents preferring streaming and non-streaming (streamed schools only)

	A-stream	B-stream	C-stream	Total
Prefer non-streaming	4(10%)	10(28%)	3 (9%)	17(15%)
Prefer streaming	35(83%)	26(72%)	27(82%)	88(79%)
Don't know	3 (7%)	—	3 (9%)	6 (6%)
Number giving information	42	36	33	111

Next, a study was made of the attitudes of parents with children above average in ability, compared with those whose children were average and below. The cut-off point was taken as a standardized score of 105 on the primary verbal test. This made possible a comparison of parents' attitudes in streamed and non-streamed schools, regardless of the stream to which pupils had been allocated.

There appeared to be an association between the child's ability and his parents' attitudes to streaming. Parents of children with above average ability definitely tended to favour streaming; parents with less gifted children were much more likely to favour non-streaming. But even in the latter group, "streamers" outnumbered "non-streamers" by almost two to one.

Table XV

Percentages of parents preferring streaming and non-streaming—according to ability of child

	Streamed schools			Non-streamed schools		
Child's test score	105 or over	Less than 105	Total	105 or over	Less than 105	Total
Prefer non-streaming	3 (7%)	14(20%)	27(15%)	6(17%)	26(34%)	32(28%)
Prefer streaming	36(88%)	52(74%)	88(79%)	27(75%)	46(60%)	73(65%)
Don't know	2 (5%)	4 (6%)	6 (6%)	3 (8%)	5 (6%)	8 (7%)
Number giving information	41	70	111	36	77	113

The 49 parents who preferred non-streaming were asked: "What do you think are the advantages of having the quicker and slower children mixed in one class?" The advantage most frequently mentioned was that it gives a sense of competition or spurs on the backward (this was mentioned by nine out of 10 B-stream parents who preferred non-streaming). Other advantages mentioned were that brighter children can help slower ones and that the feeling of differences between streams is avoided.

A similar question on advantages of streaming was put to the parents who preferred streaming. The percentages giving various responses are shown in Table XVI, with separate figures for A, B, C-streams and for two levels of ability in non-streamed schools.

Table XVI
Perceived advantages of streaming by parents preferring streaming

	Streamed schools				Non-streamed schools		
	A	B	C	Total	105 or over	Less than 105	Total
Slow ones have more attention	30(86%)	18(69%)	16(59%)	64(73%)	14(52%)	29(63%)	43(59%)
Bright child not held back by slow children	30(86%)	13(50%)	15(56%)	58(66%)	21(78%)	22(48%)	43(59%)
Slow children not made to feel slow or dunces	18(51%)	8(31%)	7(26%)	33(37%)	4(15%)	9(20%)	13(18%)
Easier for the teacher	7(20%)	5(19%)	9(33%)	21(24%)	2 (7%)	3 (7%)	5 (7%)
Number giving response	35	26	27	88	27	46	73

As Table XVI is based on the responses to an open-ended question, it is difficult to interpret the data. The numbers are small, but some trends deserve comment. In non-streamed schools, parents of bright children tended to mention mainly the advantage to the bright child, and parents of less bright children were more likely to mention advantages which would accrue to the slower child in a streamed class.

6.4 *Parents' preferences for secondary schools*

"If you had the choice, what type of secondary school would you like ...... to go to when he/she is 11?" In reply to this question 40 per cent of all parents chose the grammar school. Twenty-four per cent either had not thought about it yet or did not mind (the children were eight years old). Sixteen per cent chose technical schools, 13 per cent secondary modern schools, four per cent comprehensive schools, and three per cent other schools. None of the four areas where this research was carried out had a comprehensive school.

When asked what they thought would be the advantages of the chosen type of schools for their child, those who chose grammar schools tended to mention that it would lead to a good or better job, had good future prospects, and that there was a better standard of education and teaching.

Technical schools were thought to lead to a good job and to have a varied, interesting or wide curriculum. Those who chose secondary modern schools tended to mention mainly the varied, interesting or wide curriculum.

Parents were also asked if there was any type of secondary school which they would particularly dislike their child to go to. Seventy-seven per cent had no dislikes. The numbers mentioning a dislike are very small; suffice it to say that co-educational schools were first on the list, and secondary modern schools were second. The commonest reasons given for disliking these schools were that they contained rough, bad mannered or illiterate children and manifested bad discipline or behaviour or lax morals.

Let us now see how parents' choices were related to their children's abilities and to their socio-economic status.

In the sample, 35 per cent of children scored at or above 105 on the primary verbal test. A relatively high proportion of children from families in the upper social group obtained scores above 105, as compared with those in the lower social group. (See Table XVII below.)

Table XVII

Percentages of pupils in each social group scoring above and below 105 on the primary verbal test

	Upper group	Lower group	Total
Score of 105 or more	40%	28%	33%
Score of 104 or less	60%	72%	67%
TOTAL	100%	100%	100%
Base	89	134	223

The preferences of each of the four sub-groups were studied separately (see Table XVIII). Seventy per cent of the upper social group with bright children hoped for a grammar school, but so did 40 per cent of the upper group and 26 per cent of the lower group with less gifted children.

Evidence that social class influences to some extent the choice of school is seen in the table below. Sixteen per cent of parents of the lower social group with gifted children preferred the technical schools, which, while not chosen by parents in the upper group with bright children, were a popular choice among other parents.

The low proportion of parents actually choosing a secondary modern school bears no relation to the proportion whose children must eventually attend these schools. Again, choice of technical school was widely unrealistic when compared with availability.

Table XVIII

Percentages of parents choosing various types of secondary school

	Child's measured ability				Total all parents
	105 or over		104 or less		
Parents' social group	Upper	Lower	Upper	Lower	
Grammar school	25(70%)	20(53%)	21(40%)	25(26%)	91(41%)
Secondary modern	—	3 (8%)	6(11%)	21(22%)	30(13%)
Comprehensive	2 (6%)	—	2 (4%)	5 (5%)	9 (4%)
Technical	1 (2%)	6(16%)	9(17%)	18(19%)	34(15%)
Independent	—	—	—	—	—
Hadn't thought, don't mind	6(16%)	9(21%)	14(25%)	25(26%)	54(24%)
Others	2 (6%)	—	1 (2%)	2 (2%)	5 (3%)
Number giving information	36	38	53	96	223

Summary of Results

1. Streamed and non-streamed schools embody different philosophies (paragraph 2.8).

The streamed school seems to be more systematic in its approach, concentrates more on conventional lessons, gives more attention to the three Rs and is likely to be more "traditional". Its staff is likely to be somewhat older and more experienced, to approve of A-stream children, of 11-plus selection and of streaming. The non-streamed schools present an apparent contrast. Its younger teachers hold more "permissive" views on such things as manners, noise and cleanliness; they disapprove of streaming and A-streams, and 11-plus procedures. Their teaching tends to place more emphasis on self-expression, learning by discovery and practical experience.

Although different patterns emerge for streamed and non-streamed schools, not *all* teachers in each type conform to the predominant pattern. A minority in each type of school holds the views and opinions usually expressed by teachers in the other type of school.

Any effect which may be shown to be associated with streaming or non-streaming is unlikely to be purely and simply due to the form of organization used. Attitudes of teachers and their teaching methods may well be the critical factors.

2. A straight comparison between streamed and non-streamed schools showed that pupils in the streamed schools had slightly higher mean scores on the attainment tests (N.B.—But see conclusion, paragraph 3.4). The differences were greater the more the test reflected "traditional" educational practices; they were largest for mechanical arithmetic and smallest for reading. It may happen when the effects of teachers' attitudes and beliefs are examined, that differences between the two types of school will disappear altogether. Or that they may become larger. The differences may also disappear when the two types of school are controlled for social class.

3. A study of two contrasting groups of teachers, supporters of streaming and supporters of non-streaming, was made in *non-streamed* schools. What can be discerned at this stage is that the teachers' attitudes are just as important or perhaps even more important than the type of school organization. The teachers in non-streamed schools, *believing in streaming*, obtained a higher level of arithmetic computation from their pupils, while those *believing in non-streaming* had fewer social isolates in the class, caused less anxiety about tests and found more of their pupils a pleasure to have in the class. (Paragraph 4.4.)

4. A study was made of the characteristics of pupils allocated to, and teachers taking, the different ability streams in streamed schools. Month of birth and length of infants' schooling had a lasting effect on the educational career of children in streamed schools. (This effect is being examined in non-streamed schools.)

A steady decline in average age was seen as one proceeded from the A-streams to the lower streams. Also, children in lower streams, especially in remedial classes, tended to have had a shorter period in the infants' school. (Paragraph 5.4.)

A-streams tended to have the more experienced and, consequently, older teachers than other streams (paragraph 5.5). A-stream teachers (in three or four-stream schools) were more in favour of streaming than teachers of other streams. (Paragraph 5.8.)

5. From a study of a small sample of parents of pupils in the two types of school, it was found that the majority of parents preferred streaming to non-streaming. (Paragraph 6.3.)

Of the parents who had a preference for a secondary school, the majority preferred their child to go to a grammar school. (Paragraph 6.4.)

ANNEX 1

Details of matched pairs of schools
Initially, 50 matched pairs were selected. By the time that all the tests and questionnaires had been completed, a number of schools had changed their organization in some way which made them unrepresentative of streaming or non-streaming. They were therefore excluded from the analysis and it became necessary to re-match the remaining schools. This operation resulted in 42 matched pairs, giving a total of 84 schools for the cross-sectional study. It will be appreciated that when a number of pairs had lost one member, re-matching would not produce pairs which were as good as the original ones. An effort has been made to obtain the best possible pairs, either by re-matching or by elimination of schools which could not be re-matched.

Criteria for matching schools
(a) *Type of school:* Junior or junior-with-infants; urban or rural. (All the schools were non-denominational and all were situated in England.) The results of matching on this criterion are shown in the table below.

	Streamed schools	Non-streamed schools	Total
Junior, urban	37	37	74
Junior, rural	1	1	2
Junior-with-infants, urban	4	4	8
TOTAL	42	42	84

(b) *Number of classes in the school.* All the schools had at least eight junior classes. The two members of a matched pair could differ in size by a maximum of one class.

The 42 streamed schools had a total of 437 classes;
The 42 non-streamed had a total of 434 classes.

(c) *Average number of pupils per class.* Matched schools had approximately equal pupil/teacher ratios. A margin of ± 3 pupils was tolerated.

The average number of pupils per class were:
In streamed schools: 35·90 (standard deviation 6·27)
In non-streamed schools: 35·25 (standard deviation 4·89)
The difference was not statistically significant (C.R.=1·8). The greater standard deviation in the streamed schools was due to the tendency for A-streams to be larger than C-streams.

(d) *Geographical region: North, Midlands, South.* The two members of a matched pair were both located in the same region. The numbers of schools in each region were:

North	29
Midlands	31
South	24
TOTAL	84

(e) *Percentage of children in the local authority who attended non-selective schools.* It was felt that the forces tending to make a school concentrate on "preparing for the 11-plus" might be related to the proportion of children admitted to selective schools. We therefore matched the schools on this criterion, allowing a margin of ±5 per cent.

(f) *Predominant socio-economic status of parents.* The head teachers were asked to estimate the percentage of parents in each of five categories: professional, clerical, skilled, semi-skilled, unskilled. This information was used to form four main categories of schools. All but three pairs of matched schools were both drawn from the same category, the number of schools in each being:

Upper working class (over 50 per cent of fathers were in the skilled
category or over 50 per cent were in the clerical and skilled
categories combined)   19

Middle working class (over 50 per cent of fathers were in the
skilled and semi-skilled categories combined)   33

Lower working class (over 50 per cent of fathers were in the semi-
skilled category or in the unskilled category or over 50 per
cent were in the semi-skilled and unskilled categories combined)   24

No dominant social group (schools which did not fit into any of the
above categories)   8

TOTAL   84

(g) *Approximate matching of percentage of parents in professional, clerical and skilled occupations.* As a further precaution, matching of schools was effected within each of these socio-economic categories. The members of a pair resembled one another, both having either more or less than 10 per cent of professional parents, 20 per cent of parents in the clerical category, and 20 per cent in the category of skilled workers. This was based on the head teacher's estimate. At a later date, information, given by class teachers, for each individual child was obtained. The table below is based on the latter, more accurate information. The streamed schools in the sample were from a slightly higher socio-economic background.

Table XIX

Percentage of children in each socio-economic category, according to type of school organization

	Socio-economic categories					Total
	1	2	3	4	5	
Children in 42 streamed schools	7·4	12·8	35·7	29·2	14·9	100%
Children in 42 non-streamed schools	5·5	12·2	33·7	34·6	14·1	100%

ANNEX 2

TEST RELIABILITIES

Reliabilities of tests, calculated by the Kuder-Richardson Formula 20

Test	Junior year group	Reliability	Reliability sample size
Reading, version S.R.A.	1	0·942	99
(48 items)	2	0·949	96
	3	0·945	100
	4	0·943	98
	All	0·961	393
Reading, version S.R.B.	1	0·942	104
(48 items)	2	0·927	102
	3	0·929	106
	4	0·929	108
	All	0·951	420
Problem arithmetic, version S.P.A.	1	0·877	100
(30 items)	2	0·903	98
	3	0·916	98
	4	0·914	100
	All	0·942	396
Problem arithmetic, version S.P.B.	1	0·904	94
(30 items)	2	0·921	98
	3	0·917	100
	4	0·931	106
	All	0·950	398
Mechanical arithmetic, version S.M.A.	1	0·890	94
(35 items)	2	0·924	94
	3	0·935	100
	4	0·919	94
	All	0·948	382
Mechanical arithmetic, version S.M.B.	1	0·883	100
(35 items)	2	0·925	100
	3	0·939	106
	4	0·927	100
	All	0·950	406
English, version S.E.A.	1	0·960	88
(64 items)	2	0·966	82
	3	0·957	86
	4	0·965	86
	All	0·974	342
English, version S.E.B.	1	0·966	100
(64 items)	2	0·971	102
	3	0·968	110
	4	0·960	110
	All	0·977	422
Primary verbal I (85 items)	3 and 4	0·970	330
Verbal/Non-verbal (80 items)	4	0·940	363
ABC, general anxiety, scale A (15 items)	3 and 4	0·718	220
ABC, test anxiety, scale B (15 items)	3 and 4	0·712	220
ABC. number anxiety, scale C (15 items)	3 and 4	0·829	220

ANNEX 3

TEACHERS' ATTITUDES

Reproducibilities of Guttman Scales for Teachers' Attitudes (Questionnaire S.3)
These were calculated according to the formula proposed by Guttman. (See
S. A. Stouffer, *et al.*: *Measurement and Prediction*, Princeton, 1950. Page
117.) Values obtained from two separate random samples of 100 teachers are
given; also the minimal marginal reproducibilities (MMR), the number of
items in each scale, and the number of trichotomous items.

	Title	Reproducibility		MMR	Number of items	Number of trichotomies
		Sample 1	Sample 2			
Scale A	Permissive—obsessional	0·944	0·942	0·73	5	0
Scale B	Attitude to physical punishment	0·955	0·953	0·78	6	0
Scale D	Attitude to 11-plus selection	0·952	0·942	0·81	5	1
Scale G	Attitude to noise in the classroom	0·932	0·926	0·74	5	0
Scale H	Attitude to streaming	0·950	0·952	0·76	6	1
Scale I	Attitude to A-streams	0·936	0·942	0·75	5	1

Teachers' Attitudes—Questionnaire S.3

1. Streaming makes slow children feel inferior.
2. There is too much emphasis on cutting down noise in schools.
3. A-stream children have wider interests than other children, both inside and outside school.
4. I think a good slap in the right place at the right time does an awful lot of good.
5. Children in A-streams tend to become conceited about their abilities.
6. Children must be taught to have decent manners.
7. I don't mind a reasonably high working noise in my class.
8. Bright children should not be streamed off from the rest of their age group.
9. The 11-plus exam is an entirely fair method of assessing a child's abilities.
10. Children in A-streams worry too much about marks.
11. Physical punishment does no good at all to any child.
12. Bright children deserve a special academic course in a separate school when they are 11 years old.
13. An occasional hard slap does children no harm.
14. I cannot stand children fidgeting in class.
15. It is socially wrong to segregate children into streams.
16. The 11-plus exam can prevent slackness in junior schools and this is a good thing.
17. Teachers should demand clean hands in school.
18. I would not allow talking in a class of 35 or more children.
19. The bright children will be neglected in non-streamed classes.

20. Naturalness is more important than good manners in juniors.
21. An 11-plus exam is more fair than relying on record cards and teachers' assessments.
22. If children in my class are insolent, they have to be slapped.
23. Opportunities for self-expression through movement, painting and writing poetry, are more important than concentrating on the "three Rs".
24. In a streamed school, one gets far more done for the slow learner.
25. I'm quite prepared to spank bottoms for disobeying rules.
26. The atmosphere in A-streams is too competitive.
27. Nothing worthwhile will be achieved by a class that talks while it works.
28. Non-streaming would be impossible with large classes of 40 or more.
29. Any exam that segregates children into separate schools at 11-plus is undesirable.
30. Physical punishment is out of the question and completely unnecessary.
31. A quiet atmosphere is the one best suited for all school work.
32. Without streaming, neither the bright nor the dull get the best from what the school could offer.
33. With non-streaming, I would find it impossible to keep duller children occupied while bright children received attention.

APPENDIX 12

GYPSIES AND EDUCATION

This note was prepared at the Council's request by Mrs. B. Adams of the Sociological Research Section, Ministry of Housing and Local Government and Mr. D. M. Smith, Lecturer in Education, City of Leicester College of Education, who have made a study of gypsies in the course of their work for the Ministry of Housing and Local Government. It is reproduced here because, although the group of children involved is too small to justify a discussion of this length in the body of our Report, the children's educational needs are nevertheless extreme and largely unmet. Moreover the economic and social handicaps of the group from which they come arise to a large extent from the fact that successive generations of gypsy children are deprived of the education that would enable them to compete on equal terms with the rest of the community. Extreme as they are, the needs of gypsy children cannot be effectively met by measures of the kind we recommend for the more general problems of urban deprivation. They will require special attention and carefully planned action. At the same time, the numbers of children involved are so small that we believe a relatively small expenditure of money and effort, not confined only to the educational services, could rapidly achieve long steps towards a solution of the problems described in this Appendix.

GYPSIES AND EDUCATION

by Mrs. B. Adams, Sociological Research Section, Ministry of Housing and Local Government and Mr. D. M. Smith, Lecturer in Education, City of Leicester College of Education

1. There seems little doubt that the so-called gypsy is a descendant of members of certain wandering Indian tribes: Romany vocabulary is related to languages still spoken in northern India and traditional gypsy occupations—fortune telling, horse dealing, music, dancing, wood carving, smithery—stem from those of low-caste Indian tribes. These nomads were first noted in European countries in the fourteenth and fifteenth centuries. When they arrived in England they travelled with pack horses and lived in tents and it was not until the late eighteenth century that they adopted the covered living wagon. At first they travelled in large bands causing consternation among the settled population and repressive legislation was enacted against them, starting in 1530, which treated them as felons. Present day legislation is less repressive but the 1959 Highways Act, the Caravan Sites and Control of Development Act, 1960, and various private Acts are used by local authorities to discourage gypsies in their area.

2. Few steps have been taken to investigate the living conditions of gypsies in England and Wales. Kent Planning Authority carried out a county enquiry in 1951 which has since been followed by other counties. The investigation by the Ministry of Housing and Local Government has involved three stages.

On March 22, 1965, when most families were still in their winter quarters, a census was undertaken by the counties and county boroughs. Later in the year a survey of the sites reported in use was carried out, and a few sites were investigated in detail.

3. The census was not limited to "true gypsies" or people with Romany blood and it is important to know the criteria adopted in the definition. The persons covered were so-called gypsies and other travelling people living in caravans, huts or tents, usually isolated from the settled community. Although called "travellers", some have not left their base camp for some time. They usually make a living by dealing in scrap metal, cars, rags and other commodities, doing seasonal agricultural work, log and firewood cutting, casual labouring, hawking and begging, and they rarely take a regular job. Not included in the census were gypsies living in houses, showmen, tramps, boat-dwellers and caravan dwellers on residential sites who were typically part of the settled community.

4. It is estimated from the census that the gypsy population of England and Wales is at least 15,000* persons or about 3,400 families. The gypsies were widely scattered in almost every county and in one local authority area in three. The largest concentrations were found in the following counties:

	Families	Persons
[Kent*	325	1,363]
Worcester	197	866
Essex	164	853
Surrey	146	674
Staffordshire	109	446
Buckinghamshire	109	421
Gloucestershire	104	405
Cornwall	100	451
Hertfordshire	98	481
Herefordshire	96	459
Berkshire	85	414

5. On the day of the enquiry only 19 per cent of the families were camping on licensed or local authority sites; the rest were camping haphazardly on agricultural land, roadside verges, commons, woodlands, quarries and even on refuse tips. The facilities found to be provided were minimal and the majority of families were using stopping places with no facilities whatever. Only 33 per cent had access to running water and 35 per cent to refuse disposal facilities. Twenty-four per cent had hardstandings and 18 per cent electricity. Only 16 per cent of families had access to a water closet on their site. Conditions were generally better on the handful of sites provided by Local Authorities.

6. In the south of England the typical horse-drawn gypsy caravan and the tent have almost gone out of use though in Yorkshire and Humberside in March 1965 over a quarter of the families still lived in this type of accommodation. The trailer caravan is now the most usual dwelling. Caravans are sometimes overcrowded but some of the better off families own extremely large modern caravans with two or three apartments or have two caravans.

---

* Kent had carried out a survey on January 1, 1965 and the county was therefore excluded from the census. Figures for Kent for January 1 are included in the national total.

7. Moving from place to place is still an integral part of the life of most of these families. Approximately 60 per cent reported that they had travelled around in the preceding year and there are reasons for thinking that this is an underestimate. In March 1965 57 per cent had been on their camp site for six months or less, 21 per cent for less than a week. Travelling mainly occurs in the summer months—all but the most hardy families prefer to stay in one place for the winter, though they are not always able to do so. Twenty-six per cent of the gypsy population said they did not travel: the elderly tend to give up wandering and settle in one spot. The belief that travelling is largely economically motivated was confirmed by the census, for the majority of household heads said they had moved in search of agricultural work or other means of earning a living. However, in many cases movement was involuntary and due to the difficulty of finding a stopping place. Many of the traditional gypsy stopping places on the outskirts of towns have been closed to them since the war, in many cases by development, but in other cases by fencing, tipping or ditching to prevent access.

8. More than half of the men were dealers, mainly in scrap metal. Much of this involves house to house or factory to factory collecting, so that when supplies in one town are exhausted a move to the next is necessary. The second most important occupation was agricultural work which is seasonal and also necessitates moving from place to place. Other occupations mentioned frequently were roadwork, building work, and other labouring. Only two per cent of the men did factory work. Among the women, less than a third said that they went out to work, the largest group being hawkers. The proportion of women under 35 following this occupation was only half that among women over 65 which suggests that hawking is dying out. The relatively narrow range of occupations found among the travelling people reflects not only their traditional crafts and their unwillingness to work for others but also the fact that the vast majority are illiterate and thus unfitted for many occupations.

9. The age distribution of gypsies differs markedly from that of the total population of England and Wales in being abnormally young. It bears a marked resemblance to the age structure of the total population of the country in 1841. The age structure of the Eire tinkers is similar.†

Age	Gypsies*	Total Population of England and Wales (1965)
	%	%
0 – 4	16·7	8·7
5 – 15	24·6	15·8
16 – 34	30·6	25·0
35 – 44	11·6	13·3
45 – 64	13·1	24·9
65+	3·4	12·3
	100·0	100·0

† Report of the Commission on Itinerancy. Dublin 1963.
 Excluding the Kent gypsies, for whom age data was not collected.

10. Including an estimate for Kent, the number of children under 16 in March 1965 was over 6,000 and two households out of three contained children under 16. The high birth rate among gypsies is reflected in the proportion of children—twice the national figure for 0–4s and half as much again for the 5–15s. A forward projection of the 1965 gypsy population to 1985 suggests that the number of children is likely to double in the twenty year period.

11. The census and the site enquiry were designed solely to provide a basis for policy decisions on accommodation for gypsies. No questions on education were asked. Our information on education is therefore derived from personal experience of gypsies over many years and upon the detailed investigation of a few sites.

12. Before the war the gypsies were virtually unanimous in considering education a waste of time, harmful to health and to be avoided. Little attempt seems to have been made by the authorities at that time to get gypsy children into school.

13. This situation has not changed greatly, though some gypsy parents, probably a majority, do now want their children to go to school. Other parents had brief and unpleasant experiences at school and are determined to protect their children from similar ones. Since the majority of families still travel, staying either from choice or necessity for relatively short periods in each place, normal education is not feasible. Our evidence suggests that less than 10 per cent of the children of school age are attending school: the great majority are growing up illiterate. Some of the children who attend school do so only during the winter months when they are settled in winter quarters. There is often a conflict between the permissive attitude of primary schools, where children are usually encouraged to expand their speech and develop initiative in exploring and understanding their environment, and the child's restrictive family background.

14. Most children spend all their time in the family group and kinship bonds are particularly strong. The children are usually indulged and corporal punishment is rare. During the early months of life some children are carried by the mother when she goes hawking. Older children are left behind at the camp when the mother goes out, primarily in the care of the oldest girl and under the supervision of the other women in the extended family group. The children rarely wander from the camp and there is little or no mixing with house-dwelling children. Play tends to be non-projective and often destructive in conclusion. The increasing ownership of television sets may beneficially broaden the children's experience.

15. The children are quick to acquire certain skills. In the past they early became expert with horses or at making clothes pegs. Now, children unable to tell their right hand from their left can recognize and separate copper and alloy from base metal. Many are adept at handling money. In some families the older boys go out with their fathers collecting scrap metal and many do a full day's manual work from the age of 12 or 13.

16. As the family is almost the only socializing agency experienced by the gypsy child in its formative years, this restrictive situation, with relatively few stimulating experiences, tends to inhibit intellectual growth. A study by

Gordon (1923)* using mental and arithmetical tests showed a significant decline in mental ability with advancing chronological age in a group of gypsy children who occasionally attended school. The following figures from limited studies by students of Avery Hill College of Education give some indication of the possible intellectual growth through educational opportunity of gypsy children.

Gypsy children 12 months at school (1953)

		Age	Comprehension	I.Q.
Boy	A	10·6	67	74
Boy	B	11·3	65—	66
Girl	A	11·3	65—	71

Gypsy children with six years at school (1963)

Boy	A	10·8	85	89
Girl	A	11·5	94	84
Girl	B	10·10	81	83

17. In 1964 Leicester City Council set up a site for itinerant families at Lodge Farm, a large area of derelict land adjacent to the city refuse tips, about 2½ miles from the city centre and some three hundred yards from the nearest house. Elsan toilets and a refuse disposal service were provided, and water was delivered daily to the site. Itinerant families from several sites in the city were directed to Lodge Farm and at the beginning of 1965 there were over 30 families on the site. In some families none of the children had ever attended school, in others some of the children had attended school but not for any continuous period. While at Lodge Farm, no children attended school. The numbers on the site increased to over 60 families, but the site was closed in the autumn of 1965. Many families moved from Lodge Farm to a traditional stopping place at Anstey Gorse and in January 1966 none of the 37 (approx.) children of school age on Anstey Gorse was attending school. Four Irish tinker families had attempted to enrol their children at a local Catholic school but the waiting list was genuinely over-subscribed. All families have now been moved off Anstey Gorse; no alternative site has been provided.

18. Last year Godstone R.D.C. set up a site for gypsies and other caravan dwellers. The site has a tarmacadam road, concrete paths and hard-standings. Each pitch has a water standpipe, small shed and dustbin. There are shared toilets, ablutions block with showers, laundry room with hot water, and a washing machine. There is a resident warden, himself of travelling stock. The children can get a special bus to the local primary school where 50 per cent of the children are from the camp site. There are no special classes for gypsy children but they are sometimes given special coaching in groups. Attendance is not regular and at the slightest excuse they are absent. The headmaster reported that, without the normal home background of play and vocabulary, schooling was very difficult for the children. He is pressing for more equipment for backward children. Although there is no noticeable separation in classes, in the playground the camp children often tire of a game quickly and tend to be withdrawn. It is interesting that the higher up the school the children get, the more their appearance approximates to that of the other children.

---

* H. Gordon. Mental and Scholastic Tests among Retarded Children. Education Pamphlet No. 44. 1923.

19. South-East Buckinghamshire has traditionally accommodated considerable numbers of settled or partly settled gypsy families and at the two teacher village school at Horton several gypsy children of the second generation are now being educated. The staff are sympathetic and the school has a strong craft element. One result of the number of gypsy children in the school has been a prejudice against the school on the part of some house-dwellers. The gypsy children are wholly integrated in the two classes and to the casual visitor are undistinguishable from house-dwellers. The teachers reported that on arrival gypsy children were very withdrawn and some did not speak for three months. They appeared to understand brief verbal communications but not long sentences. However, it was usual for them to be able to read by the age of seven. One child has passed the preliminary test for the 11+, but this was exceptional and in most cases attainment is below average. Poor verbal ability persists, perhaps because few of their parents can read or write.

20. A successful attempt at settlement has been made by Eton R.D.C. who in 1964 set up a site at Iver for 32 travelling families with local ties. Each family has a fenced pitch with hardstanding and a brick storage shed. There are parking lots for lorries and rough grazing for ponies. Standpipes, w.c.s, laundries, and hot water supply are shared. The resident warden is a responsible gypsy, related to many of the residents. The standards and aspirations of the residents have risen notably since they moved on to the site and now all the children of school age are in school. They are usually taken to and from school by lorry. At the Parlaunt School at Langley, the children were originally kept in a single group in the care of a "helper" closely supervised by the headmistress. This was unsuccessful and the children were then integrated into normal classes, with several in a small remedial class. On arrival their environmental handicap was very evident: many had never used a pencil or a knife and fork and all had a very limited vocabulary. They were clean but oddly dressed. They have gradually become more interested in school work and do not stay away as much now as they did. Though they are still backward, all are making progress and there have been one or two striking successes. Most of the teachers consider the camp children to be of low intellectual capacity but the teacher of the remedial class considers that by the age of 10 or 11 some will overcome their environmental handicap and show average performances. The parents are co-operative, increasingly interested in the school, and say they are anxious for their children to be educated. Nevertheless, some take them away for Ascot week and for several months during the summer when the family goes pea-picking, fruit-picking and potato-lifting.

Conclusion

21. Of the 6,000 gypsy children in England only a small minority is attending school. These are the children living a relatively settled existence, a considerable proportion on sites provided by local authorities. Even when attending school regularly these children have to contend with a severe environmental handicap. The number of gypsy children is likely to double in the next twenty years.

In 1962 the Ministry of Housing and Local Government issued a circular urging authorities to establish sites for gypsies, but the response has been disappointing. A further circular giving the findings of the 1965 inquiry and calling for proposals for the establishment of sites is about to be issued.

APPENDIX 13

The Management of Primary Schools: Research Unit on School Management and Government, University of London, Institute of Education

This Appendix is a preliminary report prepared for the Council by the Research Unit on School Management and Government, University of London, Institute of Education. It is the first part of a more extensive study and is based mainly on the views of and information from chief education officers*. The views of teachers, managers and representatives of parental and other organizations will be sought later. Nevertheless it has helped us considerably in our study of factors affecting the status of primary education (See Vol. 1, Chapter 29). We are grateful to the Unit for making this Report at our request, particularly since they originally intended to concentrate on secondary school government.

---

*"Chief education officer" is used throughout this Report although some chief officers are called Director of Education, Education Officer or Secretary for Education.

Primary School Management: Preliminary Report submitted to the Central Advisory Council for Education (England) by the Research Unit on School Management and Government, University of London, Institute of Education. (Head of Unit: Dr. G. Baron)

This memorandum has been prepared and written by Mr. D. A. Howell, Research Officer to the Unit.

Introduction

1. The Unit's research has been concerned principally with matters relating to the government of county secondary schools but, following discussions with the Department of Education and Science and representatives of the Central Advisory Council, it was agreed that the Unit should submit what evidence it could relating to county primary school management.

2. Over the last few months visits have been paid to some seventy local education authorities. The purpose of the visits has been to discuss general questions of school management and government with Chief Education Officers and members of their departments, and the staff of the Unit have also had opportunities of studying relevant documents, such as instruments and rules of management, school bulletins, handbooks for managers and governors. It is on the basis of information gained in this way that this memorandum has been compiled.

3. We are very much aware of the limitations of this preliminary report. In particular, restrictions on time have made it impossible to discuss the main issues or to check information with head and assistant teachers or with managers. And we have not included studies of the management of voluntary controlled and aided schools whose opportunities and problems differ substantially from those of county and county borough schools. We think, however, that the information and opinions given by over two hundred administrative officers concerned with school management reflects closely the "reality" of the situation in which they work.

4. The Authorities visited to date comprise 25 County Boroughs, 18 of the Outer London Boroughs, and 27 County Councils. The County Boroughs and the Counties cannot be regarded as completely representative, but they form at least a substantial proportion of the whole. Most of the County Boroughs visited are among those with a population of 150,000 or over, but we have also visited a number of smaller boroughs. The conclusions which we draw relating to school management practice in County Boroughs may well be liable to modification if we should find that the Authorities which we have not visited (that is principally the smaller County Boroughs), display different patterns. It is unlikely, however, that any completely new arrangements will be discovered. The County Councils include most of the larger Authorities, some medium-sized counties, and a few of the smaller ones. Some of the Counties visited are administered completely through a system of Divisional Executives, others have a mixed system of administration, while yet others have no system of delegation to subordinate authorities.

5. We considered it essential to discuss our findings relating to County Councils and County Boroughs separately. It is clear that geographical facts

alone have played a considerable part in shaping overall administrative structures, and especially the school management patterns. In the County Boroughs many matters can be referred quickly and directly to the administrative branch concerned, and in more senses than one schools are nearer the Authority. It is easy for someone from the Education Office to look in at the school, or for the Headmaster to visit the Office. This point has clearly influenced the evaluation of school management in such Authorities. Great stress is laid on providing links between individual schools and members of the Education Committee, and still more with the Education Office. Relatively little importance is attached to establishing a link between the school and the local community through the recruitment of school managers who are not primarily, or to any great extent, local politicians.

County Boroughs
6. Arrangements for school management in the County Boroughs visited vary as follows:

A	Sub-committee for all schools	16 authorities
B	Grouped bodies including secondary schools	3 authorities
C	Grouped bodies for primary schools only	5 authorities
D	Separate managing bodies	1 authority

Notes
1. Group A includes one Authority with grouped bodies recruited entirely from members of the Education Committee, and one authority which operated a pilot scheme of grouped managing bodies.
2. Five Authorities in category A appoint members of the primary schools sub-committee as visitors to individual schools.
3. The Authority in category D adopts the practice of appointing one of the managers as clerk or correspondent.

County Boroughs with one managing body for all schools
7. In the Local Authorities where the sub-committee serves as the managing body for all schools, it is held that a system of separate or grouped managing bodies would be purposeless. Where the need for managing bodies is not dismissed out of hand, it is argued that the paramount need is not so much to strengthen links between school and the local community, as to ensure that schools have direct access to individual members of the Education Committee, and to the Education Office. More than one C.E.O. has said that he makes a point of visiting all the primary schools from time to time, or at least ensuring that his senior officers do. In roughly half these Authorities we are told that there is some system of visiting schools by individual Councillors, and although a few C.E.Os. think this a useless activity, the majority consider that it has many advantages. It enables Councillors to get to know their schools and to deal with local inquiries and complaints. Evidence of interest on the part of the Committee improves the morale of the school, and it enables Councillors to identify themselves with the individual schools. This is said to be particularly true where a Councillor visits one or more schools in his ward, and it is said that many schools are very proud of their Council visitor. It is also claimed that this arrangement enables a Headmaster to let off steam to a sympathetic and influential listener, but it is thought less likely that Heads will discuss their general ideas and plans for running the school, as they can so easily have informed discussions with the "Office" about such matters.

U

8. The sub-committee system often seems to be associated with the view, not uncommon in municipal government, that only elected members should be entrusted with responsibility for public institutions. We have heard claims that if elected members of the Education Committee did not form a majority on school managing bodies this would reflect a gross abdication of responsibility on their part, as non-elected members were irresponsible and might easily take embarrassing decisions. The same arguments are used to justify the sub-committee system, on the grounds that only in this way can elected members of the Borough Council, who could not attend meetings of separate or even grouped managing bodies, carry out the practice of managers. Further, and somewhat illogically, managers' meetings are not given high priority as managers have little or nothing of importance to discuss. Indeed, in some Authorities we have found that the meetings of the primary schools sub-committee are sometimes cancelled through lack of business, and elsewhere last only five or ten minutes. One or two Authorities have tried both a single sub-committee and a system of grouped managing bodies. One Authority, which replaced its grouped managing bodies by a sub-committee, felt that it could even dispense with appointing individual visitors to schools. A large Authority, which for two years ran the pilot scheme mentioned above, decided that results did not justify extending it. It is not uncommonly felt in these Authorities that managers are an unnecessary extra tier in the administrative structure, and that the requests of the schools can be dealt with expeditiously by normal administrative and committee procedure. Moreover, reference of requests to bodies meeting only once a term would be quite out of the question, and the C.E.O. and his staff are generally available anyway to discuss any general or particular question which a Head wishes to raise. It is said, further, that in these Authorities Heads have become used to the system and that they do not agitate for separate managing bodies, and that since some of these Authorities operate a closed shop system for the appointment of primary school Heads many have known no other system of school management. It is also claimed that primary Heads are less demanding than their secondary colleagues and much more inclined to take things in their stride. One Authority thinks that it has achieved a successful balance between administrative efficiency and individual interest in the schools with its system of school visitors, who are all members of the Education Committee. This visiting is taken very seriously. Heads use their visitors as sounding boards for their ideas and difficulties, and they can be asked, particularly if they are Councillors, to give a gentle prod to the Education Office. Since some of these visitors are Councillors and known locally as public persons, it is claimed that parents are not at all reluctant to approach them on any matter affecting their school, and that through their interest in the school visitors are able to perform a genuine public relations or ambassadorial function.

9. The effectiveness of this system in linking individual schools with the Education Committee and the Office was said by one C.E.O. to be more suitable for the smaller and more compact Authorities, although he claimed that a grouped system would be better for the larger Authorities. However, in the largest County Boroughs visited we found that all except one had a sub-committee system. It was one of these Authorities which had carried out the pilot scheme referred to above, but in his report on this scheme the C.E.O.

said that he could discern no benefits for the schools which had been included. He claimed that the Councillors really knew the schools and were points of reference for Heads and parents, and that they would take up the Head's grumbles with the Education Office. However, this was clearly not true in another large Authority which had a sub-committee system with visitors, where all newly appointed Heads were advised that they were not to take complaints about delays or other administrative matters to their visitor. Finally, it is generally considered in the large County Boroughs that the institution of a small grouped system would result in a top heavy organization involving considerable administrative cost with no apparent result.

County Boroughs with grouped managing bodies

10. The minority of County Boroughs visited (9) have a more highly developed system of school management. Of these, five have grouped bodies, responsible for from three to 12 schools (counting a junior and infant school on the same site as one school), three have joint bodies for primary and secondary schools, and there is one County Borough with separate managing bodies, each with one of the managers acting as clerk. In this last authority, it is said that with more than 90 primary schools it would be an impossible administrative burden for the staff of the Education Office to undertake clerking (although the number of administrative officers presumably bears some relationship to the size of the system). In general these Authorities think that they have evolved a satisfactory system with roughly the right number of schools in each group; they make the same claim as the Authorities operating a sub-committee system, that it enables a balance to be maintained between administrative efficiency and local interest and identification with individual schools. One Authority, which had tried a number of experiments, thought that there should not be more than six schools in a group. Another Authority claimed that the Heads did not mind being dealt with in larger groups, and that in fact they looked forward to their group meetings; they even regarded the waiting room as a sort of club.

11. In these Authorities the formal status of managing bodies for primary schools, as measured by provisions of the rules of management, was generally similar with that of the Authority's governing bodies for secondary schools; some six out of eight Authorities provided for the submission of estimates by individual bodies of managers, seven had identical arrangements for the appointment of Heads of primary and secondary schools, and seven again provided that in both primary and secondary schools the managers should have the general oversight of the school and its curriculum. In practice, however, these provisions are frequently dead letters. There seems to be general agreement that it is out of the question to prepare estimates for each primary school, while with regard to the general oversight of the school and its curriculum the managers are solely dependent on the Head and what he chooses to put in his report. We have not found that Heads' reports lead to managers' indulging in what the C.E.O. or Heads regard as interference; in fact, managers tend to be inhibited about voicing views on any matters relating to the school curriculum. Three of these Authorities have provision for parents to serve on managing bodies, generally through parent/teacher associations, and in another parents are said to be appointed often. One

Borough advertises in the local press for prospective managers and claims that it gets four or five applicants for every vacancy.

12. In this group of Authorities there are mixed feelings about managing bodies. It is maintained that those prepared to serve are not of high quality, that Heads find them of small help or, indeed, have little need to make use of them, or that they do not know how to deal with their managers as individuals, that operating this kind of system can mean a great deal of virtually pointless work, and that most Heads would be glad to see it ended. Yet in spite of these disadvantages, the same Authorities admit that this system is better than having one managing body for all schools. One Authority, which had changed to a grouped system, said that under a sub-committee system only the most vociferous Head had anything to say. Heads think that, under a grouped system, managers can give them more powerful support and that Councillors, especially women, enjoy their direct contact with schools. In one Borough a more positive claim is made that managers can be particularly helpful in strengthening the schools' links with the community outside. In this Authority, however, it is felt that managers are a waste of time because the town is compact and the Education Committee and the Office are in regular touch with the schools. The grouped system of school management is felt to be an over-elaborate way of establishing public relations agencies to represent the schools. Local Councillors are said to do this much better, since they are more liable to be buttonholed or harassed by the public than other managers who may be quite unknown persons. Except in the Borough which advertised for managers it is often said that it is difficult to recruit suitable people, especially in the more socially depressed areas. As far as the appointment of parents on managing bodies is concerned, there appear to be no strong feelings in general, apart from a suggestion that their interest may be too transient and subjective. In a majority of this group, all managers are appointed through party political channels, but the operation of the party system is considered to be one of the facts of life in urban local government and one which does not necessarily have pernicious effects. Political control of nominations need not depress the quality of school managers, although it is claimed that some would-be managers of good calibre are deterred from offering their services through reluctance to make themselves acceptable to one party or another. In politically marginal Boroughs it is said that there has to be a fair amount of give and take between parties in the appointment of managers. It is held everywhere that despite party interest in the appointment of managers, the matters discussed at their meetings are not such as to give rise to any great political dissensions.

13. There is recognition, albeit reluctant and qualified, that managers may have some residual function, either as a safeguard against apparently arbitrary action by the Head or the Education Office, or as a group of friends of the school. However, only in one Authority is it claimed that Heads are glad to share the responsibility of appointing staff with their managers, or at least with the Chairman. Most C.E.Os. in County Boroughs have a notice-able lack of enthusiasm for school management, and even where a grouped system exists few positive advantages are claimed for it. The same basic attitude is apparent in the steps taken by the Outer London Boroughs to inaugurate efficient systems of school management and government. Here,

apart from their sole administrative function of the appointment of Heads, and occasionally Deputy Heads, where they follow the practice of the Boroughs with a grouped system, managers are said to perform a rôle in supporting the morale of the school and its Head, in giving it a civic status through their appearance on the platform at Speech Day and other occasions, and in providing a means of greater contact between members of the Education Committee and the schools. As elsewhere, the success with which these functions are performed depends on the amount of time which managers are prepared to devote to the job. In general, however, the Outer London Boroughs have not yet considered the implications of their assessments of school management (half the Boroughs visited have a grouped system and half a sub-committee system) and this low priority itself appears to be an indication of the general lack of interest in this aspect of educational administration.

COUNTIES

Policy

14. The situation is quite different in the counties. The sheer physical distance of some individual schools from the County or Divisional Education Office tends to reinforce the case for having a body of lay support for each individual school. Indeed, we found a virtual unanimity of view in favour of school managers, and in particular of separate managing bodies wherever possible. This consensus may be highly significant since visits have been paid to a wide range of Counties, thickly and thinly populated, small and large, and of varying degrees of administrative and social complexity. A number of C.E.Os. have been emphatic that the need to have machinery for lay participation in education, and the considerations relevant to school management in villages and small towns, also apply in large measure to urban areas. They see no overwhelming reason for believing that County Boroughs and Counties have entirely different problems which it is useless to consider in the light of the same assumptions, although they are not unaware of the grounds upon which some County Boroughs reject this point of view. This insistence on the need for local participation is held particularly strongly in the more urban counties. The basic difference between the attitudes found in the two types of Authority is that the County Boroughs see a justification for school management (where they have any true system at all) in providing a direct link between the Education Committee and the schools, while Counties think that the need is to provide a link between the school and the community. Some counties are very explicit about their priorities, and have taken much more trouble than others to work out a school management scheme based on a coherent philosophy.

15. Almost all counties claim that single managing bodies are their ideal. This is said to be inevitable in rural areas, although even there grouping is not entirely unknown, and in one extreme case we have found one managing body serving no fewer than 21 schools. (This managing body was almost a divisional executive in its own right, serving a very compact and isolated area, with visiting sub-committees to ensure a greater interest in individual schools). Where grouping for management purposes does take place it is said to be the result of traditional or historical practices. On the whole it is

heartily disliked and some C.E.Os. have succeeded in establishing individual managing bodies even in fair sized towns. However, in other counties, C.E.Os. feel that they have to accept some measure of grouping, particularly where this is the wish of a large or expanding minor Authority. Indeed, most Counties are prepared to give some weight to the views of local councils on grouping policy, especially where these are former Part III Authorities. Excepted Districts virtually go their own way, even if this involves doing what the County regards as undesirable. In some cases grouping policy is associated with the arrangements for clerking managing bodies of which we will have more to say later.

Recruitment

16. Statutory practice in recruiting school managers is for the local Authority to nominate four members and the minor Authority two, for schools in areas administered directly by a County and serving the needs of one minor Authority only. When a school caters for more than one minor Authority, nominations will be made on a proportionate basis, and in Counties with a divisional system of administration the divisional executive will make nominations for two places elsewhere held by the L.E.A. These L.E.A. nominations are invariably made through local County Councillors or locally resident aldermen, who are presumed to be in touch with suitable candidates. There is some suggestion that minor Authorities tend to nominate from the ranks of their own members, and to be reluctant to consider the claims of other local residents who might have a contribution to make. Some of these minor Authorities have sought to unseat managers in mid-term if they fail to hold their seats on the local council; in these cases the Local Education Authority has had to intervene, pointing out that whatever happens to the composition of the local council, managers are there to serve their statutory term. A number of C.E.Os. expressed their concern about the numbers of elderly managers, and their apparent lack of interest in education. Nominations from County Councillors, and from minor Authorities, are often scrutinised by the Education Committee, which may have to take a formal vote on disputed appointments. Only one County of those so far visited asks for details of prospective managers' interest in education, and goes to the point of referring the nominations back, if candidates do not seem to be suitably qualified. There is said to be no general lack of people to stand, except in a few isolated areas. Both in solid working class and middle class areas people are "falling over themselves" to serve. The shortage of potential managers, so often remarked upon in County Boroughs, does not appear to be a problem in the Counties. In a few cases nominations are put forward by the C.E.O. himself, who may come across suitable people in his travels around the county. One C.E.O. who did this said that it was undemocratic but effective. He was able to hand-pick people with a positive contribution to make, and thus to produce managers of better than average calibre. Counties where the C.E.O. takes some initiative in suggesting nominations are among the less political Authorities, but in other Counties nomination can be a live political issue and is left strictly to councillors and local politicians. It is often claimed that local vicars are very much to the fore on managing bodies, especially in villages, and that they are sometimes inclined to run the school too much on their own, having to be reminded from time

to time that County schools are not the same as voluntary schools. Occasionally, would-be managers offer their services to the Chief Education Officer and in this event they are usually advised to approach their local County Councillor.

17. All Authorities were asked how desirable they thought it was to have parents on managing bodies. Four Counties have some specific provision to this effect, three of them obtaining nominations from parent/teacher associations, but only one County goes to the other extreme and expressly forbids parents to serve on the managing body of their child's school (in this Authority, a strictly constitutional view was taken that parents should voice their complaints and queries either to the Head direct or to their elected representatives); elsewhere it was reported that parents are commonly found on managing bodies and that it is almost impossible to avoid this in villages. In those Authorities where there is no formal provision for parental membership, the view is often expressed that interested groups should not be directly represented as such, and that parents should serve, like other managers, as individuals. The balance of opinion is clearly in favour of having parents serving as managers. In some Authorities, parents are regarded with enthusiasm, and efforts are made to ensure that each managing body has one or more serving on it; others give a more qualified welcome, and a few have serious reservations, generally on the grounds that parents' interest is biased and transient, and too dependent on what their child tells them, while in one case it is claimed that appointment of a representative of a P.T.A. produces the most trying relationships. However, in spite of their shortcomings, most C.E.Os. think that parents are at least more in touch with the school's basic problems than most other managers, who may have had little experience or acquaintance with local authority schools. Parents are also younger than most other managers and can produce a generally livelier discussion. It would be true to say that parenthood is often regarded as a good qualification for school managers.

Clerking.

18. There are divergent views on arrangements for clerking managing bodies, and on the merits of official versus local clerking systems. Similar counties may opt for entirely opposite arrangements. Some scattered rural counties, for example, have all primary schools clerked from the Education Office, while other much more compact Authorities attach importance to one of the managers acting as clerk. A number of Counties have hybrid systems; for example, a Divisional Officer clerks schools in his area, while a manager or other local person acts as clerk in the directly administered areas of the County. Here the C.E.O. can assess the advantages of both systems. In nine counties schools are clerked either from County Hall or from a Divisional Office. In two other Counties all schools are clerked, in principle, from County Hall, the county taking over local clerkships as these fall vacant through death, removal or resignation. Two Counties have hybrid systems and nine rely wholly or mainly on local correspondents. The arguments for central clerking are that it keeps the managers in touch with County Hall and enables authoritative answers to be given to their queries at meetings. It ensures that managing bodies meet, and is good training for the administrative

assistants in the Education Department who are sometimes used for this work. Local clerks may be unbusinesslike or, at the other extreme, legalistic, and the extra administrative cost may be justified by the wider needs of the county's administration as a whole. In favour of local clerking it is claimed that the administrative burden of official clerking would be enormous, and would not be worthwhile, since managers have very little business to transact. In contrast to the argument that it provides officials with good administrative training and an insight into the work of schools, it is dismissed as an "awful grind", and one which is wasteful of the time of high level staff. It is also said to inhibit managers' discussions and to detract from their independence if they have a man from the Office present at the meeting, whose function is perceived as being to tell them what they cannot have. One County tries to meet the acknowledged disadvantages of local clerking by giving newly appointed managers some guidance on the preparation of agenda and minutes, and on means of keeping in touch with the L.E.A. In a number of areas a modest honorarium is paid to local clerks and this is thought to remind them sufficiently of their responsibilities to the county. Even those Authorities which are in favour of local clerking agree that it is not easy to keep track of every managing body in the County and that there may well be cases where managers do not hold their statutory terminal meetings. Indeed, some managing bodies had not met for one or two years and one was said not to have met for ten. One Divisional Officer who clerked personally all meetings of managing bodies in his area argued that there was no point in having a meeting for its own sake, and that if he had too many schools to clerk, there should be fewer meetings rather than more office staff. Some C.E.Os. try to ensure that they themselves or a senior member of their staff visits all managing bodies occasionally, whether as of right or by invitation. In other Counties local clerks and correspondents consult the education office as a matter of form on the preparation of the agenda or on the taking of subsequent action. The limitations of having a completely amateur clerk can be avoided if, as happens in at least one County, members of the County Education Department act as school clerks, paid or unpaid, in their spare time. C.E.Os. with experience of both systems tend to prefer professional clerking in spite of the increased administrative costs. One C.E.O. mentioned that professional clerking does not cost much more than local clerking, especially if the latter system depends on an unbusinesslike clerk with whom correspondence over the simplest item can be protracted. Careful planning may mean that a clerk can attend two or three managing bodies in a day, even in the more scattered Counties, and deal with a number of other matters at the schools. Central clerking is said to be very successful if the representative of the Chief Education Officer regards himself at the meeting as clerk to the managers, rather than as an emissary from the Education Department, and advises them accordingly. We have spoken to a number of school clerks about the problems produced by these dual claims on their loyalties, and without exception they think that they can adapt themselves to the situation. This consideration, of course, applies just as much to school managers, who sit on County Education Committees, or indeed to anyone who sits on a parent body and one or more of its subsidiaries. There would seem to be scope for some investigation into the costs of introducing a central system. It may well be true that many local Authorities are understaffed professionally, and that if three or four additional

professional staff were recruited this might benefit County Education Departments generally as well as improving the arrangements for school management. On the whole we think that the arguments for professional clerking are
strong, in view of the importance of seeing that managers meet once a term
both to transact any necessary business, and to take a wider interest in the
life of the school. This is not "meeting for the sake of meeting".

Managers and Divisional Executives
19. Reservation on the usefulness of managers have come from the C.E.Os.
of some counties with schemes of divisional administration where there is
said to be much duplication in the membership of managing bodies and
divisional executives. In these cases managers may be nothing more than the
fifth wheel on the coach, and in some extreme cases it has been maintained
that the same people are found discussing the same issues five times (that is,
at a managers' meeting, Divisional Executive Sub-Committee, Divisional
Executive, County Education Sub-Committees, and County Education Committee). We have not as yet collected sufficient evidence to justify a substantial discussion on the relationship of managing bodies to Divisional
Executives. However, we have found that C.E.Os. are more inclined in
general to argue against Divisional Executives than against managing bodies
on the grounds that the focus of local interest should be the school and that
its links with the community should be strengthened. It may be of interest to
note that we have come across one county where Divisional Executives have
been rejected in favour of area committees consisting only of local Education
Committee members and meeting once a quarter, and another County which
scrapped its area committees, but developed greater powers on managing
bodies and increased minor Authority representation on them. At this stage
we can say only that it is essential to consider the future of managing bodies
in relation to the future of local government areas and functions as a whole.

Formal Powers
20. Why then should managers meet? We can consider this question by
reference to the formal powers which managers possess, and the functions
which they perform. If we look first at managers' formal powers, there does
not seem to be any overwhelming justification for their existence. In comparison with governing bodies, managing bodies may seem at times to be
very small beer, and even a comparative study of formal provisions in the
rules and articles of government and management provides some evidence of
their lower status. For example:

1. A Counties having identical procedures for appointment of
      Heads in primary and secondary schools   7
   B Counties with identical procedures, except for the operation
      of a promotion list for primary heads   7
   C Counties with procedures giving a smaller part to managers
      (e.g. appointment to be made by L.E.A. subject to consulta-
      tion with managers)   13
2. A Preparation of estimates by individual managing bodies   3
   B No reference to preparation by individual managing bodies   24
3. A Authorities where managers have "general oversight of the
      school and its curriculum"   5 (+2 doubtful)
   B Authorities where reference to "curriculum" is deleted   20

21. In practice the formal powers mentioned are limited by centralized procedures resulting from staffing shortages, central budgeting and bulk ordering procedures, the introduction of capitation systems, and the need to determine building programmes on an overall basis. Initial teaching appointments are generally made centrally by L.E.As., and assistant teachers and non-teaching staff are often appointed solely by the Head with, at most, the chairman of managers present. Managers are left with some share in the appointment of a headmaster, the occasional appointment of non-teaching staff, approval of school lettings, occasional closures, minor repairs and the approval of special requests by the Head for furniture and equipment as their administrative functions. While these relatively trivial matters may leave the managers some little say in running a school, they do not amount to a great deal. The most important function is that of appointing a head, but it occurs so infrequently that of itself it could not justify the existence of managing bodies. Even so, it is worthwhile taking a closer look at C.E.Os' assessments of managers' share in appointing heads. On the whole they give their managers a qualified welcome. For example, we are told that managers may be both effective judges of personality and safeguards against the appointment of "yesmen" As representatives of the community they can be concerned, in varying degrees of effectiveness, to see that the right headmaster for a particular school is appointed, but they cannot, unlike the L.E.A. representatives on the Selection Committee, be regarded in any sense as experts in interviewing. There are said to be some dangers of nepotism and of managers' playing safe. In some areas managers are said not to have the faintest idea how to interview, or to conduct themselves at meetings, even though they take their duties seriously. But if they give a unanimous vote—although this cannot always be guaranteed—this ensures that a newly appointed Head has some local backing.

22. Many of the other powers formally given to managers seem to belong to the days of the school boards, and even where they are not totally irrelevant to present day needs, they do not add up to a real job of work. Examples are rules of management which provide for managers to inspect stock books and registers and to ensure that school-keeper exercises due economy in the use of fuel and cleaning materials. It can hardly be a matter of surprise if managers complain about being frustrated, although they never seem to suggest any concrete extra powers which they might have, and they rarely carry their frustration to the point of resigning.

Informal Aspects

23. It may be more profitable to ask about the influences which managers exert, and the extent to which they act as ambassadors or public relations agents on behalf of their school. This aspect of their work is not emphasized in most rules of management, and this lack is particularly important when the rules and instruments are all which most L.E.As. ever give their managers by way of guidance. Some C.E.Os. have admitted that they might do more to develop informal aspects of managers' work, or to show them where they stand in relation to the administrative system as a whole. Five of the Counties we have visited issue handbooks. Some of these are written especially for managers, while others are intended mainly for Heads, with a special introduction emphasising how managers can show a general interest in the schools'

work in between their terminal meetings. These handbooks are said to be greatly appreciated. They certainly appear likely to give managers many excellent ideas on ways in which they can make a positive contribution to the work of the school. Two L.E.As. hold conferences for groups of managers, and the C.E.Os. have been so enthusiastic about these that it is worth quoting from our reports in some detail:

24. In Authority A, the Chief Education Officer felt strongly the danger of individual managers not having contact with the Authority and its officers. He thought there was a need for means by which chairmen of committees and he himself might meet managers informally to discuss plans and griev- ances, and to improve their interest in and information on local schools. He thought that the right kind of background would be provided by an exhibition of schools' work, where those concerned could meet for an afternoon and compare notes over tea. The system of conferences that resulted, and which have been held now for ten years, seems to have paid off. With six or seven groups of primary schools meeting at a time it takes three years to cover the County.

25. In Authority B, meetings of all managers were held after the triennial elections. This gave new managers a considerable amount of informal guidance, and old managers a chance of keeping up to date. The C.E.O. said that the event was welcomed by managers and that this was borne out by the attendance figures. Meetings were held at a school which would be especially interesting to managers, for example, a school for handicapped children, or a new comprehensive school. In the morning the managers would listen to two or three speakers, break for lunch, and in the afternoon there would be a question and answer session. The speakers would talk on matters of general educational interest. The C.E.O. in his talk might incorporate some hints on minor administrative detail (for example, the inadvisability of sending an omnibus letter on more than one subject to County Hall, as this could cause difficulties and was likely to lead to delay). It was hoped that the morning talks would spark off questions for the afternoon session, answered by a panel which included the C.E.O., the Chairman of the Education Committee, and two Heads: such questions might even include such explosive issues as "How does one sack a Head?" It was thought that this conference added to the good feeling which existed between the Com- mittee and the managers, and gave managers a chance to discuss their mutual interests and difficulties.

26. Another County issues a special bulletin to managers and governors on general educational matters twice a year, while a few others let the clerks to managing bodies see the monthly schools bulletins sent to Heads which are concerned mainly with current administrative detail.

In one County a newsletter is sent to managers by the Divisional Officers. We are told that this trouble is amply repaid, and produces keener managers who are much better informed on current developments, and able to discuss problems wider than those affecting their own school.

Relations with Heads and the public
27. C.E.Os. have been unanimous in telling us that in most cases relations between Heads and their managers are smooth and harmonious. There is the occasional domineering chairman, but there is generally great respect among managers for the headmaster, and most cases of disharmony are said to be

the fault of the Authority, or of the Head who will not make the special effort needed to gain his manager's confidence. Some Heads tend to be rightly suspicious of their managers—in one C.E.O's. words "Some of them can be quite awful"—while on the other hand, there is said to be a small minority of heads who do not appreciate the importance of carrying their managers with them. Failure to establish good relations with managers can have damaging consequences, particularly in rural areas. C.E.Os. think that the dangers of managers overstepping the mark and trespassing on the Head's professional preserves are much exaggerated. Managers are far more likely to be inhibited from asking questions relating to the curriculum, and, like their colleagues in the boroughs, to be dependent for their interest on the contents of the Head's report. When reports are full and forthcoming, and include mention of a school's shortcomings, they lead to constructive discussion, and not, as might be feared, to interference in the day to day running of the school on the part of the managers. There is bound to be some ambivalence in the attitude of C.E.Os. when considering managers' general interest in the school and the Head's professional autonomy and status, and this is reflected in the varying extent to which C.E.Os. expect to consult their chairman over "crisis" issues, for example such matters as food poisoning arising from schools' meals, the introduction of sex education, and outbreaks of bullying. While it is assumed that Heads should be able to solve most of their schools' problems on their own, C.E.Os. agree that they would be most misguided not to consult their chairman, at least with the intention of informing him of the action they propose to take. Heads can get out of touch with public feeling, and the presence of an effective and interested body of managers can help to overcome this. We are told that some village managers go to great time and trouble to give their Head useful and intelligent backing, that they can be helpful in introducing a new Head to the village, and that they can bring about a remarkably effective relationship between the parents and the school. It is not thought likely that all members of one managing body will be narrow-minded, and particularly where the Head is in a difficult school or an unreceptive area they can be a great source of encouragement to him. Heads who live in the village schoolhouse are sometimes at the mercy of angry fathers, and glad to have the managers on their side, while if the Head does not live in the village and act as its general factotum, there is said to be a greater need still for the managers to act as his eyes and ears. Even if managers are not very penetrating they often see things from the point of view of the sensible parent, which is of great benefit to both the school and the education office.

28. C.E.Os. of County Authorities are equally emphatic on the importance of managers' ambassadorial functions. We find this unanimity most impressive, particularly as it seems to be shared by their staff who are in everyday contact with managers. We do not think we have been presented with a remote and idealized view, as C.E.Os. have been very ready to talk about managers' shortcomings, examples of which have been quoted. One or two C.E.Os. say explicitly that these aspects of schools management are equally important in the towns although, as we have seen, their colleagues in the County Boroughs are, for the most part, not equally concerned. It would have been easy for C.E.Os. to content themselves with vague assertions of managers' usefulness, but we have come across numbers of instances where managers have justified

their existence ten times over, in spite of the doubtful administrative case for managing bodies. We are told that, in times of rapid change, managers can be a most potent force in presenting educational problems to the public. Service as managers has completely altered many people's attitudes to education and local administration, and they have in many cases been successful advocates of the needs of their school within the County's system of broad priorities. While they may not know much about education, they are often shrewd and active in public life and able to use their experience to the benefit of the school. They act as a first court of reference over major discipline problems. Parents are happy in knowing that local residents are involved with the school, and that managers can bring the Divisional Officer's attention to matters affecting their own children. The charge that managers can occasionally be awkward is not an argument against them, as the L.E.A. has to guard against the danger of complacency, and should be happy to welcome suggestions or criticisms from any quarter. This stress on the importance of managers is found equally in all sorts and sizes of County. One interesting regional difference appears to be that in the north there is a greater willingness for managers to concern themselves with the welfare of individual children, in additon to that of the school as a whole. Managers will, for example, have an informal word with difficult parents, or go behind the scenes to concern themselves with the needs of deprived children. This concern may be seen as a valuable legacy of previous hard times, but it is only fair to say that the opinion was expressed in other Authorities that Education Welfare Officers or Child Care Officers should be able to cope with these individual problems.

Conclusion

29. The data and views collected so far need to be treated with some considerable caution. They form only about a third, and possibly not a fully representative third, of the first stage of our research. Had we spent the last few months interviewing Heads or managers, or sitting in on meetings of managing bodies, we might now be presenting a markedly different picture. We do not, therefore, consider that we can draw more than entirely tentative conclusions at the present stage, but we think that the information and the assessments we have heard have been based on more than hearsay or second-hand evidence. Everywhere we have interviewed the staff of Education Departments directly concerned with school management, where the C.E.O. has not handled this himself. Some C.E.Os. have expounded their philosophy of school management in considerable detail, and we have been able in some places to discover how far current practice is formed by the C.E.O. or the chairman of the Education Committee. In some L.E.As. we have been confronted by a number of officers who have not been slow to disagree among themselves on almost any aspect of school management. These disagreements have been most illuminating. As the interviews have progressed, we have been better able to exploit the most promising questions, and in general we think that we have succeeded in getting C.E.Os. and their staff to ventilate their views on every important facet of school management.

30. It is quite clear that County Borough and County C.E.Os. look at school management in entirely different lights. Up to a point, this is an inevitable consequence of geographical differences, and even of different Committee

systems. In the Counties, with Committee meetings held at longer intervals and with many schools at a considerable distance from their administrative centres, there must perforce be more delegation to the individual school. The approval by the Department of Education and Science of schemes of school government which provide for large groups, with a majority of Education Committee members on the governing body, appears at least to suggest official acquiescence in the prevailing County Borough philosophy. It would seem to apply even more forcibly to managing bodies in the Boroughs. Local Authorities here are, of course, following what is allowed to them by the Education Act, 1944. It may be said that if a school has its individual visitor it is given some sort of status even when forming part of a grouped system of school management, and arguments against individual managing bodies or bodies with small groups are almost universal in the Boroughs. But is this the whole of the story? Some County C.E.Os. do not accept this, and they consider that the need to establish links between the school and the community is just as urgent in urban areas. This would seem to be supported by the minority of County Boroughs which has a working system of school management with small groups, if not with individual managing bodies.

31. Much has been made of the argument that administrative cost would prevent the establishment of more highly developed systems of school managements in the Boroughs. We think that this argument needs to be scrutinized closely, and it might also be worthwhile considering the possibility of using a manager to act as clerk, as is already done on one Borough Authority.

APPENDIX 14

NOTES ON VARIATION IN L.E.A. PROVISION*

by B. P. Davies, Lecturer in Social Administration
London School of Economics and Political Science

A. PRIMARY SCHOOL EDUCATION AND THE STUDENT YIELD OF SECONDARY SCHOOLS

1. It is in some ways useful to compare the education system with an industry which has a variety of "inputs", a number of stages, and a wide range of "outputs". Ideally, questions of resource allocation should be settled by calculating what combination of "inputs" would most effectively produce the required "output" of people of various attributes, given the technical coefficients of the production function, the relative prices of inputs and limitations or their supply. This analogy is of limited use in practice, however. There is no easy way of deciding the educational outputs required, since not only is the relative importance of different uses of outputs a controversial matter but also technical aids to judgement about the need for outputs for these uses are as yet primitive, and yield results which are unreliable. Too little is known about how inputs could best be combined to produce a given output, unless one defines output in a way that is no more than a description of the inputs. Many of the most important inputs and standards are difficult to measure. Others could be measured quite easily, but central and local authorities have not thought it worth while to do so. Thus variation in the rate of turnover of teachers or the number of secondary schools without science labs or library rooms are not recorded although the data exists for both and merely requires analysis and although the importance of both was emphasized in the Newsom Report.

2. There are very few indices of the final and intermediate output of the local authority education system. One can make rough estimates of the final output of school leavers at various ages. This is not an adequate measure of output since it takes no account of the quality of the school leavers. One cannot classify them by the number of "O" level, "A" level, O.N.C., H.N.C., C.I.S.E. and other passes in various subjects groups obtained for instance.[†] It is unfortunate that we lack indices of educational success for all types of pupils, since American studies (and British experience) have shown that systems that are relatively successful with the bright children are not necessarily those which are successful with others.[‡] Since practically the only output indices suitable

---

* Limitations of space prevent a full statement of the results of the analysis of the 100 or so standards indices, but a fuller analysis is to be published elsewhere. See BLEDDYN DAVIES. *Social Needs and Resources in Local Services*, London, 1967; and a forthcoming Occasional Paper in Social administration.

† The regional figures for numbers of "O" and "A" levels gained are based on a sample which is too small to give accurate results for individual authorities. They could perhaps be used to measure the output of individual authorities if results for several years were added together.

‡ See S. M. GOODMAN: *The Assessment of School Quality*, New York, 1959.

Table 1
Coefficients of Variation‡ of Indices of
Provision of Primary and Secondary Education (1961–62)

Variable Reference Numbers§	Index	Primary schools	Secondary schools
6, 20	Expenditure on teachers' salaries*	7·2	7·2
7, 21	Expenditure on non-teaching staff wages and salaries*	24·2	20·2
8, 22	Expenditure on upkeep of grounds and buildings*	39·3	35·0
9, 23	Expenditure of fuel, etc.*	18·8	16·6
10, 24	Expenditure on rent, rates, etc.*	29·0	22·5
127, 128	Expenditure Debt charges*	33·7	29·7
11, 28	Total cost*	8·9	7·4
12, 30	Proportion of classes oversize	53·3	16·3
15, 32	Teachers released for special advanced training†	174·9	168·2
117	Proportion of pupils aged 13 in maintained grammar, comprehensive, direct grant and independent schools	—	27·6

* £ per pupil.
† Per thousand teachers.
‡ Coefficient of variation is equal to one hundred times the standard deviation divided by the mean.
§ Variable numbers refer to the variables list shown at the end of this Appendix.

Table 2
Correlation of Indices of Standards of Provision of Primary
and Secondary School Education and Output Indices, 1961–1962

Variable reference numbers		Pupils aged 17 as % of those aged 13 four years ago 55	Total new awards to universities/population 17–19 108	Full value L.E.A. awards for non-universities/ population 17–19 37	Lesser value L.E.A. awards/population 17–19 38	Teacher training college entrants/population 17–19 39	New awards and training college/entrants population 17–19 109
	PRIMARY						
6	Cost of teachers' salaries/pupil	+0·32	+0·22	+0·22	+0·18	+0·16	+0·27
127	Debt charges/pupil	+0·17	+0·04	+0·28	−0·09	+0·19	+0·10
11	Total cost/pupil	+0·16	+0·00	+0·24	+0·01	+0·00	+0·05
12	Percentage classes oversize	−0·18	−0·17	−0·21	−0·08	−0·16	−0·20
15	Teachers released for special advanced courses/teachers	+0·04	+0·12	+0·12	+0·19	−0·13	+0·15
	SECONDARY						
20	Cost of teachers' salaries/pupil	+0·33	+0·25	+0·38	+0·15	−0·04	+0·31
128	Debt charges/pupil	−0·17	−0·03	+0·07	+0·10	−0·22	−0·03
28	Total cost/pupil	+0·14	+0·15	+0·41	+0·06	−0·20	+0·17
30	Percentage classes oversize	−0·19	−0·20	−0·19	−0·04	−0·11	−0·26
32	Teachers released for special advanced courses/teachers	−0·00	−0·12	+0·18	−0·00	+0·04	−0·11

for analysis measure the intermediate output of the system entering higher education, this note concentrates on them.

3. At first sight, it might seem that variations in standards—i.e., variations in the quantities and quality of inputs—of primary school systems might have considerable influence on the intermediate output of secondary schools going on to higher education, and the final output of pupils leaving during or after a Sixth Form course. One reason for this is that standards of provision of primary education are more unequally distributed than most aspects of standards of provision of secondary schools. This is shown in Table 1, which uses coefficients of variation.* None of the coefficients of variation for secondary schools exceeded the coefficients for the equivalent indices for primary schools and for most indices the difference between coefficient values was substantial. However the proportion of pupils aged 13 in non-selective and selective schools was more unequally distributed than other important indices of secondary school provision.

4. The correlation coefficients measuring the degree of association between certain indices of primary school provision and indices of output shown in Table 2 might also imply that variations in important standards of provision of primary schools might cause difference in output.† Thus expenditure on teachers' salaries per pupil was clearly correlated with the proportion of the cohort staying on until their 17th year, the proportion receiving awards for universities and, to a lesser extent, the proportion receiving lesser-value awards (to other branches of higher education) and the proportion entering training colleges, although the coefficients are not high. Similarly total expenditure per pupil was correlated with the proportion receiving awards for universities, and the proportion staying on. But the degree of correlation between the indices of provision of primary education and the most important output indices was generally smaller than that between the indices of primary education and the equivalent indices of secondary education. Thus expenditure per pupil on teachers' salaries in the two types of school were correlated $+0.37$, expenditure per pupil on debt changes (reflecting the proportion of school places new) were correlated $+0.22$ and total expenditure per pupil were correlated $+0.36$. The proportion of classes oversize in the two types of school were correlated $+0.18$. The equivalent indices of provision of secondary education were in general more highly correlated with the output indices than were the indices of primary education, as is shown in the bottom part of Table 2. Thus it is likely that the direct effect of the variation in standards of provision of primary education on these outputs indices is small. Multiple regres-

---

* The Coefficient of Variation is used to measure the degree of inequality of indices. The coefficient measures the relative dispersion of the scatter of readings around the mean of the readings. It is independent of the units in which the index is stated, but it can be misleading if the distribution of readings is very skewed or if the relative values of index readings in relation to zero is arbitrary.

† The correlation coefficient is used to describe the degree of association between variables. It measures the degree to which readings which are greater or less than the mean of one variable tend to be associated with readings which are greater or less than the mean of the other variables. If high readings in one variable tend to be accompanied by high readings in the other, the sign of the coefficient is positive, while if high readings in one tend to be accompanied by low readings in the other, the sign is negative. The highest value a coefficient can take is $+1.00$ or -1.00, and the lowest reading 0.00. The coefficient understates the degree of correlation if the association is non-linear.

sion analyses of the output indices on standards and socio-economic characteristics of areas support this conclusion.*

5. These results imply that it would be possible to have a slightly different pattern of variation in standards of provision between local education authority areas without affecting the pattern of variation of output of students from each authority. The pattern of variation in the yield of students, people likely to join what some have called the "clerisy", is unlikely to be affected by the small change in the pattern of variations in standards which could be achieved without a very considerable increase in the amount of re-allocable resources flowing into primary school education. Research of a different kind would be needed to test this hypothesis. These results tell one nothing about the effects of a redistribution of resources within an authority between schools attended by children who are most likely to go on to higher education and other schools. They tell one little about the effects of increasing or diminishing the total amount of resources devoted to primary school education. I argue elsewhere that a small redistribution of resources in favour of authorities with bad social conditions would leave the pattern of student yield unaffected, and that such a redistribution would be more compatible with the aim to maximise the contribution of education to economic growth than is usually thought.†

B. VARIATION IN STANDARDS OF PROVISION AND SOCIAL CONDITIONS

6. The aim of this section is to describe the variation in standards of provision of primary school education and some other services enjoyed by children of primary school age, showing how each important aspect is correlated with social conditions which make it "desirable" that services should be provided at a higher standard if one were to assume that the most important criterion for assessing the distribution of resources was the extent to which it accorded effective equality of educational opportunity. It is necessary to make some such assumption because the aims of some of the more important branches of the education service are many, some may conflict with one another, and the socio-economic attributes of local education authorities differ in relevance according to the aims considered most important.

7. The pattern of variation in standards provides some evidence about what groups of children receive resources, how area of residence influences children's opportunities, and how standards of provision in areas where a high proportion of children live in social conditions which reduce their educational opportunity compare with standards in other areas. Both the degree to which variations in standards accompany—are correlated with—variations in social conditions, and the relative inequality of standards are important. These two aspects must be considered together, since the assessments of a case in which there is a high degree of correlation between a standards index and social conditions can greatly depend on the degree of inequality of the standards index, and similarly a certain degree of inequality can have very different implications depending on the degree of correlation.

---

* These analyses will be described in the forthcoming Occasional Paper, which will also deal with the complicated and fascinating pattern of variations in standards of provision of secondary and other forms of education.

† *The Social Needs and Resources in Local Services*, Chapter 12.

Table 3—Intercorrelation of Indices of Social Conditions, 1965

Ref. Nos.	Variables	138	90	83	69	76	72	73	71	70	88	62	61	Mean	Coefficient of variation
	Social class														
60	Social class I	+0·17	−0·53	+0·39	+0·41	−0·40	+0·48	+0·29	+0·08	−0·31	−0·30	−0·78	+0·91	11·43	29·5
61	Non-manual	+0·25	−0·56	+0·37	−0·46	−0·58	+0·45	+0·46	−0·09	−0·32	−0·36	−0·78	1	28·89	24·7
62	Semi- and unskilled	−0·30	−0·56	+0·30	+0·22	+0·50	−0·50	−0·24	−0·08	+0·32	+0·40	1		27·64	18·9
	Completed family size														
88		−0·11	+0·56	−0·01	+0·22	+0·08	−0·17	+0·04	+0·07	+0·43	1			1·29	15·0
	Housing														
70	Overcrowding	+0·04	+0·41	−0·15	+0·29	+0·05	−0·17	+0·11	+0·57	1				2·74	54·3
71	Sharing	−0·40	−0·35	−0·06	+0·32	−0·60	−0·13	−0·03	1					5·15	96·5
73	Small dwellings	−0·00	+0·06	−0·06	+0·04	+0·14	−0·04	1						13·27	60·5
72	Four census amenities	−0·08	−0·03	+0·57	+0·16	−0·34	1							67·14	12·8
76	Low value dwellings	−0·35	+0·28	+0·31	+0·22	1								18·09	87·9
69	L.A. housing	−0·12	−0·48	+0·21	1									25·26	34·5
	Others														
83	Pop. increase	−0·01	+0·23	1										0·33	—
90	% pop. aged 5–11	−0·33	1											100·49	11·3
138	% pop. born in the Newer Commonwealth	1												100·54	33·7

(i) *Inter-Correlation of Social Conditions*
8. Table 3 shows the degree of inter-correlation of indices of social conditions. The indices include measures of three of the five factors distinguished by H. R. Simpson in Table A of Appendix II of *The Home and The School* as having a major influence on the educational achievement of children of primary school age. In addition to indices of social class, bad housing, and family size, there are indices of population growth, of the proportion of the population of primary school age, and of the proportion of the population born in newer Commonwealth countries.* All of these measure factors which can create additional needs for educational resources or higher standards of provision. (The tables for education welfare services include other indices of social conditions.)

9. Table 3 shows that, as Moser found,† social class indices were correlated with other socio-economic indices. Low social class, overcrowding, the absence of housing amenities, low value dwellings, and a high proportion of the population of infant and primary school age, and to a lesser extent large families and declining populations are all correlated with each other and thus interact to create an environment that obstructs educational progress. The correlation coefficients seem high enough for it to be feasible to compile an index of bad social conditions which would provide a reasonably good measure of the degree to which l.e.a.'s suffer from social conditions detrimental to the educational attainment of their pupils.‡

(ii) *Primary school provision and social conditions*
10. Table 4 shows the correlations between indices of standards of provision of primary schools and those of social conditions. The degree of correlation of most standards indices with the social conditions indices was low. Standards were, on the whole, neither strongly positive nor negatively correlated with social conditions detrimental to the educational development of primary school pupils. Moreover, most important standards indices were less variable than were social conditions indices. There is therefore little indication that the central government and local authorities have created a system which ensures positive discrimination in favour of (or against) the educationally difficult areas.

11. Expenditure per pupil on debt charges, reflecting the proportion of school places built since 1945, was more unequally distributed than total expenditure or expenditure on teachers' salaries per pupil and debt charges tended to be lowest in low social class areas. This is largely a reflection of the concentration of the building effort on areas with rapidly expanding populations. Authorities with a high proportion of their labour force in semi-skilled and unskilled jobs tended to have a higher proportion of their quota unfilled than other authorities, but the degree of variation in the proportion of the quota unfilled was very small.

12. Teachers' salaries and total cost per pupil in 1950–1 were as weakly correlated with social conditions as they were more than a decade later. This is not surprising, since patterns of provision of local authority services show

---

* J. W. B. DOUGLAS: *The Home and the School*, London, 1964, Appendix II
† C. A. MOSER and W. SCOTT, *British Towns*, London, 1961.
‡ Such an index will be presented and the extent to which it accounts for variation will be analysed in the forthcoming Occasional Paper. *Op. cit.*

Table 4—Correlation of Indices of Primary School Provision with Social Conditions

Variables*	5	6	7	8	9	10	127	11	12	13	15	100	56	58
60 Social class I	+0·01	+0·11	−0·18	−0·32	−0·29	−0·14	+0·14	−0·05	−0·09	−0·30	+0·09	+0·21	+0·09	−0·06
61 Non-manual	−0·03	+0·18	−0·19	−0·23	−0·22	−0·11	+0·15	+0·03	−0·14	−0·39	+0·13	+0·23	+0·13	+0·01
62 Semi- and unskilled	+0·00	−0·09	+0·15	+0·24	+0·14	−0·03	−0·28	−0·05	+0·14	+0·41	−0·11	−0·34	+0·13	+0·18
88 Family size	+0·14	−0·23	−0·03	−0·09	−0·08	−0·01	+0·05	−0·15	+0·30	+0·02	−0·19	−0·17	−0·10	−0·15
70 Overcrowding	+0·19	−0·15	−0·12	−0·01	−0·01	−0·05	−0·08	−0·15	+0·26	−0·07	−0·02	−0·27	−0·00	−0·10
71 Shared dwellings	−0·07	+0·30	+0·01	+0·29	+0·03	+0·03	+0·14	+0·27	−0·09	−0·28	−0·02	+0·12	+0·20	+0·15
73 Small dwellings	+0·19	−0·12	−0·28	−0·11	−0·04	−0·19	−0·03	−0·20	+0·00	−0·05	−0·03	−0·30	+0·11	−0·03
72 Four census amenities	+0·19	−0·19	−0·27	−0·43	−0·39	−0·01	+0·23	−0·21	+0·19	−0·36	+0·08	+0·10	+0·28	−0·40
76 Low value herids.	+0·05	−0·08	+0·08	+0·06	+0·09	−0·17	−0·29	−0·12	−0·05	+0·62	−0·18	−0·29	+0·14	+0·19
69 L.A. housing	+0·12	−0·24	−0·02	−0·10	+0·06	+0·29	+0·29	−0·01	+0·04	−0·00	−0·06	−0·14	−0·30	−0·27
90 % pop. aged 5–11	+0·15	−0·38	−0·14	−0·15	−0·18	+0·08	+0·04	−0·26	+0·30	−0·03	−0·01	−0·39	−0·17	−0·18
83 % increase population	+0·01	−0·14	−0·31	−0·30	−0·35	+0·12	+0·45	−0·07	+0·10	−0·41	+0·05	−0·02	−0·14	−0·24
138 % pop. born in the Newer Commonwealth	−0·13	+0·14	+0·39	+0·22	+0·30	+0·21	+0·21	+0·36	−0·11	−0·26	+0·09	+0·35	−0·08	+0·06
Coefficient of variation	5·6	7·2	24·2	39·3	18·8	29·0	33·7	8·9	53·3	18·0	174·9	2·77	9·9	10·6

Variable Key: 5. Pupils per full-time teacher, 1962.
6. Cost of teachers school wages and salaries per pupil, 1961–2.
7. Cost of non-teaching staff wages and salaries per pupil, 1961–2.
8. Cost of upkeep of buildings and grounds per pupil, 1961–2.
9. Cost of Fuel, etc., per pupil, 1961–2.
10. Rent, rate and other expenses per pupil, 1961–2
127. Debt charges per pupil, 1961–2
11. Total cost per pupil, 1961–2, excluding nursery schools.
12. Percentage of classes which are oversize (more than 30) in Junior Schools, 1961.
13. Pupils per school, 1962.
15. Number of teachers released for special advanced courses per teacher, 1964.
100. Full-time equivalent teachers as a proportion of the quota recommended by the Ministry of Education, 1961.
56. Cost of teaching salaries per pupil, 1950–1
58. Total cost per pupil, 1950–1.

great continuity. This was as true of education as in general it was of local health, welfare and children services.* Table 5 shows the same pattern in primary education. One could predict over a third of the variation in teachers' salaries per pupil in 1961–2 from the pattern in 1950–1, and over four-fifths of it from the pattern in 1958–9. Similarly, one could predict more than a quarter of the variation in total costs per pupil from the variation in 1950–1, and three-quarters of it from the variation in 1958–9. This continuity of pattern was even more striking in the case of the 53 boroughs which Professor Moser classified as "industrial".† Among these the variation of teachers' salaries in 1950–1 accounted for one-half of the variation in 1961–2, and the variation of total cost per pupil in 1950–1 accounted for 30 per cent of the variation in 1961–2. Thus patterns of expenditure on the principal items in the budget tend to persist over a long period.

Table 5

Continuity in Standards

	1958–9	1961–2	Coefficient of variation
Teachers' salaries*			
1950–1	+0·62	+0·61	9·9
1958–9	1	+0·90	7·9
1961–2		1	7·2
Total cost*			
1950–1	+0·61	+0·51	10·6
1958–9	1	+0·85	8·8
1961–2		1	8·9

* Per pupil.

13. A second feature of Table 5 is the decline in the relative inequality of the indices over time. The relative inequality of standards was slightly greater in the 83 county boroughs than in the industrial county boroughs alone, and the decline in inequality seemed to be greater. There was a similar decline in inequality of total costs per pupil up to 1958–9, but after that the tendency for inequality to decline among 83 boroughs seems to have been arrested, though the decline continued among industrial boroughs.

(iii) *Education Welfare Services and Social Conditions*

(a) *School Meals and Milk*

14. Most of the education welfare services analysed here have in common that they were provided mainly in order to assist poorer children to make more effective use of the education system. Therefore standards of provision should generally be highest where social conditions are worst. The services considered fell into five groups—school milk and meals, special education, the school medical services, nursery schools and recreation facilities. The correlation between standards of provision of school meals and milk services with social conditions indices are shown in Table 6. Variations in expenditure on meals and milk were dominated by variations in the former, the proportion receiving meals being negatively correlated (−0·26) with the proportion receiving milk.

---

* See BLEDDYN DAVIES: *Social Needs and Resources in Local Services, op. cit.*
† C. A. MOSER and W. SCOTT: *British Towns, op. cit.*

The proportion receiving dinners was highest in the high social class areas where social conditions were good. It was also high where a high proportion of the working population were women.‡ The proportion receiving milk was correlated with bad social conditions. The contrast in patterns may well have been due to the fact that a charge is imposed for meals. Thus the proportion receiving dinners tended to be low where the proportion of children in great need was high. Therefore it is likely that schools meals are not being consumed by many of those who are in most need of them. Survey research is needed to investigate whether this is so.

(b) *School Health Services*

15. Table 7 shows that standards of provision of dental services were considerably more unequal than standards of provision of medical services, and that the number of dental officers was negatively correlated with low social class. Expenditure, which measures local authorities' financial effort to provide these services, was correlated with low social class, heavy industry, bad

Table 6

Correlations of Standards of Provision of School
Meals and Milk Services with Social Conditions, 1961–1962

Variables		Expenditure on meals and milk	% pupils receiving dinners	% pupils receiving milk	Food cost per dinner
		43	45	46	47
60	Social class I	−0·15	+0·45	−0·42	−0·00
61	Non-manual	−0·15	+0·42	−0·37	+0·04
62	Semi- and unskilled	+0·19	−0·33	+0·40	−0·13
63	Females:Males in employment	+0·07	+0·40	−0·06	−0·41
70	Overcrowding	+0·00	−0·36	+0·37	−0·08
73	Housing amenities	−0·08	+0·15	−0·13	+0·11
74	Rooms per dwelling	−0·21	−0·01	−0·06	+0·16
76	Low value dwellings	+0·35	+0·07	+0·18	−0·21
88	Family size	+0·03	−0·34	+0·37	−0·02
89	% women aged 35–39 widowed	−0·06	−0·08	+0·17	−0·08
138	% population born in Newer Commonwealth	−0·09	+0·14	−0·27	+0·13
90	% population aged 5–11	+0·30	−0·40	+0·33	+0·15
91	% population aged 11–18	+0·02	−0·44	+0·17	+0·10
	Coefficient of variation	17·1	24·7	5·3	3·8

* Per thousand population.
† Pupils in nursery, primary, secondary and special schools.

‡ The correlation between low social class and women's working is very low, so that it would not be a statistical impossibility for the proportion receiving dinners to be positively correlated with both to a substantial degree.

housing, and population density, but the coefficients were low. In general, the standards of provision of school medical services were uncorrelated with indices of social conditions, as were the indices for primary schools.

(c) *Nursery Schools, Special Education, Aid to Pupils in Secondary Schools, and Recreation Facilities.*

16. Many authorities did not provide nursery schools. It can be seen from Table 8 that the more extensive the provision of schools, the higher the pupil/ teacher ratio. Thus the authorities providing nursery education on the largest scale may be using their staff most efficiently. Provision was uncorrelated with bad social conditions.*

17. Expenditure on special education was high in industrial towns and in bigger authorities. Expenditure on aid to secondary school pupils was uncorrelated with social conditions. Although expenditure on recreation facilities was high in densely populated areas. it was uncorrelated with other social conditions indices.

(d) *Inequality of Standards of Provision of Education Welfare Services*

18. Indices of standards of provision of these education welfare services were much more unequally distributed than the most important indices of standards of provision of primary and secondary education. This can be attributed partly to the fact that the authorities and those using the services both have greater scope for choice in the provision and use of welfare services than in the provision and use of education itself.

(iv) *Related Services, Education Welfare Services and Social Conditions*

19. As Table 9 shows, provision of day nurseries was uncorrelated (-0.11) with the provision of nursery school places, but was markedly correlated with the ratio of women to men in employment, population size and the proportion of live births illegitimate. There were lower positive correlations with population density and the proportion of the population born in the newer Commonwealth countries. Expenditure on Child Welfare Services by health departments correlated with standards of provision of most education welfare services, particularly expenditure on school medical services. Standards tended to be high in areas where populations had been falling, where a high proportion of adult males were in manual jobs, and where housing conditions were poor, but the correlations coefficients were low.

20. Expenditure on health visiting—less unequally distributed than the other related services by health departments—tended to be positively correlated with expenditure on medical services. Standards were correlated with the proportion of women aged 35–9 widowed, overcrowded housing, falling populations and low social class. The number of child care officers was correlated with the proportion of women working and with need correlates such as the proportion of live births illegitimate and the proportion of the population aged between 5 and 11 and the proportion of the population born in the newer Commonwealth countries. The number was, however, negatively correlated with low social class. The proportion of officers trained was also correlated with the illegitimate birth rate and the proportion of the population of school age. The

---

* An analysis of variance of the towns which provided a service also showed an absence of correlation with indices of social conditions.

Table 7

Correlation of Standards of Provision of School Health Services with Social Conditions Indices, 1961–1962

Variables	Expenditure on school medical services*	Medical Officers†	Dental Officers†	School nurses†	School nurses and nursery assistants†	Dental attendants, etc.	Child guidance centre staff*
	42	48	49	50	99	97	98
60 Social class I	−0·35	−0·05	+0·17	−0·14	−0·16	+0·05	+0·07
61 Non-manual	−0·27	+0·05	+0·18	−0·09	−0·13	+0·01	+0·07
62 Semi and unskilled	+0·20	+0·04	−0·24	+0·10	−0·10	−0·14	−0·12
63 Females: males in employment	−0·02	−0·07	+0·19	+0·14	+0·04	+0·22	+0·08
70 Overcrowding	+0·09	−0·11	−0·09	+0·15	+0·23	+0·05	−0·22
72 Housing amenities	−0·21	−0·16	+0·09	−0·16	−0·19	−0·02	+0·15
74 Rooms per dwelling	+0·07	+0·18	+0·08	−0·05	−0·02	−0·03	+0·05
76 Low rateable value dwellings	+0·07	−0·06	−0·05	−0·05	−0·05	+0·02	−0·09
88 Family size	−0·09	−0·23	−0·26	−0·14	−0·03	−0·12	−0·22
89 % women aged 35–39 widowed	+0·10	−0·06	+0·11	+0·09	+0·13	+0·05	+0·02
106 Population per acre	+0·17	−0·02	−0·10	+0·28	+0·27	−0·05	−0·19
138 % population born in Newer Commonwealth	−0·01	+0·11	+0·01	+0·13	+0·16	+0·05	+0·10
65 Heavy industry	+0·21	−0·08	−0·09	+0·07	+0·10	+0·04	−0·03
Coefficient of variation	24·3	24·9	48·6	32·8	40·8	47·8	126·0

* Per thousand population.
† Per pupil.

Note.—The correlation between Variable 42 and the Proportion of the Population aged 5–11 was +0·02 and that between Variable 42 and the Proportion of the Population aged 11–18 was +0·15.

Table 8

Correlations of Standards of Provision of Nursery School Education, Special Education, Aid to Secondary School Pupils and Recreation Facilities with Social Conditions Indices, 1961–1962

Variables	Nursery school pupils*	Expenditure on special education*	Expenditure on Aid to secondary school pupils†	Expenditure on recreational facilities*
	1	40	112	41
60 Social class I	−0·10	−0·34	+0·06	−0·12
61 Non-manual class	−0·19	−0·33	+0·13	−0·10
62 Semi and unskilled class	+0·13	+0·13	−0·00	+0·04
63 Employed females: employed males	+0·17	+0·13	+0·30	−0·03
67 Industrial occupations	+0·22	+0·36	−0·17	−0·08
70 Overcrowding	−0·04	+0·29	−0·19	+0·18
72 Housing amenities	−0·14	−0·10	+0·13	−0·15
74 Rooms per dwelling	−0·19	−0·17	−0·02	+0·00
76 Low rateable value dwellings	+0·26	+0·16	+0·04	−0·04
88 Family size	+0·04	+0·17	−0·02	+0·04
89 % women aged 35–39 widowed	−0·13	−0·04	+0·01	−0·05
106 Population per acre	−0·08	+0·21	−0·05	+0·22
87 % births illegitimate	−0·02	+0·11	−0·16	+0·11
85 Birth rate	+0·03	+0·42	−0·13	+0·15
84 % increase in population due to other than births and deaths	−0·12	−0·30	+0·13	−0·17
90 % population aged 5–11	+0·04	+0·23	−0·10	+0·06
91 % population aged 11–18	−0·06	+0·23	−0·24	+0·18
107 Population size (log transformed)	−0·08	+0·31	−0·05	+0·16
138 % population born in Newer Commonwealth	−0·18	+0·27	−0·20	+0·26
Coefficient of variation	135·8	31·0	135·0	49·3

* Per thousand population.
† Per pupil.

Table 9

Correlations of Standards of Provision of Related Social Services with Education Welfare Services and Social Conditions, 1961–1962

	Variables	Expenditure on N.H.S. day nurseries*	Expenditure on N.H.S. child welfare services*	Expenditure on health visiting*	Number of child care officers	% child care officers fully trained
		1	2	3	4	5
	(a) Related services and Education Welfare Services					
1	Nursery school pupils*	−0·11	+0·20	+0·09	+0·13	+0·17
40	Expenditure on Special Education*	+0·34	+0·28	+0·04	+0·03	+0·09
41	Expenditure on recreation facilities*	+0·03	+0·13	+0·09	+0·09	+0·04
42	Expenditure on medical inspection*	+0·07	+0·41	+0·24	−0·05	+0·06
43	Expenditure on meals and milk*	+0·23	+0·22	+0·08	−0·15	+0·02
112	Expenditure on aid to pupils in secondary schools†	+0·01	−0·18	−0·17	−0·05	−0·04
	(b) Related Services and Social Conditions					
60	Social class I	−0·09	−0·34	−0·11	+0·25	+0·13
61	Non-manual class	−0·10	−0·29	−0·11	+0·22	+0·02
62	Semi and unskilled class	+0·06	+0·23	+0·21	−0·18	−0·15
63	Employed females: employed males	+0·41	+0·06	−0·04	+0·33	−0·12
70	Overcrowding	+0·13	+0·16	+0·29	−0·12	−0·05
72	Housing amenities	−0·16	−0·22	−0·07	−0·02	+0·21
74	Rooms per dwelling	−0·19	−0·13	−0·04	+0·14	+0·00
76	% dwellings of low value	+0·13	+0·12	+0·08	−0·02	+0·01
88	Family size	−0·02	−0·09	+0·19	−0·06	−0·07
89	Women aged 35–39 widowed	+0·01	−0·04	+0·35	−0·03	−0·05
87	% births illegitimate	+0·31.	+0·13	+0·05	+0·29	+0·25
85	Birth rate	+0·19	+0·17	+0·19	−0·21	−0·13
84	% increase in population due to other than births and deaths	−0·25	−0·29	−0·23	+0·03	+0·13
90	% population aged 5–11	−0·01	+0·14	+0·19	−0·30	−0·25
91	% population aged 11–18	+0·05	+0·23	+0·03	−0·11	−0·28
107	Population size (log transformed)	+0·41	+0·12	+0·22	+0·16	+0·25
138	% population born in Newer Commonwealth	+0·23	+0·15	−0·03	+0·22	+0·18
	Coefficient of variation	95·3	40·7	32·8	43·8	87·6

* Per thousand population.

† Per population under 18.

proportion of child care officer establishment filled was less correlated with social conditions. Thus standards of provision of these related health and children's services were not more strongly correlated with bad social conditions than were education welfare services, and standards of provision of the two sets of services were in general uncorrelated.

The distribution of educational resources is not highly correlated with social conditions which generate needs for them, and the same is true for other social services for children.

EDUCATION CORRELATION MATRICES
LIST OF VARIABLES

Nursery

1. Number or pupils on nursery school registers per thousand population, 1962.

Primary

5. Pupils per full-time teacher in primary school, 1962.
6. Cost of primary school teachers' wages and salaries per pupil, 1961–2.
7. Cost of non-teaching staff wages and salaries per pupil, 1961–2.
8. Cost of upkeep of buildings and grounds per pupil, 1961–2.
9. Cost of fuel, light, cleaning materials and water per pupil, 1961–2.
10. Rent, rates and other expenses per pupil, 1961–2.
11. Total cost per primary school (excluding nursery) pupil, 1961–2.
12. Percentage of classes which are oversize (more than 30) in junior schools, 1961.
13. Average number of pupils per primary school maintained by local education authorities, 1962.
15. Number of teachers released from maintained primary schools and establishments for special advanced courses per ten thousand teachers, 1964.

Secondary

20. Cost of secondary school teachers' wages and salaries per pupil, 1961–2.
21. Cost of non-teaching staff wages and salaries per pupil, 1961–2.
22. Cost of upkeep of building and grounds per pupil, 1961–2.
23. Cost of fuel, light, cleaning materials and water per pupil, 1961–2.
24. Rent, rates, and other expenses per pupil, 1961–2.
28. Total cost secondary education per pupil, 1961–2.
30. Percentage of classes which are oversize (more than 30) in senior schools, 1961.
32. Teachers released from maintained secondary schools and establishments for special advanced courses per ten thousand teachers, 1964.

Student Yield

37. Full value local education authority awards tenable 1961–2 at non-university institutions per thousand population, average of three age groups (17, 18, 19), 1961.
38. Lesser value local education authority awards tenable 1961–2 at non-university institutions per thousand population, average of three age groups (17, 18, 19), 1961.
39. Students entering teachers' training colleges per thousand population, average of three age groups (17, 18, 19), 1961.

Other

40. Net expenditure on special schools per thousand population, 1961–2.
41. Net expenditure for facilities for recreation, etc., per thousand population, 1961–2,
42. Net expenditure on medical inspection and treatment per thousand population, 1961–2.
43. Net expenditure on provision of milk and meals per thousand population, 1961–2.

45. Proportion of pupils (nursery, primary, secondary, special) receiving dinners (day pupils only), 1961.
46. Proportion of pupils (nursery, primary, secondary, special) receiving milk (day pupils and boarders), 1961.
47. Cost of food per dinner, 1961–2.
48. Medical officers per ten thousand pupils, 1961.
49. Dental officers per ten thousand pupils, 1961.
50. School nurses per ten thousand pupils, 1961.
55. Pupils aged 17 as a proportion of those aged 13 four years before, 1962.
56. Cost of salaries of primary teachers per pupil, 1950–1.
57. Cost of salaries of primary teachers per pupil, 1958–9.
58. Total cost of primary (excluding nursery) education per pupil, 1950–1.

Occupation and Socio-Economic Class

60. Males in administrative, managerial and professional occupations as a proportion of economically active males, 1961.
61. Males in non-manual occupations as a proportion of economically active males, 1961.
62. Males in semi or unskilled occupations as a proportion of economically active males, 1961.
63. Economically active females as a proportion of economically active males, 1961.
65. Males employed in heavy industry occupations as a proportion of occupied males, 1961.
66. Males employed in light industry occupations as a proportion of occupied males, 1961.
67. Males employed in industry as a proportion of occupied males, 1961.

Housing

69. Proportion of private households rented from a local authority or New Town Corporation, 1961.
70. Proportion of private households living at more than 1½ persons per room, 1961.
71. Number of private households sharing a dwelling as a proportion of all private households, 1961.
72. Proportion of private households with exclusive use of four census amenities (hot and cold tap water, fixed bath and W.C.), 1961.
73. Proportion of dwellings with one to three rooms, 1961.
74. Rooms per dwelling, 1961.
76. Proportion of domestic hereditaments with rateable value under £10 after the 1954 revaluation.

Demographic

83. Per cent change in population, 1951–61.
84. Per cent change in population due to causes other than births and deaths, 1951–61.
85. Crude Birth Rate, average for 1960–2.
87. Illegitimate births as a proportion of live births, average for 1960–2.
88. Family size: children aged 0–14 as a proportion of all married women aged 25–54, 1961.
89. Proportion of women aged 35–39 who are widowed, 1961.
90. Population aged 5–11 per thousand population, 1961.
91. Population aged 12–18 per thousand population, 1961.

Miscellaneous

97. Dental attendant, etc., in full-time equivalents (1960) per ten thousand pupils, 1961.

98. Staff of child guidance centres, in full-time equivalents (1960) per ten thousand pupils, 1961.

99. Nurses and nursing assistants in full-time equivalents (1960) per ten thousand pupils, 1961.

100. Number of teachers in full-time equivalents as a proportion of the quota recommended by Department of Education, 1959–61.

106. Population per Acre, 1961.

107. Population size (log transformed), 1961.

108. Total number of new awards to universities per thousand population 17–19 average for 1960–2.

109. Total number of new awards (universities, plus non-universities) and training college entrants per thousand population aged 17–19 average for 1960–2.

112. Aid to pupils in secondary schools per thousand secondary school pupils, 1962.

117. Proportion of 13 year olds in grammar and comprehensive, direct grant and independent schools, 1961.

127. Cost of debt charges per primary school pupil, 1961–2.

128. Cost of debt charges per secondary school pupil, 1961–2.

129. Net expenditure on day nurseries (provided under National Health Service Act) per thousand population, 1962–3.

130. Net expenditure on Child Welfare Services (provided under National Health Service Act) per thousand population, 1962–3.

131. Net expenditure on Health Visiting (provided under National Health Service Act) per thousand population, 1962–3.

135. Total number of Child Care Officers per thousand population under 18, 1965.

136. Proportion of Child Care Officers fully trained, 1965.

138. Number of persons born in Commonwealth countries (less Canada, Australia, New Zealand and South Africa) per thousand population, 1961.

Printed in England for Her Majesty's Stationery Office by Galliard Ltd, Great Yarmouth

Dd 153490   K48